The Politics of Commercial Treaties in the Eighteenth Century

Antonella Alimento • Koen Stapelbroek
Editors

The Politics of Commercial Treaties in the Eighteenth Century

Balance of Power, Balance of Trade

palgrave
macmillan

Editors
Antonella Alimento
Dipartimento di Civiltà e Forme
del Sapere
Università di Pisa
Pisa, Italy

Koen Stapelbroek
Department of Philosophy, History,
Culture and Art Studies
University of Helsinki
Helsinki, Finland

Department of Public Administration
Erasmus University Rotterdam
Rotterdam, The Netherlands

ISBN 978-3-319-53573-9 ISBN 978-3-319-53574-6 (eBook)
DOI 10.1007/978-3-319-53574-6

Library of Congress Control Number: 2017947911

Cover illustration: Anonymous, *L'inégalité juste*, Paris, 1801, Private collection.

Printed on acid-free paper

This Palgrave Macmillan imprint is published by Springer Nature
The registered company is Springer International Publishing AG
The registered company address is: Gewerbestrasse 11, 6330 Cham, Switzerland

Acknowledgements

This collaborative volume brings together international specialists on the history of economic ideas, institutions and political thought with the aim to analyse commercial treaties in an innovative manner. It is based on two thematically focused international colloquia held at the University of Pisa, 26–27 November 2014, under the title *Treaties of Commerce. Balance of Power, Balance of Trade and the European Order of States* and at the Institute of Intellectual History at the University of St Andrews, 23–24 January 2015, entitled *Balance of Power, Balance of Trade. The Politics of Commerce in the Eighteenth Century*. Selected papers from these meetings have been thoroughly revised and complemented by additionally commissioned chapters. The editors want to thank Richard Whatmore, Carl Wennerlind, Biagio Salvemini, Guillaume Calafat and Frederik Dhondt for their papers and presentations, as well as the colleagues and students whose participation in these meetings enriched our discussions. The research and meetings for this project were funded by the Italian Government under the PRIN 2010–2011 (Progetto di rilevanza nazionale) *Libertà dei moderni. Processi di civilizzazione nel lungo illuminismo (1750–1850): commercio, politica, cultura, colonie*, coordinated by Girolamo Imbruglia (prot. 20108KZTPX_004) and the Academy of Finland Research Fellowship Project, *Historical Instruments of European Integration: The Commercial Configuration of the 'Balance of Power'* of Koen Stapelbroek. The second meeting was supported by the Institute of Intellectual History, St Andrews and the University of Chicago Center in Paris.

Contents

List of Figures

Trade and Treaties: Balancing the Interstate System

Antonella Alimento and Koen Stapelbroek

In 1787, a commentator on the Anglo-French Eden–Rayneval commercial treaty that was signed the previous year commented that 'a good treaty of commerce' was 'a masterpiece of skill' and the pinnacle of adequate diplomacy in the service of humankind. Whereas Jean-Jacques Rousseau had sarcastically criticized the development of commercial sociability into the foundation of modern politics as the 'masterpiece of our time' and highlighted the range of unresolved social-economic and political problems, this author insisted that commercial treaties were the prime instrument for ironing out whatever stood in the way of peace, domestic tranquillity and general economic development. Engaging with rival political and economic visions, the 1787 pamphlet reconstructed the accelerated creation of wealth through global trade

A. Alimento (✉)
University of Pisa, Italy
e-mail: antonella.alimento@unipi.it

K. Stapelbroek
University of Helsinki, Finland

Erasmus University Rotterdam, The Netherlands
e-mail: koen.stapelbroek@helsinki.fi

A. Alimento, K. Stapelbroek (eds.), *The Politics of Commercial Treaties in the Eighteenth Century*, DOI 10.1007/978-3-319-53574-6_1

since the mid-seventeenth century as heavily dependent upon the successful usage of commercial treaties.[1]

In contrast with this assessment of the capacity of commercial treaties to regulate peace and commerce between states, the Neapolitan Ferdinando Galiani had negatively compared the signing of trade agreements to the ritual among Native American tribes of smoking a peace pipe. Galiani judged that the latter was an act of natural justice, familiarity and liberty, but the former were almost invariably cynical attempts to manipulate and disfigure commercial relations between or within states.[2]

The difference between these two diametrically opposed assessments of the politics of commercial treaties can be explained in part by reference to political context. The author of the 1787 pamphlet sided with those British and French writers who in the 1780s promoted Anglo-French economic integration as a progressive reconfiguration of the balance of power. Galiani's resistance to accept the justice and validity of treaties stemmed from the perceived threat that along with the signing of the Bourbon Family Compact Neapolitan economic development might be sacrificed to the primacy of France in the balance of power.[3] Yet, political interest is not the full story. Underneath the diplomatic problem of negotiating trade interests, lay a set of theoretical issues. What exactly constituted a 'good treaty of commerce'? Apart from that its practical

[1] Alexander Crowcher Schomberg, *Historical and Political Remarks upon the Tariff of the Commercial Treaty: With Preliminary Observations* (London, 1787), 10–11, with reference to Postlethwayt's *Commercial Interest of Great Britain* of 1757, ii: 423. Jean-Jacques Rousseau, Preface to *Narcisse*, in: *Oeuvres complètes*, ed. Bernard Gagnebin and Marcel Raymond (Paris, 1964–1969), ii: 968, emphasized by Nannerl O. Keohane, '"The Masterpiece of Policy in Our Century": Rousseau on the Morality of the Enlightenment', *Political Theory* 6 (1978): 457–484.

[2] Ferdinando Galiani, 'Dalle Considerazioni sul trattato di commercio tra il re el il re cristianissimo', in: *Scritti di politica economica*, ed. F. Cesarano (Lanciano: Rocco Carabba, 1999), 99–100. See Koen Stapelbroek, 'The Progress of Humankind in Galiani's *Dei Doveri dei Principi Neutrali*: Natural Law, Neapolitan Trade and Catherine the Great', in: *Trade and War: The Neutrality of Commerce in the Inter-State System*. COLLeGIUM: Studies Across Disciplines in the Arts and Humanities 10, ed. Koen Stapelbroek (Helsinki: Helsinki Collegium for Advanced Studies, 2011), 161–183.

[3] Ferdinando Galiani, 'Notes au pacte de Famille', in: *Illuministi italiani. VI. Opere di Ferdinando Galiani*, ed. Furio Diaz and Luciano Guerci (Milan and Naples: Ricciardi, 1975), 704–709.

provisions had to effectively facilitate the actual trade between merchants from the signatory states, a 'good' agreement was to contribute to stable peaceful international relations through offering all states that were involved viable prospects for economic development. In other words, the negotiation of 'good' commercial treaties was not merely a matter of converting power relations into patterns of trade, but also had to be predicated upon a 'good' future vision of peaceful economic competition between nations. As will be discussed at several points in this introduction, this idea suggests that commercial treaties tended to be more than contractual arrangements on trade and taxation between merchants of different nationality, but often expressed or enacted a political will or vision on the part of contracting states to commit to the shaping of a certain international order.

The aim of this book is to clarify how the basic understanding of commercial treaties as having a structural impact on international relations developed during the eighteenth century. Merging the realms of eighteenth-century political theory and diplomatic practice, the book takes commercial treaties as a point of departure in order to help develop a new paradigm for thinking about the political economy of the international order in the eighteenth century. Yet, this by itself immediately poses a problem. From the perspective of a French diplomat, his time may have been a 'siècle de traités'.[4] Yet, the existing historiography on commercial treaties paints a very different picture, in which commercial treaties were practically absent from the eighteenth century.

This introductory chapter is therefore designed, firstly, to engage with the state of the art of the literature on commercial treaties in different academic disciplines, including the usage and role of commercial treaties in international diplomacy; secondly, to sketch and explain, with reference to the main turning points in the long eighteenth century, the conceptual development according to which treaties were adopted and rejected as instruments for regulating international trade and politics; and thirdly, to provide a compiled overview in the form of a historical table of commercial treaties signed in the period covered by the chapters in this book (see Table 1 at the end of this chapter).

[4] *Mémoire en forme de traité de droit public, contenant les extraits de tous les differents traitez de paix, treves, alliances, commerce ou navigation, conclus depuis 1648 jusques à ce jour [1736] entre la France et les puissances de l'Europe*, Bibliothèque Nationale de France, Département des Manuscrits [BNF], FF 10653, 45.

The History of Commercial Treaties and the Eighteenth Century

Before discussing the political functions of commercial treaties in the eighteenth century, one ought to consider the degree to which they were used in the eighteenth century in comparison with the general history of treaties. Here, it was observed by Edward Keene, who studied the general history of treaty-making with no specific focus on commercial treaties in order to chart the shifts in international relations over centuries, that 'treaty-making through much of the seventeenth and eighteenth centuries' was a rare activity. Moreover, 'fewer treaties were made in the first half of the eighteenth century, than during the second half of the seventeenth. The beginning of the upward trend cannot be placed earlier than the second half of the 1790s' and from there continued until the First World War. For instance, during the 1790s each year twenty to thirty treaties were signed, while in the 1890s the average number had gone up to 140 to 150.[5]

Based on the Consolidated Treaty Series compiled by Clive Parry, Keene calculated that during the later eighteenth century France concluded the most treaties, while Britain did so during most of the nineteenth. Both dominant European states together were signatories of about 15–20 per cent of all nineteenth-century treaties.[6] In general, the dynamic of treaty-making may in large part be explained by the traditional usage, developed in particular during the seventeenth century, by the great powers of the time of establishing economic ties with states that did not have large manufacturing sectors, but instead had colonies (Portugal and Spain) and were rich in gold and silver. Commercial treaties in short were tools of economic rivalry among the main commercial powers, and instruments of economic subordination between more and less powerful European states.

Another traditional function of treaty-making was the establishment of commercial common ground between European and non-European territories based on political inequality. Indeed, 'during the second half of the

[5] Edward Keene, 'The Treaty-Making Revolution of the Nineteenth Century', *International History Review* 34 (2012), 475–500: 478. Other studies of commercial treaties equally tend to focus on the nineteenth century. See Robert Pahre, *Politics and Trade Cooperation in the Nineteenth Century: The 'Agreeable Customs' of 1815–1914* (Cambridge: Cambridge University Press, 2008) and Rainer Klump and Miloš Vec, eds., *Völkerrecht und Weltwirtschaft im 19. Jahrhundert* (Baden-Baden: Nomos, 2012).

[6] Keene, 'Treaty-Making Revolution', 487.

eighteenth century intra-European treaty-making was [...] consistently overtaken by treaty-making with non-European partners'.[7] Likewise, the increase during the nineteenth century was observed by Keene to be largely due to 'colonial' treaty-making with African, Arabic and Indian rulers.[8]

Commenting on the graphs that represented the evolution of treaty-making from 1648 to 1880, Keene attributed what he called the 'treaty-making revolution'[9] of the end of that period to three principal early nineteenth-century causes: (1) changing ideas about regulatory laws made by states; (2) changes in juristic thinking and in the training of diplomats in the later eighteenth century (this era saw the publication of major collections of treaties, the use of which in diplomatic academies changed practice);[10] (3) the impact of Napoleonic codifications on the transformation of European public law.[11]

While Keene explained the later nineteenth-century increase of treaty-making in terms of early nineteenth-century factors he was all the more puzzled by the existence of a 'gap' in the eighteenth century: 'Why did states not start making more treaties during the eighteenth century?'[12] Indeed, it might be

> rather surprising in light of the standard way of thinking about the Westphalian origins and development of the modern society of states. One might have expected to see a gradual, steady increase in treaty-making from 1648 onwards, as the institutions of international society matured and as states became more closely connected with one another in emerging commercial and political systems both within and beyond Europe.[13]

[7] Keene, 'Treaty-Making Revolution', 491.

[8] Keene, 'Treaty-Making Revolution', 492, where non-European powers are called 'treaty-takers' rather than 'treaty-makers'.

[9] Keene, 'Treaty-Making Revolution', 495. Keene identified three 'spikes' in the period: the 1810s (post-Napoleon), 1830s–1870s (scramble for Africa) and the 1900s (entrance of new states into the treaty-making arena), after which multilateral agreements slowly took off.

[10] Mario Toscano, *The History of Treaties and International Politics* (Baltimore, MD: Johns Hopkins University Press, 1966).

[11] Keene, 'Treaty-Making Revolution', 496.

[12] Keene, 'Treaty-Making Revolution', 482.

[13] Keene, 'Treaty-Making Revolution', 478–479.

Given this unexplained 'gap' in the history of treaty-making, and Keene's own observation, adding to his puzzlement, that 'it is a commonplace that the eighteenth century was the golden age of balance of power politics' (and thus presumably of treaty-making),[14] a more differentiated approach to the history of treaties, specifically commercial treaties, might be helpful.

Separating War and Peace

Although the various collections of treaties published over centuries demonstrate that from the end of the fifteenth and early sixteenth century commercial stipulations were part of state diplomacy, notably in England,[15] commercial treaties became 'autonomous' in the seventeenth century, although agreements were often directly related to peace-making.[16] Stephen Neff in this respect argued that:

> by the seventeenth century, several important changes had taken place in the international relations amongst the major European states. [. . .] The concluding of treaties of friendships, commerce and navigation became, for the first time, a routine and well-nigh universal feature of relations amongst the major European maritime states—so much so that FCN treaties came in virtually standard form. The second important feature of this period was the frequency of warfare amongst the major Western European states, with rivalry between Britain and France being the single most persistent feature.[17]

According to Neff, in international legal theory the notion of war itself changed in this period from a medieval just-war 'view of war as a clash of rival national interests without general moral or legal significance for the

[14] Keene, 'Treaty-Making Revolution', 479.

[15] Giovanni Buccianti, *Accordi commerciali e di Asiento dalla Pace di Westphalia alla pace di Utrecht* (Milan: Giuffré, 1967).

[16] Stephen C. Neff, 'Peace and Prosperity: Commercial Aspects of Peacemaking', in: *Peace Treaties and International Law in European History: From the Late Middle Ages to World War One*, ed. Randall Lesaffer (Cambridge: Cambridge University Press, 2004), 365–381.

[17] Neff, 'Peace and Prosperity', 367–368; Christopher Storrs, ed., *The Fiscal Military State in Eighteenth-Century Europe: Essays in honour of P. G. M. Dickinson* (London: Ashgate, 2009); Charles Tilly, *Coercion, Capital, and European States, AD 990–1990* (Cambridge, MA: Blackwell, 1990), 72, notes that eighteenth-century European states were at war 78 per cent of the time compared to 40 per cent in the nineteenth.

international community as a whole' that was, however, also limited in scope to the realm of military–political rivalry, to a more comprehensive measuring of forces on each side.[18] This new reality can be recognized in Malachy Postlethwayt's statement in *Great Britain's Commercial Interests Explained* that 'the great object of a maritime nation should be to take advantage of any rupture with another trading state, to destroy and distress their shipping and commerce, and to cut off all resources for naval armaments'.[19]

The emergence of this total-war mentality put enormous pressure on earlier treaties such as the 1674 Anglo-Dutch commercial treaty that included the famous 'free ships make free goods' clause that was never revised, was increasingly contested, and in 1780 would trigger the outbreak of the Fourth Anglo-Dutch War.[20] Along with it came also the idea that the conclusion of peace equally required the 'normalization' of disturbed commercial relations. Initially, this 'normalization' was included in the peace settlement, such as in the Anglo-Spanish peace treaty of Madrid of 1630 and the Treaty of the Pyrenees of 1659 between France and Spain. Increasingly, the common practice became to conclude a new commercial treaty in tandem with the peace treaty itself. This was the case with the Franco-Dutch settlements at Nijmegen in 1678–1679, Ryswick in 1697 and Utrecht in 1713, and more generally at the Peace of Utrecht between other states (most famously the Franco-British treaties of 11 April 1713). However, commercial treaties could also be separated in time from the peace itself: France and Britain brought their conflict over American independence to an end in 1783 with the Treaty of Paris, three years before the conclusion of the 1786 Eden–Rayneval commercial treaty. And while not all peace settlements would be accompanied by commercial treaties (the termination of the First Anglo-Dutch War of 1652–1654 was not, nor was the peace of Ryswick of 1697 followed by a British–French commercial treaty), it remains broadly true that peace-making developed into a two-stage process, reflecting the distinction between peace in the narrow sense and the broader sense of the normalization of relations.

[18] Neff, 'Peace and Prosperity', 367–368.

[19] Malachy Postlethwayt, *Great Britain's Commercial Interests Explained* (London, 1757), i: 347.

[20] Stephen C. Neff, *The Rights and Duties of Neutrals: A General History* (Manchester: Manchester University Press, 2000), 27–43. See the chapter by Stapelbroek in this volume.

The tendency to use commercial treaties to 'normalize' political relations adds a dimension to Keene's notion that the increase of trade would be expected in the long eighteenth century to increase the intensity of treaty-making. The important question to ask at this point is what commercial treaties were used *for*. 'Normalization' on the one hand could, as was common in the course of the seventeenth century, subordinate the economies of certain nations to others. Articles 3 and 4 of the Anglo-Portuguese treaty of commerce and peace of 1642 (and the treaty of 1654 completed this process) gave English merchants the same privileges as Portuguese traders but not vice versa, instead offering Portugal naval-military protection from Spain.[21] On the other hand 'normalization' could mean the diffusion of political antagonism, such as in the case of the 1697–1699 Franco-Dutch peace and trade agreements that allowed the Dutch to benefit from special rights and tariff regulations, thus connecting the Republic commercially with France while retaining its political focus on its ally England.

Agencies and Institutions of Trade

Depending on the political functions of specific commercial treaties, certain key formulas became customary legal principles. Often newer versions of treaties reproduced the terms of abrogated ones: the Anglo-Spanish treaty of commerce of 1713 reproduced that of 1667 word for word. Usage of certain clauses also spread when other states claimed the same privileges that another state enjoyed. Thus, and along with the causes of the treaty-making revolution signalled by Keene, a cumulative practice that merged the worlds of diplomacy and trade (that had rather little to do with public law) turned into a foundation of legal practice.[22]

One could speak of a professionalization of treaty-making, when the expertise of diplomats, merchants and lawyers (and other figures, such as consuls) was combined to shape commercial relations between states from

[21] Likewise Spain's seventeenth-century treaties with England and France created an 'informal imperialism'; Stanley J. Stein and Barbara H. Stein, *Silver, Trade, and War: Spain and America in the Making of Early Modern Europe* (Baltimore, MD: Johns Hopkins University Press, 2000), 66.

[22] See the chapter by Schnakenbourg in this volume.

around the late seventeenth century.[23] At stake between these different agents, as they negotiated alternative tariff policies and political visions of trade development, were principles of nationality, royal jurisdictions, unwritten rules of early modern lobbying politics and commitments to previously established privileges and rights. The establishment of institutions such as in France the *Conseil du commerce*, in 1700 (with the aim to promote 'active commerce'),[24] and the *Bureau de la balance du commerce*, in 1713 (with an eye on the Anglo-French struggle for European hegemony),[25] provides a testimony to the institutionalization of these processes. Through the workings of committees and consultations, commercial treaties were designed with the aim to manage, control and direct foreign trade between states. While over time their nature changed from bilateral contractual deals to system-shaping agreements, the question always remained whether political agreements effectively changed previous patterns of trade, as the case of the Austrian–Spanish rapprochement shows.[26] Likewise, certain established pockets of contraband trade and legal and fiscal disputes that were treated by national boards and courts were on-the-ground realities that often proved obstinately intractable.

From this point of view, it is not surprising that modern treaty law posits a sharp distinction between the old practice of bilateral agreements and the multilateral practice that came into being in the early twentieth century. While the former is retrospectively treated as an improvised cumulative and calculating practice of mere contracts made in a political

[23] Harm Klueting, *Die Lehre von der Macht der Staaten. Das aussenpolitische Machtproblem in der 'politischen Wissenschaft' und in der praktischen Politik des 18. Jahrhunderts* (Berlin: Duncker & Humblot, 1986).

[24] David K. Smith, 'Le discours économique du Bureau du commerce, 1700–1750', in: *Le cercle de Vincent de Gournay. Savoirs économiques et pratiques administratives en France au milieu du XVIIIe siècle*, ed. Loïc Charles, Frédéric Lefebvre, and Christine Théré (Paris: INED, 2001), 31–61; Thomas J. Schaeper, *The French Council of Commerce, 1700–1715: A Study of Mercantilism after Colbert* (Columbus: Ohio State University Press, 1983).

[25] *Mémoire sur la Balance du Commerce*, Archives Nationales, Paris [AN] F/12/1834 A, in Ruggero Romano, 'Documenti e prime considerazioni intorno alla balance du commerce della Francia dal 1716 al 1780' in: Studi in onore di Armando Sapori (Milan: Istituto Editoriale Cisalpino, 1960), 1267–1299: 1295; also Loïc Charles and Guillaume Daudin, 'La collecte du chiffre au XVIIIe siècle: le Bureau de la balance du commerce et la production des données sur le commerce extérieur de la France', *Revue d'Histoire Moderne et Contemporaine* 58 (2011): 128–155.

[26] See the chapter by Lebeau in this volume.

state of nature, the latter is attributed a superior capacity to realize and control shared political and social norms normatively through public law. Even so, leaving aside the question of whether this sharp distinction is helpful or true, the old treaty system was for centuries the instrument that, however loosely, brought together diplomatic negotiation and the reality of trade on the ground and thereby meaningfully shaped the political arena of global trade relations.

An oft-discussed issue at this point is agency. Numerous economic historians in recent decades have challenged the traditional state-centred paradigm as the default mode and method for understanding the history of tariff politics. New institutional historians, differently from most diplomatic and political historians, have instead highlighted the role of rival domestic interests in shaping foreign trade policy. Thus, within the field of history the methodological preferences of International Relations and Public Choice economics became competing perspectives, particularly on the history of (British) trade policy between the Napoleonic Wars and the First World War. John Vincent Nye has called this friction between two analytical paradigms on generalizable theories of political economy and trade relations 'a real clash—almost a culture clash'.[27]

Among the merits of the neo-institutionalist approach to trade politics is the revision of the myth that commercial competition in the eighteenth and nineteenth centuries was between a liberal Britain and a protectionist France. Engaging both with the Anglo-French commercial treaty of Utrecht and the 1860 Cobden–Chevalier agreement, Nye questioned the 'fable of commercial prosperity and international integration through [British] free trade', replacing it with a focus on tariffs, taxation and political lobbying by interest groups who used public opinion and early statistical techniques to sell a political narrative.[28] The new institutional

[27] John V. C. Nye, review on EH.Net (July 2002) of Fiona McGillivray, Iain McLean, Robert Pahre and Cheryl Schonhardt-Bailey, eds., *International Trade and Political Institutions: Instituting Trade in the Long Nineteenth Century* (Cheltenham: Edward Elgar, 2002), in which Robert Pahre, 'Agreeable Duties: The Tariff Treaty Regime in the Nineteenth Century', 29–79, reconsiders Great Britain's role in trade liberalization, underlining the political support for different business interests.

[28] John Vincent Nye, 'The Myth of Free Trade Britain and Fortress France: Tariffs and Trade in the Nineteenth Century', *Journal of Economic History* 51 (1991), 23–46; 'Changing French Trade Conditions, Naval Welfare, and the 1860 Anglo-French Treaty of Commerce',

turn away from a focus on the governmental management of national economies towards underlying interests has already influenced the understanding of commercial treaties, as can be gleaned from the volume *Le négoce de la paix*, which introduced French popular satire and the campaigns of local pressure groups (acting through *Chambres de Commerce*) into the story.[29]

More specifically still, Jeff Horn's recent work has given more profound insight into the political economic debate of the 1780s in particular. While the concerned reactions by the Normandy *Chambre de Commerce* following the Eden–Rayneval treaty called for a fiscal and colonial trade reform along with a mitigation of the terms of the agreement, it did not request its abrogation. In sum, it presented an economic reform programme, not a narrow-minded protest of previous privileges. The 1786 commercial treaty, in other words, if properly implemented could be an instrument for France to 'compete with the "superior" British if the state provided the proper assistance and direction'.[30] Recognizing this aspect, and the role that other than central state institutions played, paves the way for a more complete reconstruction of the political economic reform debate than is possible by focusing merely on the political visions of Vergennes, Calonne and Dupont as the main designers of French economic policy in the 1780s.

Explorations in Economic History 28 (1991), 460–477; 'Guerre, commerce, guerre commerciale: l'économie politique des échanges franco-anglais réexaminée', *Annales. Économies, Sociétés, Civilisations* 47 (1992), 613–632; *War, Wine, and Taxes: The Political Economy of Anglo-French Trade 1689–1900* (Princeton: Princeton University Press, 2007), 44–59.

[29] Jean-Pierre Jessenne, Renaud Morieux and Pascal Dupuy, eds., *Le négoce de la paix. Les nations et les traités franco-britanniques, 1713–1802* (Paris: Société des études robespierristes, 2011), especially the chapters by Pascal Dupuy, Matthieu De Oliveira and Jeff Horn.

[30] Jeff Horn, *The Path Not Taken. French Industrialization in the Age of Revolution, 1750–1830* (Cambridge, MA: MIT Press, 2006), 51–88: 86; on the French impact Jean-Pierre Poussou, 'How, and How Not, to Use the Concept of Crisis in the Reign of Louis XVI', in: *The Crisis of the Absolute Monarchy: France from Old Regime to Revolution*, ed. Julian Swann and Joel Félix (Oxford: Oxford University Press, 2013), which questions the negative appraisal of Guy Lemarchand, *L'economie de la France de 1770 à 1830. De la crise de l'Ancien Régime à la révolution industrielle* (Paris: Armand Colin, 2008), 112–114. Likewise, based on a regionally diversified approach—also shared by Horn—David Todd, *Free Trade and Its Enemies in France, 1814–1851* (Cambridge: Cambridge University Press, 2015), analysed Franco-British trade in later times.

The Balance of Trade and the Neutrality of Commerce

The neo-institutionalist shift in the concern of the balance of trade from political competition of national wealth to internal interests, pressure groups and institutions potentially sheds new light on the nature of concrete institutions themselves. Likewise, understanding the balance of trade as a historical foil for the organization of international trade draws more realistic attention to the respective networks and contexts of negotiating agents—diplomats, financiers, administrators and political writers—such as Swift, Defoe and Davenant in the case of the Anglo-French commercial treaty of 1713.[31]

More generally, the institutional analysis of the international organization of trade opens up possibilities for new theoretical developments. Instead of sticking with the political economic caricatures of liberal Britain and protectionist France (or vice versa) that were criticized by Nye, intellectual history might be capable of bridging the gap between the political and institutional perspectives by for instance connecting endogenous processes of tariff politics to the categorization of forms of trade (active–passive, own–carrying, *économie–luxe* and further differentiations in Adam Smith or Melchiorre Gioja) from the mid-eighteenth to the early nineteenth century.

Such integrative perspectives take us beyond the legal–diplomatic–military concepts of 'normalization'—and the structural management of peace through trade agreements—as well as beyond the idea of the 'neutralization' of trade that Dutch and French authors and diplomats at times propagated in order to extend the rights of neutrals as far as possible. Different from these out-and-out political notions, the idea of the 'neutrality of trade' fits better with a new usage of the notion of 'balance of trade' that was employed by writers and political actors who continued to see bilateral commercial treaties as instruments of general peace and commercial integration.[32]

[31] Donald Cuthbert Coleman, 'Politics and Economics in the Age of Anne: The Case of the Anglo-French Trade Treaty of 1713', in: *Trade, Government and Economy in Pre-Industrial England*, ed. Donald Cuthbert and Arthur Henry John (London: Weidenfeld & Nicolson, 1976), 187–213.

[32] Stapelbroek, ed., *Trade and War*.

Unlike the influential Josiah Child, who used the term to measure and compare rival national wealth, from the early to mid-eighteenth century writers like Uztáriz, Ulloa, Véron de Forbonnais and Vincent de Gournay transformed the idea of the balance of trade into a tool to confront the challenge of designing a sustainable system of international trade that could replace the perceived British commercial hegemony in place since the end of the War of the Spanish Succession. Balancing political relations between states through trade from this point onwards generated numerous projects and visions that differed from previous political economic schemes and in which commercial treaties were innovatively used as instruments.

Within this understanding and ensuing practice of shaping the balance of trade it is important to widen the scope from a focus on individual treaty-making states to the general mosaic of modalities of trade patterns. Accordingly, the chapters in this volume not only tackle a wide range of European states, but follow in particular the attempts by different states, notably France (most consistently in different periods), but also Portugal, the United Provinces, the Habsburg Empire and the Kingdom of Sardinia, next to Great Britain, Spain, Russia and Prussia, to conclude combinations of treaties as part of comprehensive political economic visions.[33]

Increasingly, this political engagement with the balance of trade was influenced by developing analyses of the emergence of modern wealth, trade and economic development. While diplomats negotiated claims, concessions and compromises based on the principle of sovereign autonomy, the emerging system also had to be sustainable and fit with the 'rules' of commerce. It was on these terms that critiques of British commercial empire and hegemony—including by Britons like David Hume—and the analysis of the usefulness (or lack thereof) of commercial treaties intersected with the eighteenth-century debate on political economy.[34]

[33] Additionally, Sweden, Denmark, the Hanseatic League, the Ottoman Empire, the North African states and colonial rulers were included in the webs woven through bilateral diplomacy. See Antonella Alimento, 'Commercial Treaties and the Harmonization of National Interests', in: *War, Trade and Neutrality. Europe and the Mediterranean in the Seventeenth and Eighteenth Centuries*, ed. Antonella Alimento (Milan: Franco Angeli, 2011), 107–128; Spain's importance in Anglo-French relations was stressed by Hamish M. Scott, 'The Second Hundred Years War, 1689–1815', *Historical Journal* 35 (1992), 443–469: 446.

[34] Istvan Hont, *Jealousy of Trade. International Competition and the Nation-State in Historical Perspective* (Cambridge, MA: Harvard University Press, 2005).

It is crucial here to recognize what precisely divided those arguing for and against commercial treaties. Like Schomberg and Galiani at the beginning of this introductory chapter, all contributors to the debate, from the mid-eighteenth century, focused on the issue of whether making general trade development the object of political negotiation in colonial treaty-making inevitably meant defaulting to a previous form of economically suboptimal allocation of privileges to groups of people in a state. This concern was central in Adam Smith's attack on balance of trade politics and in Johann Heinrich Gottlob von Justi's attacks on both the balance of power and the balance of trade as 'chimerical'. Yet Ferdinando Galiani himself was also the architect of a Russian–Neapolitan commercial treaty in the 1780s and Adam Smith was seen as a major inspiration by William Shelburne, whose role in the conclusion of the Eden–Rayneval treaty has long been recognized. Even David Ricardo's denouncement of commercial treaties as a remnant from the trade policy 'system of retaliation' must be understood as a contribution to a longstanding discussion of the political economic reform of Britain, and not be simplified to fit better-known ideological categories.[35]

In this sense Schomberg's curious attempt to dissolve opposition in the debate on commercial treaties by coining the idea of a 'good' commercial treaty is instructive. A 'good' agreement was one that respected the mechanisms of modern wealth and the growth of trade that the world had seen since the discovery of the Americas. In addition, it assisted, based on knowledge, information and calculations (otherwise known as early statistics), in creating an integrated commercial system across states and their different relative strengths and natural and cultural resources. A 'bad' commercial treaty (which was left undefined by Schomberg) might be understood as a product of the 'system of retaliation', as Ricardo had called it. Ultimately, the only thing that separated Schomberg and Ricardo (and one might include Adam Smith's critique of the 'mercantile system'[36]) was the degree to which they believed that Britain could live up to the challenge of reforming itself.

[35] David Ricardo, *Speech on the Subject of Commercial Treaties, in the House of Commons* (London: Ridgway, 1843); *On the Principles of Political Economy and Trade* (London: Murray, 1817), Chapter 25, 'On Colonial Trade'. For an ideological misrepresentation distorting an otherwise valid argument, Olivier Accominotti and Marc Flandreau, 'Bilateral Treaties and the Most-Favored-Nation Clause: The Myth of Trade Liberalization in the Nineteenth Century', *World Politics* 60 (2008), 147–188.

[36] Book IV, Chapter VI, 'Of Treaties of Commerce' of the *Wealth of Nations* argued that treaties distorted international markets and created artificial mercantile profits, while some

Schomberg, writing in the aftermath of the conclusion of the Eden–Rayneval treaty, was more optimistic than Ricardo, who observed more than half a century later that Britain had still failed to modernize its economic and tariff policy and was 'constitutionally' turning from a leading commercial nation into a stale oligarchy.[37]

Rather than be led by quantitative analysis or ideological imposition, the chapters in this volume are developed from the insight that a more differentiated understanding of the politics of commercial treaties reconciles the fact that comparatively fewer commercial treaties were concluded during large parts of the eighteenth century than in previous and following centuries with the observation that the eighteenth century was a 'siècle de traités': the moment it was widely recognized that treaties had to be 'good' in order to function in the long-term interest of the concluding states, the treaty-producing process started to function according to a dynamic of 'waves' of new innovative political economic visions and practices. It is this moment and the development of treaty-making in this period around which the chapters in this volume are centred.[38] Recognizing the role of commercial treaties in the political economy of the international order of the eighteenth century provides a direct point of access through which to understand more clearly the relations between theory and practice, and between the realms of the political and economic without having to invent any thematic impositions similar to those that have gone in and out of fashion over recent decades.

The Peace of Utrecht as a Turning Point

The period from the Peace of Westphalia (1648) to the Treaty of Vienna (1815) can be divided up roughly into four periods as far as the usage of commercial treaties is concerned. The first is associated with the Peace of Utrecht, in our view the first attempt to use commercial treaties to regulate

agreements—like the Methuen treaty—were surrounded by misconceptions about the significance of precious metals and the balance of trade.

[37] Ricardo, *Speech on Commercial Treaties.*

[38] The chapters by Volosyuk, Lebeau, Shovlin, Alimento, Stapelbroek, Storrs and Sanz-Guasti in this volume demonstrate the trends revealed by Keene as attributable to a mutual awareness by contracting parties of the use of commercial treaties as instruments for regulating peace and trade.

international politics. During the second period, spanning the 1740s and 1750s, after the death of Cardinal de Fleury, the idea that peace could be regulated through trade in the balance of power was largely suspended and commercial treaty-making took on a different shape. The third and fourth periods, during the 1760–1770s and the 1780s–1790s, saw the re-usage of earlier institutional instruments in new combinations and a revival of the idea that peace and general economic development might be engineered through commercial regulation of the balance of power.

Nowadays, the idea that the Peace of Utrecht created a system of the balance of power and a new era in European civilization is as widespread in various parts of the historiography as the idea that this new order had its imperfections. Notably, Paul W. Schroeder forcefully argued that the international system was *not* stabilized with the Peace of Utrecht and that power politics continued, under the guise of the 'recessive', 'dangerous and counterproductive' system of the balance of power, to merely produce 'a balance of conquests'.[39] Since 'no one could agree on what a suitable balance might be; because the methods and assumptions of balance of power politics actually made anything but a temporary stability impossible [. . .] free competition would lead inevitably to the ruin of the weaker brethren'.[40] It was noted, however,

[39] Paul W. Schroeder, *The Transformation of European Politics, 1763–1848* (Oxford: Clarendon Press, 1994); Peter Krüger and Paul W. Schroeder, eds., *The Transformation of European Politics, 1763–1848. Episode or Model in Modern History?* (Münster: LIT Verlag, 2002). Also *American Historical Review*, 97 (1992), which includes articles by Paul W. Schroeder, 'Did the Vienna Settlement Rest on a Balance of Power?'; Enno E. Kraehe, 'A Bipolar Balance of Power'; Robert Jervis, 'A Political Science Perspective on the Balance of Power and the Concert'; Wolf D. Gruner, 'Was There a Reformed Balance of Power System or Cooperative Great Power Hegemony?'; and Paul W. Schroeder, 'A Mild Rejoinder'. See also Hamish M. Scott, *The Birth of a Great Power System, 1740–1815* (Harlow: Pearson, 2006).

[40] T. C. W. Blanning, 'Section II: Introduction', in: *Transformation of European Politics*, ed. Krüger and Schroeder, 85–90: 86. This perspective resembles the idea of a 'Second Hundred Years War' between 1688 and 1815: Jean Meyer and John Bromley, 'La seconde guerre de Cent Ans (1689–1815)', in: *Dix siècles d'histoire franco-britannique. De Guillaume le Conquérant au marché commun*, ed. Douglas Johnson, François Bédarida and François Crouzet (Paris: Albin Michel, 1979), 153–190; François Crouzet, 'The Second Hundred Years War: Some Reflections', *French History* 10 (1996), 432–450; Robert and Isabelle Tombs, *That Sweet Enemy: The British and the French from the Sun King to the Present* (London: Heinemann, 2006).

that Schroeder based his conclusion mainly on an analysis of the period after 1763 and paid much less attention to its formative phase.[41] In general it was not true that the entire period between Utrecht and Vienna was dominated by warfare, while, specifically after 1763, relations between European states and the Ottoman Empire intensified and were formalized in treaties.[42]

The period between the Peace of Utrecht and the 1740s, in fact, was often characterized, especially in the later eighteenth century, as a period of 'long peace' and tranquillity.[43] In different ways, recent publications by John Pocock,[44] Andreas Osiander,[45] Marc Belissa[46] and Heinhard Steiger[47] subscribe to the idea that the Peace of Utrecht heralded the formal adoption of the principles of sovereignty, equality between states and security. In addition, Hamish M. Scott underlined that the concept of 'just equilibrium of power' in relation to mutual friendship and agreement first assumed such a status in the context of a peace treaty. While the notion of the balance of power went back at least to fifteenth-century Italy, when it was used to control Venetian supremacy, it was only at Utrecht, when Europe became a unified political system, that the balance of power referred

[41] Heinz Duchhardt, 'Section I: Introduction', in: *Transformation of European Politics*, ed. Krüger and Schroeder, 25–28: 27, argued that during the period 1650–1750 and particularly 1713–1763 the system absolutely cannot be described as 'a balance of conquests'.

[42] Duchhardt, 'Section I: Introduction', 28. The latter point fits with the trend registered by Keene of agreements with states in North African and the Levant.

[43] See Frederik Dhondt, *Balance of Power and Norm Hierarchy: Franco-British Diplomacy after the Peace of Utrecht* (Leiden: Brill, 2015).

[44] J. G. A. Pocock, *Barbarism and Religion. Vol. I: The Enlightenments of Edward Gibbon, 1737–1764* (Cambridge: Cambridge University Press, 1990), 110, mentioned the Peace of Utrecht 'as having given rise to "the Europe of Enlightenment"'.

[45] Andreas Osiander, 'Sovereignty, International Relations, and the Westphalian Myth', *International Organization* 55 (2001), 251–287.

[46] Marc Belissa, *Repenser l'ordre européen (1795–1802). De la société des rois aux droits des nations* (Paris: Kimé, 2006).

[47] Heinhard Steiger, 'Was haben die Untertanen vom Frieden?' in: *Utrecht–Rastatt–Baden 1712–1714. Ein europaeisches Friedenswerk am Ende des Zeitalters Ludwig XIV*, ed. Heinz Duchhardt and Martin Espenhorst (Goettingen: Vandenhoeck und Ruprecht, 2013).

to a general system rather than a regional political tactic.[48] Interestingly, it has been suggested that the text of the preliminaries concluded by Mesnager and Bolingbroke in October 1711 represented a discursive shift in that the bilateral agreement reflected a wider concern with the aspirations of multiple actors and was an unusually general position statement at the level of European international relations.[49] Finally, the extension of the Franco-British agreement to the level of European politics has been recognized as a turning point compared with, for instance, the Peace of Westphalia in that commercial treaties were no longer integral to the peace agreements, but were separated from them as independent agreements whose structure tied together states.[50]

Regardless of their final judgement on the Utrecht balance of power system, what all these authors have in common is that they have not examined the role of these commercial treaties in the functioning of the 'Utrecht system'. There, in 1713, simultaneous to the bilateral peace treaties of which the general peace was composed, a number of commercial treaties were drafted. The commercial treaties of Utrecht were signed on the same day or in the immediate aftermath of the general peace treaty, translating into practice the separate (often secret) provisions of the peace. Such commercial treaties were signed at Utrecht between France and Great Britain, France and the United Provinces, the United Provinces and Spain and between Great Britain and Spain. Yet, the final negotiations of these treaties were primarily held by French and British representatives—who guaranteed the acceptance of these treaties by Spain and the United Provinces. Compared with the traditional use of commercial treaties by Europe's commercial powers, those stipulated at Utrecht seemingly followed a different logic, reinstating free trade among all the parties involved in the

[48] Scott, *Birth of a Great Power System*, 138–142. Also Paolo Alatri, *Le relazioni internazionali in Europa nella prima metà del XVIII secolo* (Naples: IISF, 1990); Maurizio Bazzoli, 'L'equilibrio di potenza nell'età moderna. Dal Cinquecento al Congresso di Vienna', in: *Stagioni e teorie della società internazionale* (Milan: Led, 2005).

[49] Frederik Dhondt, 'From Contract to Treaty: The Legal Transformation of the Spanish Succession 1659–1713', *Journal of the History of International Law* 13 (2011), 347–376.

[50] Andreas Osiander, *The States System of Europe, 1640–1990: Peacemaking and the Conditions of International Stability* (Oxford: Oxford University Press, 1994), 370.

preceding conflict and thus creating an economic basis for the peace itself in support of the new form of international relations that constituted the balance of power. France, Britain and the Dutch Republic mutually declared themselves the most preferred nations, thus affirming in economic terms the idea of political equality embodied by the peace treaty itself.

The fact, however, that Britain managed to obtain from Spain in 1713 the so-called *asiento*, as the obvious exception to the rule of international equality, forces one to consider more attentively the logic underlying the stipulation of commercial treaties in relation to previous negotiations and plans during the War of the Spanish Succession. Looking at the economic principles included in the peace treaties themselves one wonders why some states signed commercial treaties that were expressions of inequality in fiscal terms (France-United Provinces) or accepted terms that formally were expressions of reciprocity, but in reality were not (Great Britain-Spain). While there was an emancipation of the usage of commercial treaties from instruments of subordination and normalization to structural tools of regulating global trade, the present historiography is considerably out of step with the nature of this usage of commercial treaties, other than as simple instruments of power politics or of private economic opportunity, to recapture it.

To see how the Peace of Utrecht was actually 'configured' it is essential to recognize the previous years as a laboratory of projects and experiments devising new patterns of international trade. Before arriving in Utrecht on 29 January 1712 as the French plenipotentiary to negotiate the commercial treaty with Britain, Nicolas Mesnager, the representative of the city of Rouen on the *Conseil du commerce,* had embarked upon numerous secret diplomatic missions. At the orders of the secretary of state for war Michel Chamillart, he participated in Spain in a project of the *Junta de Restablecimiento del Comercio* between December 1704 and April 1706.[51] After briefly returning to Paris to elaborate a new tariff system for Cadiz,[52] he set off for the United Provinces in December 1707 to March 1708 to offer a separate peace including a (favourable for the Dutch) fiscal treatment based on the Peace of Ryswick.[53] In the aftermath of these missions, which gave

[51] Frederik Dhondt, *Nec pluribus impar? De campagnes en onderhandelingen van Lodewijk XIV in de Zuidelijke Nederlanden, 1707–1708* (Gent: Universiteit Gent, 2008), 319–320.

[52] 'Voyage en Espagne', December 1708, Archives du Ministère des Affaires Etrangères, La Courneuve [AAE], Correspondance Politique [CP], Espagne 183, fol. 85.

[53] AAE, CP Hollande 214, fol. 19.

Mesnager a clear perspective on the political economic puzzle that was to be solved at the end of the War of the Spanish Succession, Mesnager formulated a proposal to open up the Spanish South American trade to all nations. It was well known, as Louis XIV expressed it, that 'the main object of the present war is the Indies trade and the wealth it produces'.[54] Mesnager's solution was to end the war and create a durable peace by changing the original Franco-Spanish plan, developed in 1706, to open up trade to allied nations. During his stay in the Dutch Republic, Mesnager planned (but was denied permission from Paris to propose) the inclusion of the Dutch, and even the English, and furthermore wished to turn Cadiz into a general entrepot and even into a neutral city in wartime. Having previously attempted to reform the charter of the French Indies Company to include all nationals, Mesnager believed this visionary scheme would also be the best cure against the problem of contraband trade.[55]

Liberalizing or even neutralizing the Spanish Indies trade was a step too far for some, as Jonathan Swift remarked when the plan resurfaced in 1711:

> To think of the Spaniards living Consent to a Peace, upon Condition that the English shall have FREE TRADE to New Spain; is just as if England should make Peace with France, upon Condition that the French should

[54] *Correspondance de Louis XIV avec M. Amelot, son ambassadeur en Espagne, 1705–1709* (Paris: Aubry, 1864), ii: 120–121.

[55] *Memoire touchant le commerce de l'Amerique espagnolle et sur les moyens de l'assurer esgallement a tuttes les nations de l'Europe*, 12 January 1708, AAE, CP Hollande 214, fos. 31–32v: 31v. The originality of Mesnager's projects was first discussed by Lucien Bély, *Espions et ambassadeurs au temps de Louis XIV* (Paris: Fayard, 1990). On his missions to Spain and the Dutch Republic: Louis André and Emile Bourgeois, eds., *Recueil des instructions données aux ambassadeurs et ministres de France depuis les traités de Westphalie jusqu'à la Révolution française, XXI–XXII, Hollande* (Paris: Boccard, 1922), 159–177; Erik W. Dahlgren, *Les relations commerciales et maritimes entre la France et les côtes de l'Océan Pacifique*, I, *Le Commerce de la mer du Sud jusqu'à la paix d'Utrecht* (Paris: Honoré Champion, 1909), 566–572; Claude-Frédéric Lévy, *Capitalistes et pouvoir au siècle des Lumières*, I, *Les fondateurs dès origines à 1715* (The Hague: Mouton, 1969), 267, 322; also the chapter by Stapelbroek in this volume. On Mesnager's reform of the French India company, AN, Colonies/C/2/13, fos. 104–105 and André Lespagnol, 'Négociants et commerce indien au début du XVIIIe siècle: l'épisode des Compagnies malouines 1709–1719', *Annales de Bretagne et des Pays de l'Ouest* 86 (1979), 427–457: 452. On the contraband issue, AAE, CP Hollande 214, fos. 28–28v.

> come over hither, and lie with our Wives [. . .] New Spain is the Spouse of the Old Spain, and they will no more prostrate her to be dabauch'd in trade by us, than they, the most Jalous People in the World, should allow us to come to Bed to their Wives.[56]

Likewise in Spain the *Consulado* of Seville questioned the viability of the project.[57] And in France it directly clashed with the faction in French politics led by the secretary of state for the navy, Jérôme de Pontchartrain, whose vision (and personal interests) entailed the creation of three French overseas trade companies along with the French Asiento company (1703–1713).[58] Even Torcy de Colbert, the secretary of state for foreign affairs to whom Mesnager was especially close, only liked the project in theory, while Louis XIV thought that opening up trade in wartime could prolong the war rather than dissolve conflict.[59] Finally, divisions in the United Provinces between 'pacifists' and supporters of the 'no peace without Spain' principle obstructed the project.[60]

Apart from that of Mesnager, different projects were developed by Jan van Brouchoven, Count of Bergeyck on behalf of Philip V and by Claude-Adrien Helvétius, a French physician of Dutch origin who drafted a series of memoranda in 1705–1716 on the reform of

[56] Cited in Carl Wennerlind, *Casualties of Credit: The English Financial Revolution, 1620–1720* (Cambridge, MA: Harvard University Press, 2011), 214; although other Britons recognized free trade in the Spanish West Indies as potentially beneficial for Spain, 322n.82.

[57] Stein and Stein, *Silver, Trade, and War*, 66.

[58] Lespagnol, 'Négociants et commerce indien', 439; Charles Frostin, *Les Pontchartrain ministres de Louis XIV. Alliances et réseau d'influence sous l'Ancien Régime* (Rennes: PUR, 2006).

[59] AAE, CP Hollande 214, fol. 33.

[60] Although published in Dutch gazettes, the *Ordenanzas nuevas que se han de publicar y observar para el comercio y trafico de las Indias* of July 1708, AAE, CP Espagne 185, fos. 172–190, were never implemented. See Louis XIV to Amelot, 13 August 1708, *Correspondance Louis XIV avec Amelot*, ii: 71; Amelot to Louis XIV, 17 August 1708, AAE, CP Espagne 181, fol. 298. Also Dahlgren, *Les relations commerciales et marittimes*, I, 509–521; Lucien Bély, 'Les larmes de Monsieur de Torcy, essai sur les perspectives de l'histoire diplomatique', in: *L'art de la paix en Europe: naissance de la diplomatie moderne, XVIe–XVIIIe siècles*, ed. Lucien Bély (Paris: PUF, 2007), 431–464.

Spanish trade involving the Dutch, and who accompanied Mesnager on his mission in 1708 to the United Provinces. Bergeyck, in 1709, proposed the creation of a joint trade company that would hold the *asiento* and further neutralize the Spanish trade system. Yet this plan was rejected by the Dutch for the same reasons as Mesnager's.[61] Helvétius started from the idea that the sources of global trade conflict could be dissolved if in addition to the improved exploitation of the Spanish American trade Dutch participation in a Franco-Spanish trade company could be made properly reciprocal and mutually advantageous. A fierce critic of those who in the aftermath of Jean-Baptiste Colbert pursued policies of French commercial autonomy and whose fiscal measures had upset the manufacturing system of the monarchy, Helvétius pleaded for a return to the pre-Ryswick era in which Colbert had successfully concluded treaties with the United Provinces that promoted French economic development while using the Dutch as carriers of French goods.[62] Anticipating the idea of the 'good treaty' mentioned at the beginning of this chapter, Helvétius argued that:

> lors qu'il s'agira de faire dans la suite des traités de commerce, le seul moyen d'en dresser d'utiles et de solides est d'y proceder des deux parts avec plus de sincerité et plus de dispositions a se faire justice les uns aux autres, cette opinion, qui dans l'esprit des gens prevenus paroitra blesser des interests specieux et particuliers procurera d'ailleurs des avantages reels et universels qui rallentiront [sic !!] l'ordre et l'equité dans le commerce et le tireront de cette langueur ou les biais obliques que l'on a pris l'ont plongé depuis si longtems.[63]

[61] Archivio Histórico National, Madrid [AHN], Estado, leg. 3457, 2460. Nationaal Archief, The Hague [NA], 3.01.19, inv. 2242; correspondence between Helvétius-Nieuwpoort (1706) and van der Dussen-Bergeyck (1708) in Koninklijke Bibliotheek, The Hague [KB]: 71 H18 and 70 C24. The former comprises memoirs, letters (to Torcy and Chamillart) and manuscripts documenting Helvétius' trip in 1706, similar to AAE CP Espagne 147–149, 217 and BNF NAF 2041. Unfortunately Duivenvoorde's correspondence of 1708 (NA 3.20.87, inv. 167) went missing.

[62] See the chapter by Isenmann in this volume.

[63] *Mémoire présenté a Mgr Chamillart et a Mgr de Torcy au mois de juillet 1705*, BNF, NAF 2041, 35–91: 59v.

While the difference between the different schemes might seem to lie in whether or not Britain was included (i.e. between liberalization, and a well-constructed balance of power resting on a reform of global trade) there was an important similarity between the two approaches in that both schemes aligned an improved efficiency of American trade exploitation to the dissolution of the causes of war. However, the diplomatic mission to the United Provinces of the summer of 1705, which Helvétius embarked on at the orders of Colbert de Torcy, had also been unsuccessful.

What is certain is that Torcy, in the slipstream of his uncle, Colbert, preferred the use of commercial treaties as dual instruments of peace and economic development to the autarchic and exclusivist economic development perspective of his opponent Pontchartrain.[64] Colbert de Torcy was also behind the publication in 1703 of *Les Intérêts de l'Angleterre mal entendus dans la guerre présente* written by the abbé Dubos, in which English-style political arithmetic was used to demonstrate the damage to the English interest of the Dutch alliance.[65] Advocating the use of commercial treaties to restore order in the international system, Dubos signalled that the Anglo-Dutch alliance, in contrast with the Navigation Acts, obstructed the development of a logically functioning international trade system in which the Dutch, rather than Spain and France, were Britain's natural enemies or competitors.[66]

In a similar way, another admirer of Colbert, Jean-François Melon, argued in 1734 that national wealth depended on relations with third countries, which had to be properly reciprocal and mutually beneficial. Calling for an abandonment of the post-Utrecht Franco-Dutch economic

[64] On the continuity between the two administrative, Jacob Soll, *The Information Master. Jean-Baptiste Colbert's Secret-State Intelligence System* (Ann Arbor: University of Michigan Press, 2009), 155–156.

[65] Jean-Baptiste Dubos, *Les Intérêts de l'Angleterre mal entendus dans la guerre présente* (Amsterdam [Paris]: Gallet, 1703). See Joseph Klaits, *Printed Propaganda under Louis XIV. Absolute Monarchy and Public Opinion* (Princeton, NJ: Princeton University Press, 1976), 174–183. Dubos' work was carefully studied by members of the Gournay group; see Antonella Alimento, 'Beyond the Treaty of Utrecht: Véron de Forbonnais's French Translation of the British Merchant (1753)', *History of European Ideas* 40 (2014), 1044–1066.

[66] Dubos, *Les Intérêts de l'Angleterre mal entendus*, 162–165.

relations that copied the unequal Ryswick treaty and the conclusion of commercial treaties with other states, including Britain, Melon's political economy might be understood as an attempt to realize what the Peace of Utrecht had failed to deliver.[67]

The Treaties of Utrecht and British Hegemony

In the advent of Utrecht and apparently influenced by a refusal on the part of the Dutch to negotiate independently of Britain, the outcome of the settlement shifted in a different direction. While the commercial treaties of Utrecht still contain the language of reciprocity, the dynamic they produced was notably different and formed a mosaic of political economic mechanisms that were adapted from previous models.[68]

The most famous and intensively studied of the commercial treaties of Utrecht, the 1713 Anglo-French agreement itself is best seen as a by-product to the lapse into traditional political usages of commercial treaties. Whether or not Britain or France stood to gain from the stipulations in the very treaty that integrated the two rival economies became the subject of heated discussion in 1713.[69] Yet, more fundamentally, the treaty was both the product of previous processes and the final part of a carefully orchestrated series of negotiations that successfully cashed in on the British victories of the War of the Spanish Succession, rather than being a victory of Tory 'free trade' principles.[70]

[67] Jean-François Melon, *Essai politique sur le commerce* (1734). See the chapter by Alimento in this volume and a forthcoming collection of essays by Alimento, Shovlin, and Stapelbroek on 'Commerce vs. Conquest'. On Melon as a neo-Colbertist, Istvan Hont, 'The Early Enlightenment Debate on Commerce and Luxury', in: *The Cambridge History of Eighteenth-Century Political Thought*, ed. Mark Goldie and Robert Wokler (Cambridge: Cambridge University Press, 2006), 379–418.

[68] Notably, the commercial treaties between France–Britain, France–United Provinces, Spain–Britain, Spain–Britain, Spain–United Provinces (see Table 1) seemed instruments of reciprocal normalization. An attentive reconstruction of the pre-history of the Utrecht settlement and the political economy of peace is the subject of a forthcoming article by the editors of this volume.

[69] Doohwan Ahn, 'The Anglo-French Treaty of Commerce of 1713: Tory Trade Politics and the Question of Dutch Decline', *History of European Ideas*, special issue, *Dutch Decline in Eighteenth-Century Europe* 36 (2010), 167–180. Also the chapter by Ahn in this volume.

[70] Coleman, 'Politics and Economics in the Age of Anne'.

The Anglo-French commercial treaty of 1713, as the concluding part of a more general set-up, relied heavily on the Anglo-Spanish and Franco-Dutch trade agreements. While France, through Article 6 of its peace treaty with Britain, was excluded from commerce with the Spanish colonies, Britain was not subjected to an equal obligation, and obtained both the *asiento* and the 'annual ship', allowing limited direct trade with Spanish America.

In fact, these privileges did not deliver great profits by themselves, but functioned to support a practice that almost justified British contraband trade and smuggling. When the *asiento* was first demanded by Matthew Prior in May 1711 it took the place of the previous demand for British *places de sécurités* in Spanish America.[71] In other words, the *asiento* was not seen as a profitable enterprise, as the French knew full well and had experienced themselves,[72] but as an access point to Spanish America. Likewise, the 'annual ship' was preferred by British negotiators over the most favoured nation treatment by Spain, the reasoning being that 'the right to be treated as the most favoured nation would be contested, and it could not be denied either to the Dutch or the French', while 'we will certainly gain more by contraband'.[73]

This selective appeal to the principles of international equality and mutuality, the official discourse of the Utrecht commercial treaties, facilitated between 1713 and 1740 a constant stream of renegotiations and violations of Spain's exclusive right to trade in its colonies. In the words of the future controller general of the finances, Étienne de Silhouette, who reflected on the problems with claims by British traders to be allowed to trade freely in parts of Spanish America presumably legitimated by the terms of the Peace of Utrecht, in 1740, the violations against the Spanish exclusive rights went directly against the reason why these rights were included in the Utrecht settlement: 'C'est la jalousie reciproque des

[71] *Mémoire contenant les articles dont l'Angleterre demandoit une decision avant que d'entrer en negociation*, AAE, Mémoires et Documents [MD] Angleterre 17, fos. 51–115: 57.

[72] As exemplified by Torcy writing to Mesnager, AAE, MD Angleterre 17, fos. 51–115: 81–81v.

[73] Quoted in Léon Vignols, 'L'asiento français (1701–1713) et anglais (1713–1750) et le commerce franco-espagnol vers 1700 à 1730', *Revue d'histoire économique et sociale* 17 (1929), 403–436: 412.

nations que a fait croire que ces conditions etoient necessaire pour maintenir en Europe la ballance du commerce.'[74]

The Utrecht system of trade was established at the cost of Spain in particular and to the benefit of Britain, which also regained the fiscal privileges it had previously obtained in 1667.[75] In fact, the most important aspects, the *asiento* and the 'annual ship', that were included in the 1713 Anglo-Spanish commercial arrangements were modelled on the Treaty of Barcelona of 1707 between Charles III and Britain, which was also echoed in Articles VIII and IX of the Anglo-French treaty.[76] These articles caused the controversies due to which they were not ratified by the British Parliament. The subsequent return to a tariff war until the signing of the Eden–Rayneval treaty fit with the idea that Britain and France were 'necessary enemies'.[77]

The incorporation of South American trade in the logic of the Utrecht system thus formed a continuation of the past.[78] The way in which the *asiento* was set to be exploited by Britain made it impossible, from 1710, to reach an agreement with Britain that somehow fits with the dual logic of the previous projects entertained by Mesnager, Bergeyck and Helvétius, based on the dissolution of European conflict through a neutralization or otherwise improved efficiency of the South American trade.[79]

Britain did not only succeed in obtaining privileges from Spain. In fact, the 1707 Treaty of Barcelona, much like the 1703 Methuen

[74] AAE, CP Angleterre 407, fos. 180–189: 187.

[75] See the chapter by Sanz and Guasti in this volume. Also A. Weindl, 'The Asiento de Negros and International Law', *Journal of the History of International Law* 10 (2008): 229–258.

[76] Guillaume de Lamberty, *Mémoires pour servir à l'histoire du XVIIIe siècle, contenant les négociations, traitez, résolutions et autres documents authentiques concernant les affaires d'État liez par une narration historique des principaux événemens dont ils ont été précédez ou suivis* (Amsterdam: Mortier, 1735–1740), iv: 192–197.

[77] See the chapter by Dupuy in this volume for the Eden treaty and bibliographical indications. Also below in this introductory chapter.

[78] Allan J. Kuethe and Kenneth J. Andrien, *The Spanish Atlantic World in the Eighteenth Century. War and the Bourbon Reforms, 1713–1796* (Cambridge: Cambridge University Press, 2014), 37–40.

[79] AAE, MD Angleterre 17, fos. 51–115: 57; Antonella Alimento, 'Entre liberté et protection: les enjeux économiques du traité de commerce franco-anglais d'Utrecht et la mission d'Anisson et Fénelon en Angleterre', in: *La paix d'Utrecht (1713). Enjeux économiques, maritimes et commerciaux*, ed. Lucien Bély, Géraud Poumarède and Guillaume Hanotin (Paris: Pedone, 2017).

Treaty with Portugal,[80] was a precursor to the diplomatic strategy of the end of the War of the Spanish Succession, when Britain negotiated to reinforce its maritime commercial hegemony at the expense of its Dutch allies. The conclusion of an unequal and malfunctioning Franco-Dutch commercial treaty in 1713, based on Ryswick rather than on the true reciprocity that Torcy and Mesnager had aimed for, further sustained Britain's lead in international trade over both France and the United Provinces.

The Balance of Power Rejected

When David Hume discussed the balance of power in his essay with that title, he alluded to the Geertruydenberg negotiations to argue that 'the maxim of preserving the balance of power' required the right national spirit and policies.[81] In contrast, the 'spirit of jealous emulation' held more sway in modern Britain than that of 'prudent views of modern politics' and had caused national 'excesses' that affected both Britain's liberty and 'the fate of Europe'.[82] In another essay, *Of the Balance of Trade*, Hume suggested that Britain was the victim of its own commercial policies:

> Our jealousy and our hatred of *France* are without bounds; and the former sentiment, at least, must be acknowledged reasonable and well-grounded. These passions have occasioned innumerable barriers and obstructions upon commerce, where we are accused of being commonly the aggressors. But what have we gained by the bargain?[83]

Hume's idea of the effectiveness of the balance of power as relying upon certain conditions that would be hard to satisfy was shared by the abbé de Saint-Pierre, who is famous for his proposal for a confederation of European states as the necessary political solution for creating a lasting

[80] Alan D. Francis, *The Methuens and Portugal 1691–1708* (Cambridge: Cambridge University Press, 1966), 205–211 for Dutch protestations. See also the chapter by Cardoso in this volume.

[81] David Hume, 'Of the Balance of Power', in: *Essays Moral, Political, and Literary*, ed. Eugene Miller (Indianapolis: Liberty Fund, 1985), 332–341: 337.

[82] Hume, 'Of the Balance of Power', 339–340.

[83] Hume, 'Of the Balance of Trade', 315.

peace. Yet, that plan, far from an unrealistic utopia unconnected to reality, was conceived in immediate response and was akin to the projects negotiated by Mesnager and Bergeyck. Early drafts of the *Projet pour rendre la paix perpetuelle en Europe* circulated from the end of 1708 and the work went into small print editions after the failure of the Geertruidenberg negotiations and the Tory victory in British politics.[84] The second edition of 1712 addressed the Dutch 'peace party' and copies of a second print run were offered to Torcy and sent for comment to Pierre-Daniel Huet, the author of the influential *Grand trésor historique et politique du florissant commerce des hollandois*.[85]

The diplomatic strategy behind the *Projet pour rendre la paix perpetuelle* was a curious one. Saint-Pierre proposed the specific scenario to Torcy in 1710 that if his work was published outside of France and was first embraced by Europe's smaller and neutral states, notably the United Provinces, these states were likely to subsequently force it as a peace solution onto France, at which point Britain too might be brought on board.[86]

In opposition to the Utrecht system that was being created, the full version of Saint-Pierre's *Projet* provided a sketch of his own system of 'permanent society'.[87] Its main aim was to secure 'the Advantages of Commerce' and do justice to the way humankind had originally been created.[88] This involved a radical downscaling of the tariff system that existed in Europe.[89] Saint-Pierre's conclusion was that 'permanent society' required a permanent political structure (which would

[84] Charles Irénée Castel de Saint-Pierre, *Projet pour renderre la paix perpetuelle en Europe* (Utrecht, 1713–1717), 3 vols.; translated (and abbreviated) as *A Project for Settling an Everlasting Peace in Europe First Proposed by Henry IV of France* (London, 1714), references both the 1714 English and 1713–1717 French editions; I: ii/i–ii. [= French 1713–1717/English 1714].

[85] Maria Grazia Bottaro Palumbo, 'La Genesi dei "Mémoires pour rendre la paix perpetuelle en Europe" dell'abate di Saint-Pierre', in: *Studi politici in onore di Luigi Firpo*, ed. Silvia Rota Ghibaudi and Franco Barcia (Milan: Franco Angeli, 1990), ii: 561–588: 570. On Huet and the Franco-Dutch treaty see the chapter by Stapelbroek in this volume.

[86] MAAE, MD France 308, cc. 260r–263r; see Bottaro Palumbo, 'La Genesi dei "Mémoires"', 572–574.

[87] Saint-Pierre, *Project for settling an everlasting peace*, I: ii/i–ii

[88] Saint-Pierre, *Project for settling an everlasting peace*, I: 1–22/pp. 1–9.

[89] Saint-Pierre, *Project for settling an everlasting peace*, I: 120–121/pp. 324–325.

have Utrecht as its '*Ville de l'Assemblée*'[90]) that transcended sovereign power. Saint-Pierre appealed to the proper interest of the Dutch and British Protestant 'Allies of the House of Austria' to prevent 'that which is now treating at Utrecht' from producing a political equilibrium that kept commerce subservient to power.[91]

Saint-Pierre's work included some more (rather imprecise) suggestions concerning the European management of global commerce. Considering the pacification of interstate relations on a global scale Saint-Pierre first declared he could see a different version of his design in which extra-European states could join his 'permanent society'. While he chose not to present this cosmopolitan vision, in the preface he anticipated as an obvious and easily realizable by-product of the creation of his European union the establishment of a 'General Council' of European trade in the Indies that would neutralize relations among European traders and with native sovereigns in the Indies to make global trade more profitable and secure.[92]

Throughout his political works Saint-Pierre distinguished two categories for the organization of European affairs, 'the system of an equilibrium between two superior powers, and the system of the European diet'.[93] Next to the balance of power, which included a double hierarchy of allied states forming two military-political sides, his own system of a unified European system protected the sovereign equality of smaller states without an in-built hierarchy of protective power. Vaguely analogous to Schomberg's distinction between 'a good treaty of commerce' and its

[90] Saint-Pierre, *Project for settling an everlasting peace*, I: 359–364; II: 292–293/pp. 134–136, 151.

[91] Saint-Pierre, *Project for settling an everlasting peace*, I: 35–36/p. 14, I: xviii–xix, pp. 27–28/vii–viii, p. 11.

[92] Saint-Pierre, *Project for settling an everlasting peace*, I: xx–xxi, II: 316–319/ix, pp. 160–161: Saint-Pierre promised to explain how this Asiatic Union might function next to a European political confederacy: 'and I may some time or other prove, in another Part, that it will be much more easily formed than the European Society' (II: 319/161). Similar projects for neutralizing trade were put forward later in the century; see the chapters by Shovlin and Stapelbroek in this volume.

[93] Charles-Irénée Castel de Saint-Pierre, 'Observations sur les dernières paix', in: *Ouvrajes de politique* (Rotterdam, 1737), xi: 317–332: 321. Also 'Comparaison entre le sistême de l'Equilibre des deux principales Puissances, & le sistême de la Diète Europaine', in: *Ouvrajes de politique* (Rotterdam, 1735), x: 260–264; 'Inconvénians du sistême de l'Equilibre & Avantages du sistême de la Diète Europaine', in *Ouvrajes de politique* (Rotterdam, 1734), viii: 156–234.

'bad' counterpart, Saint-Pierre contrasted his own 'System of Equilibrium' with the 'present System of War' and its illusive faith in the 'Chimerical Equilibrium' of the balance of power:[94]

> I found that all those Means consisted in making mutual Promises, either in Treaties of Commerce, of Truce, of Peace, wherein Limits of Dominion, and other reciprocal Pretentions are regulated; or else in Treaties of Guarantie, or of League offensive and defensive, to establish, to maintain, or to re-establish the *Equilibrium of Power* between the Principal Houses; a System which hitherto seems to be the highest Degree of Prudence, that the Sovereigns of Europe, or their Ministers ever carried their Policy to.[95]

The same fundamental scepticism about commercial treaties and the balance of power remained widespread in the 1740s and 1750s, when it sparked new policies. In this period, following the death of Cardinal de Fleury, France decided not to renew the commercial treaty with the United Provinces in the late 1740s, issued only a formal declaration that confirmed previous agreements with Denmark in 1749 rather than a new treaty, refused to renegotiate with Britain the 1713 treaty, only consented in 1753 to a convention of trade with Prussia rather than a treaty, and finally, in 1760, cancelled its treaty with Hamburg.[96]

The general decline in treaty-making in the 1740s and 1750s was influenced by the rise in France of the Gournay school of political economy, which sought different strategies for turning France into a commercial monarchy and create a balance of trade. Parallel to this development, the abbé Mably also analysed the legacy of Utrecht. A diplomat himself, participating in the Breda talks in 1746 to end the War of the Austrian Succession, Mably's *Droit public de L'Europe fondé sur les Traités* of 1744 and 1746 affirmed that commercial patterns had become an object of autonomous discussion at peace negotiations only since Utrecht. In his *Principes* (1757), Mably criticized the way treaties were used to create

[94] Saint-Pierre, *Project for settling an everlasting peace*, I: vi–vii, xii, xix/iii–iv, v, viii and *passim*.

[95] Saint-Pierre, *Project for settling an everlasting peace*, I: iv–v/ii–iii.

[96] See Alimento's chapter in this volume; Cavarzere's chapter on Prussia illustrates this general tendency, while Storr's shows a parallel development—the avoidance of commercial treaties to prevent economic subordination—in Piedmont.

unequal trade conditions between citizens of different states and advocated that peace talks went accompanied by the signing of simple general conventions 'propres à assurer la liberté des mers et de la navigation'.[97] Commercial concessions reduced the sovereign independence of a state: '[the King] n'est plus maître des lois de son commerce, et il devient le tributaire de l'industrie et de l'activité de ses voisins'.[98] In his works, Mably suggested at various points that the example of the British Navigation Acts served the purposes of that state and might also serve France, in support of its own maritime commercial development and to get rid of the dependence on the Dutch carrying trade. Mably's model of British commercial sovereignty overlapped with Montesquieu's famous analysis of British liberty in the *Esprit des lois* which concluded that the British 'supremely jealous with respect to trade, [. . .] bind themselves but little by treaties, and depend only on their own laws'.[99]

These analyses of the independent sovereign foundations of Britain's commercial hegemony that were subsequently consolidated *through* commercial treaties at Utrecht chimed with the eighteenth- and nineteenth-century commonplace of the 'two Britains', which was also shared by David Hume. Although Britain's 'constitution', its incorporation of trade and financial interests into its political decision-making architecture, was superior to other states and a model for them, it sparked a fanaticism and greed that diverted global trade away from its proper channels and meant other states were forced to counteract the system Britain had created to sustain its hegemony. Like the abbé de Saint-Pierre considered Utrecht a moment of missed opportunity, the French publicist Jacob-Nicolas Moreau, in his *L'Observateur hollandais* (1755–1759) and the many volumes of his *Memoires pour servir à l'histoire de notre tems* (1757–1761), explained the origins of the Seven Years' War as lying in the British design of the Peace of Utrecht that created a situation in which underneath a formal political balance in reality there was a plan for commercial empire. With the possessions Britain gained in the Mediterranean

[97] Gabriel Bonnot de Mably, *Des Principes des Négociations pour servir d'Introduction au Droit Public de l'Europe, fondé sur les Traités* (The Hague: 1757), chapter 17, 'Des Traités de commerce. Digression sur le luxe', 231–241: 234.

[98] Bonnot de Mably, 'Des Traités de commerce. Digression sur le luxe', 234.

[99] Charles de Secondat, baron de Montesquieu, *The Spirit of Laws* (London, 1750), Book XX, Chapter 7.

and the Americas a global system of trade was created that meant that 'the whole of Europe only worked to enrich them'.[100]

While Moreau was a propagandist paid by the Foreign Ministry and weakly affiliated with the Gournay circle, the legacy of the Utrecht commercial treaties was most systematically examined by one of its key members, Véron de Forbonnais. He did so in a French translation of *The British Merchant, or Commerce Preserved*, a selection of articles originally published in a periodical that appeared after the signing of the Utrecht commercial treaties, and which he turned into three stand-alone editions that appeared in 1721, 1743 and 1748. Its three volumes displayed the British skill in using commercial treaties to undermine the economies of the very nations with which they established ties. Forbonnais' translation of 1753 made its French audience aware of the adroitness with which the British nation pursued its economic interests.[101]

Forbonnais was not just a theorist of political economy, but had first-hand knowledge of the attempts to settle the Anglo-French Acadia border dispute to prevent the outbreak of the Seven Years' War. As a theorist with experience of British politics, he was thoroughly distrustful of attempts at economic integration with Britain through treaties, as these would not create any genuine reciprocity, but at best relay privileges on each side to confirm the existing balance of trade. Like Melon, who had, however, still argued for Anglo-French economic integration through a commercial treaty, Forbonnais believed internal fiscal and economic reforms and the role of third-party neutral states were crucial in restoring balance in the interstate system.

That same awareness inspired the political economy of the Gournay group in general, whose ideas were perfectly in tune with the decision not to renew the commercial treaty with the United Provinces following the War of the Austrian Succession. While that agreement had not been reciprocal as an integral part of the Utrecht system that disadvantaged both France and the United Provinces, Vincent Gournay and his disciples lobbied for a French Navigation Act in order to compete with Britain by following the same strategy of direct trade and investment in colonial territories, creating an internal global

[100] Jacob-Nicolas Moreau, *L'Observateur hollandois* (Paris [The Hague], 1755–1756), Letter 1, 20, *passim*. Koen Stapelbroek, 'Il sistema di Utrecht, il sistema di Vattel: attraverso *L'Observateur hollandois* di Jacob-Nicolas Moreau', *Rivista Storica Italiana* (forthcoming). Also the chapter by Stapelbroek in this volume.

[101] Alimento, 'Beyond the Treaty of Utrecht'.

imperial market revolving around France. Their campaign involved the translation of British works like Gee's *Trade and Navigation of Great Britain Considered* (translated by Montesquieu's son),[102] support by the *Chambre de Commerce* of Dunkerque,[103] and meant a return to the vision first developed by the abbé Dubos now continued by the chevalier de Vivens.[104]

A different course of action from other members of the Gournay group was advocated by Forbonnais, who endorsed the commercial treaties concluded with the Hanseatic League (1716), Sweden (1741) and Denmark (1742/9) as a way to defend the neutrality of trade in wartime and create a regime of 'liberté et concurrence'. Within Forbonnais' system neutral states—including the no longer especially privileged United Provinces—competed for the French carrying trade and France could reform itself, instating a modest tariff vis-à-vis Britain, to restore the balance of trade and the balance of power.[105]

Another field where the post-Utrecht hesitation of the 1740s and 1750s to conclude commercial treaties did not occur (as was also observed by Keene, see above) was that of treaties with Mediterranean states. Similar to how Saint-Pierre imagined states in North Africa and the Levant as associate members of his European union, so France concluded commercial treaties with Tunis (1742) and Tripoli (1752), with Britain following suit with agreements with Tunis (1751/62), Algiers (1762) and Morocco (1760).[106]

[102] Joshua Gee, *Considérations sur le commerce et la navigation de la Grande-Bretagne* (Geneva: Philibert, 1750); see Antonella Alimento, 'La concurrence comme politique moderne: la contribution de l'école de Gournay à la naissance d'une sphère publique dans la France des années 1750–1760', in: *L'économie politique et la sphère publique dans le débat des Lumières*, ed. Jesús Astigarraga and Javier Usoz (Madrid: Casa de Velázquez, 2013), 213–227.

[103] *Mémoire sur le cabotage* in AN, AE, B/III/461.

[104] François de Labat, chevalier de Vivens, *Observations sur divers moyens de soutenir et d'encourager l'agriculture, principalement dans la Guyenne, où l'on traite des cultures propres à cette Province, et des obstacles qui les empêchent de s'étendre* (1756).

[105] Antonella Alimento, 'Competition, True Patriotism and Colonial Interest: Forbonnais' Vision of Neutrality and Trade', in *Trade and War*, ed. Stapelbroek, 61–94; Thierry Demals and Alexandra Hyard, 'Forbonnais, the Two Balances and the Economistes', *European Journal History of Economic Thought* 22 (2015), 445–472.

[106] See the chapter by Storrs in this volume for the argument that the Mediterranean remained an important part of the balance of trade.

The alternatives to counter the Utrecht system proposed by Gournay and Forbonnais gave way after Gournay's death in 1759 to the rise of physiocracy and a return to a vision closer to Saint-Pierre's pacifist union. Significantly, the Marquis de Mirabeau, whose 'pre-physiocratic' *Ami des hommes* advocated a 'traité de fraternité' whereby Europe's commercial states united to combat Britain and liberate Europe,[107] was convinced by François Quesnay 'to stop thinking of commerce as a state of war' and to follow the dictate of 'the natural order of commerce, wherein no motive for war nor any reservation in peace treaties can be found'.[108] This was of course no trivial pacifism, but merely an ambitious vision of turning politics into economics in which all impediments to free trade were violations of *L'Ordre naturel et essentiel des sociétés politiques*, as was the title of Le Mercier de la Rivière's physiocratic manifesto of 1767 in which he attacked the balance of power, as a self-contradictory 'projet de diviser des Puissances pour les forcer, les unes par les autres, à vivre en paix'.[109] According to the physiocratic doctrine of the 1760s there were no 'good treaties'. The notion of the balance of power and all commercial treaties were fundamentally incompatible with peace and belonged squarely to the category of 'false politics' that was characterized by 'guerres de commerce'.[110]

[107] Victor Riquetti de Mirabeau, *L'Ami des hommes* (Avignon, 1756–1760), part 3, Chapter 5, 107, 126–128, 137, 159, 208 suggests 'l'industrie et le travail' of all commercial nations should be united to oppose British aggression; see Henry C. Clark, *Compass of Society. Commerce and Absolutism in Old Regime France* (Lanham, MD: Lexington, 2007), 161–166; Michael Sonenscher, *Before the Deluge. Public Debt, Inequality, and the Intellectual Origins of the French Revolution* (Princeton: Princeton University Press, 2007). Finally, Isaac Nakhimovsky, 'The 'Ignominious Fall of the European Commonwealth: Gentz, Hauterive, and the Armed Neutrality of 1800', in: *Trade and War*, ed. Stapelbroek, 212–228 for the revival of Mirabeau's project by Hauterive.

[108] François Quesnay, 'Du commerce. Premier dialogue entre M^r. H et M^r. N.', in: *Œuvres économiques complètes et autres textes*, ed. Christine Théré, Loïc Charles and Jean Claude Perrot (Paris: INED, 2005), ii: 903–944: 929, 940; Quesnay, 'Remarques sur l'opinion de l'auteur de l'Esprit des Loix concernant les colonies',ii, 869–879: 878.

[109] Pierre-Paul Mercier de la Rivière, *L'Ordre naturel et essentiel des sociétés politiques* (London: Nourse, 1767), i: 236–237.

[110] For a clear statement, see the review by abbé Baudeau of Isaac de Pinto's Letter on the Jealousy of Commerce in the *Éphémérides du Citoyen* 10 (1771), 67, 98.

Commercial Treaties Rediscovered

Following the Seven Years' War a change of preferences in France would again influence approaches to the balance of power in Europe. Under the direction of the Duke de Choiseul, Louis XV's dominant minister and the architect of the diplomatic revolution that turned Austria into a French ally, commercial treaties were rediscovered as instruments of international politics. From 1759, Choiseul had looked to Spain as the crucial piece in the puzzle for saving 'le commerce de l'Europe' from 'l'ambition angloise dans la partie de l'Amérique' and for resisting in general the hegemony of its 'empire de la mer'.[111] Although Spain was a useless ally in wartime Choiseul hoped that a commercial alliance with France that included commercial advantages for France would serve to keep both states among the ranks of the 'commercial powers' and not let both of them irreversibly slip away to the level of Austria, Russia and Prussia. In August 1761 Choiseul signed the Bourbon Family Compact, which left the exact commercial arrangements open until 1765.[112]

In that year, in which Spain reformed its colonial trade by abolishing the Cadiz monopoly,[113] Choiseul ordered the abbé Beliardi to fix the commercial dimension of the Family Compact. Beliardi's own conviction was that France, Spain and Naples together could form an integrated self-sufficient economy that could undermine British maritime trade and industry. Beliardi thus contemplated a closed commercial block that could also include Venice and whose commerce would be regulated through a Mediterranean Navigation Act that would drive out the states of the North.[114]

Choiseul's own version of the plan was less aggressively isolationist and aimed at creating the preconditions that would guarantee commercial reciprocity, rather than subordination to Britain. Choiseul

[111] *Recueil des instructions données aux ambassadeurs et ministres de France depuis les traités de Westphalie jusqu'à la Révolution française*, vol. 12bis, *Espagne* (Paris: Félix Alcan, 1899), iii: 348–353.

[112] Allan Christelow, 'French Interest in the Spanish Empire During the Ministry of the Duc de Choiseul', *Hispanic American Historical Review* 21 (1941), 515–537: 521.

[113] See the chapter by Sanz and Guasti in this volume.

[114] *Recueil des pieces et mémoires [...] au sujet de la rupture de l'Espagne avec la cour de Londres et [...] le bien du commerce et des interets de la France et de l'Espagne*, BNF, FF 10770, fos. 153–207: 183; *Mémoire pour l'Espagne*, BNF, FF 10766, fos. 141–168.

recognized that the Family Compact had played a fundamental role in creating peace in 1763. A project of the time favoured by Choiseul explained that its power as a commercial treaty lay in the fact that it helped 'create new branches of commerce, favour agriculture and increase population' in Spain, France and Naples much more effectively than any project of perpetual peace or free trade could.[115] On this basis, Choiseul did not exclude the possibility of a commercial treaty with Britain, which in 1767 materialized in a French diplomatic mission to London to discuss Article II of the Treaty of Paris. That article, which stipulated the renewal of the Anglo-French commercial treaty of Utrecht, had been included by Bedford in 1763 on the presupposition of British commercial hegemony, yet by 1767 Choiseul was confident of having found a way to turn things around.

Choiseul's project was accompanied by a reorientation towards colonial possessions, from a focus on territory to economic productivity and population growth.[116] As part of the same vision Choiseul initiated the establishment of an all-white colony in Guyana without slave labour, in emulation of the British colonies that he believed had helped it win the Seven Years' War.[117] Rather than enforcing the territorial stipulations of Utrecht—through which Spain claimed the Falkland Islands[118]—Choiseul focused on Mediterranean trade, where the acquisition of Corsica in 1768 and the project of linking the free ports of Marseille and Trieste turned Austria into an associate member of the economic Bourbon family, thus actively reducing the market for British goods.

In 1766, when Russia signed a commercial treaty with Britain, Choiseul's diplomatic plan for a global commercial equilibrium was formalized as a treatise of political economy by Jacques Accarias de Sérionne, whose *Les intérêts des nations de l'Europe, développés relativement au commerce* was

[115] *Mémoire sur les avantages que le Pacte de Famille peut donner à la France et à l'Espagne pour le rétablissement de la marine et du commerce maritime*, BNF, FF 10767, fos. 231–256.

[116] Hamish M. Scott, 'Choiseul et le Troisième Pacte de Famille', in: *La présence des Bourbons en Europe (XIV–XIXe siècles)*, ed. Lucien Bély (Paris: PUF, 2003), 207–220: 217.

[117] On Guyana, Christopher Hodson, '"A Bondage So Harsh": Acadian Labor in the French Caribbean, 1763–1766', *Early American Studies* 5 (2007), 95–131 and *The Acadian Diaspora: An Eighteenth-Century History* (Oxford: Oxford University Press, 2012).

[118] Louis Blart, *Les Rapports de la France et de l'Espagne après le pacte de famille jusqu'à la fin du ministère du duc de Choiseul* (Paris: Félix Alcan, 1915), 88.

dedicated to Catherine the Great.[119] Sérionne's work, published in Leiden by Luzac, can be read as an invitation to all European states to join Choiseul's scheme for an interstate system based on the balance of trade. If each nation refrained from aspiring to a favourable balance and trade in India were restructured according to the neutrality of European trade, Choiseul's plan could convert jealousy of trade into pacific emulation. According to Sérionne, the quest for the balance of power on its own had caused rather than prevented conflict. The only way to establish a lasting equilibrium was to create an international economy in which states exploited their natural and cultural resources, which meant for instance that Spain and Portugal had to be agricultural economies and not attempt to be manufacturing exporters. Key to the realization of the plan was the conclusion of a commercial treaty between the two main manufacturing economies, Britain and France.[120]

Another expression of the same vision was the *Histoire des deux Indes*, published by Guillaume-Thomas Raynal from 1770 and sponsored by Choiseul. Raynal too emphasized that there should be a complementarity between 'cultivating nations' and 'manufacturers', with Spain as a main colonial power having to act upon its duty to produce cinnamon, coffee, sugar and work the mines, while a treaty of commerce between France and Britain was likewise deemed a precondition for peace.[121]

Commercial Integration and the Republican Navigation Act

Choiseul's project appears to have been continued by Charles Gravier, Count of Vergennes in the 1770s and 1780s, but with some modifications. Vergennes initiated the signing, between 1774 and 1787, of commercial

[119] The dedication may have implied the suggestion that Russia, which had been approached by Choiseul in 1761 as a prospective neutral carrier of French goods, should join the plan rather than become a British ally in the balance of power.

[120] Jacques Accarias de Sérionne, *Les intérêts des nations de l'Europe, développés relativement au commerce* (Leiden: Luzac, 1766).

[121] Antonella Alimento, 'Accarias de Sérionne, Raynal et le Pacte de Famille', in: *Autour de l'Abbé Raynal. Genèse et enjeux politiques de l'Histoire de deux Indes*, ed. Antonella Alimento and Gianluigi Goggi (Ferney-Voltaire: Centre international d'étude du XVIIIe siècle, 2017).

treaties with the United States (1778), Sweden (1784), Spain (1786), Portugal (1786), Russia (1787) and most famously the Eden–Rayneval treaty with Britain (1786). In addition, a treaty of defensive alliance including a commercial section was agreed with the United Provinces in 1785. Vergennes also continued the Family Compact vision in some way, as in 1778 Spain acceded to the treaties between France and the United States without negotiations. Interestingly, and in contrast to Choiseul, the Family Compact would be defended by Pierre-Samuel Dupont de Nemours, in line with government policy, as an open community of mutual privileges that could be joined by any other state.[122] While Choiseul's system of balance and his Mediterranean vision, next to the Bourbon core members, included Austria, Vergennes was wary of including it as an ally in his system.[123] Finally, Choiseul's strong economic profiling of states as agricultural or industrial nations was not part of Vergennes' politics.

Vergennes' policies were defended by a number of second-generation physiocrats, including the complicated figure of Dupont de Nemours, who fervently defended the Eden–Rayneval treaty.[124] Whereas earlier physiocracy rejected all commercial treaties as manifestations of the 'system of false politics' and 'guerres de commerce', the new generation was ambivalent or moved to the mainstream of French politics. Reflecting this shift, the *Encyclopédie méthodique*'s entry on 'Balance du commerce' still dogmatically differentiated between the three positions of Melon, Hume and Mercier de la Rivière, rejecting the first two as 'vulgar' and confused,[125] while the entry on 'Traité' from 1788 contrasted treaties that were and were not in accordance with the law of nature and the principles of equality and free trade.

[122] Pierre-Samuel Dupont de Nemours, *Le pacte de famille et les Conventions subséquentes entre la France & l'Espagne, avec des Observations sur chaque article* (Paris, 1790).

[123] Orville T. Murphy, *Charles Gravier, comte de Vergennes. French Diplomacy in the Age of Revolution* (Albany: SUNY Press, 1983); Thomas E. Kaiser, 'The Austrian Alliance, the Seven Years' War and the Emergence of a French "National" Foreign Policy, 1756–1790', in: *The Crisis of the Absolute Monarchy. France from Old Regime to Revolution*, ed. Julian Swann and Joël Félix (Oxford: Oxford University Press, 2013), 167–179.

[124] Pierre-Samuel Dupont de Nemours, *Lettre à la chambre du commerce de Normandie, sur le Mémoire qu'elle a publié relativement au traité de commerce avec l'Angleterre* (Rouen: Moutard, 1788).

[125] *Encyclopédie méthodique, Commerce* (Paris, 1783), i: 166–179.

It recognized the 1786 Eden–Rayneval treaty as a rare example amidst a history of chimerical politics in which the modern states that seemed commercially able 'sont encore peu avancées sur la théorie des traités de commerce'.[126]

While debate about Vergennes' commercial politics and its implementation in France tended to ask whether the Eden–Rayneval treaty was not harmful to France because it was too liberal,[127] in Britain critics of William Pitt the Younger's strategy saw it as a continuation of past practices. It has been suggested that the Eden–Rayneval treaty was in fact not just a stand-alone project but part of a wider strategy by Pitt to use treaties to continue British hegemony. Between 1785 and 1793 Pitt attempted to conclude commercial treaties with Portugal, Spain, Russia, Poland, Morocco, the United States, Prussia, Naples, the Dutch Republic, Sweden, the Ottoman Empire and Austria, but with very limited success, while Portuguese imports of Irish wool under the conditions of the Methuen treaty complicated relations with Ireland.[128] Continuing a line of argument that had emerged in the Seven Years' War about the reform of Britain's maritime imperial system,[129] a group of writers associated with Lansdowne, the Earl of Shelburne, known as the Bowood Circle criticized Pitt's commercial politics.[130]

If on a military–political scale Pitt seemed successful in creating something of a pseudo Family Compact with Prussia and the United Provinces in the later 1780s, these writers argued that British politics

[126] *Encyclopédie méthodique, Économie politique et diplomatique* (Paris, 1788), iv: 353–549.

[127] J. Holland Rose, 'The Franco-British Commercial Treaty of 1786', *English Historical Review* 23 (1908), 709–724; also the chapter by Dupuy in this volume.

[128] John Ehrman, *The British Government and Commercial Negotiations with Europe 1783–1793* (Cambridge: Cambridge University Press, 1962).

[129] Daniel A. Baugh, 'Maritime Strength and Atlantic Commerce: The Uses of "a Grand Marine Empire"', in: *An Imperial State at War. Britain from 1689 to 1815*, ed. Lawrence Stone (London: Routledge, 1994), 185–223; cf. Steve Pincus, *The Heart of the Declaration: The Founders' Case for an Activist Government* (New Haven: Yale University Press, 2017). Also the chapter by John Shovlin in this volume.

[130] Nigel Aston and Clarissa Campbell Orr, eds., *An Enlightenment Statesman in Whig Britain. Lord Shelburne in Context, 1737–1805* (Woodbridge: Boydell & Brewer, 2011); Stephen Conway, 'Bentham versus Pitt: Jeremy Bentham and British Foreign Policy 1789', *Historical Journal* 30 (1987), 791–809.

was self-contradictory and formed a 'system of Machiavellism'.[131] The phrase was coined by Jeremy Bentham, whose own 'Plan for an Universal and Perpetual Peace' was based on a contrast between Britain's Hanoverian continental politics including the Prussian alliance, which he detested, and a course of action that was pro-Russian, yet without any need or desire ('better no arrangements at all') for a commercial treaty with Catherine the Great.[132] International trade was central to Shelburne and Bentham's vision. Although the Eden–Rayneval treaty was maybe a step in the right direction (Shelburne did not hesitate to call it 'perfectly agreeable to my principles'[133]) it was much too limited and did not break down established monopolies or promote reciprocal trade. What was required both to create the foundation for a lasting peace and to reform Britain's national economy was a new system of international relations based on the neutrality of trade. From 1782–1783 onwards Shelburne promoted at various points the creation of a periodical entitled 'the Neutralist', which was to be edited by Jeremy Bentham, Richard Price or the abbé Morellet.[134] One problem with Britain's 'mercantile system'—Bentham shared Smith's vision on this—was that the Navigation Acts and the subsequent strategy of commercial treaty-making had created a fanatic belief in the possibility of competing on the global market beyond its own natural and cultural resources.[135] Shelburne was equally critical of commercial treaties as hindrances to peace and claimed, in line with this logic that 'a peace is good in the exact proportion that it recognizes [. . .] the great principle of free trade'.[136] Anxious that some 'secret little motive' to sabotage parliamentary approval might be operated, he was

[131] Conway, 'Bentham versus Pitt', 802.

[132] Conway, 'Bentham versus Pitt', 799–800.

[133] Richard Price, *Letters To and From, 1767–1790* (Cambridge: Wilson, 1903), 98. In the same letter, 22 November 1786, he approved of the US–Prussian 1785 commercial treaty.

[134] Conway, 'Bentham versus Pitt', 794; Price, *Letters*, 99–100; Lord Fitzmaurice, *Life of William, Earl of Shelburne* (London, 1912), ii: 306–308.

[135] Proposition III of Jeremy Bentham, 'A Plan for an Universal and Perpetual Peace, Essay IV, Principles of International Law', in: *The Works of Jeremy Bentham*, ed. John Bowring (Edinburgh: William Tait, 1843), ii: 535–540.

[136] Fitzmaurice, *Life of Shelburne*, ii: 220.

puzzled when in 1786 the 'French treaty' was set to include 'the principles of Arm'd neutrality'.[137]

Those principles had been formulated by Catherine the Great in 1780, during the War of American Independence when she launched the initiative of the League of Armed Neutrality.[138] The political theory behind the principles remains elusive but was discussed indirectly by Ferdinando Galiani in 1782, in support of the Neapolitan accession to the League.[139] However, if one part of the commercial treaties concluded during the 1780s can be ascribed to Vergennes' efforts, and a few other treaties to Pitt's, there remain a number of other commercial treaties between states that participated in the League (particularly Russia) whose language resembled the discourse of equality that was central to the League. For states like Naples and Portugal, the armed neutrality signalled a way out of a balance of power where they were forced to play the role of an economic auxiliary. From the point of view of British and French advocates of economic integration through the balance of power (which would produce the Vergennes treaties, including the Eden–Rayneval agreement) it looked like a staged Austrian–Russian attempt to overhaul the existing global trade system.[140]

Bentham's use of Saint-Pierre's phrase of 'Perpetual Peace' came at a moment of perceived crisis, just as Immanuel Kant would use it in the midst of the French Revolution. In the same way the Chevalier d'Hénin, posing as the translator of the 'Marquis Galliani' (Ferdinando Galiani's brother) revisited the issue of treaty-making with extra-European states in his *Mémoire concernant le système de paix et de guerre que les Puissances européennes pratiquent à l'égard*

[137] Price, *Letters*, 98–99.

[138] On the diplomatic emergence of the armed neutrality, Isabel de Madariaga, *Britain, Russia and the Armed Neutrality of 1780. Sir James Harris's Mission to St. Petersburg During the American Revolution* (London: Hollis & Carter, 1962).

[139] Koen Stapelbroek, 'The Progress of Humankind in Galiani's *Dei Doveri dei Principi Neutrali*: Natural Law, Neapolitan Trade and Catherine the Great', in: *Trade and War*, ed. Stapelbroek, 161–183.

[140] Honoré-Gabriel de Riquetti de Mirabeau, *Doutes sur la Liberté de l'Escaut: reclamé par l'Empereur* (London, 1784). Also the chapter by Stapelbroek in this volume.

des Régences barbaresques, in 1787. Invoking Saint-Pierre's distinction between a 'system of war' and 'system of peace' Hénin argued that separate treaties by France and Britain with North African states precluded the possibility of a general peace. The only solution was a European–North African multilateral agreement. A Europe that united in this respect, parallel to what the League of Armed Neutrality purported to do, would civilize itself along with its extra-European treaty partners.[141]

While international political crisis intensified in the 1790s the entire range of available options for regulating global trade and European peace had been presented in previous decades. Thus, with the system designed by Vergennes in the background, the collected works by Mably in 1794–1795 restated his view that even commerce with the enemy should not be stopped in wartime, while Forbonnais in 1796 republished his *Elémens du commerce* as a sceptical statement about free trade and commercial treaties.[142] Yet, Republican France opted, in September 1793, for a Navigation Act that connected France and her colonies and all other republican states in a system of 'commercial diplomacy'.[143] Based on the earlier projects advocated by Gournay and the early Mirabeau, the republican system sparked a debate about the relative merits of a (Russian-led) League of Armed Neutrality versus a (French-led) Republican Navigation Act system that included the neutral powers of the continent.[144] As these scenarios were discussed and crisis escalated, they were to give way to the Continental System. The time had effectively passed to defend the conception of commercial neutrality of Vergennes' system of the 1780s along with Mably, as the article 'Europe' in the *Dictionnaire universel* in Year VIII attempted.[145]

[141] Étienne-Félix Hénin de Cuvillers, *Mémoire concernant le système de paix et de guerre que les Puissances européennes pratiquent à l'égard des Régences barbaresques* (Venice, 1787).

[142] Gabriel Bonnot de Mably, 'Le Droit public de l'Europe fondé sur les Traités', in: *Collection complète des œuvres de l'abbé de Mably* (Paris: Desbriere, 1794–1795), v: 61.

[143] See the chapter by Belissa in this volume.

[144] Nakhimovsky, 'The 'Ignominious Fall of the European Commonwealth'.

[145] *Dictionnaire universel de la géographie commerçante* (Paris: 1799–1800), iv: 36–99.

It was out of this meltdown of the international political system that the Congress of Vienna put together a new state system, the ingredients of which were all very familiar to participants of the later eighteenth-century debate about peace and trade. If the ultimate attempt to get rid of the balance of power had involved a declared rejection of commercial treaties, the nineteenth century hailed them as instruments for regulating relations between states on the grounds of principles that sounded like those defended by the Bowood circle and Vergennes. These principles had been accepted by Friedrich von Gentz, Gerard de Rayneval and others whose treatises became the new orthodoxy. This did not mean that entrenched commercial structures in the global economy could easily, or at all, be reformed.[146] In this sense it was logical that French writers like Ambroise Marie Arnould during the revolutionary period looked back to the history of the balance of trade to understand how the system might be transformed or overcome.[147] The big question remained whether the new official discourse of international trade was also matched in practice by a reform of what Adam Smith had called the 'mercantile system'. Here David Ricardo, as we saw, criticized the conclusion of commercial treaties in his time as a continuation of an earlier tradition—one that had been innovatively scrutinized in all of its aspects, in theory and practice, during the eighteenth century.

[146] See the chapter by Cheney in this volume. Likewise French–American trade after 1778 created no new trade patterns: Paul Cheney, 'A False Dawn for Enlightenment Cosmopolitanism? Franco-American Trade during the American War of Independence', *William and Mary Quarterly* 3/62 (2006), 463–488.

[147] Ambroise Marie Arnould, *Système maritime et politique des Européens: pendant le dix-huitième siècle; fondé sur leurs traités* de *paix, de commerce et de navigation* (Paris: 1797); *De la Balance du Commerce et des Relations Commerciales Extérieures de la France, dans Toutes les Parties du Globe* (Paris: 1791).

Table 1 Commercial treaties concluded 1641–1800

1641–1650

State	*Year*	*With*, Type	*Details*
SPAIN	1645	DENMARK *Comm*	3 February, Madrid Ratification treaty of commerce concluded in Madrid on 20 March 1641
	1648	UNITED PROVINCES *Comm, Navig*	30 January, Münster Treaty of peace and commerce; separate article on navigation and commerce
		HANSEATIC LEAGUE *Comm*	24 June Treaty of commerce following Treaty of Münster of 11 September 1647
	1650	HANSEATIC LEAGUE *Comm*	12 August, Hamburg Treaty of commerce following Treaty of Münster of 11 September 1647
		UNITED PROVINCES *Comm, Navig, Mar*	17 December, The Hague Treaty explicating separate article of Münster, 4 February 1648
UNITED PROVINCES	1649	(VOC and) ATJEH *Comm*	6/9 November, Tijco Agreement
ENGLAND	1642	PORTUGAL *Comm*	29 January, London Articles of peace and commerce
1651–1660			
ENGLAND	1654	SWEDEN *Comm*	11 April, Uppsala Treaty of amity and commerce, followed by a convention, Uppsala, 8 May
		PORTUGAL *Comm*	10 July 1654, Westminster Treaty of peace, confederation and commerce
		UNITED PROVINCES *Comm*	30 August Regulation between India companies, related to Treaty of Westminster of 5 April 1654

Table 1 (continued)

State	*Year*	*With*, Type	*Details*
		DENMARK *Comm*	15 September, Westminster Treaty of amity and commerce
	1655	FRANCE *Comm*	3 November, Westminster Treaty of peace and commerce
	1660	SPAIN *Comm*	11 September, Madrid Restoration of treaty of peace and commerce of 15 November 1630
UNITED PROVINCES	1651	(VOC and) BASRA *Comm, Trade*	9 May/17 August 1651, Basra Notes for the regulations of trade and commerce
	1660	(VOC and) BANTAM *Comm*	8 August, Sillebaar Agreement
		(VOC and) INDRAPURA *Comm*	16 August, Indrapura Agreement
FRANCE	1655	BREMEN, LUBECK, HAMBURG *Comm, Mar*	10 May, Paris Treaty of alliance and commerce
	1659	SPAIN *Comm*	7 November, Pheasant Island Treaty of peace and commerce (Treaty of the Pyrenees)
1661–1670			
ENGLAND	1661	UNITED PROVINCES *Navig*	11 April, London Agreement and convention for regulation of trade posts
		SWEDEN *Comm*	21 October, Whitehall Treaty of friendship and commerce
	1662	TUNIS *Comm*	5 October, Tunis Treaty of peace and commerce
	1663	BREMEN (?) *Trade*	May, Westminster Declaration Charles II concerning rights of trade for citizens of Bremen

(*continued*)

Table 1 (continued)

State	*Year*	*With*, Type	*Details*
	1665	SPAIN *Comm*	17 December, Madrid Treaty of peace and commerce
	1666	SWEDEN *Comm*	16 February, Stockholm Treaty
	1667	SPAIN *Comm*	11/23 May, Madrid Treaty of restoration of peace, alliance and commerce
		UNITED PROVINCES *Comm*	21/31 July 1667, Breda Articles of commerce and navigation
	1668	UNITED PROVINCES *Comm, Navig*	17 February, The Hague Treaty of navigation and commerce
	1669	SAVOY *Comm*	19 September, Florence Treaty of amity and commerce
	1670	DENMARK *Comm*	11 July, Copenhagen Treaty of peace and commerce
UNITED PROVINCES	1661	PORTUGAL *Comm*	6 August, The Hague Treaty of peace, alliance and free trade
	1662	FRANCE *Comm, Navig*	27 April, Paris Treaty of amity, confederation, commerce and navigation
	1664	(VOC and) MALABAR *Comm*	11 February, Cannanore Treaty of friendship and commerce
		(VOC and) COLACTRIA *Comm*	21 and 22 July Agreement
		(VOC and) BANDJARMASIN *Comm*	7 September Agreement
		(VOC and) ANDRAGIRIJ *Comm*	28 October, Andragirij Agreement
	1669	PORTUGAL *Comm*	30 July, The Hague Treaty of alliance and commerce

Table 1 (continued)

State	*Year*	*With*, Type	*Details*
FRANCE	1662	SWEDEN *Comm*	20 (30) December, Stockholm Treaty
	1663	DENMARK *Comm, Navig*	16 February, Paris Treaty of alliance, commerce and navigation
	1666	TUNIS *Comm*	2 August Treaty of commerce
OTTOMAN EMPIRE	1665	GENOA *Comm*	30 October, Adrianople Treaty
MUNSTER	1669	EMDEN *Comm*	24 October, Assendorp Treaty of commerce and good correspondence
1671–1680			
UNITED PROVINCES	1674	ENGLAND *Mar, Nav, Comm*	1 (10) December, London Treaty
	1675	SPAIN *Mar*	25 November, Brussels Provisional agreement elucidating maritime treaty of 1650
		SWEDEN *Comm*	26 November, Stockholm Treaty
		ENGLAND *Comm*	30 December, The Hague Explicatory declaration of maritime treaties of 17 February 1667/8, 1 December 1674
	1676	(VOC and) MADURAI *Comm*	2 July Transaction
		SPAIN *Mar*	25 November, Brussels Provisional declaration respecting maritime treaty of 1650
	1678	ENGLAND *Comm, Navig*	10 August, Nijmegen Treaty
			15 August

(continued)

Table 1 (continued)

State	*Year*	*With*, Type	*Details*
		(VOC and) ONY/ ONIH (New Guinea), *Trade*	Treaty of peace and regulation of slave trade
	1679	ALGIERS *Comm*	30 April, Algiers Treaty of peace and commerce
		SWEDEN *Comm, Navig*	2 (12) October, Nijmegen Treaty
ENGLAND	1676	TRIPOLI *Comm*	5 (15) March, Tripoli Articles of peace and commerce
		TRIPOLI *Comm*	1 May, Tripoli Treaty of peace and commerce
	1677	FRANCE *Comm, Navig*	24 February, Saint-Germain-en-Laye Treaty
FRANCE	1675	SPAIN *Comm*	25 October, Freyr Conventions for the restoration of trade on the Meuse and Sambre and in the Southern Netherlands
1681–1690			
ENGLAND	1682	ALGIERS *Comm*	10 April, Barberia Articles of peace and commerce
	1686	ALGIERS *Comm*	5 (15) April, Algiers Treaty of peace and commerce
		TUNIS *Comm*	2 October, Tunis Treaty of peace and commerce
	1689	UNITED PROVINCES	12/22 August, London Convention concerning the prohibition of trade with France
UNITED PROVINCES	1683	MOROCCO *Navig, Comm*	26 May, The Hague Treaty of peace, navigation and commerce
	1684	MOROCCO *Navig, Comm*	5 May Treaty of peace, navigation and commerce
	1686	(VOC and) BANTAM *Comm*	15 February, Batavia Castle Political and commercial treaty

Table 1 (continued)

State	*Year*	*With*, Type	*Details*
FRANCE	1685	TUNIS *Comm*	28 August, Tunis Treaty of commerce with *Compagnie du Cap Nègre*
	1686	LIÈGE *Comm*	5 April, Versailles Treaty of commerce
BRANDENBURG	1688	RUSSIA *Comm*	20/21/28 January, Moscow Treaty of commerce and friendship
1691–1700			
FRANCE	1691	TUNIS *Comm*	16 December, Tunis Treaty of peace and commerce
	1693	TRIPOLI *Comm*	27 May, Tripoli Treaty of peace and commerce
	1694	SPAIN *Comm*	24 August, Isle of Pheasants Treaty of commerce and good correspondence
	1697	UNITED PROVINCES *Comm, Mar, Navig*	20 September, Rijswijck Treaty of commerce and navigation
	1699	UNITED PROVINCES *Comm, Navig*	29 May, Paris Tariff agreement following Treaty of Ryswick of 20 September 1697
		TUNIS *Comm*	28 June, Tunis Acts conferming treaty of peace and commerce of 30 August 1685
ENGLAND	1691	DENMARK and UNITED PROVINCES *Navig, Comm*	20 (30) June, Copenhagen Provisional navigation and commerce treaty regarding subjects in France or elsewhere
	1698	RUSSIA *Comm*	16 April Treaty of commerce
	1700	ALGIERS *Comm*	17 August, Algiers Treaty of peace and commerce

(*continued*)

Table 1 (continued)

State	*Year*	*With*, Type	*Details*
		(Merchants GB and) Magistrates SANTANDER, *Trade*	12 September, Santander Treaty
DENMARK	1691	SWEDEN *Comm, Navig*	10 March, Stockholm Treaty to protect commerce and navigation
	1692	HAMBURG *Trade*	16 August, Copenhagen Treaty
	1693	SWEDEN *Trade*	17 March, Stockholm Treaty concerning measures for maintaining free trade
UNITED PROVINCES	1698	BAVARIA *Comm*	28 August, Bruxelles Treaty of protection and commerce
1701–1710			
ENGLAND	1703	AUSTRIA and UNITED PROVINCES *Comm*	11 April, The Hague Convention for prohibition of commerce and exchange of correspondence with France
		ALGIERS *Comm*	28 October (8 November), Algiers Articles of peace and commerce
		PORTUGAL *Comm*	27 December, Lisbon Treaty
	1706	DANZIG *Comm*	22 October, Danzig Treaty
	1707	SPAIN *Comm*	10 July, Barcelona Treaty of peace and commerce
FRANCE	1703	SPAIN *Comm*	15 March, Bruxelles Convention on trade in the Southern Netherlands
	1710	TUNIS *Comm*	16 December, Tunis Treaty of peace and commerce
UNITED PROVINCES	1701	DENMARK *Comm*	15 June, Copenhagen Treaty of amity and commerce
	1703	TRIPOLI *Navig, Comm*	15 December, Tripoli Treaty of peace, navigation and commerce

Table 1 (continued)

State	*Year*	*With*, Type	*Details*
	1704	TUNIS *Navig, Comm*	24 March, Tunis Treaty of peace, navigation and commerce
	1705	PORTUGAL *Comm*	7 August, Lisbon Treaty
FRANCE	1703	SPAIN *Comm*	15 March, Bruxelles Convention on trade in the Southern Netherlands
	1710	TUNIS *Comm*	16 December, Tunis Treaty of peace and commerce
SPAIN	1701	PORTUGAL *Comm*	18 June, Lisbon Convention on the Asiento
1711–1720			
GREAT BRITAIN	1713	SAVOY, TWO SICILIES *Comm*	25 February/8 March 1712/1713, Utrecht Rights and privileges of British merchants in the Two Sicilies
		SPAIN *Comm*	26 March, Madrid Treaty of Asiento
		FRANCE *Comm, Navig*	11 April, Utrecht Treaty
		UNITED PROVINCES *Comm*	15/26 July, Utrecht Provisional regulation on trade in the Southern Netherlands
		SPAIN *Comm, Navig*	28 November/9 December, Utrecht Treaty
	1715	AUSTRIA *Comm*	26 July, London Convention on silk exports to the Southern Netherlands
		SPAIN *Comm*	14 December, Madrid Explanation of articles of Treaty Utrecht of 28 November/9 December 1713
	1716	SPAIN *Comm*	15/26 May, Madrid Explicatory convention of the Asiento

(*continued*)

Table 1 (continued)

State	*Year*	*With*, Type	*Details*
		TRIPOLI *Comm, Navig*	19 July, Tripoli Treaty of peace, commerce and navigation
		TUNIS *Comm*	30 August, Tunis Treaty of peace and commerce
		ALGIERS *Comm*	29 October, Algiers Treaty of peace and commerce
UNITED PROVINCES	1712	ALGIERS *Navig, Comm*	18 June, Algiers Treaty of peace, navigation and commerce
	1712	TUNIS *Comm, Navig*	17 August, Tunis Treaty of peace, commerce and navigation
	1713	TRIPOLI *Comm, Navig*	s.d., Tripoli Treaty of commerce and navigation
		FRANCE *Comm, Navig*	11 April, Utrecht Treaty
	1714	SPAIN *Comm*	26 June, Utrecht Treaty
FRANCE	1715	PERSIA *Comm*	13 August, Versailles Treaty
	1716	HANSEATIC LEAGUE *Comm, Navig*	28 September, Paris Treaty
	1720	TUNIS *Comm*	20 February, Tunis Treaty
AUSTRIA	1716	*Comm*	20/31 August Declaration concerning trade in the Austrian Netherlands
	1718	OTTOMAN EMPIRE *Comm, Navig*	27 July, Passarowitz Treaty
RUSSIA	1713	HAMBURG *Trade*	4 (15) June, Hamburg Convention
	1713	DANZIG *Trade*	16 (27) October, Marienwerder Convention

Table 1 (continued)

State	*Year*	*With*, Type	*Details*
1721–1730			
GREAT BRITAIN	1721	MOROCCO *Comm*	23 January, Fez Treaty of peace and commerce
	1728	MOROCCO *Comm*	14 January, Mequinez Articles of peace and commerce
	1729	ALGIERS *Comm*	18 March, Algiers Treaty of peace and commerce
		UNITED PROVINCES *Comm*	21 November Separate article on East India trade following Treaty of Seville of 9 November 1729
	1730	CHEROKEE *Comm*	20 (30) September Treaty of peace and commerce
FRANCE	1722	PERSIA *Comm*	1 May Ordinance by the Shah in favour of French trade
	1727	UNITED PROVINCES *Comm*	1 January, The Hague Cession treaty concerning island of Arguin and African trade
	1728	TUNIS *Comm*	1 July Treaty of peace and commerce
	1729	TRIPOLI *Comm*	9 June/2 August, Tripoli Treaty of peace and commerce
SWEDEN	1724	*Navig*	10 November Ordinance concerning navigation towards Sweden and Finland
	1726	*Navig*	28 February Declaration concerning ordinance of 10 November 1724
	1729	ALGIERS *Comm*	16 April, Algiers Treaty of peace and commerce
AUSTRIA	1725	SPAIN *Comm, Navig*	1 May, Vienna Treaty
	1725	TUNIS *Navig, Comm*	23 September, Tunis Treaty of peace, navigation and commerce

(*continued*)

Table 1 (continued)

State	*Year*	*With*, Type	*Details*
UNITED PROVINCES	1728	TRIPOLI *Comm*	4 October, Tripoli Treaty of peace and commerce
PRUSSIA	1728	SAXE *Comm*	16 October, Leipzig Treaty of commerce
1731–1740			
UNITED PROVINCES	1731	DENMARK *Comm*	3 September, Copenhagen Convention of ratification of treaty of commerce of 15 June 1701
	1737	(VOC and) SURAT *Comm*	23 June Agreement
	1739	FRANCE *Comm, Navig, Mar*	21 December, Versailles Treaty
GREAT BRITAIN	1734	RUSSIA *Comm*	2 December, St Petersburg Treaty
		MOROCCO *Comm*	15 December Treaty of peace and commerce
OTTOMAN EMPIRE	1737	SWEDEN *Comm, Navig*	10 January, Constantinople Treaty
	1740	TWO SICILIES *Comm*	7 April, Constantinople Treaty
DENMARK	1731	RUSSIA *Navig*	30 October/10 November, Mosca Treaty
FRANCE	1733	DANISH West India Company	15 June, Copenhagen Contract of sale and cession of the island of St Croix
1741–1750			
FRANCE	1741	SWEDEN *Comm, Navig*	25 April, Versailles Preliminary convention of commerce and navigation
	1742	DENMARK *Comm, Navig*	23 August, Copenhagen Treaty
		TUNIS *Comm*	9 November Treaty of peace and commerce

Table 1 (continued)

State	*Year*	*With*, Type	*Details*
	1743	TUNIS *Comm*	24 February, Tunis Additional articles of treaty of 9 November 1742
	1744	GREAT BRITAIN *Comm*	April Convention concerning articles Utrecht treaty of commerce
	1745	*Comm*	31 December Revocation of commercial treaty of 1739 with United Provinces
	1749	DENMARK *Comm*	30 September, Versailles Declaration renewal treaty of commerce 23 August 1742
TRIPOLI	1741	SWEDEN *Comm, Navig*	15 April, Tripoli Treaty of peace, commerce and navigation
	1741	TWO SICILIES *Comm, Navig*	3 June, Tripoli Treaty of peace, commerce and navigation
	1749	AUSTRIA *Comm, Navig*	27 January Treaty of peace, commerce and navigation
	1749	TUSCANY *Comm, Navig*	27 January Treaty of peace, commerce and navigation
TWO SICILIES	1742	SWEDEN *Comm, Navig*	30 June Treaty
	1748	DENMARK *Comm, Navig*	16 April, Madrid Treaty
TUSCANY	1747	OTTOMAN EMPIRE *Comm*	25 May Treaty of peace and free trade
	1748	TUNIS *Comm, Navig*	23 December, Tunis Treaty of peace, commerce and navigation
DENMARK	1742	SPAIN *Comm, Mar, Navig*	18 July, San Ildefonso Treaty of commerce, navigation and marine
	1751	*Comm*	26 March Ordinance concerning commerce with Greenland

(*continued*)

Table 1 (continued)

State	*Year*	*With*, Type	*Details*
AUSTRIA	1748	ALGIERS *Comm, Navig*	8 October, Algiers Treaty of peace, commerce and navigation
		TUNIS *Comm, Navig*	23 December Treaty of peace, commerce and navigation
UNITED PROVINCES	1743	(VOC and) TERNATE *Comm*	4 July, Ternate Agreement
	1744	(VOC and) KARTASURA *Comm*	24 September Agreement
SPAIN	1750	GREAT BRITAIN *Comm*	5 October, Madrid Treaty of indemnity and trade, following Article 16 of Treaty of Aix-la-Chapelle
1751–1760			
GREAT BRITAIN	1751	ALGIERS *Comm*	3 June, Algiers Treaty of peace and commerce
		TUNIS *Comm*	19 October, Bardo Treaty of peace and commerce
		TRIPOLI *Comm*	19 September, Tripoli Treaty of peace and commerce
			19 October Decree concerning abolition of commerce with Hamburg
	1752	*Comm*	14 November Decree for the re-establishment of commerce with Hamburg
	1753	*Comm*	26 August Decree concerning abolition of commerce with Denmark
	1756	(EIC and) CHERICAL *Trade*	Treaty
		(EIC and) MAHRATTAS *Trade*	12 October, Poona Treaty

Table 1 (continued)

State	*Year*	*With*, Type	*Details*
	1757	(EIC and) BENGAL *Trade*	9 February Treaty
		(EIC and) BENGAL *Trade*	15 July Treaty
	1759	(EIC and) HYDERABAD *Trade*	14 May Treaty
		(EIC and) COTIOTE *Trade*	23 August Treaty
	1760	MOROCCO *Comm, Navig*	28 July, Fez Treaty of peace, commerce and navigation
DENMARK	1752	TRIPOLI *Comm*	22 January, Tripoli Treaty of peace and commerce
	1753	MOROCCO *Comm*	18 June Treaty of peace and commerce
		Comm	22 October Ordinance prohibiting commerce with Spain
		GENOA *Comm, Navig*	13 March, Paris Treaty of amity, commerce and navigation
		SWEDEN *Comm, Navig*	12 July, Stockholm Convention to protect commerce and navigation
		OTTOMAN EMPIRE *Comm, Navig*	14 October, Constantinople Treaty of friendship, navigation and commerce
		Comm	12 November Edict re-establishing commerce with Spain
	1757	SPAIN *Comm*	22 September, The Hague Agreement of renewal of amity and commerce
	1760	RUSSIA, SWEDEN *Navig*	17 March, St Petersburg Accession to convention of 9 March 1759

(*continued*)

Table 1 (continued)

State	*Year*	*With*, Type	*Details*
FRANCE	1751	MAINZ, PALATINATE *Navig*	28 April, Munich Convention on navigation of the Rhine
	1752	TRIPOLI *Comm*	30 May, Tripoli Explicatory articleof treaty of peace and commerce of 2 August 1729
	1753	PRUSSIA *Comm, Navig*	14 February, Paris Preliminary treaty
	1759	RUSSIA, SWEDEN *Comm, Navig*	9 March, St Petersburg Convention concerning protection of trade and navigation in Baltic Sea
UNITED PROVINCES	1752	MOROCCO *Comm, Navig*	21 November, Tetouan Treaty of peace, commerce and navigation
	1753	TWO SICILIES *Comm*	27 August, The Hague Treaty
	1760	ALGIERS *Comm*	26 May, Algiers Additional articles to 1757 treaty of commerce
		(VOC and) NATTER (Sumatra) *Comm*	6 October, Padang Agreement
SPAIN	1751	*Comm*	19 October Decree concerning abolition of commerce with Hamburg
	1752	*Comm*	14 November Decree for the re-establishment of commerce with Hamburg
	1753	*Comm*	26 August Decree concerning abolition of commerce with Denmark
AUSTRIA	1751	SARDINIA *Comm*	4 October, Milan Treaty for the establishment of commerce
	1757	HOLY SEE *Comm*	30 November/24 December, Rome/Milan Treaty of commerce for Austrian Lombardy

Table 1 (continued)

State	*Year*	*With,* Type	*Details*
ALGIERS	1751	HAMBURG *Comm, Navig*	22 February, Algiers Treaty of peace, commerce and navigation
1761–1770			
GREAT BRITAIN	1761	(EIC and) JAFFRABAD *Trade*	3 January, Bombay Agreement
		(EIC and) MAHRATTAS *Trade*	14 September, Bombay Articles of agreement
		(EIC and) CARTINAAD *Trade*	30 December Articles of agreement
	1762	ALGIERS *Comm, Navig*	14 May, Algiers Treaty of peace, commerce and navigation
		TUNIS *Comm, Navig*	22 June, Bardo Treaty of peace, commerce and navigation
		TRIPOLI *Comm, Navig*	22 July, Tripoli Treaty of peace, commerce and navigation
	1763	(EIC and) BUSHIRE (Persia) *Trade*	12 April Agreement
		(EIC and) BENGAL *Trade*	10 July, Fort William Treaty and additional articles
		MOROCCO *Comm*	5 August Treaty of peace and commerce
	1765	(EIC and) BENGAL *Trade*	20 and 25 February, Fort William Articles
		(EIC and) BHONSLA (Bowncello, Savantvadi)	7 April 1765, Raree Articles of agreement
		ALGIERS *Comm*	3 August, Algiers Articles of peace and commerce

(*continued*)

Table 1 (continued)

State	*Year*	*With*, Type	*Details*
		(EIC and) BENGAL *Trade*	16 August, Illiabad Treaty
	1766	(EIC and) COLAPORE *Trade*	12 January Articles of agreement
		SWEDEN *Comm*	5 February, Stockholm Treaty
		RUSSIA *Comm, Navig*	20 June (1 July), St Petersburg Treaty of amity, commerce and navigation
		(EIC and) BHONSLA (Savantvadi) *Trade*	24 October, Raree Articles of agreement
	1767	*Comm*	10 March *Mémoire* concerning commercial relations with Portugal
	1768	(EIC and) DECCAN *Trade*	23 February, Fort St George Treaty of perpetual friendship and alliance
	1769	(EIC and) MYSORE *Trade*	3 April, Fort St George/ Madavaram Treaty of perpetual friendship and alliance
	1770	(EIC and) BENGAL *Trade*	21 March Treaty
		Trade	12 July Document statement concerning neutral states against pirates
		(EIC and) MYSORE *Trade*	8 August, Bombay Treaty
FRANCE	1766	NASSAU-SAARBRUCK *Exch*	15 February, Bouquenom Boundary and exchange treaty
	1767	MOROCCO *Comm*	28 May, Morocco Treaty of peace, amity and commerce
		LIÈGE *Comm*	9 October, Fontainebleau Boundary and trade convention

Table 1 (continued)

State	*Year*	*With*, Type	*Details*
	1768	SPAIN *Comm, Mar, Navig*	5 January, Madrid Treaty
	1769	HAMBURG *Comm, Mar, Navig*	1 April, Hamburg Treaty and tariff
	1770	TUNIS *Comm*	13 September, Bardo Treaty of peace and commerce
		NASSAU-SAARBRUCK *Exch*	26 October, Fontainebleau Supplementary convention to treaty of 15 February 1766; separate article
PRUSSIA	1761	OTTOMANS *Comm*	22 March, Constantinople Treaty of amity and commerce
	1762	SWEDEN *Comm*	7 April, Ribnitz Convention of commerce
	1766	SAXE *Comm*	18 June, Halle Commercial convention
	1769	BREMEN *Comm, Navig*	26 August, Bremen Agreement of commerce and navigation concerning the town of Minden
MOROCCO	1763	SWEDEN *Comm, Navig*	16 May Treaty of peace, commerce and navigation
	1767	SPAIN *Comm*	28 May Treaty of peace and commerce
	1767	DENMARK *Comm*	25 July, Morocco Treaty of peace and commerce
DENMARK	1766	PORTUGAL *Comm, Navig*	26 September, Lisbon Trade convention
HAMBURG	1768	HOLSTEIN *Trade*	27 May, Gottorp Agreement
PERSIA	1763	*Trade*	2 July Privileges for the EIC
UNITED PROVINCES	1766	CEYLON *Comm*	14 February, Colombo Treaty of peace and commerce

(*continued*)

Table 1 (continued)

State	*Year*	*With*, Type	*Details*
1771–1780			
FRANCE	1772	GENOA *Comm*	3 February, Genoa Declaration on French investments in free port of Genoa and against contraband
		LIÈGE *Comm*	24 May, Versailles Commercial and boundary treaty
	1774	SPAIN *Comm, Navig*	27 December, Versailles Interpretive convention on treaty of commerce and navigation of 5 January 1768 Madrid against contraband
	1776	NASSAU-WELLBURG *Exch*	24 January, Nancy Exchange and boundary treaty
		RAGUSA *Comm, Navig*	2 April, Ragusa Convention of commerce and navigation
		LIÈGE *Comm*	6 July, Versailles Additional articles to treaty of 24 May 1772
	1778	USA *Comm*	6 February, Paris Treaty
		SPAIN and PORTUGAL *Comm*	11 March, Madrid Treaty
		Trade	28 March Ordinance concerning captured ships
		TREVES *Exch*	1 July, Versailles Exchange and boundary convention
		Navig	26 July Regulation for neutral navigation
	1779	MECKLEMBURG-SCHWERIN,*Comm*	18 September, Hamburg Treaty

Table 1 (continued)

State	*Year*	*With*, Type	*Details*
		Trade	8 November Regulation concerning captured ships
		Navig	13 November Modifications to neutral trade regulation of 1763
	1780	*Navig*	8 May Ordinance concerning regulation of neutral navigation
		Navig	25 May Reply to Danish declaration on navigation of Baltic Sea
GREAT BRITAIN	1771	(EIC and) CAMBAY *Trade*	22 October Agreement
		(EIC and) BAROACH *Trade*	30 November, Bombay Castle Treaty
	1772	*Comm, Navig*	1 May Document about navigation and commerce of neutrals
	1775	(EIC and) MAHRATTAS *Trade*	6 March, Surat Treaty
		EGYPT *Navig, Comm*	7 March, Cairo Treaty
		POLAND *Trade*	15 March, Warsaw Separate acts concerning treaties of 1768 and 1773 on rights of ceded countries, commerce etc.
	1776	(EIC and) MAHRATTAS *Trade*	1 March, Poorundah Treaty
		Comm	Ordinance suppressing commerce with American colonies

(*continued*)

Table 1 (continued)

State	*Year*	*With*, Type	*Details*
	1780	*Navig*	17 April Declaration to United Provinces suspending special terms for Dutch navigation
		DENMARK *Comm*	4 July Explanation of Article 3 of commercial treaty of 1670
DENMARK	1772	ALGIERS *Comm*	16 May, Algiers Treaty of peace and commerce
	1776	*Comm*	18 March Ordinance concerning commerce with Greenland
		Comm	1 April Ordinance concerning commerce with Iceland
	1780	RUSSIA *Mar, Comm, Navig*	28 June–9 July, Copenhagen Maritime convention on free and neutral navigation and trade, with separate articles
	1789	GENOA *Comm*	30 July, Genoa Renewal of the treaty of amity, commerce and extradition of 1756
SWEDEN	1775	*Comm*	15 August Edict on the establishment of a free port in Marstrand
	1778	*Exch*	20 June *Mémoire* to German Empire about exchange treaty of 1773 between Denmark and Russia
	1779	*Comm, Navig*	March Ordinance about neutral commerce and navigation
	1780	RUSSIA *Comm, Navig*	1 August, St Petersburg Maritime convention on free and neutral commerce and navigation, and separate articles

Table 1 (continued)

State	*Year*	*With*, Type	*Details*
		Navig	9 September Accession to the maritime convention between Russia and Denmark of 9 July 1780
SPAIN	1772	GENOA *Comm*	2 May, Genoa Declaration expanding Article 11 of treaty of 1 May 1745
	1778	PORTUGAL *Comm*	24 March, (El Pardo) Treaty
	1780	*Navig*	13 March Regulation of neutral navigation
		MOROCCO *Comm*	30 May, Aranjuez Agreement of amity and commerce
OTTOMAN EMPIRE	1771	AUSTRIA *Comm*	6 July, Constantinople Boundary and trade convention
	1774	*Comm*	Firman suppressing English commerce in Suez
	1780	*Navig*	12 February Declaration concerning neutral navigation within seas of Ottoman States
POLAND	1775	RUSSIA *Comm*	15 March, Warsaw Separate acts concerning treaties of 1768 and 1773, about subjects and trade with ceded territories
	1775	AUSTRIA *Comm*	16 March, Warsaw Separate articles concerning commerce and subjects of ceded territories
		PRUSSIA *Comm*	18 March, Warsaw Separate acts concerning commerce
TUSCANY	1778	MOROCCO *Comm*	6 February Treaty of peace and commerce
		Navig	1 August Regulation concerning neutral navigation

(*continued*)

Table 1 (continued)

State	*Year*	*With*, Type	*Details*
HAMBURG	1778	*Navig*	18 September Regulation concerning neutral navigation
TWO SICILIES	1778	*Comm, Navig*	19 September Regulation of neutral commerce and navigation
USA	1778	*Navig*	9 May Congress proclamation concerning neutral navigation
HOLY SEE	1779	*Comm, Navig*	4 March Edict concerning neutral commerce and navigation
GENOA	1779	*Comm, Navig*	1 July Edict concerning neutral commerce and navigation
VENICE	1779	*Comm, Navig*	9 September Edict concerning neutral commerce and navigation
RUSSIA	1780	*Navig*	19 May Ordinance concerning navigation
UNITED PROVINCES	1780	*Mar*	20 November Accession to maritime convention between Russia, Denmark and Sweden of 9 July and 1 August
1781–1790			
FRANCE	1781	UNITED PROVINCES *Comm*	1 May, Versailles Treaty on captures
		TRIPOLI *Comm*	20 May, Tripoli Additional articles with treaty of 2 August 1729
		LEYEN *Exch*	22 September, Bliescastel Treaty of exchange and boundaries

Table 1 (continued)

State	*Year*	*With,* Type	*Details*
	1784	SWEDEN *Comm, Navig*	1 July, Versailles Provisional convention explicating convention of commerce and navigation of 25 April 1741
	1785	EGYPT *Comm, Navig*	9 January, Cairo Treaty
		UNITED PROVINCES *Comm*	10 November, Fontainebleau Defensive alliance including articles on trade
	1786	PORTUGAL, SPAIN *Comm*	30 January, Madrid Convention of trade along the Cabinda coast
		GREAT BRITAIN *Comm, Navig*	26 September, Versailles (Eden–Rayneval Treaty) Treaty
		SPAIN *Comm*	24 December, Madrid Conventions of commerce against contraband
	1787	RUSSIA *Comm, Navig*	11 January, St Petersburg Treaty
		GREAT BRITAIN *Comm, Navig*	15 January, Versailles Conventions concerning treaty of 26 September 1786
		GREAT BRITAIN *Comm, Navig*	31 May Suspension of treaties of 26 September 1786 and 15 January 1787
		GREAT BRITAIN *Comm*	31 August, Versailles Explicatory convention on articles of 1783 treaty of peace concerning India trade
	1789	HAMBURG *Comm, Navig*	17 March, Hamburg Agreements on extension treaty of 18 September 1779
RUSSIA	1781	UNITED PROVINCES	3 January, St Petersburg

(*continued*)

Table 1 (continued)

State	*Year*	*With*, Type	*Details*
		Mar	Accession to maritime convention between Russia, Denmark and Sweden of 9 July, 1 August 1780
		PRUSSIA *Comm, Navig*	8 May, St Petersburg Convention concerning free and neutral commerce and navigation, with separate articles
		AUSTRIA *Comm*	9 October Act of subscription to Russian propositions concerning free, neutral commerce and navigation
	1782	PORTUGAL *Comm, Navig*	13 July, St Petersburg Maritime convention on free and neutral commerce and navigation
		DENMARK *Comm*	8–19 October, St Petersburg Treaty of amity and commerce, and explicatory declaration
	1783	COURLAND *Comm*	10 (21) May, Riga Treaty of commerce
		OTTOMANS *Comm*	21 June, Constantinople Treaty of commerce
	1784	*Trade*	22 February Ukaz in favour of foreign merchants around Black Sea
		GREAT BRITAIN *Comm*	22 February, St Petersburg Free trade edict concerning Black Sea
	1785	*Comm, Navig*	1 November Edict concerning commerce and navigation of Austrian subjects
		AUSTRIA *Comm, Navig*	1/12 November, St Petersburg and Vienna Treaty concerning commerce and navigation of Russian subjects

Table 1 (continued)

State	*Year*	*With*, Type	*Details*
	1787	TWO SICILIES *Comm*	17 January, Zarskoje Selo Treaty of commerce
		PORTUGAL *Comm, Navig*	20 December, St Petersburg Treaty
	1789	*Trade*	6 May Declaration of neutral trade in the Baltic Sea
PRUSSIA	1781	*Comm*	30 April Ordinance concerning neutral commerce
		Comm, Navig	3 November/8 December Ordinances concerning neutral commerce and navigation
	1783	*Comm*	29 April Declaration establishing commerce between Poland and Koenigsberg and Memel
	1785	DANZIG *Comm, Navig*	22 February, Warsaw Convention of commerce and navigation
		USA *Comm*	9/28 July, 5 August, 10 September Treaty
	1790	POLAND *Comm*	Plan for a treaty of commerce and cession
		AUSTRIA, GREAT BRITAIN, UNITED PROVINCES, *Trade*	10 December, The Hague Convention concerning the Southern Netherlands, including restoration of trade
MOROCCO	1783	GREAT BRITAIN *Comm*	24 May Additional articles of peace and commerce
	1786	UNITED PROVINCES *Trade*	25 February Opening of the port of Larrache
		Comm	15 May Ordinance concerning foreign commerce in ports of Tangier and Larrache

(continued)

Table 1 (continued)

State	*Year*	*With*, Type	*Details*
	1787	USA *Comm, Navig*	25 January Treaty of amity, commerce and navigation, with additional article
	1789	*Comm*	20 October Declaration concerning Spanish commerce
SPAIN	1782	OTTOMANS *Comm*	14 September, Constantinople Treaty
		OTTOMANS *Comm*	24 December, Madrid Treaty
	1784	TRIPOLI *Comm*	10 September Treaty of peace, amity and commerce
UNITED PROVINCES	1781	*Mar*	Declarations to Denmark and belligerent powers, accession to maritime conventions of 1780
	1782	USA *Comm*	8 October, The Hague Convention concerning captures and reprisals
USA	1783	SWEDEN *Comm*	3 April Treaty of amity and commerce and separate articles
		Comm	25 September Proclamation concerning execution of the treaty with Sweden of 3 April
AUSTRIA	1784	*Trade*	27 August Decree restricting import of foreign manufactures
		TUSCANY *Comm*	4 December Commercial convention concerning possessions in Italy
DENMARK	1789	GENOA *Comm*	30 July, Genoa Renewal of treaty of amity, commerce and extradition of 1756

Table 1 (continued)

State	*Year*	*With*, Type	*Details*
COURLAND	1783	*Comm*	22 May Declaration concerning boundary and trade treaty of 21 May
GREAT BRITAIN	1788	BENGAL *Comm*	25 July Treaty
OTTOMANS	1784	*Comm*	24 February *Sened* in favour of Austrian commerce
SWEDEN	1788	*Trade*	8 July Regulation concerning captures
1791–1800			
FRANCE	1791	MÜLHAUSEN *Comm*	22 September, Convention of commerce and transit
	1792	MÜLHAUSEN *Comm*	15 March, Additional articles to convention of 22 September 1791
	1793	*Navig*	21 September Act of navigation
	1796	HAMBURG *Comm*	24 June, Paris Secret treaty for the restoration of commerce
		GENOA *Comm*	9 October, Paris Convention on closure Genoese ports to Britain, and protection Genoese trade
		Trade	31 October Law prohibiting import and sale of English merchandise
	1797	*Trade*	2 March Document concerning ships carrying enemy merchandise
	1798	*Trade*	18 January Law on ships carrying English merchandise

(*continued*)

Table 1 (continued)

State	*Year*	*With,* Type	*Details*
		CISALPINE REPUBLIC *Comm*	21 February, Paris Treaty
	1799	SWITZERLAND *Comm*	30 May, Paris Treaty
		Comm	9 October Document establishing embargo on Hamburg ships
	1800	*Trade*	17 June Exemption from captures of English fishing vessels
		USA *Comm, Navig*	30 September, Paris Treaty of peace, amity, commerce and navigation
RUSSIA	1793	*Comm*	8 February Edict suspending 1787 treaty of commerce with France
	1793	GREAT BRITAIN *Comm*	25 March, London Commercial convention
		Trade	19 April Edict prohibiting import of French merchandise
	1797	GREAT BRITAIN *Comm*	21 February, St Petersburg Treaty of commerce
	1798	PORTUGAL *Comm, Navig*	27 December, St Petersburg Treaty of amity, navigation and commerce
	1800	*Trade*	7 November Embargo on English ships
		SWEDEN *Mar*	16 December, St Petersburg Maritime convention for armed neutrality
		DENMARK *Mar*	16 December, St Petersburg Maritime convention for armed neutrality
		PRUSSIA *Mar*	18 December, St Petersburg Maritime convention for armed neutrality

Table 1 (continued)

State	*Year*	*With*, Type	*Details*
SPAIN	1791	TUNIS *Comm*	9 July, January Treaty of peace, amity and commerce
	1795	USA *Navig*	27 October, San Lorenzo el Real (ratification 25 April 1796, Aranjuez) Treaty of amity, boundaries and navigation
	1799	MOROCCO *Comm, Navig*	1 March, Mequinez Treaty of peace, amity, navigation and fishery
USA	1794	GREAT BRITAIN *Comm, Navig*	19 November, London Treaty of amity, commerce and navigation; additional article commerce and navigation
	1795	GREAT BRITAIN	24 June Conditional ratification of treaty of 19 November 1794; additional article
		ALGIERS *Navig*	5 September Treaty of friendship and navigation
	1796	GREAT BRITAIN	4 May Clarifying article concerning treaty of 19 November 1794
		TRIPOLI *Navig*	4 November, Tripoli Treaty of amity and navigation
	1797	TUNIS *Comm, Navig*	August, Tunis Treaty of amity, commerce and navigation
	1799	PRUSSIA *Comm*	11 July, Berlin Treaty of amity and commerce
SWEDEN	1792	ALGIERS *Comm*	25 May Renewal of treaty of peace and commerce of 16 April 1729

(*continued*)

Table 1 (continued)

State	*Year*	*With*, Type	*Details*
	1793	*Navig*	23 April Ordinance concerning navigation in wartime
	1794	DENMARK *Comm, Navig*	27 March, Copenhagen Convention to protect commerce and navigation
		Comm	22 May Ordinance of free entrepot for the port of Gothenburg
	1800	*Navig*	23 December Regulation for neutral navigation
GREAT BRITAIN	1791	MOROCCO *Comm, Navig*	8 April Treaty of amity, commerce and navigation
	1794	*Comm*	26 March Declaration on free imports from USA
	1800	ALGIERS *Comm*	3 September, Algiers Treaty of peace and commerce
PORTUGAL	1796	*Trade*	13 May Declaration of Lisbon as free port
		Trade	17 September Decree concerning neutrality in Portuguese ports
	1799	TRIPOLI *Comm*	14 May Treaty of peace, amity and commerce
DENMARK	1793	*Comm, Navig*	22 (25) February Royal ordinance concerning navigation and commerce in wartime
	1794	*Comm*	28 March Document concerning neutral trade

Table 1 (continued)

State	*Year*	*With*, Type	*Details*
OTTOMAN EMPIRE	1795	*Comm*	Firman concerning free commerce of Austrian citizens in Moldavia

Sources: Coded from Frédéric Léonard, *Recueil des Traités de Paix, de Trêve, de Neutralité, de Confédération, d'Alliance & de Commerce faits par les Rois de France* (1693), Adriaan Moetjens, *Recueil de divers Traités de Paix, de Confédération, d'Alliance, de Commerce, &c faits depuis soixante ans entre les Etats souverains de l'Europe* (1707), Jean Dumont, *Corps universel diplomatique du droit des gens* (1726–1731), José Álvarez de Abréu y Bertodano, *Coleccion de los tratados de paz* (1751–1752), *Coleccion de los tratados de paz, alianza, comercio* (1796), Charles Jenkinson, *A Collection of All the Treaties of Peace, Alliance, and Commerce Between Great Britain and Other Powers* (1785), George Chalmers, *A Collection of Treaties Between Great Britain and Other Powers* (1790), Georg Friedrich von Martens, *Recueil des traités d'alliance, de paix, de trêve, de neutralité, de commerce* (1791–1808), Holger Christian de Reedtz, *Répertoire historique et chronologique des traités conclus par la couronne de Dannemarc* (1826), Alexandre Jehan Henry de Clerq, *Recueil des traités de la France* (1864), *Treaties and Conventions Concluded Between the United States of America and Other Powers* (1871), Clive Parry, *Consolidated Treaty Series 1648–1919* (1969–1980) and the *Institut für Europäische Geschichte Mainz*, www.ieg-friedensvertraege.de.

Note: The order of treaty-making parties per decade is decided based on which state concluded the most agreements per decade, filtering down to less 'active' states. The table does not include the vast number of treaties that were planned but never concluded, some of which are discussed in this book.

Antonella Alimento is an Associate Professor in Modern History at the University of Pisa specializing in European eighteenth-century political and economic history. Among her key publications are *Réformes fiscales et crises politiques dans la France de Louis XV* (2008; first Italian edition 1995), *Finanze ed amministrazione. Un'inchiesta francese sui catasti nell'Italia del Settecento (1763–1764)* (2008) and the edited volume *War, Trade and Neutrality. Europe and the Mediterranean in the Seventeenth and Eighteenth Centuries* (2011).

Koen Stapelbroek is an Academy of Finland Senior Research Fellow at the University of Helsinki and Associate Professor at Erasmus University Rotterdam. He received his PhD from the University of Cambridge (2004). He has published *Love, Self-Deceit and Money. Commerce and Morality in the Early Neapolitan Enlightenment* (2008) and many articles and edited volumes on eighteenth-century political thought. He is completing a monograph on European perceptions of the rise and fall of the Dutch trade republic.

Égalité, réciprocité, souveraineté: The Role of Commercial Treaties in Colbert's Economic Policy

Moritz Isenmann

Introduction

Historians portray Jean-Baptiste Colbert as a paradoxical figure.[1] Born into a family of wealthy cloth merchants,[2] as a young man he seemed at first destined to become a *négociant.* To that end, after attending the Jesuit school in his home town of Reims he went as an apprentice to Lyon, where, in the office of the Mascranni family—associates of the

[1] This essay draws on my habilitation thesis entitled 'Der "Colbertismus" und die Ursprünge des wirtschaftlichen Liberalismus. Französische Außenhandelspolitik im Zeitalter Ludwigs XIV'. The following abbreviations have been used: Archives Nationales de Paris (AN), Affaires Étrangères (AE); Archives du Ministère des Affaires Étrangères (AAE); Bibliothèque national de France (BnF); Correspondance politique (CP). All translations from French are mine.

[2] For Colbert's family background, see Jean-Louis Bourgeon, *Les Colberts avant Colbert. Destin d'une famille marchande* (Paris: Presses Universitaires de France, 1973).

M. Isenmann (✉)
University of Cologne, Germany
e-mail: moritz.isenmann@uni-koeln.de

A. Alimento, K. Stapelbroek (eds.), *The Politics of Commercial Treaties in the Eighteenth Century*, DOI 10.1007/978-3-319-53574-6_2

Colberts—he trained in international banking.[3] Then, from 1651, he served for almost ten years as the personal intendant to the then most powerful man in France, first minister Jules Mazarin, and thereby, even before he rose to power in the French administration, he added intimate knowledge of international politics to his business experience. Finally, as a minister, he is characterized as having been avid in gathering as much information as possible in order to base his actions on knowledge.[4]

Here lies the paradox: for all that he had a more than solid business background and had gained significant insight into the relationship between France and other European countries, Colbert is said to have completely misunderstood the workings of international economy. Jean Jacquart, for example, stated in an article published in 1996 that Colbert's commercial policy was at once the 'most spectacular and most fragile aspect' of his work, for it was based on 'a mistaken analysis of the economic realities in Europe of the time'.[5] Colbert's tariff policy is considered to have been especially misguided. Citing a famous note of Colbert dating from 1664, Jacquart wrote:

> 'All trade consists in lowering the import duties on goods needed by manufacturers, charging incoming manufactured goods, lowering export duties on nationally manufactured goods.' At the base of all this there is an undeniable tendency towards autarky. A reasoning so simple that it is simplistic, because it haughtily ignores the realities of international trade and the functioning of rival economies.[6]

Thus the failure of Colbert's plan to turn France into a first-rate economic power is blamed on his allegedly 'simplistic' reasoning. His pursuit of autarky, it is argued, inevitably provoked reprisals from 'all damaged

[3] Emphasized most recently by Jacob Soll, *The Information Master. Jean Baptiste Colbert's Secret State Intelligence System* (Ann Arbor: University of Michigan Press, 2009), 34–35.

[4] In addition to Soll's study, mentioned in the previous note, see, for example, Jean Meyer, *Colbert* (Paris: Hachette, 1981), 221–226.

[5] Jean Jacquart, 'Colbert', in: *L'État classique. Regards sur la pensée politique de la France dans le second XVIIe siècle*, ed. Henri Méchoulan and Joël Cornette (Paris: Vrin 1996), 196.

[6] Jacquart, 'Colbert', 196.

nations', which in turn enacted protectionist measures that had deleterious effects on French trade.

As I want to show in this chapter, however, Colbert was far from 'haughtily ignoring' how international commercial competition operated. The problem is rather that historians have an oversimplified view of his commercial policy. Contrary to what Jacquart, Henri Hauser, Jean Meyer and many others have to say, Colbert's aim was not to turn France into a 'closed system with only two doors, one to let raw materials in, and the other to let manufactured products out'.[7] Indeed, his ingenuity was such that he fully expected other countries to shut their own doors if France pursued a path of strict self-sufficiency, for which reason his policy was instead guided by the acute awareness that trade had to a certain extent to be 'free' and competition permitted if France were to be allowed to sell her many agricultural and industrial products abroad. He had a twofold objective: to keep trade generally open while at the same time reducing imports into France and increasing the kingdom's share of world trade.

But how could he achieve those two goals? Colbert knew that implementing appropriate measures within France would not by itself be enough but had to go hand-in-hand with somehow obstructing the likely retaliation of other states. Contemporaries of Colbert, such as Thomas Hobbes and Samuel von Pufendorf, formulated a theory of interstate relationships with a construct of the state of nature within which each sovereign nation had 'natural equality' and an imperative duty to defend its right to self-preservation, a right moreover which legitimized whatever measures were needed to secure that end. The only possibility of acquiring rights over another state and thus restricting its freedom of action, was (apart from brute force) to conclude treaties which, being part of natural law, then had to be honoured according to the maxim *pacta sunt servanda* (agreements are to be honoured).[8]

[7] Henri Hauser, *Les débuts du capitalisme* (Paris: Félix Alcan, 1927), 181; Meyer, *Colbert*, 232.

[8] See, for example, Peter Schroeder, 'Natural Law, Sovereignty and International Law: A Comparative Perspective', in: *Natural Law and Civil Sovereignty. Moral Right and State Authority in Early Modern Political Thought*, ed. Ian Hunter and David Saunders (Basingstoke: Palgrave Macmillan, 2002), 204–218.

Accordingly, Colbert tried to negotiate commercial treaties containing legal—rather than economic—principles that would ensure a kind of international economic competition which would ultimately work in France's favour. Unfortunately, due to their near-exclusive concentration on his economic work, historians have lost sight of those principles. In Colbert's mind, however, economic and legal principles were inextricably interwoven.

Thus, in the period from the end of the 1650s until the outbreak of the Dutch War in 1672, two different phases are distinguishable. First, one in which Colbert used traditional principles of the law of nations to ensure fair competition, and then one in which he tried to change the character and focus of that competition. The first centred on shipping and trade, and the second on industrial development within France. However, before considering these two focal points, and more specifically their role in Colbert's trade policy, it is important to outline briefly the broader economic and intellectual context of French commercial aspirations in the seventeenth century.

France at the Beginning of Louis XIV's Reign and the Providential Foundations of Commerce

The commercial policy of France during the reign of Louis XIV can only be understood by bearing in mind the situation in which the kingdom found itself at the end of the 1650s. Since the start of the religious wars of the second half of the previous century, France had been almost constantly torn by internal troubles and external conflicts, while, at the same time, fiscal pressure on the population intensified to an unprecedented degree. While this period had witnessed the rise of the United Provinces and of England as commercial powers, France's economic development had waned. With an end of the long conflict with Spain—which had continued after the Peace of Westphalia—finally in sight, the French administration began to tackle the problem of the discrepancy between the economic potential of the kingdom and its subordinate role in international trade.[9]

[9] See Alain Guery, 'Industrie et colbertisme: origine de la forme française de la politique industrielle?', *Histoire, économie et société* 8 (1989), 300.

This discrepancy, as well as the influence that other nations had exerted over the French economy during the past decades, was made all the more irritating for many Frenchmen by not according with their concept of the role of trade in the world's divine order. The common view was that the origins of trade and its ultimate goal had to be seen in the way the Creator had distributed the wherewithal for human survival amongst different countries. Human beings were therefore obliged to interrelate and to establish a peaceful trading system.[10] During the seventeenth century, this rationale for the origins of trade, which dated from late antiquity, merged with the Aristotelian notion of autarky as the absolute ideal of every polity and the gauge for measuring its degree of perfection. The union of these two ideas led every country to evaluate its divine blessings in line with the variety and wealth of goods at its disposal and the level of self-sufficiency which they made possible. This intellectual construct can be found in many European countries of the time.[11] Thomas Mun, for example, in his *England's treasure by Forraign Trade*, published posthumously in 1664, wrote that England disposed of all the means 'to sit as Master of a Monarchy'.[12] But the conviction of being especially favoured by nature was particularly widespread and deeply rooted in France, simply because of its comparative wealth of natural resources. In many French writings, from Claude de Seyssel's *Grande Monarchie de France* (1519) onwards, France was depicted as the only country which could 'do without all the other countries', none of which, however, could manage without France. Indeed, at the beginning of the seventeenth century Antoine de Montchrestien's *Traicté de l'Œconomie politique*

[10] See, for example, Jean Bodin, *La response de Jean Bodin à M. de Malestroit (1568)*, ed. Henri Hauser (Paris: Armand Colin, 1932), 34. For other examples, see Jacob Viner, *The Role of Providence in the Social Order. An Essay in Intellectual History* (Philadelphia: American Philosophical Society, 1972), 27–54, and Andrea Finkelstein, *Harmony and the Balance. An Intellectual History of Seventeenth-Century English Economic Thought* (Ann Arbor: University of Michigan Press, 2009), 94–95.

[11] See, for example, Edmund Silberner, *La guerre dans la pensée économique du XVIe au XVIIIe siècle* (Paris: Sirey, 1939), 113–114.

[12] Thomas Mun, *England's Treasure by Forraign Trade* (London: Thomas Clark, 1664), 176–177.

(1615) defined France as the 'most complete kingdom the sun gets to see between its rising and setting'.[13]

However, it was a Carmelite monk from Nantes called Jean Eon who expounded more eloquently and elaborately than any other the many natural advantages of the country. France, he explained in his tract entitled *Le commerce honorable*, published in 1646,[14] possessed an abundance of natural goods which other countries needed: wine, brandy, grain, hemp and salt, to name just a few. What was more, its geographical situation at the centre of Europe saved it from exposure to extreme climatic conditions while making it particularly suited to commerce since it had both Mediterranean and Atlantic coastlines. The monk accordingly concluded that the French must at long last exploit by means of commerce the many gifts they had received from God, and other countries must respect the particular position assigned to France by Providence.

Eon's arguments were directed in particular at the Netherlands, the only country in Europe without a claim to some form of divine enrichment and yet one whose trading companies and enormous shipping power gave it a strong hegemony, not least over French commerce, which in the eyes of Eon and many others left the kingdom in a position of intolerable servitude. In addition, the Carmelite not only repeated and reinforced the notion of France's particular chosenness compared to other, supposedly less wealthy countries, but he also made concrete proposals for the development of France's huge economic potential and for breaking free of foreign domination. He stressed the need to establish large trading companies in the style of the Dutch and the English, and to prohibit the export of French commodities on anything other than French ships.[15] It is not surprising, then, that the Dutch tried

[13] Antoine de Montchrestien, *Traicté de l'Œconomie politique*, ed. François Billacois (Geneva: Droz, 1999), 60. For further examples, see Lionel Rothkrug, *Opposition to Louis XIV. The Political and Social Origins of the French Enlightenment* (Princeton, NJ: Princeton University Press, 1965), 95–102.

[14] Jean Eon, *Le commerce honorable ou Considérations politiques contenant les motifs de nécessité, d'honneur et de profit qui se trouvent à former des Compagnies de personnes de toutes conditions pour l'entretien du Négoce de mer en France* (Nantes: Guillaume Le Monnier, 1646), esp. 210–219.

[15] Eon, *Le commerce honorable*, 230–253.

to block the dissemination of the cleric's bulky tract, efforts that were only partly successful for in 1659 an extract of it, containing all its key points, was published in Paris.[16]

Eon's ideas proved to be highly influential, becoming a major source of inspiration for the French government which, from the late 1650s onwards, sought to strengthen the kingdom's economy. The first measures were put in place in 1657 with the foundation of a company granted the exclusive right to sell whaling products in France (*Compagnie pour la pêche à la baleine*) and, two years later, on 15 March 1659, with the prohibition of exporting French goods on foreign ships. However, since the French did not yet have a fleet of its own capable of meeting the needs of its exporters, the prohibition was temporarily substituted just two weeks later by a 'shipping duty' (*droit de tonneau*), a special tax of 50 *sous* per tonne of freight capacity imposed on all foreign vessels arriving at and leaving French ports or sailing from one French port to another.[17]

On 10 April 1661, only one month after Mazarin's death and the commencement of Louis XIV's personal rule of France, a decree (*arrêt*) was published which set out the programme and fundamental principles of future French economic and commercial policy.[18] It bemoaned the decline of French shipping and the kingdom's manufacturing base and complained of the part supposedly played by other states in this downturn. By drawing the 'capital of their subsistence' from trade, those countries had sought to become the ubiquitous 'masters of commerce' and to deny France its share. It was a situation that had to change—not least by acquiring the facility that foreign countries had in matters of commerce, but which had long been neglected in the French kingdom—'in order to take the just and appropriate measures to reinstate it in the possession of

[16] *Extrait du livre intitulé Considerations politiques sur le Faict du Commerce de France. Composé par un Habitant de la Ville de Nantes & Imprimé en ladite Ville en 1646* (Paris: no publisher, 1659). The Dutch efforts to impede the dissemination of the *Commerce honorable* were reported by the French ambassador to The Hague, see AAE, CP, Hollande 66, fos. 54–54v.

[17] AN, Marine, A1 5, fos. 175–177.

[18] AN, E 1718, fos. 47–48v: 'Arrest du Conseil d'Estat, pour le retablissement du commerce tant au dedans qu'au dehors du Royaume'. The *arrêt* had been prepared jointly by Fouquet and Colbert.

that part of commerce, which is promised to it by the law of nations and nature itself seems to have intended for it'.[19]

The 'Law of Nations', National Treatment and the Principle of Most Favoured Nation (1659–1665)

Of what did this 'law of nations' referred to by the *arrêt* of April 1661 consist? In the seventeenth century, as in ancient and medieval times, the 'law of nations' (*ius gentium, droit des gens*) still represented a universal law of divine origins rather than a body of law composed of different agreements assembled over time. It was a code the rightness of which was evident to all people endowed with reason, since it contained the fundamental rules that alone made possible the peaceful coexistence of men. As far as the relations between individual states were concerned, the 'law of nations' obliged them to perform a juggling act. The first rule of the law was the right to self-preservation, according to which a state was entitled to do everything in its power to guarantee the well-being of its subjects. But, on the other hand, it was forbidden to harm other states arbitrarily through measures that damaged their interests without procuring advantages for one's own citizens.[20] Also, nations were not allowed to discriminate against specific states by excluding them from benefits conceded to others.[21] Within this framework, the central tenet of the law of nations was 'reciprocity'. Antoine de Montchrestien, in his *Traicté de l'Œconomie politique* confirmed the validity of this rule in the economic sphere by stating explicitly that between equals treatment itself had to be equal: 'He who wants to obtain more than he is willing to concede, claims more than is due to him. [. . .] What we do for ourselves we must allow others to do for themselves, or we are unjust!'[22]

In addition to reciprocity, another important principle inherent in commercial treaties since the second half of the fifteenth century was what in modern terminology is called 'national treatment'. This *égalité de traitement*, as it was known in seventeenth-century France, revolved around the

[19] AN, E 1718, fol. 48.

[20] See, for example, Francisco de Vitoria, *Relectio de Indis recenter inventis* (1539), ed. Walter Schätzel (Tübingen: Mohr, 1952), III 3.

[21] De Vitoria, *Relectio*, III 4.

[22] Montchrestien, *Traicté*, 283.

precept of non-discrimination of foreign merchants apropos import and export duties and other taxes. National treatment was included, for example, in the Anglo-Spanish treaties of 1466 and 1499.[23] The merchants of the Hanseatic League enjoyed national treatment in France from 1483, a privilege which was periodically renewed over the following centuries, for example by Henri IV in 1604 and Louis XIV in 1655. It was also conceded to the Dutch in the treaties of 1596 and 1608.[24]

A third important principle inherent in these treaties was that trade in every sort of commodity—with the traditional exception of 'wares of contraband', that is, military equipment—would be permitted. However, such treaties contained no specific clauses relating to the level of customs duties, which in effect was a discretionary charge decided by respective governments, albeit on the understanding that they were to be applied equally to foreigners and natives.

From the late 1650s onwards trade relations between France and the Netherlands became particularly tense. The French whaling company and the *droit de tonneau* hurt vital Dutch commercial interests. Furthermore, since in 1648 the United Provinces concluded in Münster a separate peace with Spain, disregarding an explicit clause inserted in the Franco-Dutch guarantee agreement of 1644 prohibiting such a separate peace, the French government no longer felt obliged to do anything to stop French privateers attacking Dutch ships, and this became a serious problem for the Dutch during the 1650s. Attempts to force the French to withdraw these measures by boycotting French products did not work, partly because of the economic egotism of Dutch merchants and partly because other countries refused to join in, which meant that the boycott would only have diverted French commerce to England and the Hanseatic towns. Thus, in 1660 the Estates General decided to dispatch Coenraad van Beuningen as head of a special delegation to Paris, tasking him with negotiating a new treaty of commerce with France. The deliberations took up the early months of 1661, in part as a result of the political situation in Europe, which had been shaken by the return of Charles II to the English

[23] Andrea Weindl, *Wer kleidet die Welt? Globale Märkte und merkantile Kräfte in der europäischen Politik der Frühen Neuzeit* (Mainz: Philipp von Zabern, 2007), 73–74.

[24] Jean Dumont (ed.), *Corps universel diplomatique du droit des gens* (Amsterdam: Brunel et al., 1728), V/I: 540.

throne in May of the previous year, an event which made a new alliance advisable for both sides.

The Dutch envoys arrived in Paris with instructions to have three conditions included in the treaty: that privateering would be stopped, that France would not establish any more exclusive trading companies that contravened the 'law of nations', and that the *droit de tonneau* would be withdrawn since it violated the principle of 'national treatment' established in previous Franco-Dutch treaties.[25] The French, however, had no intention to listen to Dutch lectures on 'freedom of trade'. Hence in their opening conversation, the French Secretary of State for Foreign Affairs, Brienne, told van Beuningen that everyone was 'master in his own state' and could therefore take steps in line with the national good. He further warned the Dutch diplomat not to seek an agreement in which the 'advantages, which have to be common, lean completely to one side'.[26]

The negotiations for the Franco-Dutch commercial treaty were the first in which Colbert was deeply involved. He had been appointed intendant of finances shortly after Mazarin's death in March 1661 and would become the leading figure in the financial and economic administration after the disgrace of the superintendent of finances, Nicolas Fouquet, in September of the same year. It may be argued that the negotiations were formative for him, in that they allowed him to observe at first hand the behaviour and tactics of the Dutch and thereby gain an understanding of what to expect from them in the future.

Since reaching their agreement with the Spanish at Münster the Dutch had a reputation in France of being inveterate turncoats. Henri Brasset, a long-term French 'resident' in The Hague and eyewitness to the change in Dutch allegiances, wrote a long memorandum to help prepare the French negotiators for their task: 'according to their good habits they exploit everything which is of use to them and afterward refuse to anyone else to do the same'.[27] Dutch conduct seemed to confirm Brasset's negative account, particularly in trade affairs. The Dutch had managed—through

[25] AAE, CP, Hollande 66, fos. 12–14.

[26] *Lettres et négociations entre Mr. Jean de Witt conseiller pensionnaire et garde des sceaux des provinces de Hollande et de West-Frise et Messieurs les plénipotentiaires des provinces unies des Pais-Bas aux cours de France, d'Angleterre, de Suède, de Danmarc, de Pologne etc.*, vol. II (Amsterdam: Janssons-Waesberge, 1725), 22.

[27] AAE, CP, Hollande 66, fos. 24–24v.

the use of an exclusive trading company and flagrant violence—to monopolize whaling along the coasts of Greenland and the trade in its products for decades. Moreover, they had restricted 'liberty of commerce' to their ports in Europe, barring the French from the places and ports held by the *Vereenigde Oostindische Compagnie* (VOC) in East India.[28] The Estates General had engaged a young lawyer from Delft, Hugo Grotius, to give their actions a semblance of legality. In relation to both issues he first turned to natural rights arguments in favour of 'free trade' to challenge the dominance of others operating in those markets, while using the self-same arguments in reverse when defending the Dutch position as dominant force.[29]

It is practically unthinkable that Grotius' line of reasoning convinced anyone outside of the Netherlands, and it certainly missed the mark in France. Responding to a draft treaty provided by the Dutch envoys in March 1661, the French king insisted on the principle of reciprocity. He indicated his willingness to withdraw the *droit de tonneau* if the Dutch in turn opened their overseas ports to French merchants. As for the Dutch request for the French to cease establishing any trading companies—a particularly hypocritical suggestion to French ears, since such companies had long been key to Dutch dominance over world trade, being used by them to oust foreign competition—Louis commented dryly that 'since in their own country they had established such companies it must be equally allowed to the King to establish them in his countries'. Furthermore, he emphasized tellingly, that he had 'no intention at all to diminish their [that is, Dutch] commerce, but to augment that of his subjects by just and reasonable means as much as possible'.[30]

The negotiations dragged on for another year, the Dutch insisting that the French abolish the shipping duty and their whaling company,

[28] Indeed, the prohibition on exporting French goods on anything other than French ships emanated on 15 March 1659 and, as a consequence, also the imposition of the *droit de tonneau* had been explicitly justified by the discrimination shown towards French merchants in the ports of other countries, by which the latter sought to 'attract all the profit of commerce by Sea'; AN, Marine, A1 5, fol. 175.

[29] See Martine van Ittersum, *Profit and Principle. Hugo Grotius, Natural Rights Theories and the Rise of Dutch Power in the East Indies, 1595–1615* (Leiden: Brill, 2006); 'The Long Goodbye: Hugo Grotius' Justification of Dutch Expansion Overseas (1615–1645)', *History of European Ideas* 26 (2010), 386–411.

[30] AAE, CP, Hollande 66, fos. 182–183.

but with limited success. Van Beuningen was told that the Estates General in the United Provinces, as regards their initiatives in trade and shipping, 'had in mind the special interest of their people without regard to that of the others, so that it was only natural that the French king did the same'.[31] The Treaty of Paris was eventually concluded in April 1662 (but not ratified until a year later) and the principle of free trade within Europe of all sorts of commodities 'which are not generally prohibited to both, nationals and foreigners' was confirmed, as were those of national treatment and national jurisdiction over taxation (Dutch trade was subjected to the same fiscal regime as French). Exceptions to these rules were made for the whaling company and the 'tonnage duty', which still set apart Dutchmen from Frenchmen.[32] However, van Beuningen and his fellow envoys did not go home empty-handed, since a separate clause was agreed according to which the Dutch had to pay the *droit de tonneau* only when leaving France and for the actual freight, while another stipulated that this would be halved for the transport of salt. Moreover, it was expressly stated that the Dutch had the right to impose tonnage duties at the same level.

These concessions were probably granted because Louis XIV, having already cast an eye on the Spanish Netherlands, did not want to alienate the Dutch completely. Nevertheless, the Dutch were far from satisfied with what they had obtained, and in March 1663 ambassador Boreel even wrote to the Grand Pensionary of Holland, Johan de Witt, that the shipping duty had dealt a 'mortal blow' to Dutch commerce.[33] This was obviously an exaggeration, although Colbert believed that the remaining *droit de tonneau* would be enough to give French shipping an advantage when competing with the lower costs of Dutch ships and would also allow France to replace the Dutch carrying trade with a merchant fleet of its own.[34]

With the treaty with the United Provinces concluded, Colbert turned his attention to establishing direct trade with the Baltic States: Baltic trade was vital to both the United Provinces and France. Jonathan Israel, arguing

[31] *Lettres de Witt*, 222–223.

[32] See Articles 19 and 20 of the treaty, Dumont, ed., *Corps universel diplomatique*, VI/I: 412–416: 414.

[33] *Lettres de Witt*, 512.

[34] See his memorandum for the newly founded *Conseil de commerce* in 1664. Colbert, *Lettres*, II/I: cclxvii.

against Fernand Braudel, has maintained that bulk trade to the Baltics declined considerably in importance during the second half of the seventeenth century at which time the key to profitable commerce shifted to colonial luxury trade.[35] But here Israel misses the crucial point that successful Baltic trade was a precondition for successful overseas trade, since it supplied the trading nations with shipbuilding materials. To maintain the strength of its commercial fleet, the Netherlands had to replace 400 to 500 vessels of various sizes every year.[36] Likewise, if France wanted to build up a merchant fleet and trade on an equal footing with its competitors, it needed the materials necessary for the construction of ships, in particular wood from Denmark, Norway and Prussia. In addition, the Baltic region was an important market for French agricultural goods such as wine, vinegar, brandy, salt and grain, above all in times of good harvests. Reduced exports led to falling prices, thus depriving a large part of the French population of income.

Negotiations started on 30 December 1662 and a treaty was concluded with Sweden that established direct reciprocal trade for a restricted number of domestic goods.[37] It was more important, however, to broker an agreement with Denmark (then in possession of Norway), which controlled the passage linking the North Sea to the Baltic Sea, and levied a toll on ships passing through the Øresund. The Dutch had been granted privileged toll terms in 1645 with the Treaty of Christianstad and, in order to trade successfully in the region, French merchants required the same concessions.

A similar problem had existed in relation to markets controlled by Spain, which had long since conceded preferential treatment to the United Provinces and to England. In the Treaty of the Pyrenees (1659), France was ensured that its citizens would not have to pay higher duties and taxes 'than those which have been paid by the

[35] Jonathan I. Israel, *Dutch Primacy in World Trade, 1585–1740* (Oxford: Clarendon Press, 1989), esp. 213–224. See also the discussion of this problem by Jan T. Lindblad, 'Foreign Trade of the Dutch Republic in the Seventeenth Century', in: *The Dutch Economy in the Golden Age. Nine Studies*, ed. K. Davids and L. Noordegraaf (Amsterdam: NEHA, 1993), 231–238.

[36] Jan de Vries and Ad van der Woude, *The First Modern Economy. Success, Failure, and Perseverance of the Dutch Economy, 1500–1815* (Cambridge: Cambridge University Press, 1997), 297.

[37] See AN, Marine, B7 485, fos. 201–215.

English [. . .] or which are at present paid by the inhabitants of the United Provinces of the Netherlands, or other strangers, who are treated most favourably'.[38] Now, with a treaty eventually concluded in 1663, Colbert also made sure that French merchants would not be charged more for passing through the Øresund than 'other nations, and especially the Dutch'.[39] This toll was fixed for decades to come, but both nations remained free to impose whatever duties they wished and, furthermore, as in the Franco-Dutch treaty, national treatment was established.

By 1663 France held favourable commercial treaties with all the major European commercial powers except England. Considering the Franco-Dutch treaty of 1662 to be highly advantageous for the Dutch because of the national treatment it included, the English approached the French ambassador to London, the Count of Comminges, to propose a treaty modelled on that of Paris. Margaret Priestley has written that grievances on both sides showed a 'remarkable similarity',[40] although this was confined to the wording. Both sides called for 'reciprocity', but meant something quite different by it. Colbert hoped to obtain reciprocal national treatment, which he thought would be of great advantage to French merchants. Louis XIV explained to his ambassador in London that 'the whole question of this treaty consists in knowing if the French in England will be treated as the English, and reciprocally the English in France as the French'.[41] In English legislation, however, discrimination against non-nationals was deeply rooted. Traditionally, they had to pay higher import and export duties on commodities than 'natural born subjects'. The Navigation Acts of 1651 and 1660 likewise put foreign traders at a disadvantage by excluding them from all forms of intermediary and colonial trade. On top of that, free trade in certain products, such as high-quality woollens (in French *drapéries*), was restricted by import prohibitions enacted in the late fifteenth and early sixteenth centuries and never revoked.

[38] The treaty established furthermore 'free trade' with all sorts of commodities apart from military equipment (Arts. 11–13) as well as a strict reciprocity of treatment of merchants in both countries (Art. 20). See Dumont, ed., *Corps universel diplomatique*, VI/II: 246–283.

[39] AN, Marine, B7 485, fos. 240v–250.

[40] Margaret Priestley, 'Anglo-French Trade and the "Unfavourable Balance" Controversy, 1660–1685', *Economic History Review*, 2nd ser. 4 (1951), 37–52: 37.

[41] AAE, CP, Angleterre 78, fol. 371. See also fol. 393v.

Modern scholars normally date the beginning of English protectionism from 1689, when duties on French products were raised markedly. Ralph Davis, for example, has written that without these longstanding prohibitions seventeenth-century trade would have hardly looked any different.[42] French contemporaries, on the contrary, saw these import prohibitions and other discriminatory measures against foreign merchants as a serious impediment to French commerce with England and a thoroughly unjust state of affairs. Antoine de Montchrestien, who knew the English laws well from his time as an exile at the English court, had already complained bitterly about them in his *Traicté de l'Œconomie politique.*[43] Several memoranda dating from the beginning of the 1660s angrily denounced the 'difference of treatment' and called on France to respond in kind.[44]

While the French pressed the claim for reciprocal national treatment and freedom of trade, Charles II requested that English merchants be treated in France in the same way as other foreign merchants, while French merchants in England would 'reciprocally' continue to be treated like those of other countries. Louis XIV warned the English not to try to 'establish one of these societies called leonine, in which the whole advantage is on one side'.[45] In point of fact, the English conception of 'reciprocity' was that French merchants would be discriminated against in England whereas English traders would be treated like nationals in France. Comminges was soon frustrated by his counterparts in the negotiations and complained to his king that 'nothing seems just to them which does not serve their interests, and if you want to be their friend, you are not supposed to contradict them'.[46]

The negotiations ran on until the end of 1664 without making any real progress. In a note he handed to Louis XIV on 20 December 1664, the English ambassador to France, Lord Denzil Hollis, used somewhat acrobatic arguments to lay out the English position and referred to an

[42] Ralph Davis, 'The Rise of Protection in England 1689–1786', *Economic History Review* 19 (1966), 306–317.

[43] Montchrestien, *Traicté*, 338–345.

[44] See AN, Marine, B7 486, fos. 15–32.

[45] AAE, CP, Angleterre 78, fol. 392v.

[46] AAE, CP, Angleterre 80, fol. 82v.

Anglo-Dutch treaty concluded in 1662 to explain why the English request was justified:

> The Dutch have not conceded to the subjects of the Most Christian King more than to all other strangers, who in Holland do not pay more taxes than the Dutch themselves; with the consequence that the subjects of the King of Great Britain, who has not concluded such a treaty with them, receive the same advantages as the French. Also, the Dutch when concluding two years ago their treaty with His Majesty in London have neither requested nor even proposed to receive greater privileges than the other foreigners, because they know well that they treat them all the same way in their own country. For this same reason all strangers can request to receive the same advantages as the Dutch, and specially the subjects of the king of Great Britain, who would be inconsolable if he had to see that the Dutch were being treated here better than all other nations.[47]

This must have sounded exactly like a 'leonine treaty' to the French king. Indeed, no good came of it and the negotiations were eventually interrupted by the outbreak of the Second Anglo-Dutch War.

The Development of Manufacturing in France and the Problem of Sovereignty (1667–1672)

During the early years of his activity, Colbert had tried to establish rules for fair competition with neighbouring countries, among these being the non-discrimination of foreign merchants, reciprocity, and the most favoured nation principle. Supposed transgressions of these rules were used to implement equal measures in France which gave French merchants some advantage over foreign rivals. Colbert's main focus had been shipping and international trade, but now, while the war effort held the attention of the Dutch and English governments, he worked on the second part of his plan for the economic recovery of the French kingdom: the promotion of manufacturing.[48] Between 1664 and 1667 he gave

[47] AAE, CP, Angleterre 83, fos. 126–126v.

[48] See especially his *Discours sur les manufactures du royaume* (1663), in: Colbert, *Lettres*, II/I: cclvii–cclxii; Charles W. Cole, *Colbert and a Century of French Mercantilism*, 2 vols. (New York: Columbia University Press, 1939), vol. 1: 132–137.

support to a great variety of industries with financial subsidies and other special concessions.

Manufacturing—particularly textiles—was an important part of his project, because it offered work to vast numbers of people, produced goods of greater value than agriculture and was not susceptible to the vagaries of the weather which could play havoc with harvests. In April 1667, while the Netherlands and England were still discussing the terms for a peace settlement, Colbert enacted a new tariff regime that raised import duties on several items, including textiles. He had known from the beginning that some kind of protection against foreign competition would be necessary, on top of the privileges granted by the king. But given that in the early years French production had not been sufficiently developed to meet the high demand for certain products, he had refrained from curbing imports, since to do so would have triggered a rise in prices and hurt the people.[49] Thus, in the first tariff list issued by Colbert in September 1664, import duties on foreign manufactures had been raised only moderately. But now, with the new tariff, they were doubled: those on *drapéries*, for example, rose from 40 *livres* to 80 *livres*.

Historians have labelled the tariff list of 1667 'ultra-protectionist' and 'frankly prohibitive',[50] with Charles W. Cole branding it a 'fighting tariff'.[51] These interpretations are highly misleading insofar as they infer that the tariff was equivalent to an actual import prohibition. But this was not the case. In the tariffs, duties were given as actual amounts, not in percentages *ad valorem*. Even so, from the early eighteenth century it has been attested that the tariff of 1664 raised taxes on the import of foreign manufactures from 5 to 10 per cent of their real value. And by doubling the duties on foreign *drapéries*, the tariff list of 1667 elevated them to 20 per cent.[52] This, however, was far from being an import

[49] See Colbert, *Lettres*, VII: 241–242.

[50] Pierre Goubert, *Louis XIV et vingt millions de Français* (Paris: Fayard, 1967), 94; Rothkrug, *Opposition*, 199.

[51] Cole, *Colbert*, vol. 1: 428.

[52] BnF, MS fr. 21773, fol. 169; AN, F12 1910 (25 March 1703). This corresponds roughly with a document dating from 1686 in which a piece of *draps d'Angleterre* was estimated at a value of 330 *livres* (AN, G7 1697, n.188). Margaret Priestley, who has analysed the impact of the tariff on English exports, writes that English mercantile propaganda 'launched upon Colbert's tariffs an attack out of all proportion to their actual effects': 'Anglo-French Trade', 48.

prohibition, especially with regard to luxury goods such as high-quality textiles. As many contemporaries pointed out, such commodities were purchased by wealthy people who were not deterred from buying them by their high price, so the increase in cost caused by the import duty normally fell on consumers such as they. Moreover, in some cases, the popularity of such goods was even enhanced by their expensiveness. To be really sure that certain foreign manufactures did not enter the country (at least legally), an outright import prohibition would be required.[53] As a matter of fact, before Colbert took office France had periodically issued import prohibitions on foreign textiles,[54] the last such measure being applied in 1648 when the guild of Parisian cloth manufacturers pressured the king to issue an import ban on woollen and silk cloth.

Why, then, did Colbert not resort to import prohibitions as his predecessors had done and the English continued to do, but chose instead to raise import duties? The answer is that he deemed a general freedom of trade vital to the exportation of French goods, as he stated as early as 1651 in a letter to Mazarin:

> Although the abundance with which God has endowed most provinces of this kingdom seems to place it in a position to be self-sufficient, Providence has put France in such a situation that without trade, which brings from one province to another and even to foreign countries the things that the one needs from the other, its own fertility would be of no use and often even a burden.[55]

Colbert wanted to keep the Dutch and English markets open for French agricultural and manufactured goods, deliberately avoiding any action that might prompt the Dutch and English to prohibit the import of French wine into their countries by way of reprisal. This was a lesson that the English had taught Colbert in 1649 when, after the aforementioned French import ban on woollen and silk cloth, England retaliated by

[53] BnF, MS fr. 14294, fol. 195v.

[54] The rise in import tariffs enacted by Fouquet in 1654 is generally considered to have been a measure of economic protectionism. However, Fouquet's intention remained mostly fiscal, for he raised import duties on raw materials required by French manufactures, too. Colbert, on the contrary, combined high duties for the import of manufactures with low duties for the import of raw materials and the export of manufactured goods.

[55] Colbert, *Lettres*, II/II: 405.

banning (the import of French woollens already being prohibited) the import of French silk and wine. The French ambassador to London, who claimed that the English would not be able to do without French wine, was told that if England had managed without a king, contrary to what many had thought, it could easily cope without French wine.[56]

It has become a commonplace of economic history that Colbert did not invent anything, but merely pursued with great tenacity principles devised by others long before him.[57] This is not quite accurate for in fact the actions of the Comptroller-General were essentially new. To preclude reprisals that might damage the French export economy, he substituted import prohibitions with a system that required the preservation of competition in the trade of all commodities, while simultaneously shifting competition away from price—made pointless by the import duty—to the quality of goods. At the same time he did his best to ensure, with his *règlements* for textiles of 1669 and 1670, which reinforced and systematized the traditional manufacturing standards of France that dated back to the Middle Ages, that French industry would do well in a competition centred on quality.[58]

In doing so, Colbert debunked the old French dreams of self-sufficiency and the time-honoured adage that other countries could not do without France, a fantasy that, not least, his great role model Richelieu had often indulged in.[59] When Colbert himself stated that other countries 'could not do without' certain French products, he meant something quite different from his predecessors: he was never naive enough to think that others could need French products to such a degree that they would not be able to prohibit their import. What he meant was that foreign nationals would keep buying French goods if import regulations made them available, and they would do so if such goods, whatever their price, were either unique or of better quality or style. This policy thus promoted an alliance between Colbert's France and foreign 'consumers'

[56] *Recueil des instructions données aux Ambassadeurs*, vol. 24.1: *Angleterre 1648–1665* (Paris: Centre National de la Recherche Scientifique, 1929), 86.

[57] See, for example, Jacquart, 'Colbert', 188.

[58] For quality controls, see especially Philippe Minard, *La fortune du colbertisme. État et industrie dans la France des lumières* (Paris: Fayard, 1998).

[59] Richelieu, *Maximes d'état et fragments politiques*, ed. Gabriel Hanotaux (Paris: Imprimerie nationale, 1880), 67. Cf. Cole, *Colbert*, vol. 1: 140–141.

against their governments, but the alliance could be formed only if he was able to conclude commercial treaties with foreign governments that, besides protecting the principles of reciprocity and 'national treatment', also ensured that no nation could impose a blanket ban on the import of commodities, while not preventing a ruler from levying duties in a way that in his mind best suited his subjects.

With regard to the Dutch, Colbert thought that Articles 19 and 20 of the Treaty of Paris had settled everything satisfactorily. There thus remained only the problem of England with which negotiations for a commercial treaty were reopened in 1669. In line with his plans, Colbert told his younger brother, the Marquis of Croissy, who led the French delegation, that the keystones of the treaty should be *égalité de traitement* and the freedom of both kings to impose the customs duties they desired, provided that what applied to non-nationals applied equally to their own people.[60] The English Secretary of State for Foreign Affairs, Arlington, assured the French ambassador that the treaty would be formulated in compliance with the principle of reciprocity, but the draft plan he finally handed over to Croissy fell well short of Colbert's expectations: freedom of commerce was still restricted to Europe, many French commodities continued to be excluded from import into England, and tax discrimination against French merchants was maintained, along with the Navigation Act. Colbert responded angrily by declaring that the English had protected the 'appearance' of reciprocity, but in truth had 'completely destroyed it'.[61] Furthermore, English merchants requested for their textiles to be exempt from quality controls before entering France, thereby allowing them to import low-quality products, undercut their French rivals and undermine the newly established industries. And perhaps most importantly, they insisted that France must return to the import duties established by the tariff list of 1664.

For almost three years Colbert stood firm over this last question, referring to princely sovereignty in matters of duties and the most favoured nation principle, which would oblige the French king to make the same concession to all other nations with whom he had concluded commercial treaties: 'The King cannot agree to this point, which would cause his subjects great prejudice and would despoil him of the right and

[60] Colbert, *Lettres*, vol. II/II: 492.

[61] Colbert, *Lettres*, vol. II/II: 816.

the liberty to impose such duties in his kingdom as he deems right', he explained his brother. Such a thing had 'never been requested from any king' and was a 'grace which He would necessarily have to concede equally to the Spaniards, the Dutch, the Swedes and the Hanseatic towns'.[62] It is noteworthy that when referring to princely sovereignty in matters of taxation Colbert used an old legal argument while at the same time changing its character to support his new economic system. Duties were traditionally regarded as an integral part of the Prince's sovereignty because they generated revenue and were therefore legally considered to be a part of his *domaine*, which—according to French jurists such as Jean Bodin and Jean Domat—could not be alienated without damaging his sovereignty.[63] What possibly irritated the Dutch and the English was that Colbert persisted in making this legal argument while no longer using duties to generate revenue, but to shape economic policy.

Following the advice of the Parisian merchants he had consulted for the negotiations, in April 1672 Colbert was almost prepared to give up the 1667 tariff. The merchants were of the opinion that, although a return to the tariff list of 1664 would impact badly on French manufacturing, overall the deal would be a good one if in return the same treatment as for English merchants was accorded to French merchants in England. Colbert maintained that he had already agreed to most of the English requests and to concede more would not be possible 'without changing the form of this state'.[64] A few weeks later, however, the negotiations with England failed definitively because the concessions Colbert was willing to make were not enough for the English: they continued to claim the same treatment for their merchants in France as Frenchmen, but were not willing to grant the same to French merchants in England. A memorandum dating from the end of the seventeenth century gave this report of the end of the negotiations: the English negotiators told Croissy that the French had no reason to complain about the way they were treated in England because other nations were treated in the same way, and the English in France equally were not treated any better than citizens of other

[62] Colbert, *Lettres*, vol. II/II: 816.

[63] For the broad notion of *domaine*, see Gaston Zeller, *Les institutions de la France au XVIe siècle* (Paris: Presses Universitaires de France 1948), 251–252.

[64] AN, Marine, B7 55, fol. 126.

countries. The French ambassador allegedly replied: 'This is true, Gentlemen, but the difference is that in France we treat you all well, whereas here you treat us all badly.'[65]

Things did not go as smoothly as Colbert had hoped with the Dutch as well. At the very same time that Croissy was negotiating with Arlington in London, the French ambassador to The Hague, Arnauld de Pomponne, was confronted with requests by Johan de Witt for the tariff of 1667 to be revoked. While de Witt tried to make his case in economic terms, emphasizing that France would suffer by its move since all the other countries would imitate its new policy of self-sufficiency, Pomponne stayed firmly on jus naturalistic grounds: by raising import duties the king simply wanted to promote the sale of French manufactured products by protecting them from the unfair competition of a 'great abundance' of low-price foreign products. The tariff was not intended to damage the Netherlands, he said, but to give employment to French subjects and to offer them some means of subsistence. He thereby emphasized that 'this care was worthy of the King's benevolence for his people, and that this primary concern could not be reprimanded by those which He left in the second rank'. In addition, he told de Witt that the tariff did not infringe the treaty of 1662 in any way, since this had left both governments free to raise duties on the import of foreign commodities.[66] Initially, the Grand Pensionary of Holland tried to contend that it was at least a circumvention of the principle of national treatment, for only foreign commodities were involved, but according to Pomponne he had to eventually admit that this did not qualify as a breach of the treaty.[67]

The weakness of Colbert's approach was, however, that the treaty's wording was open to interpretation and treaties never proved to be a sufficient constraint when a nation's vital economic interests were at stake. This became evident over the course of the next two years. First, in 1669 Colbert provoked a Dutch outcry by awarding the *Compagnie du Nord*—which had finally established direct economic exchanges between France and the countries bordering on the Baltic and the North Sea—a subsidy of three *livres* for each barrel of brandy and four *livres* for each

[65] AN, Marine, B7 499, fos. 468–468v.

[66] AN, A.E., BI 619 (14 March 1669).

[67] AN, A.E., BI 619 (8 November 1669).

tonne of all other commodities exported.[68] In this way, Colbert attempted to protect the *Compagnie* against the price-dumping to which the Dutch would assuredly resort in order to bring about its ruin. De Witt argued that the move constituted a violation of the clause of national treatment while Colbert, on the other hand, was of the opinion that the French king had every right to give 'gratifications' to his subjects.[69]

The real confrontation, however, came in autumn 1670 when, in order to force Louis XIV to revoke the tariff of 1667, the Estates General resorted to reprisals in the form of an import duty of 50 per cent *ad valorem* on many French manufactures as well as salt and a blanket ban on brandy imports. De Witt quickly explained to Pomponne that these measures did not in any way constitute a violation of the treaty with France since the import of brandy had generally been prohibited from all countries and on all other French commodities only import duties had been raised.[70] For Colbert, however, this act did indeed imply such a contravention because it singled out French products with the clear aim of weakening the kingdom's economy. This intention was explicit in relation to duties on French manufactures, and implicit in the import ban on brandy, which was imported exclusively from France. 'You see', he wrote to Pomponne,

> that the States General are much more temerarious than is our King. Hitherto His Majesty has always honoured the treaties and only favoured the commerce of his subjects with different ordinances regarding import and export duties, which has never been denied to any sovereign. The States General, on the contrary, since their very first steps have had no regards for the treaties, which they pass over and destroy without the slightest consideration.[71]

Pomponne emphasized the importance of the 'spirit' of the treaty in his discussions with de Witt: this left countries free to favour the well-being of their own citizens but never to the detriment of specific countries. In fact,

[68] For Colbert's plans concerning trade with the Baltic States and the foundation of the 'Northern Company', see Prosper Boissonnade and Pierre-Jacques Charliat, *Colbert et la Compagnie de commerce du Nord (1661–1689)* (Paris: Marcel Rivière 1930).

[69] Colbert, *Lettres*, vol. II/II: 496.

[70] AN, A.E., BI 619 (27 November 1670).

[71] Colbert, *Lettres*, II/II: 603.

the French tariff lists only made reference to different commodities, and not their provenance. The same commodity was subject to the same level of duty whatever its place of origin, something that implicitly observed the most favoured nation principle.

Louis XIV now felt justified in transgressing the boundaries of the treaty, and the conflict thus escalated further. Since the Dutch had only prohibited the import of brandy into the Netherlands but continued to transport it to the North so as not to lose the profit of freightage, in the early weeks of 1671 the French king banned its export from France on Dutch ships. At the same time, he also raised import duties on herring and spices transported by Dutch ships.[72] These measures were interpreted by the Dutch as an infringement of the treaty of 1662, for they discriminated against Dutch merchants vis-à-vis those of other nations, but Pomponne showed just cause for the measure by pointing to the Dutch duties that disfavoured French products and salt. However, the French ambassador reported: 'Although these things are very similar [. . .] our points of view were too distant to be able to reach an agreement on this question.'[73]

Despite these setbacks, until the autumn of 1671 Colbert's policy continued to work reasonably well. The measures taken by the Dutch did not substantially hurt French trade. The tax of 50 per cent on French products, high though it was, did not impede the sale of those commodities in the Netherlands, and the States General eventually fell back on severely stigmatizing those who continued to buy them.[74] As far as brandy was concerned, the import ban mainly damaged the United Provinces themselves, since it did not curb the French exports, which were simply taken over by ships from England, Denmark and Hamburg, as Colbert noted with some satisfaction in March 1671.[75] Consequently, in early November 1671, the Dutch regents took even more drastic steps and totally suspended the importing of French wine, vinegar, paper and sail canvas into the Netherlands. In prohibiting the import of French wine they calculated that the other countries together lacked the requisite number of ships and adequate storage facilities to transport French wine and expected that, as Jonathan Israel has written, 'France's exports would

[72] Colbert, *Lettres*, II/II: 599.

[73] AN, A.E., BI 620 (29 January 1671).

[74] AN, Marine, B7 207, fol. 92v.

[75] Colbert, *Lettres*, II/II: 609.

now slump and a severe depression grip France's wine-producing regions, which, in turn, would depress noble and ecclesiastical rents.'[76]

No information about Colbert's reaction to these final measures taken by the United Provinces has been handed down. But it is reasonable to assume that he was outraged. Indeed, having been for a long time reluctant to support Louis' preparations for war against the Dutch—a reluctance that almost amounted to insubordination—during the *conseil d'en haut* one week after the Dutch prohibition of French wine he declared himself in favour of a military strike on the United Provinces and explained how it could be financed. Paul Sonnino has argued that Colbert's volte-face should be attributed to the fear of potential disgrace for not making the necessary financial resources available to Louis XIV.[77] But he thus misses the point that with the Dutch import ban on French wine the main reason for Colbert's opposition to the war had ceased to exist since his entire economic system could not work if countries utilized such tactics.

It is an integral part of the legend built around Colbert that during the favourable military situation in the first months of the military campaign he had 'already sold the skin of the bear', that is, of the Netherlands.[78] A close reading of the two remaining memoranda he wrote for Louis XIV during the war instead shows that he still adhered to his legally framed view of international commerce and maintained that by laying an import prohibition on French brandy and wine, the Dutch had broken the treaty with France: 'for commerce has to be free, with the only exception of wares of contraband'.[79]

Conclusions

The aborted negotiations for a commercial treaty with England, the Dutch import prohibition on French wine and the beginning of the Dutch war marked the collapse of Colbert's trade policy. It did not break down,

[76] Israel, *Dutch Primacy*, 291.

[77] Paul Sonnino, 'Jean-Baptiste Colbert and the Origins of the Dutch War', *European History Quarterly* 13 (1983), 1–11.

[78] Goubert, *Louis XIV*, 95. See also Jean-Christian Petitfils, *Louis XIV* (Paris: Perrin, 1995), 372; Cole, *Colbert*, vol. 1: 372.

[79] Colbert, *Lettres*, II/II: 677.

however, because it was based on wrong economic principles, as has often been claimed, but rather because Colbert was unable to persuade France's two major competitors to abide by the legal conditions which were a necessary precondition for France's economic regeneration. Without taking into account the legal principles—including reciprocity, national treatment, the most favoured nation clause and sovereignty in matters of customs duties—around which Colbert tried to construct his economic policy, the latter remains incomprehensible and Colbert inevitably appears to be an economic incompetent, as many historians have portrayed him.

It should also be noted that the Comptroller-General's trade policy was far more original than is commonly admitted and quite distant from the unsubtle protectionism it is often said to be. The originality lay in the new way that Colbert combined the old principle of 'liberty of commerce' and that of 'sovereignty' over customs: every country had the right to protect its industry by manipulating import duties but had no right to prohibit the import of foreign products completely. He thereby sought to place international trade competition on a middle path between open market rivalry, which France could not have withstood, and outright protectionism as practised in the past, which would have caused a slump in economic activity to the detriment of all nations, including France.

After the foundering of the treaties, England and the Netherlands shared the same objectives: to force France to surrender the principle of sovereignty in matters of import duties and to commit to binding treaties that enshrined an unalterable scale of duties. This would allow them to move the standard of evaluation of products back onto price levels rather than quality standards, as Colbert had wanted, and to dominate the French market. The Dutch were the first to succeed. As a consequence of the Treaty of Rijswijk Louis in 1699 agreed to a binding Franco-Dutch tariff list.

English efforts remained unsuccessful until 1786. While the damage done to French industry caused by the tariff list of 1699 was limited, the Franco-English commercial treaty known as the 'Eden Treaty' would prove to be a short-term disaster for the French manufacturing sector and then would exacerbate the financial and economic crisis which the French monarchy faced shortly before its fall.

Moritz Isenmann is a Lecturer at the University of Cologne. He received his PhD from the European University Institute (Florence), and was a Humboldt

Fellow at the German Historical Institute and École des Hautes Études, Paris. He published *Legalität und Herrschaftskontrolle (1200–1600)* (2010) and edited *Merkantilismus. Wiederaufnahme einer Debatte* (2014). His habilitation thesis discussed Colbert's foreign trade politics. Currently, he researches the rise of liberal economic thinking in the Enlightenment.

The Anglo-Portuguese Methuen Treaty of 1703: Opportunities and Constraints of Economic Development

José Luís Cardoso

Introduction

The trade treaty signed between Portugal and England on 27 December 1703 is one of the most succinct documents in the entire history of commercial diplomacy. Nevertheless, with three simple articles, occupying just one folio, a treaty was written whose significance and interest extend far beyond the history of trade relations between the two contracting parties.

Commonly known by the name of the ambassador responsible for the English negotiations and agreements that preceded its signing, this treaty was not the only one to be associated with John Methuen. In fact, in May 1703, Portugal had sealed its commitment to a treaty of defensive and offensive adherence to the powers of the Grand Alliance, in the context of the political, diplomatic and military manoeuvring relating to the War of the Spanish Succession. Methuen also played an important part in ending the neutrality that had been maintained until then by the Portuguese court, which is why the commercial treaty that he negotiated should be seen as the

J.L. Cardoso (✉)
Institute of Social Sciences, University of Lisbon, Portugal
e-mail: jcardoso@ics.ulisboa.pt

A. Alimento, K. Stapelbroek (eds.), *The Politics of Commercial Treaties in the Eighteenth Century*, DOI 10.1007/978-3-319-53574-6_3

culmination of strategic choices and orientations that had implications and consequences in political, diplomatic, military and economic terms.

This chapter will take an in-depth look at the historiography of the Methuen treaty, using two main groups of documents as the subject of analysis. First of all, are the interpretations that were produced, in both Portugal and England, shortly after the treaty came into force. Attention will focus on the main trails opened up in the eighteenth century by authors who clearly understood the importance of a commercial treaty as a basis for reflecting on more general questions concerning the ways and means of government affairs, in particular economic policy. It is therefore opportune to first give a brief explanation of the broad context of the signing of trade agreements, such as the Methuen treaty, within a more general framework of the development of mercantilist economic policies in the period under review.

The second group of documents comprises texts resulting primarily from a genuine historical interest in studying the Methuen treaty, and these will be examined with a view to highlighting the diplomatic, political and economic problems associated with them. This historical interest was clearly prompted by a certain ideological desire to decipher the good and bad aspects which the treaty contained in the opinion of those who interpreted it after its signing. Here there will be a discussion of the theses and ideas most apparent in contemporary historiography, drawing conclusions and lessons which—without in any way wishing to claim that they are consensual—will hopefully make a contribution to the renewed historical attention that the Methuen treaty merits.

A Contextual Approach to the Historical Meaning of the Methuen Treaty

The most conventional interpretation of the Methuen treaty is the common-sense view which presents it as clear-cut evidence of the dominance of English economic interests over Portuguese ones, a situation which seems to have been the corollary of a long-lasting commercial relationship regulated by mutually favourable treaties.[1] Having no choice but to accept the economic consequences of a political alignment with England,

[1] The study of the activities of the British community of merchants in Portugal has been the subject of several studies, including H. E. S. Fisher, *The Portugal Trade. A Study of Anglo-Portuguese Commerce, 1700–1770* (London: Methuen, 1971), and L. M. E. Shaw, *The*

Portugal could not reject the permissive terms of treaties of commerce that preserved England's political sovereignty, notwithstanding the conditions of commercial reciprocity enshrined in them.

It must, however, be mentioned that this interpretation is based on testimonies offered from the Portuguese side, while a different perspective is given by the British side. In order to gain an unbiased explanation of the treaty's real meaning, one needs to reach a better understanding of the historical context in which the treaty was signed, namely Portugal's negotiating capacity in the context of bitter rivalry between European powers, especially between France and England during the period from 1689 to 1713.[2]

In 1689, Portugal was confronting the harsh reality of its weakened condition in the aftermath of the War of Restoration against Spain, which followed a period of dynastic union between the Iberian kingdoms from 1580 to 1640. Thus the War of the Spanish Succession, which broke out just twelve years later, in 1701, represented a threat to Portuguese hopes of securing the country's independence from the claims of Philip, Duke of Anjou, and his supporters. This small state, while fully intending to fend for itself by exploiting its own territorial resources, was well aware of the difficulties it faced in a political arena dominated by major powers with global influence and big ambitions.

It is important to remember that, after a first alliance with France and the United Provinces, which had supported the political movement towards Restoration and ensured the integrity of the Brazilian Empire, the renewed Portuguese kingdom came under the influence of the English in 1654 when they conceded it certain economic privileges in a quite unusual way. The English community living in Portugal were granted religious freedom and the right to free circulation and trade in continental Portugal and its colonies, in particular Brazil. And the ample reparations paid for damage caused by conflicts with English merchants and, in particular, the confidential article establishing custom duties (23 per cent

Anglo-Portuguese Alliance and the English Merchants in Portugal, 1654–1810 (Manchester: Manchester University Press, 1988).

[2] On the polarization between France and England at the end of the seventeenth century see Michael Braddick, 'The English Government, War, Trade and Settlement, 1625–1688', in: *The Oxford History of the British Empire, Vol. I. The Origins of Empire*, ed. Nicholas Canny (Oxford: Oxford University Press, 1998), 286–308.

ad valorem) on goods traded by English merchants that were equal to those paid by the Portuguese, were further signs of the predominance of English interests in Portugal and Brazil.

Seven years later, the humiliation imposed by Cromwell was slightly amended by the treaty of 1661, fulfilling the preconditions for the marriage of Catherine of Bragança to Charles II. This time, despite the transfer of Bombay and Tangier to English possession, the terms of the treaty gave Portugal new defensive military guarantees in a context that already showed signs of growing tension with its former allies—France and the United Provinces—despite the fact that they had ceased to engage in territorial disputes in Brazil.[3]

In the midst of such political turmoil, the military and diplomatic alignments were naturally followed by commercial agreements that confirmed the pertinence of trade to the securing of political ends.[4] According to the best doctrines and practices of mercantilism, it had always been deemed judicious to underline the instrumental nature of customs duties, protection rights for national industries, privileges granted to favoured interest groups, selective and differentiated taxation on imported goods, and other converging economic policies aimed at reinforcing the power of individual nations.

For most mercantilist authors, the binomial of wealth and power represented the central core of economic and political concerns. Power meant money, and the profits of a rich and powerful nation were estimated in terms of superiority over other nations, at the military level, but also commercially. Maintaining a positive balance of trade was seen as a priority, around which economic policy measures and instruments were set out to achieve that aim.

The policies of providing incentives and subsidies for the export of manufactured goods, restricting and imposing heavy customs duties on imports of the same type of goods, retaining raw materials and heavily

[3] For a detailed description of this international political context, see Leonor F. Costa, 'Da Restauração a Methuen: ruptura e continuidade', in: *O Tratado de Methuen (1703). Diplomacia, Guerra, Política e Economia*, ed. José Luís Cardoso (Lisbon: Livros Horizonte, 2003), 31–49. See also Violet M. Shillington and Beatrice W. Chapman, *The Commercial Relations of England and Portugal* (London: Routledge, 1907).

[4] On the intersection between trade and conflict see Lucia Coppolaro and Francine McKenzie, eds., *A Global History of Trade and Conflict since 1500* (Basingstoke: Palgrave Macmillan, 2013).

taxing their export, were just some of the expedients that were universally contemplated and regularly put into practice.[5] These were combined with the more elaborate ways in which fundamental economic activities were organized and structured, namely the creation of trading companies designed specifically for overseas trade, operating in colonial markets through the institutionalization of monopoly practices and exclusive privileges, as well as the signing of bilateral agreements and conventions formulated to establish mutually agreed rules and the sharing of benefits, even if in reality these were markedly unequal.[6]

Bilateral agreements could better serve the needs of friendly nations, even when established through unequal power relations. The Methuen treaty shows precisely the ambivalence of an unequal balance of power that, nevertheless, brought undisputed mutual advantages. The issue at stake for the two nations was not only that of gaining space in which to sell their wares: granting English textiles permanent and convenient access to the Portuguese market in return for lower tariffs on wine imported from Portugal. For England, the scope of the treaty was much wider in the sense that it would have a favourable effect on its commercial rivalry with France—whose wines were not only of a better quality, but could also be obtained at a more convenient price—as well as on the possibility of English merchants having right of entry to the Portuguese colonial empire. As for Portugal, apart from guaranteeing political sovereignty, the Methuen treaty also provided an inducement for the modernization and maximization of its wine sector.

Bilateral trade agreements between Portugal and England, of which the Methuen treaty can be considered the prime example, show how difficult it was for less developed countries to maintain a political neutrality that

[5] For a synthetic approach to mercantilist doctrines and economic policies, as well as the range of different interpretations that these have given rise to in the historiography of economic thought, see Lars Magnusson, *Mercantilism. The Shaping of an Economic Language* (London and New York: Routledge, 1994). A good example of the continuation and updating of studies of national cases relating to mercantilism is given by Andrea Finkelstein, *Harmony and the Balance. An Intellectual History of Seventeenth-Century English Economic Thought* (Ann Arbor: University of Michigan Press, 2000).

[6] On the ideological foundations of colonial enterprise throughout the mercantilist era see David Armitage, *The Ideological Origins of the British Empire* (Cambridge: Cambridge University Press, 2001).

would serve the purpose of multilateral commercial relationships.[7] Apart from having to take into account the vested interests of economic players, there were also national political considerations that virtually determined the implementation of policies. England, after all, had the power to control a small state's capacity to preserve the autonomy of its political and commercial institutions and could thus impose on it trade conditions that generated imbalances in the interstate system.[8]

It is in this context that we should place interpretations of the Methuen treaty. Of course, if we could momentarily ignore the political and diplomatic atmosphere that prevailed at the time of its signing, and if we could also put to one side the matter of the personal interests of those who, with greater or lesser enthusiasm, gave their approval and let their name be associated with the signing of the treaty, we could simply conclude that what we are faced with here is a negotiated trade settlement based on a series of undertakings and responsibilities, freely entered into as a gesture of sovereign will.

But the fact is, we already know about the adverse conditions that were normally linked to the signing of bilateral trade agreements during that period. We know it was a time when the different European nations were focused on devising strategies for industrial development and trading supremacy which would have an inescapable impact on disputes, competition and rivalry. Hence it seems unavoidable that we should admit that each of those nations possessed different advantages and capacities that greatly reduced the possibility of obtaining genuinely reciprocal commercial benefits by dint of the treaties they concluded. Consequently, we must see that it would be difficult for Portugal to derive any immediate advantage from a treaty that essentially amounted to a certified seal of approval for an external political alignment that could generate security for the maintenance of territorial and political sovereignty.

[7] On the issue of neutrality and trade, see Antonella Alimento, 'Commercial Treaties and the Harmonization of National Interests: The Anglo-French Case (1667–1713)', in: *War, Trade and Neutrality. Europe and the Mediterranean in the Seventeenth and Eighteenth Centuries*, ed. Antonella Alimento (Milan: Franco Angeli, 2011), 107–128.

[8] See Koen Stapelbroek, 'The Rights of Neutral Trade and its Forgotten History', in: *Trade and War: The Neutrality of Commerce in the Inter-State System*, ed. Koen Stapelbroek (Helsinki: Helsinki Collegium for Advanced Studies, 2011), 3–13.

British Testimonies about the Treaty

Immediately after the signing of the treaty, at a time when its implementation was not yet the subject of intense political debate, several British merchants published anonymous pamphlets to explain why they nurtured expectations about the benefits of increased trade with Portugal.[9] Needless to say, these were voices that spoke in defence of particular interests. It is curious to observe, however, that, from the very beginning, concerns were also expressed in the public sphere, seeking to gain support for the Methuen treaty since it offered advantages to both British wine importers and cloth exporters. The development of long-distance trade, including colonial trade with Brazil, was also good news for the British merchant navy, a factor not overlooked by the treaty's supporters, as would later be recognized and elucidated in relevant historical approaches.[10]

The Methuen treaty was regularized and effectively came into force only after 1711. In fact, during the first years of its existence, it was either given little attention or purposely disregarded. The debates that took place at that time in the British Parliament and newspapers suggest that the English were initially satisfied with its provisions. In a speech delivered to the House of Lords in 1713 in Methuen's honour Charles Montagu, 1st Earl of Halifax, declared his delight over the substantial rise in British profits thanks to the Anglo-Portuguese treaty, and proposed that in each British trading city a

[9] Excerpts from these pamphlets are commented on by John V. C. Nye, *War, Wine, and Taxes. The Political Economy of Anglo-French Trade, 1689–1900* (Princeton, NJ: Princeton University Press, 2007), 52–53.

[10] On the role of Portugal as a gateway to the wider colonial market of Brazil, see François Crouzet, *La guerre économique franco-anglaise au XVIIIe siècle* (Paris: Fayard, 2008). According to Crouzet, Portugal was the third country in the ranking of British exports in the early eighteenth century and, throughout the first half of this same century, the overall increase in British exports to Portugal contrasted with its relatively moderate performance with other commercial partners (Crouzet, *La guerre économique*, 160–161). British imports from Portugal were equal to the total imports of all the other nations, throughout the first half of the eighteenth century. As to the importance of the discoveries of gold and diamonds in Brazil (especially after 1720) in furthering Portuguese trade with England, according to Crouzet (*La guerre économique*, 164), England received 30 per cent of the amount of gold mined in Brazil between 1700 and 1760, which was used to pay for merchandise bought by Portugal in the British markets.

statue of Methuen should be erected as a sign of the people's gratitude for his remarkable feat.[11]

Discussions about the pros and cons of the treaty later became a source of political tension when, in 1713, the Tory government, in the context of ongoing negotiations that culminated in the signing of the Treaty of Utrecht, put forward a new policy of trade expansion that required the celebration of peace agreements and the suspension of restrictions on trade with France. Former enemies were now seen as potential allies, contributing to the prosperity and power of Britain. The defence of this shift in commercial relationships and the Tory plans for free trade with France implied an attack on the Methuen treaty and a reduced estimation of what it meant for British interests. To support this new policy orientation—which did not succeed as expected—the Tory government deployed powerful journalists and men of letters, namely Jonathan Swift and Daniel Defoe, who wrote several articles and pamphlets denouncing the terms of the Methuen treaty, accusing Portugal of breaking the terms of the trade agreements, and hinting that Methuen himself was financially involved in the treaty when negotiating in 1703.[12] The Whig arguments, favouring the economic interests of the supporters of the Methuen treaty, were channelled through the pages of the *British Merchant* with great public impact, outsmarting the defenders of open trade relations with France.

Opinions about the trading interests associated with the import of wines and the export of cloth rose and fell, being swayed by the public pressure of short-term commercial benefits.[13] It therefore pays to concentrate attention on the more consistent arguments and reflections advanced by authors equipped with scholarly skills, such as Adam Smith.

Smith used the example of trade between Portugal and Britain to criticize the model based on preferential relations of a mercantilist nature that did nothing to promote British commercial interests. In the chapter

[11] See the transcription of this speech in A. D. Francis, *The Methuens and Portugal, 1691–1708* (Cambridge: Cambridge University Press, 1966), 354–355.

[12] On this topic, see Paul Duguid, 'The Making of Methuen: The Commercial Treaty in the English Imagination', *História* 4 (2003), 9–36.

[13] For a global understanding of the relationship between the strategic behaviour of merchants and the representation of political interests in the mercantilist era, from the mid-sixteenth to the mid-seventeenth century, see Robert Brenner, *Merchants and Revolution. Commercial Change, Political Conflicts and London's Overseas Traders, 1550–1653* (Princeton, NJ: Princeton University Press, 1991).

of *The Wealth of Nations* that he devoted to a critical discussion of the relevance of trade treaties,[14] he began by considering whether the advantages of favouring certain foreign interests to the detriment of others (by including specific purposive clauses in bilateral agreements) might be cancelled out by increased prices in the internal market. In other words, whether eliminating free competition between nations that supply certain consumer goods might harm domestic trade.

To Smith's mind, the Methuen treaty had not been a good deal for Britain, for two reasons. First, because the gold that Portugal used to pay off its balance of trade deficit could have been obtained by means of skilful trade with other nations. And second, because British consumers were obliged to make sacrifices owing to the politically expedient favouring of Portuguese wines. Although he did not actually say so, Smith left the idea hovering in the air that the preferential treatment of Portuguese wines, based on a price–quality ratio, had not been made in the best interests of British consumers. Despite the highly nationalistic stance that he adopted when assessing British losses, Smith highlighted the key political issue that had justified the signing of the treaty, in other words, the guarantee to defend a country that held an enviable geo-strategic situation.

An almost identical stance was adopted by Sir Philip Francis when he commented on some of the economic policy measures implemented by the Marquis of Pombal, namely the creation of monopoly companies for the growing of vines in the Douro and for trade with Brazil, which obviously threatened established British interests.[15] For this British author, there should not be any doubt over the importance of the alliance for Portugal's continued political independence. It would therefore be wrong to think that the union established in the Methuen treaty should have been based on a mutual exchange of identical trade advantages; even

[14] Adam Smith, *An Inquiry into the Nature and Causes of the Wealth of Nations* (1776) (Glasgow Edition, Oxford: Oxford University Press, 1976), Book IV, Chapter VI.

[15] Sir Philip Francis, '[Final note to] Letter on the Jealousy of Commerce by Monsieur De Pinto', in: *Essay on Circulation and Credit*, ed. Isaac de Pinto (London: J. Ridley, 1774), 241–242. For political reasons, Sir Philip Francis, the author of the translation and notes to the English edition of this book by Isaac de Pinto, caused his name to be replaced by that of a relative of his, Reverend S. Baggs, which appears in the foreword to the work. This detail is recounted and explained by Richard H. Popkin, 'Isaac de Pinto's Criticism of Mandeville and Hume on Luxury', *Studies on Voltaire and the Eighteenth Century* 154 (1976), 1705–1714: 1712.

so, the fact was that, through it, Portugal had gained an outlet for selling its wines that seemed propitious.

The commercial facilitations granted by Portugal were in fact the only way in which the English had been compensated for their commitment to political support. For this reason both Francis and Smith believed that the treaty should be pared back to its original premises of providing economic advantages for England and political security for Portugal. Both of them understood that the treaty represented a valuable bargaining chip for both countries, with the added advantage for Portugal that it had procured a marketplace and means of motivation for its wine producers.

The Portuguese Position: From Dom Luís da Cunha to the Marquis of Pombal

Among those who wrote conventional interpretations of the treaty, Dom Luís da Cunha (1662–1749) is generally considered to have been the first to denounce its negative effects on Portugal.[16] But was that in fact his position? It seems undeniable that in many of his writings Cunha advanced clear-cut arguments that would suggest that it was so. His *Testamento Político*, for example, famously conveyed his views on the matter: to his mind, three circumstances combined to confirm the disgraceful nature of the treaty: Dom Pedro II's desire to 'please the Queen of England'; the fact that Methuen, the English ambassador in Portugal, was the brother of a prominent cloth merchant and so had sought to feather his own nest; and the fact that the same ambassador had somehow convinced wine makers and merchants of the profitability of marketing their product in England (since French vintners had to pay a third more in duties).[17]

Cunha's opposition to what the treaty represented had been voiced early on, well before it was actually signed. In fact, at the beginning of his diplomatic mission to London in 1697, he wrote in his official reports for

[16] Dom Luís da Cunha was the Portuguese ambassador in London when the treaty was signed. A central figure in Portuguese diplomacy, he distinguished himself through the attributes that he displayed as a political adviser to the king, Dom João V.

[17] Dom Luís da Cunha, *Testamento Político ou Carta Escrita ao Senhor Rei D. José I Antes do Seu Governo* (1748) (Lisbon: Impressão Régia, 1820), 38.

the court about the presumed potential for developing the Portuguese wine trade by exporting to England and the false claims of English cloth manufacturers, according to whom the import of wines would have to be offset by the export of their products under equally advantageous conditions. But, for him, the main point of concern was the inordinate number of products that England was already exporting to Portugal, which meant that suspending the laws that protected Portuguese manufacturing would greatly exacerbate the negative balance in the country's trade relations with England.

However, despite constantly reiterating his reservations about the treaty and how it had been negotiated, he submitted that it should be adhered to, albeit with a straightforward explanation of its provisions. And his pragmatism and political realism were manifest when he admitted the historical inevitability of the treaty, categorically stating that 'we have no choice: instead, we are obliged to preserve the perpetual defensive alliance that we have with England, even though it remains subject to the inconstancy of that nation, the deliberations of its parliament, the difficulties in providing aid, because of the delay in their embarking, and accidents at sea'.[18]

Similar mildly critical reservations about the nature of the treaty were voiced by the Marquis of Pombal in his various writings and the letters that he composed when serving as the Portuguese ambassador to London.[19] By referring to the imperatives of diplomatic and political balance which dictated the Portuguese strategies of international alignment, he unequivocally stated that: 'As far as external interests are concerned, that treaty signed in 1703 was granted to a natural and necessary ally for our own sustenance: such that what we give them always ends up being the (expensive) price of our own safety […] Furthermore, the said treaty is thought to have been established so that we are not in trouble with anyone.'[20] Moreover, Pombal acknowledged the political and diplomatic inevitability of a commercially disadvantageous treaty in his personal papers and reports.

[18] Dom Luís da Cunha, *Instruções Políticas a Marco António de Azevedo Coutinho* (1736) (Lisbon: Comissão Nacional para as Comemorações dos Descobrimentos Portugueses, 2001, ed. Abílio Diniz Silva), 276.

[19] Sebastião José de Carvalho e Melo, *Escritos Económicos de Londres, 1741–1742* (Lisbon: Biblioteca Nacional, 1986, ed. José Barreto).

[20] Carvalho e Melo, *Escritos Económicos de Londres*, 131.

Historiographical Theses and Revisions

As I have tried to document and demonstrate, the theses that seek to attribute to Cunha and Pombal the initial arguments that blame the treaty for the deceleration of Portuguese industrial development (in the eighteenth century) are not entirely convincing. The myth that the Methuen treaty lay at the root of Portugal's process of dependent development began to spread much later and in a rather diffuse fashion, having started in the first phase of the construction of the liberal state.

It was, in fact, within the context of the relatively fervent and nationalistic anti-British feeling that surrounded the preparations for the 1820 Revolution and the work of the constitutional *Cortes* in 1821–1822 that the first signs of renewed interest in the application of economic recipes and protectionist policies began to appear. Blame was placed on the British occupancy of many important positions both in the military and in public administration, as a concomitant of the help given to Portugal during the Napoleonic Wars, which ended with the signing of the Treaties of Friendship and Commerce of 1810, largely favourable to British economic interests. The symbolic pedestal on which the mythical figure of Pombal came to be placed proved the esteem reserved for heroes who, in the heated debate of the time, had sought to throw off the British yoke. It should be noted that it was also during this period that Cunha's *Testamento Político* was first published and given a place in the corpus of authoritative arguments against the British oppression.

The word-pictures that were painted at that time of the perfidious nature of the Methuen treaty (in shades darker than what might justifiably have been painted of the 1810 Treaties of Friendship and Commerce) were frequently reproduced throughout the nineteenth century. And these criticisms were enthusiastically espoused by historians and writers who, regardless of the time when they were formulating their prophecies, were committed to demonstrating that the political and commercial relations between Portugal and England, patently asymmetrical in nature and resulting in Portugal's inauspicious dependence, constituted the original sin of Portuguese economic development.

We cannot ignore the importance of this traditional interpretation of the treaty, which, curiously, reached its peak in the work of an author who, since he was not Portuguese, cannot be accused of excessive nationalistic sentiment. In fact, for Sandro Sideri, the Methuen treaty can be explained as the decisive cause of Portugal's humiliating relationship of economic and political dependence on Britain and also of the long delay in beginning the process of industrialization in Portugal.[21] Sideri's thesis remains a recurrent interpretation of the Methuen treaty, as the scattered references still to be found in the international bibliography on this subject demonstrate.

Not surprisingly, then, whenever scholars have begun a serious study of the clauses, precedents and consequences of the Methuen treaty, they have been confronted with a mass of unhelpful evidence supporting the impressions that popular opinion has inexplicably perpetuated.[22] Even so, and despite the echoes of Sideri's thesis in popular discourse, not to mention its propagation in pre-university school textbooks over many generations, it is pleasing to see that the most relevant Portuguese historiography on the Methuen treaty presents points of view that contradict the negative interpretations which link Portugal's economic malaise to the treaty.

Thus, the historiography which has remained most faithful to the historical significance of the treaty has chosen to underline the instrumental nature of a preferential agreement that did not entirely exclude the competition of other countries, but merely restricted it through the privileged treatment that the contracting parties accorded each other. In other words, the treaty was not the instrument of a policy of commercial monopoly (Portuguese wines in England and English textiles in Portugal): indeed, the competition of other countries continued to make itself felt. Moreover, the treaty did not establish completely binding rules, since it provided for the possibility of the preferential practices one day ending.

And neither did the treaty lead to the establishment of a new policy. In fact, it did no more than extend the 1654 treaty that had created the conditions for permanent English involvement in the export of Douro wines and established clear benefits for English cloths and manufactured products, namely through a confidential clause that, in practice, allowed

[21] See Sandro Sideri, *Trade and Power. Informal Colonialism in Anglo-Portuguese Relations* (Rotterdam: Rotterdam University Press, 1970).

[22] Among the authors who most contributed to the formation of this group of historiographers who proved capable of looking at the Methuen treaty without the customary nationalist fervour, attention is drawn in particular to: João Lúcio de Azevedo, *Épocas de Portugal Económico. Esboços de História* (Lisbon: Livraria Clássica Editora, 1928); Luís Teixeira de Sampaio, 'Para a história do Tratado de Methuen', *O Instituto* 76/1 (1928), 125–141; and Francisco António Correia, 'O Tratado de Methuen', *Revista do Instituto Superior de Comércio de Lisboa* 24 (1930), offprint.

English products imported by Portugal to be declared at artificially low prices in order to qualify for lower duties.

At the time when the Methuen treaty was signed, most of the efforts that had been invested in the manufacturing policy of the late seventeenth century were beginning to flag. The presence of foreign technicians, labour and equipment was not enough to achieve the standard of workmanship that would make Portuguese products competitive domestically. That could only be achieved through protectionist measures which understandably aroused the fury of English industrialists and merchants. The shortage of raw materials, smuggling practices, and politico-religious restrictions on raising capital for production purposes, were all factors that exacerbated the difficulty of successfully implementing the process of industrialization.[23]

At this point, it is also important to bear in mind the political and diplomatic context of the signing of the Methuen treaty, which resulted from the strategic option of aligning with the English–Austrian–Dutch alliance against France and its designs for dominance over the Iberian Peninsula during the War of the Spanish Succession. What is more, the signing of the treaty did not imply that one country could be considered to be a winner and the other a loser. The advantages of the treaty were mutual and particularly beneficial to Portugal, given the influx of English capital that supported the development of the Douro region. Although not recorded in the balance of trade, such productive investments were also important for the exploitation of sources of wealth in other economic sectors.

New Historiographical Developments

The theses countering the idea that the Methuen treaty was the chief cause of Portugal's dependence upon Britain and for the transfer of Brazilian gold to Britain prefaced the well-documented opinion elaborated by Jorge Borges de Macedo in his studies of eighteenth-century Portuguese industry. In a synthetic text dedicated to the Methuen treaty,[24] he challenged

[23] See Carl A. Hanson, *Economia e Sociedade no Portugal Barroco, 1668–1703* (Lisbon: Publicações Dom Quixote, 1986), 287–300.

[24] Jorge Borges de Macedo, 'O Tratado de Methuen', in: *Dicionário de História de Portugal*, ed. Joel Serrão (Lisbon: Iniciativas Editoriais, 1966, Tomo III), 48–55.

the unilateral interpretations of the treaty that can be traced back to Cunha and Alexandre de Gusmão. For Macedo, the supposed superiority and excellence of Portuguese wines—the crucial reason for the growing demand for them in the British market—were far from proved. He also disputed the idea that the treaty per se could be held responsible for the stagnation of industry in Portugal. In order to dismantle this argument, he raised a series of questions that have proved decisive in the investigation of Portuguese industrial history and which essentially relate to the types and sectors of industry supposedly covered by the treaty, as well as to the regions and social groups it affected. Even in the sector that was directly referred to in the treaty, Macedo's conclusion was that 'both before and after the Methuen treaty, the wool industry in Portugal enjoyed a widespread and steady consumption'.[25]

His explanation for the weakness of Portuguese industry in the eighteenth century centred on the role played by the gold from Brazil, which, by providing an easy solution for the balance of trade problem, meant that fewer initiatives involving industrial risk were taken. His analysis led him to conclude that the Methuen treaty merely enshrined a de facto state of affairs brought about by Portugal's inability to sustain the development of industrialization process at the end of the seventeenth century. Hence the easy solution.

In another synthetic text,[26] which dealt with a different situation, Macedo raised some controversy when discussing the simplistic explanations which imputed the processes of dependence and underdevelopment to the English alliance and the 1703 treaty, such notions being popularized by the above-mentioned book by Sideri. For Macedo, the political and diplomatic background to the signing of the treaty was fundamental to understanding how it did not represent 'an imposition of force, but rather an economic compensation designed to guarantee the great transformation that Portugal had just made, by distancing itself, with great effort, from the French-Spanish pressure'.[27]

[25] Borges de Macedo, 'O Tratado de Methuen', 53.

[26] Jorge Borges de Macedo, 'Diplomacia, agricultura e comércio transitário: factores subalternizados no estudo do Tratado de Methuen', in: *Nova Economia em Portugal. Estudos em Homenagem a António Manuel Pinto Barbosa* (Lisbon: Universidade Nova de Lisboa, 1989), 75–93.

[27] Borges de Macedo, 'Diplomacia, agricultura e comércio transitário', 77.

The prevailing idea was that the treaty functioned as a reliable instrument in the distribution of advantages, costs and concessions. Thus Portugal and the Atlantic played a strategic role not only in British trade policy, but also in the political decisions of Austria and Holland. Some facts about the Portuguese economy in the first half of the eighteenth century help us to understand why the treaty did not, in reality, have a deleterious effect on Portugal: the fact that woollen cloths made up only a fraction of British trade with Portugal and were primarily used for bringing foodstuffs into the country, and that wine was the main commodity of Portuguese overseas trade, being the only area in which it could maximize an advantage.[28]

Most of the arguments advanced by Macedo were based on the detailed empirical evidence studied and discussed in the books and preparatory articles that A. D. Francis dedicated to the Methuen treaty, its antecedents and outcome.[29] This is without doubt the most thorough and complete work on Methuen's time in Portugal, based on unpublished documentation (mostly official and private correspondence) that had never been subjected to systematic study. Francis' study in fact makes it possible to follow Methuen's career from the first phase of his appointment as English ambassador to Portugal between 1691 and 1696, and the influence that he succeeded in exerting over prominent figures in the court of Dom Pedro II, where he enjoyed direct and easy access to the Portuguese king. His activities in Lisbon were continued by his son Paul from 1697 to 1702, an important period for the management of Portuguese neutrality on the international diplomatic scene. But it was Methuen himself who, once more settled in Lisbon from May 1702 onwards, played a crucial role in the Portuguese political realignment with the powers of the Grand Alliance. The pressure he applied and his direct political involvement in the negotiations were decisive (particularly in late 1702) in reversing Portugal's neutrality, overcoming the country's hesitations and preventing an alliance with France. In the difficult diplomatic context of the War of the Spanish Succession, Methuen displayed great skill and commitment when making an economic case for consolidating England's strategic alliance with Portugal.

[28] See Jorge Pedreira, 'Diplomacia, manufacturas e desenvolvimento económico. Em torno do mito de Methuen', in: *O Tratado de Methuen (1703)*, ed. Cardoso, 131–156.

[29] A. D. Francis, *The Methuens and Portugal, 1691–1708* (Cambridge: Cambridge University Press, 1966).

The documentation analysed by Francis reveals England's eagerness to have privileged access to the Portuguese colonial market, which would certainly have been facilitated by the signing of a treaty of trade and friendship. That had been a concern expressed by Methuen ever since the beginning of his diplomatic mission in Lisbon in 1691. Although there is no documentary evidence that he ever discussed the problem of abolishing the pragmatic laws against luxury or the difficulties of finding an outlet for British manufactured products, the instructions received by Cunha, when he became established in London in 1797, mention some of the efforts that Methuen made with the aim of changing the bilateral trade relations.[30] In other words, the direct role that Methuen played in the final months of 1703 corresponded in some way to what occurred in earlier initiatives when the much desired strengthening of the friendly relationship between Portugal and England was sealed by agreeing mutual trade concessions.[31]

Concluding Remarks

In 1703, Portugal signed two highly significant international treaties. The first was the agreement to align itself defensively and offensively with the Grand Alliance formed by England, Holland and Austria against the French intentions in the War of the Spanish Succession. The second was the commercial treaty signed with England, known by the name of English ambassador who negotiated its various clauses.

The two 1703 treaties correspond to the natural outcome of a process of diplomatic alignment with high costs for Portugal, due to the French–Spanish axis being a threat to national sovereignty. The price paid for the guaranteed defence of the country's sovereignty by the powers of the Grand Alliance, England in particular, inevitably had an adverse impact on the economy.

We should remember that the increase in wine exports to England was not an immediate result of the 1703 treaty. In fact, from the last

[30] Francis, *The Methuens and Portugal*, 187–192.

[31] It should be borne in mind that Methuen did not act only on behalf of the English public cause. His own personal and family interests were bound up with the treaty, since his brother was a cloth manufacturer in Bradford-on-Avon, England, a son-in-law (Humphrey Simpson) was a wine importer, and he, John Methuen, dedicated himself to the production of wine in Portugal (see Francis, *The Methuens and Portugal*, 204).

two decades of the seventeenth century onwards, especially after the intensification of the military conflict between England and France in 1689, Portuguese wine exports to England had been on the rise. The same was true for the export of textiles from England to Portugal: the protection of the Portuguese wool industry could not prevent English textiles from entering Portugal and, via Portugal, also Brazil. Therefore, the advantages guaranteed to the English in the form of an outlet for their woollen manufactures was neither a novelty nor a substantial change to the trade agreements and commercial privileges already established in previous treaties (1654 and 1661) concluded by the two countries. Such advantages, however, were not of use to just one of the parties. Besides having its political security guaranteed in the complicated international arena, Portugal also benefited from conditions that stimulated its wine industry.

The disturbing assertion that bribery preceded the signing of the treaty can neither be proved nor disproved by documentation. And to claim that the absence of such evidence shows that it was destroyed serves only to appease theorizers who have scant regard for the rigour of actual proof. It seems, however, reasonable to surmise that in this case there may have been some exchanges of diplomatic gratification deemed indispensable for the maintaining good relations between the decision-makers.

The Portuguese authors who are normally considered the main inspiration of opposition to the Methuen treaty (Cunha and Pombal) were well aware of the delicacy of the political situation and ended up accepting the inevitability of the agreements that were signed. The divisive use made of their testimonies gave rise to the interpretation which is determined to perceive the Methuen treaty as a diplomatic and political ambush with dire economic consequences. Despite this, Portuguese historiography has shown itself to have sufficient maturity to demonstrate that the treaty was not, and never could have been, an irremovable stigma, the original sin of Portuguese industrial development.

More important than knowing whether industry stagnated in consequence of the treaty is actually discovering whether there existed solid structural conditions for a more rapid industrial development than the one which in the event happened. Or whether Portuguese wines would have succeeded in gaining an important foothold in the British markets if their export had not been expressly regulated by the treaty. But addressing these imponderables is far beyond the scope of this brief chapter.[32]

Although there is no mention of such an idea in the terms of the Methuen treaty, the classical English economist David Ricardo used the treaty as a pretext for demonstrating the benefits of a productive specialization based on a system of comparative advantages. His model for international trade is illustrated by Portugal and Britain and their exchange of two products (wine and cloth). And so, paradoxically, a mercantilist treaty designed to regulate converging interests between courtiers and businessmen, ended up serving the aims and arguments of a system of laissez-faire in economic relations on an international scale.

Epilogue

A great deal of animosity towards the Methuen treaty was caused by the unequal conditions imposed by the Anglo-Portuguese Treaties of Friendship and Commerce of 1810, in the context of the Napoleonic Wars. The conflict in which France and Britain were the two main opponents obliged Portugal to once again face the repercussions of an impossible neutrality. The Methuen treaty served as a scarecrow representing the fears of a new situation in which the maintenance of political sovereignty, vis-à-vis the Franco-Spanish threat, necessitated the acceptance of new forms of economic dominance by Britain, Portuguese's faithful and powerful ally.

In 1810, however, the situation become rather negative for Portuguese economic interests, especially as regards the control of the colonial market following the opening of Brazilian ports in 1808, an upshot of the military aid provided by British troops in the fight against the Napoleonic army that had invaded Portugal at the beginning of 1808 and forced the Portuguese king and his court to move to Rio de Janeiro. Until then, foreign commercial activities in Brazilian ports had only been allowed in exceptional situations of enforced docking, when, due to insufficient means of payment, expenses had to be defrayed through the sale of the goods transported by such vessels. The opening up of the ports decreed at

[32] For an approach to all of these implications, see the texts gathered together in *O Tratado de Methuen (1703)*, ed. Cardoso.

the end of January 1808 was the precursor of the much greater economic liberalization that was shortly to follow.

In keeping with a free-trade ideology and the sound principles of political economy, Portugal had lost control of its important colonial trade and opened its internal market to British manufactures imported at very low tariffs, leaving no competitive possibilities for Portuguese industrial goods. Indeed, the 1810 treaty stipulated that the tariffs on British goods transported by British or Portuguese ships were 15 per cent *ad valorem*, whereas the tariffs on Portuguese or foreign goods transported by Portuguese ships were 16 per cent *ad valorem*, and 24 per cent *ad valorem* on other foreign goods carried on foreign ships. Such was the price to be paid for the integration of Portugal into a stable international order.

The effects of the 1810 treaty would prove to be extremely harmful to the aspirations of industrial development in Portugal throughout the nineteenth century. And although it had been signed one century earlier, the Methuen treaty—smeared and defamed—was also associated with the same undesirable fate of a nation condemned to serve British interests. Myths cannot be explained away with historical evidence. But their persistence offers a good excuse for understanding their meaning, as this historiographical essay has tried to demonstrate.[33]

José Luís Cardoso is Research Professor of the Institute of Social Sciences, University of Lisbon. He has published and edited books on the Portuguese history of economic thought from a comparative perspective, with special emphasis on the study of the processes of diffusion and assimilation of economic ideas. He has published articles in the main international journals on the history of economic thought. His most recent edited book is *The German Historical School and European Economic Thought* (2016).

[33] I am grateful to the editors of this volume, Antonella Alimento and Koen Stapelbroek, for the comments and suggestions provided at the different stages of the preparation of this chapter.

The Anglo-French Treaty of Utrecht of 1713 Revisited: The Politics of Rivalry and Alliance

Doohwan Ahn

Introduction

On 9 April 1715, James Stanhope, Secretary of State for the Southern Department, presented to the House of Commons a motion for appointing a secret committee to investigate the conduct of the late Tory ministry during the last phase of the War of the Spanish Succession.[1] Four days later, twenty-one members were chosen by way of balloting, including, alongside Stanhope himself, such staunch Whigs as Robert Walpole, Sir Richard Onslow, William Pulteney, and Thomas Coningsby. Later that day, Walpole, the Paymaster of the

This work was supported by the Ministry of Education of the Republic of Korea and the National Research Foundation of Korea (NRF-2016S1A3A2924409).

[1] William Cobbett, *The Parliamentary History of England from the Earliest Period to 1803, Vol. VII. A.D. 1714–1722* (London: T. C. Hansard, Peterborough-Court, Fleet-Street, 1811), cols. 53–57. Hereafter *Parliamentary Debates.*

D. Ahn (✉)
Department of Politics and International Relations, Seoul National University, South Korea
e-mail: dhwahn@snu.ac.kr

A. Alimento, K. Stapelbroek (eds.), *The Politics of Commercial Treaties in the Eighteenth Century*, DOI 10.1007/978-3-319-53574-6_4

Forces, was elected chairman, and began to ransack all the seized instructions and papers of the negotiations with France that led to the 'Woeful' Treaty of Utrecht of 11 April 1713.[2] It was the start of a purge. On 10 June, Robert Harley, Earl of Oxford and Mortimer (Lord High Treasurer) and Henry St John, Viscount Bolingbroke (Secretary of State for the Southern Department) were convicted of high treason, respectively by Coningsby and Walpole.[3] 'The worthy chairman of the Committee', Coningsby stated triumphantly on the occasion, 'has impeached the hand, but I do impeach the head; he has impeached, the clerk, and I the justice; he has impeached the scholar, and I the master'.[4] Oxford was sent to the Tower of London, and Bolingbroke, despite his earlier assurance to Francis Atterbury, Bishop of Rochester that 'I am not in the least intimidated from any consideration of the Whig malice and power', had already fled to France.[5] Within two months the Tory party's leadership was replaced by the Whig oligarchy.[6] Worse yet, the harshness of the Whig indictment left the Tory party with no other choice than to side with the Old Pretender. In a letter to his trusted colleague Sir William Windham composed a year later, Bolingbroke groaned, 'If milder measures had been pursued, certain it is, that the Tories had never universally embraced Jacobitism.'[7] Bolingbroke himself was no exception. Upon arriving in France in late March, he joined the exiled Stuart court and helped James as his Secretary of State to organize the Jacobite rising of 1715.[8] This finally sealed the fate of the Tory party, not to mention

[2] Anon., *The Woeful Treaty; or the Unhappy Peace. An Ode* (London: J. Harrisson and J. Billingsley, 1716), 11.

[3] *Parliamentary Debates*, col. 66.

[4] *Parliamentary Debates*, col. 67.

[5] 'Lord Bolingbroke to the Bishop of Rochester (1714)', in: *The Miscellaneous Works of Bishop Atterbury*, 5 vols. (London: John Nichols, 1798), 5: 255.

[6] William Coxe, *Memoirs of the Life and Administration of Sir Robert Walpole, Earl of Orford*, 3 vols. (London: T. Cadell, Jun. and W. Davies, 1800), 1: 109–117.

[7] Bolingbroke, 'A Letter to Sir William Windham', in: *The Works of the Late Right Honourable Henry St. John, Lord Viscount Bolingbroke*, 8 vols. (London: J. Johnson, 1809), 1: 38.

[8] Daniel Szechi, *1715: The Great Jacobite Rebellion* (New Haven, CT: Yale University Press, 2006), 84–86.

that of Bolingbroke. The stage was perfectly set for a Walpolean smear campaign that painted all Tories as Jacobites.[9]

With regard to his Jacobite intrigue, Bolingbroke publicly expressed his great regret, though only after his dismissal by the Old Pretender in March 1716. In a lengthy open letter to Windham, he confessed that 'I own the crime of having been for the pretender', and went on to swear that 'if ever I return home, as far as I am able, to promote the national good of Britain without any other regard'.[10] But for the Utrecht Treaty of Peace, Bolingbroke was determined to stand up. 'No man will deny', he proclaimed in the same place: 'The importance of succeeding, in the work of the peace, was equally great to Europe, to our country, to our party, to our persons, to the present age, and to future generations.'[11] He was ready to concede that 'The means employed to bring it about were in no degree proportionable.'[12] But this was due in the main to the Whig intransigence. From the very start to the end, Bolingbroke contended with much bitterness, 'no one measure possible to be taken was omitted to traverse every advance that was made in this work, to intimidate, to allure, to embarrass every person concerned in it'.[13] 'This was done without any regard either to decency or good policy', he angrily concluded.[14]

The continued Whig accusation of betrayal notwithstanding, the verdict of posterity on the Treaty of Utrecht has been overwhelmingly favourable to the Tory ministry of Oxford and Bolingbroke. Most famously, perhaps, John Robert Seeley in his *Expansion of England* (1883) identified the Treaty of Utrecht as marking 'the beginning of England's supremacy'.[15] 'The Treaty of Utrecht', he declared, 'left England the first state in the world', and 'ever since that no state is more powerful than England […] in wealth and commerce and in

[9] Simon Targett, 'Government and Ideology during the Age of Whig Supremacy: The Political Argument of Sir Robert Walpole's Newspaper Propagandists', *The Historical Journal* 32/2 (1994), 289–317.

[10] Bolingbroke, 'A Letter to Sir William Windham', 105, 109.

[11] Bolingbroke, 'A Letter to Sir William Windham', 18–19.

[12] Bolingbroke, 'A Letter to Sir William Windham', 19.

[13] Bolingbroke, 'A Letter to Sir William Windham', 20.

[14] Bolingbroke, 'A Letter to Sir William Windham', 20.

[15] John Robert Seeley, *The Expansion of England*, 2nd edn. (London: Macmillan, 1914), 153.

maritime power'.[16] More recently, J. G. A. Pocock went on to approve the Tory peace plan as having given rise to 'the Europe of Enlightenment'.[17] 'Utrecht', Pocock pronounced, 'had achieved a Europe that had outgrown barbarism, fanaticism, and conquest'.[18] 'It was the first attempt to construct a European order', or to be more specific, 'a republic or confederation of states held together by treaties to which wars were merely auxiliary, and by a common system of civilised manners communicated everywhere by commerce'.[19] Seen in this light, the impeachments of the Tory ex-ministers, as David Hume famously remarked in his 1752 essay called 'Of the Balance of Power', were comparable to the Ostracism of Athens.[20] Bolingbroke and Oxford were simply victims of the rage of party, which had dominated Queen Anne's reign.[21]

If one admits that the political purge in 1715 was the culmination of more than a decade of violent partisan politics, identifying exactly on what grounds Oxford and Bolingbroke among others were charged of high treason, as well as their vindications, becomes a prerequisite for understanding the Tory–Whig divide over foreign policy.[22] This chapter, by taking Walpole and Stanhope's arguments for impeachment as a point of reference, seeks to revisit the partisan struggle between Tory and Whig over the conduct of British foreign policy from 1710 to 1713. It is shown that the primary factor in the political storm over the peace of 1713 was the role of trust in international politics. While the Tories justified a

[16] Seeley, *Expansion of England*, 153–154. In the same vein, more recently, see Jonathan Scott, *When the Waves Ruled Britannia. Geography and Political Identities, 1500–1800* (Cambridge: Cambridge University Press, 2011), 139.

[17] J. G. A. Pocock, *Barbarism and Religion. Vol. I: The Enlightenments of Edward Gibbon, 1737–1764* (Cambridge: Cambridge University Press, 1990), 110.

[18] J. G. A. Pocock, 'What do We Mean by Europe?' *The Wilson Quarterly* (Winter, 1997), 23.

[19] Pocock, 'What do We Mean by Europe?', 23.

[20] David Hume, 'Of the Balance of Power', in: *Political Essays*, ed. Knud Haakonssen (Cambridge: Cambridge University Press, 1994), 155–159.

[21] J. H. Plumb, *The Growth of Political Stability in England, 1675–1725* (London: Macmillan, 1967), 129–158.

[22] For a recent reappraisal of the traditional dichotomy of the Whig continental commitment and Tory isolationism, see Jeremy Black, 'Foreign Policy and the Tory World in the Eighteenth Century', in: *The Tory World. Deep History and the Tory Theme in British Foreign Policy, 1679–2014*, ed. Jeremy Black (Farnham: Ashgate, 2015), 33–68.

separate peace negotiation with France by defining European diplomacy as the harsh world of power politics, in which states had to be permanently on their guard, the Whig pursuit to sustain the anti-Bourbon system of alliance took a moralistic approach and urged to abide by the law of nations. The conflict, at bottom, was one between two conflicting *Weltanschauungs*, that of rivalry and that of alliance.[23]

The Impeachments in 1715: Charges and Defences

On 7 July 1715, after three months of intense scrutiny, Walpole's parliamentary committee reported the articles of impeachment against Oxford and Bolingbroke, followed a month later by those against James Butler, 2nd Duke of Ormond, who, succeeding John Churchill, 1st Duke of Marlborough, had served as Captain-General and Commander-in-Chief of the Forces from 1711 to 1714. In total, twenty-two articles (sixteen initially and six added) were drawn up against Oxford, and six each against Bolingbroke and Ormond. The task Walpole set himself was considerable. Wanting to indict them under the Treason Act of 1351 (25 Edward III), Walpole was to prove they had conducted peace negotiations with France without specific orders from Queen Anne.[24] Unsurprisingly, as soon as the charges were laid, Edward Harley, Oxford's younger brother, came forward with rebutting evidence, protesting that his brother had 'done nothing but by immediate commands of the late Queen'.[25] Similarly, the famous Country economist Archibald Hutcheson defended his patron Ormond by recording that 'in the whole course of his late conduct, he had but obeyed the late Queen's commands'.[26] Evidently expecting such a move,[27] and with the intention of relating the trial to a wider context of European

[23] In contrast, Steve Pincus has recently reframed the controversy as a battle between two competing models of empire, that of a territorial empire espoused by the Tories and that of an integrated commercial empire conceived by the Whigs; see his 'Addison's Empire: Whig Conceptions of Empire in the Early 18th Century', *Parliamentary History* 31/1 (2012), 99–117.

[24] *Parliamentary Debates*, col. 67.

[25] *Parliamentary Debates*, cols. 67, 73.

[26] *Parliamentary Debates*, col. 68. Hutcheson served as a legal adviser to the duke in around 1710. He was appointed to the position of the Lord Commissioner of the Board of Trade in late 1714, but resigned in early 1716 as a protest to the impeachment.

[27] *Parliamentary Debates*, cols. 211–222.

politics, Walpole redirected his focus and commenced his impeachment speech by reminding the initial agreements between England, the Dutch Republic and the Austrian Empire made on 7 December 1701.[28] Walpole did not simply enumerate the original objectives of the allies; probably following Stanhope's expert advice, he made every effort to highlight the sanctity of treaties and alliances.[29]

Walpole's strategy of accusing the Tory government of violating the principle of good faith was a double-edged sword. On the one hand it enabled him to justify the Whig policy of 'No Peace without Spain'. After the failure of the Geertruidenberg negotiations in July 1710 and the subsequent Tory landslide election victory three months later, the Whig party became more insistent on continuing the war. Next December, Walpole in the Commons and Daniel Finch, 2nd Earl of Nottingham, in the Lords, orchestrated a move to request Queen Anne to announce that there would be 'No Peace without Spain'.[30] They demanded that unless Spain and her colonies, including the Spanish Netherlands, were in the hands of the Habsburg candidate King Charles III, as had been promised in the Second Partition Treaty of 1700, no general peace conference should be commenced. Walpole condemned Oxford and Bolingbroke, first and foremost, because they lured Queen Anne to break the oath she had made to the members of the Grand Alliance. By the 1701 Treaty of The Hague, Walpole prompted, England had pledged not 'to treat peace with the enemy, unless jointly and by a communication of counsels'.[31] This provision, he added, had been reaffirmed two years later in the Treaty of Methuen with Portugal: 'That no peace nor truce shall be made, but by the mutual consent of all the confederates.'[32] Such was the emphasis Walpole's committee placed on the duty of mutual trust and confidence that the first article of impeachment

[28] *Parliamentary Debates*, cols. 74–82.

[29] Stanhope was the only one in the Whig committee who had extensive experience in diplomatic missions. Basil Williams, *Stanhope. A Study in Eighteenth-Century War and Diplomacy* (Oxford: Clarendon Press, 1932), 169–175.

[30] Geoffrey Holmes, 'The Commons' Division on "No Peace without Spain", 7 December 1711', *Bulletin of the Institute of Historical Research* 33 (1960), 223–234; Clyve Jones, 'The Debate in the House of Lords on "No Peace without Spain", 7 December 1711: A New Source', *Parliamentary History* 28/1 (2009), 191–199.

[31] *Parliamentary Debates*, col. 76.

[32] *Parliamentary Debates*, col. 78.

against the two Tory ex-ministers began stating they had 'no regard to the honour or safety of her late majesty or her kingdoms, or to the many solemn engagements she was under to the old and faithful allies of this nation, or to the common liberties of Europe'.[33] The new Whig ministry indicted Oxford and Bolingbroke for high treason primarily because they set on foot 'a private, separate, dishonourable, and destructive negociations of peace between Great Britain and France', 'in defiance of the solemn and mutual assurances [...] to act in perfect concert with them, in making peace, as in making war'.[34] In Article III against Oxford, Walpole was more specific on this point. By Oxford's 'most wicked counsels', he affirmed, referring also to Thomas, 3rd Earl of Strafford and Matthew Prior, both of whom represented Britain at Utrecht:

> That unquestionable truth and sacredness, which, by the laws of nations, ought to accompany and constitute the instructions of public ambassadors to princes in friendship and confederacy against the common enemy, was most vilely prostituted to the most dangerous purposes, to deceive and mislead her majesty's good allies in matters of the greatest importance to their own interests; and the interests of these kingdoms, the honour of her majesty's sacred person, and of the imperial crown of these realms, which had been raised to the highest pitch of glory abroad, and had been justly held in veneration with her good allies, was scandalously debased and betrayed.[35]

In other words, it was in keeping with the law of nations that the Whig party resolutely pursued the 'No Peace without Spain' policy. Herein lay a crucial difference between the conferences held at Geertruidenberg and those convened at Utrecht. Unlike the latter, Walpole stressed, the former was conducted with the agreement of, and in consultation with, 'her good and faithful allies'.[36] For the Whig committee, it was Britain's honour that mattered most. On it rested her safety and not the other way around.

The great Whig Bishop Gilbert Burnet, too, upheld the inviolability of treaties. In a speech prepared in early May 1713 in case the House of

[33] *Parliamentary Debates*, cols. 82, 131–132.

[34] *Parliamentary Debates*, cols. 82–83, 130–131.

[35] *Parliamentary Debates*, col. 85. Prior was taken into custody on 17 June, and on 31 August Strafford was impeached for high crimes and misdemeanours.

[36] *Parliamentary Debates*, cols. 80–81.

Lords moved for approval of the Treaty of Peace with France, Burnet deployed his knowledge of 'Grotius, Puffendorf, and others who have wrote of the law of nations' to protest against it.

> [They] lay this down for a rule, that the nature of a treaty, and the tie that arises out of it, is not altered by the having or not having an oath; the oath serves only to heighten the obligation. They do also agree in this, that confederacies do not bind states to carry on a war to their utter ruin; but that princes and states are bound to use their utmost efforts in maintaining them; and it is agreed by all who have treated of these matters, that the common enemy, by offering to any one confederate all his pretensions, cannot justify his departing from the confederacy; because it was entered into with that view, that all the pretensions upon which the confederacy was made, should be insisted on or departed from by common consent.[37]

On the other hand, in his opening speech and throughout the articles of impeachment, Walpole made frequent use of such terms as 'evil', 'wicked', 'treacherous' and 'malicious' to describe the Oxford–Bolingbroke ministry. Given the high level of partisan conflict, there was nothing new in this, but on this occasion it equipped him to make Queen Anne a perfectly innocent victim of the Tory plot. Whether she had ordered to negotiate with France independently and secretly was of no relevance. The blame was placed squarely on her two Tory ministers. From the very start, Walpole alleged, Oxford and Bolingbroke had no intention of keeping their oaths of allegiance and the trust of Queen Anne. With the single purpose to 'disunite the confederacy', they obtained access to Queen Anne, and then, in the summer of 1710, 'by their evil counsel and advice', they prevailed on her to dismiss the Godolphin administration.[38] Eventually, as stated in the seventh article against Oxford, 'by the influence of his evil counsels, her majesty was prevailed on to accept, and finally to conclude and ratify, a treaty of peace with France'.[39] Throughout, the

[37] Gilbert Burnet, *The History of His Own Time, from the Restoration of King Charles II to the Conclusion of the Treaty of Peace at Utrecht, in the Reign of Queen Anne*, 4 vols. (London: J. Nunn, 1818), 1: 328–329.

[38] *Parliamentary Debates*, col. 80.

[39] *Parliamentary Debates*, col. 89.

Tory leadership had acted in bad faith towards Queen Anne, as they had towards her allies.

To Walpole's committee, the Tory party had a natural affinity with the French. They both were untrustworthy and devious. Especially since December 1701 when Louis XIV contravened the will of Carlos II of Spain and announced that his grandson Philippe, Duc d'Anjou (later Philip V of Spain) remained eligible for the succession to the French throne, the duplicitous nature of French diplomacy became a prominent theme in Whig polemic.[40] For example, in 1702, Henry Maxwell, a staunch Irish Whig and MP for Bangor, County Down, averred in his pamphlet called *Anguis in Herba: or the Fatal Consequences of a Treaty with France*, 'That the Principles whereby the French King governs himself, will not allow him to observe any Treaty longer than it is for his Interest to break it.'[41] 'Every single Treaty of Peace' Louis had made was a subservient to 'his great Design of Empire', Maxwell cautioned, adding:

> That all those must grosly deceive themselves, that treat with such a Prince, out of a prospect that he will religiously and *bonâ fide* observe the Treaty; for that would stand in his way between him and his great Design of Empire: Therefore it is evident that such a Prince never enters into a Treaty, but with a real Design to deceive others, and to reap the solid Advantages of every such Treaty himself; such as are, generally to break or prevent Confederacies against him, to disarm and divide his Enemies, to secure new Conquests or Accession of Dominion, or lastly, to put the Revenues, &c. of his own State in a better condition.[42]

[40] See Mark A. Thomson, 'Louis XIV and the Origins of the War of the Spanish Succession', and 'Louis XIV and the Grand Alliance', in: *William III and Louis XIV. Essays 1680–1720 by and for Mark A. Thomson*, ed. Ragnhild Hatton and J. S. Bromley (Liverpool: Liverpool University Press, 1968), 140–161, 190–212; John B. Wolf, *Louis XIV* (Toronto: W. W. Norton, 1968), 491–577; Paul Sonnino, 'The Origins of Louis XIV's Wars', in: *The Origins of War in Early Modern Europe*, ed. Jeremy Black (Edinburgh: John Donald, 1987), 112–131; William Roosen, 'The Origins of the War of the Spanish Succession', in: *Origins of War*, ed. Black, 151–175; John A. Lynn, *The Wars of Louis XIV, 1667–1714* (Harlow: Pearson Education, 1999), 266–360

[41] Henry Maxwell, *Anguis in Herba: or the Fatal Consequences of a Treaty with France* (London: A. Baldwin, 1702), 1.

[42] Maxwell, *Anguis in Herba*, 64, 5.

This became more pronounced when the Tory party took power in late 1710. In 1711, the anonymous author of *The Old French Way of Managing Treaties* related Philippe de Commine's memoir of the Treaty of Picquigny of 1475 between Edward III and Louis XI to the effect that 'England was trick'd by the French King's Perfidiousness and Cunning', 'our Allies were abus'd and ruin'd', and eventually, 'the exorbitant Power of France was founded, tho' England was in a Capacity to have prevented it'.[43] In the same year, the Duke of Marlborough's wartime chaplain and Whig polemicist Francis Hare brought up the same point in his poignantly entitled tract, *A Clear View of the French King's Bona Fide: or Sacred Regard to His Most Solemn Promises and Oaths in Treaties of Peace.* As Hare noted in the preface, it was composed as 'a general Account of the French King's Violation of all the Treaties yet made with him for securing the Quiet of Christendom'.[44] In a similar vein, the unknown writer of *The Friendship of King Lewis always Fatal* (1712) concluded his detailed survey of how Louis had exploited alliances with all the major European powers, including Britain, with the statement that 'no People under the Sun are at this Day so noted for Treachery and Cruelty, as the French'.[45] Likewise, in his *Secret History of Europe* (1712), John Oldmixon, a celebrated Whig colonialist, called Louis 'a King, who thinks it for his glory not to be bound by such mean things as Promises and Treaties'.[46] No wonder that the Whig

[43] Anon., *The Old French Way of Managing Treaties* (London: A. Baldwin, 1711), 19. It is noteworthy that Commine's *Mémoires* (1524) was translated into English in 1712 by Robert Uvedale, a friend of John Tilotson, Archbishop of Canterbury during the reign of William III; see *The Memoirs of Philip de Comines*, 2 vols. (London: John Phillips). Comparing Louis XIV with Louis XI was a common Whig propaganda strategy; see Anon., *The Interest of Europe, with Respect to Peace and War* (London: S. Popping, 1712), 35–38.

[44] Francis Hare, *A Clear View of the French King's Bona Fide: or Sacred Regard to His Most Solemn Promises and Oaths in Treaties of Peace* (London: J. Baker, 1711), 3.

[45] Anon., *The Friendship of King Lewis Always Fatal* (London: A. Baldwin, 1712), 3. It comes as no surprise that the marriage contract between Louis and the Spanish Infanta received a special focus in Whig propaganda; see Anon., *The Breach of Publick Faith Exemplify'd: or, the Contract of Marriage between Lewis XIV of France, and the Most Serene Infanta of Spain, Eldest Daughter of the Catholick King: Concluded the 7th of Nov. 1659* (London: A Baldwin, 1712).

[46] John Oldmixon, *The Secret History of Europe* (London: no publisher, 1712), 44.

government had steadfastly demanded at the Geertruidenberg conference that Louis assist Britain and the Dutch Republic militarily in case the Duc d'Anjou declined to evacuate Spain within two months.[47]

The Whig emphasis on what Oldmixon termed 'the Law of Alliance' explains, firstly, the way in which Jonathan Swift opened his highly influential ministerial tract, *The Conduct of the Allies, and of the Late Ministry, in Beginning and Carrying on the Present War* (1711).[48] In consultation with Oxford, the Tory polemicist began his argument by outlining the nature of power politics.[49] While recognizing that 'a War should be undertaken upon a just and prudent Motive', he was careful to note that except for *pro aris et focis*, 'no Monarch or Commonwealth did ever engage beyond a certain Degree'.[50] 'A Prince', Swift maintained, 'ought maturely to consider the Condition he is in when he enters on it' and when 'to receive the Overtures of a Peace'.[51] Earlier that year, Archduke Charles had succeeded his brother Joseph I as Emperor Charles VI. The spectre of a Habsburg universal monarchy suddenly began to loom large.[52] Besides, the situation in the Spanish theatre of war since the Battle of Malplaquet in September 1709 turned in favour of the French.

It was in much the same way that Oxford formulated his defence in 1715. To Walpole's accusation of betraying the allies, he responded, likewise pointing to the death of the emperor and the change it brought about in the European power structure: 'It is a known and an allowed rule by the

[47] John C. Rule, 'France and the Preliminaries to the Gertruydenberg Conference, September 1709 to March 1710', in: *Studies in Diplomatic History. Essays in Honour of David Bayne Horn*, ed. Ragnhild Hatton and M. S. Anderson (London: Longman, 1970), 97–115. See also Francis Hare, *The Negociations for a Treaty of Peace, In 1709. Consider'd, in a Third Letter to a Tory-Member. Part the First*, 2nd edn. (London: A. Baldwin, 1711); *The Negotiations for a Treaty of Peace, from the Breaking off of the Conferences at the Hague, to the End of Those at Gertruydenberg, Consider'd, in a Fourth Letter to a Tory-Member, Part II* (London: A. Baldwin, 1711).

[48] Oldmixon, *The Secret History of Europe*, 18–19.

[49] J. A. Downie, 'Polemical Strategy and Swift's *Conduct of the Allies*', *Prose Studies* 4/2 (1981), 134–145.

[50] Jonathan Swift, *The Conduct of the Allies*, ed. C. B. Wheeler (Oxford: Clarendon Press, 1916), 5.

[51] Swift, *Conduct of the Allies*, 5–6.

[52] Swift, *Conduct of the Allies*, 59–61.

law of nations, in reference to leagues between princes, That if there happens a material change in what was the principal ground and cause of the treaty, the obligation thereof ceases.'[53] More tellingly, in his concluding speech, Oxford challenged the legality of the charges brought against him by specifically pointing out that:

> It is in most of them built chiefly on the supposed infraction of certain treaties and alliances with foreign princes and states; and he conceives, that such infractions of public treaties, where they do not particularly affect the interests of Great Britain, being cognizable by the laws of nations only and not by those of the realm, are not wont to be examined into here at home, and prosecuted as criminal.[54]

Oxford pleaded that during the Utrecht negotiations he had 'give[n] reasonable satisfaction to her allies', and hence 'none of them did afterwards complain to her majesty [. . .] of any hardships imposed upon them in it'.[55] Likewise, Bolingbroke in his *Letters on the Study and Use of History* (1735–1736) vindicated himself by rewriting the history of modern Europe from a power political perspective. While observing that the balance of power between the Houses of Bourbon and Habsburg was the key to European peace and prosperity, Bolingbroke called attention to the unreliable nature of alliances.[56] The disunion of the Grand Alliance, which he assigned to Dutch recalcitrance, was no exception.[57] Lamenting 'how unequally we were burdened, and how unfairly we were treated by our allies', Bolingbroke implored that the guiding principle of foreign policy should be that of *raison d'état*, or, in Horace's maxim, '*Nec Deus intersit, nisi dignus vindice nodus Inciderit*'.[58] By the same token, and contrary to the popular belief, Bolingbroke had earlier praised Queen Elizabeth, primarily because of her firm grasp of the cruel reality of

[53] *Parliamentary Debates*, col. 160.

[54] *Parliamentary Debates*, col. 208.

[55] *Parliamentary Debates*, cols. 164, 208.

[56] Bolingbroke, *Defence of the Treaty of Utrecht: Letters VI–VIII of the Study and Use of History*, ed. G. M. Trevelyan (Cambridge: Cambridge University Press, 1932), 17–18, 84, 88.

[57] Bolingbroke, *Defence of the Treaty of Utrecht*, 124–139.

[58] Bolingbroke, *Defence of the Treaty of Utrecht*, 137, 147.

power politics, and secondarily because of her policy of maritime expansion. In his *Remarks on the History of England* (1743), first published in the Country journal *The Craftsman* (1730–1731) in the form of pseudonymous letters, Bolingbroke proclaimed that 'the first and fundamental Principle, by which Queen Elizabeth govern'd herself in all foreign Affairs' was that:

> She consider'd the Interest of no Kingdom, no State, nor People, no not even the general Interest of the Reformation, as zealous a Protestant she was, nor the Preservation of a Ballance of Power in Europe, as great an Heroine as she was, in any other Light than relatively to the Interest of England. She assisted, or opposed, she defended, or attack'd, just as this Interest directed; and the Degree, to which it was concern'd, was the exact and constant Measure, to which she proportion'd her good, and her ill Offices, her Friendship, and her Enmity.[59]

Furthermore, Britain's geographical situation, Bolingbroke repeatedly stressed, made a ruthless policy of national interest most suitable to her. Britain 'can have no Necessity, in the ordinary Course of Affairs, to take up the Policy of the Continent; to enter into the System of Alliances', or, to be more specific, 'to be Mediators, Arbitrators, or, which is infinitely worse, Guaranties; to be contracting Parties in preliminary, provisional, or explanatory Treaties; in defensive, or offensive Alliances'.[60] She only needed 'to act any other Part than that of a friendly Neighbour and a fair Trader'.[61] Perfidious Albion, in a word, was Bolingbroke's Tory dream.

Surely, as is commonly accepted, Swift and his two Tory patrons heavily resorted to anti-Dutch rhetoric to smother the Francophobia of the Whigs.[62] Equally noticeable, however, is the difference in the kinds of language each party had employed. While the Whigs, or 'our English Dutch', as the Tories often called them, resolutely defined the Grand

[59] Bolingbroke, *Remarks on the History of England*, 2nd edn. (London: R. Franklin, 1747), 176–177 (Letter XV).

[60] Bolingbroke, *Remarks*, 190–191 (Letter XVI).

[61] Bolingbroke, *Remarks*, 190–191 (Letter XVI).

[62] Douglas Coombs, *The Conduct of the Dutch. British Opinion and the Dutch Alliance during the War of the Spanish Succession* (The Hague: Martinus Njihoff, 1958).

Alliance as amounting to a legally binding agreement, the Tory ministers, or as one Whig pamphleteer astutely named them 'our Mock Machiavellians', countered it by recalling the logic of power politics.[63]

The Economics of Alliance and Rivalry

While perhaps the most enduring legacy of the Treaty of Utrecht was to be found in the clauses that concerned Britain's trade and colonies, they appear to be of less importance to the Whig committee of secrecy than the Tory betrayal of the allies. Out of sixteen original articles of impeachment drawn up against Oxford only one (Article XIII) pertained to the commercial clauses of the Treaty of Peace, and, more surprisingly, none out of six against Bolingbroke.[64] This, of course, is neither to suggest that the Whig party, as the Tory propaganda machine had persistently claimed, had little, if any, interest in procuring economic benefits, nor, of course, that they were largely pleased with what the Tory government had acquired. Rather, it is to place the economic aspect of the Treaty of Utrecht into perspective.

To begin with, Walpole and Stanhope, as if to vindicate their party from the popular Tory accusation of warmongering, commenced the article in question by reaffirming that 'the riches, power, and strength of these kingdoms, depend entirely on the flourishing condition of trade and navigation'.[65] For much the same reason, while thanking Queen Anne for the care and consideration she had shown to her people reeling under the burden of war, they professed that they too wanted 'a good peace'.[66] To be sure, as Daniel Defoe made clear in his

[63] Anon., *A Search after Dutch Honesty: Or, the Old Use and Custom of That Nation to Their Friends and Allies* (London: no publisher, 1712), iii; Anon., *The Dismal State of the Nation: With Remarks on the Articles of Gertruydenberg and Utrecht* (London: J. Roberts, 1715), 56–58.

[64] *Parliamentary Debates*, cols. 95–98, 129–137. On 2 August, Walpole's committee produced six more articles against Oxford, additionally charging the Tory chief minister for misuse of public money. Because Bolingbroke had already fled to France, they decided to concentrate their criticism on Oxford. Clyve Jones, 'The Opening of the Impeachment of Robert Harley, Earl of Oxford, June to September 1715: The "Memorandum" of William Wake, Bishop of London', *Electronic British Library Journal* 4 (2015), 1–14.

[65] *Parliamentary Debates*, col. 95.

[66] *Parliamentary Debates*, col. 95.

Tory pamphlet called *An Essay at a Plain Exposition of That Difficult Phrase A Good Peace* (1712), they had a very different understanding.[67]

What mattered to Walpole and Stanhope, however, was less that the Tory government had negotiated poorly, but rather that it had betrayed and let down the Dutch Republic.[68] That this was so can be inferred from the ease and confidence with which Oxford refuted their charge of 'sacrificing the commerce of Great Britain to the aggrandisement of France'.[69] The Whig committee indicted him on two counts. In the first place, and as expected, they attacked Oxford for having advised the ninth article of the Commercial Treaty of Utrecht. Oxford, they claimed, had instructed Prior to make Britain's demands 'in loose, general, and insufficient terms' so as to insert 'that fundamental principle of treating and being treated as *gens amicissima*', which had been persistently requested by the French.[70] To this, Oxford answered bluntly, imputing it to Bolingbroke, 'that nothing is positively stipulated in that article; but the whole is conditional, and left to be determined by the wisdom of parliament', adding that it should not be taken as 'an act of treachery, to refer any article of any treaty to the judgment and consideration of parliament'.[71] Secondly, Walpole and Stanhope reproved Oxford for having conceded the French the right to fish and dry fish on Newfoundland and the Isle of Cape Breton.[72] Oxford found no difficulty in rebutting these two charges as well. For not only the Isle of Cape Breton but also the part of Newfoundland yielded was not, as Walpole claimed, 'the ancient territories of the crown of Great Britain', not to mention the fact that they were occupied by the French at the time of the Treaty of Utrecht.[73] Oxford, then, boastfully listed the gains achieved by the Tory government, from the *asiento* contract for thirty years, the cession of Acadia, the bay and straights of Hudson, the islands of St Christopher and St Peter, Newfoundland across the Atlantic on the one

[67] Daniel Defoe, *An Essay at a Plain Exposition of that Difficult Phrase a Good Peace* (London: J. Baker, 1711).

[68] Jonathan Swift, *The History of the Four Last Years of the Queen*, ed. Herbert Davis (Oxford: Basil Blackwell, 1951), 51–52.

[69] *Parliamentary Debates*, col. 180.

[70] *Parliamentary Debates*, cols. 96–97.

[71] *Parliamentary Debates*, col. 180.

[72] *Parliamentary Debates*, col. 97.

[73] *Parliamentary Debates*, cols. 97, 181–182.

hand, and on the other to the demolition of Dunkirk and the cession of Port Mahon and Gibraltar in Europe, resulting in 'the flourishing condition of the trade and navigation of these kingdoms, since the conclusion of and by the means of the late peace'.[74]

Most revealingly, Oxford did not deny the accusation that the Tory ministry had purposefully broken faith with the Dutch. But Walpole and Stanhope took special care to recall Queen Anne's Commons speech delivered in June 1712 that 'none of the confederates would envy her share in the glory and advantage of the peace'.[75] What they had in mind was the Second Treaty of the Grand Alliance in which it was agreed that:

> (Article VIII) Full Liberty be granted unto the Subjects of the King of Great Britain, and the States-General, to exercise and enjoy all the same Privileges, Immunities, and Franchises of Commerce by Sea and Land, in Spain, the Mediterranean, and all Lands and Places which the King of Spain, last deceas'd, did possess at the time of his Death, as well as in Europe as elsewhere [. . .]
>
> (Article IX) The Confederates shall agree among themselves, about all the Things they shall think necessary for maintaining the Navigation and Commerce of the Subjects of his Majesty of Great Britain, and the States-General, in the Countries and Places they may acquire, and that was possess'd by the late deceas'd King of Spain, and also in what manner the States-General may be secur'd by the aforesaid Fence and Barrier.[76]

Walpole himself had reiterated these two clauses verbatim in his opening speech against Oxford.[77] Perhaps still wary of anti-Dutch sentiment, effectively mobilized by the Tory administration against the Whig Barrier Treaty of 1709 and henceforth,[78] no further comments were submitted. But considering the importance the Godolphin ministry had placed on cooperating and coordinating with the Dutch Republic in

[74] *Parliamentary Debates*, cols. 181, 183.

[75] *Parliamentary Debates*, col. 95.

[76] 'The Fundamental Treaty of the Grand Alliance between the Empire, Great Britain, and the United Provinces, 1701', in: *The Compleat History of the Treaty of Utrecht, as also That of Gertruydenberg*, 2 vols. (London: A. Rober, 1715), I: 6.

[77] *Parliamentary Debates*, cols. 76–77.

[78] See Jonathan Swift, *Some Remarks on the Barrier Treaty, between Her Majesty and the States-General* (London: John Morphew, 1712); John Oldmixon, *Remarks upon Remarks; or, the*

securing the Spanish Indies trade at Geertruidenberg (Article VII),[79] it is clear that integral, if not central, to Whig economic thought was the maintenance of the anti-Bourbon system of alliance.

In this respect, not only did Hare and other Whig scribblers try hard to persuade the wavering public that the Dutch were in destitute circumstances, and that the French were wholly untrustworthy. But more crucially, they took great pains to explain why having Archduke Charles on the Spanish throne was the safest way to secure the Spanish American trade to Britain, to say nothing of the balance of power in Europe. In other words, they had to provide a reasonable answer to the Tory apprehension of a Habsburg universal monarchy since the death of Joseph I. 'Even, tho' the King of France should come and say to us, that his Grandson was ready to Evacuate Spain, to lay down his Pretensions, and give up the Possession of the Crown, as we formerly Desired and Demanded', a Tory pamphleteer noted in late 1711, 'we are now uncertain whether we had best take it or no, and if we should accept it, are still more Doubtful to whom we should give it, or in brief what we should do with it'.[80] Hence, in addition to supplying evidence of the Imperial commitment to the rule of *pacta sunt servanda*, especially since the formation of the Grand Alliance,[81] they pointed out that the situation in Europe had changed dramatically from the time of Charles V. 'In the Days of Cha. Vth', as one Tory critic succinctly put it:

> Neither Holland was a State, or France in any Figure, nor was there any Naval Power Superior to the Emperour; whereas now should the Emperour attack any of them all, either France, or Holland, or Britain, are able to Cut off his

Barrier Treaty and the Protestant Succession vindicated (London: A. Baldwin, 1711); Francis Hare, *A Full Answer to the Conduct of the Allies* (London: no publisher, 1712); *Remarks on the Barrier-Treaty vindicated* (London: John Morphew, 1713).

79 'The Articles Preliminary to the Treaties of a General Peace, agreed between the Allies and France, 1709', in: *The Compleat History of the Treaty of Utrecht, as also That of Gertruydenberg*, I: 20.

80 Anon., *The Ballance of Europe: or, An Enquiry into the Respective Dangers of Being the Spanish Monarchy to the Emperour as Well as to King Philip, with the Consequence that may be Expected from Either* (London: John Baker, 1711), 4–5.

81 See Francis Hare, *A Full Answer to the Conduct of the Allies: To which is added, Some Observations on the Remarks on the Barrier Treaty* (London: no publisher, 1712), 13–14; *The Allies and the Late Ministry defended against France, and the Present Friends of France* (London: E. Sanger, 1712), 33.

> Communication with the Indies; nay even with Spain it self, and with all the Islands; so that the Power of the Empire is nothing to what it then was. This and much more, make up what they [Whigs] allege for their Opinion.[82]

Indeed, when the news of Joseph's death broke, Arthur Maynwaring, a Whig MP and confederate of Sarah Churchill, stood up to the Tory government and questioned:

> The Greatness of the House of Austria might be troublesome to their Neighbours on the Continent, but what have we to apprehend from them? Can, they, be they as great as they will, affect us in our very Vitals, and ruin our Commerce, as France may do? Can we suppose the House of Austria could have a superior Fleet drop out of the Clouds? Or can they disturb our Trade without a Fleet? What then is it we pretend to be afraid of? But, alas! the very Supposition of their Greatness is all a jest.[83]

Maynwaring added with emphasis, 'The addition of the Spanish Monarchy will be a Burden to him [Charles VI] rather than any Advantage for many years, tho a Burden he would be glad to bear, rather than it should fall into the hands of France, to whom Spain and the Indies would be infinitedly more useful than they can ever to him.'[84] Put otherwise, it was in his interest to yield the Spanish American trade to the two maritime powers, Britain more especially, 'For the stronger and richer we are, the more able we shall be to support him against France.'[85] Besides, as the anonymous writer of *The Ballance of Power: Or, a Comparison of the Strength of the Emperor and the French King* (1714) remarked, the economy of the Austrian Empire was too underdeveloped to take advantage of the Spanish market, let alone the Portuguese market which was already in British hands by the Treaty of Methuen. 'Since his Spanish Subjects cannot furnish those Colonies with such Manufactures as are wanted there', the emperor will not be able to 'possess himself of the Riches of Peru and Mexico', 'nor can the rest of the Imperial Dominions furnish

[82] Anon., *The Ballance of Europe*, 14–15.

[83] Arthur Maynwaring, *A Vindication of the Present M—y, from the Clamours rais'd against them upon occasion of the New Preliminaries* (London: no publisher, 1711), 34.

[84] Maynwaring, *Vindication*, 35–36.

[85] Maynwaring, *Vindication*, 36.

Spain'.[86] 'Peru and Mexico', he concluded, 'must have the Goods of England, France and Holland; and therefore England, France and Holland will come in for their Shares of that Mony', and of the three countries France was most formidable, militarily as well as economically, and Holland the weakest.[87]

While much has been discussed about the Tory press campaign against the Dutch on the eve of the parliamentary vote on the Treaty of Commerce with France, surprisingly little attention has been devoted to that against the Austrian Empire. Yet, since the Whig economic vision as embodied in the policy of 'No Peace without Spain' was ultimately premised on the Imperial cooperation, if not approval, the Tory ministry was no less determined to shatter the Whig faith in the empire. So much so that Oxford ordered his penman Defoe to tackle this issue head on, providing him with necessary information.[88] In his *Imperial Gratitude, drawn from a Modest View of the Conduct of the Emperor Ch . . . es VI and the King of Spain Ch . . . es III* (1712), Defoe took a more provocative and confrontational approach than did Swift in his *Conduct of the Allies* which appeared in the previous year. Moreover, by effectively weaving together lengthy quotations from diplomatic correspondence of the Austrian Empire and detailed accounts of the Imperial forces under British pay during the last ten years, Defoe made his arguments more convincing. Yet, as he made clear, Defoe was 'not so much stating an Account of Debtor and Creditor as to Money, but a Debt of Gratitude, and Ingratitude, in which the Money disburst, the Blood and Lives lost, in his Quarrel, and Services done for his Person, stand on the one Side to his Debt in Account'.[89] In surveying every major battle fought and funded by Britain in support of the Archduke Charles of Austria, from Marlborough's victory at Hocksted in 1704 to Count von Guido Strahemberg's success at Sarragossa six years later, Defoe took care to point out that 'he has not yet indeed given us

[86] Anon., *The Ballance of Power: Or, a Comparison of the Strength of the Emperor and the French King* (London: A. Baldwin, 1714), 13.

[87] Anon., *The Ballance of Power*, 13.

[88] J. A. Downie, *Robert Harley and the Press. Propaganda and the Public Opinion in the Age of Swift and Defoe* (Cambridge: Cambridge University Press, 1979), 146–147.

[89] Daniel Defoe, 'Imperial Gratitude, drawn from a Modest View of the Conduct of the Emperor Ch . . . es VI and the King of Spain Ch . . . es III', in: *Political and Economic Writings of Daniel Defoe. Vol. 5: International Relations*, ed. P. N. Furbank (London: Pickering & Chatto, 2000), 199.

many Verbal Acknowledgements of, at least that are made Publick'.[90] Should Britain, questioned Defoe by way of conclusion, 'carry on the War to oblige, and in dependence upon, the Promises of Such an Ally?'[91] Here again, the point at issue was doubtless the Whig emphasis on the principle of honour and good faith.

The policy implication was obvious. It was better to negotiate with France over the spoils now than to rely on the Austrian Empire for trading privileges in the Spanish colonies, even if the Grand Alliance would succeed in expelling the French from the Iberian Peninsula. 'Well may King Charles, and the Emperor, his Father, call Her Majesty Mother; for the Treatment he has receiv'd from hence has gone beyond even the manner of Fathers in this Age; the King of France has not acted thus even with his own Flesh and Blood', Defoe remarked suggestively.[92] To drive home his message, Defoe referred to an episode in the summer of 1711 when Charles VI was alleged to have said, upon hearing of Bolingbroke's Quebec Expedition, 'Sure the English could not be so Insolent.'[93] That is to say, the emperor had no intention of complying with Article VI of the Treaty of the Second Grand Alliance, which Defoe reproduced word by word in the same place:

> It shall be lawful for his Royal Majesty of Great Britain, and the Lords, the States General, by common Advice, and for the Benefit and Enlargement of the Navigation and Commerce of their Subjects, to seize by their Forces what Lands and Citys they can, belonging to the Spanish Dominions in the Indies; and whatsoever they so take, shall be their own.[94]

While it has been customary to distinguish Tory from Whig understandings of political economy on the basis of their contrasting attitudes on the Financial Revolution of the 1690s, respectively in favour of the landed and moneyed interests,[95] not much effort has been made

[90] Defoe, 'Imperial Gratitude', 198.

[91] Defoe, 'Imperial Gratitude', 220.

[92] Defoe, 'Imperial Gratitude', 199.

[93] Defoe, 'Imperial Gratitude', 200.

[94] Defoe, 'Imperial Gratitude', 200.

[95] See J. G. A. Pocock, *The Machiavellian Moment. Florentine Political Thought and the Atlantic Republican Tradition* (Princeton, NJ: Princeton University Press, 1975), 423–461;

to incorporate the Commercial Treaty of Utrecht into this picture other than the Tory venture to open free trade with France (Articles VIII and IX) and the Whig protectionist opposition to it.[96] Yet the central thread that ran through the Whig criticism of the Commercial Treaty of Utrecht in the 1715 impeachment was the Tory betrayal of the Grand Alliance. To be more specific, it was the Tory exclusion of the Dutch from the Spanish New World that Walpole and Stanhope's committee of secrecy found most unacceptable. Conversely, in the sceptical eyes of the Tory politicians, the Whig reliance on the Austrian Empire for Britain's economic future, to say nothing of their underestimation of, if not sympathy for, the Dutch, was simply delusional and irresponsible.

Conclusion: The Aftermath of the Treaty of Utrecht

In 1716, only a year after the triumphant celebration of their political victory over the Tory party, the Whigs found themselves in an awkward position. In a sudden turn of events, Britain entered into a defensive alliance with France. With hesitation and reluctance, the Dutch Republic joined the next year, followed by the Austrian Empire in 1718. Formed just in time to suppress Elizabeth Farnese's revisionist Spain, the central objective of the Quadruple Alliance was the maintenance of the Utrecht settlement. The War of the Quadruple Alliance ended two years later in 1720 by the Second Treaty of The Hague, which basically reconfirmed the Treaty of Utrecht. Was, then, the Whig clamour against the Peace of Utrecht merely driven by party politics, as Oxford and Bolingbroke strongly complained?

Istvan Hont, 'Free Trade and the Economic Limits to National Politics: Neo-Machiavellian Political Economy Reconsidered', in: *Jealousy of Trade. International Competition and the Nation-State in Historical Perspective* (Cambridge, MA: The Belknap Press of Harvard University Press, 2005), 185–266.

[96] W. J. Ashley, 'The Tory Origin of Free Trade Policy', *Quarterly Journal of Economics* 11/4 (1897), 335–371; D. A. E. Harkness, 'The Opposition to the 8th and 9th Articles of the Commercial Treaty of Utrecht', *Scottish Historical Review* 21/83 (1924), 219–226; D. C. Coleman, 'Politics and Economics in the Age of Anne: The Case of the Anglo-French Trade Treaty of 1713', in: *Trade, Government, and Economy in Pre-Industrial England. Essays presented to F. J. Fischer*, ed. D. C. Coleman and A. H. John (London: Weidenfeld & Nicolson, 1976), 187–211.

True, with the Hanoverian succession in 1714 and the establishment of the Regency of Philippe d'Orléans in the following year, the power structure in Europe had radically changed. But they were not wholly unexpected. Louis XIV was well over seventy years old, and Queen Anne's health had been fragile for some years. Besides, though George I joined with Peter the Great of Russia against Charles XII of Sweden only after his accession to the British throne, and that as the Elector of Hanover, the Great Northern War had been going on for more than a decade.[97] Tellingly, however, it was not until two years later, in 1718, that the Whig press began to grapple with the thorny issue of the Anglo-French Treaty of 1716. Understandably so, for it was, as Walpole's subsequent resignation together with Charles, Viscount Townshend, Secretary of State for the Northern Department, attests to, signed principally with a view to enhancing the security of Hanover.[98] In this regard, the outbreak of the Spanish war in 1718 temporarily saved the new Whig ministry of Stanhope and Charles Spencer, 3rd Earl of Sunderland, by providing belated justification for the Treaty of Alliance with France. Insofar as it served to keep Gibraltar, a commercial and military outpost obtained by the Whig Godolphin government, under British control, and the Regent firmly in power, the strategic cooperation with France was explicable, if not excusable. Or at least so believed John Trenchard and Thomas Gordon, the two eminent co-editors of the journal *Cato's Letters* (1720–1723). Welcoming the Whig Treaty of The Hague, they argued, the Defensive Treaty with France was concluded with the Regent, who 'can never conspire against us, without conspiring against himself', emphatically adding:

> He [Philip V of Spain] has the interests of the Regent, of all Germany, Italy, the states of Holland, and indeed of all Europe, against him, as well as the united interest of his own subjects, who will not be contented to be a province to France; and I may venture to assert, that whilst we keep the possession of Gibraltar, and make a proper use of it, he can neither effect the

[97] J. F. Chance, *George I and the Northern War. A Study of British-Hanoverian Policy in the North of Europe in the Years 1709 to 1721* (London: Smith, Elder, & Company, 1909).

[98] W. A. Speck, 'The Whig Schism under George I', *Huntington Library Quarterly* 40/2 (1977), 171–179; Derek McKay, 'The Struggle for Control of George I's Northern Policy, 1718–1719', *Journal of Modern History* 45/3 (1973), 367–386.

> one nor the other; namely, he can never make himself King of France, nor the Pretender King of England.[99]

Not unexpectedly, the Whig Hanoverian entente with France had its ramifications. Most of all, it alienated the Austrian Empire. So much so that in late April 1725 the Emperor Charles VI entered into a secret agreement with the Spanish King Philip (the first Treaty of Vienna) to help him to regain Gibraltar and Minorca from Britain in exchange for his recognition of the Pragmatic Sanction as well as his cooperation in the development of the Imperial Ostend Company.[100] Worse still, they concurred to arrange the marriages of their children in the near future.[101] Shocked and terrified by such a volte-face, the Whig ministry hurriedly approached the courts of France and Prussia and managed, five months later in September, to form the Alliance of Hanover.[102] The collaboration with the Regent, however, did not last long in the face of increasing evidence of the resurgence of French power and ambition, [103] not least the restoration of Dunkirk.[104] In March 1731 Britain signed the Treaty of Vienna with the Austrian Empire and returned to the 'Old System' of alliance against Bourbon France.

This was Bolingbroke's *Schadenfreude* moment. He concluded his *Letters on the Study and Use of History* by drawing a contrast between his

[99] Trenchard and Thomas Gordon, 'The Vain Hopes of the Pretender and His Party', in: *Cato's Letters: Or, Essays on Liberty, Civil and Religious, and Other Important Subjects*, ed. Ronald Hamowy, 2 vols. (Indianapolis: Liberty Fund, 1995), 604–606 (No. 83, Saturday, 30 June 1722).

[100] Jeremy Black, 'Anglo-Austrian Relations, 1725–1740: A Study in Failure', *Journal for Eighteenth-Century Studies* 12/1 (1989), 19–45; Gerald B. Hertz, 'England and the Ostend Company', *English Historical Review* 22/86 (1907), 255–279.

[101] Frederick Dhont, 'Law on the Diplomatic State: The 1725 Ripperda Treaty', in: *Die Inszenierung des Rechts. Law on Stage*, ed. Viktoria Draganova, Helmut Landerer, Stefan Kroll and Ulrike Meyer (München: Meidenbauer, 2011), 303–324.

[102] G. C. Gibbs, 'Britain and the Alliance of Hanover, April 1725–February 1726', *English Historical Review* 73/288 (1958), 404–430; J. F. Chance, 'The Treaty of Hanover', *English Historical Review* 29/116 (1914), 657–688.

[103] Jeremy Black, *The Collapse of the Anglo-French Alliance, 1727–1731* (Gloucester: Alan Sutton, 1987); Arthur M. Wilson, *French Foreign Policy during the Administration of Cardinal Fleury, 1729–1743. A Study in Diplomacy and Commercial Development* (Cambridge, MA: Harvard University Press, 1936), 42–239.

[104] Bolingbroke, *The Case of Dunkirk Faithfully Stated and Impartially Considered* (London: A. Moore, 1730).

foreign policy and that of the Whigs before, and especially after, the peace treaty of 1713. First, he was, as expected, highly critical of the Whig policy of 'No Peace without Spain', describing it as 'a rage of warring'.[105] Nevertheless, he admitted in retrospect that it had brought some benefits. 'The rage of warring confirmed the beggary of our nation', 'but then it gave, in the last war, reputation to our arms, and our councils too'.[106] While the Henry St John of 1710–1712 dreamed of Perfidious Albion, the Bolingbroke of 1735–1736 came to appreciate the Whig politics of alliance based on the principle of good faith and mutual trust.

More important, Bolingbroke took extra care to distinguish the negotiations with France under the Tory government from those under the Whig. 'The rage of negociating began twenty years ago, under pretence of consummating the treaty of Utrecht; and, from that time to this, our ministers have been in one perpetual maze', he taunted.[107] In Bolingbroke's judgement, the Quadruple Alliance was more reproachable than the Grand Alliance. For even though Stanhope and Sunderland successfully preserved stability in Europe, they not only failed to pay off debts, but, more seriously, 'They have made themselves and us, often, objects of aversion to the powers on the continent; and we are become at last objects of contempt, even to the Spaniards.'[108] 'This is grievous, and the more so to any man, who has the honour of his country, as well as her prosperity at heart', Bolingbroke continued. 'Because we have not, in this case, the airy consolation we had in the other.'[109] Turning the tables on the Whigs, the Tory statesman criticized their negotiations with the Regent as having been conducted 'without any part of that deciding influence which we ought to have'.[110] In the last analysis, Bolingbroke as before took as his point of reference the principle of *raison d'état*. 'The rage of negociating' attests the Whig incomprehension of the kaleidoscopic nature of diplomatic *realpolitik*, even more so than 'the rage of

[105] Bolingbroke, *Defence of the Treaty of Utrecht*, 145.

[106] Bolingbroke, *Defence of the Treaty of Utrecht*, 145.

[107] Bolingbroke, *Defence of the Treaty of Utrecht*, 146.

[108] Bolingbroke, *Defence of the Treaty of Utrecht*, 146.

[109] Bolingbroke, *Defence of the Treaty of Utrecht*, 146.

[110] Bolingbroke, *Defence of the Treaty of Utrecht*, 147.

warring', because it provided Britain's arch-rival, France, with ample time to recover and regain her strength.

Fortunately, Britain was given one last chance. 'By Reason of some lucky Circumstances at this Juncture we have no Cause to apprehend any instant Danger from France', Bolingbroke's protégé George Lyttelton noted on the eve of the War of Jenkins' Ear of 1739, adding, 'What can be expect by delaying it longer, but to draw on farther Insults, farther Wrongs, farther Contempt, to be treated on all Occasions as a Province of France?'[111] The war against Spain, to Bolingbroke's circle, was a pre-emptive war against the united House of Bourbon. Or, as Hugh-Hume Campbell, 3rd Earl of Marchmont, declared in 1740, 'The Treaty of Utrecht opened very wisely a Dispute concerning the Encroachments of the French on the Spanish Colonies', and it was high time to complete this unfinished business.[112] The underlying legacy of the Tory Treaty of Utrecht in British history, in a nutshell, is that it introduced, in the crudest manner, the modern world of economic power politics.

Doohwan Ahn is Assistant Professor at the Department of Politics and International Relations at Seoul National University. He obtained his PhD from the University of Cambridge (2012), co-edited *Fénelon in the Enlightenment. Traditions, Adaptations, and Variations* (2014) and published 'From Hanover to Gibraltar: *Cato's Letters* (1720–23) in International Context' (2016) and 'The Anglo-French Commercial Treaty of 1713: Tory Trade Politics and the Question of Dutch Decline' (2010). He is completing a monograph on Henry St John, Viscount Bolingbroke.

[111] George Lyttelton, *Considerations upon the Present State of Our Affairs, at Home and Abroad, in a Letter to a Member of Parliament from a Friend in the Country*, 2nd edn. (London, 1739), 18, 29.

[112] Hugh-Hume, 3rd Earl of Marchmont, *A State of the Rise and Progress of the Disputes with Spain* (London: H. Goreham, 1740), 52.

The Treaty of *Asiento* between Spain and Great Britain

Virginia Léon Sanz and Niccolò Guasti

The *Asiento* Treaty and the War of the Spanish Succession

To fully comprehend the significance of the Treaty of Asiento that was signed on 26 March 1713,[1] it is important to recall that during the conflict Great Britain reached an agreement with Charles III of Austria, who, with the backing of the allies, established his court in

[1] 'Asiento ajustado entre las dos Majestades Católica y Británica sobre encargarse la Compañía de Inglaterra de la introducción de Esclavos Negros en la América española', AGI, Indiferente, General, leg. 2799. This publication was prepared within the framework of the project MINECO HAR2015-65987-P: Redefinition of the European and Mediterranean Spaces in the Eighteenth Century. Politics, Diplomacy and Conflict.

V. Léon Sanz
Department of Modern History, Complutense University Madrid, Spain
e-mail: virgleon@ucm.es

N. Guasti (✉)
Department of Humanistic Studies, University of Foggia, Italy
e-mail: niccologuasti@yahoo.com

A. Alimento, K. Stapelbroek (eds.), *The Politics of Commercial Treaties in the Eighteenth Century*, DOI 10.1007/978-3-319-53574-6_5

Barcelona in 1705.[2] Queen Anne instructed James Stanhope, her envoy at the Catalonian court and future Secretary of State under George I, to negotiate the commercial advantages England would obtain at the end of the war. Stanhope convinced Charles to agree to the British demands by taking advantage of Charles' weakened claim to the Spanish throne after the Battle of Almansa in April 1707.[3] The *asiento* of black Africans with the court of Barcelona, like the previous *asiento* held by France from May 1702 to May 1712,[4] was to last ten years and permitted the English to ship 4,800 slaves to the Indies each year.[5] The English would pay 200,000 *escudos* in advance, around £45,000, at a fixed exchange rate. The terms took into account Catalan aspirations to participate in the America trade. Among other concessions, it was approved that four ships annually would be sent to the Indies and a council would be established for the development of the *Compañía Náutica Mercantil y Universal*. Consequently, in 1709, a group of Catalans led by S. Feliú de la Penya founded the *Companya Nova de Gibraltar*, with the aim of breaking the Cadiz monopoly on the America trade by taking advantage of the British seizure of Gibraltar.[6] Originally, the Company was intended to continue for three years, with a capital of 11,200 Catalan pounds, divided into sixteen participations of 700 pounds.

The 1713 *asiento* signed by Philip V was, however, based on the French model, copying several of its articles. It was to last thirty years and was also formally different from previous treaties signed by Portugal and France. The

[2] J. Albareda, *La Guerra de Sucesión de España (1700–1714)* (Barcelona: Crítica, 2010); V. Léon Sanz, *El Archiduque Carlos y los austracistas. Guerra de Sucesión y exilio* (Sant Cugat: Arpegio, 2014).

[3] D. W. Jones, *War and Economy in the Age of William III and Marlborough* (Oxford and New York: Blackwell, 1988).

[4] BN. 76224, 'Assiento ajustado entre las dos Majestades Cathólica y Cristianísima con la Compañía Real de Guinea establecida en el Reyno de Francia'; R. Fernández Durán, *La Corona española y el tráfico de Negros* (Madrid: Ecobook, 2011), 39–59; C. Malamud Rikles, *Cádiz y Saint Malò en el comercio colonial peruano (1698–1725)* (Cádiz: Diputación Provincial, 1986).

[5] NA SP 108/471, 'Treaty between her Majesty and the King of Spain', Barcelona 1707, analysed by Fernández Durán, *La Corona española*, 93–95.

[6] P. Vilar, *Le 'Manual de la Companya Nova de Gibraltar'* (Paris: SEVPEN, 1962). After the war, the Company continued its activities, using Gibraltar as a base, until 1723.

commercial agreement that contained the 1713 *asiento* was part of a peace treaty, whereas the Portuguese one was signed in the presence of a notary public, and the French by the monarchs with the Guinea Company. Moreover, in the case of the British licence, the Spanish crown participated in the *asiento* trade. Never before had the Spanish monarchy directly exploited slave trading. Since the early sixteenth century it had granted the exploitation rights to varied contractors, Portugal, Genoa and later France.

The 1713 *asiento* stipulated that the Queen of England and the King of Spain each held a quarter share. As such it was a Hispano-British mixed merchant company with a shared profit potential. Regardless of dynastic change and post-war impositions, this would explain the choice of granting the *asiento* to a British company.[7] Yet, the Spanish crown never held 25 per cent of the company. Instead Philip V bore responsibility for a quarter of the costs of the *asiento*. Furthermore, Philip V was by statute the last in line to receive a share in the profits from the *asiento*, but was responsible for any losses. Finally, he neglected the opinion of the Council of the Indies (*Consejo de Indias*) which warned that trafficking in slaves had never been profitable: the contractors made money from smuggling goods, just like the French Guinea Company profited from contraband in Spanish America, particularly in the Pacific.[8] Arguably, the Treaty of Asiento signed by Charles III was more favourable to Spain than that signed by Philip V. And if the negotiations of the Treaty of Asiento went badly for Spain, so did the renegotiations in 1716, which saw the interest rate move from 8 per cent to 6 per cent and the crown's capital share increase while officials at the Bourbon court, except for Minister José Grimaldo, seemed unaware of the content of the treaties.

Such unawareness was never to be observed on the British side, where the *asiento* was always part of a broader strategy. On 10 July 1707, Queen Anne and Charles III, as King of Spain, signed a commercial treaty in Barcelona that was ratified on 9 April 1708, which included the *asiento*. In the same treaty, Stanhope and his Spanish counterparts agreed to reduce the duty on

[7] J. M. Delgado, 'El impacto de Utrecht en la organización del comercio colonial español (1713–1739)', in: *El declive de la Monarquía y del Imperio español*, ed. J. Albareda (Barcelona: Crítica, 2015), 123–172.

[8] Fernández Durán, *La Corona española*, 45–91; E. W. Dahlgren, *Les relations commerciales et maritimes entre la France et les côtes de l'Océan Pacifique* (Paris: Champion, 1909); C. Yuste, *Emporios transpacíficos. Comerciantes mexicanos en Manila, 1710–1815* (México: UNAM, 2007).

English goods and recognize all privileges granted to English merchants, specifically those in the 1667 agreement. The treaty, moreover, included a secret article that stipulated the creation of an Indies trade company with only Spanish and English shareholders. Once 'His Catholic Majesty [took] possession of the Court of Madrid', English subjects enjoyed the same rights and freedoms as Spaniards, paid the same duties and the joint Company would be granted permission to send via Cadiz ten 500-ton ships to ports in the Indies. According to the agreement, the French would be prohibited from trading with the Indies, as would the Dutch, whose exclusion from the treaty caused great tension among the allies during the war.[9]

Compared with the 1707 treaty, the one signed at Utrecht on 9 December 1713 differed significantly, particularly in that the creation of a joint trade company was abolished, while the 1707 permission to send ten company ships turned into the well-known 'annual ship' (*navío de permiso*) clause. Having achieved his main diplomatic objective, to convince Philip V to renounce the French throne, Lexington had stayed another six months at the Spanish court to defend the general goals of Queen Anne's government and her allies and negotiate the preliminary Commercial Treaty that was signed along with a Peace and Friendship Treaty on 13 July 1713.[10] In the Utrecht treaty, Philip V recognized British sovereignty of Gibraltar and Menorca, while demanding that the Roman creed be preserved in both places. The British on their part made demands on the customs duty and the statute of the city of Santander.[11] Spain retained all of its territories in America and obtained the British promise of assistance in restoring

[9] R. Donoso Anes, *El asiento de esclavos con Inglaterra: su contexto histórico y sus aspectos económicos y contables* (Sevilla: Universidad de Sevilla, 2010); J. O. McLachlan, *Trade and Peace with Old Spain, 1667–1750* (Cambridge: Cambridge University Press, 1940).

[10] 'Tratado de paz y amistad entre sus Majestades el rey de España y la reina de Inglaterra…concluido en Utrecht el 13 de julio de 1713' and 'Tratado preliminar de comercio entre las coronas de España e Inglaterra, concluido en Madrid el 13 de julio de 1713', in: *Tratados, convenios y declaraciones de paz y comercio*, ed. A. del Cantillo (Madrid: Imprenteria de Alegria y Charlain, 1843), 75–87 and 115–127. See C. Storrs (Lord Lexington's mission to Madrid), L. Bély (Mesnager's diplomatic arbitration) and J. Albareda (French Spanish relations), in: *1713. La Monarquía de España y los Tratados de Utrecht*, ed. V. Léon Sanz, Cuadernos de Historia Moderna. Anejos XII (2013).

[11] BN 1/6853, 'Tratado de amistad y comercio ajustado entre las Coronas de España y de Inglaterra, concluido en Utrecht, el 9 de diciembre de 1713'.

the original borders, which, indirectly but powerfully, helped strengthen the exclusive character of British trade privileges. The eventual Commercial Treaty may be interpreted as an implementation of what had been agreed by France and Britain at the London preliminaries on 8 October 1711, where the objective of French diplomacy had been to avoid concessions at the expense of Spain; as the Duke of Osuna wrote: 'Spain relinquished all that was relinquishable'.[12]

The Evolution of the *Asiento* Until the Treaty of Vienna

Thus, Britain obtained its long-desired advantages in the Spanish Indies which were further confirmed in a series of complementary treaties on 14 December 1715, 26 May 1716 and the Treaty of Madrid of 13 June 1721.[13] While the British ambassador in Madrid, Richard Keene, was very aware of the interests of the South Sea Company, his Bourbon counterparts in London tended to show little interest or otherwise failed to control the income and profits the Company generated for the Spanish crown. The exception was Tomás Giraldino from Jerez, whose capable directorship of the Company in London fits with Keene's comment that it was hard to find 'a more fair or honest man'.

The *asiento* granted to the South Sea Company and the contraband carried out under cover of the *asiento* brought more riches to private individuals than to the Company. With the passage of time the earlier problems of piracy and privateering transformed into an unbridled growth of British smuggling from Jamaica. In fact, the British authorities protected this practice by pointing to the rights established in several agreements with Spain between 1670 and 1713, thus using the *asiento* as

[12] NA SP 105/258. R. Fernández Durán, 'Asiento de Negros con Inglaterra. Marzo 1713. Una sociedad buscadora de rentas', in: *Los tratados de Utrecht. Claroscuros de la paz. La resistencia de los catalanes*, ed. C. Mollfulleda and N. Sallés (Barcelona: Museu d´Història de Catalunya, 2015), 177–178.

[13] BN VC/852/27, 'Tratado de Declaración y Explicación sobre algunos artículos del antecedente ajustado en Utrecht, entre esta Corona y la de Inglaterra, sobre la Paz y el Comercio, concluido en Madrid en 14 de Diciembre de 1715'; 'Tratado declaratorio de algunos artículos del asiento de negros que se pactó el 26 de marzo de 1713, concluido en Madrid el 26 de mayo de 1716'; 'Tratado particular de paz y amistad entre las Coronas de España y de Inglaterra, firmado en Madrid el 13 de junio de 1721', in: *Tratados*, ed. Cantillo, 174–191 and 198–201.

an instrument to develop legal and illegal trade in Spanish America. This while Spain attempted to maintain the trade monopoly and keep Spanish American commerce 'clean'. Bernardo de Tinajero, who had participated in the *asiento* negotiations, had already warned Philip V that, without the profit from the smuggling of goods, the black slave trade simply was not a lucrative business. According to his analysis, the greatest problem would arise from the establishment of factories in Veracruz, Portobello, Cartagena, Panama, Havana and Buenos Aires, through which British merchants could control the fairs and the internal trading of the various American territories.[14]

In this way the *asiento* developed fairly quietly between 1713 and 1718 (the main institutional change was the transfer of the *Casa de Contratación* from Seville to Cadiz in 1717), while the following years saw conflicts between Spain and Britain culminate in warfare and the *asiento* trade and annual ship interrupted until 1721. It was in this period that Spanish reforms of the South America trade were first debated and initiated with the passing of the *Real Proyecto de Flotas y Galeones* in 1720. The renewal of the ratification of the British *asiento* in 1721 and the 1724–1726 Ripperda interlude only postponed further initiatives to reorganize colonial trade.[15] Of special significance was the attempt by Ripperda to align the Hispano-Austrian reconciliation and the 1725 Treaty of Vienna, with an overhaul of the global trade regime through Spanish support for the Company of Ostend. On 1 May 1725, a day after the Treaty of Vienna was signed, a Commercial Treaty was concluded that provocatively (with explicit reference to the Treaty of Münster which the Dutch cited to suppress the new company) used the most favoured nation principle to give the Ostend Company the same rights as

[14] Delgado, 'El impacto de Utrecht', 147–156; G. J. Walker, *Spanish Politics and Imperial Trade, 1700–1789* (London: Macmillan, 1979), 149–205.

[15] A. García-Baquero González, *Cádiz y el Atlántico (1717–1778)*, 2 vols. (Seville: Escuela de Estudios Hispano-Americanos de Sevilla, 1976); A. Crespo, *La Casa de la Contratación y la Intendencia General de la Marina de Cádiz (1717–1730)* (Cádiz: Universidad de Cádiz, 1996). The 1720 Project which meant a return to the fleets and galleons, was a disaster: after that only three escorted fleets were sent to New Spain (in 1721, 1723 and 1730): see J. M. Delgado Ribas, *Dinámicas imperiales (1650–1796). España, América y Europa en el cambio institucional del sistema colonial español* (Barcelona: Bellaterra, 2007), 97–140.

the British—in their treaties of 1667, 1670 and 1713—and the Dutch—in their treaties of 1648, 1650 and 1714.[16]

War and the Elimination of the *Asiento*

Within months of the Treaty of Vienna, Ripperda fell and was replaced by José Patiño.[17] Following an unsuccessful Spanish siege of Gibraltar in 1726–1727 and the cession of the Ostend Company, the relationship with Vienna came to an end. The Treaty of Seville of 9 November 1729 restored the situation prior to 1725.[18]

If the conclusion of the Treaty of Seville improved relations between Madrid and London, its negotiation and the previous Hispano-Austrian interval also brought to light the true dimensions of the problem with the *asiento* and the annual ship, over which the Spanish government now demanded greater control. In 1726–1728, again during a conflict with Britain, an attempt had been made to reform the Indies trade, although it was not until the Patiño government, in 1730–1732, that the workings of the Company of the *asiento* were really understood.[19] The Secretary of

[16] 'Tratado de paz y amistad entre el rey Católico don Felipe V y el emperador de Alemania Carlos VI; concluido en Viena el 30 de abril de 1725'; 'Tratado de comercio entre su Majestad imperial Carlos VI y Su Majestad Católica Felipe V, concluido en Viena el 1 de mayo de 1725', in: *Tratados*, ed. Cantillo, 202–216 and 218–228, especially Articles 26 and 47. See A. Mur Raurell, *Diplomacia secreta y paz. La correspondencia de los embajadores españoles en Viena Juan Guillermo Ripperda y Luis Ripperda (1724–1727)*, 2 vols. (Madrid: Ministerio de Asuntos Exteriores, 2011); V. Léon Sanz, 'La diplomacia de la Corte Borbónica: Hacia la Paz con Austria de 1725', in: *La Corte de los Borbones. Crisis del modelo cortesano*, ed. J. Martínez Millán, C. Camarero and M. Luzzi (Madrid: Polifemo, 2013), 529–558.

[17] I. Pulido Bueno, *José Patiño. El inicio del Gobierno político-económico ilustrado en España* (Huelva: Artes Gráficas Andaluzas, 1998); A. F. Kuethe and K. J. Andrien, *The Spanish Atlantic World in the Eighteenth Century. War and the Bourbon Reforms, 1713–1796* (Cambridge: Cambridge University Press, 2014), 31–157; A. J. Pierce, *The Origins of Bourbon Reform in Spanish South America, 1700–1763* (New York: Palgrave Macmillan, 2014).

[18] 'Tratado de paz, unión, amistad y alianza defensiva con las Coronas de España, Francia e Inglaterra, ajustado y concluido en Sevilla el 9 de noviembre de 1729', IX, in: *Tratados*, ed. Cantillo, 247. See L. Bély, *Les relations internationales en Europe (XVIIe–XVIIIe siècles)* (Paris: PUF, 1992), 441; and V. Léon Sanz, *Carlos VI. El emperador que no pudo ser rey de España* (Madrid: Aguilar, 2003), 301–320.

[19] Walker, *Spanish Politics*, 159–173; Delgado Ribas, *Dinámicas imperiales*, 124–140. On the Anglo-Spanish diplomatic relations between1728 and 1739, see A. de Béthencourt, *Relaciones de España bajo Felipe V* (Alicante: AEHM, 1998).

State, Orendain, Marquis of the Paz, requested a report from Varas Valdés, the President of the *Casa de la Contratación*, who had analysed the main evils of the *asiento* and argued for its termination. Valdés pointed out that arrival of the ships should never coincide with the fairs of Portobello and Veracruz. Likewise, in 1732, Tomás Giraldino attempted to clear up the doubts on the *asiento* accounts in London, with a policy for greater control carried out by Orendain and Patiño.[20] Scrutiny of the *asiento* accounts revealed not only the increase in British smuggling, which also involved highly placed civil servants, but moreover the collaboration of bribed representatives of the Spanish king.

Guided by these insights, the early 1730s saw new negotiations between Company shareholders and the Spanish government which nearly ended the *asiento* treaty, and in 1735 the idea of eliminating the annual ship was discussed.[21] In fact, the merchants and shareholders of the British Company were happy to negotiate with Spain as they too considered the *asiento* unprofitable. In 1732 the merchants of Cadiz offered a pay-off sum of 2 per cent of the annual dividend from profits of the fleets and galleons as compensation. According to Ozanam, Newcastle and Walpole only refused this deal because the *asiento* was part of the popular understanding of the British victory at Utrecht.

Under these awkward circumstances, aggravated by increased smuggling and repeated British obstructions to allow Spanish officials access to the accounts of the South Sea Company, the War of Jenkins' Ear (known as the War of the Asiento in Spain) emerged in 1739.[22] Most historians,

[20] L. de Luxan Hernández and S. de Luxan Menéndez, 'Las dificultades de funcionamiento del Asiento de Negros británico en el imperio español, 1713–1739: la misión de Tomás de Geraldino en Londres', *Colonial Latin American Historical Review* 1/3 (2013), 273–307. About Varas Valdés, see R. Antúnez Acevedo, *Memorias Históricas sobre legislación y gobierno* (Madrid: Sancha, 1797).

[21] Fernández Durán, *La Corona española*, 267–289; S. J. Stein and B. Stein, *Silver, Trade and War. Spain and America in the Making of Early Modern Europe* (Baltimore, MD: Johns Hopkins University Press, 2000).

[22] Something similar had occurred with the French *asiento*. In 1713, Grimaldo asked the Duke of Alba, the Spanish ambassador in Paris, to request the accounts of the South Sea Company and of the *asiento* through reserved channels. In 1734, France had not yet settled the accounts, but had repeatedly demanded compensation from Spain, which in this case had the support of Britain; see Fernández Durán, *La Corona española*, 87. This is one of the conclusions reached by S. Carmona, R. Donoso and S. P. Walker in work focusing on clarifying the accounts of the *asiento*, although, in spite of their efforts to apply a

like G. H. Nelson, agree that its main cause was the damage caused to Spanish commercial interests by uncontrolled British trade under cover of the *asiento*, which 'threatened to destroy the whole trading structure of the Spanish Empire'.[23] Focusing on the conceptual clash between the economic model of the colonial monopoly that was defended by Spain and the unbridled exploitation of commercial privileges by Britain, Temperley judged that the war was 'waged solely for balance of trade rather than for balance of power'. However, Zeller has stressed that British public opinion agitated by the influence of mercantile griefs reignited traditional anti-Spanish sentiments.[24] Additional—internal—causes lay in Patiño's attempts to interfere in complex local interests in Cadiz, Mexico and Peru, mishaps of the fleet in 1735 and of the galleons in 1737, the ongoing investigation from 1737 by the *Junta de Medios* into the *asiento*'s functioning and the wider context of fiscal-financial crisis of the Treasury.[25]

As the war with Britain gave way to the War of the Austrian Succession, from 1741 the main figures in Spanish politics were Campillo, Carvajal

methodology based on international accountancy and the impact of globalization, they find that the way the Company accounts were registered did not differ much from those of a private individual and admit their difficulty in coming to conclusive results, in 'Accounting, International Relations and Treaty Verification: Britain, Spain and the Asiento', *Accounting, Organizations and Society* 35 (2010), 252–273.

[23] B. L. Brown, 'The South Sea Company and Contraband Trade', *American Historical Review* 4 (1926, XXXI), 662–678; G. H. Nelson, 'Contraband Trade under the Asiento, 1730–1739', *American Historical Review* 51 (1945–1946), 55–67; Fernández Durán, *La Corona española*, 289–294; C. A. Palmer, *Human Cargoes. The British Slave Trade to Spanish America, 1700–1739* (Urbana: University of Illinois Press, 1981).

[24] G. Zeller, 'Los tiempos modernos', in: *Historia de las relaciones internacionales*, ed. P. Renouvin (Madrid: Akal 1984); H. W. V. Temperley, 'The Causes of the War of Jenkins Ear, 1739', *Transactions of the Royal Historical Society* 3 (1909), 197–236; J. Cerdá Crespo, *Conflictos Coloniales. La Guerra de los Nueve Años 1739–1748* (Alicante: Universidad de Alicante, 2010).

[25] Delgado Ribas, *Dinámicas imperiales*, 141–171; J. M. Delgado Barrado, *Aquiles y Teseos. Bosquejos del reformismo borbónico (1701–1759)* (Granada: Universidad de Granada/ Universidad de Jaén, 2007), 90–110. From the coincidence of the outbreak of the War of Jenkins' Ear, with the bankruptcy of the Spanish Treasury, the government clearly saw that reforming the Atlantic trade would be profitable for the finances of the crown; see P. Fernádez Albadalejo, 'El decreto de suspensión de pagos de 1739: análisis e implicaciones', *Moneda y Crédito* 142 (1977), 51–73.

and the Marquis of Ensenada.[26] They witnessed how the Franco-Spanish Treaty of Fontainebleau, also known as the Second Bourbon Family Compact (1743), drew attention away from the Indies towards Italy, until the death of Philip V in 1746, when Gibraltar, the Indies and trade become the focus again.

While it was initially agreed at Aix-la-Chapelle in 1748 that Spain and Britain restored the previous borders and Britain would, as compensation for the interruption during the war, regain the *asiento* for four more years, Carvajal's decision to terminate the *asiento* materialized on 5 October 1750, as part of a new commercial treaty with Britain.[27] Article 1 stated that Britain ceded to Spain 'her right to use of the *Asiento* and the annual ship', in exchange for a compensation of £100,000 and the renewal of the articles of the 1667 and 1715 treaties on the tariffs, exceptions and privileges enjoyed by British merchants.

The *Proyectistas* and the 'Legacy' of Utrecht (1713–1750)

In the course of events every aspect of the legacy of Utrecht was analysed in published political economic treatises.[28] The common starting point was the Spanish political and economic decline that had occurred during the reign of Charles II of Habsburg.[29] The loss of Jamaica to Britain in

[26] J. L. Gómez Urdáñez, *El proyecto reformista de Ensenada* (Lleida: Milenio, 1996); J. Molina Cortón, *Reformismo y neutralidad. José de Carvajal y la diplomacia de la España preilustrada* (Mérida: Junta de Extremadura, 2003) 218–278.

[27] 'Tratado de indemnizaciones y comercio entre las coronas de España y de la Gran Bretaña, concluido y firmado en Madrid el 5 de octubre de 1750 para la ejecución del artículo 16 del Tratado de Aquisgrán', in: *Tratados*, ed. Cantillo, 409–412.

[28] For the sake of brevity, we will limit our analysis to economic treaties, in print or manuscript form, circulated between the 1720s and 1750s, which are the most relevant on the debate on the legacy of Utrecht. This type of literature has been named *proyectismo*: cf. J. Muñoz Pérez, 'Los proyectos sobre España e Indias en el siglo XVIII: el proyectismo como género', *Revista de Estudios Políticos* 81 (1955), 169–195; P. Álvarez de Miranda, 'Proyecto y proyectistas en el siglo XVIII español', *Boletín de la Real Academia Española* 65 (1985), 409–429; A. Domínguez Ortiz, 'Estudio Preliminar', in: F. M. Moya Torres y Velasco, *Manifiesto universal de los males envejecidos que España padece* [. . .], ed. A. Domínguez Ortiz (Madrid: Instituto de Estudios Fiscales, 1992), vii–lviii, especially xiii–xvii.

[29] L. García Fuentes, *El comercio español con América, 1650–1700* (Sevilla: Excma. Diputación Provincial de Sevilla, Escuela de Estudios Hispanoamericanos, CSIC, 1980).

1655 decisively ended Spain's trade monopoly over the Caribbean–Mexican region, and thereby the entire American continent, and left Spain as a mere administrator of its own colonial empire to the benefit of Britain, Holland and France. Among the most salient of such measures were the *real cédula* of 31 March 1660, which substituted the principal *ad valorem* customs tariffs with duties based on the cubic volume occupied by the goods being transported, and the undue tax relief granted in 1666 by the head of customs in Cadiz, Francisco Báez Eminente, to British merchants. Such 'graces' had been officially ratified in the Anglo-Spanish trade agreement of 1667, whose key articles were then transcribed word-for-word in the treaties of Utrecht and those of Madrid of 14 December 1715 and 26 May 1716.[30]

All *proyectistas* and commentators of the early eighteenth century began their reflections on Atlantic trade from an understanding of the urgent need to regain full sovereignty over the Spanish colonies given that America was a potentially huge market which the primary and secondary sectors of the mother country—i.e. agriculture and manufacturing—needed once again to exploit as an exclusive right. This required the cancellation, or at least the renegotiation, of existing commercial treaties and the formulation of a coherent tariff policy.[31]

The opinions of economic writers also concurred that the *asiento* and the *navío de permiso* had produced an exponential increase in contraband stimulated by the merchants and officials of the South Sea Company. It was calculated that the volume of illicit trade conducted by the factors of the *asiento* and the annual ships was quite minor compared to the smuggling carried out directly by the British colonies, above all by Jamaica. Spanish authorities, merchants and economic writers had fully understood that these two privileges were

[30] Cantillo, ed., *Tratados*, 170–174; on the adjustment to British advantage of the Utrecht treaty in subsequent years, see McLachlan, *Trade and Peace*, 20–73.

[31] On the long eighteenth-century debate on America and the Spanish colonial empire see the classic works by R. Ezquerra, 'La crítica española de la situación de America en el siglo XVIII', *Revista de Indias* 87–88 (1962), 159–287; M. Bitar Letayf, *Economistas españoles del siglo XVIII. Sus ideas sobre la libertad del comercio con Indias* (Madrid: Ediciones Cultura Hispánica, 1968); M. Artola, 'América en el pensamiento español del siglo XVIII', *Revista de Indias* 115–118 (1969), 51–77; J. A. García Baquero González, *El comercio colonial en la época del absolutismo ilustrado. Problemas y debates* (Granada: Universidad de Granada, 2003).

destroying the little amount of Atlantic trade still managed autonomously by Spanish subjects.[32]

Three different perspectives may be distinguished within the debate on the legacy of the Utrecht treaties that took off in the 1720s. The main representatives of the first perspective were Gerónimo da Uztáriz and Bernardo de Ulloa, who argued for the restoration of the Spanish trade monopoly over the Indies: the system of escorted fleets, the use of a single loading port (Seville), and a differentiated customs scheme based on *ad valorem* tariffs.[33] In order to respond to the manufacturing based and protectionist trade politics of the main European commercial powers,[34] Uztáriz and Ulloa believed that the *Carrrera de las Indias* and the *Casa de Contratación*, when brought back to Seville, could regenerate Spanish Atlantic trade and Castilian manufacturing. Their economic reform programme was premised on the idea that 'active trade' fuelled political power and derived from the export of manufactured goods, particularly textiles. Castilian manufacturing had undergone a recent crisis caused by a mistaken regime of indirect taxation (especially the *alcabala* sales tax, which raised production costs) and the corrupted tariff that worked for the personal greed of customs contractors in Cadiz, especially Báez Eminente, rather than for the state.[35] Next to fiscal exemptions to favour producers and traders of domestic manufactured goods,

[32] McLachlan, *Trade and Peace*, 81–83; Walker, *Spanish Politics*, 111–113.

[33] G. de Uztáriz, *Theórica y Práctica de comercio y de marina [. . .]* (Madrid: n.p., 1724; 1742^2; 1757^3) (the second edition was reproduced anastatically by Gabriel Franco (Madrid: Aguilar, 1968); B. de Ulloa, *Restablecimiento de las fábricas y comercio español [. . .]* (Madrid: A. Marín, 1740). I use the edition by Gonzalo Anes (Madrid: Instituto de Estudios Fiscales, 1992) which also includes the third unpublished part of the treatise. On the life of Uztáriz cf. R. Fernández Durán, *Gerónimo de Uztáriz (1670–1732). Una política económica para Felipe V* (Madrid: Minerva Ediciones, 1999).

[34] Despite the anti-English attitude of the *Theórica* and the *Restablecimiento*, the two Bourbon officials admired the effectiveness of the Navigation Act, the text of which they knew through the translation-summary provided by J.-B. Dubos in *Les intêrets de l'Angleterre mal entendus dans la guerre présente* (Amsterdam: Gallet, 1704), 308–317. Dubos' treatise, which was also extremely important to transmitting the methodology of the English political arithmetic in France and Spain, was undoubtedly a point of reference for all the Iberian *proyectistas* and reformers of the early eighteenth century.

[35] Eminente had justified the drastic decrease in customs tariffs in Cadiz, which he himself administrated, with the need to stamp out contraband, given that it was the elevated duties charged in Seville (30 per cent *ad valorem*) that incentivized it: cf. García Fuentes, *El comercio español*, 60–62 and 74.

Uztáriz and Ulloa advocated a protectionist policy that shielded Iberian products from foreign competition. Moreover, for both men the establishment of a merchant navy on the British or Dutch model, with national crews and charters, was essential for the recovery of Spain's economy. However, unlike the Dutch and British joint stock trading companies, Uztáriz and Ulloa preferred to finance Spain's chartered trade through the rigid corporatism of the Cadiz and Seville merchants and the Andalusian commercial monopoly.[36] Pointing to the bankruptcy of John Law's Indies Company in France, Uztáriz and Ulloa were suspicious that limited companies could spiral out of control and had a natural tendency to restrict monarchical sovereignty. Joint stock companies in their opinion suited mercantile republics or parliamentary regimes, but not absolute monarchies such as Spain.

A key part of the perspective of Uztáriz and Ulloa was their analysis of the legacy of Utrecht, especially the commercial treaties concluded with Britain between 1713 and 1716: Spain had mortgaged the possible reform of its colonial trade, including the restoration of sixteenth- and seventeenth-century rules and practices. The insistence with which Britain had promoted the principle of 'free trade' provided a cover for the exploitation of contraband trade from British ports or from Jamaica.[37] The challenge Uztáriz and Ulloa identified was to restore the Spanish king's sovereign rights through protectionist laws, tariffs and regulations to combat smuggling, while preserving peace with Britain in the absence of sufficient naval forces to enforce these policies. This line was followed to some extent during the administration of José Patiño. Although Patiño clashed with Uztáriz on several occasions, the reorganization of the fleets envisaged in the *proyecto* of 1720 and the development of the *guardacostas* (a force of licensed warships guarding against foreign interlopers) between Cuba and the *Tierra*

[36] Ulloa nevertheless argued for the need to facilitate the freedom of non-Andalusian and non-Castilian merchants to add their capital to the *Carrera*. Furthermore, compared to Uztariz, Ulloa was more disposed to recognize the usefulness of trading companies, in particular in organizing traffic towards those parts of the monarchy that remained isolated or to conquer new colonial territories, like in Asia. Cf. Ulloa, *Restablecimiento*, 165–176, 196–198, 337–355.

[37] Ulloa, *Restablecimiento*, 130, 151–152, 159, 177, 183–184, 191–192, 215, 274, 338, 386–387.

Firme were in keeping with the policy measures recommended by Uztáriz.[38]

In the same period, a second perspective emerged. Different from Uztáriz and Ulloa, its proponents argued for the establishment of privileged or joint stock companies, and numerous attempts at such were made: from 1728 to 1755 four trading companies were formed (and at least two others, one being the Ostend Company, remained at the planning stage): the Compañía Guipuzcoana de Caracas (1728), the Honduras Company (1734), the Real Compañía de San Cristóbal de la Habana (1740) and the Real Compañía de Barcelona (1755).

On one level, these companies served to connect regions of Spain directly with parts of the empire that were otherwise supplied through foreign contraband. The Real Compañía de Barcelona, for instance, traded in San Domingo, Puerto Rico and Santa Margarita. Patiño thus intended these new companies not to interfere with the fleet system. On another level, Spanish officials envisaged the new companies to bypass Cadiz's monopoly and thereby remove profits from foreign merchants of Cadiz, who used Andalusian traders as mere figureheads and who were the staunchest supporters of the status quo of the *Carrera de las Indias*.[39] Of the new companies, only the Guipuzcoana,

[38] Pulido Bueno, *José Patiño*, 33–34, 44–53, 57–58, 210–214; Fernández Durán, *Gerónimo de Uztáriz*, 116–117, 199–224, 285, 288–290; Delgado Ribas, *Dinámicas imperiales*, 99–140. The clash between the two, apart from being based on specific issues like the transfer of the *Casa de Contratación* from Seville to Cadiz, the profitability of royal manufactures and the level of effectiveness of the 1720 *Proyecto* (which had maintained, in compliance with the trade treaties, a system of taxation based on the cubic size and not the value of goods), originated essentially from their different and opposed vision of the economic future of the Spanish monarchy: while for Uztáriz Spain needed to return to being a nation that produced textiles to export mostly towards the American market, Patiño, more realistically, believed that it was more important simply to reactivate exports of any type, even those of agricultural products (primary materials and foodstuffs), without considering too much the Colbertist principle according to which final, manufactured products, being more valuable, represented a guarantee of obtaining an active balance of trade. Not by coincidence, the 1720 *Proyecto* contained a general decrease in customs duties on export goods, without however establishing a clear 'qualitative' difference between manufactured goods and raw materials. Walker justly underlined that at the heart of this attempt to stimulate the volume of exports there was nevertheless a desire to increase tax revenues: *Spanish Politics*, 110–111.

[39] Lynch, *Bourbon Spain 1700–1808* (Oxford and Cambridge, MA: Basil Blackwell, 1993^2), 148–149; J. M. Delgado Barrado, 'Reformismo borbónico y compañías privilegiadas para el comercio americano (1700–1756)', in: *El reformismo borbónico. Una visión interdisciplinar*, ed. A. Guimerá (Madrid: Alianza, 1996), 123–143. On the changing definition, between the second half of the

founded by Patiño, achieved any real success, managing to do harm to British, Dutch and French interests in the Antilles, especially in the cocoa trade (and, to a smaller extent, that of tobacco, indigo and cotton).[40]

While holding different views on the specific nature and number of companies, authors like Legarra, Zavala y Auñón, Santa Cruz de Marcenado, Amor de Soria, Argumosa y Gándara, Carvajal, Dantini and Gutiérrez de Rubalcava saw them as the most propitious instrument for recovering commercial sovereignty. Potentially, they could open up new colonial markets to increase the competitiveness of the entire Iberian economy.[41] Where Uztáriz and Ulloa

sixteenth century and the start of the nineteenth, of 'centre' and 'periphery' within the Spanish Imperial area, cf. L. L. Johnson and S. Migden Socolow, 'Colonial Centers, Colonial Peripheries, and the Economic Agency of the Spanish State', in: *Negotiated Empires. Centers and Peripheries in the Americas, 1500–1820*, ed. C. Daniels and M. V. Kennedy (New York: Routledge, 2002), 59–77.

[40] R. D. Hussey, *The Caracas Company, 1728–1784* (Cambridge, MA: Harvard University Press, 1934); R. Rico Linage, *Las Reales Compañías de comercio con América. Los órganos de gobierno* (Sevilla: CSIC, 1983); M. García Ruiperez, 'El pensamiento económico ilustrado y las compañías de comercio', *Revista de Historia Económica* 4/3 (1986), 521–548; M. Gárate Ojanguren, *La Real Compañía Guipuzcoana de Caracas* (San Sebastian: Grupo Camino Doctor de Historia Donostiarra/Sociedad Guipuzcoana de Ediciones y Publicaciones, 1990); M. Gárate Ojanguren, *Comercio ultramarino e Ilustración. La Real Compañía de la Habana* (San Sebastian: Departamento de Cultura del País Basco, 1993); J. M. Delgado Barrado, *Fomento portuario y compañías privilegiadas. Los 'Dialogos familiares' de Marcelo Dantini (1740–1748)* (Madrid: CSIC, 1998); M. E. Rodríguez García, *Compañías privilegiadas de comercio con América y cambio político (1706–1765)* (Madrid: Banco de España, 2005); Delgado Ribas, *Dinámicas imperiales*, 150–156.

[41] J. de Legarra, *Representación [. . .] sobre el estado actual de los comercios de España e Indias* (manuscript no. 4666 in Biblioteca de la Real Academia de la Historia de Madrid); M. Zavala y Auñón, *Representación al Rey N. Señor D. Phelipe V dirigida al más seguro aumento del Real Erario y conseguir la felicidad, mayor alivio, riqueza y abundancia de su Monarquía* (n.p.: n.p., 1732) (later in Pamplona: A. Espinosa, *Miscelánea económico-política* (1749), 7–180, from which I cite); Á. Navia Osorio y Vigil de Quiñones, marqués de Santa Cruz de Marcenado, *Rapsodia económico-política monárquica [. . .]* (Madrid: A. Marín, 1732) (anastatic edition Oviedo: Instituto de Estudios Asturianos, 1984), especially 211–228; J. Amor de Soria, 'Enfermedad crónica, y peligrosa de los reinos de España y de Indias (1741)', in: J. Amor de Soria, *Aragonesismo austracista (1734–1742)*, ed. E. Lluch (Madrid: CSIC, 2000), 73–375, especially 304–316; T. V. Argumosa y Gándara, *Erudición política [. . .]* (Madrid: n.p., 1743), 143 ff.; M. Dantini, 'Diálogos familiares de la agricoltura indiana [. . .]', in: *Fomento portuario y compañías privilegiadas*, ed. Delgado Barrado; J. M. Delgado Barrado, *José de Carvajal y Lancáster. Testamento politico o idea de un gobierno catolico* (Córdoba: Universidad de Córdoba, 1999), 111–130; J. Gutiérrez de Rubalcava, *Tratado histórico, político y legal del comercio de las Indias Occidentales [. . .]* (Cadiz: Imprenta Real de Marina, 1750); Anon., 'Representación hecha al

intended to create a profitable balance of trade and flourishing Spanish manufacturing through protectionist customs, these writers attacked the *Carrera de las Indias* and the Andalusian monopoly itself. They fervently defended the aspirations of elites elsewhere, such as the textile entrepreneurs of Catalonia, whose cotton industry would enjoy rapid growth in the late eighteenth century, against the corrupted monopoly exercised by the *consulados* of Cadiz, Mexico City and Lima.

These *proyectistas* were well aware of the political obstacles hindering the creation of companies. Both within the Iberian Peninsula and through British diplomacy there was insurmountable resistance to their visions.[42] Hence, whatever arguments they developed to justify their different proposals remained arbitrary, politically largely inconsequential and often mutually contradictory: while Carvajal affirmed that one of the twelve companies he envisaged, the one based in Cadiz, maintained its control over the bulk of Atlantic commerce trade including the slave trade, based on an undisputed 'right of primogeniture on the part of Cádiz to the Indies trade', Zavala invoked the law of nations to link Spanish monarchical sovereignty to the creation of new companies as the new natural form of the old colonial trade monopoly.[43]

The third perspective proposed a domestic liberalization of Atlantic trade and was predicated upon a different political economy. It emerged in the 1720s with Melchor Rafael de Macanaz and in the early 1740s was supported by José del Campillo y Cosío after the War of Jenkins' Ear had further undermined the old organization of the

Ex.mo Sr. Marqués de la Ensenada [. . .]' in: *Semanario Erudito*, vol. XIV (1788), 257–284. On the numerous manuscripts of the late 1740s by authors (and functionaries of the Bourbon administration) who proposed the creation of trading companies see Delgado Barrado, *Aquiles y Teseos*, 165–187.

[42] Many Spanish functionaries, diplomats and ministers, starting from Carvajal, display a certain understanding of the functioning of the English political system, in particular regarding the link between the press campaigns promoted by the British merchant classes (first of all those of the powerful pressure group of the South Sea Company) and the positions taken by Parliament, to whose authority the British government often and willingly had to bend. Furthermore, they were also perfectly aware of the different foreign policy positions taken by the Whigs and Tories: cf. Molina Cortón, *Reformismo y neutralidad*, 239, 258, 261–262, 267, 269, 274.

[43] Zavala y Auñón, *Representación*, 132–173; Delgado Barrado, *Carvajal y Lancáster*, 111–130.

Atlantic monopoly.[44] Its starting point was not the problem of British smuggling or any malfunctioning of the monopoly, which were only symptoms of the problem, but the fundamental structure of the Spanish economy.[45] It was necessary to think about reorganizing the *Carrera de las Indias* as part of a comprehensive reform of the American territories of the monarchy.[46]

The first step to properly unlock the vast American market was to open up colonial market to merchants of all the Iberian provinces, starting with the Catalans, rather than to either stick with the Cadiz monopoly or develop new company monopolies by its side.[47] In addition to the customs reform that was generally supported by all *proyectistas*, they proposed to extend the

[44] G. M. de Macanaz, *Discurso sobre la America española* (manuscript no. 9-26-7/4998 in Biblioteca de la Real Academia de la Historia de Madrid); G. M. de Macanaz, 'Auxilios para bien gobernar una monarquía católica [. . .],' *Semanario Erudito*, vol. V (1787), 215–303. Cf. Stein and Stein, *Silver, Trade, and War*, 221–226. Even the three main works of José del Campillo y Cosío (secretario de Hacienda from 1739, and then of Guerra, Marina e Indias from November 1741 to April 1743), written in the early 1740s, circulated in manuscript form: *Lo que hay de más y de menos en España, para que sea lo que debe ser y no lo que es* (1741); *España despierta [. . .]* (1742); *Nuevo sistema de gobierno económico para la América [. . .]* (1743) (Madrid: B. Cano, 1789; I use the edition edited by M. Ballesteros Gaibrois, Oviedo: GEA, 1993). The first works were published in J. del Campillo y Cosío, *Dos escritos politicos*, ed. D. Mateos Dorado (Oviedo: Junta General del Pricipado de Asturias, 1993). On the life and work of Campillo cf. V. García Caso, *El ministro Campillo* (Llanes: El Oriente de Asturias, 1988).

[45] Many of the criticisms directed towards the Bourbon administration by Campillo about the American territories (starting from the corruption of the functionaries in charge, at different levels, of customs and the fight against contraband) and about the miserable socio-economic conditions of the *indios*, were similar to those set out in the same years by J. Juan and A. de Ulloa in their *Noticias secretas de América* (Madrid: Dastin, 2002, first edn. 1826).

[46] Campillo, who at the start of the 1720s had lived in America, insisted on several occasions on underlining that the territories of the New World were fully part of the 'mystical body' of the Spanish monarchy (and therefore the Creole and indigenous subjects had to be granted the same treatment as those of the peninsula). He therefore avoided using the term 'colonias', preferring 'provincias': Campillo, *Nuevo sistema de gobierno*, 68, 78, 219–224, 239. Furthermore he often defined the Spanish monarchy using the term 'impero': Campillo, *Nuevo sistema de gobierno*, 65, 108, 184.

[47] Thus the *proyectistas* of the period made a clear distinction between the gradual process of liberalization of the traffic towards the Iberian motherland and the colonies (reaffirming the monopoly of Spain) from the concept of 'free trade'. They in fact argued that foreign politicians and treatise writers (especially British ones) used the rhetoric of 'free trade' to argue for the legitimacy of their illegal trading practices: cf. for example, D. de Alcedo y Herrera, *Aviso*

registros sueltos, the licence registration for individual ships independent of the *flotas*, to all Spanish ports. While this was a longstanding small-scale practice that was used to occasionally supply isolated corners of the empire that were excluded from the main commercial channels (that ran along the Mexico City–Veracruz–Portobello–Lima axis) with Iberian goods, the political and financial crisis of 1739–1748 gave it new relevance.[48] Andalusian *flotistas* had always claimed that the *registros sueltos* did not counteract but replicate the effects of foreign smuggling by saturating the American market for goods carried by the annual fleets. Macanaz and Campillo proposed to turn this exceptional practice that infringed on the Seville–Cadiz monopoly into a standard one, thus overhauling the existing system.

Thus voicing the interests of the elites of Catalonia, Galicia, the Basque countries, as well as the Río de la Plata and Honduras, they called for a greater number of ports in the motherland to be opened to direct trade with America. Yet, while questioning the traditional economic mentality of the monarchy, counteracting contraband and denouncing the peace and trade treaties that had facilitated and institutionalized the system, these officials also changed the economic reflection on the Spanish colonial system, which they conceived as an integrated imperial space to economically develop, rather than to monopolistically exploit. As politicians, Macanaz and Campillo accepted compromises and openly expressed the belief that their reforms could only be realized in future once the legacy of Utrecht had been

histórico, político, geográphico, con las noticias más particulares del Perú, Tierra-Firme, Chile, y Nuevo Reyno de Granada […] (Madrid: D. Miguel de Peralta, 1740), 348–368; Delgado Barrado, *José de Carvajal y Lancáster*, 21, 99, 115. They were aware that foreign politicians and treatise writers (especially the British and Dutch) used the literature of natural law (Grotius, Selden, Pufendorf, etc.) to give legal and rhetorical force to their desire to continue trading in contraband goods in Spanish America: cf. Delgado Barrado, *José de Carvajal y Lancáster*, 98; D. Ozanam, *La diplomacia de Fernando VI*, 154 and 163; Anon., *Representación hecha al Ex.mo Sr. Marqués de la Ensenada*, 247–249.

48 Campillo, *Nuevo sistema de gobierno*, 76–78, 204, 207–216, 223, 228–229, 300–302, 311. In the second half of the seventeenth century the mercantile and political authorities of Bilbao, Malaga and the Canaries, as well as those of a number of colonial centres (Guatemala, Buenos Aires, Cartagena), had asked the Council of the Indies for permission to set up direct trade links through occasional *registros* between the two sides of the Atlantic: all these petitions were rejected by the *consulado* of Seville since it was clear that such measures would have destroyed the monopoly of Seville and Cadiz from within. Cf. García Fuentes, *El comercio español*, 70–72, 85–103, 171–172.

overcome, yet their influence transcended the reforms they themselves were able to initiate.[49]

Conclusion: Beyond the Legacy of Utrecht and the Cadiz System

The War of Jenkins' Ear provided supporters of the liberalization of trade between Spain and America with clear evidence of their views. British naval expeditions were formidable between 1740 and 1743 and coincided with the beginning of the phase of British imperialism that culminated in the Seven Years War and aimed directly at the annexation of Spanish and French colonial territories to expand the market for British products.[50]

Britain's aggressive trade politics thus forced the Spanish government to take countermeasures to preserve its colonial empire in America and motivated the liberalization of its Atlantic trade through the *registros sueltos*. Its implementation during the war of 1739–1748 produced significant and long-term stabilizing effects: (1) an exponential increase in Atlantic traffic, amounting to 753 single vessels crossing the Atlantic between 1739 and 1754;[51]

[49] A clear supporter of the *navíos de registro* was Domingo de Marcoleta (the future translator of the *Intérêts des Nations de l'Europe* by J. Accarias de Serionne): as a representative of the mercantile class of Buenos Aires in Madrid, in 1750 he wrote two *representaciones* to Ferdinand VI in which he argued that this system was preferable to the trading companies (which he criticized using the same arguments as Uztáriz) and to the fleet system managed by the *consulado* of Cadiz. His argument was based, in any case, on the practical desire to make Buenos Aires into the American focal point for Atlantic traffic instead of Veracruz, Jalapa, Cartagena or Portobello: whichever system the government intended to adopt, the Río de la Plata would be used as the central point of redistribution of goods from the mother country to the whole of South America. Cf. *Representación que hace al Rey Nuestro Señor [...] Don Domingo de Marcoleta [...]. Apoderado de la ciudad de Buenos-Aires [...]* (Madrid: Imprenta Mercurio, 1750); *Nueva representación que hace a S. M. Don Domingo de Marcoleta, apoderado de la ciudad de Buenos-Aires [....]* (Madrid: Imprenta Mercurio, 1750.

[50] Up to then, Great Britain (like France) had preferred to benefit 'indirectly' from American trade, in other words leaving formal sovereignty over South America, and with it the burdens of the administration of these territories, to Spain, managing their respective traffic sometimes using the open breach of the 1713 treaties, sometimes through contraband, and sometimes through the Andalusian merchants who re-exported English products using the *flotas, galeones* and *registros sueltos*.

[51] García Baquero, *Cádiz y el Atlántico*, 164–174; Walker, *Spanish Politics*, 210–214; Lynch, *Bourbon Spain*, 152–153. During the years 1739–1743 some 120 register ships sailed from Cadiz, despite the fact that much of the merchandise transported in them was foreign,

(2) the consolidation of new sea routes (such as between the Iberian peninsula and Buenos Aires, and with Peru via Cape Horn); and (3) a gradual change in the quality of Spanish supplies, since the export of agricultural products, in particular Catalan ones, exceeded that of Castilian manufactures.

The final aspect is particularly significant. The war with Britain, which itself was inspired by the new principles of British global commerce, made patently clear that the American vice-royalties acquired their textiles from foreigners and that the only 'national' products for which there was a colonial market were wines and spirits, foodstuffs and some luxury and traditional items (such as metal objects).[52] Although this did not stop Spanish writers in the late eighteenth century from echoing Uztáriz' pleas for encouraging textile manufacturing as an export industry, it did provide a greater understanding of the trade potential of Iberian agricultural products.

After the war, the *registro suelto* remained in use and enabled Spanish merchants to access new slices of the American market that hitherto were supplied by contraband from other European powers. Even the backlash of the old monopolist-corporatist system in October 1754, three months after the fall of the Marquis de la Ensenada, was effectively nullified by the then established practice that tended towards 'national' liberalization of the Atlantic trade.[53] As Campillo had predicted, this liberalization could only be realized once the *asiento* and the *navío de permiso* had been revoked, which was sanctioned by the Anglo-Spanish treaty of 1750, promoted by

particularly French. The development of the *registros sueltos*, even during the early years of the conflict, was also witnessed by Ulloa, *Restablecimiento*, 320–321.

[52] Stein and Stein, *Silver, Trade, and War*, 191–199; Molina Cortón, *Reformismo y neutralidad*, 223–278; Delgado Ribas, *Dinámicas imperiales*, 157–171. It was noteworthy that the Seville *consulado*, from the moment that it started formally managing the trade monopoly with America, had not been at all insensitive to the interests of Andalusian landowners (which included nobles belonging to the Castilian *Grandeza*), to the extent that the management of the *flotas* and *galeones* called for at least one-third of cargo space to be reserved for Andalusian agricultural exports: cf. García Fuentes, *El comercio español*, 26, 72, 239.

[53] Walker, *Spanish Politics*, 220–224; Lynch, *Bourbon Spain*, 154; Gómez Urdáñez, *El proyecto reformista*, 119; Delgado Ribas, *Dinámicas imperiales*, 186. Between 1757 and 1776 seven more *flotas* set sail from Cadiz, but by then the fleet system had lost the

Carvajal.[54] The officials of the time of Charles III, however, ignored the essence of Carvajal's company system,[55] preferring the vision of Macanaz and Campillo. And so, when in 1789 Campillo's *Nuevo sistema económico para América* was first published (having been 'plagiarized' by various authors including Bernardo Ward),[56] many of its reforms had already been implemented between 1765 and 1778 by Campomanes, Floridablanca and Gálvez.[57] The legacy of Utrecht thus was relegated to the past.

Virginia Léon-Sanz is Professor of Modern History at the Complutense University Madrid. Her research interests include the War of the Spanish

importance it had held before, and remained a residual practice promoted irregularly by the merchants of Cadiz.

[54] Cantillo, ed., *Tratados*, 409–410.

[55] It nevertheless remained true that the nine ports allowed, by the 1765 decree, to trade directly with America were chosen from the twelve that Carvajal had named in his *Testamento* as the headquarters of new companies: Cadiz, Seville, Malaga, Cartagena, Alicante, La Coruña, Santander, Barcelona and Gijón.

[56] B. Ward, *Proyecto económico [. . .]* (Madrid: J. Ibarra, 1779). See the version edited by J. L. Castellano (Madrid: Instituto de Estudios Fiscales, 1982), 279–352.

[57] M. Artola, 'Campillo y las reformas de Carlos III', *Revista de Indias* 50 (1952), 685–714; C. Martínez Shaw, *Cataluña en la Carrera de Indias* (Barcelona: Crítica, 1981); V. Lombart, *Campomanes, economista y político de Carlos III* (Madrid: Alianza, 1992), 129–147; V. Lombart, 'Estudio preliminar', in: P. Rodríguez de Campomanes, *Reflexiones sobre el comercio español a Indias* (Madrid: Instituto de Estudios Fiscales, 1988), xi–xlv; L. Navarro García, 'El falso Campillo y el reformismo borbónico', *Temas Americanistas* 12 (1995), 5–14. On the *real decreto* of 16 October 1765 (which revoked Cadiz's trade monopoly in favour of the main Spanish ports), on the decree of 2 February 1778 and on the *Reglamento y Aranceles Reales para el comercio libre de España a Indias* of 12 October 1778 cf. J. Muñoz Pérez, 'La publicación del reglamento del comercio libre de Indias', *Anuario de Estudios Americanos* 4 (1947), 615–664; A. M. Bernal (coord.), *El 'Comercio libre' entre España y América (1765–1824)* (Madrid: Fundación Banco Exterior, 1987); G. Anes and A. de Castrillón, 'La economía española en el siglo XVIII', in: *Economía y economistas españoles*, ed. E. Fuentes Quintana (Barcelona: Galaxia Gutenberg/Círculo de Lectores, 2000), vol. 3 (*La Ilustración*), 91–173, especially 167–170; C. Martínez Shaw and J. M. Oliva Melgar, eds., *El sistema atlántico español (siglos XVII–XIX)* (Madrid: Marcial Pons, 2005); S. J. Stein and B. H. Stein, *Apogee of Empire. Spain and New Spain in the Age of Charles III, 1759–1789* (Baltimore, MD: Johns Hopkins University Press, 2003); G. B. Paquette, *Enlightenment, Governance, and Reform in Spain and its Empire 1759–1808* (New York: Palgrave Macmillan, 2008); Lynch, *Bourbon Spain*, 317–324 and 329–366; Fernández Durán, *La corona española*, 312–315; Delgado Ribas, *Dinámicas imperiales*, 228–456; Kuethe and Andrien, *The Spanish Atlantic World*, 157–301.

Succession, Spanish exiles in Vienna and early eighteenth-century diplomatic history. She has published *Carlos VI. El emperador que no pudo ser rey de España* (2003) and *El Archiduque Carlos y los austracistas. Guerra de Sucesión y exilio* (2014) and is director of the project *Redefinition of the European and Mediterranean Spaces in the Eighteenth Century* (2016–2018).

Niccolò Guasti is Assistant Professor in Early Modern History at the Department of Humanistic Studies of the University of Foggia. His research interests include the eighteenth-century history of the Jesuits and economic reform debates in the Iberian and Neapolitan contexts. He has published three monographs on the expulsion of the Spanish Jesuits, editions of economic texts by Antonio Genovesi (2008) and Lorenzo Normante y Carcavilla (2013) and articles on the diffusion of economic ideas and enlightened reform projects between Spain, France and Italy.

Negotiating the Balance of Power: Russian–Spanish Commercial Relations in the Early Eighteenth Century

Olga Volosyuk

Anglo-Russian Relations: The War of the Spanish Succession

Although England had historically been Russia's trade partner in the Baltic region, in the early eighteenth century Anglo-Russian relations were put under pressure by the combination of the geopolitical importance of an English alliance with Sweden in the War of the Spanish Succession and in the Northern War in which Sweden fought Russia.

It was in the context of this crisis that Queen Anne initiated the creation of a permanent diplomatic mission to Russia by sending Charles Whitworth there in 1704. England was ready 'to enter into a closer alliance of friendship with [Peter the Great] for the mutual benefit of trade and commerce' and, in relation to the negotiation of

O. Volosyuk (✉)
National Research University 'Higher School of Economics' , Moscow, Russia
e-mail: olgavolosiuk@yahoo.com

A. Alimento, K. Stapelbroek (eds.), *The Politics of Commercial Treaties in the Eighteenth Century*, DOI 10.1007/978-3-319-53574-6_6

peace, would 'not neglect his interest upon that occasion'.[1] During Whitworth's first meeting with Chancellor Count Fyodor Golovin, however, the latter made known the Czar's desire to enter into an alliance with England, promising commercial advantages and proposing that the two countries conclude a trade agreement. While Golovin thus made Russia's entry into the Grand Alliance the object of a commercial agreement, the English diplomat tartly responded that 'the substance of this alliance of friendship was understood to consist in removing those hardships which obstructed our commerce at present and in allowing Her Majesty's subjects to export the product of the Czar dominions'.

The conflation of geopolitical and commercial reasoning did not stop here, as Golovin desired to know 'whether those stores were to be fetched from Archangel or from the Baltic Sea, from which place the passage would be nearer and the transport of those commodities more convenient'.[2] The catch, then, was that the transfer of trade to the Baltic Sea would *ipso facto* acknowledge the validity of Russian conquests in the region.

Whitworth favoured cooperating with Russia, 'for the Czar is so bent on beginning a trade thereabouts, that I might hope to procure all manner of stores for Her Majesty's navy either without or on a very inconsiderable custom during this war without any further obligation'.[3] Furthermore, 'the court of Russia would willingly obtain from Her Majesty [. . .] a treaty of commerce; for hitherto they have no engagements with England except by offices or letters of common civility, and as they are changing by degrees all the old customs, so they would likewise come more into fashion in respect of foreign alliances, whereof they begin to see the advantage and reputation'.[4] To secure the commercial partnership, he insisted that another treaty was required, as the Russians 'are apt to suspect we have great want of

[1] Instructions to Charles Whitworth, 29.9.1704, *Diplomaticheskaya perepiska angliyskikh poslov i poslannikov pri russkom dvore (gody s 1704 po 1708)* Sbornik Imperatorskogo Russkogo Istoricheskogo Obshchestva, ed. A. A. Polovtsev, 39 (St Petersburg: Tip. Imp. Akad. Nauk, 1884), ii: 5.

[2] Whitworth to Harley, Moscow, 28.2/11.3.1705, ibid., 37–38.

[3] Whitworth to Harley, Moscow, 2.5/13.5.1705, ibid., 83–84.

[4] Whitworth to Hedges, Moscow, 23.5/6.7.6.1705, ibid., 98.

their commodities, but little esteem for their force and friendship'.[5] Whitworth wondered 'how far it may be the interest of England and Holland to let the Czar into affairs and the trade of Europe by this door'.[6] In the event of peace 'between the allies and the king of France before the northern war is ended' the Czar 'in his private conversations' feared 'England and Holland would be at liberty to turn their eyes this way [and] agree with Sweden to shut him out from the East-sea'.[7]

In May 1707, Andrei Matveyev was sent from The Hague as ambassador to England to raise the question of an alliance between Russia and England. Matveyev spoke of the readiness of Peter to enter into the Grand Alliance and send Russian troops wherever Alliance members saw fit. Russia moreover was willing to assume responsibility for delivering shipbuilding materials to maritime states. The Russian embassy wanted England to mediate a peace treaty with Sweden on the condition that Russian conquests along the Gulf of Finland and the Neva River were recognized.[8] Again, England was invited to sign a commercial agreement on favourable terms on the proviso that trade would shift from Arkhangelsk to the Baltic Sea. In the autumn of 1707, the Duke of Marlborough, the leader of the allied forces of the Grand Alliance, gave firm instructions to reject the deal without offending the Czar, a decision reiterated in a meeting with the Austrian commander Prince Eugene of Savoy and Dutch representatives that took place in April 1708 at The Hague.[9]

If, in Whitworth's terms, 'the Czar's offer of entering into the grand alliance' appeared 'an indigested proposal, disadvantageous and impracticable in the present juncture' and 'the chief design in their proposing a treaty was not to promote the good of commerce in general', the Russian defeat of Sweden at Poltava of 27 June 1709 forced a change of perspective.[10] The British *chargé d'affaires* Ludwig Weisbrod wrote: 'It is

[5] Whitworth to Hedges, Moscow, 23.5/3.6.1705, ibid., 100.

[6] Whitworth to Harley, Moscow, 23.1/3.2.1706, ibid., 222.

[7] Whitworth to Harley, Grodno, 20.10/31.10.1705, ibid., 176.

[8] Whitworth to Harley, Moscow, 26.11/7.12.1706, ibid., 334.

[9] V. A. Timiryazev, 'Russkiye diplomaty XVIII stoletiya v Anglii', *Istoricheskiy vestnik* 72 (1898), 248; T. K. Krylova, 'Rossiya i "Velikiy Soyuz"', *Istoricheskiye zapiski* 13 (1942), 127.

[10] Whitworth to Harley, Moscow, 10/21.3.1708, *Diplomaticheskaya perepiska*, 39: 459.

true a long time will be required to this nation to attain to such a height of perfection in politeness and good constitution of government [. . .] yet they grow every day wiser' while the Czar himself 'is able enough to pick out what may serve his end and interest':

> In making himself master of good sea-ports in the East-sea, His Majesty may be able to build a fleet, and by it to increase and maintain trade, to protect his dominions, and make a considerable figure in Europe, as well with their own power, which will very much increase in establishing the trade to the benefit of his subjects.[11]

When talks about Russia's entry into the Grand Alliance were resumed and made conditional on a reconciliation with Sweden, the imminent Peace of Utrecht blocked the Czar's counterproposal for Russia to act as an intermediary in negotiations to end the War of the Spanish Succession, while agreeing to Britain's mediation in the Great Northern War.[12] The conclusion of the Treaty of Utrecht opened a new era in Anglo-Russian relations. While both Whig and Tory governments had tried to strike a balance between Sweden and Russia before the Congress of Utrecht in order to obtain the greatest advantages for their country, British policy became more anti-Russian.

The Turn to Spain: Russia in the Balance of Power (1714–1719)

English reluctance to discuss Russia's trade and northern conquests as a package deal had earlier induced Peter to seek a rapprochement with France. In October 1705, France 'offered [to Matveyev] to make a treaty of commerce for the future', causing some alarm at the English court and a greater willingness by 'Her Majesty' to avoid 'occasions of coldness'

[11] Weisbrod to St John, Moscow, 18/29.10.1711, ibid., 61: 58, 66.

[12] Whitworth to Henry St John, 2/13.10.1711, *Diplomaticheskaya perepiska angliyskikh poslov i poslannikov pri russkom dvore, CH. 5 (gody s 1712 po 1719)*, Sbornik Imperatorskogo Russkogo Istoricheskogo Obshchestva, ed. A. A. Polovtsev (St Petersburg: Tip. Imp. Akad. Nauk, 1888), 61: 25.

towards the Czar.[13] Early in 1715 Mackenzie reported rumours that 'the French king will consent to the Czar's retaining the ports His Majesty has in the province',[14] and that the Czar had offered French commissioners commercial opportunities that, although of no interest to Britain, were of 'advantage to the French' and 'must certainly in time put the king of France in better credit, than happily he has been at this court hitherto'.[15] In 1715 the French marine commissioner and consul Henry La Vie reported from St Petersburg that the Russian Czar considered trade with France and Spain to be most advantageous for his nation and his subjects.[16]

How did this situation come about? As Tatiana Krylova wrote, 'the main incentive prompting the Spaniards to establish direct trade with Russia at that time consisted in the hope of receiving cheap Russian shipbuilding materials for reconstructing its navy'.[17] Ever since the War of the Spanish Succession, Spanish representatives had been hard at work, trying to obtain arms and munitions abroad on account of the foreign policy of Philip V, who considered the ceding of Italian territories to Austria to be 'temporary'. Cardinal Alberoni's project to revive the Spanish navy, for which vessels were to be built in new docks in Cadiz and Barcelona, explains why Spanish emissaries came to Paris in late 1715 for talks with Konon Zotov, Russia's commercial agent.

In late 1715, Zotov was met by two Spanish traders Noli and Marqueli who proposed that two Russian ships be sent to Spain 'with military goods for armies. If they come to Cádiz, their goods shall be immediately bought, and the ships shall be loaded with Spanish goods, if Russia so desires.' Marqueli even asked 'whether the Czar would allow him to

[13] Whitworth to Harley, Moscow, 24.7/4.8.1706, ibid., 291; Whitworth to St John, Carlsbad, 2/13.10.1711, ibid., 26–27.

[14] Mackenzie to Townshend, Petersburg, 17/28.1.1715, ibid., 343.

[15] Mackenzie to Townshend, Petersburg, 11/22.2.1715, ibid., 353–354.

[16] La Vie to d'Uxelles, St Petersburg, 28.3.1714, *Doneseniya frantsuzskikh poslannikov i poverennykh v delakh pri Russkom dvore. Poveleniya pravitel'stva i otchety o prebyvanii russkikh poslov, poslannikov i diplomaticheskikh agentov, nakhodivshikhsya vo Frantsii, s 1681 po 1718 god.*, Sbornik Imperatorskogo Russkogo Istoricheskogo Obshchestva, ed. A. A. Polovtsev, A. F. Bichkov and G. F. Shtendman (St Petersburg: Tip. Imp. Akad. Nauk, 1881), 34: 106.

[17] T. K. Krylova, 'Otnosheniya Rossii i Ispanii v pervoy chetverti XVIII veka', in: *Kul'tura Ispanii*, ed. A. Deborin (Moscow: Academy of Sciences, 1940), 338–339.

build ships in Russia for the Spanish king'.[18] After consulting with Secretary of the Cabinet Alexey Makarov, Peter decided that, 'he would allow not just five ships with goods for building and arming ships to be sent to Marqueli and Noli but as many as eighteen if a peace treaty is concluded with Sweden'.[19]

Zotov's subsequent negotiations with the Spanish ambassador to France Antonio del Giudice, prince of Cellamare, were based on a shared understanding of the political terms through which 'trade with Russia would be advantageous to both nations'.[20] While Russia consented to building three battleships for Spain in St Petersburg and providing cannon, Cellamare voiced his hopes that the Northern War would soon end and offered Spain's services as mediator in the person of the Italian baron Bonmazari. With respect to this Zotov said, 'I greatly hope that he will be very useful for concluding a peace treaty with the Swedes' and recommended him to the Czar as an aide for conducting business and concluding trade agreements with Spain.[21]

Russia's courting of Spain coincided with a deterioration of relations with Hanoverian Britain, with France temporarily serving as a diplomatic pivot in the balance of power. By early 1716, George I's programme in the Northern War, reflected in the Treaty of Greifswald with Russia, had been fully implemented and a military and political union with Russia thereby became superfluous—indeed, even harmful in view of Britain's strategic aims.[22] George I's concerns about the threat posed to his Hanoverian territories by 'Russian expansion' into Northern Germany, the possibility of Franco-Russian rapprochement, and fears of a Jacobite invasion made him enter a defensive alliance with Austria and sign an Anglo-French treaty in 1716.[23] In response,

[18] Rossiyskiy Gosudarstvennyy Arkhiv Drevnikh Aktov (RGADA), Peter the Great Cabinet, series I, 56, fol. 179.

[19] Krylova, *Otnoshenia*, 339; RGADA, Peter the Great Cabinet, series I, 62, fol. 508; 56, fos. 178–179.

[20] Ibid., series II, 32, fol. 482.

[21] RGADA, Peter the Great Cabinet, series I, 62, fol. 22; series II, 27, fos. 901–902.

[22] L. A. Nikiforov, *Vneshnyaya politika Rossii i posledniye gody Severnoy voyny. Nishtadskiy mir* (Moscow: Academy of Sciences, 1959), 39.

[23] L. A. Nikiforov, 'Rossiya v sisteme yevropeyskikh derzhav v pervoy chetverti 18 v.', *Rossiya v period reform Petra I* (Moscow: Nauka, 1973), 30. Kurakin managed to procure a copy of

Alberoni adopted a pro-Stuart policy and sided with Charles XII's Sweden, which recognized James III's claims to the English throne. Meanwhile, the British diplomats Norris and Whitworth continued to believe that Peter's 'chief aim is to draw Great Britain into the war by the guaranty of his conquests and the price he proposes is a treaty of commerce, which must be precarious as long as the whole market is in his own hands'.[24]

Already before the forming of the Triple Alliance in January 1717, Peter had feared interference in the Northern War against Russia and had sought to reach an alliance with France, to which end he personally visited Paris in April 1717 to meet with Philip of Orleans.[25] In order to 'harmonize the plans' of Spain, José de Grimaldo decided to 'pay the Czar a visit' almost immediately after Peter's arrival in Paris and push, through the agency of the prince of Cellamare, for a new system of 'friendship and correspondence', which comprised the conclusion of a Franco-Russian defensive treaty, plus a solution for the Russian–Swedish conflict, and—to sweeten the deal—a trade agreement in which the Czar gave consent 'for four French ships to be permitted to load naval stores in his country'.[26]

The Transformation of Trade Relations in Russian–Spanish Diplomacy

Commercial agreements remained an object of negotiation between Peter and Alberoni, whose military and political aims dovetailed harmoniously. While Spain needed Russia to rebuild its navy, Prince Boris Kurakin,

the secret articles of the treaty and noted that England guaranteed France that 'in the event of the death of the French king, it would not allow the Spanish king to take over the French crown and allow it to devolve to the Duke of Orleans, while the Duke of Orleans promises to support the House of Hanover in England and not allow the pretender to the throne'. RGADA, Relations between Russia and Holland, 1718, 5, fol. 187.

[24] Norris and Whitworth to Sunderland, Amsterdam, 10.8.1717, *Diplomaticheskaya perepiska*, 61: 407, 408.

[25] See P. Pekarsky, *Nauka i literatura v Rossii pri Petre Velikom* 1 (St Petersburg: T-vo 'Obshch. pol'za', 1862), 160–161.

[26] RGADA, Relations between Russia and Holland, 1717, 6, fol. 165; M. Kovalevsky, 'Novyye dannyye o prebyvanii Petra v Parizhe, pocherpnutyye iz ispanskikh arkhivov', *Russkaya mysl'* 1 (1884), 106, 110; Norris and Whitworth to Sunderland, Amsterdam, 10.8.1717, 17.8.1717, 31.8.1717, *Diplomaticheskaya perepiska*, 61: 403, 405, 410, 432.

writing from The Hague, pointed out to Peter that 'as long as Spain is armed and at war with the Emperor, the maritime powers and France will be unable to interfere in northern affairs.'[27] Indeed, Cellamare and Beretti-Landi alternately signalled to Kurakin that Spain 'would not accept the plan devised in England [. . .] and is able to continue the war' in Italy and that trade between Russia and Spain was essential in this respect.[28] Hence, when at the Congress of Åland in May 1718 Peter received notice of Spain's commitment to war in Italy, the news was 'not unpleasant for him'.[29] His active diplomacy thus kept the maritime powers at bay in the Baltic and weakened Austria near the Black Sea, while Spain anticipated an anti-British alliance between Russia and Sweden to lure the English navy from the Mediterranean.[30] Aware of the need to prevent France and the Dutch Republic being drawn into the Italian war and to counter British attempts to frustrate the emerging Russian–Swedish–Spanish coalition, Kurakin and Johann Christoph Schleinitz worked 'in close cooperation with the Spanish ambassador', who in turn took advantage of the same threat 'to enter into a close alliance' with Russia.[31]

Russian enthusiasm for a close military and political alliance with Spain, Sweden and also France, was however severely affected by the defeat of the Spanish fleet at the Battle of Cape Passaro in August 1718. Immediately, Peter decided to prioritize peace with Sweden over negotiations with Madrid,[32] and by November 1718 Alberoni's proposals, which mixed dynastic, military, commercial and financial interests, seemed less attractive.[33] Meanwhile, the death of Charles XII and the rise of pro-British sympathies

[27] RGADA, Relations between Russia and Holland, 1718, 5, fol. 254; see also *Istoriya Ispanii*, ed. O. Volosyuk, M. Lipkin and E. Yurchik, vol. 2: *S nachala XVIII veka do nashikh dney* (Moscow: Indrik, 2014), 124–125.

[28] RGADA, Relations between Russia and Holland, 1718, 5, fol. 169; see N. N. Bantish-Kamenski, *Obzor vneshnij snoshenii Rossii (po 1800 g.)* (Moscow: Tip. Imp. Akad. Nauk, 1894), 164 for the initial Spanish invitation to a deal.

[29] La Vie to d'Uxelles, St Petersburg, 27.5.1718, *Doneseniya frantsuzskikh poslannikov*, 343.

[30] RGADA, Relations between Russia and France, 1718, 5, fol. 187.

[31] RGADA, Relations between Russia and Holland, 1718, 4, fol. 320; 5, fol. 114, 266; Relations between Russia and France, 1718, 4, fol. 49; 5, fol. 187.

[32] RGADA, Relations between Russia and France, 1718, 5, fos. 77–78.

[33] RGADA, Peter the Great Cabinet, series II, 36, fol. 207; Relations between Russia and Holland, 1718, 5, fos. 438–439; Relations between Russia and France, 1718, 4, fol. 512; Bantish-Kamenski, *Obsor*, 165.

in Sweden, combined with the signing of a 'defensive' pact against Russia by Austria, Saxony and Hanover in Vienna on 5 January 1719, dissuaded France. Indeed, Dubois made it clear that if Russia did not abandon plans to ally with Sweden, this would trigger a war with the Triple Alliance. Likewise, Schleinitz warned Peter that 'in the present conditions' any talk of an alliance with Spain would 'give occasion for creating a strong alliance against Your Majesty'.[34]

In view of the new situation, Kurakin was initially instructed 'not to give cause for displeasure to the Emperor and England, [. . .] comport yourself circumspectly with the Spanish ambassador and not promise him anything anymore'.[35] Yet when British diplomacy went on the offensive and concluded pacts with Prussia and Sweden,[36] Peter turned once again to Spain.[37] At first, the aim was to revive Alberoni's offers and develop a comprehensive military, commercial and financial alliance to influence the course of events in south-western Europe. But after December 1719, when Alberoni fell from grace and Spain withdrew from the war, Kurakin was instructed to 'stop all correspondence with the Spanish ambassador'.[38] At this point Peter reverted to the idea of a few years earlier, to bring Spain closer by establishing commercial relations in a more indirect fashion.

In the summer of 1721 the Russian diplomat and trade agent in Lubeck, Petr Beklemishev, was sent to Cadiz with instructions to gather information about the state of Spanish trade, especially that with the American colonies. He promptly reported that trade with the Americas was strictly forbidden and recommended opening a Russian office in Cadiz to facilitate direct trade with Spain.[39] In the same year Peter sent another representative, Captain Petr Bredahl, to France, Spain and Holland with letters from himself informing the

[34] RGADA, Relations between Russia and France, 1718, 4, fol. 512.

[35] RGADA, State Archive, coll. 15, 5, fol. 13; 12, fol. 13.

[36] L. A. Nikiforov, *Russko-angliyskiye otnosheniya pri Petre I* (Moscow: Gospolitizdat, 1950), 211, 220–221.

[37] Peter the Great to Kurakin, in: *Bumagi knyazya Borisa Ivanovicha Kurakina*, 1676–1727, Arkhiv knyazya F. A. Kurakina, ed. M. I. Semevski (St Petersburg: Tip. V. S. Balasheva, 1890), i: 11.

[38] RGADA, State Archive, coll. 15, 12, fol. 15.

[39] Krilova, *Otnoshenia*, 338–339.

governments of the end of the Northern War and the conclusion of a peace with Sweden. Following a visit to Paris in January 1722, Bredahl arrived in Madrid on 8 February, giving Grimaldo the Czar's message that expressed the wish 'for friendship and kind correspondence [so that], amiable commerce can flourish between our two States to the mutual advantage and to the benefit of our subjects'.[40] He also advised Grimaldo in person that 'there is an opportunity for the two Nations to conduct generous commerce'.[41] When it emerged that Spain shared this view,[42] Peter decided in that same year to send a permanent Russian diplomatic representative to Madrid, namely Prince Sergei Golitzin.

Golitzin's mandate, beyond gathering political information, specifically required him to report on 'what Russian goods and materials were needed there and what goods could be bought from Spain cheaper than from other States'.[43] Trade per se had to be a profitable activity for both countries rather than a mere bargaining tool used to forge closer ties and allow Russia to enter European politics. Spanish merchants were dependent on French trade, then stagnant: 'The merchants here who trade with the French are in dormancy, for they would otherwise have to supply goods at a loss to themselves, and the merchandise which is the pillar of French trade, cannot be brought here, for the credit of the French is in very low standing.'[44] And yet Spanish traders in general had only a dim awareness of the opportunities offered by trade with Russia and therefore took no initiatives in that direction. A rare exception was Simon Bregante, a merchant from Cadiz. On 22 July 1723 he asked Golitzin for authorization to build a trade house in St Petersburg that would do business with Italy, Spain and the Levant, exchanging their imports for Russian exports.[45] Following the meeting with Bregante, the Russian diplomat sent his first report containing information on Spanish

[40] Arkhiv Vneshnei Politiki Rossiiskoi Imperii (AVPRI), Relations between Russia and Spain, 58, fol. 1.

[41] Ibid., 62, fos. 1–5; 12, fos. 1–2.

[42] Bantish-Kamenski, *Obzor*, 164.

[43] *Corpus diplomático hispano-ruso (1667–1799)*, ed. Manuel Espadas Burgos (Madrid: Ministerio de asuntos exteriores, 1991), i: 60.

[44] AVPRI, Relations between Russia and Spain, 76, fol. 90.

[45] Ibid., 68, fos. 42–43.

trade to the Secretary of the Cabinet Makarov, and a copy to the College of Foreign Affairs. He noted that according to the peace treaties representatives of all nations in Spain enjoyed equal trade privileges, and levies were determined by special officials.[46] The Russian Chancellor Gavriil Golovkin wrote to Golitzin in January 1724: 'Concerning the merchant who intends to form a company and trade with Russia, you have been sent a decree allowing that merchant to come to Russia and establish commerce.'[47] In September 1723 Golitzin was informed that Peter approved of Bregante's proposition and wished to begin negotiations with Spain on the conclusion of a trade pact.[48] On 19 August 1723 Andrey Osterman informed Golitzin:

> Your Excellency's dispatch [. . .] about the restoration of commerce with Spain, has been duly received, and His Imperial Majesty will be informed of its contents. I deem it opportune to remind Your Excellency by the present letter, that you should diligently inquire into the movements of the Spanish Navy [. . .]. You are also kindly requested to take upon yourself the travail of ascertaining whether the treaty known as 'aciento' has been concluded between the Spanish and French Courts; and if this is the case, from this it is possible to see, that Spain and France are closely obligated, with the ensuing exclusion of England.[49]

It thus appears that Russian diplomacy had started to think in a somewhat different way about attaining its political ends through commerce, by treating it not as subservient, but as parallel to the patterns of political relations in the balance of power.

Ivan Shcherbatov and the Domestic Development of Russian Commerce

In November 1723 Peter issued a personal decree on the establishment of direct trade relations with Spain and the designation of a consul in Cadiz. Prince Ivan Shcherbatov was chosen by the Senate to head a temporary

[46] *Corpus diplomático*, 63; V. A. Ulianitzkii, *Russkie consulstva za granitzei v XVIII veke* (Moscow: Tip. G. Lissnera i A. Gegelya, 1889), i–ii: 114.

[47] *Osmnadzatii vek. Istoricheskiy sbornik*, ed. P. Bartenev (Moscow: Tip. T. Ris, 1869), iii: 140.

[48] Ulianitzkii, *Russkie consulstva*, 114.

[49] *Osmnadzatii vek*, 134.

mission to establish a consulate, identify trade opportunities and obtain for Russia the status of 'most preferred nation'.[50] Writing from London in 1719, the young prince had offered his services to the Czar.[51] During his stay in Britain, Shcherbatov had become hugely impressed with the 'system' of John Law[52] and, being convinced of the importance of introducing his views to Russian readers, had translated the *Considérations sur le numeraire et le commerce par J. Law* in late 1719 and early 1720.

Shcherbatov's translation of Law's treatise—133 pages long and dated 27 February 1720—included the first five chapters and the beginning of Chapter 6, and was preceded by a dedication to Peter the Great. In addition to the translation, Shcherbatov wrote an '*Opinion of Prince I.A. Shcherbatov about the establishment of banks and paper money for the development of commerce in Russia*', 44 pages that were also inscribed to Peter the Great.[53] Shcherbatov's 'Opinion' was inspired by Law's ideas, which probably also led in the 1750s to his plan for the establishment of banks for the nobility. The 'Opinion' had three sections: the first on the need to set up banks and introduce paper currency in Russia (twenty-two articles); the second on the organization of a merchant company (twenty-two articles); and, in conclusion, a brief summary of Law's views on the role played by money and trade in stimulating public wealth.

According to Shcherbatov, public revenues in Russia could be improved by an increase in the money supply, and the best way to promote trade was to establish banks in trading towns and a central Russian bank in St Petersburg. The bank would issue banknotes in different denominations on special paper, adhering to a model described by Shcherbatov; they would be legal tender used for payment of all taxes and fees, and would gradually replace coinage.[54]

[50] Ulianitzkii, *Russkie consulstva*, 114–115.

[51] AVPRI, Cabinet Affairs, 42, fol. 589.

[52] Antoine E. Murphy, *John Law. Economic Theorist and Policy-Maker* (Oxford: Oxford University Press, 1997), 138–148, 153–155, 164–165, 167–172.

[53] According to the title page, the Law translation was corrected by Shcherbatov in 1724. Rossiyskaya Natsional'naya Biblioteka, Otdel rukopisei, Hermitage Collection, coll. 885, 122a, fos. 1–22. Cf. I. A. Shcherbatov, 'Opinion of Prince I. A. Shcherbatov about the establishment of banks and paper money for the development of commerce in Russia', *Franko-russkiye ekonomicheskiye svyazi* (Moscow: Nauka, 1970), 122–132, and S. M. Troitsky, '"Sistema" Dzhona Lo i yeye russkiye posledovateli', *Franko-russkiye*, 91–121.

[54] Shcherbatov, 'Opinion', 123–124.

The state itself would orchestrate and implement these monetary reforms, approving the issuing of the banknotes, setting deadlines for replacing metal coins with paper money, and punishing those who defied the plan. There was a practicality to Shcherbatov's project, since the heavy coins in circulation were hard to transport and count and thus hindered commercial development. Other visionary aspects of Shcherbatov's plan for the development of Russian commerce included a recommendation that twenty-four men should be selected 'from among the nobles and merchants who understand domestic and foreign trade' to discuss and decide, together with government officials, the formation and running of a new merchant company.[55] The company was a political attempt to integrate the business affairs of the nobles with those of the citizenry, and Article 8 of its draft constitution foresaw it accepting cash investments of at least a hundred roubles. With a similar aim in mind, Peter had issued a decree in 1711 authorizing and urging nobles to engage in commerce.

Shcherbatov's proposal was for a joint stock company with capital provided by shareholders, who would exchange all their coins for banknotes held by the bank. His recommendations were modelled on measures taken by Law when establishing his bank in Paris and the India Company. Crucially, Shcherbatov believed that the new company would not only expand commerce with Russia's longstanding trading partners, such as Persia and China, but would also help secure similar relations with Spain and Portugal, whose commercial empires supplied Europe with gold and silver. In pursuit of the same objectives Peter had promulgated decrees 'on expanding trade with France, Spain, and Portugal'.[56] Shcherbatov's vision was based on a specific understanding of the interrelationship of global trade, finance and national economic development: revitalized by a domestic financial project and an economic reform project, he believed Russia could insert itself into the core of the global trade system. He cited Law's assertion that 'a state's power and wealth depend on the size of the population and foreign and domestic trade, while trade is based on money', adding that to be 'powerful and wealthy' Russia had to have as much money in circulation as other European states. Once that key requirement was met, the number of people producing goods suitable

[55] Ibid., 125–126.

[56] Ibid., 126.

for sale in Russia's domestic and foreign markets would grow.[57] As for global trade, he advised that the trade company should develop a consular network of commercial agents in the principal trading cities.

Shcherbatov's political economy restated the main principles of John Law's view of the global trade system by considering money as the main source of wealth and its increased circulation as a means of stimulating foreign trade. He further contended that establishing a credit system was of the essence. Once the entire Russian economy was reformed on the basis of his financial-commercial project the entire population, and the estates owned by the nobility, would benefit: for when crafts and trade were developed, revenues from estates would be paid on time and agricultural potential could be further unlocked. Although Shcherbatov's projects for setting up banks and introducing paper currency were never actually implemented, it is important to recognize their relation to his mission to Cadiz.

After completing his translation of Law's treatise, Shcherbatov sent it to the Czar on 1 March 1720, through Johannes van den Burgh, Russia's trade agent in Amsterdam. On the same day, he sent a letter to the Secretary of the Cabinet Makarov with a request to submit his translation to Peter as soon as possible, explaining that he had had the 'temerity to present the Czar with a translation of the book of J. Law, inspired by the desire to seek favour with the Czar', knowing of his propensity 'towards the establishment of fine arts and commerce as well as sciences'.[58] On 4 March 1720, Shcherbatov, mistrusting the post, sent Makarov a copy of the initial letter of 1 March.[59] Worrying about the fate of his work, he transmitted, on 19 April 1720, a third letter to Makarov from London through Amsterdam, asking him once again to give the translated treatise to the Czar at the earliest opportunity.[60] When both the letter and the manuscript failed to reach Peter, Shcherbatov dispatched his servant Fyodor Nekhayev to St Petersburg on 12 June 1720, carrying another letter to the Secretary of the Cabinet along with a copy of the translated treatise and his 'Opinion' for the Czar.[61] However, when Peter did finally

[57] Ibid., 131–132.

[58] Shcherbatov to Makarov, London, 1.3.1720, *Franko-russkiye*, 133.

[59] RGADA, State Archive, coll. IX, series II, box 3, 49, fol. 122.

[60] Ibid., fol. 115.

[61] Shcherbatov to Makarov, London, 12.6.1720, *Franko-russkiye*, 133.

receive Shcherbatov's works in September or early October 1720, Law had already fled to Brussels after the failure of his own project, a series of events about which Schleinitz had kept Peter fully informed.[62]

Despite this setback, Shcherbatov's proposals appear to have influenced a number of moves subsequently made by the Russian Czar. In March 1721 he ordered that Law be invited to Russia, promising to make him a prince, give him 2,000 serf households and the right to build a town of his own that would be populated with 'foreign artisans and craftsmen', allow him to keep 100 guardsmen, and accord him many other privileges. He wanted Law to build towns and villages, build plants and factories, and attract foreign colonists to populate 'eastern Russia around the Caspian Sea'. If Law agreed to enter the service of Russia and 'to create and found Russian mining works and a Persian Trade Company in the Russian State', Peter would lavish him with new favours, including the titles of Grand Marshal of the Court, Active Privy Councillor, and Collegiate President, the Order of St Andrew, and so forth.[63] Peter was particularly interested in Law's ability to organize trade companies and develop foreign commerce in France, as he himself had actively sought to do for Russian industry and trade for more than two decades.

Shcherbatov returned to Russia in September 1721 and obtained a position at the College of Foreign Affairs, transferring the following year to the College of Commerce, where he was appointed Counsellor. In November 1723 Peter decided to send him to Spain as his commercial representative[64] with two subordinates under his direction: Alexey Veshniakov and Yakov Evreinov, who were sent to Cadiz soon after his arrival.[65] Each had identical Consular Patents from the College of Foreign Affairs, and were given identical instructions.[66] However, Shcherbatov had to choose who to name consul and send to Madrid to present his Letters of Investiture at court. He himself was to stay in Cadiz to collect

[62] RGADA, State Archive, coll. IX, series II, box 4, 57, fol. 1115; AVPRI, Relations between Russia and France, 1720, 5a, fol. 55.

[63] Pekarsky, *Nauka*, 247.

[64] V. N. Aleksandrenko, *Russkie diplomaticheskie agenti v Londone v XVIII veke* (Warsaw, 1897), 28.

[65] AVPRI, Relations between Russia and Spain, 69, fos. 1–14.

[66] *Corpus*, 64–66.

information on Spanish goods and make necessary contacts and acquaintances before returning to Russia.[67]

While in Cadiz Shcherbatov wrote *An Introduction to Russian Commerce* in which—article by article in alphabetical order—he collated all manner of information about Russian commerce, drawing from a compilation of decrees printed in 1719, Admiralty Regulations, and the Code of Marine Commerce and Tariffs. The work was introduced by a covering article 'On Russian Commerce' that contained references to publications with information on Russian trade that he had used.[68]

Shcherbatov's *An Introduction to Russian Commerce* began in the twelfth and thirteenth centuries, recalling that the centre of Russian trade had initially been the Swedish city of Visby, then a Russian merchant quarter. Russian ships sailed as far as Gibraltar and Russians also traded with Italians, especially the Genoese when the latter controlled Kaffa and the Crimea. Oriental trade passed through Astrakhan before the discovery of a sea route from India along the Indus and Oxus Rivers to the Caspian Sea and then along the Volga and Don to the Black Sea, from where goods were taken all over Europe by the Venetians and the Genoese. Trade with western countries passed through the free cities of Novgorod, which had a trade agreement with the Hanseatic towns, and Pskov. Trade with Persia passed through Astrakhan and Bukhara. Caravans of merchants departed from Tobolsk in Siberia to different parts of China. Commerce with northern countries began in 1533 when the English opened their first office in Arkhangelsk, yet 'the Dutch seized the opportunity to get a share of this trade; for some time, they shared it with the English yet soon got the upper hand, so that the English virtually abandoned it altogether'.[69]

Shcherbatov noted that the centre of Russian trade became Arkhangelsk, which had connections with Amsterdam. Here foreign merchants—at first mainly the English, then the Dutch—made the

[67] Ulianitzkii, *Russkie consulstva*, 115–118.

[68] Russkii biograficheskii slovar, 24 (St Petersburg: Tip. Glavnogo upr. Udelov, 1912), 99. This manuscript is currently housed in the National Library of Russia. In his 'Description of the Manuscripts of Count Tolstoy', Pavel Stroyev attributed this article to Prince Sergei Golitzin, yet Pekarsky, *Nauka*, 248, asserted on the basis of handwriting that it was written by Shcherbatov.

[69] Pekarsky, *Nauka*, 565.

highest profits on the export of furs, leather, hemp, ropes, flax, fish glue and Russian leather, while importing gold and silver, silk and woollen fabrics, metals, weapons, gunpowder, spices, olive oil, wines and grape liquors.[70] Shcherbatov's historical and geographical account and inventory of the Russian balance of trade profile presumably served as a reference point while reorienting its direction when negotiating with Spain.

Francisco Perats' Draft Commercial Treaty

On 24 January 1724, Golitzin received a letter from Grimaldo containing a draft trade agreement between Spain and Russia. The text had been drawn up by Francisco Perats, a clerk of Spain's Junta of Commerce. Perats' judgement was that under Peter Russia had become a mighty European power, whose vast territories and natural riches, combined with the stimulus the Czar had given to mechanics and science made it attractive not only for Spain to ally 'with its strong army, both at sea and on land', but 'also [to] attach trade issues to political problems'.[71]

Leaving the 'political problems' to the Secretary of State, Perats focused on identifying mutually advantageous trade opportunities. He stressed that 'the great reputation of the state depends on the wealth of merchants', pointing to the example of Holland, which 'does not occupy large territories and is pinched by many rivers and canals, but in just over a hundred years, only through trade obtained such power, that in future can claim almost European dominance'.[72] A native of Cadiz, Perats had never been to Russia but had studied historical and geographical works about the country and talked to the crews of convoys sent from different Swedish ports that were near the frontier Russian ports. In this way he gleaned information about goods that Spain could get from Muscovy[73] and was able to assess 'the advantages of incalculable forests, of different species of wood carried by so many rivers to very low price and so useful for different uses in the national economy'. He also listed other products of Russia, such as metals, wax, linen, furs and crops. Spain,

[70] Ibid., 564–567.
[71] *Corpus*, 73–74
[72] Ibid., 75.
[73] Ibid., 74–75.

however, was rich in salt, vines, soaps, olive oil, lemons, sugar, almonds and olives: 'while all these things and fruits originate from this country; Moscow is poor in these things'.[74]

Perats explained that it was necessary 'to establish my proposal without delay because the subjects of the two countries will gain a lot from it and profit, the same as the Dutch and the cities of Hamburg, Lubeck and Bremen now do by negligence, thanks to having prosperous merchants'.[75] Perats' plan was aimed at cutting out the trading nations of the North and establishing direct trade between Russia and Spain by agreeing mutually favourable conditions, including declaring each other the most preferred nation. As he wrote:

> If you [Philip V] are to ensure the Russians other privileges, on the arrival and departure of ships, the same as exist for other Northern nations, [. . .] the Czar, having numerous merchant ships, will send them directly to these ports under the convoy of warships to sell merchandise in your state and to buy those that he needs (since he can do it without the help of intermediaries), and he will not need the above-mentioned nations, which until now used trade with the Czar by necessity.[76]

During an audience arranged on 25 January, Grimaldo invited Golitzin to reflect on a trade agreement that 'would be beneficial for Russia and how it was possible to embark on it'.[77] After consideration of Perats' draft in the College of Commerce and the College of Foreign Affairs, on 1 August 1724 Golitzin received instructions to declare to the Spanish court that:

> We are ready to begin this commerce [. . .] and, as is accurately stated in the draft, subjects on both sides will profit from direct commerce between the two states. For our part, we shall open up all opportunities for subjects of His Catholic Spanish Majesty, allowing them all the privileges that other most favoured nations enjoy in our state.[78]

[74] Ibid., 75–76.

[75] Ibid., 77.

[76] Ibid., 78.

[77] Ibid., 71–72; AVPRI, Relations between Russia and Spain 74, fos. 5–6.

[78] Ibid., fos. 12–13, 28–29.

Curiously, the draft of the commercial treaty prepared by Perats was shelved. It seems reasonable to assume, as was suggested by Vicente Palacio Atard, that the political substance of a privileged trading company sending some merchant ships to Spain, or some Spanish ships to Riga, was too small to warrant the conclusion of a commercial treaty.[79]

Russian–Spanish Commercial Relations after Peter the Great

When in early 1724 the two Russian consular nominees arrived in Spain the presentation of their Letters of Investiture was delayed by the abdication of Philip V. After the death of Louis I and Philip's return to the throne, Yakov Evreinov was confirmed as Russian Consul in Cadiz,[80] and in November 1724 he set off for his destination. Meanwhile, on 18 September 1724 reports by Shcherbatov from Spain and by the Russian Consul Alekseev in France were considered at a session of the Senate. Consequently, on 4 December, Peter decreed that three ships with Russian goods be sent to Spain and one to France, and instructions were duly given to the Admiralty on 24 December 1724 and 20 January 1725.[81] Simultaneous to the imminent departure of the ships, Golitzin was instructed to request the Spanish government to accord Russian traders the same rights as merchants from other countries, and this was granted in April.[82] On 4 May 1725 Peter's widow, who ascended the Russian throne under the name of Catherine I, issued 'Instructions to Fleet Skipper Ivan Mikhailov' and on 12 May three Russian ships, loaded with hides, wax, canvas and other traditional Russian export products, set sail for Cadiz from Revel.[83] When they dropped anchor in the Spanish port on 28 August, Philip V immediately issued a decree ordering the 'opening [of] free commerce with Russia in the provinces'. Russian–Spanish trade was thus placed on a new footing, although Golitzin had to remind the Spanish court that Russia should

[79] Vicente Palacio Atard, 'Una ignorada misión diplomática a Rusia en 1741', in: *Homenaje académico a D. Emilio García Gómez* (Madrid: Real Academia de Historia, 1993), 274.

[80] *Corpus*, 98. See also Ulianitzkii, *Russkie consulstva*, 118–125, 138.

[81] *Corpus*, 82–83; AVPRI, Relations between Russia and Spain 87, fos. 7–13.

[82] Ulianitzkii, *Russkie consulstva*, 145–147; AVPRI, Relations between Russia and Spain 87, fol. 72.

[83] AVPRI, Relations between Russia and Spain 87, fos. 13–72.

not be the object of restrictions, as were Sweden and Denmark, but should receive more favourable treatment.[84]

In the absence of a formal commercial treaty, the first Russian Consulate in Spain did not last long. Peter's vision of Russia entering the European state system in which Spain played a key role evaporated, and by September 1726 the College of Commerce questioned the viability of the Consular Offices in Cadiz, partly in view of losses incurred by the trade of the first Russian ships, and in September 1727 they were closed.[85]

The Russian withdrawal from Cadiz and the foundering of the project of linking domestic economic development to global trade coincided with the disruption of the European political equilibrium in 1725. The creation of the Austrian–Spanish Treaty of Vienna and the Anglo-Franco-Prussian Hanover Alliance triggered Spanish diplomatic activity to bring Russia into its political sphere of interest.[86] At the beginning of 1726 negotiations to that end were initiated in Madrid by Baron Ripperda and Shcherbatov, and Russia joined the Viennese Alliance on 6 August 1726.[87] To support the alliance with Russia, at the end of 1726 the Spanish court sent Jacobo F. Stuart, Duke of Liria and Xerica, as permanent representative to Russia.[88] His instructions of 22 January 1727 underscored the importance to Spain of drawing Russia into a war against Britain and gave him free rein to provide assurances to the Russian government on questions of trade while heaping praise on the mutual advantages of direct commerce.[89]

In Russia, however, the Treaty of Vienna was seen merely as a means of dealing with Turkish aggression, and when Spain, with the Treaty of Seville of 1729, defected from the Vienna alliance, Russia was left with Austria as its sole partner. In April the Russian Empress Anna Ioannovna notified Philip V of the recall of Shcherbatov.[90]

[84] Archivo General Simancas, Estado, Leg. 6.610.

[85] AVPRI, Relations between Russia and Spain 105, fos. 1–3; 101, fol. 29. Also Ulianitzkii, *Russkie consulstva*, 150–152.

[86] A. M. Schop Soler, Las *relaciones entre España y Rusia en la época de Carlos IV* (Barcelona: Universidad de Barcelona, 1971), 11–12; N. A. Nekrasov, *Rol' Rossii v yevropeyskoy mezhdunarodnoy politike 1725–1739* (Moscow: Nauka, 1976), 12–13.

[87] *Corpus*, 89–90.

[88] AVPRI, Relations between Russia and Spain 104, fos. 1–62.

[89] *Corpus*, 98–99.

[90] Nekrasov, *Rol' Rossii*, 204.

Thus the protracted enterprise of concluding a Russian–Spanish commercial treaty came to an end, as also did the modernizing vision in Russia in which global commerce and domestic economic reforms were structurally and institutionally connected. Political and geographical factors, the unsuccessful experience of the first commercial convoy of 1725, active opposition of Dutch merchants who prospered on the resale of Russian goods to Spain and Spanish wines to Russia, and the refusal of the Spanish Royal Council to grant Russia the most preferred nation clause conspired to bring about such a result. In point of fact, the Royal Council made that refusal partly because of diplomatic pressure from France, which obstructed Russian–Spanish rapprochement in every possible way, but the main reason for it was the lack of sustained political interest on the part of both Spain and Russia.[91] And it was not until the 1780s that rulers of the two countries—namely, Carlos III and Catherine II—attempted to revive the original vision and discuss the possibility of signing a commercial treaty, just as Ferdinand VII and Nicholas I later tried to achieve the same objective. This was done finally, in 1876, when the first commercial treaty between Spain and Russia was signed, to be followed by another in 1885 and a third in 1887.

Olga Volosyuk is Professor of History at the Faculty of World Economy and International Affairs, National Research University 'Higher School of Economics' Moscow. She is the author of two monographs on Russian–Spanish relations in the eighteenth century and edited the first Russian publication of the *History of Spain*. Currently she is researching the diplomatic and commercial relations between Russia and Spain in the nineteenth century.

[91] *Corpus*, 98.

Reinventing the Dutch Republic: Franco-Dutch Commercial Treaties from Ryswick to Vienna

Koen Stapelbroek

Introduction: Dutch Independence and the Neutrality of Trade

The history of the relation between the politics of the Dutch Republic and the institutional form of commercial treaties cannot be told without identifying the Peace of Utrecht and the negotiations taking place during the War of the Spanish Succession as a key turning point. Since its emergence following the revolt against Habsburg Spain, the Dutch state had conducted its foreign trade both to defend and to justify its political independence (particularly and most self-consciously during the period of the 'True Liberty' under Jean de Witt and the writings of the brothers De la Court). More recently, it shaped its foreign policy and trade alongside its British ally, despite that nation forming

K. Stapelbroek (✉)
University of Helsinki, Finland

Erasmus University Rotterdam, The Netherlands
e-mail: koen.stapelbroek@helsinki.fi

A. Alimento, K. Stapelbroek (eds.), *The Politics of Commercial Treaties in the Eighteenth Century*, DOI 10.1007/978-3-319-53574-6_7

its main commercial competitor.[1] Since 1678 and particularly following the 'Glorious Revolution' that put William III on the British throne, Dutch Grand Pensionaries like Heinsius followed the anti-French containment doctrine of the Protestant or Grand Alliance. Through the entire period, Dutch trade politics and the role of the Dutch state in the interstate system derived from a condition of commercial independence, where the Dutch were 'the common Carriers of the World' as William Temple famously put it.[2]

After 1713 this direct linkage of political and commercial independence disappeared, or rather, turned into the challenge to relay it via a different state that acted as a guarantor to Dutch interests. Parallel to the familiar narrative of Dutch decline after 1700, the prospects for the survival of Dutch political independence became conditional on the principles upon which Europe's main territorial monarchies chose to organize their respective commercial empires and devised their institutional and fiscal infrastructure to fit with weaker states in the balance of power. That 'selection' of principles itself was the object of recurrent warfare about trade and colonial possessions in the eighteenth century. In the case of the Dutch, the highly charged and polarizing question from 1713 onwards was whether France or Britain offered the best commercial-political package to secure the future of the Republic. The period following the War of the Spanish Succession then also can be characterized, from a Dutch perspective, as a sequence of debates and projects through which the previous function where the Dutch played an independent role in the interstate system might be restored through securing the neutrality of international trade on a general level. Some Dutch positions developed in the period from 1713 to the end of the Republic in 1795 were coloured by patriotic sentiment and a naive longing for restoring a mythical past of Dutch glory. This chapter suggests that Dutch diplomacy and particularly its attitude towards commercial treaties with France played an important role in the history of global trade politics between the seventeenth and the later eighteenth century. It shows that among the plethora of visions

[1] Ragnhild Hatton, *Diplomatic Relations between Great Britain and the Dutch Republic, 1714–1721* (London: Anglo-Netherlands Society, 1950); Hugh Dunthorne, *The Maritime Powers 1721–1740. A Study of Anglo-Dutch Relations in the Age of Walpole* (New York: Garland, 1986).

[2] William Temple, *Observations upon the United Provinces of the Netherlands* (London, 1673), 187.

brought forward in Dutch pamphlets, journals and treatises published in the later eighteenth century, the more serious Dutch ideas about international trade politics and commercial treaties were associated with some of the most advanced political economic theories of the time.

Ryswick, the 1699 Tariff and Utrecht: Defeating France?

In 1713 a Franco-Dutch treaty of commerce was drawn up, signed (at Utrecht, on 11 April, the same day as the Anglo-French treaty and the Franco-Dutch peace treaty) and ratified by the respective signatories and representative bodies. The content of the treaty was not spectacularly new in a technical sense. The terms and conditions and height of the respective duties formed a revival of the treaty of 1697 and the tariff of 1699 that had been agreed between Willem Nieuwpoort (1647–1729)—who had been the Rotterdam *admodiateur der convooien en licenten* from 1688 and who was appointed as special commissioner by the States-General[3]—and the French negotiators. The 1699 tariff agreement, signed on 29 May in Paris, followed an extended series of painstaking negotiations that lasted over two years, during which the gap between 'les demandes de Monsr. de Pontchartrain' and 'mes offres pour le nouveau Tarif' was very slowly bridged.[4] Following the Peace of Ryswick, which had seen the conclusion of a commercial treaty negotiated between Caillières and Boreel and Dijkveld, Nieuwpoort and his French interlocutors engaged in a series of exchanges to specify what had been prepared in the actual treaty.[5] Article XII there stipulated that 'there shall be a new Tariff established [...] in the space of three Months' during which period the 1667 rates were applied.[6] Subsequently, the generally lower, albeit more extensive in the goods it

[3] On the negotiations, Nationaal Archief The Hague [NA] 3.01.19, inv. 2164.

[4] NA 3.01.19, inv. 2164.

[5] On Ryswick, Heinz Duchhardt, Matthias Schnettger and Martin Vogt, eds., *Der Friede von Rijswijk, 1697* (Mainz: von Zabern, 1998); J. Z. Kannegieter 'Amsterdam en de vrede van Rijswijk', *Bijdragen en Mededeelingen van het Historisch Genootschap* 48 (1927), 99–135; Marjorie Bowen, *Engeland bij den Vrede van Rijswijk* (The Hague: Daamen, 1924); William Thomas Morgan, 'Economic Aspects of the Negotiations at Ryswick', *Transactions of the Royal Society* 14 (1931), 225–249.

[6] *A treaty of commerce, navigation, and marine affairs, concluded and agreed on at Reswick [...] With some account of the proceedings since between the French and Dutch commissioners relating to the tariff* (London, 1699).

covered, 1664 tariff (which was more advantageous from the Dutch point of view) would be restored until a new one was agreed upon.

The two main characteristics of the 1697 treaty were the degree to which Dutch merchants were allowed to trade freely in French goods and the abolition, through the separate article following the treaty, of the *droit de fret* duty of fifty *sols* per ton levied upon imports into France. These two measures together meant that the 1697 commercial treaty established the Dutch trade republic in formal terms as the prime privileged carrier of French imports and exports. In fact it became pretty hard to legally distinguish between own citizens and Dutch merchants.[7] These stipulations went far beyond the later standardized most favoured nation clause and the formulas of harmonization that were stipulated in the Utrecht treaties.[8]

When, in 1709, Torcy de Colbert and Pierre Rouillé met with the same regents who earlier had rejected alternative projects for a general peace (see below) they were humiliated according to Voltaire:

> Louis XIV, who had already made some advances toward a peace, determined under these fatal circumstances to send his chief minister, the marquis Torci Colbert, to The Hague, assisted by the president Rouillé. This was a humbling step. They first met at Antwerp, with two burgomasters from Amsterdam, named Buis and Vanderhussen [i.e. Buys and Van der Dussen], who talked like conquerors, and returned to the ministers of the proudest of all princes all the arrogance with which they themselves had been treated in 1672.[9]

If in 1709 Torcy had not much of a negotiating position, it seemed also unthinkable to him that the Dutch would be adamant that the peace had to include the victorious commercial terms of the Ryswick Treaty. When handed the Dutch *Articles Préliminaires pour servir aux Traités de la Paix Générale*, Torcy was confident that mutual interest could be restored in the negotiation of the final terms, as he commented with Article XXV, which claimed the conditions of Ryswick: 'We propose suitable expedients to remove by mutual agreement those difficulties which might hamper

[7] Articles VII, VIII and XXVIII.

[8] And were equally far-reaching on neutral and belligerent trade. Articles XVIII, XXVII.

[9] Voltaire, 'Age of Louis XIV', in: *The Works of Voltaire* (New York: DuMont, 1901), xii: 74.

trade between the French and the Dutch, and these will be agreed amicably at the conclusion of the peace.'[10] Yet, this would not be the case.

Voltaire's judgement of the emotions on the part of the Dutch negotiators in 1709 hit the same registers as David Hume's declamation against the British decision (inspired by a 'spirit of jealous emulation' rather than 'prudent views of modern politics'[11]) not to accept the Geertruydenberg conditions of a general peace. Describing how Dutch magistrates bossed around their German pet princes, Voltaire saw the Dutch claim to the barrier towns as another sign of their greed for 'superiority', explained how without a stadtholder who hated Louis XIV their politics had turned into vanity and concluded that 'the republican spirit is in the main fully as ambitious as the monarchical'.[12]

Ryswick and Utrecht as the End of 'True Liberty'

While in the aftermath of Ryswick the manoeuvrings between the 1664 and 1667 tariffs were the object of correspondence between Nieuwpoort, the States-General and the Grand Pensionary, an English publication of the 1697 commercial treaty noted that 'the business of setling the Tariff between Holland and France has been so long in agitation, so generally talked of, and yet so little understood'.[13] Emphasizing 'how Just and Equitable the Dutch Pretentions' were in the light of the 1697 treaty, it was 'a mere sham' for the French 'to say, They understood not what they did, when they agreed to it'.[14] Warning his countrymen that the French 'can never be bound too fast [...] when we come to treat with that nation', the British translator played on the theme of French deceitfulness and ambition to establish universal monarchy.[15]

Anglo-French distrust as displayed in these phrases was also an ingredient of Voltaire's account in which he depicted the Dutch as the greedy victors of

[10] Jean Baptiste Colbert marquis de Torcy, *Memoires pour servir à l'histoire des négociations depuis le traité de Riswick jusqu'à la paix d'Utrecht* (Paris, 1828), i: 319.

[11] David Hume, 'Of the Balance of Power', in: *Essays Moral, Political, and Literary*, ed. Eugene Miller (Indianapolis: Liberty Fund, 1985), 339–340.

[12] Voltaire, 'Age of Louis XIV', xii: 74–75.

[13] *A treaty of commerce*, 'Preface to the Reader', n.p.

[14] *A treaty of commerce*, 'Preface to the Reader', n.p.

[15] *A treaty of commerce*, 'Preface to the Reader', n.p.

Utrecht. Having exploited the English 'spirit of freedom' against France 'the Dutch wanted to reap all the fruits of the war, not only at the expense of France, but also at that of the house of Austria, whose cause they had been fighting'.[16] Yet, the dominant French perception of Ryswick and Utrecht was that the true victors were the British and that the Franco-Dutch commercial treaty made neither of the contracting states better off.

How this could possibly work was explained by Daniel Defoe in his *Considerations upon the eighth and ninth articles of the treaty of commerce and navigation* of 1713. Defoe defined commercial treaties as 'exceptions' to the general logic of a state defining its own general import and export duties vis-à-vis all other states: 'in several Treaties of Commerce there have been Agreements made, and Articles enter'd into, especially between France and the States-General, by which the Duties of Merchandises have been adjusted respectively'.[17] The main example he thought of was the treaty following '*Reswick*' of 1699.[18] Just like that particular treaty created a channel for the increase of Franco-Dutch profit, and thereby power, parallel to considerations regarding the 'Interest of the Kingdom, respecting Peace and War', so 'Considerations of Trade' had to be made to sometimes make 'Trade run in a different Channel, and [alter] the Balance' between states.[19] Political economy was a game of optimizing relative profit and power vis-à-vis other states using commercial treaties as instruments. Such a rivalrous competition-based outlook on channelling trade was potentially at odds with creating a long-term sustainable system of trade that optimized general economic growth.

A number of accounts focused on the way the Dutch had organized their trade until the time of William III and contrasted the time of the 'True Liberty' with the style of treaty-making that the Dutch adopted since Ryswick. In 1787, Alexander Crowcher Schomberg, a commentator on the Eden–Rayneval treaty of the preceding year made a contrast between the growth of modern wealth between the Peace of Westphalia and 1700 and the entire eighteenth century. The plan in the 1780s on his understanding was to turn recent history around and shift back to the practice of

[16] Voltaire, 'Age of Louis XIV', xii: 74–75, 292–293.

[17] Daniel Defoe, *Considerations upon the eighth and ninth articles of the treaty of commerce and navigation* (London, 1713), 4.

[18] Defoe, *Considerations*, 5.

[19] Defoe, *Considerations*, 9.

the later seventeenth century. What had been central to the growth of modern wealth since the Peace of Westphalia, according to Schomberg was not or not only the discovery of overseas territories and Dutch company trade, but the fact that the Dutch Republic had engaged in trade and created commercial treaties with other states that had spread and generalized the benefits of global trade. In particular, Schomberg praised the Franco-Dutch commercial treaties that were concluded between Colbert and De Witt.[20]

Following the Peace of Westphalia, the financial struggles of the Dutch West Indies Company, the declaration of the English Navigation Act and the First Anglo-Dutch War, Dutch trade policy became organized according to a logic that was praised in Pieter De la Court's *Interest of Holland* of 1662.[21] This book, which appeared in French in 1709 as the *Mémoires de Jean de Witt, grand pensionnaire de Hollande*, explained that if only the Dutch took good care of their wealth derived from carrying trade, fishery and limited colonial possessions there would be no grounds for other states to vie for trade and compete against each other aggressively.[22] Having the Dutch carry other states' goods was not only beneficial for the Dutch economy, but for European states at large, and created an international system in which power and trade were separated. This structure was much to be preferred to the alternative of balancing states by means of war or treaties, which offered no real security, De la Court insisted.[23] If states behaved in their true interest, not the interest of their monarchs, the world had no need for alliances or political treaties, which were also not in line with the maxims of a trading nation.[24]

[20] Alexander Crowcher Schomberg, *Historical and political remarks upon the tariff of the commercial treaty: with preliminary observations* (London, 1787). See also the chapter by Isenmann in this volume.

[21] Pieter De la Court, *The True Interest and Political Maxims of the Republick of Holland and West-Friesland* (London, 1702) based on the *Aanwysing der heilsame politike gronden en maximen van de republike van Holland en West-Vriesland* (Leiden, 1669), an earlier version of which was published as the *Interest van Holland, ofte gronden van Hollands-Welvaren* (Amsterdam, 1662). See also Koen Stapelbroek, 'The Dutch Debate on Commercial Neutrality 1713–1830', in: *Trade and War: The Neutrality of Commerce in the Inter-State System*, COLLeGIUM: Studies Across Disciplines in the Arts and Humanities 10, ed. Koen Stapelbroek (Helsinki: Helsinki Collegium for Advanced Studies, 2011), 114–142.

[22] De la Court, *Interest of Holland*, 204, also 133, 195.

[23] De la Court, *Interest of Holland*, 216–219.

[24] De la Court, *Interest of Holland*, 311, 393–397.

Yet, De la Court also signalled that regents neglected their duty to actively consider the common good and created a problem that ultimately went beyond the fate of the Republic. The Republic had to modernize fiscally, financially and institutionally and reform its outdated laws and political ideas that resembled those of the 'warlike Roman republic'.[25] One of the presuppositions of the *Interest of Holland* was that the time of Republican glory—the Golden Age—in the interstate arena was over and the Republic had to accept and adapt to this new reality. The status of the Dutch East India Company's maritime power had declined and the Dutch interest no longer dovetailed seamlessly with Grotian natural law doctrine and its concept of justice. Instead, the flourishing of Dutch trade had come to hinge more delicately than before on general policies on foreign political treaty arrangements so as to align the Dutch interest and a wider and general separation of the world of trade from the world of power politics.

The picture painted by Schomberg was that the Dutch Republic under Johan de Witt was successfully playing this role. Using commercial treaties to balance and mediate France and Britain, these treaties were a successful antidote and response to the English Navigation Act, Schomberg suggested, which promoted a suboptimal system of global trade. Likewise, in the same decade in which Schomberg reflected upon the history of treaty-making and identified the role of the Dutch as crucial, Jeremy Bentham mentioned the negotiations between Temple and De Witt, which had already been praised by Hume as well:

> Temple and De Wit, whose confidence in each other was so exemplary and so just—Temple and De Wit were two of the wisest as well as most honourable men in Europe, [. . .] Since then, the world has had upwards of a century to improve itself in experience, in reflection, in virtue. In every other line its improvements have been immense and unquestioned. Is it too much to hope that France and England might produce not a Temple and a De Wit.[26]

From this point of view it becomes possible to understand the French confusion and disappointment with the Dutch decisions of Ryswick and

[25] De la Court, *Interest of Holland*, 108.

[26] Jeremy Bentham, 'A Plan for an Universal and Perpetual Peace, Essay IV, Principles of International Law', in: *The Works of Jeremy Bentham*, ed. John Bowring (Edinburgh: William Tait, 1843), ii: 553–554.

in the lead-up to Utrecht to substitute the principle of reciprocity and the trade policy of the 'True Liberty' period for the political economic package-deal of the Protestant Alliance.[27] It also explains the commissioning, presumably at the end of the Nine Years War, by Colbert de Torcy and Louis XIV to Pierre Daniel Huet and the French diplomat and ambassador to the United Provinces François d'Usson, marquis de Bonrepos (or Bonrepaus) to write a history of Dutch trade.[28] The manuscript that became known as Huet's *Memoirs of the Dutch trade in all the states, empires, and kingdoms in the world*, published posthumously in 1712, argued that the Dutch discovery of global company trade during the revolt and its audacious deployment in the service of national power, wealth and glory had been a revolution in the history of humankind. France had no choice but to emulate the Dutch and thereby protect itself from being overrun by Britain in Europe. Bonrepos' narrative of the rise of Dutch trade ran parallel to Huet's, but reads as a manual for the completion of the process of turning the Dutch Republic intro a neutral carrying state by seizing its empire and subsequently creating a Franco-British balance of power supported by the 'services' of the Dutch. Interestingly, both Huet's and Bonrepos' manuscripts on the history of Dutch trade ended on a similar note: Bonrepos finished his piece with a few comments on the tariff negotiation following the Peace of Ryswick, while Huet's manuscript was published in 1718 in Amsterdam 'augmentée de plusieurs mémoires & du tarif general d'Hollande'.[29]

Franco-Dutch Trade Relations from 1713

Whether the Dutch became monarchical or whether the republican spirit was by itself prone to over-ambition, was unclear in Voltaire's account. De la Court's analysis in the 1660s that institutional inertia played a role in the mindset of republican regents could equally count. Recent research does

[27] See the introductory chapter by Alimento and Stapelbroek in this volume.

[28] Their placement in the Archives du Ministère des Affaires Etrangères [AAE] also gives reason to make this connection: Huet's text (not attributed to him in the catalogue) is entitled 'Etat du commerce des hollandois dans toutes les parties du monde' and dated 1697 (Mémoires et Documents [MD], Hollande 49), followed by three copies of Bonrepos' piece ('Mémoire concernant le commerce des Hollandois depuis leur establissement jusques en la présente année 1699', AAE MD, Hollande 50–52).

[29] Pierre-Daniel Huet, *Mémoires sur le commerce des Hollandois, dans tous les Etats et empires du monde* (Amsterdam, 1718).

indeed point in the direction that the failure of Utrecht to establish a lasting peace and general economic development through trade agreements has to do with the role of Dutch diplomacy. In the years leading up to Utrecht, different schemes proposed by Mesnager, Helvétius and Bergeyck for the Franco-Spanish-Dutch integration, joint incorporation or neutralization of overseas trade as part of the peace settlement were consistently rejected by Buys, Van der Dussen and others.[30] Interestingly, part of the process appears to have been overseen by Nieuwpoort, in whose home in Overschie Helvétius and the Dutch negotiators met in 1705–1716 and who remained involved in Dutch commercial politics as an apologist of Stadtholderly rule until at least 1716.[31]

Chronologically located 'between the treaties of Nimeguen (1678) and Utrecht (1713)' the Treaty of Ryswick was once called 'in fact, a commentary upon the former and a prelude to the latter'.[32] What the author of this statement alluded to was the demise of Louis XIV's power and the rise of Britain as a commercial empire. Yet, the significance of Ryswick is completely overlooked here. What happened, as argued above, is that the reciprocity in Franco-Dutch trade was lost. Even if Louis XIV was the first to propose the reduction of the fifty *sols* duty in order 'to drive an economic wedge between the English and Dutch', the tenacity with which the Dutch clung to the deal created a skewed pattern of trade that was compounded by the failure in the same years (under the circumstance of political infighting on the newly created Board of Trade) to conclude an Anglo-French treaty.[33]

[30] See also the introductory chapter in this volume and forthcoming work by Alimento and Stapelbroek.

[31] Correspondence between Helvétius and Nieuwpoort in Koninklijke Bibliotheek The Hague [KB]: 71 H18. Jan Wagenaar, *Vaderlandsche Historie* (Amsterdam, 1758), xviii: 128: Nieuwpoort argued in 1716 that the Admiralty Boards might not respect fiscal order unless overseen by a Stadtholder.

[32] Morgan, 'Economic Aspects of the Negotiations at Ryswick', 226.

[33] Morgan, 'Economic Aspects of the Negotiations at Ryswick', 239. For the longer history of the failure to create an Anglo-French commercial treaty and political infighting without any apparent ideological differences on foreign trade, Antonella Alimento, 'Commercial Treaties and the Harmonisation of National Interests: The Anglo-French Case (1667–1713)', in: *War, Trade and Neutrality. Europe and the Mediterranean in the Seventeenth and Eighteenth Centuries*, ed. Antonella Alimento (Milan: Franco Angeli, 2011), 107–128.

From the aftermath of Ryswick to the aftermath of Utrecht, Dutch commentators started to question the desirability of the advantageous deal with France. If the commercial treaty of Ryswick provided advantageous fiscal privileges, these could be interpreted (and were by some) as a formal legal-political confirmation of the mythical idea of the Dutch as the natural carriers of the world's goods. Yet, clearly they were due to political and military causes. One Dutch pamphleteer saw already before Ryswick that the preservation of the basis for Dutch commercial primacy required a careful reform of the fiscal and institutional foundations of the Dutch economy.[34]

A pamphlet published in 1714, *Korte Schets Van 'sLands welwezen door de laatste Vrede*, indicated the wider dynamic in which the Franco-Dutch commercial treaties played a role. While there was a current in British pamphleteering that focused on the Dutch 'greed' with which they had claimed the barrier,[35] this pamphlet too criticized the war effort and the alliance with England as inspired by monarchical-territorial 'envy' and 'lust for war', but rejected the significance of the barrier.[36] Echoing De la Court, the *Korte Schets* noted that the United Provinces counted enough merchants and sailors to carry on the world's entire trade. However, most of them had been excluded from the Indies companies, which wanted to make a few large profits, rather than own the world's trade and be content with smaller margins.[37] The company-based organization of Dutch foreign trade had left space for other states to turn to trade, which ultimately led to the conclusion of politically inspired commercial treaties that reinforced Dutch decline.[38] The recently concluded Anglo-Spanish commercial treaty showed the danger of this development that turned trade directly into an object of reason of state: who held the South American trade determined the balance of power.[39] Thus, the rise of Britain as a

[34] *Consideratien over de huydendaagsche commercie met bygevoegde speculatien over 't werk der transitoire goederen* (s.l., s.d.). Datings of the pamphlet differ, but probably 1687–1688.

[35] Douglas Coombs, *The Conduct of the Dutch. British Opinion and the Dutch Alliance during the War of the Spanish Succession* (The Hague: Nijhoff, 1958), after the pamphlet by Jonathan Swift that was the basis of the Tory campaign.

[36] Anon., *Korte Schets Van 'sLands welwezen door de laatste Vrede, Nevens eenige Aanmerkingen op het stuk van de commercie en Barriere* (s.l. 1714), 4–5.

[37] Anon., *Korte Schets*, 7–12.

[38] Anon., *Korte Schets*, 35–37.

[39] Anon., *Korte Schets*, 14–17.

commercial empire and the decline of Dutch trade represented a lapse from a naturally optimal situation to a politicized global trade system.

The *Korte Schets* was right to immediately identify Utrecht as a turning point. The settlement converted the territorial and military gains of the Alliance into a set of commercial privileges for Britain and left the Republic with the barrier and an unequal commercial treaty with France.[40] If from the negotiations of the Peace of Ryswick one could see the contours of an Anglo-French struggle for commercial empire emerging, Utrecht fixed it as the dominant trait of international relations in the eighteenth century. While the British aims at Ryswick had concerned colonial possessions outside Europe, at Utrecht the system of British commercial hegemony was institutionalized through commercial treaties.

What changed in and after 1713 was that the Anglo-Dutch alliance as it had functioned was effectively disbanded and the conditions for promoting Dutch trade became directly dependent upon Franco-Dutch relations. Echoing Torcy, Mesnager, Helvétius and Saint-Pierre, a French manuscript from 1716 bemoaned the loss of reciprocity, justice and equality in these relations.[41] Between Utrecht and the 1740s a range of Dutch translations—promoted by Dutch Huguenots—of foreign political works helped to understand the new system of global trade and the restrictions that now existed to reinventing the Dutch trade republic.[42] One of those conditions, as Jean Dumont, the Huguenot publisher of the greatest collections of treaties at the time, put it in a well-known pamphlet, was that the political economy of Britain had changed when it pushed out the Dutch, sustained its colonial empire and on top of it all created commercial ties with France. This unleashed apprehension and anxiety all-around, but particularly among Dutch Huguenots:

[40] See the introductory chapter by Alimento and Stapelbroek in this volume.

[41] NA 3.01.19, inv. 2167; 1.02.07, inv. 77 shows the French perspective on Dutch opinions, in 1714, on the newly agreed Franco-Dutch commercial treaty in the form of a newsletter from The Hague.

[42] Koen Stapelbroek, 'Between Utrecht and the War of the Austrian Succession: The Dutch Translation of the *British Merchant* of 1728', *History of European Ideas* 40 (2014), 1026–1043. On the post-Utrecht Republic, C. H. Th. Bussemaker, 'Een memorie over de Republiek uit 1728', *Bijdragen en Mededeelingen van het Historisch Genootschap* 30 (1909), 96–197; 'De Republiek der Vereenigde Nederlanden in hare staatkundige betrekkingen gedurende de eerste jaren na den vrede van Utrecht, 1713–1721', *De Gids* 63/3 (1809), 32–88.

> We Foreigners now look for *Great Britain* in *Great Britain* and can scarce believe we have found it. The State, indeed, is the same, but the Spirit, and the Conduct have a different Aspect. Other Measures and Maxims have Succeeded in the Place of former Counsels, and we cannot but be apprehensive, that, unless Providence prevent it, her former Allies may have the Dissatisfaction of seeing her Enemies become her Friends.[43]

Profit not the Mother of Alliance: Neutrality and the 'Stationary Trading State'

The unequal commercial treaty of 1713 was agreed for twenty-five years, would be revised in 1717 and was renewed after negotiations between Amelot and van Hoey in 1739.[44] In 1745 when the Dutch lent succour to Britain in the War of the Austrian Succession the treaty was abolished and never renewed despite long and repeated attempts of negotiations since the peace-making process of 1748.[45] From 1739 the treaty had started to assume new functions that France wanted it to have and Franco-Dutch commercial relations—even after the treaty—reflected the reigning preferences in French politics. Although the renewal in 1739 meant that Fleury still opted for Dutch traders as the privileged carriers of French merchandise, the terms had changed. In 1739, a Dutch commentator noted, with reference to Pierre Daniel Huet and reflecting on Franco-Dutch trade since 1648, that owing to a great number of concessions the new conditions were more beneficial for the French than the Dutch.[46] Yet, after 1739 attitudes quickly changed. If earlier French writers bemoaned the loss of reciprocity in Franco-Dutch trade, and French politics for a few decades resigned to the reality of an unequal trade that never became an alliance, in the 1730s writers like Jean-François Melon had started to devise radically different ways out of this situation from simply negotiating better treaty conditions. Rather than accept the Dutch as privileged

[43] Jean Dumont, Baron de Carlscroon, *Les soupirs de l'Europe, etc, or, The groans of Europe at the prospect of the present posture of affairs* ([London], 1713), 4; the *Corps universel diplomatique du droit des gens* was the standard work on peace, commercial and other treaties.

[44] For the renegotiation of 1717, NA 3.01.19, inv. 2167.

[45] Johannes Hovy, *Het voorstel van 1751 tot instelling van een beperkt vrijhavenstelsel in de Republiek. (Propositie tot een gelimiteerd porto-franco)* (Groningen: Wolters, 1966).

[46] Hovy, *Propositie porto-franco*, 318 on Gerard Westerwijck's reflection.

carriers, one strand within French politics preferred France to adopt a Navigation Act and develop its own merchant fleet, while another preferred to make the French trade a subject of competition between a wider range of states, notably Sweden and Denmark.[47] When Jacob Gilles and later Dirk Marselis and Isaac de Larrey in 1748–1749 and again in 1754 attempted to negotiate an agreement with Trudaine, they concluded that the conditions Dutch merchants had enjoyed since Nijmegen and particularly since Ryswick and Utrecht were not on the menu anymore.[48]

From 1740 until the 1780s, the nature of Franco-Dutch trade became part of an extended and increasingly polarized Dutch pamphlet debate about the rights of neutral states to trade in wartime and about questions of the neutrality of trade in general.[49] When Grand Pensionary Anthonie van der Heim in 1742 contemplated the conclusion of a separate treaty of

[47] See Antonella Alimento, 'Competition, True Patriotism and Colonial Interest: Forbonnais' Vision of Neutrality and Trade', in: *Trade and War*, ed. Stapelbroek, 61–95; see also the chapter by Alimento and the introductory chapter by Alimento and Stapelbroek in this volume. Pieces in AAE MD 1 Hollande ('Considerations sur le renouvellement and Mémoires sur le renouvellement du traité de commerce entre la France et les Provinces-Unies'), MD 73 Hollande; earlier texts of MD 137 Hollande; and Trudaine, BNF NAF 20541 ('Mémoire sur le commerce de la Hollande') show the French turn of opinion.

[48] Hovy, *Propositie porto-franco*, 321–327; NA 1.02.14, inv. 6–7, 34–36, 375; 1.01.47.27, inv. 488; 1.10.29, inv. 1549; 1.10.105, inv. 43; On 1754–1755: 1.01.50, inv. 253 (cf. with 1.01.50, inv. 563, Project for a commercial treaty with Britain 1753). Interestingly, 3.01.24, inv. 302 (no. 20) includes pessimistic musings by Marselis from 30 January 1754 (that fit with BNF FR 5371, fos. 266–281, correspondence later that year by Trudaine and Rouillé on the rejection of a 'Mémoire envoyé par la Hollande pour le renouvellement d'un traité de commerce avec la France'). NA 3.01.24, inv. 302–332 forms a series of studies and documentation made by Steyn in 1756 of the usages and formulas of treaties of commerce from the later seventeenth century onwards, exactly at the time of the debate with d'Affry, Bonnac and Yorke.

[49] For a Dutch perspective on deteriorating relations with France from 1740, J. Z. Kannegieter, 'Rapport, op 22 September 1747 aan H.H.M. uitgebracht, door Mr. Abraham van Hoey, gewezen gezant onzer Republiek in Frankrijk', *Bijdragen en Mededeelingen van het Historisch Genootschap* 51 (1930), 1–21; on the general debate Koen Stapelbroek, 'Neutrality and Trade in the Dutch Republic (1775–1783): Preludes to a Piecemeal Revolution', in: *Rethinking the Atlantic World. Europe and America in the Age of Democratic Revolutions*, ed. Manuela Albertone and Antonino De Francesco (Basingstoke: Palgrave Macmillan, 2009), 100–119; Koen Stapelbroek, 'Economic Reform and Neutrality in Dutch Political Pamphlets, 1741–1779', in: *Pamphlets and Politics in the Dutch Republic*, ed. Femke Deen, David Onnekink and Michel Reinders (Leiden: Brill, 2011), 173–204; Koen Stapelbroek, 'The Emergence of Dutch Neutrality: Trade, Treaty Politics and the Peace of the Republic', in: *War, Trade and Neutrality*, ed. Alimento, 129–145.

neutrality with France and pondered the feasibility and consequences of alienating Britain he was exactly where his French interlocutors wanted him to be.[50] While the French (d'Affry and Vauguyon) and British (Yorke) ambassadors participated actively in this debate with their own published pamphlet interventions it was not simply the case that the Republic had to make a political choice between 'roast beef' or 'onion soup', as one pamphleteer put it at the start of the Seven Years War, or to the famous image of a puppet theatre play where behind the scenes French and British diplomats pulled the strings in Dutch politics.[51] This whole debate was not about Anglophile Orangists versus Francophile Patriots, but about the various scenarios for the development of interstate trade and the remaining options for the reform of the Dutch Republic.

Reinventing the Dutch Republic was also the object of the 1751 'Proposal for a general free port' supported by Stadtholder William IV, who had come into power in 1748. Immediately when the Dutch negotiators returned from Paris with news that in the aftermath of the end of the War of the Austrian Succession, despite long negotiations, the 1713 treaty would not be renewed various scenarios for changing the Dutch tariff and economic structure of the country were discussed.[52] Treaty-based privileged trade with France and the 1751 'Proposal' were alternatives for Dutch economic development based on different principles of how France and Britain shaped interstate trade patterns. If the first option was the leftover result of British manoeuvrings at the end of the War of the Spanish Succession and was neither in the French nor even the Dutch interest, the second was an attempt to convert what was left of the Dutch potential to carry the world's trade into a redeveloped 'stationary trading state'.[53] Its main manifesto picked up the arguments that De la Court and the author of the *Korte Schets* had made and argued for a fiscal reform programme that in some sense turned the entire Republic into a free port,

[50] NA 3.01.22, 706.

[51] H. T. Colenbrander, *De Patriottentijd. Hoofdzakelijk naar Buitenlandsche Bescheiden* (The Hague: Nijhoff, 1897), i: vii–ix.

[52] Hovy, *Propositie porto-franco.*

[53] *Proposals made up by His late Highness the Prince of Orange [...] for redressing and amending the Trade of the Republick* (London, 1751); see Koen Stapelbroek, 'Dutch Commercial Decline Revisited: The Future of International Trade and the 1750s Debate about a Limited Free Port', *Annali della Fondazione Feltrinelli* 43 (2009), 193–221.

without leaving the manufacturing and agriculture of the inland provinces entirely vulnerable to foreign competition. In a sense, the 1751 'Proposal' was a domestic commercial treaty between the different provinces in order to tidy up the economic system of the Republic, reform its finances and fiscal structures and discipline price levels and the cost of labour.[54]

A main figure involved in the development of the new strategy was the Amsterdam financier and political writer Isaac de Pinto, whose first unpublished writings stem from the late 1740s. The author of the 'Proposal', Thomas Hope, was a close ally of Pinto and both were main figures in the attempted reforms of the Dutch WIC and VOC that were also part of the same overall attempt to renew the economic foundations of the Republic. A brief summary of Pinto's manuscripts and later works shows the wider vision of the reform project of the late 1740s and the continuity with earlier ideas.

In his 'Tribut Patriotique' manuscript of 1748, dedicated to William IV, Pinto sketched how the development of the American and Asian trade by European states and their East India Companies had given rise to a global system of economic development. The Dutch in particular, Pinto explained, by way of their East India Company were the first to almost accidentally tap into a major resource for changing the face of the earth through trade. It was by means of this company that one had found the 'secret' of how a sterile country could survive and flourish. Many people still failed to understand the sheer impact of this discovery, Pinto asserted. After the discovery of America and the development of intercontinental currents of capital and goods streams, Europe had become infinitely richer and become universally opulent.[55]

Pinto argued that the Dutch by means of trade, rather than through political alliances, were tied to the territory of other states whose reliance on the Dutch for their trade gave the Dutch state a special function and viability in interstate politics. This conclusion was also drawn in the 1751

[54] It is easy to see why the 'Proposal' was controversial and—also due to the untimely death of William IV—was never adopted; Stapelbroek, 'Dutch Commercial Decline Revisited'.

[55] Isaac de Pinto, *Tribut patriotique présenté avec le plus profond respect à Son Altesse Sérénissime Monseigneur le Prince d'Orange et de Nassau*, NA 2.21.005.39, inv. 165. On Pinto, see Koen Stapelbroek, 'From Jealousy of Trade to the Neutrality of Finance: Isaac de Pinto's "System" of Luxury and Perpetual Peace', in: *Commerce and Peace in the Enlightenment*, ed. Bela Kapossy, Isaac Nakhimovsky and Richard Whatmore (Cambridge: Cambridge University Press, 2017), 87–109.

'Proposal', which confidently stated that 'neighbouring Nations will be more or less concerned, in the Conservation of our Trade, as their commerce chiefly consists in the Vending of their own Products; and will therefore rather protect than obstruct ours, which has such a Connection with their own, that it may not improperly be called a Part'.[56]

Yet, for Pinto trade was only the beginning, not the end, of the development of the modern state. Following the *facheux* Peace of Utrecht Dutch politicians had failed to adapt the fiscal, financial and commercial structures of the state to the evolving requirements of the interstate commercial system.[57] Pinto's writings from the 1760s and 1770s shifted the perspective from that of the Dutch Republic to that of the commercial state in general and the dynamics of international competition. Overseas commerce had triggered within Europe the invention of new production methods and had allowed for the major increase of manufacturing improvement, parallel to which the 'intrinsic power' of states had become linked with the management of public credit.[58] The connections that had thus arisen between 'circulation' and 'credit' acted as checks to the development of complementary exchange relationships between states, each drawing upon its own characteristics and relative competitive strengths in international trade.[59] For Pinto the eighteenth-century problem of 'jealousy of trade' was primarily the result of the fact that modern politics did not understand how the world had changed. The paradox was that the division of comparative advantages made at Utrecht had created a situation in which 'each European power enjoys more or less the possessions of its neighbours'—effectively there *was* a joint European trading system that extended to the entire world. At the same time, 'chimerical commercial jealousies', as Pinto called them, caused repeated warfare.[60] Although Pinto was not a balance of power theorist, he did believe that one had better leave intact the current 'balance of Europe, purchased with the blood of our ancestors [that] is now so well

[56] *Proposals for redressing the Trade of the Republick* (London, 1751), 59.

[57] Pinto, *Tribut patriotique.*

[58] Isaac de Pinto, *An essay on circulation and credit: in four parts; and a letter on the jealousy of commerce* (London, 1774), 26–30, 44–47; *Letters on the American Troubles Translated from the French* (London, 1776), 44, 63–64, 73, 80–89.

[59] Pinto, *Circulation and credit; jealousy of commerce*, 44.

[60] Pinto, *Letters on the American Troubles*, 40–41.

established'. Any attempt to conquer 'commerce[,] the apple of discord' caused the 'destruction of trade' itself.[61]

The Balance of Power and the End of the Dutch Republic

Pinto was no balance of power theorist in that he did not see the idea of balance as central or necessary for a functioning interstate system. This was different for Elie Luzac, who in 1766 published Jacques Accarias de Serionne's *Les intérêts des nations de l'Europe, développés relativement au commerce*, the main manifesto of Choiseul's scheme to orchestrate international peace through a bipolar hierarchy of states with Britain and France at the top connecting to each other with a commercial treaty.[62] Lower-level states in the hierarchy were to occupy themselves with providing agricultural supplies and support the manufacturing economies of the dominant states that competed with each other for market shares on a global level.[63]

Going into the 1780s, the opposition between these two visions was publicly overshadowed by that between 'Patriots' and 'Orangists' (both Pinto and Luzac were in the latter category). The economic dimensions of Dutch 'Patriotism(s)' have never properly been clarified, yet the more Anglophobe 'Patriots' during the War of American Independence advocated a capital strike on the British debt and a cheap loan to John Adams in the hope of securing trade privileges with independent America.[64] The Dutch–American commercial treaty of 1782, which was earlier

[61] Pinto, *Circulation and credit; jealousy of commerce*, 228.

[62] On Pinto, Luzac, Accarias and Raynal, Koen Stapelbroek, 'Raynal et Pinto: le commerce mondial et l'histoire et la constitution de l'état commercial', in: *Autour de l'Abbé Raynal. Genèse et enjeux politiques de l'Histoire de deux Indes*, ed. Antonella Alimento and Gianluigi Goggi (Ferney-Voltaire: Centre international d'étude du XVIIIe siècle, 2017).

[63] See also the introductory chapter in this volume.

[64] See respectively Koen Stapelbroek, 'The Haarlem 1771 Prize Essay on the Restoration of Dutch Trade and the Emergence of the Oeconomische Tak of the Hollandsche Maatschappye der Weetenschappen', in: *The Rise of Economic Societies in the Eighteenth Century. Patriotic Reform in Europe and North America*, ed. Koen Stapelbroek and Jani Marjanen (Basingstoke: Palgrave MacMillan, 2012), 257–284 and Koen Stapelbroek, 'Trade, Treaties and Political Virtue: The Machiavellian Legacy at the End of the Republic', in: *Machiavelli's Heirs. Humanism, Tacitism and Reason of State in the Dutch Republic*, ed. H. W. Blom (Leiden: Brill, forthcoming).

concocted unofficially by Amsterdam regents and merchants, was largely the fruit of their work.[65]

These Dutch 'Patriots' also advocated a Dutch accession to a League of states that acted in opposition to Britain, but it is unclear whether theoretically they preferred the Dutch Republic to join a League of Armed Neutrality, such as was established by Catherine the Great in 1780 and which created tensions that caused the Fourth Anglo-Dutch War,[66] or opted for a commercial confederative alliance that operated as one side within a balance of power.

There was definitely some affinity between Luzac and these 'Patriots'. Unlike Pinto, Luzac did not recognize the British depredations of Dutch ships in the War of American Independence as rightful,[67] although he fiercely opposed the attempts by Dutch merchants to exploit their neutral status in wartime. Luzac judged the interruption of general trade in wartime cost Dutch traders far more than any fleeting extra profits from neutral trade in wartime.[68] What was needed was a secure political structure within which the Dutch enduring culturally based competitive advantage in the international carrying trade was protected.[69]

It appears that what Luzac had in mind was a Dutch accession to the project that Choiseul had developed and that in a different form was continued by Vergennes.[70] In that context fits the rapprochement of the 1780s between Dutch and French diplomacy. Following a curious interaction of offers and demands for a commercial treaty, where the Dutch were initially hoping for a revival of the Utrecht terms, a defensive alliance was

[65] Next to a huge pamphlet debate, NA 1.01.50, inv. 793; 1.10.29, inv. 1464–1465; 1.10.26, inv. 76–83; 3.01.09, inv. 108. For an account and overview of the literature on this episode, Stapelbroek, 'Neutrality and Trade in the Dutch Republic'; also 'Trade, Treaties and Political Virtue'. NA 1.10.26, inv. 11 shows that in 1781–1782 a clandestine attempt to agree a commercial treaty with France inspired an unsuccessful mission to Brest.

[66] NA 1.01.47.27, inv. 500; Stapelbroek, 'Economic Reform and Neutrality' and the references in the previous note.

[67] Luzac joined those who called the English rights discourses chimerical under the pseudonym Reinier Vryaart, *Openhartige brieven, om te dienen tot opheldering en regte kennis van de vaderlandsche historie* (Leiden, 1781–1784), v: 120–121.

[68] Jacques Accarias de Serionne, *La Richesse de la Hollande* (Amsterdam, 1768), ii: 205, which was transformed into Elie Luzac, *Hollands rijkdom, behelzende den oorsprong van de koophandel* (Leiden, 1780–1783).

[69] Cf. Pinto, *Circulation and credit; jealousy of commerce*, 213–214, 220.

[70] See the introductory chapter in this volume.

agreed at Fontainebleau on 10 November 1785 (the day after the peace treaty between Austria and the United Provinces, arranged through Vergennes, was signed at Fontainebleau) that included articles on neutral trade (Article VIII), the most favoured nation clause and the resolution to conclude a Franco-Dutch commercial treaty (Article XIII).[71] What happened in Franco-Dutch trade practice after the conclusion of this treaty and subsequently following the 1787 'Patriot Revolt' when the Triple Alliance—itself a pseudo Family Compact—voided the defensive alliance is unclear. The commercial treaty was never concluded. Yet, it is interesting from a theoretical point of view to note that exactly at the moment that Luzac published his adaptation of Accarias' *Richesse de la Hollande* and when treaties were concluded between Austria, France and Russia (Accarias himself was in the pay of Austria and dedicated his work to Catherine the Great), Pinto in his last (unpublished) writings of the 1780s expressed his distrust of Austrian and Russian initiatives in arbitrating and proposing an international regime of commercial neutrality. Just like in his pamphlets published during the War of American Independence, Pinto showed himself very concerned that the dysfunctional element in the British party-political system that had given rise to chaos and confusion would trigger a European antipathy and punitive desire.[72] The consequences if that desire was acted upon in commercial-political and financial respects would have wider geopolitical consequences that went beyond Britain itself and would backfire upon the entirety of Europe.

In a pamphlet from 1779, Pinto compared the situation to the point in human history when Rome and Carthage battled for global hegemony. The world stood at the crossroads and the outcome of this present war, Pinto stated, was to decide about the future well-being of all nations on earth.[73] It was the same association that was invoked in the declaration of the French Navigation Act of 1793, whose direct aim was the destruction of

[71] NA 3.01.25, inv. 386–389, show Bleiswijk guessing Vergennes' motivations. See also Dumas on this: NA 1.10.26, inv. 22. For the history of the treaty, Christophe Guillaume de Koch and Frédéric Schoell, *Histoire abrégée des traités de paix entre les puissances de l'Europe depuis la paix de Westphalie* (Brussels, 1837), i: 490–491.

[72] Archivio di Stato di Torino, inv. 100, 2a addizione, Olanda, mazzo 4 addizione, fascicolo 2 (anonymous and probably dated too early [1779]). An earlier version is KB: 130 D3/ J, entitled 'Examen impartial des intérêts actuels de la République par rapport à une alliance', dated 1783, attributed to Pinto.

[73] [Isaac de Pinto], *Second discours d'un Bon Hollandais à ses compatriotes* (s.l., 1779), 12.

the Eden–Rayneval treaty, but which meant a lot more:[74] just like 'hatred of Kings and of Carthage founded the constitution of the Roman republic [so] the hatred of […] the English, must consolidate the French constitution'.[75] And while a Dutch history of Rome, also published in 1793, claimed it was 'alleraanmerkelijkst', on the authority of Polybius, that in 507 BC a commercial treaty was concluded between Rome and Carthage, this symbolism was too nuanced for its time.[76] Finally, if the arrangements of Vienna changed anything in shaping a new international regime, it certainly did not prevent Garonne in 1814 and 1817 from presenting a history of Franco-Dutch trade, comparing Vienna as highly similar to Utrecht and proposing a new Franco-Dutch commercial treaty as part of a continental alliance to correct the system that had triumphed.[77]

Koen Stapelbroek is an Academy of Finland Senior Research Fellow at the University of Helsinki and Associate Professor at Erasmus University Rotterdam. He received his PhD from the University of Cambridge (2004), and has published *Love, Self-Deceit and Money. Commerce and Morality in the Early Neapolitan Enlightenment* (2008) and many articles and edited volumes on eighteenth-century political thought. He is completing a monograph on European perceptions of the rise and fall of the Dutch trade republic.

[74] See the chapter by Belissa in this volume.

[75] *American State Papers. Documents, Legislative and Executive, of the Congress of the United States* (Washington: Gales and Seaton, 1833), i: 317. In 1791–1792 an Anglo-Dutch commercial treaty had been projected 1.10.29, inv. 1540.

[76] Martinus Stuart, *Romeinsche geschiedenissen* (Utrecht, 1793), ii: 65–66

[77] N. N. Garonne, *Considérations politiques sur l'état actuel de l'Europe, sur la nécessité de changer le système de nos relations commerciales* (Paris, 1814); *Essai sur la possibilité d'un traité de commerce entre la France et le Royaume des Pays-Bas: tendant à démontrer l'avantage qu'auraient tous les gouvernemens du continent à s'unir entr'eux par des traités* (Gand, 1817); also at the end of AAE MD 137 Hollande; cf. NA 2.05.47, inv. 129 for the Dutch initiative for a commercial treaty with France (though not the kind Garonne had in mind).

The Conditions of Trade in Wartime: Treaties of Commerce and Maritime Law in the Eighteenth Century

Éric Schnakenbourg

Real commercial treaties were first concluded in the Middle Ages mainly in Mediterranean Europe,[1] becoming common practice in the sixteenth century and, to a greater extent, in the seventeenth.[2] While the chief aim of the earliest treaties had been the removal of trade restrictions,[3] by the sixteenth century their primary objective was the defining of the conditions of bilateral exchange. The differences of power between the signatories made each treaty a specific case, whether it dealt with customs tariffs or free trade or wartime shipping regulations. But during the seventeenth

[1] François-Louis Ganshof, *Le Moyen Âge. Histoire des relations internationales du Moyen Âge à 1789*, part 1 (Paris: Hachette, 1994), 52, 114–117.

[2] Stephen Neff, 'Peace and Prosperity: Commercial Aspects of Peacemaking', in: *Peace Treaties and International Law in European History*, ed. Randall Lesaffer (Cambridge: Cambridge University Press, 2004), 367.

[3] Mohamed Ouerfelli, 'Les enjeux commerciaux dans les traités de paix et de commerce entre Pise et les Etats du Maghreb au Moyen Age (XIIe–XIVe siecle)', in: *Les territoires de la Méditerranée XIe–XVIe siècle*, ed. Annliese Nef (Rennes: Presses Universitaires de Rennes, 2013), 205–215.

É. Schnakenbourg (✉)
University of Nantes, France
e-mail: eric.schnakenbourg@univ-nantes.fr

A. Alimento, K. Stapelbroek (eds.), *The Politics of Commercial Treaties in the Eighteenth Century*, DOI 10.1007/978-3-319-53574-6_8

and eighteenth centuries the function of treaties evolved concomitantly with the European governments' increasing interest in commerce, an interest which triggered a remarkable growth in trade. Between 1610 and 1715, for example, France concluded thirty-two international conventions (equal to one every 3.3 years) that related in some way to commerce, but between 1715 and 1789 there were sixty such treaties: one for every 1.2 years.[4] This rise occurred in line with the changing role of commerce in international relations. While in the seventeenth century the world had been seen as an arena in which trade wars could be used to weaken rivals and favour military success,[5] in the eighteenth century commerce often served as a means of drawing nations together, as an expression of cosmopolitanism and as a basis for peace. In this context commercial treaties helped to regulate international rivalries intensified by the 'jealousy of trade',[6] and to protect trade in wartime.

The eighteenth century produced significant theoretical reflections on international relations aimed at denouncing war, promoting commerce and encouraging a legal international order.[7] As a result, trade treaties included provisions that set out the principles, prohibitions, rights and safeguards required by commerce, ensuring that trading was regulated by the law of nations and thereby helping to create a civil society of states. According to the entry on 'Europe' in Jean-Baptiste-René Robinet's

[4] This count is based on Pierre Louis d'Auterive and Ferdinand de Cornot de Cussy, *Recueil des traités de commerce et de la navigation de la France*, 3 vols. (Paris: P. J. Rey, 1844).

[5] Colbert clearly underlined the connection between commercial wars and military struggles at the very heart of the mercantilist doctrine: 'Commerce is the source of finance, and finance is the sinews of war', quoted by Céline Spector, 'Le concept de mercantilisme', *Revue de métaphysique et de morale* 39 (2003), 294. See also Edmund Silberner, *La guerre dans la pensée économique du XVIe au XVIIIe siècle* (Paris: Sirey, 1939), 33–38.

[6] Istvan Hont, *Jealousy of Trade. International Competition and the Nation-State in Historical Perspective* (Cambridge, MA: Harvard University Press, 2005), 5–24. 'Commerce had become one of the main objects which disturb and divide them [the nations and the sovereigns]', wrote Accarias de Sérionne, *Intérêts des nations de l'Europe dévelopés relativement au commerce* (Leyden: Elie Luzac, 1766), vol. 2, 299. All translations of French sources are by the author. See also John Sholvin, 'War and Peace: Trade, International Competition, and Political Economy' in: *Mercantilism Reimagined. Political Economy in Early Modern Britain and Its Empire*, ed. Philip J. Stern and Carl Wennerlind (Oxford: Oxford University Press, 2013), 305–327.

[7] Marc Belissa, *Fraternité universelle et intérêt national (1713–1795): les cosmopolitiques du droit des gens* (Paris: Kimé, 1998).

Dictionnaire universel (1781), the continent was governed by numerous conventions that defined and supported interstate relations.[8] International trade and maritime treaties joined the interstate system and thus were part of broader reflections on how to create lasting peace.

This explains the interest displayed by authors like Gabriel Bonnot de Mably, Emer de Vattel, Eobald Toze and Mathieu-Antoine Bouchaud who investigated how and to what extent trade treaties covered maritime and commercial issues, as well as the range and limits of free trade. Such authors were particularly interested in wartime trade, when the normal business between neutral states was interrupted by belligerents. This chapter examines commercial treaties through the lens of the provisions agreed between those parties, and will explore how philosophers and legal specialists analysed them along with the role of trade in international relations. The aim is to see if the various provisions of these treaties of commerce constituted a sort of international law of commerce that established an order designed to ensure peace between nations or, at least, to cushion the impact of war.

Treaties and the Natural Right to Trade

Trade was of great interest to Enlightenment thinkers,[9] who thought it capable of counteracting the unequal distribution of natural resources and thus contributing to the prosperity of states and human well-being. 'Our century is too Enlightened to need to prove that a nation cannot be happy & flourishing without commerce',[10] declared Mably in 1746. The idea of *doux commerce*, propounded mainly by Montesquieu, spelt out the duty of assistance that the universality of the human race required of all nations, while it also supported the efforts of states seeking peace with their aggressors.[11]

[8] Article 'Europe', in: *Dictionnaire universel des sciences, morale, économique, politique et diplomatique* (London: Libraires associés, 1781), vol. 18, 578.

[9] Michel Bottin, 'Commerce', in: *Dictionnaire européen des Lumières*, ed. Michel Delon (Paris: PUF, 2007), 279–282.

[10] Gabriel Bonnot de Mably, *Le droit public de l'Europe fondé sur les traités* (La Haye: Jean van Duren, 1746), vol. 2, 230.

[11] 'Peace is the natural effect of trade. Two nations who traffic with each other become reciprocally dependent; for if one has an interest in buying, the other has an interest in selling; and thus their union is founded on their mutual necessities', Montesquieu, *De l'esprit des Lois*

Commercial treaties thereby shifted from their seventeenth-century purpose of managing the continual rivalries between countries to that of facilitating trade for the greater good. Thus it became part of a new, broader concept of international relations.

During the decades following the War of the Spanish Succession, there was sharp criticism of war policies that always involved an aggressive approach to commerce. On the contrary, choosing peace was generally emulated, and stimulating trade was considered to be useful for peoples and states alike. Commerce could not flourish without freedom and safety.[12] According to Mably, therefore, the 'considerable' importance of trade for Europe made it necessary 'to submit it to laws'.[13] For Vattel, commercial treaties helped reconcile the general need for free trade and the particular interests of states, which sometimes needed to control or even curb the activities of a rival while supposedly advocating trade expansion.[14] In a manner of speaking, then, the treaties were seen as an agreement that clarified the conditions of commercial exchange, especially in extraordinary situations such as wartime. They served to confirm principles of natural law, to explicate obscure issues, and to mould imperfect natural law into a constraining conventional law.[15] However, as Mably stressed, commercial treaties usually incorporated two types of provision: recurrent general ones, such as the right to carry goods or confiscate cargo, and those dealing with specific circumstances.[16] By harmonizing general principles and individual requirements, the treaties became a valuable frame of reference.

In the late eighteenth century a different concept of commercial treaties became widespread with authors like Jacob Friedrich von Bielfeld, Eobald

[1748] (Paris: Garnier Flammarion, 1979), vol. 2, 10; Céline Spector, *Montesquieu et l'émergence de l'économie politique* (Paris: Honoré Champion, 2006), 181–183.

[12] Simone Meyssonnier, *La balance et l'horloge. La genèse de la pensée libérale en France au XVIIIe siècle* (Montreuil: Éditions de la passion, 1989), 137–157.

[13] Bonnot de Mably, *Le droit public de l'Europe fondé sur les traités*, vol. 2, 270.

[14] Emer de Vattel, *Le droit des gens ou principes de la loi naturelle, appliqués à la conduite & aux affaires des Nations & des souverains* (London: 1758), vol. 1, 274–278. Vattel's opinion on the natural and compulsory character of commerce between nations may also be found in the work of authors such as Charles de La Maillardiére, *Précis du droit des gens, de la guerre, de la paix et des ambassades* (Paris: Quillau, 1775), 78, 82–83, 114–115.

[15] Vattel, *Le droit des gens*, vol. 1, 86–87 and 271–273.

[16] Bonnot de Mably, *Le droit public de l'Europe fondé sur les traités*, vol. 2, 270.

Toze and George Frédéric de Martens reputing them to be political acts that chiefly served the interests of their signatories. Although aspects of natural law remained, such authors contended that a state's interests should be safeguarded by stipulations in treaties.[17] For Bielfeld, treaties were the result of negotiations in which each party used 'all his art & all his skill, to have all the advantages of the negotiation on his side'. The text of the treaty should allow for potential difficulties[18] and the changing character of commerce pointed to the need for expiry dates to avoid later becoming hostage to disadvantageous terms.[19] In the third edition of his *Droit public de l'Europe fondé sur les traités* (1764), Mably argued against seventeenth-century commercial treaties, which contained 'eternal commitments', and in favour of those concluded after the Peace of Utrecht, which were limited to two or three decades.[20]

Most of the commercial treaties from Louis XIV's reign onwards were concluded alongside peace accords. This was the case for those signed by England and Spain in 1630, 1667 and 1713, by France and the United Provinces in 1678, 1697 and 1713, and for the peace treaty brokered between France and Spain in 1659, which contained no less than twenty-three articles on trade and shipping.[21] The simultaneity of agreements on peace and trade shows the will to re-establish a normal state of relations between two countries that had just finished fighting each other. In the eighteenth century, however, the distinction between these two kinds of treaties revolved around the belief that trading nations should live in amity. Peace treaties therefore served to secure a lasting cessation of hostilities, while commercial treaties settled all the thorny business issues.

[17] Eobald Toze, *La liberté de la navigation et du commerce des nations neutres, pendant la guerre considéré selon le droit des gens universel, de celui de l'Europe et les traités. Essai historique et juridique pour servir d'éclaircissement aux différends entre les puissances belligérantes et les États neutres au sujet du commerce maritime* (London and Amsterdam: 1780), 29; George Frédéric de Martens, *Précis du droit des gens moderne de l'Europe* (Gottingen: de Dietrich, 1789), vol. 1, 171.

[18] Jacob Friedrich von Bielfeld, *Les institutions politiques* (La Haye: Pierre Gosse, 1760), vol. 1, 307.

[19] Bielfeld, *Les institutions politiques*, vol. 1, 307; Vattel, *Le droit des gens*, vol. 1, 278.

[20] Bonnot de Mably, *Le droit public de l'Europe fondé sur les traités*, vol. 2, 563.

[21] Henri Vast, *Les grands traités du règne de Louis XIV* (Paris: Alphonse Picard, 1893), vol. 1, 97–107.

In eighteenth-century thought commercial treaties not only established mutual rights and reviewed trade conditions but also formed a framework in which natural law defined how states should coexist, particularly on the high seas where there was no sovereignty. Thus by regulating international sociability they reduced the risk of conflict between competing states. This interpretation no longer regarded commerce as a natural, peaceful relationship, but rather as one of intense rivalry between powers: 'a jealousy of trade'. Commercial treaties were therefore indispensable in wartime, which wreaked havoc on free trade. Indeed, the escalation of marine warfare, which involved attacks on merchant fleets, necessitated an expansion of the functions of the treaties.

Treaties of Commerce and Maritime Law in Wartime

The number of treaty provisions relating to maritime law and neutral countries rose in the first half of the eighteenth century,[22] reflecting changes in the conduct of marine warfare. After the Anglo-Dutch wars of the 1652–1674 period, enemy merchant ships were attacked to a degree hitherto unknown,[23] and in subsequent conflicts between France, England and the United Provinces such episodes became common. As George Clark has stated: 'The more of the enemy's ships you captured or sank and the fewer of your own you lost, the better for your trade: that seemed to be the gist of the matter.'[24] In consequence of this, neutral shipping found itself in a precarious situation since it undermined a

[22] However, the ratio changed according to the identity of the signatories. Whereas only 13–15 per cent of the articles of the Franco-Dutch and Franco-British treaties of commerce of 1713 dealt with the conditions of wartime commerce, the proportion reached two-thirds in the Franco-Hanseatic Treaty of 1716; Éric Schnakenbourg, 'La guerre de Succession d'Espagne et la réflexion française sur la navigation neutre', presented at the workshop *La paix d'Utrecht (1713): enjeux économiques, maritimes et commerciaux*, organized by Guillaume Hanotin and Géraud Poumarède, Bordeaux, December 2013.

[23] Leos Müller, 'Nordic Neutrals and Anglo-French Wars, 1689–1815', presented at The Northern Mediterranean, XIVth International Economic History Congress, Helsinki, 2006, www.helsinki.fi/iehc2006/papers1/Muller36.pdf, 4; Steve Murdoch, Andrew Little and A. D. M. Forte, 'Scottish Privateering, Swedish Neutrality and Prize Law in the Third Anglo-Dutch War, 1672–1674', *Forum navale* 59 (2003), 37–65.

[24] George Clark, 'War Trade and Trade War, 1701–1713', *Economic History Review* 2 (1928), 267.

belligerent's efforts to paralyse an enemy's economy. Commercial treaties therefore began to establish safe-conduct measures for non-belligerents in periods of war, the only time when a country could legally disrupt another's trade. The priority was to limit damage to belligerents alone. Thus, as George Frédéric de Martens observed, commercial treaties no longer had the exclusive aim of furthering economic interests[25] but also made rulings on issues at the core of neutral maritime trade, such as contraband and goods of warring nations transported under neutral flags.

Since the ability of neutral countries to transport goods belonging to belligerent powers depended on safeguards, these duly became a recurrent proviso of commercial treaties. At the end of the Middle Ages, the rule known as the 'Consulate of the Sea' decided the fate of seized cargo on the basis of provenance, which meant that enemy goods were a legitimate target while those of neutrals were untouchable.[26] This rule could still be found in a few treaties of the seventeenth century but by then it had been superseded by the principle whereby enemy merchandise conveyed under neutral flags was protected while the cargo of neutrals transported by enemy vessels was lawful prey. Such a rule had in fact existed since the end of the Middle Ages in Northern Europe, and had spread thanks to the growing commercial influence of the Dutch. Shipping, trade and neutrality were so important to the Dutch that they took great care about whose goods they carried.[27]

The treaties of commerce concluded by the United Provinces with France (1646), Spain (1650) and England (1674) contained explicit safeguards for cargo on neutral ships.[28] The English, however, were not always so clear: they accepted the principle of 'free ships, free goods' in the treaties signed with Portugal (1654), France (1667) and the United Provinces (1674),[29] but took a different position with Sweden (1661) and Denmark (1670),

[25] Martens, *Précis du droit des gens moderne de l'Europe*, vol. 1, 179.

[26] Stanley S. Jados, *Consulate of the Sea and Related Documents* (Tuscaloosa: Alabama University Press, 1975), chapter 276: 'A Merchantman Intercepted by an Armed Vessel', 191–194.

[27] Duco Hellema, *Neutraliteit & Vrijhandel. De geschiedenis van den Nederlandse buitenlandse betrekkingen* (Utrecht: Het Spectrum, 2001), 19.

[28] Jean Dumont, *Corps universel diplomatique du droit des gens* (Amsterdam, 1728), vol. 6, part 1, 342 and 571.

[29] George Chalmers, *A collection of treaties between Great Britain and other powers*, 2 vols. (London: J. Stockdale, 1790), vol. 1, 177 for the Anglo-Dutch treaty and vol. 2, 280 for the Anglo-Portuguese one. For the Franco-English treaty see P.-L. d'Hauterive and F. de Cussy,

affirming that the transportation of enemy merchandise 'to the prejudice of the other confederate' could justify its seizure.[30] The provisions of the Anglo-Russian treaties of 1734 and 1766 were less explicit. Free trade was reasserted and privateers were ordered to act with the Russians 'as far as may be, [accordingly to] the principles and maxims of the law of nations, that are generally acknowledged' (Art. 10 of the treaty of 1766).[31] The appeal to good faith and the law of nations in this provision was peculiar given that the British did not apply the same rule with all foreign nations and the fate of enemy goods thus depended on the nationality of the neutral vessel. Rather than expound a clear law, the different provisions of the various treaties merely formed an incoherent hotchpotch of bilateral agreements.

Although during the eighteenth century the sanctity of the neutral flag was not always observed in practice, there were no new treaties of commerce with provisions allowing the sequestration of enemy cargo carried by a non-belligerent. This reflected an evolution in legal doctrine, since most of the scholars interested in law of nations theory endorsed the inviolability of neutral ships. During the seventeenth century only a few authors, notably Hugo Grotius and Richard Zouche, were interested in the fate of neutral merchandise found aboard enemy ships, but in the eighteenth century the main theorists of that law (Bynkershoek, Abreu, Hübner, Galiani, but not Vattel) acknowledged that enemy goods were protected if transported under a neutral flag but that an entire cargo could be confiscated if shipped under enemy colours.[32] The provisions of the treaties and contemporary thought had converged because of two factors. Firstly, many Enlightenment thinkers shared the ambition of making shipping and trade neutral activities by keeping them separate and protecting them from the impact of war.[33] Secondly, safeguarding cargoes under

Recueil des traités de commerce et de la navigation de la France (Paris: P. J. Rey, 1844), vol. 2, 28–29.

[30] Chalmers, *A collection of treaties*, vol. 1, 53 and 86–87.

[31] Chalmers, *A collection of treaties*, 7; Charles Jenkinson, *A collection of treaties of peace, commerce and alliance between Great Britain and other powers from the year 1619 to 1734* (London: J. Debrett, 1781), vol. 1, 77.

[32] Éric Schnakenbourg, *Entre la guerre et la paix. Neutralité et relations internationales, XVII–XVIIIe siècles* (Rennes: Presses Universitaires de Rennes, 2013), 96–99.

[33] Koen Stapelbroek, 'Universal Society, Commerce and the Rights of Neutral Trade: Martin Hübner, Emer de Vattel and Ferdinando Galiani', in: *Universalism in International Law and*

a neutral flag reduced the grounds of dispute between neutrals and belligerents by limiting the range of suspect goods and thereby reducing the duration of on-board searches: such searches thereafter came to be a hunt for contraband, as mutually defined by the two parties.

In the seventeenth century the notion of contraband turned into a key issue of commercial treaties, which dealt with it in divergent ways. Hence the need, and the sustained effort, to define contraband goods precisely. While most French commercial treaties excluded naval supplies from contraband, those concluded in 1655 with the Hanseatic cities and in 1742 with Denmark included them.[34] On the English side, however, only a handful of seventeenth-century treaties considered that sort of merchandise to be contraband, and the treaty concluded with the United Provinces in 1674 explicitly allowed freedom to trade in naval supplies even in wartime.[35] But English treaties with Sweden (1661) and Denmark (1670) actually defined contraband as military supplies and added, in the Danish case, '*aut alia bello gerundo apta et necessaria*'.[36] On the whole, even though there had been no general ban on trading in naval supplies during a period of war, the provisions of the main European commercial treaties of the seventeenth and eighteenth centuries showed a clear tendency to treat them as contraband,[37] the 1725 treaty between the emperor and Spain being the single exception. Legal thinkers were more uncertain. Mably and Abreu relied upon the terms of commercial treaties to defend the free trade

Political Philosophy, ed. Petter Korkman and Virpi Mäkinen (Helsinki: Collegium for Advanced Studies, vol. 4, February 2008), 63–89, available online.

[34] Article 2 of the Franco-Hanseatic treaty of 1655 included riggings and canvas in the contraband category, but the treaty of 1716 between the same powers permitted the transport of naval supplies. Article 26 of the Franco-Danish treaty of 1742 added hemp and tar to contraband goods; Hauterive and Cussy, *Recueil des traités de commerce et de la navigation de la France*, vol. 3, 404–405 and vol. 1, 318.

[35] Dumont, *Corps universel diplomatique*, vol. 5, part 2, 480; Chalmers, *A collection of treaties*, vol. 1, 179.

[36] '[. . .] and other items equipment necessary for war', Laurs Laursen, ed., *Danmark-Norges Traktater 1523–1750* (Copenhagen: Carlsbergfondet, 1923), vol. 6, 319.

[37] Carl Kulsrud, *Maritime Neutrality to 1780. A History of Main Principles Governing Neutrality and Belligerency to 1780* (Boston, MA: Little, Brown and Company, 1936), 284. The Turks also regarded naval stores as contraband goods, 'Mémoire sur le commerce de la mer Noire par le comte de Vergennes', Constantinople, 29 January 1767, AAE [Archives des Affaires Étrangères, La Courneuve], MD [Mémoires et Documents], Russia, vol. 7, fol. 198.

of naval supplies, while other authors, like Bynkershoek, Vattel and Hübner, considered the question from the point of view of natural law and the law of war and therefore formed a more balanced opinion and allowed that, under certain circumstances, some naval supplies could be regarded as contraband.[38]

The many treaty provisions concerning the fate of sequestered cargoes and contraband goods, as well as the concern of several authors for such matters, underlined the importance of defining neutral rights. And the treaties helped to mark out the line between war and peace, even while ongoing conflicts showed the boundary between belligerency and neutrality to be often blurred.

Treaties and the Jurisprudence of International Commerce

The belief that recurring treaty provisions of a similar nature constituted a kind of de facto law for European nations gained widespread acceptance in the first half of the eighteenth century, as shown by the publication of collections of international treaties.[39] In his *Droit public de l'Europe fondé sur les traités*, first published in 1746, Mably set out to study the 'common law of nations on seas and the general conditions which are the basis for all treaties of shipping and commerce'. He intended to make his work distinctive by providing an 'accurate analysis' of treaty dispositions dealing with diplomacy and primary legal principles so as to deduce their general order and meaning. He observed the diffusion of certain principles, such as the definition of contraband as military supplies and the ban on neutral shipping entering a blockaded harbour, but he did not take a clear position on safeguarding enemy merchandise transported on neutral vessels, despite this being specified in most treaties.[40] In contrast, other

[38] Schnakenbourg, *Entre la guerre et la paix*, 103–111.

[39] The first major publication was the *Codex Juris gentium diplomaticus* by Leibniz in 1693, and the most famous is the *Corps universel diplomatique du droit des gens* by Jean Dumont published in eight volumes between 1726 and 1731.

[40] Bonnot de Mably, *Le droit public de l'Europe fondé sur les traités*, vol. 2, VI, 270 and 272–275. However, Mably judged as lawful the seizure of neutrals' goods under an enemy flag, which theoretically meant that the non-belligerent flag was a guarantee of the safeguarding of the cargo.

contemporary authors, such as the Dutchman Cornelius van Bynkershoek and the Spaniard Felix Joseph de Abreu, used a similar approach based on the scrutiny of the provisions included in the main international treaties of commerce to argue for the removal of naval supplies and foodstuffs from the definition of war contraband.[41]

This interest in the main principles of commercial treaties came to the fore in disagreements on practical outcomes. A famous example of this is the dispute that arose between Britain and Prussia during the War of the Austrian Succession. In the absence of a treaty of commerce between the two countries, the British government assured the Prussians that the neutrality of their ships would be observed in accordance with the rules embedded in the treaties concluded between the maritime powers.[42] Thus, in adherence to the provisions of the Anglo-Dutch treaty of 1674, Frederick II allowed his subjects to carry naval supplies and French goods, but after 1745 a number of Prussian ships bound for France loaded with timber and other wares were seized and condemned by British courts. Then, in 1748, eighteen Prussian ships and thirty-three other vessels freighted partially or totally by Prussian subjects were seized by British privateers.[43]

Following these losses, a heated dispute broke out regarding what principles of international law existed between two countries that had not negotiated a bilateral commercial treaty. The British claimed that since no commitment had been made to permit the transportation of enemy merchandise, the instructions given to privateers to treat naval supplies as contraband were legitimate.[44] The Prussians, on the other hand, based their protests on the principle of free trade enshrined in

[41] Cornelius van Bynkershoek, *A Treatise of the law of war* (translation of 'De rebus bellicis' book I of *Quaestiones Juris Publici*, 1737) (Philadelphia, 1810), 76–77; Felix Joseph de Abreu y Bertodano, *Traité juridico-politique sur les prises maritimes et sur les moyens qui doivent concourir pour rendre ces prises légitimes* (1st Spanish edition 1746; French translation, Paris, 1758), 140.

[42] Andrié to Frédéric II, 29 May and 9 June 1744; Charles de Martens, *Causes célèbres du droit des gens* (Leipzig: Brockhaus, 1858), vol. 2, 98–100.

[43] The list of arrested ships can be found in 'Exposition des motifs fondés sur le droit des gens universellement reçu . . . ' (Berlin, 1752), 37, 59.

[44] Frederic Pratt, *The law of contraband of war* (London: Benning, 1856), 109–115; Reginald Marsden, ed., *Law and Custom of the Sea* (London: Publications of the Naval Record Society, 1916), vol. 2, 336–337 and 429.

the law of nations, which enabled them to argue for a narrow definition of contraband and the sanctity of the neutral flag.[45] According to them, the fact that the provisions made in all existing treaties of commerce converged around the same principles inferred that they amounted to a general law applicable to all nations. Consequently, the Prussians restricted their definition of contraband goods to gunpowder, weapons, cannons and ammunition, and asserted their right to carry French goods.[46] The controversy finally ended in 1756 when the British agreed to compensate the Prussian merchants for their losses.

France adopted similar reasoning in their negotiations with the British in the hope of receiving reparation for French property confiscated from Dutch ships during the War of the Austrian Succession. In 1753, in his *Mémoire sur les prises de mer*, the French Secretary of State for Foreign Affairs insisted that the protection of cargo under a neutral flag had to be acknowledged in accordance with 'the uniform provisions of the treaties which could perhaps be considered as a kind of jurisprudence accepted by the European powers', a point equally applicable to the definition of contraband.[47] The same idea was used in Sweden during the Seven Years War, when the Swedish government declared that the accumulation of corresponding provisions in international treaties created 'a kind of general convention in Europe'.[48] This cumulative and analytic construal of treaty provisions allowed these parties to extrapolate a general law from practice, since the provisions converged. In other words, the bilateral commitments, when taken together, were seen to provide the raw material out of which a general law on neutral shipping and trade could be moulded.

This approach changed during the eighteenth century through the influence of advocates of the liberalization of trade and because of the outbreak of the Seven Years War. In 1753, the publication of the article

[45] Friedrich Ehrenreich Behmer, 'Exposition des motifs fondés sur le droit des gens universellement reçu . . . ', 18–19 and 24–25. Behmer came back to this affair in a later publication, *Observation du droit de la nature et des gens, touchant la capture et la détention des vaisseaux et effets neutres en temps de guerre, jusqu'à quel point elle doit être censée licite* (Hamburg, 1771), 4–10.

[46] Ernest Satow, *The Silesian Loan and Frederick the Great* (Oxford: Clarendon Press, 1915), 22.

[47] 'Mémoire concernant les prises sur mer', 20 April 1753, by Saint Contest, AAE, MD, France, vol. 2021, fos. 183–184.

[48] Riksarkivet [Stockholm], Diplomatica, Gallica, vol. 403, report to the ambassador of Naples, of Sardinia, of Venice and to the Duke of Choiseul, 10 December 1759.

'Commerce' in the second volume of the *Encyclopédie*, and the French translation of the *British Merchant* (under the title *Le Négotiant Anglais, Ou Traduction Libre du Livre intitulé The British Merchant*), both by Véron de Forbonnais, opened up a new era of thinking about trade in general and commercial treaties in particular. The author emphasized that it was in France's interest to conclude treaties of commerce, which played an important role in the field of international relations.[49] At the end of the Seven Years War, the French condemned Britain's 'tyranny of the seas'[50] because of the superiority of its navy and in this context the establishment of comprehensive international maritime law was seen as a potential obstacle to the worldwide 'despotism' that the British was seeking to impose. For these reasons, the freedom of neutral shipping and trade had to be seen as a key element of treaties of commerce, leading the reviewer of Vattel's *Droit des gens* (1758), in the May 1759 issue of the *Journal de Commerce*, to reproach Vattel for having conceded too many rights to belligerents.[51] In the following year, however, reviews of Martin Hübner's *De La saisie des Batimens Neutres* published in the February 1760 issue of the *Journal de Trévoux* and in three issues of the *Journal de Commerce* (March, April, May 1760) praised the clarity of the text and declared it to be a touchstone for the law of neutrality.[52]

The increase of provisions included in treaties of commerce created a melange of bilateral agreements that impeded comprehensive thinking about an international organization of trade. A holistic approach of that kind was, nevertheless, precisely what Mably had in mind in the third edition of his *Droit public de l'Europe fondé sur les traités*, published in 1764. In this, he reflected further on a law of international commerce based on the treaties and studied their ill-defined commitments, albeit this

[49] Antonella Alimento, 'Beyond the Treaty of Utrecht: Véron de Forbonnais's French Translation of the *British Merchant* (1753)', *History of European Ideas* 40 (2014), 1044–1066.

[50] Schnakenbourg, *Entre la guerre et la paix*, 219–222.

[51] *Journal de Commerce*, May 1759, 41–60.

[52] *Journal de Trévoux ou Anonyme. Mémoires pour l'histoire des sciences et des beaux-arts*, February 1760, 393 and *Journal de Commerce*, March 1760, 89–126; April 1760, 46–70; May 1760, 53–76. Éric Schnakenbourg, 'From a Right of War to a Right of Peace: Martin Hübner's Contribution to the Reflection on Neutrality in the Eighteenth Century', in: *War, Trade and Neutrality. Europe and the Mediterranean in the Seventeenth and Eighteenth Centuries*, ed. Antonella Alimento (Milan: Franco Angeli, 2011), 203–216.

time he also took account of new developments inspired by the recently concluded war. He wrote about the 'Empire of the seas', favoured the neutralization of trade in wartime and denounced privateering;[53] furthermore, in the light of recent events he endorsed liberalization as a prerequisite for trade development. Previously, in his *Principes des négociations* of 1757, he had asserted that commercial treaties should only include provisions based on the law of nations that were aimed at 'strengthening the freedom of seas and shipping'. The creation of a general framework that would assist the flourishing of trade should, he then thought, be the only objective of the treaties.[54] Human greed had, however, led inevitably to a great number of obligations being inserted in the treaties that multiplied prohibitions on commercial exchange,[55] and so, instead of creating propitious conditions for trade, the treaties acted as constraints. In the field of commerce, Mably recommended listing the frequently used provisions that had, by constant repetition, 'acquired the same authority between nations as the civil laws between the citizens in their common country'.[56] In general, criticisms voiced in the 1760s focused not so much on the actual contents of the treaties as on their usage, either because they made too heavy an impact or because they were not applied in the spirit originally intended. The issue at stake was not whether to annul such treaties, but rather how to use them wisely in order to facilitate the liberalization of trade.

The changing attitude towards commercial treaties in the 1750s and 1760s belonged to a broader reflection on how to transform bilateral agreements into components of an international order. Mathieu-Antoine Bouchaud's *Théorie des traités de commerce entre les nations* (1777) was written with this aim in mind.[57] Although he was not the first author to reflect on commercial treaties, he was the first to devote

[53] Bonnot de Mably, *Le droit public de l'Europe fondé sur les traités*, 422–428, 467–472.

[54] Gabriel Bonnot de Mably, *Des principes des négociations, pour servir d'introduction au Droit public de l'Europe fondé sur les traités* (1757), ed. Marc Bélissa (Paris: Kimé, 2001), 147–148.

[55] Bonnot de Mably, *Le droit public de l'Europe fondé sur les traités*, 458, 561–563.

[56] Bonnot de Mably, *Le droit public de l'Europe fondé sur les traités*, v.

[57] Mathieu-Antoine Bouchaud, *Théorie des traités de commerce entre les nations* (Paris: Veuve Duchesne, 1777). It is sometimes possible to find 1773 as the date of publication, but there was no edition in that year. It seems that 1777 was the actual year of the original edition.

an entire book—490 pages of main text and forty in the appendix—exclusively to the subject. A man of letters and friend of d'Alembert, Bouchaud (1719–1804) had had four articles concerning ecclesiastical and canon law[58] published in the *Encyclopédie*, but after receiving sharp criticisms for them, he severed relations with the main philosophers of his time and devoted himself to the study of Roman jurisprudence, becoming a professor of law in 1768.

In 1774, he became the first professor of the chair of Law of Nature and of Nations established in the Collège de France.[59] His *Théorie des traités de commerce entre les nations* was his sole study of the law of nations, and he seemed to have worked on it with little enthusiasm. The work was at first intended to form part of the first volume of his 'Mémoires', published by the Collège de France, but as the text grew in length he decided to make it a book on its own, not least because he felt that the topic had never been adequately investigated.[60] Unlike other authors of this period, like Mably, who published a fourth edition of his *Droit public de l'Europe fondé sur les traités* in 1776, Bouchaud did not base his reasoning primarily on the provisions of important commercial treaties. For him, international agreements were secondary and the sum and substance of his sources were historical and legal books from three categories of authors: those of antiquity (Thucydides, Cicero, Virgil and Polybius), those from the seventeenth century (Grotius, Zouche and Marquard) and some of his contemporaries. Of the last-mentioned he quoted Johan Mascov, author of a brief study on commercial treaties,[61] Bynkershoek, Réal de Curban and, in particular, Mably.

Bouchaud held that the prime purpose of commercial treaties was to confirm the natural rights of commerce: freedom, safety and ease of

[58] The articles were 'Concile', 'Décret', 'Décrétales' and 'Décrétales (fausses)'.

[59] The biographical information on Mathieu-Antoine Bouchaud can be found in Frank A. Kafker, *The Encyclopedists as Individuals: A Biographical Dictionary of the Authors of the Encyclopédie* (Oxford: Voltaire Foundation, 1988), 45–47; *Biographie universelle ancienne et moderne* (Paris: Michaud frères, 1812), vol. 5, 263–266; 'Notice historique sur la vie et les ouvrages de M. Bouchaud', *Magasin encyclopédique, ou Journal des sciences, des lettres et des arts* (April 1805), 318–332.

[60] Bouchaud, *Théorie des traités de commerce entre les nations*, vii–viii. In his '*avertissement*' Bouchaud told his readers that he wrote his book to fulfil his duties as a professor law of nature and nations, but he did not highlight the importance of his topic.

[61] *De Foederibus Commerciorum*, 1735, republished in 1751, only fifty pages long.

trade.[62] They had to be effective in reminding people of the main principles underpinning commerce between civilized nations, defending them from states inclined to neglect those values in pursuit of their own interests.[63] He regretted that most of the authors who had studied commercial treaties had attempted to further their own countries' advantages, but nevertheless accepted that the basic principles of trade should be subject to some restrictions, including two at the heart of neutral trade: the definition of contraband and the question of the nationality of a ship and its cargo.

Bouchaud began by trying to justify the ban on a neutral trading with a belligerent, not because the activity would be contrary to the legitimate objective of harming the enemy, but rather because of the risks involved for neutral merchants.[64] He then studied the goods forbidden to neutrals, a 'question which had raised strong quarrels between Kings and Republics, and these quarrels had often degenerated into a bloody war'. After analysing several examples and concluding that individual cases did not permit the deduction of a general rule, he returned to Grotius' classic tripartite division of merchandise (those used only in war, those of no use in war, those used in both wartime and peacetime). The third category (foodstuffs, money, naval supplies) was the most problematic. Bouchaud discussed Grotius' assertion of the legitimacy of seizing neutral merchandise of no use in war and arrived at a clear rule: that all items which could strengthen the enemy or help him to bolster his defences could be seized lawfully.[65] Although Bouchaud did not quote him, his opinion was close to Vattel's when he wrote that neutrals should not deliver any goods—such as naval supplies—that were likely to render a warring party 'formidable'.[66]

[62] Bouchaud, *Théorie des traités de commerce entre les nations*, 103, 133, 411.

[63] 'The reciprocal need of good offices, must not inspire a blind confidence in the good faith of nations', Bouchaud, *Théorie des traités de commerce entre les nations*, 31.

[64] Bouchaud, *Théorie des traités de commerce entre les nations*, 246–247.

[65] 'Yet, who can deny, that foodstuff, money, and ships and all useful material for their fitting, does not less contribute to the increasing of enemy forces than a supply of weapon. Consequently, nothing is more lawful than the possibility of intercepting these merchandise', Bouchaud, *Théorie des traités de commerce entre les nations*, 277–278. The only exception admitted by the author is the explicit renunciation on which two countries agree.

[66] Vattel, *Le droit des gens*, vol. 2, 88.

Bouchaud's views on contraband were less favourable to neutrals than the provisions of the commercial treaties, which generally did not include foodstuffs, money and naval supplies in their definition of it.[67] The connection between a ship's nationality and the fate of its sequestered cargo (contraband excepted) was a major issue for Bouchaud. He denounced the 'hostile infection' rule, which permitted the seizure of a neutral ship and its cargo if any enemy goods were found on board. He then dealt with neutral merchandise carried under the flag of the enemy, asserting that there was no justification for confiscation: neither the nationality of the owner, nor the nature of merchandise, nor the simple fact of it being onboard a belligerent ship gave grounds for it. On the other hand, since the law of war allowed for the sequestration of all enemy goods, the neutral flag offered no protection.[68] Bouchaud continued to follow the rules of the 'Consulate of the Sea', also adhered to by the British, and it must be stressed that he stood in contrast to the prevailing tendency of his time, when the 'free ships, free goods' rule was applied generally as, for example, in the Franco-American treaty of 1778.[69]

Bouchaud's opinion on the two major issues relating to neutral shipping was also held in opposition to the general doctrinal trend and to French jurisprudence, and the nature of his thinking explains why: he was interested in developing an overall theory for commercial treaties, one for which 'the principles of good reason and of universal jurisprudence'[70] were fundamental. Indeed, the originality of Bouchaud's little-known work lies not in its choice of subject matter, but in the author's determination to tackle it at a theoretical level. He did not adopt a 'from below' approach, as his contemporaries usually did, identifying comparable treaty provisions and trying to work out a general rule from them, but instead he began 'from above', considering a priori the commitments that should be present in every treaty. He frequently based his thinking on Roman

[67] Article 26 of the Franco-American treaty of friendship and commerce, 6 February 1778, clearly excluded foodstuff and naval stores from contraband; Hauterive and Cussy, *Recueil des traités de commerce et de la navigation de la France*, vol. 1, 471–473.

[68] Bouchaud, *Théorie des traités de commerce entre les nations*, 365–367.

[69] Article 25 of the Franco-American treaty of 1778 acknowledged the safeguard of enemy properties under a neutral flag; Hauterive and Cussy, *Recueil des traités de commerce et de la navigation de la France*, vol. 1, 470–471. For Vattel see *Le droit des gens*, vol. 2, 60.

[70] Bouchaud, *Théorie des traités de commerce entre les nations*, 273.

jurisprudence in order to determine the fair use of commercial treaties, but unlike other authors, such as Hübner, he gave little thought to the practical consequences of his conclusions. As the title of his book indicates, he was concerned above all with the abstract principles required for an ideal treaty of commerce so as to devise a single model that would bring durable equilibrium to the field of international relations generally, and even to wartime trade.

From the Seven Years War onwards, the contradictory claims of neutrals and belligerents led to a call for clearer rules on marine warfare. Accarias de Sérionne denounced the heavy losses suffered by neutral shipping because of the sometimes inconsistent constraints imposed by warring states, and hoped that one day it would be possible to develop 'a real code of humanity [. . .] able to form a basis for the tranquillity and the prosperity of empires'.[71] One of the most enthusiastic supporters of the consolidation of maritime law was the Mecklenburg jurist Eobald Toze, who on the whole was sceptical about commercial treaties, declaring that they did not facilitate trade but instead hindered it by imposing so many boundaries that liberty of commerce 'had almost been annihilated or at least truly reduced'.[72]

Toze believed that even though treaties obligated only their signatories, the reiteration of common principles meant they ended up being deemed 'universally acknowledged' and helped 'to prove the European law of nations about commercial matters'.[73] For this reason, he supported the Prussians in their dispute with the British, judging that the right to seize enemy property transported under a neutral flag had in reality been abolished. To his mind, the British government could only justify its seizures with reference to two treaties (1661 with Sweden and 1670 with Denmark), while no less than thirty treaties stated the opposite: 'It is consequently true that these ones made the rule and the former the exception, all the more since these ones are new and the former old.'[74] In line with this reasoning, Toze established forty points common to the treaties of commerce that he thought ought to form the basic legal tenets regarding neutral shipping and trade. These included the rigidly restricted

[71] Accarias de Sérionne, *Intérêts des nations de l'Europe dévelopés relativement au commerce*, 51.

[72] Toze, *La liberté de la navigation et du commerce des nations neutres*, 74.

[73] Toze, *La liberté de la navigation et du commerce des nations neutres*, 109–110.

[74] Toze, *La liberté de la navigation et du commerce des nations neutres*, 193–197.

definition of contraband as military supplies, the safeguarding of an enemy's goods on neutral ships and the right to seize all cargo carried under enemy flags. In other words, he asserted the 'free ships, free goods' doctrine in the name of principles that had consistently been recognized by all the maritime powers since the mid-seventeenth century.[75]

Toze's thinking was closely linked to the contemporary context of the early years of the American Revolutionary War, during which the British tried to restrict neutral trade and shipping. His work, however, was not simply a reaction to events, since he wanted neither to defend the liberty of neutrals caught up in that conflict nor neutral rights as a whole. His objective was instead to ascertain what conditions were required for a lasting commercial and political balance among the European powers. For this reason, he complained that the provisions of commercial treaties were often contrary 'to equality and justice as well', since they were the result of negotiations in which the stronger party could impose its will on the weaker.[76] His desire was to inject some cohesiveness into these numerous provisions in order to stabilize the international system.

In the second half of the eighteenth century it became widely accepted that the accumulation of treaties aided the emergence of a general rule. This was not just the opinion of legal experts, for it was also expressed in a report sent to Sartine, the French Secretary of State for the Navy, during the American Revolutionary War, by an anonymous author who asserted that 'particular treaties together make a universal code' and that public law 'is only the result of similar dispositions included in the greatest number of particular conventions'. The minister himself reckoned that taken together treaties enabled the 'establishment of a rule and a kind of common law'.[77] George Frédéric de Martens, the most important compiler of treaties in the late eighteenth century, considered new laws to be based on the 'presumed' will of states as expressed in parallel clauses of commercial treaties.[78]

[75] Toze, *La liberté de la navigation et du commerce des nations neutres*, 111–123.

[76] Toze, *La liberté de la navigation et du commerce des nations neutres*, 108.

[77] 'Mémoire sur la navigation des neutres', AN [Archives Nationales, Paris], Marine, B7/515, fos. 38–39, 27 November 1778 and AAE, B1/63, fol. 31, Sartine à Leseurre, 16 January 1780.

[78] Martens, *Précis du droit des gens moderne de l'Europe*, 50 and 69. In 1801, in the second edition, Martens stressed that the presumed will of states emerges from 'the uniformity of the acts already existing till now with similar cases', Martens, *Précis du droit des gens moderne de l'Europe*, 79.

Applying this reasoning to the conditions of wartime trade, he observed that commercial treaties had been abolished (with a few exceptions), as had the seizure of ships carrying contraband goods, and took this as the basis of the principle of '*frey Schiff frey Gut, verfallen schiff verfallen Gut*' thinking that it could be claimed by all neutral nations.

With Bouchard's expanded conception of contraband and rejection of the protection of the neutral flag on the one hand, and the opposing views taken by Toze and Martens on the other, it may seem that the eighteenth century ended without any agreement on the role of commercial treaties in the formation of maritime law. Nevertheless, the three authors shared the same ambition: that of establishing a norm to serve as a point of reference so that all commercial treaties would converge on the same general principles. This was deemed to be the only way of providing a uniform code of procedure for the protection of neutral trade and shipping which would displace the heterogeneity of the provisions in bilateral agreements. Fundamentally, the aim was to rethink international trade relations so that they would no longer be driven by the self-interest of individual nations and the principle of 'might makes right', but instead be guided by genuine equality that would render impossible the concession of specific advantages to one particular nation. According to Mably, powerful nations took advantage of their privileges to create monopolies, while nations that felt left out of the spoils resorted to threats to improve their situation. Moreover, the concessions initially granted with reluctance by a weaker state often became a law, to the detriment of that state's economy and the benefit of its competitors.[79] Clearly, a consistent trade framework was required to limit disputes between commercial nations, and also to ensure that each of them remained masters of their own trade.

The calls to establish a universal maritime code may appear to have been as fruitless as the earlier, forgotten plans of authors who had dreamed of limiting the damage of war or guaranteeing respect for the rights of neutrals. On 8 March 1780, however, the Russian Empress Catherine II issued a declaration to the courts of London, Versailles and Madrid containing a set of principles that formed the groundwork of the League of Armed Neutrality.[80] In terms of the focus of this

[79] Bonnot de Mably, *Le droit public de l'Europe fondé sur les traités*, 562.

[80] These principles were: the liberty of neutral shipping, the safeguard of enemy goods under neutral flags (contraband excepted), the definition of contraband goods accordingly to the valid treaties, and the ban on neutral ships from entering a blockaded harbour. See James

chapter, the foundations of her claims are interesting, for they were based on 'the principles imbedded in the primitive law on which every nation is entitled to rely, and which the belligerent Powers cannot ignore without violating the laws of neutrality, and without disavowing the maxims they have adopted, notably, in different treaties and public engagements'.[81] In the name of the universality of the treaty provisions, Catherine II justified not only the right of her subjects but also that of all other non-belligerents to neutral shipping, and even signed an Act with Joseph II, the Holy Roman Emperor, containing a commitment 'to secure the permanent establishment of the principles on the rights of neutrality' laid down in the treaties of the League of Armed Neutrality and make them a universal rule for future maritime conflicts.[82] Catherine's most enthusiastic contemporaries, amongst whom were Toze and Simon Linguet, believed the association of neutral powers to be a necessary precursor to the foundation of the universal code of which they dreamed.[83]

Treaties of Commerce, an Imperfect Source of Law

It comes as no surprise that commercial treaties included unclear provisions which gave rise to divergent interpretations, and in fact their ambiguity, insofar as it was deliberate, was condemned on moral grounds since their *raison d'être* was to quash conflict and encourage agreement between powers.[84] Moreover, without infringing on the sanctity of the treaties, which was recognized as vital for the very existence of an interstate society,

Brown Scott, *Extracts from American and Foreign Works on International Law concerning the Armed Neutrality of 1780 and 1800* (Washington, DC: Carnegie Endowment for International Peace. Division of International Law, 1917), 641–642.

[81] Scott, *Extracts from American and Foreign Works*, 273.

[82] Scott, *Extracts from American and Foreign Works*, 409.

[83] Schnakenbourg, *Entre la guerre et la paix*, 264–270.

[84] 'Putting ambiguous and insidious terms in a treaty means preparing the seeds of war for the future, it is putting kegs of gunpowder under the houses were one lives', Fénelon, 'Examen de conscience sur les devoirs de la royauté', in: *Oeuvres de Fénelon* (Paris: Auguste Desrez, 1837), part 3, 341. Vattel also denounced clearly the bad faith of the deliberate ambiguity of treaties, *Droit des gens*, part 2, 260–261. Marc Belissa, 'Peace Treaties, *Bonne Foi* and European Civility in the Enlightenment', in: *Peace Treaties and International Law in European History*, ed. Lesaffer, 241–253.

the signatories were free to interpret the imprecise provisions in ways that best suited them. At the beginning of the nineteenth century, the British lawyer and politician Robert Plumer Ward said that since 1642 there had been seventy-two treaties of commerce containing provisions that were either opposed to the safeguarding of enemy cargo on neutral ships or did not mention the issue at all, and only thirty-five that explicitly confirmed the principle. From this data he deduced that the protection of non-contraband merchandise by a neutral flag could not be deemed a universal principle.[85] However, while he held that only an explicit negation of this principle was valid, it was quite possible for someone else to turn the argument around and claim that the lack of negation inferred the principle's general validity.

In reality, the interpretation of a provision was sometimes induced by a real-life case of a sequestered cargo. For example, in 1744, the Swedish ship *Med Guds Hielpe* loaded with a cargo of pitch and tar bound for France was arrested by a British privateer, and the Swedes argued that the commodities it carried were not among the contraband goods listed in the Anglo-Swedish treaty of 1661. Judge Henry Penrice, however, still condemned the cargo on the grounds that: 'Pitch and tar are not enumerated in the 11th article of the Swedish treaty but I rather think those enumerated were mentioned rather for example than by way of exclusion.'[86] He thus passed judgement on the provision in a somewhat partial way without actually contradicting the letter of the treaty.

The crux of the matter was clearly the ambiguous nature of commercial treaties: were goods not expressly mentioned as free to be automatically considered contraband? Or were the goods that neutral ships were forbidden to carry only those clearly mentioned in the treaties? A situation similar to the Swedish incident arose in relation to the Anglo-Danish treaty of 1670, in which contraband was again loosely defined. And during the years of the American Revolution the British imposed their concept of contraband to limit the freedom of neutrals in line with their own interests. It was in fact not until 1780 that an Anglo-Danish convention

[85] Robert Plumer Ward, *A Treatise of the Relative rights and duties of belligerent and neutral powers in maritime affairs: in which the principles of armed neutralities and the opinions of Hubner and Schlegel are fully discussed* (London: Butterworth, 1801), 152.

[86] Edward Stanley Roscoe, ed., *Reports of Prize Cases determined in the High Court of Admiralty, 1745 to 1859*, vol. 1: *1745–1808* (London: Stevens and Sons, 1905), 1–3.

specified that naval supplies had to be treated as contraband and that transporting them was therefore forbidden.[87] Also in 1780, the inability of the British government to justify the restriction of Dutch neutral rights as mentioned in the 1674 treaty led to a war with the United Provinces.[88] The construal of the terms of treaties of commerce, as with all international acts, therefore amounted to a question of power. Indeed, if such agreements ever created laws and rights, these were likely to be revised de facto when the balance of power between the signatories changed.

This potential instability was one of the main weaknesses of transitioning from a perceived law, derived from commercial treaties, to a genuine international law. The most sceptical author in this respect was the Danish jurist Martin Hübner. He conceded the validity of law based on treaties, but maintained that it was subordinate to the universal principles of the law of nations, which was the only immutable one.[89] Indeed, the obligations of a treaty were only compulsory for the signatory parties who were at liberty to alter the provisions as they saw fit so long as both sides were in agreement, whereas 'the universal law of nations compels all the peoples on Earth and forever'.[90] Hübner's criticisms concerned the uncertain, sometimes even incoherent, character of conventional law, as shown by several treaties concluded by Denmark: the 1742 agreements with France and Spain defined some naval supplies as contraband, while these were explicitly allowed in the 1748 treaty with the King of Sicily and the 1756 treaty with Genoa.[91]

[87] 'Pour ne laisser aucun doute sur ce qui doit être entendu pour le terme de contrebande, on est convenu qu'on entend sous cette dénomination [. . .] le bois de construction, le goudron ou la poix résinée, le cuivre en feuille, les voiles, chanvres, cordages, et généralement tout ce qui sert directement à l'armement des vaisseaux', 'Convention entre sa Majesté Danoise et sa Majesté Britannique à Londres, 4 July 1780 pour expliquer le traité de commerce entre ces deux puissances de 1670', AAE, CP [Correspondance Politique], Denmark, vol. 163, fol. 127.

[88] Victor Enthoven, '"The Unlimited Cupidity of the Dutch Merchants": St. Eustatius and Anglo-Dutch Controversy over Neutral Rights, 1680–1780', in: *Neutres et neutralité dans l'espace atlantique durant le long XVIIIe siècle (1700–1820). Une approche globale/Neutrals and Neutrality in the Atlantic World during the Long Eighteenth Century (1700–1820). A Global Approach*, ed. Éric Schnakenbourg (Becherel: Les Perseides, 2015), 269–297; Neff, 'Peace and Prosperity: Commercial Aspects of Peacemaking', 368.

[89] Martin Hübner, *De la saisie des batimens neutres ou du Droit qu'ont les Nations Belligérantes d'arrêter les Navires des Peuples Amis* (La Haye, 1759), vol. 2, 131–132.

[90] Hübner, *De la saisie des batimens neutres*, vol. 2, 125–126.

[91] Hübner, *De la saisie des batimens neutres*, vol. 2, 168–171.

Hübner's argument is all the more relevant when related to the League of Armed Neutrality. Every convention concluded by Empress Catherine II stated that provisions should be regarded as permanent and a basis for a future 'law' or 'rule' on the rights of neutral nations.[92] In Prussian and Imperial conventions the signatories accepted the safeguarding of neutral cargoes and the definition of contraband as found in Articles 10 and 11 of the Anglo-Russian treaty of 1766.[93] The adoption of a single rule was possible because neither Frederick II nor Joseph II had signed valid commercial treaties with belligerents. Consequently, they agreed to extend to their subjects commitments contained in a treaty between two foreign powers. The members of the League of Armed Neutrality that had unexpired treaties with belligerents had, however, to continue to adhere to those commitments, each abiding by the definitions of contraband contained in them. For example, the treaties signed by the Danes prohibited them from transporting naval supplies (except wood for the French), while the Russians could do so lawfully. The League of Armed Neutrality was based on provisions included in certain treaties, some of which were very old and imprecise and lacked consistent definitions of contraband. The League, built by Catherine II, had not been established on a universal law for non-belligerent commerce but was instead a multifaceted legal structure. As such, it serves as an example of the impracticability of using the terms of commercial treaties to realize the dream of producing a single general law.

Conclusion

'The modern nations which seem the cleverest, have still made little progress on the theory of treaties of commerce. All the powers seek to get the monopoly of a few countries [. . .] they seek to help their allies at the expense of their rivals; the allied people always treat themselves as enemies on a few points.'[94] The opening lines of the article 'Traités de commerce' published in the *Encyclopédie méthodique* in 1788 expressed regret that a commercial treaty—an international act—was habitually used

[92] Scott, *Extracts from American and Foreign Works*, 648, 655, 662, 666, 668, 671.

[93] Scott, *Extracts from American and Foreign Works*, 661 and 665.

[94] Jean Nicolas Démeunier, ed., *Encyclopédie méthodique ou par ordre de matières* (Paris: Panckoucke, 1788), part 4, 358.

by the participating parties more as a tool to satisfy their own interests than as a means to create a peaceful framework for mercantile exchange.

In other words, commercial treaties did not move beyond the bilateral terms of a trading relationship to create a general law. This was a key point of eighteenth-century thought, as made clear by Bouchaud who described his study as a 'piece of the law of nations' in the opening line of his work. Indeed, commercial treaties outlined the rights, privileges and prohibitions that merchants and ships' officers had to observe or could enjoy. Since international treaties were public acts they were known to all, and the most favourable provisions contained in them created a kind of jurisprudence that became a natural reference point for all countries as they sought to obtain, during negotiations, the most advantageous outcome for their subjects. So far as wartime trade was concerned, all neutral states wanted the benefit of the widest possible commercial freedom, which explains why a majority of the treaties converged on the same priorities, namely the right to transport all the goods of belligerents and a narrow definition of contraband.[95]

On these points, the accumulated provisions of seventeenth- and eighteenth-century commercial treaties led jurists to deduce certain vague, broad principles that contributed to creating the law of nations through the propagation and standardization of rules concerning wartime maritime law. In this sense, the treaties contributed to the building of an international order inclined towards the ideals of international relations promoted by Enlightenment thinkers. The multiplication of disputes and incidents between countries that had signed commercial treaties testified, however, to the limited efficacy of such international conventions. The similarity of their provisions could be seen as a sign of evolution and of an outline of a tendency, but that alone could not produce a conventional law. Establishing a legal order that claims to be universal requires much more than aggregating different parts. A sovereign power could only be committed to a provision by giving its word explicitly, and thereafter remained free to interpret it and the principles of the law of nations opportunely. In consequence, commercial treaties, which played an important part in the maturing of the international system, fell short as legal sources.

[95] I would add the question of blockades, which was quite common in the treaties of commerce. Globally, however, this issue has raised fewer controversies; Schnakenbourg, *Entre la guerre et la paix*, 112–114.

The second half of the eighteenth century was a time of considerable reflection on the role of commercial treaties in the interstate system, and their qualities were examined in a context generally favourable to the real equality of nations and the development of rules that would allow commerce to flourish. Treaties were supposed not only to contain bilateral commitments, but also to be part of the framework of international order. This issue drew the attention of legal specialists as well as of governments and merchants: which is to say, it was relevant to both the theory and practice of international relations.

This fact reflects the dual nature of commercial treaties which, on the one hand, had to abide by general principles and, on the other, had to contain convenient and practical provisions for merchants. Trade treaties were all the more important since they were the only international conventions that enabled competing parties to reach agreement on wartime shipping and commerce. From this point of view, their purpose was less to define the concrete conditions of mercantile exchange than to ensure its feasibility. For all these reasons, a broad approach to studying treaties of commerce is required: an approach that allows us to go beyond simply examining individual provisions as part of a relationship between two countries and to analyse the terms of commercial treaties within a political, economic and legal frame of reference.

Éric Schnakenbourg is Professor of Early Modern History in the University of Nantes and Member of the *Centre de Recherche en Histoire Internationale et Atlantique*. His main interest is seventeenth- and eighteenth-century international relations in Europe and the Atlantic, particularly the themes of neutrality and international maritime law. He has published *Entre la guerre et la paix. Neutralité et relations internationales, XVIIe–XVIIIe siècles* (2013) and edited *Neutres et neutralité dans l'espace atlantique durant le long XVIIIe siècle* (2015).

From Privilege to Equality: Commercial Treaties and the French Solutions to International Competition (1736–1770)

Antonella Alimento

Introduction

Between 1736, the year in which the definitive edition of Jean-François Melon's *Essai politique sur le commerce* was published, and 1748, the year in which the Aix-La-Chapelle peace treaty was signed, French political and economic culture underwent profound changes. In the first part of this chapter I will reconstruct the political and cultural context within which the decision not to renew the navigation and trade treaty with the United Provinces at Aix-La-Chapelle was made: this decision was the result of collaboration between merchants about to become administrators (such as Vincent de Gournay and Étienne de Silhouette), administrators already in office (such as Daniel Trudaine), young diplomats (such as the Abbé de Mably), and well-known farmers (such as Jean-Joseph La Borde), who brought to bear the concepts of reciprocal advantage and of balance of trade, as put forth in the works of Melon, to challenge the preferential economic treatment conceded in 1739 by André Hercule, Cardinal de Fleury, to the United Provinces.

A. Alimento (✉)
University of Pisa, Italy
e-mail: antonella.alimento@unipi.it

A. Alimento, K. Stapelbroek (eds.), *The Politics of Commercial Treaties in the Eighteenth Century*, DOI 10.1007/978-3-319-53574-6_9

The non-renewal of the treaty was part of a broader strategy aimed at transforming France into a monarchy that could assure the balance of power in Europe by virtue of its ability to compete on European and colonial markets. Among the protagonists of this political change, some, like Gournay and Silhouette, argued for the need to establish a Navigation Act based on the British model. Gournay's appointment in 1751 to the post of intendant of commerce gave substance to the guiding role now exercised by this new generation of intellectual-administrators, who linked their destiny to the aim of modifying the arrangements set down at Utrecht and of establishing a balance of trade between the major colonial powers.

The decision to break the navigation and trade treaty with the United Provinces gave the French government fresh options that led to a complete rethinking of the nation's treaty strategy as a whole: Trudaine, the controller-general of finances Jean-Baptiste Machault and some other members of the government and administration insisted on the need to win back the 'grand cabotage' without actually resorting to a Navigation Act and decided to stimulate competition between all the merchant navies interested in marketing French raw materials and manufactured goods. They also publicly debated the practicality of activating the commercial treaty that France had signed with Britain at Utrecht in 1713, as the British government had requested from 1749.

In the second part of the chapter, I will examine the debate on the nature of commercial treaties that, starting with the French translation of the *British Merchant* by Véron de Forbonnais (1753), took place in France. As a result of the contribution of Forbonnais—a leading representative of the Gournay group who did not believe it possible to secure an agreement advantageous to both parties—navigation and trade treaties were no longer generally considered to be political or instrumental but rather, as Lacombe de Prézel, the editor of the *Dictionnaire du Citoyen*,[1] wrote openly, were regarded as a trade-off of advantages voluntarily entered into by two nations. If they were uneven, commercial treaties made economies subservient to political matters, but they could nevertheless serve as potent peace-making instruments if entered into by independent nations with the intention of acquiring market share from any

[1] *Dictionnaire du Citoyen, ou Abrégé historique, théorique et pratique du commerce* (Amsterdam: 1762), entry 'Traité', 228–232.

power that aimed to monopolize international trade, as clearly explained by Véron de Forbonnais' *Réflections sur la nécessité de comprendre l'étude du Commerce et des Finances dans celle de la politique* (1755),[2] Victor de Mirabeau's *L'Ami des hommes* (1755)[3] and Emer de Vattel's *Le droit des gens* (1758).[4]

Appealing to the principle of perfect reciprocity, Henri Bertin, the controller-general of finances charged with raising the funds needed for the hugely expensive Seven Years' War, opposed the request put forward by the British government to include the Utrecht trade treaty in the Paris peace settlement (1763). Instead, he, in the name of perfect equality, proposed the introduction of a law to increase French navigation and commerce while effectively countering the British Navigation Act with a similar measure.

This aggressive view of reciprocity was opposed by the Choiseul clan, in particular Étienne-François, the Duke of Choiseul—France's foremost minister until 1770, when he was forced into retirement—who used trade treaties as the key instrument of his policy of combating British supremacy without turning to military conflict.

In the third part of this chapter I will analyse the attempt made by Choiseul to defuse the feud with Britain by negotiating a fair commercial treaty with the 'natural and necessary enemy' and creating an integrated economic space composed of France, the Austrian Empire, Spain and Portugal and their respective colonies, for the purpose of counterbalancing and containing British hegemony. Rather than pass a Navigation Act, Choiseul sought to improve the productivity of the French economy in order to make it competitive on the American market, which he thought would then be revitalized by the availability of French raw materials and manufactured goods. This approach accorded with the plan proposed in *Les intérêts des nations de l'Europe* in 1766 by Accarias de Sérionne[5] and

[2] *Réflexions sur la nécessité de comprendre l'étude du Commerce et des Finances dans celle de la politique*, published in the second edition of *Considérations sur les finances d'Espagne* (Dresden and Paris: 1755).

[3] Victor Riquetti de Mirabeau, *L'Ami des hommes* (Avignon: 1756–1760).

[4] Emer de Vattel, *Le droit des gens ou Principes de la loi naturelle appliqués à la conduite et aux affaires des nations et des souverains* (London [Neuchâtel]: 1758).

[5] Jacques Accarias de Sérionne, *Les intérêts des nations de l'Europe, développés relativement au commerce* (Leiden: 1766).

taken up in 1770 by Abbé Raynal in the *Histoire des deux Indes*,[6] a work in fact commissioned by Choiseul.

I conclude my analysis by advancing the hypothesis that Choiseul's strategy was followed closely by Charles Gravier, Count of Vergennes, the foreign minister who strenuously defended the Family Compact and made arranging commercial treaties his defining characteristic.

From Privilege to Reciprocal Advantage: The Rejection of the Franco-Dutch Treaty of Commerce

David Bindon, the Irish translator of the *Essai politique sur le commerce*, remarked in 1738 that 'the Temper of [French] People were changed. And the Rigour of their arbitrary Government were abated, since the Writers of that Nation are endeavouring to inculcate Principles, which tend to the Improvement of the Arts of Peace'.[7] Chapter 7 of the *Essai*, entitled 'Of Military Government', in which Melon asserted that 'the Spirit of Conquest, and the Spirit of Commerce, mutually exclude each other, in a Nation' (1738, 136) fully justified the translator's assertion. What is important to understand is that Melon linked the rejection of the use of arms to a very specific social and economic project: since the spirit of commerce was opposed to the spirit of conquest, the French government had to reformulate its priorities and social hierarchies, giving peace-making pre-eminence over warmongering.

This violent attack on the military vocation of the French nobility in the midst of the War of the Polish Succession (1733–1738) explains why the *Essai* was brought out anonymously, without divulging where and by whom it had been edited and published, but merely stating that it was printed in 1734.[8] The final edition, published in 1736, had an additional

[6] Guillaume-Thomas Raynal, *Histoire philosophique et politique des établissements et du commerce des Européens dans les deux Indes* (Amsterdam: 1770).

[7] *A Political Essay upon Commerce* (Dublin: 1738), vi, remark by David Bindon, the translator.

[8] [Jean-François Melon], *Essai politique sur le commerce* (n.p.: n.p., 1734); the work was suppressed on 5 September 1736, without punishment for the author: see Jean-François Melon, *Opere*, ed. Onofrio Nicastro and Severina Perona (Pisa: Libreria testi universitari, 1983), I: 65–67.

seven chapters[9] in which Melon discussed the conditions that the legislator needed to put in place if he wished to transform a monarchy, like that of France, into a commercial power. The abandonment of a military strategy needed in fact to be accompanied by specific measures relating to agricultural and manufacturing production, with particular regard to commerce and navigation. The rejection of the universal monarchy project pursued with arms by Louis XIV did not in any way imply the adoption of the agrarian solution offered by François Fenélon.[10]

Unlike John Law, whom he served as secretary, Melon held that France could not reach the level of production required to play the role of a great power on the international stage without interacting with other nations. Law's plans were intended to make France self-sufficient: with the creation of a national bank 'France will no longer need other powers', he wrote to the Regent in support of his project.[11] Melon, however, was convinced that national self-sufficiency was unattainable because relations between nations were subjected to the same forces that shaped those between the nation's internal divisions. He was persuaded that 'there is such an intimate connection among the parts of society that you cannot strike one part without provoking a counterstrike in all the others'.[12] The same interplay of strikes and counterstrikes informed international relations. The problem he addressed was that of how a search for internal power and a search for international recognition could be undertaken in combination.

Indeed, to Melon's mind trade required an act of harmonizing mediation on the part of the legislator: in Chapter 10, 'De l'exportation et de l'importation' (which did not appear in the English edition), he analysed the systems that made exchange possible and came to a negative conclusion about that of free trade because this presupposed 'that all Europe

[9] [Jean-François Melon], *Essai politique sur le commerce* (n.p.: 1736).

[10] Lionel Rothkrug, *Opposition to Louis XIV. The Political and Social Origins of the French Enlightenment* (Princeton: Princeton University Press, 1964) and Istvan Hont, 'The Early Enlightenment Debate on Commerce and Luxury', in: *The Cambridge History of Eighteenth-Century Political Thought*, ed. Mark Goldie and Robert Wokler (Cambridge: Cambridge University Press, 2006), 377–418.

[11] John Law to Philippe d'Orléans, in: John Law, *Oeuvres complètes*, ed. Paul Harsin, 3 vols. (Paris: Librairie du Recueil Sirey, 1934), II: 266–267.

[12] [Melon], *Essai politique sur le commerce*, 1734, 10.

would adopt such a general vision, a vision that is in high contrast with particular interests'. While the system of free trade was unrealistic, a highly self-protectionist fiscal system that used duties and excises to safeguard domestic manufactured goods while excluding foreign ones was at odds with the search for internal power, which in his view depended on foreign demand for raw materials and manufactured products.

Melon took as an example the buying and selling that took place between France and Britain to contend that 'if foreign manufactured items—such as British cloths—are cheaper than domestic ones, and the foreign nation providing this manufactured items could, in exchange, buy French national *surplus*—such as wines—it would be useful not to prohibit this commerce'. Thus he clearly perceived how the interests of nations could be reconciled by concluding, in times of unforced peace ('paix non forcée', 1736, 143), voluntary bilateral treaties. But he went further: given that agreements made during peacetime ensured 'mutual advantage' ('l'avantage réciproque', 1736, 143), they should be adhered to even in times of war since preserving the relationship did not imply an alteration of the original state of reciprocity: 'by maintaining previous agreements in time of war [. . .] both nations would gain and lose at the same time' ('les percussions sont réciproques', 1736, 144).

Focusing on the research of reciprocal advantage, Melon, who in 1726 had returned to private life after the collapse of Law's bank,[13] carved out an entirely original space in the political and economic panorama of the time. Melon rejected the theory of free trade advocated by Pierre de Boisguilbert and shared in the 1720s by the Abbé de Saint-Pierre, and members of the Entresol Club,[14] declaring it to be unrealistic, and he denounced the protectionist system of its most extreme version—enacted France in 1701 against the English[15]—as damaging. Instead, he recognized that the most effective way of harmonizing national interests was through voluntary commercial agreements.

[13] Melon, *Opere*, I: 49–58.

[14] On the Club de l'Entresol, Nick Childs, *A Political Academy in Paris, 1724–1731: The Entresol and its Members* (Oxford: Voltaire Foundation, 2000).

[15] Antonella Alimento, 'Commercial Treaties and the Harmonisation of National Interests: The Anglo-French Case (1667–1713)', in: *War, Trade and Neutrality. Europe and the Mediterranean in the Seventeenth and Eighteenth Centuries*, ed. Antonella Alimento (Milan: FrancoAngeli, 2011), 107–128: 121–124.

But for these agreements to be truly advantageous neither partner must ever seek to unilaterally exploit the wealth of the other, as the United Provinces did. Underlining the importance of choosing one's trade partners with great care, Melon became the interpreter of the doubts circulating in many sectors of society, the administration and the government, which were then coping with the costs imposed on the French economy by the navigation and tariff privileges granted to the United Provinces with the 1713 Utrecht treaty. Just as the militarism of the sabre-rattling nobility had to be restrained, so too had the favourable economic treatment that France traditionally gave the United Provinces, in an attempt to sever its alliance with Britain, to be revised. Instead of exempting them from the charge of fifty *sols* payable by all other foreign vessels and continuing to allow them the tariff of 1699 as had occurred in Utrecht, the legislator had to encourage its merchants to buy raw materials and manufactured goods directly from the producer countries and to sell the nation's commodities and products without using wholesalers.[16] In short, France had to regain control of the 'grand cabotage' through the passing of a Navigation Act, which Melon extolled in Chapter 10 of his book.

Melon was not the only one to hold these views: in 1738 the *Réflexions politiques sur les finances et le commerce*[17] was published and its author, Nicolas Dutot, the former *commis* of the Compagnie des Indes, while having little regard for Melon's ideas on the beneficial effect of monetary inflation,[18] shared his conviction that the balancing function of France should be exercised not through war but with the weapons of peace.[19] In the *Réflexions*, Dutot sided with the pacifist approach of Fleury, who in that very year was formally ending the War of the Polish Succession after the cessation of hostilities in 1735, following the French recognition of the Pragmatic Sanction. Dutot, who, like Melon, linked the economic development of the monarchy to its ability to recover the 'grand cabotage', openly criticized France's strategy of allowing the United Provinces economic concessions in the hope of drawing it into its political orbit, and

[16] [Melon], *Essai politique sur le commerce*, 1736, 136–137.

[17] Nicolas Dutot, *Réflexions politiques sur les finances et le commerce* (The Hague: 1738).

[18] See François R. Velde, 'The Life and Times of Nicolas Dutot', *Journal of the History of Economic Thought* 34/1 (2012), 67–107.

[19] Dutot, *Réflexions*, II: 231–232.

openly called for Article 7 of the Treaty of Nijmegen renewed in the Utrecht treaty of 1713, which gave them national parity on tariffs, not to be renewed after its expiry (in 1738).[20]

The navy minister, Count Maurepas, would not have been unaware of these two works. Both Melon and Dutot closely linked the economic success of France and its balancing function to the abandonment of the assumption that had shaped government's actions from the times of Colbert: namely, that the profitable marketing of French produce and agricultural surplus abroad depended of necessity on Dutch intermediation. In a *mémoire* entitled *Situation du Commerce extérieur* presented to the Conseil du commerce in 1730,[21] Maurepas had criticized the clause by which the Utrecht treaty had granted most favoured nation status to the Dutch and argued for the need to increase the naval budget and to put French traders in a position to reacquire the cabotage profits lost to the Dutch by reason of the privileges they enjoyed. To his mind, granting the Dutch the same tariff treatment as French nationals was incompatible with the protection that French commerce had a right to expect.

There is no definite proof that Dutot's *Réflexions* was authorized by the government, but, according to Silhouette, British public opinion seemed to believe it was so.[22] This information is particularly interesting given that it came from a man destined to become the controller-general of finances during the time of the Seven Years' War. After studying law and commerce in Leyden, Silhouette had moved to London in 1733 to work as a tobacco buyer, but while there also served as a political consultant and commercial adviser to the secretary of state for foreign affairs, Germain Louis Chauvelin, and his eventual successor Amelot de Chaillou, as well as to Fleury himself.

In fact, the proposal set out in the *Réflexions* and the *Essai* concurred with the objectives that Maurepas was on the verge of achieving by

[20] Dutot, *Réflexions*, II: 226–228.

[21] 'Situation du Commerce exterieur', Paris, Bibliothèque Nationale de France [BNF], Fonds Français [FF] 11332, fols. 663–701, published by Maurice Filion, *Maurepas. Ministre de Louis XV (1715–1749)* (Montreal: Leméac, 1967), 157–172.

[22] Letter signed by Silhouette, London, 31 December 1739 N[ew]S[tyle], Archives du Ministère des Affaires Étrangères, La Courneuve [AAE] Correspondance Politique [CP] Angleterre 405, fols. 394–399v: 398. Nicolas Dutot, *Histoire du Systême de John Law (1716–1720)* (Paris: INED, 2000).

launching the first Family Compact. The Treaty of El Escorial of 9 November 1733, not only accorded France most favoured nation status (Article XII), but also foresaw the establishment of a trade treaty. In 1739 the treaty, which regulated the duties payable by French merchants and granted favourable terms to French coffee,[23] was on the point of being signed when the negotiations, conducted by Louis Pierre de La Marck, the French ambassador to Madrid, were suddenly suspended by the French.[24] According to Maurepas himself,[25] Fleury had decided to renew the commercial treaty with the United Provinces to prevent the Dutch from siding with the British should they interpret the expedition of the Marquis of Antin as evidence that France had decided to join Spain in its war with Britain.[26] Wishing to reassure Holland, Fleury decided to block the signing of the trade treaty with Spain, which had been strongly supported by those sectors of government and the administration which, in order to avoid military conflict, had hoped for the concluding of a commercial treaty with Spain and Portugal while being opposed to the renewal of the treaty with the United Provinces. Among those who made the strongest objections to the renewal was Daniel Trudaine, the state councillor who tried in vain to restrict the privileges enjoyed by the Dutch in the Levant trade, where they enjoyed equal treatment to French merchants.[27]

Despite the economic concessions they obtained in 1739, the United Provinces adopted an ambiguous attitude during the War of the Austrian Succession and therefore, on 31 December 1745, at the instigation of the war minister, the Marquis of Argenson, Louis XV retaliated by unilaterally

[23] *Recueil des instructions données aux ambassadeurs et ministres de France depuis les traités de Westphalie jusqu'à la Révolution française*, XII bis, Espagne, 3, 1722–1793, avec une introd. et des notes par A. Morel-Fatio et H. Léonardon (Paris: Alcan, 1899), 201–202; and Alfred Baudrillart, *Philippe V et la cour de France d'après des documents inédits* (Paris: Firmin-Didot, 1890), IV: 525–531.

[24] *Exposé abrégé de ce qui s'est fait... novembre 1738–15 février 1741* by La Mark in *Recueil des instructions*, 214–238.

[25] 'Observations Sommaires sur un Mémoire du Sr Fondiere', 28 April 1749, BNF, Nouvelles Acquisitions Françaises [NAF] 20541, fos. 152–153v.

[26] Philip Woodfine, *Britannia's Glories: The Walpole Ministry and the 1739 War with Spain* (Woodbridge: Boydell & Brewer, 1998).

[27] 'Réflexion sur le renouvellement du traité de commerce avec les Etats généraux des Provinces Unies', BNF, NAF 20541, fol. 72.

breaking the treaty of 21 December 1739.[28]In the course of the negotiations leading to the peace treaty, Maurepas requested, following the example 'of what Britain and Holland had done in the Utrecht treaty, the protection of French commercial interests'.[29] Those charged with achieving this were—apart from the foreign secretary (from 12 January 1747 to 11 September 1751), Marquis Puisieulx—Mably,[30] a young diplomat, and Gournay, an established merchant. Both men had taken part in the negotiations of Bréda, which were interrupted in 1747 when France invaded Dutch territory.

While participating in the negotiations, Mably published a book, *Le Droit public de l'Europe fondé sur les Traités*, in which he pointed out that bad economic policy choices—such as that which had essentially turned French merchants into commercial agents of the Dutch—threatened the solidity of France, despite the natural advantages that the country enjoyed. He pressed the navy minister to encourage French commercial shipping and, as Melon had done earlier, requested the passing of a Navigation Act in order to curb the Dutch who grew rich at the expense of the agriculture of all European nations.[31]

Gournay's economic thinking matured in the course of the Bréda negotiations.[32] Having been involved in the negotiations for the commercial treaty with Spain,[33] he had first come into contact with Maurepas in 1743 when, finding himself in Cadiz to take care of the business interests of the Vincent family, he had taken charge of the repatriation of the gold earned by French commerce in Spanish America.[34] During the

[28] *Recueil des instructions données aux ambassadeurs et ministres de France*, XXIII, *Hollande (1730–1788)*, ed. Louis André and Emile Bourgeois (Paris: Boccard, 1924).

[29] 'Mémoire sur les intérêts commerciaux et sur les moyens de les protéger à la conférence de Paix', Filion, *Maurepas*, 53.

[30] Gabriel Bonnot de Mably took part in the negotiations in his role as secretary to the Minister of Foreign Affairs, Pierre Guérin, Cardinal of Tencin.

[31] Gabriel de Mably, *Le droit public de l'Europe fondé sur les traitez conclus jusqu'en l'année 1740* (The Hague: 1746), II: 238–239.

[32] Gustave Schelle, *Vincent de Gournay* (Paris: Guillaumin, 1897), 24.

[33] Antonella Alimento, 'Beyond the Treaty of Utrecht: Véron de Forbonnais's French Translation of the *British Merchant* (1753)', *History of European Ideas* 40 (2014), 1044–1066.

[34] For his sojourns in Cadiz (from 1729 to 1744), Simone Meyssonnier, *La balance et l'horloge. La genèse de la pensée libérale au XVIIIe siècle* (Montreal: Éditions de la Passion, 1989), 170–174.

negotiations, Gournay argued for maintaining a hard-line position against the United Provinces.[35]

Silhouette agreed with this stance. From the time of his stay in London he had contended that the best way to weaken British power was to grow the French economy and establish a 'commercial equilibrium' between the two countries.[36] Back in France in 1740, he participated in the drafting of the decision not to renew the commercial treaty with the United Provinces, endorsing the selective use of the British Navigation Act: a ban on non-British ships arriving in France would prompt French traders to increase their own activity, and if these were then to regain control of the cabotage, they would immediately cause the Dutch economy to suffer huge losses.[37]

The considered opinions of Mably, Gournay and Silhouette influenced economic policy-making to such an extent that the 1748 peace treaty did not make any reference to the treaty of commerce between France and the United Provinces, despite the Dutch having requested its renewal for another twenty-five years.

From the Navigation Act to the Rejection of the Commercial Treaty

The Dutch government reacted by sending two negotiators, Thomas Isaac de Larrey and Dirk Marsellis, to Paris with the aim of winning a new commercial treaty. Trudaine, who in a series of memoranda written in 1748 argued for the need not to grant rights relating to fishing[38] and refined sugar to the United Provinces,[39] was put in charge of the negotiation the

[35] 'Mémoire sans titre' (1747–1748?), in: Claude-Marie Vincent de Gournay, *Mémoires et lettres de Vincent de Gournay*, ed. Takumo Tsuda (Tokyo: Kinokuniya, 1993), 3–12.

[36] Letter signed by Silhouette, 21 December 1733 to 1 January 1734, to Chauvelin, AAE, CP Angleterre 383, fol. 8.

[37] 'Observations sur les finances, la navigation et le commerce d'Angleterre', AAE, Mémoires et Documents [MD] Angleterre 46, fos. 45–88, on which see Paul Cheney, *Revolutionary Commerce. Globalization and the French Monarchy* (Cambridge, MA: Harvard University Press, 2010), 32–34.

[38] 'Mémoire', 8 August 1748, BNF, NAF 20541, fos. 148–149.

[39] 'Observations sur un mémoire concernant le traité de commerce avec la Hollande', 29 November 1749, BNF, NAF 20541, fos. 159–160v.

following year.[40] During the process, which lasted up to 1761, Trudaine, now intendant of commerce, was given strong support for his uncompromising approach[41] by the other negotiator, the farmer-general La Borde and by Gournay, who in 1751 had officially entered the administration as intendant of commerce. Although they all agreed not to grant privileges to the United Provinces, they viewed certain other points differently.

The passing of a Navigation Act was a central axis in the plan drawn up by Gournay to turn France into a trading monarchy: indeed, the abolition of internal monopolies and of all constraints that held back individual initiative was supplementary to the protection of the French navy ('liberté et protection').[42] The *Remarques* written by Gournay as a commentary to Josiah Child's translation concluded, tellingly, with an *Extrait du Traité de navigation et de commerce conclû à Utrecht en 1713 entre la France et les Etats Généraux*. In these notes Gournay contended that free exchange and the treatment of national parity enjoyed by the United Provinces were a threat to the security of France insofar as the Dutch navy, strengthened by the privileges it received, could readily be made available to its British ally. To prevent the renewal of the treaty and to press for the launch of a Navigation Act, Gournay orchestrated a public campaign: 1750 saw the publication of a translation of the work by Joshua Gee[43]—one of the most influential proponents of British protectionism—to which the translation of the most important articles of the English Navigation Act of 1660 was appended. This translation was followed in 1754 by the publication of Pierre-André O'Héguerty's *Essay*[44] and in 1756 by *Les*

[40] See 'Mémoire', in AAE, MD Hollande 137 (1758–1829), fos. 37–42v.

[41] See the autograph letter by Trudaine to Rouillé, 'à Paris ce 6 décembre 1754' in BNF, FF 5371, fol. 65; Alimento, 'Beyond the Treaty of Utrecht', 1048–1049.

[42] Antonella Alimento, 'Competition, True Patriotism and Colonial Interest: Forbonnais' Vision of Neutrality and Trade', in: *War and Trade. Neutrality of Commerce in the Inter-State System*, ed. Koen Stapelbroek (Helsinki: Helsinki Collegium for Advanced Studies, 2011), 61–94.

[43] Joshua Gee, *Considérations sur le commerce et la navigation de la Grande-Bretagne*. Ouvrage traduit de l'Anglois de Mr. Joshua Gee, sur la quatrième édition (Geneva: 1750).

[44] [Pierre-André O'Héguerty], *Essai sur les intérêts du commerce maritime* (1754), in *Discours politiques de Mr. Hume traduits de l'anglois par Mr. De M[auvillon]* (Amsterdam, 1756–1761).

intérêts de la France mal entendus by Ange Goudar,[45] which carried the English Navigation Act in French.[46]

Despite the strong pressure exercised by Gournay and some members of his group, the plan formulated by La Borde[47] and Trudaine[48] won the day: instead of directly attacking Dutch commerce by means of a Navigation Act, both suggested weakening it indirectly by putting Dutch trade on the same level as that of Sweden, the Hanseatic cities and Prussia, and thereby placing it in competition with them. In this way France would increase its wealth while acting as a balancing power.

La Borde and Trudaine's perspective of economic development and international relations consolidated the plan of action adopted by Machault to resolve the problem of the dependency of French colonies on the Dutch navy, which had become acute with the outbreak of the Seven Years' War. Machault's influence was decisive in pushing the government to put pressure on the neutrals to demand that the right to protect with their flag the cargoes transported for third parties be respected (free ships, free goods).[49]

In 1756, as an authoritative member of the Gournay group, Forbonnais had an *Essai sur l'admission des navires neutres dans nos Colonies* [50] published anonymously. In this he supported the edict of that same year, which, thanks to pressure exerted by Machault, had made French colonial trade accessible to the neutral countries. Son of an industrialist of Le Mans, and a merchant before his move to Paris in 1747, where he met Diderot and began to collaborate on the *Encyclopédie*, Forbonnais was well aware that the European interstate

[45] Ange Goudar, *Les intérêts de la France mal entendus dans les branches de l'Agriculture, de la Population, des Finances, du Commerce, de la Marine, et de l'Industrie* (Amsterdam: 1756).

[46] Antonella Alimento, 'La concurrence comme politique moderne: la contribution de l'école de Gournay à la naissance d'une sphère publique dans la France des années 1750–1760', in: *L'économie politique et la sphère publique dans le débat des Lumières*, ed. Jesús Astigarraga and Javier Usoz (Madrid: Casa de Velázquez, 2013), 221–223.

[47] 'Mémoire sur le commerce concernant differentes Puissances de l'Europe', by Mr. de La Borde, 15 January 1748, A[rchives] N[ationales], A[ffaires] E[trangères], /B/III/461.

[48] 'Mémoire sur le traitement à faire aux hollandois, pour leur commerce, à la prochaine paix', May 1748, BNF, NAF 20541, fos. 143–147.

[49] Éric Schnakenbourg, *Entre la guerre et la paix. Neutralité et relations internationales, XVIe–XVIIIe siècles* (Rennes: PUF, 2013), 182–190, 226–229.

[50] On which see Alimento, 'Competition, True Patriotism and Colonial Interest'.

system was governed by commerce, and opened his *Préface du traducteur* to *Le Négotiant anglois* by writing: 'Europe has recognized that a balance of trade is veritably a balance of powers',[51] and thus being conscious of the need to finally realize a trade balance between the major European powers, he opposed the renewal of the trade treaty with the United Provinces. He had initially agreed with Gournay's objective of establishing reciprocity between France and the United Provinces to the point of supporting calls for a Navigation Act,[52] but changed his original plan—summed up as 'liberté et protection' and centred on the Navigation Act—while translating the *British Merchant*, espousing instead a plan based on 'liberté et concurrence'. By 1754 he was a supporter of Machault's approach and aligned himself with the plan to form a maritime union which was eventually instituted, under pressure from the French, in 1756, albeit only to be dissolved in September 1757 when Sweden went to war on the side of the French.

Forbonnais upheld this position by citing a Scottish author, David Hume, whom he had discovered while working on his translation of the *British Merchant*. Forbonnais proposed using merchant ships belonging to the minor European countries to transport French goods, appropriating Hume's idea that in order to establish a European peace it was essential to ensure the existence of competing small states.[53] Forbonnais made this point explicitly in the *Réflexions sur la nécessité de comprendre l'étude du Commerce et des Finances dans celle de la politique* (1755), a text in which he clearly distanced himself from the plan to transform France into a commercial nation by means of a Navigation Act. In his opinion, such an Act would keep France separate from other countries, whereas if the

[51] *Le négotiant anglois, ou traduction libre du livre intitulé The British Merchant, contenant divers mémoires sur le commerce de l'Angleterre avec la France, le Portugal et l'Espagne. Publié pour la première fois en 1713* (Paris: 1753), I: ij.

[52] See the annotation attributed to Forbonnais by Meyssonnier, in Vincent de Gournay, *Traités sur le commerce de Josiah Child suivis des Remarques de Jacques Vincent de Gournay*, ed. Simone Meyssonnier (Paris: L'Harmattan, 2008), 217.

[53] On Forbonnais' reaction to Hume's *Of the Rise and Progress of the Arts and Sciences*, see Antonella Alimento, 'Entre animosité nationale et rivalité d'émulation: la position de Véron de Forbonnais face à la compétition anglaise', in: *Governare il mondo. L'economia come linguaggio della politica nell'Europa del Settecento*, ed. Manuela Albertone (Milan: Feltrinelli, 2009), 125–148: 146.

minor states were allowed to trade on behalf of France, all the nations involved would be enriched and peace in Europe would be preserved.[54]

In essence, Forbonnais was able to call into question the special treatment granted to the Dutch navy by setting out a reformist project that profoundly changed the way of conceiving the balance of power in Europe. Without resorting to the establishment of an aggressive Navigation Act, France could become the guarantor of a new balance between the European powers by simultaneously enriching the neutral countries and itself. He therefore invited the legislator to reverse its priorities and create the conditions that would lead to a real balance of trade.

Bearing in mind this highly original politico-economic conception, it is not surprising to note that there was a significant convergence between the ideas of Forbonnais and those of the Marquis de Mirabeau. Butel-Dumont, a close collaborator of Forbonnais, in fact gave a copy of his *Acte du parlement d'Angleterre, connu sous le nom d'Acte de Navigation, passé en 1660, traduit littéralement de l'Anglois, avec des notes* (1760) to the author of the *Ami des Hommes* (1755). In his book, published anonymously, Butel-Dumont used certain passages of the *Elémens du commerce* by Forbonnais to demonstrate that a Navigation Act would be economically disadvantageous seeing that it would impede the beneficial evolvement of competition.[55] To counter the danger that the British Navigation Act presented to the law of nations, the 'pre-physiocratic' Mirabeau in his *Ami des hommes* had proposed the creation of a 'Traité de fraternité' between the states 'that live solely on industry'; this treaty would allow the exclusivist spirit of the British to be repulsed with the weapons of commerce. He who, unlike Forbonnais, recognized the usefulness of the function carried out by the United Provinces, assigned to France, given its natural characteristics, the role of protector of the right that nations had to trade freely in Europe and the colonies. He was convinced that the implementation of the 'plan for the universal protection of commerce'

[54] *Réflexions sur la nécessité de comprendre l'étude du Commerce*, 68.

[55] *Acte du parlement d'Angleterre, connu sous le nom d'Acte de Navigation, passé en 1660, traduit littéralement de l'Anglois, avec des notes* (Amsterdam and Paris: 1760) on which, Alimento, 'La concurrence comme politique moderne', 221–223; regarding the delivery of the book to Mirabeau, François Quesnay, *Œuvres économiques complètes et autres textes*, ed. Christine Théré, Loïc Charles and Jean Claude Perrot (Paris: INED, 2005), II: 1190—1193: 1190.

under French leadership would shield the 'industry and labour' of all trading nations from British aggressiveness.[56]

Forbonnais' ideas also proved crucial in transforming, in a comprehensive economic and political strategy, the proposals put forward by the vast circle of intellectual-administrators, like Trudaine, who were no longer disposed towards conceding special treatment in duty and tariff matters to Britain and yet were reluctant to return to the 'law of the duel', as Forbonnais called the mutual reprisals that the two countries habitually made.[57] In a series of memoranda written in response to the British request to introduce watchmaking and metalworking in France in exchange for lifting the ban on importing cambric and lowering the high taxation on French wines, Trudaine spelt out the need to establish reciprocal treatment and emulation between the two countries. In his opinion, the British request should be accepted because national goods, protected by a moderate system of custom duties, had to compete with British products and secure consumer preference.[58]

Forbonnais accepted the challenge launched by Trudaine and used his translation of the *British Merchant* to explain publicly how to overcome the problem posed by commercial treaties. Borrowing Melon's notion of reciprocal advantage, in *Le Négociant anglois* he distinguished between peace treaties, which were binding, and commercial treaties, which were voluntary. While the former obligated, the latter were free acts by which treaty partners chose not to use their legitimate power to prohibit the consumption or circulation of goods that might damage the economy of their countries; hence when a nation believed that a concession no longer met its needs, it had every right to break the treaty,[59] and in *Le Négociant anglois* Forbonnais used this proposition to reject the possible renewal of the trade treaty with Britain. Differently from what Melon had claimed, the two nations could not agree a tariff accord due to the different levels of economic progress that each had reached, Forbonnais contended, adding that if they—both exporters of

[56] Mirabeau, *L'ami des hommes*, 107, 126–128, 137, 159, 208.

[57] *Réflexions sur la nécessité de comprendre*, 60.

[58] 'Mémoire sur la proposition de la cour britannique de faire lever la prohibition sur les Cambrays à condition de donner la libre entrée à l'horlogerie anglaise, 4 janvier 1752 par M. Trudaine', AAE, MD Angleterre, 49, fos. 48–55v.

[59] *Le Négociant anglois*, II, 193, note (a); II, 198–99, note (a); II, 200–01, note (a).

raw materials and manufactured goods—ever came to an equal agreement, they would surely do so by damaging the interests of their respective consumers, since entire productive sectors would have been removed from emulative competition. In preference to a renewed treaty, he proposed the adoption of a system of duties that allowed domestic manufactured goods to compete with foreign ones of equal quality, without having recourse to a system of prohibitions.[60] While Forbonnais did not transform opposition to the signing of a commercial treaty with Britain into a closed and exclusivist system, others reached different conclusions.

During the negotiations entered into after the peace of Aix and thwarted by the start of the Seven Years War, La Borde proposed confirming only the navigation rules decreed by the Treaty of Utrecht, without granting Britain any favour in relation to customs matters.[61] In 1751 the conviction arose that France should not be bound to commercial treaties and related tariffs that automatically extended to the contracting party measures taken in favour of the national economy.[62] The general convention agreed with Prussia on 4 February 1753 thereupon became the model to imitate[63] since, as Mably wrote in the *Principes* (1757),[64] once 'the freedom of the seas and of navigation' was secured—in other words, once the 'conventions regarding the right of nations' were established—no other issue should be negotiated. Although it had the same objective—that is, the priority of establishing a balance of trade—the isolationist solution advanced by Mably[65] was in direct opposition to the logic of competitive emulation advocated by Trudaine and Forbonnais.

[60] See Antonella Alimento, 'Between Mercantilism and Physiocracy: Forbonnais's "Est modus in Rebus" Vision', in: *The Economic Turn: Recasting Political Economy in Enlightenment Europe*, ed. Steven Kaplan and Sophus Reinert (London and New Delhi: Anthem, forthcoming).

[61] See 'Mémoire sur le commerce concernant differentes Puissances de l'Europe'.

[62] 'Sur les Tarifs, Mars 1751', AAE, MD Angleterre 69, fol. 150.

[63] 'Mémoire sur les traités de commerce en general et avec l'Espagne en particulier', BNF 10768, fos. 33–40 and the chapter by Cavarzere in this volume.

[64] Gabriel Bonnot de Mably, *Des Principes des Négociations pour servir d'Introduction au Droit Public de l'Europe, fondé sur les Traités* (The Hague: 1757), ch. XVII, 'Des Traités de commerce. Digression sur le luxe', 231–241: 234.

[65] Mably, *Des Principes des Négociations*: 'Chaque puissance, à cet égard, ne doit dépendre que d'elle-même', 233.

The 'No Territory Policy' of Choiseul, the Family Compact and the Neutralization of Spanish Colonial Trade

The decision not to conclude commercial treaties in order to avoid conceding preferential treatment in areas of tariffs and trade, widely accepted in the 1750s, was severely tested by the outcome of the Seven Years' War: the British government demanded, as a non-negotiable condition for peace, the renewal of the commercial Treaty of Utrecht,[66] which Bertin—the controller-general of finances—rejected out of hand.[67] British society and government, in his opinion, would never accept the conditions of parity on which a trade treaty should be founded: the terms of the British Navigation Act did not provide for the establishment of relations based on 'perfect equality' and 'strict reciprocity'.[68]

During the negotiations which took place in London, the considerations of Bertin went unheeded, not only because it had become critical to agree a truce without delay but also because Choiseul (the chief negotiator who had chosen to disregard Bertin)[69] did not want to subordinate achieving peace to obtaining 'perfect equality' and 'strict reciprocity'. He had set himself a different agenda, which he had adhered to from the time of his appointment to the ministry of foreign affairs in 1758.

Although accused of being a secret agent for the Austrians,[70] partly because he was born in Lorraine and had links to Mathias Nettine, the

[66] See the Duke of Bedford's letter to the Count of Egremont, Paris, 24 December 1762, *Correspondence of John, fourth Duke Bedford* (London: Longman, 1846), III: 173–183: 177 and the letter from M. de Bussy to M. Durand, 7 June 1766, AAE, MD Angleterre 49, fol. 184.

[67] 'Sur la demande de l'exemption du droit de fret de la part de la Cour d'Angleterre', 26 December 1762, AAE, MD Angleterre 69, fol. 243.

[68] 'Mémoire sur le traité de navigation et de commerce convenu a Utrecht le 11 avril 1713 et qui n'a pas eu d'exécution, joint a la lettre de M. le Contrôleur général du 25 décembre 1762', AAE, MD Angleterre 49, fol. 176.

[69] 'Copie de la Note de M. de Choiseul, écrite de sa main à la marge du "Mémoire sur le traité de navigation"', AAE, MD Angleterre 49, fol. 178.

[70] Thomas E. Kaiser, 'The Austrian Alliance, the Seven Years' War, and the Emergence of a French "National" Foreign Policy, 1756–1790', in: *The Crisis of the Absolute Monarchy: France from Old Regime to Revolution*, ed. Julian Swann and Joël Félix (Oxford: Oxford University Press, 2013), 167–179: 171.

Catholic banker who bankrolled the reversal of alliances,[71] Choiseul worked to ensure that French economic interests were not subject to the military objectives of the House of Austria, and in 1758 and 1759 he aimed to renegotiate the alliance so strongly desired by Louis XV.[72] Thanks to the Third Treaty of Versailles (20 March 1759), he obtained a large reduction in the subsidies stipulated in the Second Treaty and also broke free of the obligation, previously agreed, to remain at war until Austria had regained control of Silesia.

Furthermore, he obtained the right to keep separate the Anglo-French and Prusso-Austrian conflicts, thus making it possible to hold negotiations with Britain.[73] From March 1761, having reached an impasse with Pitt, he broke off the negotiations over the borders of North America, accepting the principle of *uti possidetis*: in other words, he opted to lose Canada.[74] At the same time, he brought Spain into play, having since 1759 gathered information on the state of its economy. As John Fraser Ramsay has shown,[75] for Choiseul the military aspect of the alliance with the Bourbons of Spain was inseparable from the economic one: from the Third Family Compact (1761), Choiseul had hoped for the creation of an integrated economic space in which Spain, the Kingdom of Naples and France could exchange raw materials and manufactured goods, thus weakening British trade.

[71] Antonella Alimento, *Réformes fiscales et crises politiques dans la France de Louis XV. De la taille tarifée au cadastre général* (Brussels: Peter Lang, 2008), 28.

[72] Edmont Dziembowski, *La guerre de Sept Ans 1756–1763* (Paris: Perrin/Ministère de la Défense, 2015), 340–354.

[73] On the attempt to invade Britain by taking advantage of the Jacobite Restoration, see Claude J. Nordmann, 'Choiseul et la dernière tentative Jacobite de 1759', *Revue d'histoire diplomatique* 3–4 (1979), 223–246; and Daniel Baugh, *The Global Seven Years' War, 1754–1673: Britain and France in a Great Power Contest* (Harlow: Pearson, 2011), 422–431. Silhouette agreed with the invasion plan: see the original 'Mémoire', 15 July 1759, AAE, MD Angleterre 54, fos. 147–147v.

[74] This decision was accompanied by a strenuous defence of the right to fish in the waters of Newfoundland; see John G. Reid, 'Imperialism, Diplomacies, and the Conquest of Acadia', in *The Conquest of Acadia, 1710: Imperial, Colonial, and Aboriginal Constructions*, ed. John G. Reid et al. (Toronto: University of Toronto Press, 2004), 101–123.

[75] John Fraser Ramsey, *Anglo-French Relations, 1763–1770: A Study of Choiseul's Foreign Policy* (Berkeley: University of California Press, 1939).

Convinced, like Forbonnais, that the balance of power depended on that of trade,[76] Choiseul put pressure on Spain to accord the French the treatment enjoyed by the British and the Dutch. At the same time, he resisted every effort that might reignite hostilities with Britain, which was why he rejected the edict that the controller-general of finances put to him in 1764: this provided for the suppression of the *droit de fret* for direct trade and that of first sale but, wishing to preserve 'the balance of commerce through the reciprocity of rights that foreign nations impose on our subjects', he tightened the levy on British ships that docked in French ports.[77] The aim of this act of 'perfect reciprocity' coincided with what Gournay had tried to attain in the 1750s through the adoption of a Navigation Act: if passed, the proposal would have revived the system of reprisals initiated by the *arrêt* of September 1701.[78]

To check this vision of 'exact reciprocity', the argument made by Melon in 1736 was used: that it was dangerous to close the ports to nations that did not offer reciprocal navigation arrangements because, if their goods were cheap enough, their entry would favour the sale of the national surplus. Instead of aiming to enlarge the navy by dint of a punitive measure, the legislator should rather promote the growth of agriculture and manufacturing. The free export of grains and an increased competitiveness of French manufactured goods would stimulate the creation of a national navy and shipowners. Only in this way would it be possible to renegotiate the trade treaty with Britain and to obtain proper acceptance of the 'reciprocal treatment of our vessels'.[79]

We do not know whether Melon's consideration was brought back by Trudaine or by the minister of war himself, but what is certain is that, while he refused to increase French colonial possessions by military means,[80] Choiseul strengthened the state's control over existing colonies

[76] Choiseul's letter to d'Affry, 28 October 1759 in Alfred Bourguet, *Études sur la politique étrangère du Duc de Choiseul* (Paris: Plon, 1907), 113–114.

[77] 'Edit du Roi concernant le commerce et la navigation française Remis par M. le Contrôleur général le 4 mars 1764', AN, AE/B/III/461.

[78] 'Le projet d'Edit, Mars 1764', AN, AE/B/III/461.

[79] 'Suitte d'observations sur le Projet d'Edit concernant la navigation', 19 November 1763, AN, AE/B/III/461.

[80] Hamish M. Scott, *Choiseul et le Troisième Pacte de Famille. La présence des Bourbons en Europe (XIV–XIXe siècles)*, ed. Lucien Bély (Paris: PUF, 2003), 207–220: 217 and Lucien Bély,

so as to increase their productivity.[81] In short, he pursued his 'no territory policy'[82] by endeavouring to boost the competitiveness of the national economy: the enactment in 1764 of the measure that liberalized the export of grains was part of this strategy.

Supported by Jean Charles Trudaine de Montigny in his attempt to modernize the French economy, in 1767 Choiseul pushed the French ambassador to London to sound out the willingness of the British government to establish a new commercial treaty. The formal negotiations with Britain[83] were conducted in parallel to those for a treaty with Spain: Abbot Béliardi, Choiseul's man, had been sent to Madrid between 1765 and 1767 to achieve precisely this objective.[84]

The practical implementation of Article 24 of the Family Compact would allow an integrated market to be formed between France, Spain and the Kingdom of Naples, in line with the prospect presented by Accarias de Sérionne's *Les intérêts des nations de l'Europe* (1766), and brought again to public attention by a work commissioned by Choiseul. This was the *Histoire des deux Indes* (1770) by Raynal who adopted the two initiatives that Sérionne believed were indispensable to achieving an economic balance between the nations of Europe and thereby obviating new military conflicts. Sérionne held that in order to secure peace in Europe two changes were fundamental: the signing of a Franco-British commercial treaty, which would bring about conditions that would help all nations make progress, and the transformation of the Spanish colonies into a market for European

'Le duc de Choiseul, la Cour de France et la politique étrangère française, 1761–1770', *Revue d'histoire diplomatique* 118 (2004), 281–300; cf. Paul W. Mapp, *The Elusive West and the Contest for Empire, 1713–1763* (Chapel Hill: University of North Carolina Press, 2011), 374–390.

[81] Eugene Daubigny, *Choiseul et la France d'outre mer d'après le traité de Paris* (Paris: Hachette, 1892); Jean Tarrade, *Le commerce colonial de la France à la fin de l'Ancien Régime. L'évolution du régime de l'Exclusif de 1763 à 1789* (Paris: PUF, 1972).

[82] François-Joseph Ruggiu, 'Falling into Oblivion? Canada and the French Monarchy, 1759–1783', in: *Revisiting 1759. The Conquest of Canada in Historical Perspective*, ed. Philip Buckner and John G. Reid (Toronto: University of Toronto Press, 2012), 69–94.

[83] 'Mémoire sur l'Execution du Traité de commerce entre la France et l'Angleterre signé à Utrecht le 11 Avril 1713', 1767, AAE, MD Angleterre 46, fos. 129–132v.

[84] On Béliardi's mission, see Pierre Muret, 'Les papiers de l'abbé Béliardi et les relations commerciales de la France et de l'Espagne au milieu du XVIIIe siècle (1757–1770)', *Revue d'histoire moderne et contemporaine* 4 (1902–1903), 657–672.

manufactured goods by guaranteeing it purchasing power through the sale of goods sought by the manufacturing nations.[85] The fact that this solution was proposed by Sérionne, a French businessman who had obtained an important position in Vienna, a capital linked to France not only by a political alliance but also by commercial interests, is not surprising because the strategy devised by Choiseul for arriving at a balance of trade between the European states implied the involvement of the empire.

Béliardi did not see the full picture of Choiseul's project, but the objective of placing the empire in the integrated economic space ensured by the Family Compact was, however, clearly understood by the party that forced the retirement of the most prominent minister in 1770.[86] The purchase of Corsica (1768), the only territorial acquisition truly desired by Choiseul, was in fact a detail of a much broader economic strategy that aimed to redefine the economic role of France in the Mediterranean through the exploitation of the free port of Trieste once it had formed an association with the free port of Marseilles.[87]

Had Choiseul's ultimate goal been, as Malachy Postlethwayt believed, a Catholic confederation under French leadership which would make a stable peace in Europe impossible? To counter this danger, the translator of Savary des Brûlons's *Dictionnaire Universel du Commerce* (1751–1755), proposed to the Duke of Newcastle a plan for a global peace centred on a Protestant trade federation. Conceived in part as a military-alliance-cum-customs-union, this league would control the coasts of Africa and seize the colonial trade with America, leaving Britain with the lion's share of the territories.[88] Or did Choiseul simply wish to create,

[85] On Raynal's re-proposition of the suggestion put forward by Sérionne, see Antonella Alimento, 'Accarias de Sérionne, Raynal et le Pacte de Famille', in *Autour de l'Abbé Raynal. Genèse et enjeux politiques de l'Histoire de deux Indes*, ed. Antonella Alimento and Gianluigi Goggi (Ferney-Voltaire: Centre international d'étude du XVIIIe siècle, forthcoming).

[86] The *parti dévot* attacked the Family Compact because it saw it as a way to enable Austria to enter into relations with Spain. Kaiser, *The Austrian Alliance*, 172–175.

[87] F. Pomponi, 'Les îles du Bassin Occidental de la Méditerranée et la "redécouverte" par la France d'une politique Méditerranéenne (1769–1799)', *Cahiers de la Méditerranée* 57 (1998), 1–32; Marie Thérèse Combet, *L'alliance franco-autrichienne sous le consulat de Choiseul (1756–1770)* (Paris: Thèse de l'école nationale des chartes, 1964).

[88] Malachy Postlethwayt, *The sequel to considerations upon the measures necessary to be taken by the court of Great Britain to obtain a very good and a very durable peace* (1768), British Library, Additional MS 33053, fos. 323–330.

without in fact actually doing so,[89] an integrated economic space in order to extract some shares of the market from the power that aspired to monopolize international trade? Such had been the wish of Vattel, as outlined in his *Droit public de l'Europe* (1758), a work which circulated in France thanks to the protection of Chrétien Guillaume de Malesherbes, the director of the *Librairie*, and which was used by the *commis* of Choiseul to denounce the lack of loyalty of the negotiators of the Utrecht accords.[90]

What is certain is that the use of commercial treaties as an instrument to harmonize, by balancing them, the interests of the European nations and to avoid the outbreak of new wars did not cease after Choiseul's fall from grace on 24 December 1770.

In keeping with the aim of countering British economic hegemony, the new foreign minister Vergennes, a tenacious supporter of the Family Compact, never attempted to recover Canada[91] while signing between 1774 and 1787 no fewer than six commercial treaties: apart from that with Britain (September 1786), he concluded treaties with the United States (February 1778), Sweden (July 1784), Spain (December 1786), Portugal (January 1786) and Russia (January 1787). As Jeffrey Horn has underlined, this diplomatic offensive had a clear objective, 'to facilitate the continuation of peace and provide opportunities for France to improve its economic competitiveness'.[92] Significantly, Pierre-Samuel Du Pont de Nemours entered the fray in defence of both the Anglo-French treaty of September 1786[93] and the maintenance of the Family Compact,[94] a perspective that the

[89] Stanley J. Stein and Barbara Stein, *Apogee of the Empire. Spain and New Spain in the Age of Charles III, 1759–1789* (Baltimore: Johns Hopkins University Press, 2003).

[90] Antonella Alimento, 'Tra strategie editoriali e progettualità riformista: la circolazione in Francia de *Le droit des gens* di Emer de Vattel', *Rivista Storica Italiana* 109 (2017), 536–573.

[91] Jacob Osinga, 'The Myth of the Treaties of February 6, 1778: A Case of Beautification of the Reality', in: *La Révolution américaine et l'Europe*, ed. Claude Fohlen and Jacques Godechot (Paris: CNRS, 1979), 371–384: 378.

[92] Jeff Horn, *The Path Not Taken. French Industrialization in the Age of Revolution, 1750–1830* (Cambridge, MA: MIT Press, 2006), 66.

[93] Pierre-Samuel Dupont de Nemours, *Lettre à la chambre du commerce de Normandie, sur le Mémoire qu'elle a publié relativement au traité de commerce avec l'Angleterre* (Rouen: 1788).

[94] Dupont de Nemours, *Le pacte de famille et les Conventions subséquentes entre la France & l'Espagne, avec des Observations sur chaque article* (Paris: Imprimerie Nationale, July 1790).

Republic discarded, preferring to turn to the passing of a Navigation Act, now said to be an international instrument of fraternity.[95]

Antonella Alimento is an Associate Professor in Modern History at the University of Pisa specializing in European eighteenth-century political and economic history. Among her key publications are *Réformes fiscales et crises politiques dans la France de Louis XV* (2008; first Italian edition 1995), *Finanze ed amministrazione. Un'inchiesta francese sui catasti nell'Italia del Settecento (1763–1764)* (2008) and the edited volume *War, Trade and Neutrality. Europe and the Mediterranean in the Seventeenth and Eighteenth Centuries* (2011).

[95] See the chapter by Belissa in this volume.

Securing Asian Trade: Treaty Negotiations between the French and English East India Companies, 1753–1755

John Shovlin

An uncertain peace came to the Coromandel Coast in the closing days of 1754.[1] After years of war, officials of the French and English East India companies signed a treaty suspending hostilities between them: each company promised in the future to recognize the possessions of the other and to permit its rival to trade freely in South Asia, and both agreed to withdraw from the Indian power struggles that had enmeshed them in conflict. A provisional accord, the deal would have to be ratified in Europe where, for a year and a half, the two bodies had negotiated the terms of a permanent settlement.[2] Following an initial approach from the East India Company in February 1753, the French proposed a treaty to exempt the settlements and vessels of both organizations

[1] Thanks to Antonella Alimento and Koen Stapelbroek for their advice; thanks also to Elizabeth Cross, Felicia Gottmann, and Pernille Røge for helpful criticism.

[2] Archives du Ministère des Affaires Étrangères, La Courneuve [AAE], Correspondance Politique [CP] Angleterre [Ang] 435, fol. 350, Gaston-Pierre de Lévis, duc de Mirepoix to François-Dominique de Barberie, marquis de Saint-Contest, 10 February 1753.

J. Shovlin (✉)
New York University, USA
e-mail: john.shovlin@nyu.edu

A. Alimento, K. Stapelbroek (eds.), *The Politics of Commercial Treaties in the Eighteenth Century*, DOI 10.1007/978-3-319-53574-6_10

from attack in case of future wars in Europe, to commit the companies to disengage from Indian politics, and to create an alliance between them to resist Indian princes who threatened their establishments or trade. Had these proposals been adopted, Franco-British commercial competition east of the Cape of Good Hope would, effectively, have been demilitarized, and the Anglo-French relationship in South Asia recast as a kind of security cartel to manage relations with Asian powers.

Neither this prospective accord nor the provisional deal signed in India was a commercial treaty in the ordinary sense of the term. In Europe, treaties of commerce were used to create a political framework to secure the trade of a state's subjects in spaces under the control of another sovereign. The sovereign in question agreed to permit and protect the commerce of foreign nationals, and sometimes to allow them a limited self-government under consuls. In parts of the world where rulers had no regular interaction with the European states system, as was the case with China and the Mughal Empire, making such governance arrangements fell to the chartered companies which monopolized trade between Europe and the East. In an Indian context, the companies typically secured *farmans*—grants of privileges and rights of self-government—from the Mughal emperor. However, a departure from these standard arrangements was entailed in the treaty negotiations which are the subject of this chapter. Here it was an agreement between the companies themselves that was at issue, aimed at establishing a political structure to secure Asian trade independent of Indian sovereigns, while also disentangling the companies from Franco-British geopolitical rivalry.

What has seemed important about the treaty to most scholars is the fact that it failed. After two years of talks, the best the companies could achieve was an anodyne declaration that they were "commercial" organizations, not "warlike or conquering" ones; the provisional treaty signed in India became a dead letter.[3] In the course of the war that followed, the East India Company crushed the French, and laid in Bengal the foundations for a new territorial empire. It is these violent events that have engrossed our attention. The preceding, abortive effort to direct history along a different path features prominently only in biographies of Dupleix, the French Governor General who set out to extend the territories controlled by the

[3] Philippe Haudrère, *La Compagnie française des Indes au XVIIIe siècle*, 2nd edn., 2 vols. (Paris: Les Indes savantes, 2005), II: 743.

Compagnie des Indes before he was recalled in 1754 as part of the search for peace. For French historians of an imperialist bent, this was the fatal moment when their forefathers let slip a world historical opportunity to found a great French empire in India.[4]

But it is not only for the way it made, or broke, the fortunes of European empires to be, or not to be, that the treaty negotiations between the two companies are worth examining. Indeed, to treat this moment as an episode in the history of European empire formation may occlude as much as it reveals. What is striking in the perspective of the companies is their wary attitude toward imperial control and domination, the shared sense that conquest and commerce might be incompatible. Each company wished to prevent its rival from establishing a territorial empire in India, but each sought also to avoid this fate itself. The companies advanced different, less familiar solutions to the problems of security and governance they faced—neutralization of European trade in Asia, and political cooperation to manage relations with Indian rulers. These impulses are often treated, anachronistically, as a failure of (imperial) vision on the part of the companies. In fact they reflect ambitious and sweeping prospects for remaking the geopolitics of the Indian Ocean region that deserve to be understood on their own terms.

We must take seriously as political thinkers the company directors and public officials who proposed and managed the treaty negotiations in 1753.[5] The companies had long been creative sites of political economic reflection, fostering, *inter alia*, ideas for remaking geopolitical rivalries on more peaceful lines. These visions are critical to understanding the 1753 initiative and are the principal subject of the chapter. In elaborating such perspectives, company insiders contributed to wider debates in the first half of the eighteenth century concerned with pacifying and stabilizing the international order by recasting the relationship between trade and power politics. These debates were occluded by the transformations in European political economy which occurred in the late 1750s and 1760s, and which

[4] On the theme of "l'Inde perdue," see Kate Marsh, "Territorial Loss and the Construction of French Colonial Identities, 1763–1962," in: *France's Lost Empires. Fragmentation, Nostalgia, and La Fracture Coloniale*, ed. Kate Marsh and Nicola Frith (Lanham, MD: Lexington Books, 2011), 1–14.

[5] Philip J. Stern, *The Company-State. Corporate Sovereignty and the Early Modern Foundations of the British Empire in India* (Oxford: Oxford University Press, 2011), 14.

introduced new ways to imagine a world of peaceful, competing, commercial states. It is only recently that we have begun to rediscover the intellectual richness of the earlier period.[6] Examining the treaty initiative of 1753 enhances our understanding of how early eighteenth-century Europeans imagined the possibilities for peaceful geopolitical transformation by taming "jealousy of trade." It also shows how such ideas could enter concretely into the practice of global politics. To be sure, they could do so only in a very particular political context, and it is to this context we turn first.

Indian Geopolitics and Restive Shareholders

The conditions that impelled the companies to negotiate a treaty in 1753 are to be found in the geopolitical context and above all in Indian politics. The India companies supplied a legal, political, and defense framework to foster trade in zones where the sovereignty of their home polities did not extend. By managing political relationships and negotiating trade and tax privileges with Asian powers, companies created a space in which the activities of European merchants and their Asian partners could be pursued profitably. This governance structure had major liabilities. Defense costs had to be borne directly by trade; they could not, except in special circumstances, be shifted onto taxpayers. Security spending ballooned disastrously during the 1740s and 1750s in the face of political instability in India and war in Europe. The negotiations begun in 1753 were intended to address this problem by coordinating the behavior of the French and English companies and by erecting a firewall between trade and politics.

Until the mid-1740s, the French and the British mostly managed to avoid clashes in South Asia. But when war broke out between the two kingdoms in the midst of the Austrian Succession struggle in Europe, conflict soon followed in India. French Governor General Joseph-François Dupleix hoped at first to preserve a state of peace between

[6] See, notably, Istvan Hont, *Jealousy of Trade. International Competition and the Nation-State in Historical Perspective* (Cambridge, MA: Belknap Press, 2005); Paul Cheney, *Revolutionary Commerce. Globalization and the French Monarchy* (Cambridge, MA: Harvard University Press, 2010); and Sophus A. Reinert, *Translating Empire. Emulation and the Origins of Political Economy* (Cambridge, MA: Harvard University Press, 2011).

the French and English settlements in the Coromandel, but the British refused the truce he proposed. Naval attacks quickly dried up the French company's trade and in 1746 Dupleix seized Madras, hoping to swap it for territories closer to Pondicherry from which the French could raise revenues. He had come to believe that the *Compagnie des Indes* could finance its operations only if it acquired a tax base in India.[7] To gain the necessary concessions from Indian powers, he threw the forces of the company behind the claims of Chanda Sahib and Muzafar Jang, who sought to become, respectively, nawab of Arcot and nizam of Hyderabad.[8] The strategy paid off to the degree that the French won new revenue farming rights in the Carnatic, and commercial and tax concessions at Machilipatnam, on the island of Divi, and in the Northern Circars. But the gain proved pyrrhic as the French were unable to make good on these acquisitions, or to defeat rival claimants to rule Arcot and Hyderabad, who received money and troops from the English company.[9] Indeed the French suffered major defeats in 1752 when Chanda Sahib was killed and a French army surrendered at Tiruchchirappalli to Indian and British forces.

The actions of Dupleix were impelled by geopolitical and regional political shifts—shifts also critical to understanding the desire of the companies to reach an agreement with one another. As the authority of the Mughal Empire waned, successor regimes emerged in several regions of South Asia including Bengal, the Carnatic, and the Deccan. New pressures and new opportunities arose for men like Dupleix and Robert Clive: pressures to adapt to an unstable political terrain, and opportunities to profit by joining in Indian struggles, backing one or another of the contenders for power in the successor states.[10] Geopolitically, war demonstrated that the French company could not carry on its commerce in the teeth of British naval attacks. It seemed unlikely, moreover, that

[7] Bibliothèque Nationale de France [BNF] Nouvelle Acquisitions Françaises [NAF] 9335, fos. 343–347; AAE Mémoires et Documents [MD] Asie 4, fos. 44–62.

[8] Haudrère, *Compagnie française des Indes*, II: 730–737.

[9] Catherine Manning, *Fortunes à Faire. The French in Asian Trade, 1718–48* (Aldershot: Variorum, 1996), 197–214.

[10] P. J. Marshall, "The British in Asia: Trade to Dominion, 1700–1765," in: *The Oxford History of the British Empire*, vol. II: *The Eighteenth Century*, ed. P. J. Marshall (Oxford: Oxford University Press, 1998), 487–507.

Franco-British relations would return to their prewar stability. The war left in its wake a range of potential flash points—in America, in Germany, and of course in India. The possibility of new wars in the future thus seemed very real.

Against this background, leaders of the companies in London and Paris concluded that the conflict between them in India must end. The most urgent impetus for peace was financial. Dupleix's initiatives were expensive. His wars cost the French company over twenty million *livres*, and struck at its commerce by drying up funds for trade.[11] For the East India Company, too, conflict with the French came at a high cost. The directors estimated in 1756 that the annual expenses of the company in India had increased by 60 percent since the fall of Madras, and that they had spent half a million pounds on the conflict with the French.[12] These losses dampened stock prices. The declaration of war with France in 1744 had triggered a sharp decline in the value of company shares; the fall of Madras prompted another slump.[13] The outbreak of a new war would surely bring similar results. Indeed, the Seven Years War, when it came, entailed the century's longest period of depressed East India stock values. It is telling that the peak share price for the entire period between early 1744 and mid-1766 occurred in June 1753, when a deal with the French seemed imminent.

After the fall of Madras, the directors of the East India Company were criticized for failing to accept a neutrality agreement proffered by the French company in 1744. The proposed accord stipulated that "In the event of war in Europe between the two Powers, there will be none in the East Indies between the French and the English." Neither were vessels of the companies to be permitted to attack one another at sea. The proposal was vetoed by Henry Gough, the dominant figure in the English company, who wanted scope to attack French shipping in the Indian Ocean.[14] Gough's action would later attract the ire of company servants involved in the defense of Madras, who felt they had been blamed for a loss that was

[11] Alfred Martineau, *Dupleix et l'Inde française*, 5 vols. (Paris: E. Champion, 1920), III: 26.

[12] British Library [BL] Egerton [Eg] MS 3487, fos. 185–186, Secret Committee of the East India Company to Robert Darcy, Earl of Holdernesse, 21 December 1756.

[13] John Castaing, *Course of the Exchange*, reproduced in European State Finance Database, http://esfdb.websites.bta.com/Database.aspx.

[14] BL Add MS 35906, fos. 180–181.

the consequence of London's choices. The Madras President, William Monson, attacked the direction for its "ill judged Parsimony, or stupid Neglect, to say no worse." In order to inflate the dividend, he charged, the directors failed to fortify Madras adequately or to maintain sufficient troops. The leadership should have accepted the neutrality offered by the French: "What could a Set of Merchants have desired or wished for more, than to carry on their Trade free from any additional Expence or Fear of Danger; at least in those Parts where they were most exposed?"[15] Monson's pamphlet was reissued in French translation—perhaps in an effort to invite renewed negotiation with the *Compagnie des Indes.*[16] Indeed that same year the French company weighed a new approach to its rival to secure a treaty of "perpetual neutrality."[17]

In Paris, a shareholder revolt was brewing against the policies of Dupleix. Syndic Joseph-Philippe Narcis complained in October 1751 that the funds sent to India to buy merchandise were diverted to warfare, crippling the company's trade.[18] Falling profits ate up dividends and depressed share values. A decline in the price of company stock set in from 1751. Rumors of new hostilities in India, well-founded or not, triggered drops in the share price. "It is said publicly that Pondicherry is invested by the Indians, supported by English in disguise," wrote one correspondent from Paris in the summer of 1753. In consequence, "The shares of the company have fallen by nearly 150 livres and it is not doubted but they will fall further every day. This news furiously alarms the poor share-holders."[19]

The nightmare scenario from the French point of view was that hostilities in India would trigger war in Europe. Could Dupleix be unaware, asked director Gabriel Michel, of "the public outcry against a company of merchants which dares [...] to abandon its trade to give itself over to a

[15] [William Monson], *A Letter to a Proprietor of the East-India Company* (London: T. Osborne, 1750).

[16] *Lettre écrite à un actionnaire de la Compagnie des Indes Orientales d'Angleterre* (London: T. Osborne, 1750).

[17] AAE MD Asie 12, fol. 228, "Sur le Projet d'un Traitté de Neut.$^{\acute{e}}$ perp.^{lle} entre les Comp.^{ies} des Indes de France et d'Ang.^{re}," October 1750.

[18] Archives Nationales, Paris [AN] Colonies [Col] C^2 44, fos. 48–60.

[19] Essex Record Office, Chelmsford, Mildmay Papers, D/DM/O1/27, unidentified to William Mildmay, 17 July 1753.

spirit of conquest, and does not fear to provoke a rupture with our neighbors?"[20] From the perspective of the directors, geopolitical stability was necessary to make a profit, indeed to keep the company afloat. The company prospered during the Franco-British peace of the 1720s and 1730s: the volume of its shipping and trade expanded; profits and share prices rose. After 1744, by contrast, it suffered major losses; its trade dried up; shareholders were pressed to recapitalize the company, and dividends went unpaid—leading to a revolt of the stockholders in 1745 and a reorganization of the direction.[21]

Against the background of shareholder disaffection with Dupleix, one of the syndics of the company, Pierre-Claude Delaître, proposed in 1752 that a treaty be made with the English company, not only to end the conflict in Asia, but to place the relationship between the two on a more cooperative footing. War between the companies had to end, Delaître argued: it had ruined trade; it exposed both companies to manipulation by Indian rulers; it risked teaching European military discipline to Indian powers, which in time might jeopardize the European presence in Asia; and it created an opening for interlopers like Prussia's new Embden Company. Strife among the companies also exposed them to being exploited by their own servants, who pursued private political and financial ambitions at their employers' expense. This last theme was a frequent complaint directed against Dupleix and his lieutenants, as it would later be against Clive and other English "nabobs."

Delaître proposed a treaty allying the French and English companies, to which the Dutch might later be invited to accede. The companies should agree to fix the rights and possessions of each, renouncing forever any claims against the possessions of the other. Each company should guarantee the holdings of its rival in case of attack by a third party—make common cause, that is, against Indian rulers. The companies should cease meddling in the wars of Asian powers and, in case of war in Europe, the vessels and settlements of both should be exempt from attack. They should enjoy freedom to trade in all parts of India, and no new establishments should be made tending to exclude the trade of the other company. What Delaître proposed, in effect, was a cartel between the

[20] BNF NAF 9150, fos. 22–23, Gabriel Michel to Joseph-François Dupleix, 21 January 1754.

[21] Haudrère, *Compagnie française des Indes*, I: 126–127.

companies for their collective security, and the neutralization of a vast zone east of the Cape of Good Hope from European geopolitical struggles.[22] His proposal embodied the central elements of the initial French negotiating position in the summer of 1753.

Commerce not Conquest: The Geopolitics of the *Compagnie des Indes*

Delaître's proposal went beyond earlier calls for wartime neutrality deals between the European companies, or truces between adjacent settlements, and harkened back to more ambitious schemes for the permanent pacification of European long-distance trade floated in the opening decades of the century. In his 1713 plan for "perpetual peace," the abbé de Saint-Pierre had suggested that Europeans, including the India companies, should have freedom to trade in Asia under the auspices of a body established by the European federation he proposed, which would provide security and manage diplomatic relations with Asian powers.[23] This idea for a common European cartel to secure and pacify trade to the East Indies echoes schemes for the joint management of trade to Spanish America fostered in the same period by France's chief commercial diplomat, Nicolas Mesnager. As Koen Stapelbroek has shown, Mesnager worked fruitlessly between 1705 and 1711 to convince Spanish, Dutch, and English counterparts that an international cartel of European merchants would offer the best framework to manage trade to the Spanish Empire.[24] As in Delaître's later proposal for the East Indies, the trade was to enjoy neutrality in wartime. Mesnager's vision was not forgotten. It was the basis for a plan to reorganize the Spanish American trade developed in the early 1730s by France's *contrôle général*, the ministry which also supervised the

[22] "Mémoire sur les inconvénients pour les trois Compagnies françoise, angloise et hollandoise de leur mésintelligence dans l'Inde, sur les avantages communs à ces trois Comp.[es] qui resulteroient de leur Union," 30 July 1752, AN Col C2 38, fos. 74–81.

[23] Charles Irénée Castel de Saint-Pierre, *Projet pour rendre la paix perpétuelle en Europe*, 3 vols. (Utrecht: A. Schouten, 1713–1717), I: ix; II: 264–269.

[24] Koen Stapelbroek, "'The Long Peace': Commercial Treaties and the Principles of Global Trade at the Peace of Utrecht," in: *The 1713 Peace of Utrecht and Its Enduring Effects*, ed. A. H. A. Soons (Leiden: Brill, forthcoming).

Compagnie des Indes.[25] The outlook of Saint-Pierre, too, had its partisans within the company: the director Pierre Saintard would publish a peace plan inspired by it on the eve of the Seven Years War.[26]

A second and different strain of political economic thought, identified by Istvan Hont as "neo-Colbertist," also came into play in 1753.[27] Writers associated with the *Compagnie des Indes* had played a key role in the development of this line of analysis. Indeed the founder of the modern company, the Scottish financier John Law, has some claim to be viewed as its originator. Law had an ambitious agenda to pacify Europe under a benign French hegemony. Had his "System" survived, he later claimed, it "would have conserved the peace of Europe."[28] Law toyed with the idea of European trading companies operating cooperatively in Asia, though it was never central to his thinking.[29] While converging with Saint-Pierre's views on the value of peace, the spirit of Law's thinking was different. The abbé wanted the structures of international politics bent to the needs of trade, while, for Law, commerce—albeit peaceful commerce—continued to be the handmaiden of power. His *Compagnie des Indes* and Banque Générale would endow France with such a degree of economic preponderance, he argued, as to make coalition warfare against it unwinnable. The result would be a peaceful Europe rather than universal monarchy, according to Law, because France would have no further interest in conquest—indeed, it "would weaken itself by expanding."[30] For the Scot, peace was condition as well as consequence of his System's success. He supported the French alliance with Britain negotiated by the abbé Guillaume Dubois, believing it would shelter his System while it took root. Tensions with Britain would ease in any case as the paper money

[25] Bibliothèque de l'Arsenal MS 6193, "Mémoire sur le commerce de l'Amérique, par M. Malet," February 1732.

[26] [Pierre Saintard], *Roman politique sur l'état présent des affaires d'Amérique, ou Lettres de M*** à M*** sur les moyens d'établir une paix solide & durable dans les colonies, & la liberté générale du commerce extérieur* (Amsterdam: Duchesne, 1756).

[27] Hont, *Jealousy of Trade*, 28–30.

[28] Bibliothèque Méjanes, Aix-en-Provence, MS 614 (355), John Law to M. de Rosemberg, 15 May 1722.

[29] John Law, "Réponse aux deux lettres, sur le Nouveau Système des Finances," in: *Œuvres complètes*, ed. Paul Harsin, 3 vols. (Paris: Librairie du Recueil Sirey, 1934), III: 115.

[30] BNF MS français 21750, fos. 4–5, Law to Philippe d'Orléans, undated.

Law's bank issued reduced French dependence on Spanish American silver, and thus devalued the struggle for New World trade.[31]

Law's ideas shaped subsequent debate in French political economy, especially debates within and on the edges of the *Compagnie des Indes.* After the Scot was disgraced in 1720, his enemies took over and reorganized the company, yet a circle of major shareholders continued to sympathize with Law's ideas. In this milieu, the most influential theorist was Law's one-time secretary, Jean-François Melon. In his *Essai politique sur le commerce* (1734), Melon claimed that "the spirit of conquest and the spirit of commerce are mutually exclusive in a nation," a formula which, echoing Law, rejected territorial expansionism and war, and valorized economic development as the sole route to security and power. Melon's political economy was pacific in spirit, concerned with containing the threat of British commercial power by developing French manufactures and agriculture.[32] He believed a commercial empire could play a role in generating wealth, but he rejected territorial empires, such as that of Spain, based on extraction rather than trade, and requiring large numbers of colonists and soldiers to secure. Another of Law's former lieutenants, Nicolas Dutot, while differing with Melon in many respects, also believed that peaceful commercial expansion was the key to success. "An end to those victories won by ruinous efforts," Dutot wrote. "France, superior by the advantages of her trade will make known to neighboring states that she is as capable of increasing her power by peace as by war."[33]

Dutot's call for aggrandizement through peaceful commercial expansion appealed to the young Étienne de Silhouette, who would go on to be royal commissioner of the *Compagnie des Indes* in the 1750s. Invoking Dutot, Silhouette argued that the British feared the pacific projects of the French more than their military ones, because "it is in fact more by the arts of peace than by those of war that France is in a position to ruin this rival

[31] See John Shovlin, "Jealousy of Credit: John Law's 'System' and the Geopolitics of Financial Revolution," *Journal of Modern History* 88 (2016), 275–305.

[32] Istvan Hont, "The 'Rich Country–Poor Country' Debate Revisited: The Irish Origins and French Reception of the Hume Paradox," in: *David Hume's Political Economy*, ed. Margaret Schabas and Carl Wennerlind (London: Routledge, 2008), 243–322; 263.

[33] Nicolas Dutot, *Réflexions politiques sur les finances, et le commerce*, 2 vols. (The Hague: Frères Vaillant & N. Prevost, 1738), II: 403–404. Dutot had been a cashier of the company under the System. See François Velde, "The Life and Times of Nicolas Dutot," *Journal of the History of Economic Thought* 34 (2012), 67–107.

and enemy nation."[34] He reiterated this claim in a widely read memorandum of 1747 where he argued that the key strategic challenge was to prevent the emergence of a British monopoly of American trade.[35] Silhouette helped manage French relations with Britain in the 1750s as a diplomat regulating territorial disputes in America, and subsequently as commissioner of the *Compagnie des Indes*, where he also directed the unfolding negotiation with the East India Company.

In this role, Silhouette favored peaceful commerce over territorial aggrandizement in India, and put himself at the head of the anti-Dupleix party. In 1752 he told Dupleix that in Paris "peace is generally preferred to conquests." Territorial concessions would only drag the French into internecine Indian struggles. "We do not wish to become a political power in India," Silhouette wrote, "we want only a few establishments to aid and protect trade."[36] This position was echoed by several of the writers associated with intendant of trade, Jacques-Claude Vincent de Gournay, with whom Silhouette was allied. According to François Véron de Forbonnais, the establishments of European nations in India "would deviate from their original purpose if they were to become conquering."[37] Commerce rather than conquest in India was also the preference of Silhouette's superior, *contrôleur général des finances* Jean-Baptiste Machault d'Arnouville—the most influential minister in the French government. Machault wanted financial retrenchment, for which peace was essential. "One cannot desire too much the end of the troubles in India," he wrote in March 1753, adding that he hoped the pacific overtures of the East India Company "will be followed by a happy success."[38]

[34] AAE CP Ang 405, fos. 394–399, Étienne de Silhouette to André-Hercule, Cardinal Fleury, 31 December 1739.

[35] AAE MD Ang 46, fos. 45–88, "Observations sur les finances, la navigation & le commerce de l'Angleterre."

[36] BNF NAF 9150, fos. 266–267, Silhouette to Dupleix, 13 September 1752.

[37] François Véron de Forbonnais, *Élémens du commerce*, 2 vols. (Leiden: Briasson, 1754), I: 355. See also [Louis-Joseph Plumard de Dangeul], *Remarques sur les avantages et les désavantages de la France et de la Grande Bretagne, par rapport au commerce, & aux autres sources de la puissance des États*, 3rd edn. (Paris: Frères Éstienne, 1754), 237.

[38] AAE CP Ang 436, fol. 7, Machault to Saint-Contest, 1 March 1753.

Thus, for the French, the negotiation undertaken in 1753 constituted a convergence of two positions. It emerged from a line of thinking long associated with the company arguing that peace best served French geopolitical interests because it favored the commercial expansion which underpinned power—a view tending to value commerce over conquest. This position was allied to proposals for neutralizing trade, which had their origin early in the century. In the interests of profits and financial stability, trade must be sheltered from war, if need be through some kind of cartel with commercial rivals to neutralize it. Views with affinities to these, though derived from different intellectual roots, also spurred the peace party in the English company and its supporters in the British government. Indeed it was this convergence that opened the way for negotiation between the two companies. Thus with support from Silhouette and the leaders of the company, director Pierre Duvelaer and his brother the comte du Lude traveled to London in April 1753 to conduct negotiations with the Secret Committee of the East India Company.

Containing France by the Arts of Peace

The negotiations initiated in 1753 by the East India Company reflected the intellectual traditions of the company and must also be situated within currents of thinking and action oriented to recasting British relations with France. The War of the Austrian Succession ended in stalemate. Great Britain gained nothing from it, and was left with a ballooning national debt. The conflict bolstered the conviction that France was Britain's most dangerous rival, but left unresolved how the British might best respond to the French challenge. Some Britons, especially among the former "patriot" critics of Walpole, looked with equanimity on the prospect of a new war, concentrated against French naval power and colonies. Others, even among the patriots, reflecting on the futility of the preceding struggle, and the alarming inflation of the public debt, sought more peaceful ways to contain French power.

These tendencies were reflected in the government, a coalition of forces originally loyal to Walpole with others from patriot opposition ranks.[39] Walpole's stance in foreign relations had been notably pacific, a proclivity shared by his successor, Henry Pelham, Prime Minister

[39] John B. Owen, *The Rise of the Pelhams* (London: Methuen, 1957).

from 1743 until his death in 1754. Pelham pushed for an end to the War of the Austrian Succession as early as 1745, and, in 1748, looked forward to a peace which would permit economies and lower taxes.[40] His pacific inclinations were shared by the patriot Duke of Bedford, and by Lord Holdernesse, the two ministers who successively oversaw relations with France in this period. Lord Chancellor Philip Hardwicke was decidedly a member of the peace camp, as was Pelham's brother, the Duke of Newcastle, though less reliably so.[41] Those who sought to check France without war could draw on a range of political economic perspectives offering blueprints for a less bellicose, if still unremittingly competitive, relationship.

A proposal to liberalize trade with France was popularized by the most widely read English political economist of the 1740s, Sir Matthew Decker. A former chairman of the East India Company, Decker was the latest in a line of influential political economic writers associated with the company.[42] He argued that a freer trade was the best means to enrich Britain and to reduce thereby the relative power of its rival. The failure to confirm the commercial treaty signed at Utrecht in 1713, he argued, was mistaken. The British could have ousted the Dutch as the carriers of French goods, and benefited from low-priced French linens. Britain would have no trouble winning an economic struggle with France if the price of labor were contained. To achieve this end, Decker called for reform of the tax system and the transformation of Great Britain into a general free port. The customs duties funding the national debt strangled trade, he argued, while excises drove up the cost of labor, pricing British manufactures out of foreign markets. Freer trade, too, would diminish labor costs—a more effective mode of protecting British industries than high duties which encouraged smuggling.[43]

[40] Newcastle (Clumber) Collection [Ne(C)], University of Nottingham, 389/1–2 Henry Pelham to William Stanhope, Earl of Harrington, 12 July 1745; Ne(C) 1290 Pelham to Thomas Pelham-Holles, Duke of Newcastle, 12 May 1752; Ne(C) 1291 Pelham to Newcastle, 25 May 1752.

[41] William Coxe, *Memoirs of the Administration of the Right Honourable Henry Pelham*, 2 vols. (London: Longman, 1829), I: 32, 39.

[42] Philip J. Stern, "Companies: Monopoly, Sovereignty, and the East Indies," in: *Mercantilism Reimagined. Political Economy in Early Modern Britain and its Empire*, ed. Philip J. Stern and Carl Wennerlind (Oxford: Oxford University Press, 2013), 177–195.

[43] [Sir Matthew Decker], *An Essay on the Causes of the Decline of the Foreign Trade* (London: John Brotherton, 1744).

Given Decker's biography, it is tempting to link his political economy to the initiative of the East India Company to reach an accommodation with its French rival. Decker had been the dominant figure in the company from the 1720s through the early 1730s, a period when the two bodies avoided the clashes that marked their relationship in the 1740s. Having died in 1749, he played no part in the negotiations, but he would likely have approved of them had he lived. His staunchest City allies worked to shape a less bellicose Franco-British relationship in the 1740s, and would do so again on the eve of the Seven Years War. In 1745, Decker's friend, Gerard Van Neck—another erstwhile East India director—played a role in unofficial diplomacy seeking to end the war.[44] Ten years later, his brother Joshua Van Neck worked to head off the coming conflict by serving as a back channel between the peace camps in France and Britain. He was supported by his business partner and son-in-law, Thomas Walpole (nephew of Sir Robert), a sitting director of the Company.[45]

Yet Decker's call for freer trade was not embraced by the leadership of the company when the idea of reviving the 1713 commercial treaty with France was raised in 1749 by the Duke of Bedford. Bedford claimed that those elements of the 1713 treaty not vetoed by the House of Commons in 1713 ought still to govern trading relations between the two powers, a position the French rejected.[46] Nevertheless, with some support from Pelham and Holdernesse (who replaced Bedford as secretary for the southern department in 1751), efforts were made to liberalize trade with France. The British relaxed the duty imposed on French ships in English ports, and pushed the French to reciprocate. They sought to open French markets to British hardware and clocks. Some within the French

[44] AAE CP Ang 421, fos. 57–60, Jean-Baptiste Fournier to Jean-Ignace de La Ville, 7/18 June 1745.

[45] BL Add MS 32861, fos. 118–119, Thomas Walpole to Horatio Walpole, 28 November 1755; BL Add MS 32862, fol. 279, unidentified to Newcastle, 29 January 1756.

[46] John Russell, Duke of Bedford to Willem Anne van Keppel, Earl of Albemarle, 3 August 1749, in: *Correspondence of John, Fourth Duke of Bedford*, ed. Lord John Russell, 3 vols. (London: Longman, 1844–1846), II: 40–44; AAE MD Ang 69, fol. 17, François-Marie Durand to Louis-Philogène Brulart, marquis de Puysieulx, 17 July 1749. As Antonella Alimento has shown, Forbonnais underlined the dangers of unequal trade treaties in this context: "Beyond the Treaty of Utrecht: Véron de Forbonnais' French Translation of the *British Merchant* (1753)," *History of European Ideas* 40 (2014), 1044–1066.

administration were open to a measure of liberalization.[47] The sticking point was a British law passed in 1745 to ban the importation of fine French linens.[48] Pelham introduced a bill to repeal the exclusion in 1753 but gave it only lukewarm support. In fact, the bill was anathema to some of the government's most loyal supporters, including William Baker, chairman of the East India Company, who came out strongly against it.

Ultimately the company's position on negotiating with the French in 1753 owed less to Decker's position on trade liberalization than to his conviction that the best way to beat the French geopolitically was to undersell them. This general perspective was shared by many in the Pelhamite camp. Lord Hardwicke and his sons, Philip, Charles, and Joseph Yorke, cultivated a circle of writers and political economists broadly sympathetic to Walpole and sharing his skepticism that Britain could be the economic gainer by war. In letters to Philip Yorke, Thomas Birch discussed Voltaire's *Anti-Machiavel* and the abbé de Saint-Pierre's judgment of the work, while excoriating the aggressive foreign policy of Frederick II.[49] The younger Yorkes befriended Isaac de Pinto, a leading critic of jealousy of trade.[50] The Hardwicke nexus also drew in Josiah Tucker, who held that Great Britain must strike at France not through war but via peaceful commercial competition. Tucker opposed fighting to extend the British Empire into the interior of North America. He urged that Britain check its enemy "by ye Arts of Peace."[51] Its rulers must expand trade, manufactures, and navigation, to "increase his Majesty's Revenue, and do everything that is necessary to make a Nation great and powerful; without involving us in any Disputes with France or any other Power."[52]

Pelham, Hardwicke, and Holdernesse patronized officials who shared their outlook. One such was William Mildmay, appointed as a royal

[47] AAE MD Ang 69, fos. 151–152, Philibert Trudaine de Montigny to Puysieulx, 27 May 1751.

[48] AAE MD Ang 69, fos. 4–162.

[49] BL Add MS 35396, fos. 35–36, Thomas Birch to Philip Yorke, 27 October 1741.

[50] BL Add MS 35918, fos. 1, 4–12, 15–19, 23–33, 75, Pinto to Charles Yorke; fol. 82, Joseph Yorke to Pinto; BL Eg MS 1749, fos. 317–318, Pinto to William Bentinck, 20 July 1765.

[51] BL Add MS 4319, fol. 260, Josiah Tucker to Birch, 30 November 1756.

[52] [Josiah Tucker], *The Case of the Importation of Bar-Iron, from Our Own Colonies of North America* (London: Thomas Trye, 1756), 15.

commissioner to accommodate Franco-British differences in America. Against the hardline position of his fellow commissioner, William Shirley, Mildmay supported a pragmatic partition of disputed territories in America.[53] He viewed trade as a field of struggle between nations but believed that, if the confrontation with France could be limited to an economic terrain, Britain must prevail, given the burdens imposed on the French by their "constitution."[54] In political economic works published in the 1760s he argued that while natural endowments were important, it was intelligent economic policy that would decide the contest between states.[55] Mildmay took a lively interest in the India negotiations, and hoped for a peaceful accommodation. From Paris he reported that "All sensible people in this Country, as well as in ours, are convinced that a flourishing Commerce cannot be carried on by either Side without a mutual agreement to keep Peace with one another."[56]

A similar view was taken by Alexander Hume, an influential East India shareholder, MP, and ally of Pelham and Holdernesse, who was to play the leading role in company negotiations with the French. As a former agent of the Ostend Company in Bengal, Hume had experience of managing a profitable India trade without troops and fortifications, but also understood the decisive character of European politics for the companies. After the Ostend operation was terminated under the Treaty of Vienna in 1731 the East India Company recruited him, and he served in the direction during the War of the Austrian Succession.[57] There he experienced the downside of military confrontation with the French. Hume saw little advantage to acquiring more territory on the Coromandel Coast. "We desire no Conquests upon the French in India," he argued. "They would be of no use to Us."[58]

[53] BL Eg 3456, fol. 203, Mildmay to Holdernesse, 22 April/3 May 1752.

[54] BL Eg 3456, fos. 254–255, Mildmay to Holdernesse, 19/30 June 1752.

[55] William Mildmay, *The Laws and Policy of England, Relating to Trade, Examined by the Maxims and Principles of Trade in General* (London: T. Harrison, 1765). Mildmay was a longtime student of political economy. See Essex Record Office, Mildmay Papers, D/DM/O1/19, 27–28, 42.

[56] William Clements Library, University of Michigan, Mildmay Papers, vol. 3, Mildmay to William Mildmay, Earl Fitzwalter, 13 February 1754.

[57] BL Add MS 73965, fos. 27–28, John Drummond to Horatio Walpole, 12 August 1737.

[58] BL Eg MS 3484, fos. 45–50.

But he appreciated the menace that a militarized French presence there represented to the interests of the English company. Its other vulnerability was the threat to its balance sheet of any shock in India—a hazard that extended to public credit, given the role the company played in the management of the public debt. These were issues to which Hume was sensitive, both as a major stockholder, and as one of Pelham's closest City allies in the management of the government's credit.[59]

The solution to these problems was the separation of the India trade from global Franco-British military competition. Hume was the principal champion in the British company of the neutrality treaty proffered by the French—a neutrality to extend not only to settlements and trade in India, but to the shipping of the two companies. Neutrality would resolve the problems of the company in India by rechanneling Anglo-French competition into a more purely commercial form, while benefiting British security at home by saving the Admiralty from sending a squadron to the Indies in any future war.

Territorial Parity and Commercial Competition

Despite the support for an accommodation between the companies, a deal proved elusive. While the companies favored the neutralization of trade, the divergent interests of the two governments stymied an agreement extending to shipping. Neither was the English company prepared to go as far as the French in matters of security cooperation in India. There were other hitches. While the French were in earnest about abandoning the strategy pursued by Dupleix, they were reluctant to give up all the territorial gains he had made, which inspired British mistrust that they still sought territorial empire. Despite these hurdles a deal might have been possible; indeed, a preliminary agreement was actually signed late in 1754 in the Coromandel. Ultimately, it would be clashes in America that rendered these efforts futile.

The Secret Committee of the East India Company took up Hume's arguments in favor of neutralization. In the Duke of Newcastle's words, "our Directors now press the neutrality extremely."[60] The companies

[59] BL Add. MS 33055, fos. 265–268, "Memorandum relating to Mr. H[ume]," 10 December 1760.

[60] BL Eg MS 3484, fol. 17, cabinet minute, 30 May 1753.

wished to assume a neutral stance in future Franco-British wars; their wartime position would be analogous to small, commercially vulnerable polities hoping to shelter their trade in a time of conflict. For the two governments, on the other hand, this meant circumscribing the domain in which future conflict might be conducted.[61] The discussion of a neutrality agreement continued over the summer, but while the cabinet approved a neutralization of settlements in Asia, it refused to extend it to French vessels at sea.[62] The Admiralty opposed the measure, wanting to take advantage of British naval superiority.[63] The French were understandably uninterested in any agreement that did not cover their shipping.[64]

If it scuttled the neutrality deal, the cabinet nevertheless favored an accord to end hostilities in India. The conflict threatened to drag in the two powers, and English public credit was hostage to the fortunes of the company. The talks focused henceforth on ending the fighting and preventing future struggles by fixing the possessions of the two companies and committing both to withdraw permanently from Indian politics. The companies accepted that they should cooperate in the future on security matters. The French proposed an alliance in India.[65] The more minimal formula settled on by the English was that each company would seek the good offices of the other in case of a dispute with an Indian power.[66] While both parties agreed to withdraw from Indian politics, settling outstanding succession struggles was a thornier problem. The English wanted the French to recognize their claimant in Arcot, Mahomed Ali Khan.

[61] The distinction is between *neutrality* and *neutralization*. See Éric Schnakenbourg, *Entre la guerre et la paix: neutralité et relations internationales XVIIe–XVIIIe siècles* (Rennes: Presses Universitaires de Rennes, 2013), 10–11.

[62] BL Eg MS 3484, fos. 34–35, Newcastle to Joseph Yorke, 26 June 1753; fos. 43–45, Secret Committee to Newcastle, 18 July 1753; fos. 74–75, Newcastle to Joseph Yorke, 14 September 1753.

[63] AAE CP Ang 436, fos. 193–196, Mirepoix to Machault, 8 June 1753.

[64] BL Eg MS 3484, fos. 27–29, copy of a letter to Duvelaer, 16 June 1753.

[65] BL Eg MS 3484, fol. 59, "Extrait des articles d'un projet de neutralité envoyé par M. Duvelaer, le 23 May 1753 avec des observations par le Comité Secret de la Compagnie des Indes de France."

[66] BL Eg MS 3484, fos. 122–123, "Heads of Articles," 26 October 1753.

The French refused. Duvelaer agreed to a compromise allowing the Mughal emperor to designate a nawab, but he was overruled by Paris.[67] The French were worried about losing credibility in India.

The more fundamental difficulty, however, which absorbed the negotiators for much of 1754, was the disposition of territories and settlements. Initially, the English proposed that both companies withdraw to their prewar limits. This was unacceptable to the French who, if they disavowed the strategy of Dupleix, wished to salvage from his acquisitions whatever seemed compatible with future peace.[68] The East India Company next proposed that the French retain new acquisitions near Pondicherry, while ceding to the English equivalent territories near Fort St. George.[69] This too was unacceptable in Paris. Silhouette wanted to preserve gains in the Northern Coromandel.[70] Ultimately the French aspired to territorial parity with the English company.[71] For their part, the English negotiators worried that the French had not broken with the spirit of Dupleix, that they still sought large territorial concessions and tax revenues.

Ultimately, the English company wished to separate trade from "political" sources of profit or advantage. In language adopted by the Secret Committee, Hume proposed that the two companies should have the right to establish any factories they pleased on the Coromandel Coast or in the Deccan, "provid'd such new Establishments or Factories do not by their Extent, Situation, Revenues or other Profits (excepting Those to be obtain'd by Commerce only) give just Cause of Umbrage to either Company." Neither company was to be permitted to develop a tax base, nor was either to be allowed to fortify or garrison new establishments "beyond what may be necessary to secure their own Persons & Property."[72] Neither company should use political means to close off trading opportunities to the other. The model here may have been the

[67] AN Col C[2] 41, fos. 114–115, Duvelaer to the Secret Committee of the *Compagnie des Indes*, 2 May 1754.

[68] BL IOR/I/1/4, "Narrative of what formerly passed towards effecting an Accommodation between the English and French Companies."

[69] BL Eg MS 3484, fos. 122–123, "Heads of Articles," 26 October 1753.

[70] AN Col C[2] 39, fol. 97, Silhouette, "Mémoire sur les affaires de l'Inde."

[71] BL Eg MS 3484, fos. 280–284, Machault to Mirepoix, 11 March 1754.

[72] BL Eg 3486, fos. 119–120, draft proposal for revised 5th article. See also fol. 121, Alexander Hume to Holdernesse, 30 October 1754.

smaller European companies, which managed to trade—and seemingly to profit—without the large investments in security that threatened the balance sheets of the English and French. Alexander Hume, it will be recalled, had made his fortune in the Ostend Company.

As the talks dragged on, each company feared the other was playing for time, angling to strengthen its military position in India. At Silhouette's behest, the French sent 2,000 men to India under director Charles Godeheu, who was to replace Dupleix as the leading French official. Godeheu was authorized to negotiate a provisional settlement with the servants of the East India Company. On learning of the large force traveling with him, however, the English directors demanded a naval squadron to protect British settlements.[73] By the end of 1754, Hume was beginning to doubt that negotiation could resolve the outstanding issues and was contemplating military solutions.[74] This was a second best strategy, but a treaty with the French appeared increasingly out of reach.

All hope was not yet lost though. On his arrival, Godeheu quickly concluded a truce and provisional treaty with Thomas Saunders, the Madras president, which embodied aspirations articulated by both sides in the preceding years. The two officials agreed to withdraw from the quarrels of Indian princes. During the truce, the two "nations" were to make common cause against any Indian ally that disturbed the peace. The treaty made a preliminary territorial division based on the principle of parity between the companies. So, for example, they decided that Machilipatnam and Divi should be "neuter" until London and Paris decided on a final partition, with each side eventually to receive one settlement or the other. Trade was to be "free," in the sense that neither side would obstruct the other, throughout the Carnatic and in the countries to the north of the Coromandel.

When word of its signing arrived in Europe, the Godeheu–Saunders Treaty revived hope for a permanent agreement. While Hume criticized the treaty as "loose and imperfect," if revised it might serve as the basis for a deal.[75]

[73] BL Eg MS 3484, fos. 70–72, Court of Directors to Holdernesse, 14 September 1753; BL Eg MS 3484, fol. 98, cabinet minute, 27 September 1753; AAE CP Ang 437, fos. 25–26, Mirepoix to Saint Contest, 17 January 1754; BL Eg MS 3484, fol. 136, council minute, 17 January 1754.

[74] BL Eg 3486, fol. 193, Hume to Holdernesse, 1 December 1754; fos. 210–213, "Plan humbly offered for the Support of the British Possessions Trade & Privilidges [sic] in the East Indies."

[75] BL Eg MS 3487, fol. 72, Hume to Holdernesse, 8 June 1755; fos. 76–77, Hume to Holdernesse, 26 June 1755.

Holdernesse congratulated Hume on "the appearance there now is of bringing about an accommodation between the English and French E. I. Comp[s]."[76] The Indian treaty seemed set to revive the negotiation in London. But just at this moment it became clear that military conflict between French and British forces in America was imminent.[77] Frontier clashes in the Ohio country in the summer of 1754 had broadened by 1755 into an undeclared war pitting British regulars against French colonial troops and their Native American allies. With a formal state of war now fast approaching, the Godeheu–Saunders deal became a dead letter.[78]

Coda: Trade and Geopolitics after the Seven Years War

The Seven Years War transformed the context of Franco-British relations in India. By the end of the conflict, the East India Company had established the foundations of a territorial empire in Bengal, and decisively defeated the French on the Coromandel Coast. At the peace, the *Compagnie des Indes* ceded all the territories it had gained since 1749. But if the scene had shifted, the challenge of securing Asian trade persisted. For the East India Company, it was unclear if the costs of territorial empire in Bengal could be sustained on the basis of its new privileges. "So large a sovereignty may possibly be an object too extensive for a mercantile company [. . .] without the nation's assistance," worried Clive. Laurence Sulivan warned of the dangers of territorial empire for a trading company, remarking that the conquests of Dupleix had been a prelude to French ruin.[79] Clive's acquisition of the *diwani* for the company in Bengal would not resolve this dilemma. The problem of balancing revenues with administrative and military costs plagued the

[76] BL Eg MS 3487, fos. 112–113, Holdernesse to Hume, 11 July 1755.

[77] BL Eg MS 3487, fol. 83, Secret Committee to Holdernesse, 27 June 1755; BL Add MS 32856, fol. 113, Roger Drake to Newcastle, 22 June 1755; BL Eg MS 3487, fos. 134–135, Secret Committee to Henry Fox, 18 August 1756.

[78] BL Eg MS 3487, fos. 116–117, Secret Committee to Sir Thomas Robinson, 30 July 1755.

[79] Robert Clive to William Pitt, 7 January 1759, cited in *Fifth Report from the Select Committee of the House of Commons on the Affairs of the East India Company* (New York: A. M. Kelley, 1969 [1812]), clvi; BL IOR/H/808, fol. 186, Laurence Sulivan to Pitt, 27 July 1761.

company for decades, and gradually drew the crown into stewardship over the company's domain in India.[80]

If the problem of balancing profit with security persisted for the English company, it was more acute—and the postwar debate correspondingly more searching—in the *Compagnie des Indes.* The company was reorganized in 1764, and in 1769 the crown stripped it of its monopoly and reconstituted it as the manager of the Indian *comptoirs* necessary to sustain a "free" French trade. These reforms and the arguments they elicited have been ably described elsewhere.[81] My objective here is simply to situate the debate of the 1760s in relation to the 1753 treaty initiative and the thinking it reflected.

The principal point is that the terms of the postwar debate constituted a partial rupture with the political and intellectual traditions of the company—a breach which eventually effaced earlier peacemaking efforts. Some of the impulses that distinguished the prewar period faded. Neutralizing trade receded as a solution to the problems of French commerce in Asia. Proposals for security cooperation with the British disappeared; only in the 1780s, with the foundation of the *Nouvelle Compagnie des Indes*, did the idea of a cartel resurface, and then in a different form.[82] The efforts of the company to reach an accommodation with its British rival were gradually forgotten, while the notion that the companies favored war in the interests of trade began to take root. This process of rupture and occlusion occurred in part because debate on the problem of securing Asian trade moved outside the company, into the public sphere, and came to be dominated by individuals without ties to the organization—indeed hostile to its existence. The war years had given birth to Physiocracy, which disdained

[80] H. V. Bowen, *Revenue & Reform. The Indian Problem in British Politics 1757–1773* (Cambridge: Cambridge University Press, 1991); H. V. Bowen, *The Business of Empire. The East India Company and Imperial Britain, 1756–1833* (Cambridge: Cambridge University Press, 2006).

[81] Kenneth Margerison, "Commercial Liberty, French National Power, and the Indies Trade after the Seven Years' War," *Historical Reflections/Réflexions Historiques* 35 (2009), 52–73; Kenneth Margerison, "The Shareholders' Revolt at the Compagnie des Indes: Commerce and Political Culture in Old Regime France," *French History* 22 (2006), 25–51; Anoush Fraser Terjanian, *Commerce and Its Discontents in Eighteenth-Century French Political Thought* (Cambridge: Cambridge University Press, 2013), 137–181.

[82] Holden Furber, *John Company at Work: A Study of European Expansion in India in the Late Eighteenth Century* (Cambridge, MA: Harvard University Press, 1948), 32–35.

most previous political economic reflection as little more than mercantile lobbying. The Physiocrats favored an agricultural empire based on free trade, and deplored a colonial system predicated on monopoly, whether the national monopoly of the *Exclusif* in the Atlantic, or the company monopoly of Asian trade.[83] They and other critics received a hearing because the *Compagnie des Indes* appeared to be a broken institution—the challenges it faced in Asia nearly insuperable. The postwar conversation was dominated by new proposals: to shift defense costs from the company to the crown; to develop the Mascarene Islands as a base to protect French commerce, free of Indian political pressures; and to end the company's monopoly.[84]

Once it became clear that the Godeheu–Saunders Treaty had failed, a range of competing free trade schemes emerged promising to render French trade in Asia peaceful and prosperous. In June 1755, Vincent de Gournay suggested that the trade be opened to all French merchants, and that the *Compagnie des Indes*, funded by a duty on India goods, maintain the forts and establishments necessary to sustain the trade. Free trade would be greater in volume, more competitive in price, and—free of defense costs—more economical. The tax revenues it would generate would fund a security umbrella in the shape of the reformed company.[85] In 1756 Delaître, too, proposed that the company's monopoly be broken. The trade could be conducted from Mauritius, he suggested, if the island were developed as a military colony and entrepot.[86] At the end of the war critics of the status quo returned to the charge. The future Physiocrat, Nicolas Baudeau, suggested that the company be reconstituted as a carrier of French goods to and from the Indian Ocean, but that the trade be opened to all French subjects. Military and agricultural colonies in the Mascarene Islands, defended by the crown, would secure this commerce. More sweeping reform was staved off in 1764 with a

[83] Pernille Røge, "A Natural Order of Empire: The Physiocratic Vision of Colonial France after the Seven Years' War," in: *The Political Economy of Empire in the Early Modern World*, ed. Sophus Reinert and Pernille Røge (Basingstoke: Palgrave Macmillan, 2013), 32–52.

[84] Emma Rothschild, "Global Commerce and the Question of Sovereignty in the Eighteenth-Century Provinces," *Modern Intellectual History* 1/1 (2004), 3–25.

[85] Jacques-Claude Vincent de Gournay, "Observations sur le rapport fait à M. le Contrôleur-Général, par M. de S.*** le 26 juin 1755, sur l'état de la Compagnie des Indes," in: André Morellet, *Mémoire sur la situation actuelle de la Compagnie des Indes* (n.p., 1769), x–xxiv.

[86] AN Col C^2 43, fos. 174–225, "Mémoire sur le commerce de l'Inde," 31 October 1756.

recapitalization of the company, a renewal of its trade, and the transfer of sovereignty over the Mascarenes to the crown. The champion of this restructuring, Jacques Necker, argued that the company's difficulties stemmed from bearing the costs of defending French trade in Asia. If these could be reduced or passed to the crown, the trade might yet flourish.[87]

As the company moved toward a new financial crisis in the late 1760s, the ministry decided to revoke its monopoly and employed the abbé Morellet to make the case for reform. Morellet offered a revived version of Gournay's 1755 proposal: free trade, with the *Compagnie des Indes* to continue to operate the *comptoirs* necessary to sustain it.[88] Under pressure from critics, he later suggested that the trade could be carried on without maintaining the establishments of the company in India, a position previously sketched by the abbé Roubaud, a Physiocratic fellow traveler, who looked to Indian powers to protect merchants.[89] Without fortifications and troops, French trade would be less likely to arouse the jealousy of rival nations. The most radical position in the 1769 debate was taken by François Quesnay's protégé, Pierre-Samuel Dupont, who argued that the French trade could never be secured; that the effort to compete in Indian Ocean commerce had been a continual source of jealousies and wars; that France would be better off buying India goods from other Europeans and establishing on this basis a reciprocal trade in French commodities.[90]

Each of these free trade schemes, in their different ways, embodied the impulse to separate trade altogether from "political" functions, or the provision of organized violence, and in this sense represented a retooling of the older notion that commerce and conquest were incompatible. The ethos of the prewar *Compagnie des Indes* was appropriated, in transformed fashion, for the new paradigm. It continued to be axiomatic in the postwar climate that conquests in India be avoided. Indeed, under the leadership of the duc de Choiseul, François-Joseph Ruggiu suggests, a policy of

[87] AN Col C^2 47, fos. 53–60, "Discours de M. Necker, banquier" (1764).

[88] Morellet, *Mémoire sur la situation actuelle.*

[89] André Morellet, *Examen de la réponse de M. N.** au mémoire de M. l'abbé Morellet, sur la Compagnie des Indes* (Paris: Desaint, 1769); Pierre-Joseph-André Roubaud, *Le politique indien, ou considérations sur les colonies des Indes orientales* (Paris: Lacombe, 1768).

[90] Pierre-Samuel Dupont, *Du commerce et de la Compagnie des Indes* (Paris: Delalain, 1769).

avoiding extensive territorial acquisitions was extended to the whole French Empire.[91] Eclipsed and cannibalized in this fashion, the pacific Colbertism of the prewar decades was destined to recede from view, the victim of its own failure either to keep the peace or to aggrandize the monarchy.

The swansong of this tradition, we can see in retrospect, was the 1753 effort to reach an accommodation between the two India companies. In the aftermath of global Franco-British war and in the midst of a sweeping reconfiguration of Indian politics, the perennial problem of balancing the costs of security with the profits of trade in South Asia had become acute. The French company proved most imaginative in offering solutions to this challenge, perhaps because it had a model in the initiatives to reorganize the Spanish trade by cartel and neutralization during the War of the Spanish Succession—a model which the abbé de Saint-Pierre proposed extending to the East Indies as early as 1713. But both companies had fostered traditions of political thought in which the "arts of peace" were conceived as an effective substitute for war in the struggle of states for power. This perspective was appealing to politicians and officials in a period of exhaustion and financial restructuring following the stalemated War of the Austrian Succession. Yet the British government was not prepared to concede wartime immunity to French East India shipping, and in the wake of this impasse, the negotiations focused on less ambitious goals—ending the conflict between the companies; disentangling both from Indian politics; forging an understanding on security cooperation in Asia; and agreeing on a permanent division of establishments and territories in India.

One might argue that there was a contradiction at the heart of the 1753 initiative. The thinking that shaped it was rooted in the very jealousy of trade whose destabilizing consequences the leaders of the companies wished to transcend. Company directors and shareholders wanted to create a pacified space in which Asian commerce could flourish with greater safety and predictability. But they also represented

[91] François-Joseph Ruggiu, "India and the Reshaping of the French Colonial Policy (1759–1789)," *Itinerario* 35/2 (2011), 25–43. Also, Sudipta Das, *Myths and Realities of French Imperialism in India, 1763–1783* (New York: Peter Lang, 1993). For a contrasting view, see Kenneth Margerison, "French Visions of Empire: Contesting British Power in India after the Seven Years War," *English Historical Review* 130/544 (2015), 583–612.

peace as necessary to foster the wealth that would aggrandize their respective sovereigns. The companies were key sites for the articulation of such a viewpoint because, on the one hand, they stood to bear the costs of the imbrication of commerce with geopolitical competition, while, on the other, they were important elements in the military-fiscal apparatuses of major powers. Did this tension doom the 1753 negotiations to failure? I do not think so. The treaty negotiations were victims of events, not intellectual contradictions—it was the entanglement of the India accord with a separate imperial conflict in America that finally wrecked it. Only, perhaps, from the perspective of the new paradigm which crystallized in the aftermath of that failure can the early eighteenth-century geopolitical traditions of the India companies be found wanting.

John Shovlin is an Associate Professor of History at New York University. He is the author of *The Political Economy of Virtue. Luxury, Patriotism, and the Origins of the French Revolution* (2007), and editor of *The Bordeaux–Dublin Letters, 1757. Correspondence of an Irish Community Abroad* (2013), along with Thomas M. Truxes and Louis M. Cullen. With support from the National Endowment for the Humanities, he is currently writing a book on capitalism and international order in eighteenth-century Europe.

The Rise of a Trading Nation: Prussia and the *Convention préliminaire de commerce* with France (1753)

Marco Cavarzere

For a long time historians examined the foreign policy of Frederick II, King of Prussia, according to the categories of nineteenth-century *Machtpolitik*. In the worst of cases, his victories were used as propagandistic justifications for further plans of conquest; in the best, his economic choices were considered not per se but as a necessary means for him to achieve desired military glory.[1] This analysis reflected an anachronistic view of eighteenth-century politics and led to a long-lasting misunderstanding of Frederick's strategies and objectives. Only recent research has shown the vitality of Frederick's reign and of Prussian society as a whole.[2] This shift in perspective was the result of more general changes in the domain of political and intellectual history. Nowadays, concepts such as

[1] Wolfgang Neugebauer, 'Preußen in der Historiographie. Epochen und Forschungsprobleme der Preußischen Geschichte', in: *Handbuch der Preußischen Geschichte*, ed. Otto Büsch and Wolfgang Neugebauer (Berlin: de Gruyter, 2009), I: 3–109.

[2] First of all, Christopher Clark, *Iron Kingdom. The Rise and Downfall of Prussia 1600–1947* (London: Allen Lane, 2006).

M. Cavarzere (✉)
Goethe-University, Frankfurt am Main, Germany
e-mail: cavarzere@em.uni-frankfurt.de

A. Alimento, K. Stapelbroek (eds.), *The Politics of Commercial Treaties in the Eighteenth Century*, DOI 10.1007/978-3-319-53574-6_11

those of 'universal monarchy', 'balance of power' and 'jealousy of trade' seem more proper keys for appreciating the complex game of eighteenth-century politics than the idea of *Machtpolitik*.[3] As far as Prussian history is concerned, this debate has given birth to a thorough reconsideration of Frederick's actions. Writings previously read as almost utopian fantasies, such as the *Anti-Machiavel* (1740), have accordingly acquired deeper and clearer meanings, whereas political decisions, which Frederick's biographers teleologically regarded as the expression of his aspirations for *agrandissement* and *gloire*, are finally finding more consistent explanations.[4]

The War of the Austrian Succession was one of the most badly misinterpreted events of Frederick's reign. On the one hand, nationalistic historians distorted its meaning by extolling Frederick's legendary fame as an intrepid general and his will to affirm German supremacy over Europe. On the other hand, scholars deemed Frederick's ambition as the only political reason for the quick invasion of Silesia, which had entailed a consistent fracture with Prussian political tradition and the sudden betrayal of all those theories about a peaceful European order that Frederick himself had proposed in the *Anti-Machiavel*.

It is useless to ignore or to try to disguise the inner contradictions of Frederick's behaviour; at the same time, the problem cannot be solved by portraying the image of the *prince-philosophe*, who did not practise what he preached. To exclusively focus on the Silesian wars, *guerres d'interêt*, as Frederick would define them, does not help to understand the framework in which they took place. The first section of this chapter aims at showing how Frederick's idea of a balance of power based on trade—an idea that he

[3] On 'universal monarchy', see John Robertson, 'Empire and Union: Two Concepts of the Early Modern Political Order', in: *A Union for Empire. Political Thought and the British Union of 1707*, ed. John Robertson (Cambridge: Cambridge University Press, 1995), 3–36; on 'jealousy of trade', Istvan Hont, *Jealousy of Trade. International Competition and the Nation-State in Historical Perspective* (Cambridge, MA: Harvard University Press, 2005); and, more generally, on the debate about these categories, with a perceptive definition of 'balance of power', see, most recently, Isaac Nakhimovsky, 'Envisioning Europe after Utrecht. Voltaire and the Historiography of the Balance of Power', in: *The 1713 Peace of Utrecht and Its Enduring Effects*, ed. A.H.A. Soons (Leiden: Brill, 2017).

[4] On the *Anti-Machiavel*, see, in particular, Hont, *Jealousy of Trade*, 22–36, and Isaac Nakhimovsky, 'The Peaceful Prince and the Future of Europe: Frederick and Voltaire's Anti-Machiavel of 1740', in: *Commerce and Peace in the Enlightenment*, ed. Bela Kapossy, Isaac Nakhimovsky and Richard Whatmore (Cambridge: Cambridge University Press, 2017), 44–77.

had first outlined in the *Anti-Machiavel*—became the cornerstone of his administration from the mid-1740s until the Seven Years War: that is, from the Treaty of Dresden (1745), which substantially recognized Prussia's annexation of Silesia and East Frisia, to the end of the political equilibrium established at the beginning of the century. In order to describe this evolution, a case in point is provided by the negotiations for a commercial treaty with France, held between 1747 and 1753. The importance of these diplomatic consultations does not reside in their results, which finally proved to be unsatisfactory and short-term. Instead, they attest to the wearying attempts made by the Prussian government to carve itself a niche as a trading power within an interstate order inspired by the new 'science of commerce'.

In the second place, the analysis of a forgotten *convention de commerce* contributes to better understanding eighteenth-century diplomatic practice. In general, Frederick did not trust in treaties.[5] The trade treaty with France was a *unicum* in his politics of the 1740s and 1750s and has to be interpreted as consequence of the tight political and commercial links between Prussia and France. Engaging in the diplomatic talks with the Bourbon kings, Frederick took advantage of the role that trade treaties played in asserting economic and political equality between powers holding the same rank. After the Peace of Utrecht (1713), trade treaties were no longer instruments through which Britain or France could bind weaker allies to themselves, but served to forge a more equal international system. In the Prussian case, the achievement of a treaty with France implied a change in status for Frederick's country and a rebalance of power in the apparently solid alliance between the two kingdoms.

However, this treaty was an exception. While negotiating with France, Frederick followed further methods to assert himself in the political and economic competition, above all trying to enforce Prussia's position as a neutral power. Parallel negotiations with Britain and the confrontation with the Dutch Republic in 1750s show that Frederick was seeking recognition for Prussian neutrality and make clear that neutral trade was

[5] Frederick II of Prussia and Voltaire, *Anti-Machiavel* (*The Complete Works of Voltaire*, vol. 19), ed. Werner Bahner and Helga Bergmann (Oxford: Voltaire Foundation, 1996), 252–253.

becoming an important strategy for 'small states', which desired to play an active role on the political stage.[6]

With its plans of transforming Prussian shipping into a carrier of goods in the Northern seas and into a transoceanic trader, Frederick's policy bears witness to the transition occurring both on the macro-scale of the European political order and in the micro-context of the Prussian 'composite monarchy'. After a detailed presentation of the diplomatic exchanges between Berlin and Paris regarding a treaty of commerce, the focus will move on to the ongoing debates in the Prussian territories, in an attempt to consider the influence exerted by society—and not only by Frederick and his advisers—on the shifting Prussian economic policy.

The Theoretical Foundations of Frederick's Policy

The argumentative structure of the *Anti-Machiavel* owed large intellectual debts to several authors: Fénelon's interpretation of Machiavelli; the political views of d'Argenson's milieu within the French court; the economic literature on luxury, with its emphasis on the importance of commerce as the founding principle of a European commonwealth. The 'bon gouvernement' described in this book was accordingly a political course capable both of patronizing the *beaux arts* and of awakening the mercantile and industrial skills of the country.[7] Although Frederick still considered agriculture an important aspect of state wealth, he no longer saw it as its primary resource, while trade appeared to be a fundamental branch of the economy, as the example of the Dutch Republic perfectly demonstrated.

If we look ahead at the following years, it is evident that the *Anti-Machiavel* became an effective programme of government for Prussia during the 1740s and 1750s, providing a number of pragmatic suggestions for economic reforms. Apart from general indications about the duties of sovereigns, the *Anti-Machiavel* presented distinctive and concrete economic ideas, which the Prussian government put into practice during the early years of Frederick's reign.

In his book, Frederick discussed the financial problems which might arise from trade and from the exchange of luxury products induced by the

[6] Antonella Alimento, ed., *War, Trade, and Neutrality. Europe and the Mediterranean in the Seventeenth and Eighteenth Centuries* (Milan: Franco Angeli, 2011).

[7] Frederick II and Voltaire, *Anti-Machiavel*, chs. V, XVI and XXI.

increase of commercial activities. Following the traditional economic theory, Frederick stated that a high level of imports would result in an excessive outflow of money. The question was solved by differentiating big empires from small states: while luxury was necessary in an empire because it allowed the circulation of goods, it ultimately brought a small state to collapse, causing a disproportionate drain of wealth.[8] The strengthening of industries was one of the ways in which it was possible to attract money from other countries without compromising the internal equilibrium of the state. As Frederick wrote, 'on the one hand, they (i.e. manufactures) prevent money from leaving the country; on the other, they bring it in'. But manufacturing could not be the result of a mere state intervention. Although a prince's duty was to give financial support to industrial development, he was like the heaven, which provides the earth with dew and rain.[9]

When this theoretical presentation had to come to terms with the reality of the 1740s, the clear-cut differentiation between empires and small countries immediately lost its cogency. Prussia was a small country compared to the commercial powers of its time, but, if it wanted to reach the rank of a 'grand royaume', it had to commit itself to manufacturing and to sustaining the demand for luxury goods. Consequently, Frederick was convinced that, after the Silesian wars, it was essential to avoid the mortal bleeding of money that he had feared in the *Anti-Machiavel* and to hinder the intermediation of commercial states like the Dutch Republic. Considering that Prussia was not an empire, the only solution left was to import directly both manufactured and natural products from their countries of origin. The plan was advantageous for exporting countries as well. As the *Anti-Machiavel* had shown, countries that based their wealth on wheat and grapes should in fact improve the means of transportation for these goods, trying to spend less money on delivery and to sell them at a better price.[10]

[8] Frederick II and Voltaire, *Anti-Machiavel*, 192–193.

[9] Frederick II and Voltaire, *Anti-Machiavel*, 227 (on the role played by industries); the translation is that provided by Frederick of Prussia, *The Refutation of Machiavelli's Prince or Anti-Machiavel* (Athens: Ohio University Press, 1981), 134. On the image of the prince as heaven, see Frederick of Prussia, *Refutation*, 195. On Frederick's support for Prussian manufacturing, see Florian Schui, *Early Debates about Industry. Voltaire and His Contemporaries* (Basingstoke: Palgrave Macmillan, 2005), 35–78.

[10] Frederick II and Voltaire, *Anti-Machiavel*, 226–227.

Some of the problems posed by the *Anti-Machiavel* were more concretely treated in Frederick's *Political Testament* of 1752, which testifies to the substantial continuity of his economic thought. This writing was drafted during the final phase of the diplomatic talks between Prussia and France and, in comparison with the other testaments that Frederick wrote in the course of his long life, it appeared to be considerably focused on economic issues.[11] The debate on economy conducted in the 1752 *Political Testament* mirrored the same concerns about trade and luxury as the *Anti-Machiavel*. Twelve years after the publication of this book, Frederick declared once again that 'the founding principle of trade and manufactures is to prevent money from going abroad and to help it to return to the country'.[12] In brief, Frederick's economic thought continued to ground itself on a monetary theory that regarded trade as a potential danger to the internal balance of state. At the same time, such a theoretical approach carefully mixed the old dogmas of economic doctrine with the novelties of the 'science of commerce'.

As the *Political Testament* made clear, trade was a vital part of a nation's economy. The recipe that Frederick suggested to his heir obviously concentrated on Prussia and on the political strategies pursued by his government. Prussian merchants should learn to 'trade on their own'; only by abandoning any form of intermediation, was it possible to save money and preserve the balance of trade. In fact, Frederick explained that, while the Prussians paid one *écu* (a crown) in exchange for Spanish goods bought from merchants of 'Hambourg et de Holland', they would have only paid one florin, if they had purchased them directly in Spain.[13] The reference to these two states—Hamburg and Holland—was not at all accidental: on the one hand, Hanseatic cities, namely Bremen, Lübeck and above all Hamburg, which was placed at the estuary of the River Elbe, were the gateways to German trade; on the other hand, the Dutch Republic was the most important trader in Northern seas and

[11] Cf. *Die politischen Testamente der Hohenzollern*, ed. Georg Küntzel (Berlin: Hobbing, 1920), II: 1–109; for a comparison between the 1752 testament and the subsequent one, drafted in 1768, see Bernd Sösemann, 'Lo spirito dell'Illuminismo e la politica. Contorni e confini del progetto politico di Federico II', in *Stato e cultura in Prussia sotto Federico II*, ed. Edoardo Tortarolo (Naples: Edizioni scientifiche italiane, 2013), 1–22.

[12] *Die politischen Testamente*, ed. Küntzel, 24.

[13] *Die politischen Testamente*, ed. Küntzel, 24–25.

a traditional carrier of French goods. It was their models of economic growth that Prussia had to imitate.

The other important way of maintaining a healthy balance of commerce consisted in the development of the industrial sector. The state should be involved in this process through indirect support, for instance through the building of new infrastructures, the 'dew and rain' of trade. The 1752 *Political Testament* proudly remembered Frederick's works in this field, especially his investments in water transport. Frederick recalled the construction of new channels between the rivers Oder and Havel and the Havel and Elbe, channels that built up a communication system around the different parts of his kingdom and allowed the equalization of customs rights all over this area. It was evident that these works were not sufficient. Frederick's desires went beyond these first projects: he invited his successor to consolidate the connections between Stettin and Emden, the eastern and western poles of the kingdom, and to establish stable relationships with Moravia, Bohemia and Poland.[14] The choice of these countries perfectly corresponded with Frederick's ideas about trade balance: they all lacked a manufacturing base and thus offered great opportunities for a nation that wanted to relaunch its internal production.

This emphasis on trade quite patently uncovered the influence of recent economic theories, which tried to reconcile the defence of the commercial balance with freedom of trade. There are considerable traces of Frederick's interest in this new literature. In comparison with the *Anti-Machiavel*, inspired by Voltaire and his 1736 apology of luxury *Le Mondain*, the *Political Testament* relied on a massive amount of new reading. In 1749 Frederick dedicated his time to studying Melon's *Essai politique sur le commerce*, which reflected similar concerns both for internal manufacturing and for trade possibilities.[15] At the same time, the inventory of Frederick's library confirms a great interest in the most recent European

[14] *Die politischen Testamente*, ed. Küntzel, 16–17, and, in general, the overview by Friedrich-Wilhelm Henning, 'Die Entwicklung der Verkehrsinfrastruktur in Brandenburg/Preußen als Teil der Staatsbaukunst von 1648 bis 1850', *Forschungen zur brandenburgischen und preußischen Geschichte* 7 (1997), 211–232.

[15] Cf. Reinhold Koser, *Geschichte des Friedrich des Grossen* (Stuttgart: Cotta, 1921–1925), II: 158; Karl Heinrich Born, *Wirtschaft und Gesellschaft im Denken Friedrichs des Großen* (Mainz: Akademie der Wissenschaften und der Literatur, 1979), 15; Ingrid Mittenzwei, *Friedrich II von Preußen: eine Biographie* (Cologne: Pahl-Rugenstein, 1983), 159–164.

literature on trade. It is well known that library catalogues may be slippery sources: they do not say when books were bought, why they became part of the collection and, above all, if they were actually read. However, it is significant that the editions of economic texts registered among the king's personal belongings had been all published between 1750 and 1755 and promoted the same cultural and political reforms. Frederick, a renowned Francophone, kept in his library, beyond Melon's treatise, Forbonnais' French translation of the *Theórica de comercio y de marina* by Uztariz (Hamburg, 1753); Plumard de Dangeul's translation of the *Restablecimiento de las fábricas y comercio español* by Bernardo de Ulloa (Amsterdam, 1753); Forbonnais' translation of the *British Merchant*, the *Négociant anglais* (Amsterdam, 1755); and Vincent de Gournay's translation of *A new discourse of trade* by Josiah Child (Amsterdam, 1755).[16] Moreover, Frederick's library possessed a copy of the second 1755 edition of Forbonnais' *Considérations sur les finances d'Espagne* and *Elémens du commerce*, a work which was gaining great success throughout Germany. Among the few titles regarding economic matters (the above-mentioned books more or less form the whole collection of economic texts present in his library), one can recognize all the translations promoted by the so-called Gournay group, the Parisian circle that gathered the most prominent supporters of Bourbon reformism.[17]

While it is difficult to exactly determine what Frederick learnt from this economic literature, there is little doubt that the middle of the century witnessed a change of pace in Prussia's commercial policy. It is Frederick himself who informs us about the shift in his interests and to crown himself as the discoverer of trade in Prussia, an opinion shared amongst European public opinion.[18] In the *Mémoires pour servir à l'histoire de la maison de*

[16] For the catalogue of Frederick's library, see Bogdan Krieger, *Friedrich der Große und seine Bücher* (Berlin: Giesecke und Devrient, 1914), for the economic texts see 174–176. Frederick's readings are analysed in *Friedrich der Große als Leser*, ed. Brunhilde Wehinger and Günther Lottes (Berlin: Akademie Verlag, 2012), where no attention is given to economic books.

[17] On this circle, see *Le cercle de Vincent de Gournay. Savoirs économiques et pratiques administratives en France au milieu du XVIIIe siècle*, ed. Loïc Charles, Frédéric Lefebvre and Christine Théré (Paris: Institut National d'études démographiques, 2011).

[18] See the comments of the British media in the 1750s: Manfred Schlenke, *England und das Friderizianische Preußen. 1740–1763. Ein Beitrag zum Verhältnis von Politik und öffentlicher Meinung im England des 18. Jahrhunderts* (Munich: Alber, 1963), 303–315.

Brandenbourg, a traditional dynastic history that he was writing in the same years, he made clear that at the time of his ancestors 'our trade was not born yet'; it was instead his own political will that had allowed a great improvement in this field and had created new economic chances for the country.[19]

Such a 'discovery' of trade was conducive to a different idea of interstate relationships. Between the 1740s and 1750s, Johann Heinrich Gottlob von Justi, the most important innovator in the eighteenth-century cameralistic sciences and a strong supporter of Frederick's politics, clearly expressed Prussian views on the subject. As has been recently underlined, Justi's journal *Ergetzungen der vernünftigen Seele aus der Sittenlehre und der Gelehrsamkeit überhaupt* (1745–1749) contained unambiguous stances in favour of Prussian policy.[20] In particular, Justi's articles mainly focused on the right of Prussia to become a carrier of goods and to enjoy the status of a neutral power. Justi further developed his eulogy of neutrality during the disruptive period of the Seven Years War by publishing his *Chimäre des Gleichgewichts von Europa* (1758) and *Chimäre des Gleichgewichts von Handlung and Schiffahrt* (1759).[21] These writings described neutrality as a decisive political weapon in an intrinsically unequal balance of powers. It is, however, worth noting that Justi's chimeras had abandoned the model offered by the Dutch Republic, which had been highly praised in the *Anti-Machiavel*, considering it no longer viable. The United Provinces, which in the meantime had become Prussia's primary economic rival, were replaced by the example given by the Danish fleet: that is, by the neutrality of a little country, which had found its way in the crowded European scene thanks to its wise politics.

[19] Frederick II of Prussia, *Mémoires pour servir à l'histoire de Brandenbourg* (s.l., 1750), 85. The same opinion was expressed in a memorandum that Frederick wrote to the director of the Fifth Department Faesch in 1749: see Reinhold Koser, 'Ein handelspolitisches Programm Friedrichs des Großen', *Hohenzollern-Jahrbuch* 5 (1901), 270–271. In general, on the importance of trade in Frederick's foreign policy, see Ulrike Müller-Weil, *Absolutismus und Aussenpolitik in Preussen. Ein Beitrag zur Strukturgeschichte des preussischen Absolutismus* (Stuttgart: Steiner, 1992), 100–108 and 282–294.

[20] Ere Nokkala, 'Just and Unjust Neutrality. J. H. G. von Justis Defence of Prussian Maritime Neutrality (1740–1763)', in: *Trade and War. The Neutrality of War in the Inter-State System*, ed. Koen Stapelbroek (Helsinki: Helsinki Collegium for Advanced Studies, 2011), 42–60.

[21] On these works, see Ulrich Adam, *The Political Economy of J. H. Justi* (Bern: Peter Lang, 2006), 70–92.

Justi's statements coincided with a change in Frederick's economic plans, which resulted in a different course of his politics from that foreseen before the Seven Years War. At the time of the French–Prussian negotiations for a treaty of commerce in 1747–1753, the role of peaceful go-between suggested by Justi at the end of the 1750s could not fit with the king's plans, which were then far more ambitious than the replication of the Danish model.

The French–Prussian Treaty and other Options at Stake

Between the *Anti-Machiavel* and the 1752 *Political Testament* some important events occurred, which influenced the economic policy of the Prussian government. The transition from the written page to political practice needs to be reconstructed through the analysis of the contingent situation that characterized Prussian economy in the 1740s and 1750s. The negotiations between Prussia and France for a commercial treaty provide a robust thread, capable of unwinding the complex series of actions taking place in those years. During these diplomatic discussions, luxury, trade and neutrality—central themes of Frederick's economic theories—became a matter of everyday politics.

Quite unexpectedly, it was the French government that convinced Frederick to engage himself in a more intense economic policy. Everything started when the diplomatic crisis with the United Provinces came to a head as a consequence of the 1747 Orangist Revolution. Fearing that the Dutch, traditional shippers on behalf of French merchants, might decide to boycott the French traffic with Northern Europe and the Baltic Sea, the Bourbons addressed the Prussians.[22] Their intention was to reach a trade agreement that would allow the French merchants to embark their goods on Prussian ships and to distribute them through Prussian harbours. The project seemed to be the natural consequence of the new geographical position occupied by the Prussians during the war. Prussia had in fact conquered both East Frisia, a region bordering the Low Countries with a famous harbour, Emden, and

[22] The first attempts made by the French diplomats to reach a trade agreement date back to the end of September 1747, when Puyzieulx sent clear instructions on this matter to the French ambassador at the Prussian court, the Marquis de Valori: see Paris, Archives du Ministère des Affaires Étrangères [MAE], Correspondance Politique Prusse 149, fos. 149v–150r.

Silesia, an important territory for its strategic location. Keeping Silesia implied dominating the course of the River Oder and having privileged access to the Polish market. Although the war was not yet over, it was already clear that Prussia was becoming a regional power, destined to take control of Central Europe.

This evolution had not passed unnoticed either on the French or on the Prussian sides. Already in 1743 a first project of trade treaty was sent to the court of Versailles. Its author was Monsieur d'Eguilles, the brother of Frederick's chamberlain.[23] The difficulties inherent in his proposal were well known to the French ministries. As an anonymous reviewer of the project rightly pointed out,[24] problems arose both from a merely geographical point of view and at the economic level. On the one hand, the Prussians lacked the essential infrastructures for large-scale trade: they did not have sufficient know-how and their fleet was too small. Besides, many Prussian harbours could not be used most of the year because of rigid weather conditions, not to mention the fact that Prussia was still an aggregate of distant regions, devoid of a good infrastructure network. On the other hand, the two countries had rival interests. The most contentious issue concerned the linens produced in Silesia, products of little value and low price, which posed a serious threat to the French industry.[25] To open French harbours to the Prussians could thus cause serious damage to the French linen manufactories.

In Berlin, the discussion was similarly lively. In August 1746, the most important Prussian banker, David Splittgerber, wrote a letter to the king underlining the bad treatment that the Prussian merchants suffered in French harbours in comparison with Dutch tradesmen.[26] In Splittgerber's eyes, the conditions existed for negotiating a better settlement with France. In fact, it was time to claim for a treaty of commerce between France and

[23] This first draft of a treaty of commerce, issued on 17 March 1743, is preserved in MAE, Mémoires et Documents Prusse 4, fos. 275r–298v. Other documentation can be found in *Die Handels-, Zoll- und Akzisepolitik Preußens*, ed. Hugo Rachel (Berlin: Parey, 1928), III/2: 571–572.

[24] MAE, Mémoires et Documents Prusse 4, fos. 301r–304v.

[25] On Silesian linens, see William Henderson, *Studies in the Economic Policy of Frederick the Great* (London: Cass, 1963), 136–152.

[26] Friedrich Lenz and Otto Unholtz, *Die Geschichte des Bankhauses Gebrüder Schickler. Festschrift zum 200 jährigen Bestehen* (Berlin: Georg Reimer, 1912), 76–80.

Prussia, as other of Splittgerber's letters made clear; the new political strength of the reign allowed it to take a determined stance with France and to reach a position of parity. Despite this call to arms, Frederick's response was prudent, searching instead for an accommodation in order to partially satisfy Splittgerber's requests.

The possibility of a trade agreement between France and Prussia materialized only a year later, in 1747, when the Dutch turmoil had aggravated the problem of the Northern trade and the considerable territorial expansion of Prussia had transformed the country into a reliable market for French colonial goods. In the view of the Paris government, the main goal of the agreement should be the strengthening of Emden at the expense of the Dutch harbours and its transformation into a new base for French shipping. If this was the focal point of French interests, there were also other options to be taken into consideration. First of all, it seemed profitable to establish *maisons de commerce* and consular missions in Stettin, at the mouth of the River Oder, and even further east, in Königsberg. Through this capillary action the French planned to reach the Polish market and the internal areas of the empire, such as Silesia, Bohemia and Saxony, another state with which France was tightening its relationships.

In order to convince Frederick to accept the agreement, the French offered the Prussian merchants who wanted to trade with the French coasts exemption from paying the *droit de fret*, a tax on shipping that charged fifty *sols* per ton of cargo transported on foreign ships. These generous conditions and the interest shown by the French for trade with Eastern and Northern Europe find a logical justification from a long-term perspective. It was from the beginning of the eighteenth century that France was weaving an intricate diplomatic net, designed to ensure the Eastern markets for its colonial goods and manufactured products.[27] In 1716, France had signed a treaty with the Hanseatic cities; in 1739, a treaty with the Low Countries had followed and two other treaties with Sweden and with Denmark had been concluded in 1741 and 1742. Moreover, in the same years France was attempting to win the favour of the Russians and to sign a treaty of commerce with them, which could be

[27] On this first phase, see Eric Schnakenbourg, *La France, le Nord et l'Europe au début du XVIII*[e] *siècle* (Paris: Honoré Champion, 2008).

fruitfully compared with the Prussian one in its scope.[28] In fact, this treaty would have aimed at reducing the intervention of 'broker countries', such as the United Provinces and the Hanseatic cities, and presented the same conditions accorded to the Prussians: the French asked both Russia and Prussia to take charge of the commercial relationships with France. Even the typology of goods that could be traded were very similar: the French offered their wines and products in exchange for raw materials. In particular, from the Prussian agreement the French government expected to obtain an increase in the imports of wax, wood and meat and to develop the export of French wares, such as wine, spirit, olives, soap, coffee, sugar and spices.[29]

In their negotiations with the Prussians, French diplomats underlined that the conditions proposed contained the same articles as those present in the treaties signed with the Hanseatic cities and with the Low Countries. In other words, they intended to underline that the French government considered Prussia a trade power on the same footing as these countries. The truth was slightly different. As seen above, the main concerns of the French court regarded a possible embargo of French goods by the Dutch harbours and fleet, while the possibilities opened up by the new Prussian geopolitical conditions still seemed too uncertain. Accordingly, as soon as the war ended, the French lost interest in the agreement. After the Peace of Aachen (1748), all the requests made by the Prussians about a trade treaty went unheeded.[30]

[28] Cf. the unpublished doctoral dissertation by Frank Fox 'French–Russian Commercial Relations in the Eighteenth Century and the French–Russian Commercial Treaty of 1787', presented at the University of Delaware in 1966; on the period 1726–1761 and on the 1745 and 1761 projects of treaty of commerce, see esp. 46–104.

[29] These expectations were made clear in the memoranda prepared at that time by different consultants of the French Foreign Office: see MAE, Mémoires et Documents Prusse 3, fos. 151–163.

[30] In September 1748, the French ambassador in Berlin was summoned in order to receive a formal riposte to the Prussian proposal of a treaty of commerce. Attempts to reach a trade agreement of any kind were equally unsuccessful: see Berlin, Geheimes Staatsarchiv Preussischer Kulturbesitz [GStA], I. HA, Rep. 11, Geheimer Rat, Auswärtige Beziehungen, Akten Nr. 2763, fos. 133–164. In March 1750, the Prussians proposed, to their French allies, that Stettin, a city-member of the Hansa in the thirteenth century, should be treated like the other Hanseatic cities with which France had already signed a treaty. The idea encountered opposition from the French side: cf. GStA, I. HA, Rep. 11, Geheimer Rat, Auswärtige Beziehungen, Akten Nr. 2777, fos. 10–17.

At the beginning of the negotiations, Frederick the Great looked with great suspicion at French requests. First of all, the real reason underpinning the French move appeared largely unclear. Frederick and his counsellors were afraid (and rightly so) that France had no other intention than overcoming the temporary difficulties that it was experiencing in the Low Countries.[31] The risks that a trade treaty with France would bring were considered much higher than the potential benefits and entailed a fracture in the Prussian policy of neutrality. It is in fact impossible to divide the history of the trade treaty with France from a general view on the Prussian policy of the time, which primarily aimed at affirming the kingdom's neutrality. Already in 1744, Berliner diplomats had attempted to sign an agreement with the British cabinet in order to gain British recognition of its status as a neutral country. However, the oral guarantees offered were completely ignored the following year, after France had started to rely more heavily on neutral carriers for its own commerce. In accordance with British policy of hindering any kind of trade 'for' the enemy, in 1745–1747 some Prussian vessels were seized by the British authorities under the accusation that they carried French goods. Consequently, a long quarrel started between London and Berlin about their maritime relationships.[32]

In the meantime, Frederick faced the competition of the United Provinces. After the Peace of Aachen, France opened an official negotiation with the Dutch Republic in order to re-establish profitable commercial relationships. The Prussian government took very seriously the political moves of the United Provinces, and tried to counter them at any cost. A larger perspective, which takes into account the Dutch policy,

[31] The Prussian reactions to the French proposal were expressed in different memoranda, now preserved in GStA, I. HA, Rep. 11, Geheimer Rat, Auswärtige Beziehungen, Akten. Nr. 2763, fos. 5r–v, 8–9. See also Frederick's letters, published in *Politische Correspondenz Friedrichs des Grossen* (Berlin: Verlag von Alexander Duncker, 1879–1939), V: 514–515, 518–521, 547–548.

[32] The accounts on these confiscations rely on Georg Friedrich von Martens, *Causes celèbres du droit des gens* (Leipzig and Paris: Brockhaus-Ponthieu, 1827), 1–88, and on Reinhold Koser, *Preußische Staatsschriften aus der Regierungszeit König Friedrichs II.* (Berlin: Dunckler, 1885), II: 433–498. See also Ernest Satow, *The Silesian Loan and Frederick the Great* (Oxford: Clarendon Press, 1915). On the British policy of neutral trade, see Richard Pares, *Colonial Blockade and Neutral Rights, 1739–1763* (Oxford: Oxford University Press, 1938), 148–225.

throws new light both on the diplomatic talks between Prussia and France and, more generally, on the economic views of the Prussian government.[33] The parallel activity of Dutch diplomats in Paris served as a reference point for Prussian ministers, who continuously compared their initiatives to those of the representatives of the United Provinces. The question was twofold: on the one hand, the Dutch government was prone to making further concessions to France with respect to the previous 1739 Franco-Dutch trade treaty, which Berlin considered the model for an agreement with France—in other words, Dutch negotiations were weakening the Prussian position; on the other hand, the difficulties which the United Provinces were encountering in Paris made the treaty with Prussia more attractive from a French standpoint.[34] Not surprisingly, the French government, until then reluctant to sign a treaty with Prussia, asked the Prussians to intensify the diplomatic consultations from 1750 onwards, when the two Dutch negotiators had substantially failed their mission.[35]

But the commercial treaty with France was not the only measure taken by Prussia in direct riposte to the Dutch threat. As recent research has stressed,[36] in 1751 important circles of Dutch merchants were endorsing economic projects aimed to rescue Dutch economy from decline through the creation of a free port area and the diminution of taxes on import goods. Such a project would have allowed Dutch merchants to be once again the primary carriers of goods in Northern Europe, overcoming the competition of other minor powers, such as the Hanseatic cities,

[33] On the Dutch policy of the time, compare the chapter by Koen Stapelbroek in this volume.

[34] See the letter of Frederick to the Prussian envoy in Paris D'Ammon on 13 February 1751 and the letter from D'Ammon on 28 November 1751: GStA, I. HA, Rep. 11, Geheimer Rat, Auswärtige Beziehungen, Akten Nr. 2778, fos. 59 and 367ff. (a copy of the letter sent on 28 November is also held GStA, I HA, Rep. 11, Geheimer Rat, Auswärtige Beziehungen, Akten Nr. 2789, fos. 23–25).

[35] On their mission, see Johannes Hovy, *Het Voorstel van 1751 tot instelling vane en beperkt vrijhavenstelsel in de Republiek (propositie tot een gelimiteerd porto-franco)* (Groningen: Wolters, 1966), 316–332. In August 1750, some months after the Dutch envoys had left Paris, the French court accepted the Prussian proposal of a treaty and asked to send to France an envoy in order to write the trade treaty: see GStA, I. HA, Rep. 11, Geheimer Rat, Auswärtige Beziehungen, Akten Nr. 2777, fos. 24–26, and see below.

[36] Koen Stapelbroek, 'Dutch Commercial Decline Revisited: The Future of International Trade and the 1750s Debate about a Limited Free Port,' in: *Governare il mondo. L'economia come linguaggio della politica nell'Europa del Settecento*, ed. Manuela Albertone (Milan: Feltrinelli, 2009), 227–255.

Denmark, Sweden and Prussia itself. Frederick's government was kept well informed about these plans. In August 1751, the king received the French translation of an as yet unpublished report, in which the Zeeland's Admiralty board openly criticized the project of a *porto franco.*[37] Only three months later, in November 1751, while still trying to conclude the trade treaty with France, Frederick granted Emden the privilege to become a free port and to host French, Dutch and Prussian ships, eventually becoming an attractive station for the whole Northern European area of trade. This sudden decision did not directly follow the charter of a Prussian Asiatic Company, already established a year earlier, but should more properly be seen in the context of economic competition with the United Provinces.

To sum up, the commercial treaty with France, the expansion of Prussian trade routes and the economic rivalry with the United Provinces all went hand-in-hand. Even the project of an East Frisian free port and of an Asiatic Company reveals a connection to the Franco-Prussian negotiations of the 1740s.[38] If Emden was so relevant to French interests, why was it not possible to circumvent the French merchants themselves and to create direct trade connections with export countries? In this respect, the foundation of the Asiatic Company of Emden was a consequence of an intricate political strategy, fuelled by Frederick's economic ideas and which aimed to transform Prussia into a trading nation.[39] Its charter in fact reflected the will to free Prussia from the intermediation of other mercantile fleets and find its own way into world trade, thus balancing the internal production (the Silesian linens) and the demand from outside (the colonial wares). Emden seemed to be an ideal place to realize such projects: sited between France and the eastern parts of the Prussian kingdom, it could become a bridge between Northern Europe and the rest of the world.

[37] See the translation and the letter which accompanies it in GStA, I.HA Rep. 96, Geh. Zivilkabinett, ältere Periode (bis 1797), Nr. 76.B, fos. not numbered. The document has already been quoted in Schui, *Early Debates*, 59. The document prepared by the Zeeland Admiralty Board was published a year later, in the 1752 issue of the *Nederlansche Jaerboeken*: see Stapelbroek, *Dutch Commercial Decline Revisited*, 245 n.83.

[38] Viktor Ring, *Asiatische Handlungscompagnien Friedrichs des Grossen. Ein Beitrag zur Geschichte des preussischen Seehandels und Aktienwesens* (Berlin: Heymann, 1890), 40–48.

[39] Florian Schui, 'Prussia's "Trans-Oceanic Moment": The Creation of the Prussian Asiatic Trade Company in 1750', *The Historical Journal* 49 (2006), 143–160.

Coming back to the negotiations with France, they need to be considered within a much more comprehensive frame. From Frederick's point of view, if France wanted to join an agreement, it had to give substantial guarantees; the temporary solution foreseen by the French in 1747 had to be replaced with a formal treaty of commerce, which would put Prussia on the same footing as France. In other words, Prussia was determined not to become a colonial or sub-colonial territory of the French crown. Instead of expanding its commercial network in Frederick's kingdom through the foundation of new trade bases, France should contribute to forging a new mercantile class of Prussians, capable of responding to the French needs. According to the Berliner politicians, Emden was only one of the harbours that expected to receive strong support. Stettin and the cities on the Baltic coast of Prussia were the other poles of a developing programme to embrace both the western and the eastern parts of the Prussian monarchy.

Frederick's comprehensive plans come to refute the judgement by the Marquis de Valori, the French ambassador in Berlin, who wrote that the king had no profound knowledge of economics and did not even understand what the potentialities of the new Prussian kingdom might be.[40] Valori's perception was wrong. It was instead true that at the Berliner court the void of technical competencies and the lack of reliable data were still remarkable. The main efforts made in the months following the first French proposal of a trade agreement were directed at filling this gap. In particular, Frederick imposed his bureaucracy to gather new information about Emden and the commercial situation of Prussia; furthermore, in 1747, he sent Christoph Heinrich von Ammon (or D'Ammon) to Amsterdam, charged to report exact quantitative data on the conditions of French–Dutch trade and on the harbour of Emden.[41] Part of his mission also consisted in convincing Dutch merchants to move to Emden and to revitalize the activity of that city. D'Ammon's survey proved to be very encouraging and

[40] See Valori's letter of 17 February 1748 to Puyzieulx in MAE, Correspondance politique Prusse 149, fos. 227v–229r. About Valori, see *Mémoires des négociations du Marquis de Valori* (Paris: Firmin Didot, 1820); his correspondence from Berlin is partially edited in Reinhold Koser, 'Aus der Korrespondenz der französischen Gesandschaft zu Berlin 1746–1756', *Forschungen zur brandenburgischen und preußischen Geschichte* 6 (1893), 451–481, and 7 (1894), 71–96. In these works, however, economic issues are neglected.

[41] On D'Ammon, see Rolf Straubel, *Biographisches Handbuch der preußischen Verwaltungs- und Justizbeamten* (Munich: Saur, 2009), I: 9.

induced the king both to look more closely at the French project and, finally, to propose a treaty in forty-two articles, which was sent to Paris in April 1748.[42]

This project pivoted on the recognition of the reciprocity between Prussia and France, on the exemption from the *droit de fret* and on other facilities, which the French government would guarantee to the Prussian merchants (for example, the possibility of storing Prussian goods in the royal depositories). Moreover, in case one of the contracting parties had declared war on a third nation, the treaty would have not required any military support from the other ally, whose neutrality was thus protected. Such a treaty was obviously very advantageous for the Prussians, while it encountered strong reactions in Paris. The French government did not want to make such large concessions to the Prussian fleet and above all did not accept that the treaty could be considered valid also for the colonies.[43] Despite this, France did not want to break the ties that so closely linked it to Prussia. Instead of criticizing the project and officially rejecting it, the tactic adopted by the French court was dilatory and successfully stifled the whole affair for the following years.

In concomitance with the official creation of the Company of Emden (August 1750), the Prussians drafted a new project for a treaty of commerce with France.[44] In the new version of the treaty, Frederick demanded that the Company of Emden should be officially recognized and supported by the French.[45] However, the reason given for the reopening of the negotiations

[42] D'Ammon's memorandum dated 28 November 1747 (GStA, I. HA, Rep. 11, Geheimer Rat, Auswärtige Beziehungen, Akten Nr. 2763, fos. 42–46); the projected treaty sent to Paris is held in MAE, Mémoires et documents Prusse 3, fos. 175ff.

[43] See the briefings prepared as a riposte to the Prussian project, MAE, Mémoires et documents Prusse 3, fos. 189–195.

[44] The French were informed about the new treaty of commerce a month before the Company of Emden was founded. See MAE, Correspondance politique 158, fol. 422, letter of M. de Tyrconnell dated 27 June 1750 (a copy of the same letter is also MAE, Mémoires et documents Prusse 3, int. 45, fos. 222ff.). Tyrconnell was the successor of M. de Valori as French ambassador in Prussia; on his mission in Berlin, see Marc Serge Rivière, 'The Earl of Tyrconnell's Impact on Franco-Prussian Relations (1750–2)', *Eighteenth Century Ireland* 15 (2000), 120–138.

[45] Frederick II underlines this point in his correspondence with D'Ammon several times: see *Politische Correspondenz Friedrichs des Grossen*, VIII: 381–382, 398–399, 405–406.

was not linked to the creation of the Asiatic Company. In the diplomatic correspondence, it was explained that Frederick had just come back from a visit to Königsberg and had realized how much Prussia could improve its trade and make the fortune of French merchants. Frederick was ready to reconsider some of his requests in order to convince the French government. For example, he was willing to concede a semi-monopoly to the French wines in Silesia, by imposing higher tariffs and customs duties on the Hungarian wines coming from the hereditary lands of the Habsburgs.[46] Such an offer was particularly intriguing for the French, although many other aspects of the treaty did not please them, starting from the Prussian wish to interfere with its transoceanic trade.

The general situation had changed after the failure of the Franco-Dutch negotiations. This time, the French crown officially invited the King of Prussia to send to Paris an envoy, empowered to prepare a treaty of commerce. Again, the choice came down to D'Ammon, who had followed the negotiations with France from their very beginning.

The key problem for the French government concerned the introduction of Silesian linens into the colonial market: the treaty had to be considered valid only in the French mainland. Apart from that, France was particularly cautious about making further concessions to the Prussians, frightening their economic growth. After more than a year of intense negotiations, D'Ammon informed Frederick that the French government refused to sign a treaty and proposed subscribing a *convention de commerce* or a mere *déclaration*. Frederick was particularly annoyed by this sudden change of plan, but he accepted it for the good of Prussia.[47] In particular, the failure of the negotiations led to a rupture between D'Ammon and the Berliner court: the *convention de commerce* was actually presented by the Chevalier de la Touche, at that time French ambassador in Berlin, and did not involve D'Ammon, who always remained very

[46] On the issue of Hungarian wines, see GStA, I. HA, Rep. 11, Geheimer Rat, Auswärtige Beziehungen, Akten Nr. 2777, fos. 78–79 and 118–121; the question was very important for the French too: see the letter of M. Tyrconnell quoted in n. 50 and the letter of 25 August 1750 in MAE, Correspondance politique Prusse 159, fos. 164v–165v. The problems of customs tariff in Silesia finally gave rise to a commercial war between Austria and Prussia in 1753: Koser, *Geschichte*, II: 182–185.

[47] See Frederick's letter to his envoy in Paris, dated 18 April 1752, in *Politische Correspondenz Friedrichs des Grossen*, IX: 90–91.

critical about its content.[48] Finally, in February 1753, a ten-year-long *convention préliminaire de commerce* was signed in Versailles by the representatives of the two states.

The result was quite meagre, if compared with the long pre-history of this treaty. Of the forty-two articles of the 1748 plan, only seven remained in the final agreement.[49] And yet the content of the *convention* was not devoid of important achievements. The Prussians had obtained the exemption from the *droit de fret*—but this exemption was valid only in case of direct trade between Prussia and France and did not include the coastal navigation services offered by the Prussian ships between French harbours—and the exemption from the *droit d'aubaine*, namely a royal right of escheat, which allowed the king to confiscate the inheritance of a foreigner who died in France. Moreover, Prussia was finally recognized as the *nation la plus favorisée* by the French, something to which it had always aspired. *In extremis*, Frederick managed to introduce in the *convention* a specific article which explicitly equated Prussia with the Low Countries and the Hanseatic cities, although the terms of the agreement were still very vague. The French could be satisfied: they had avoided accepting too cogent engagements with the Prussians, while (apparently) tightening the links that bound them to France. The Prussians had to be pleased as well: although they did not manage to sign a trade treaty, they had made important steps further on the way to become a trading nation.

The Prussian Trading Nation

In 1750, the *Berlinische Nachrichten von Staats- und Gelehrten-Sachen* announced the charter of the Asiatic Company in Emden.[50] The journal in which the information was published was Frederick's official newspaper, founded in 1740, after he had just ascended the throne. The

[48] The correspondence between Frederick and D'Ammon dating back to 1752–1753 reveals their strong disagreements: see GStA, I HA, Rep. 96, Geh. Zivilkabinett, ältere Periode (bis 1797), Nr. 25 E and F.

[49] Different drafts of the convention are preserved in MAE, Correspondance politique Prusse 167, fos. 257–258 and Correspondance politique Prusse 168, fos. 65r–69v, while the signed *convention du commerce* has been published in Friedrich August Wilhelm Wenck, *Codex iuris gentium* (Lipsiae: Weidmann, 1781–1795), II: 722–725.

[50] *Berlinische Nachrichten von Staats- und gelehrten Sachen*, n. 117, 29 September 1750. The journal comes back to the Emden trade activities in n. 130, 29 October 1750.

announcement devoted to Emden, which reported in great detail the *Octroi* granted by the king to the Company, showed that the 'trading nation' had to take part in the economic development of the country. But was there such a thing as a 'trading nation' in Prussia? In opposition to its traditional image of authoritarianism and social immobility, recent research has shown that Prussia presented a good degree of economic vivacity. In particular, the analysis of mercantile families and groups has attested a deep gulf within Prussian territories in terms of economic development.[51] While Berlin experienced a stronger state influence, exerted in many different ways (a more efficient web of communication, the presence of the court, larger investments), the economy of other provinces was still controlled by local ruling classes, which could impose their will to a certain extent even on Frederick's own policies.[52]

East Frisia was certainly one of the most independent and economically lively regions of the Prussian monarchy. After it was annexed to Prussia in 1744, the estates immediately founded a local *Intelligenzblatt*, the *Wochentliche Ostfriesische Anzeigen und Nachrichten*, and tried to reorientate their activities in the new Prussian order.[53] Furthermore, merchants from Eastern Frisia, as well as the *Commercium-Collegia* of other important trading cities, played an active role in the negotiations with France. During D'Ammon's mission to Frisia and to the Dutch Republic in 1747–1748, the above-mentioned Frisian *Intelligenzblatt* summoned all the merchants, who had trade relationships with France, to the Prussian authorities in order to give and receive information about the state of French–Frisian commerce.[54] In 1747, similar consultations occurred in

[51] Rolf Straubel, *Kaufleute und Manufakturunternehmer. Eine empirische Untersuchung über die sozialen Träger von Handel und Großgewerbe in den mittleren preußischen Provinzen (1763 bis 1815)* (Stuttgart: Franz Steiner, 1995).

[52] See the famous case of the Prussian *Régie*, a centralized agency of revenue that raised large opposition in the whole country: Florian Schui, *Rebellious Prussians. Urban Political Culture under Frederick the Great and his Successors* (Oxford: Oxford University Press, 2013), ch. 4, and Edoardo Tortarolo, 'Opinione pubblica e opposizione in Prussia sotto Federico II', in *Stato e cultura in Prussia*, 137–165, esp. 156–165.

[53] Johannes-Hendrik Sonntag, *Die preußische Wirtschaftspolitik in Ostfriesland (1744–1806/1813–1815) unter besonderer Berücksichtigung der Stadt Emden und des Emsverkehrs* (Aurich: Verlag Ostfriesische Landschaft, 1987).

[54] *Wöchentliche Ost-friesische Anzeigen und Nachrichten von allerhand zum gemeinen Besten überhaupt, auch zur Beförderung Handels und Wandels, dienenden Sachen* 1 (1747), 78, 86.

Königsberg and Stettin, i.e. the eastern bulwarks of Prussian trade. From these reports it clearly emerged that it was common opinion among the different merchants' communities that the second-hand trade was an obstacle for Prussian development.[55] In particular, Stettin, who was directly interested in French trade, exerted direct pressures on the diplomatic talks. While D'Ammon was in Paris, Stettiner merchants asked and obtained exemption from paying the *droits de fret* before any agreement was concluded.[56]

There is no reason to over-emphasize the influence of the mercantile class. The negotiations with France and, more generally, Frederick's economic policy were shaped by the ultimate will of the king.[57] The decision to create a free port in Emden was independently taken by the Prussian government; and, if it is undeniable that Berliner archives are filled with a consistent amount of requests and economic projects about Emden and other colonial enterprises, many of these plans were presented by 'subsidy-hunters', who did not have any clear idea about commerce and usually failed after a few years.[58] However, Frederick needed the involvement of a modern mercantile class in order to support this new economic course: after all, there is no trade without skilful traders. The announcement in the *Berlinische Nachrichten* about the Asiatic Company was part of a royal campaign in favour of commerce, which found its natural completion in the theoretical works of Prussian cameralists. As has already been seen, Justi contributed to the king's campaign outside Prussia, but the major support

[55] *Die Handels-, Zoll- und Akzisepolitik*, III/2: 573–574.

[56] In March 1752, the French government conceded the exemption from the *droits de fret* to Prussian merchants. The decision was taken after Stettiner merchants complained about the treatment they had received in French harbours. See GStA, I. HA, Rep. 11, Geheimer Rat, Auswärtige Beziehungen, Akten Nr. 2778, fos. 437–438; other documentation GStA, I HA, Rep. 96, Geh. Zivilkabinett, ältere Periode (bis 1797), Nr. 25 F.

[57] Hamish M. Scott, 'Prussia's Royal Foreign Minister: Frederick the Great and the Administration of Prussian Diplomacy,' in: *Royal and Republican Sovereignty in Early Modern Europe. Essays in Memory of Ragnhild Hatton*, ed. Robert Oresko, Graham C. Gibbs and Hamish M. Scott (Cambridge: Cambridge University Press, 1997), 500–526.

[58] See primarily Heinrich Berger, *Überseeische Handelsbestrebungen und koloniale Pläne unter Friedrich dem Grossen* (Leipzig: Gustav Fock, 1899); on the Prussian 'subsidy-hunters', see Wilhelm Treue, *Preußens Wirtschaft vom Dreißigjährigen Krieg bis zum Nationalsozialismus*, in: *Handbuch der Preußischen Geschichte*, ed. Büsch and Neugebauer, II: 449–604, esp. 479–483.

came from state universities. The one who took the challenge in 1751 was the professor of state law (*Staats-Recht*) and history at the University of Königsberg, Carl Friedrich Pauli, with his *The Interest of the Prussian States in the Profitable Trade, especially in the Maritime One*.[59]

This sixteen-page booklet started by recognizing the success achieved by the United Provinces in the last decades and the role played in the process by trade. However, the Dutch monopoly could no longer persist. The 'true sources of wealth' had become known to everyone and other states were trying to 'make their subjects happy' by trading. In particular, Prussia had recently discovered the importance of commerce and started to threaten Dutch supremacy. Pauli underlined that Prussia occupied a geographical position that allowed it to trade on two seas, the Northern and the Baltic one, and to reach 'all the other parts of the world'. Furthermore, Prussian harbours were growing fast and an internal network of channels and rivers permitted the shipment of goods 'without passing through the lands of any foreign sovereigns'; consequently, Poland and Saxony did not have any other choice than to deal with Prussian merchants. The last gift with which nature had provided Prussia was the wealth of its agricultural products: barley, wheat, rye and, above all, amber.

In Pauli's eulogy, natural products were only one aspect of the Prussian trading potentialities. In the same years, Frederick was implementing important reforms and sustaining manufacturers throughout the country. In Prussia, this was possible because labour was cheap and no religious persecutions hindered the economic development. The Silesian linens were already well known, while the silk industry would become stronger when new trading relationships were established with Persia and China. So far Pauli dealt with exportations, but he was obviously conscious that Prussia also needed to import many products, such as wines, spices, silk and cotton. This was another important route to trade and especially to first-hand trade. Prussia had to create connections with colonial countries such as Spain, Portugal and even France and Britain, and to trade with the Far East in order to exchange its own goods with those which it needed.

Pauli's goal was to support Prussian reforms in a practical way: the last part of the work bears witness to this objective and makes very concrete proposals, which went well beyond the economic field. In fact, in his view, trade did not

[59] Pauli's *Die Vortheile derer Preussischen Staaten zum einträglichen Handel, sonderlich zur See* was published in Halle im Magdeburgischen in 1751 by Johann Friedrich Grunert.

require only harbours, storehouses and channels, but a well-working judicial system and 'good dispositions of police' (*gute Policey-Anstalten*), that is: an efficient post system, public safety and a reliable classification of weights and measures. Most of all, Pauli praised the freedom that Frederick II had guaranteed to Prussia and which could ensure wider possibilities for trade.

Understandably, Pauli never mentioned trade treaties. Diplomatic talks and agreements were kept jealously secret in the governmental bureaus and, even after the *convention de commerce* was signed, it continued to remain unknown to general public. The message that the writing had to convey concerned the general framework in which trade treaties and Frederick's economic initiatives should take place. Some pamphlets published in the early 1750s shared with Pauli's work the same intention to convince Prussian public opinion about the need of trade and the importance of free, first-hand one.

Two further examples can be discussed here: the first is an advertising pamphlet, which was issued in 1750 in order to convince potential investors to buy stocks of the newly established Asiatic Company; the second is a speech contemporarily held at the German society of Königsberg, a literary academy endorsed by the court.[60] The two different typologies of texts were intended to reach a wide spectrum of readers involved in trade activities or, at least, interested in such a topic. The literary genres of these works were completely different. On the one hand, the advertisement of the Prussian Company was presented as a letter of a British merchant to a Berliner one, in which a British tradesman asked for some explanations about this new business; a reply written by the Prussian trader followed, strongly supporting the ambitions of the Company. On the other hand, the academic speech amounted to a traditional dynastic celebration of the Hohenzollern, which attempted to include trade among their glorious deeds. Clearly, the audiences that these texts addressed were completely different, but, at the same time, the economic discourse laid on the same presuppositions and aimed at

[60] See the *Schreiben eines Englischen Negotianten an einen Kaufmann in Berlin, die königliche Preußische Handlungcompagnie betreffend. Nebst der Antwort* (London 1750), and *Die Vorrechte der preußischen Länder zur Handlung nach China*..., in: *Der königliche deutschen Gesellschaft in Königsberg eigene Schriften*... (Königsberg: Johann Heinrich Hartung, 1754), 160–179. The two works are almost simultaneous—the fictitious letters dated October and November 1750, while the speech was delivered on 21 November 1750; both works are anonymous, although Pauli uncovers the authorship of *Die Vorrechte*, whose author was a member of the Königsberg Academy named Schröder.

the same goal. Both texts started with an analysis of the trading possibilities of Prussia: the presence of important harbours, the wealth of relevant goods and manufactures, the attitude to free trade. These parts of the texts mirrored each other and closely resembled Pauli's book, which in fact quoted them at length. Apart from that, the general tone of the two pamphlets changed according to the different audiences: the exchange of commercial letters published in the first pamphlet was characterized by a more technical language and gave practical details about goods and trade routes; the academic speech had a more erudite appeal and recollected (presumptive) seventeenth-century precedents for Frederick's policies.

All in all, Pauli's writing and these two other pamphlets were part of the same strategy, which the court itself was supporting. Although the Asiatic Company of Emden was a private enterprise, the Prussian government was directly implicated in its activities. At the beginning of 1751, on the way to Paris for his diplomatic mission, D'Ammon passed through Amsterdam, Brussels and Antwerp in order to convince local merchants to buy stocks of the Company on behalf of the court.[61] To some extent, this diplomatic mission appears as the development of the press campaign, represented by the *Schreiben eines Englischen Negotianten*, into the domain of politics. Furthermore, these works published in German and intended to reach the Prussian public also had an international counterweight, which better show the political relevance of the topic. In fact, both the French–Prussian treaty and the charter of the Asiatic Company were seen as direct attacks against Dutch supremacy, attacks which Dutch journalists immediately tried to drive back. In 1752, while the negotiations between France and Prussia were still ongoing, a libel, probably due to Genu Soahalt de Mainvilliers, was published in The Hague against the Prussian envoy in Paris D'Ammon and, after the *convention de commerce* was signed, Dutch authorities tried to undermine the treaty's authenticity in order to divert French and other merchants from carrying their goods on Prussian ships.[62] As a riposte to these false conjectures, the Berliner court planned to unofficially publish the text of the *convention* itself using Dutch journals.

[61] GStA, I. HA, Rep. 11, Geheimer Rat, Auswärtige Beziehungen, Akten Nr. 2778, fos. 49–53.

[62] On the libel, see GStA, I HA, Rep. 96, Geh. Zivilkabinett, ältere Periode (bis 1797), Nr. 25 E, fol. 195, and F, fol. 3. About the Dutch opposition to the plan, see GStA, I HA, Rep. 11, Geheimer Rat, Auswärtige Beziehungen, Akten, Nr. 2789, fol. 99.

Despite the wide appeal that the Prussian discussions about trade gained, the interest arising from Frederick's projects of 1750s was destined to result in a great disappointment. The outbreak of the Seven Years War put an end both to the Company of Emden and the *convention de commerce* between France and Prussia. Already before the war, the *convention* had shown some critical flaws: in 1753 and 1754 the French and Prussian courts already had to solve several conflicts about the article concerning the *droit d'aubaine*.[63] But it was above all the belligerent events of 1756–1763 that came to remind Frederick that commerce was a much more difficult subject to handle than his military campaigns. The critical situation that Frederick faced during those years forced him to reshape his economic projects, which started to more closely follow the old path traced by his father and grandfather. As they were used to advising, the first duty of a king was not to trigger innovative economic strategies, but to guarantee the government budget.

Marco Cavarzere is research fellow at the Goethe-University of Frankfurt. He gained his PhD from the Scuola Normale Superiore Pisa and has published *La prassi della censura nell'Italia del Seicento. Tra repressione e mediazione* (2011), 'The "New Science of Commerce" in the Holy Roman Empire: Véron de Forbonnais's *Élémens du commerce* and its German Readers' *History of European Ideas* (2014) and 'Land and Nation: The Ancient Modernity of National Geography (Piedmont, 1750–1800)' *Journal of the History of Ideas* (2016).

[63] GStA, I. HA, Rep. 11, Geheimer Rat, Auswärtige Beziehungen, Akten, Nr. 2791.

War, Neutrality and Commercial Treaties: The Savoyard State 1660–1789

Christopher Storrs

Introduction

The rise between 1648 and 1815 of an elite of so-called great powers—Austria, Britain, France, Prussia and Russia—was accompanied by that of various secondary powers which exploited the competition between their more powerful neighbours but also had to accommodate themselves, politically and economically to a world increasingly shaped by them.[1] These inferior powers included, in Italy, the Savoyard state, a composite polity united by allegiance to the House of Savoy. The dynasty's ancestral territories comprised the principality of Piedmont—the largest, most populous and richest territory—the duchy of Savoy, the duchy of Aosta and the county of Nice. New territories were added between 1690 and 1748 by Victor Amadeus II (1675–1730) and his son and successor Charles Emanuel III (1730–1773). Their state also acquired a new standing in Europe due in large part to its military participation in the Nine

[1] Derek McKay and H. M. Scott, *The Rise of the Great Powers 1648–1815* (Harlow: Longman, 1983).

C. Storrs (✉)
University of Dundee, UK
e-mail: c.d.storrs@dundee.ac.uk

A. Alimento, K. Stapelbroek (eds.), *The Politics of Commercial Treaties in the Eighteenth Century*, DOI 10.1007/978-3-319-53574-6_12

Years War and the Wars of the Spanish, Polish and Austrian Successions and for its diplomatic skill.[2]

This remarkable success story was accompanied by various challenges, political and economic. What efforts were made in Turin to take economic advantage of the bigger changes in Europe between 1660 and 1800? To what extent did these rely on commercial treaties? Were prince and ministers aware of the later decades of the eighteenth century as a period characterized by a new preoccupation on the part of other European states with the negotiation of such treaties? Or did they prefer to use instruments of policy such as tariffs independently from commercial treaties? How far was neutrality a deliberately pursued political and economic option? Last, but by no means least, what does the experience of the Savoyard state say about the relative importance of the Atlantic and the Mediterranean in this period? The flurry of interest in the Atlantic and globalization in recent decades has been based upon a belief that the Mediterranean was a backwater in the eighteenth century. This was far from the reality: the Mediterranean—and the Levant beyond—remained of enormous importance to Europe's commerce and its policy-makers.

In what follows, I seek to show that the court of Turin made frequent efforts to stimulate domestic economic growth, but was unwilling—especially after 1748—to conclude trade treaties not least because it was determined in a more dangerous international political climate not to commit itself for the long term and found it difficult to separate commercial and political ties. Instead, and in part driven by other pressures—notably the debt incurred in the wars fought between 1690 and 1748—the Court of Turin preferred to conclude a number of narrower agreements which removed some lesser obstacles to trade and thus facilitated improved commercial relations and economic growth without restricting its freedom of political manoeuvre.

[2] Christopher Storrs, *War, Diplomacy and the Rise of Savoy, 1690–1720* (Cambridge: Cambridge University Press, 1999); Geoffrey Symcox, *Victor Amadeus II. Absolutism in the Savoyard State 1675–1730* (London: Thames & Hudson, 1983); Christopher Storrs, 'The Savoyard Fiscal-Military State in the "Long" Eighteenth Century', in: *The Fiscal-Military State in the Eighteenth Century. Essays for P. G. M. Dickson*, ed. Christopher Storrs (Farnham: Ashgate, 2009), 201–235; Guido Quazza, *Il Problema, Italiano e l'Equilibrio Europeo 1720–1738* (Turin: Diputazione di Storia Subalpina, 1965); Jeremy Black, 'The Development of Anglo-Sardinian Relations in the First Half of the Eighteenth Century', *Studi Piemontesi* 12 (1983), 48–59.

An Abortive Trade Treaty

Following the 'restoration' of the Savoyard state at the conclusion of the so-called 'Italian Wars' (1494–1559), successive dukes of Savoy sought to rebuild their state, economically and politically.[3] Under Charles Emanuel II (1638–1675), this policy found expression in various projects, including a treaty of friendship and commerce with England which was concluded—reflecting the lack of formal contacts between the two courts—not in Turin or London, but in Florence in September 1669.[4] The preamble declared that the agreement aimed to 'superadd the new tie of mutual commerce to those of family', while the first article asserted the link between trade and peace, declaring—something more frequently asserted in elite circles in Europe a century later—that 'commerce was always the companion of peace'. It was hoped to achieve peace and trade by attracting English merchants and trade to the port complex of Nice (declared a free port by Charles Emanuel), Villefranche and San Ospizio. The county of Nice was difficult of access from Piedmont—communications obstructed by the Alps—but was at least adjacent to it whereas the tiny territory of Oneglia, the only other Savoyard coastal possession, was enclaved within Genoese territory, access to which was made difficult by the often tense relations between the court of Turin and the republic of Genoa. To stimulate trade through Nice, Charles Emanuel was prepared to extend the privileges already enjoyed there by English merchants. Just how far those merchants were attracted to Nice by the treaty is unclear. However, subsequent discussions (below), suggest it had little impact; English trade with Italy continued to be oriented towards Leghorn and Sicily.[5]

The treaty of 1669 was not the only attempt to insert the Savoyard economy into a bigger commercial framework before 1690. Equally striking, and equally unsuccessful, were the efforts of Charles

[3] Pierpaolo Merlin, Claudio Rosso, Geoffrey Symcox and Giuseppe Ricuperati, *Il Piemonte Sabaudo. Stato e Territori in Età Moderna* (Turin: UTET, 1994).

[4] Carlo Contessa, 'Aspirazioni commerciali intrecciate ad alleanze politiche della Casa di Savoia coll'Inghilterra nei secoli XVII e XVIII', *Memorie della Reale Accademie delle Scienze di Torino*, ser. II, 64 (1914), 1–50; Comte Solar de la Marguerite, *Traités publics de la Maison Royale de Savoie* (Turin: L'Imprimerie Royale, 1838–61), II: 91–103.

[5] Federico Sclopis, *Delle Relazioni Politiche tra la dinastia di Savoia ed il governo britannico 1240–1815* (Turin: Stamperia Reale, 1854), 14–15; Gigliola Pagano de Divitiis, *English Merchants in Seventeenth-Century Italy* (Cambridge: Cambridge University Press, 1997).

Emanuel's widow, Jeanne Baptiste de Nemours. As regent for her infant son, Victor Amadeus II, she sought to marry him to her niece, the *Infanta* of Portugal, thus gaining access to Portugal's overseas empire and trade which were being rebuilt around Brazil. This project, which reflected the Savoyard state's alignment with Bourbon France against Habsburg Spain—Louis XIV approving the project—also reflected the regent's desire to retain power in Turin by removing her son to Lisbon. A Piedmontese company to trade with Portugal was established in 1681, when a formal trade treaty was concluded between the two courts. Unfortunately for the regent and for this attempt to stimulate the economy of the Savoyard territories, the scheme did not succeed, not least because of the opposition of her son and of a substantial portion of the Savoyard elite.[6]

However, other possibilities emerged at the end of the 1680s as Victor Amadeus both exploited and contributed to the emergence of a new configuration of power in Europe. In the generation or more before 1690, the Savoyard state was a French satellite, helping to underpin French influence in north Italy. But Victor Amadeus resented his subordinate role and in 1690 joined the Grand Alliance against the Sun King. While the duke was attracted by the subsidies paid by England, Spain and the Dutch Republic to compensate the loss of revenues from territorial occupation or devastation by Louis XIV's forces, the subsidy-paying states devised an alternative project which would have fundamentally reoriented the political and commercial relations of the Savoyard state with important implications for the European balance.

By 1695, the English subsidy to the duke of Savoy strained the English finances,[7] while the duke of Savoy obtained cloth for army uniforms from

[6] Carlo Contessa, 'Progetti economici della seconda Madame Reale fondati sopra un contratto nuziale (1678–1682)', *Miscellanea di Storia Italiana* 48 (1915), 121–179; Toby Osborne, '"Notre grand dessein": il progetto di nozze fra Vittorio Amedeo II e l'infanta Isabella Luisa (1675–82)', in: *Portogallo e Piemonte. Nove secoli (XII–XX) di relazioni dinastiche e politiche*, ed. Maria Antonia Lopes and Blythe Alice Raviola (Rome: Carocci, 2014), 159–180; Symcox, *Victor Amadeus*, 82–90.

[7] D. W. Jones, 'The Economic Consequences of William III', in: *Knights Errant and True Englishmen. British Foreign Policy, 1660–1800*, ed. Jeremy Black (Edinburgh: John Donald, 1989), 24–40; Geoffrey Symcox, 'Britain and Victor Amadeus II: or, The Use and Abuse of Allies', in: *Britain's Rise to Greatness 1660–1763*, ed. Stephen Baxter (Berkeley: University of California Press, 1983), 151–184; Christopher Storrs, 'Diplomatic Relations between William III and Victor Amadeus II of Savoy 1690–1696', unpublished PhD thesis,

France. The English government proposed that the duke should receive cloth instead of cash. But the thinking behind the project went further. The economy of the duke's territories was closely tied to that of France, which took many of the Savoyard state's exports and provided many of its imports. It was believed in English and Dutch circles that this relationship helped Louis XIV raise tax revenues and fund his military domination of Western Europe. By establishing new commercial links between Savoy and its new allies, above all England, Louis would not be able to threaten his neighbours as he had done before 1688. The English Lustring Company, which was to oversee the scheme and to export cloth to Piedmont in return for silk, oil, soap and paper, sent an agent to Turin in the summer of 1695 with samples of cloth.

The project formulated a close relationship between economic, military and political power. Unfortunately for those proposing it, the scheme—whose existence suggests the failure of the treaty of 1669—proved unworkable. Victor Amadeus was by no means hostile to the project, but wanted the English (and Dutch) to take more Piedmontese exports (including rice). Also, Piedmontese merchants had many French contacts, but few or none in England, and vice versa (apart from the consul in Nice). Nothing had come of the cloth for subsidies scheme when in 1696 Victor Amadeus abandoned the Grand Alliance. In 1699, when William III sent Richard Hill to Turin to congratulate the duke on the birth of a son, the envoy noted that the economy of Victor Amadeus' states was still closely tied to that of France. Hill also noted that while England had concluded a trade treaty with the duke of Savoy—that of 1669—'I see very little trade driven that way'. As instructed, Hill raised the question of duties imposed upon English ships contrary to that treaty but was told the treaty had been a purely temporary measure.[8]

The War of the Spanish Succession, when England again paid Victor Amadeus a subsidy,[9] saw renewed efforts to stimulate trade between the two states. The treaty of alliance and subsidy which was

University of London (1990), 322–330; Christopher Storrs, '"Grosse Erwartungen": Britische Subsidienzahlungen an Savoyen im 18. Jahrhundert', *Historische Zeitschrift* 56 (Munich: Oldenbourg, 2012), 87–126.

[8] W. Blackley, ed., *The Diplomatic Correspondence of the Right Hon Richard Hill* (London: John Murray, 1845), II: 803–813.

[9] Franco Venturi, 'Il Piemonte ai primi decenni del Settecento nelle relazioni dei diplomatici inglesi', *Bollettino Storico Bibliografico Subalpino* 54 (1956), 229–30.

concluded in 1704 sought—at the suggestion of the English ministers—to encourage trade links by easing the duties on the transit of English goods through the Savoyard state.[10] In 1709, the English representative in Turin, Chetwynd, suggested the restructuring of commercial relations between Turin and London to the disadvantage of France. The idea found support in London, not least from the Lustring Company, but foundered on the perennial problem of poor communications between Nice and Piedmont.[11] Nevertheless, trade between Piedmont and France declined during the war years, while English cloth imports into Piedmont rose.[12] In that sense, the adjustment of the Savoyard state's place in the state system between 1690 and 1713 had been accompanied by some adjustment of its economic relations, but without major formal commitments.

The peace settlement of 1713 offered more opportunities. The duke's interests had been well looked after by Queen Anne's Tory ministers. This owed something to the fact that Victor Amadeus' duchess was Anne's cousin, with a claim on the English and Scottish crowns which had been set aside in the Act of Settlement of 1701, something to his claim on the Spanish succession, and something to the fact that as a member of the Grand Alliance he shared in the spoils of victory. But the precise nature of the gains those ministers secured for him was shaped in part by England's Mediterranean commercial interests. By giving the duke the island kingdom of Sicily they ensured that Victor Amadeus, who had no navy to speak of in 1713, would in the short term at least depend on English help at sea. His dependence would contribute to the security of England's Levant trade through the Mediterranean.[13] Some English ministers had a vision of a new relationship in which Piedmont offered an alternative route to Venice for English goods entering Italy, with Piedmont cast in the role of another

[10] The treaty is in Blackley, ed., *Diplomatic Correspondence*, II: 770–797, 929–955.

[11] Venturi, 'Il Piemonte', 229–231.

[12] Symcox, 'Britain and Victor Amadeus II', 174–175.

[13] H. N. Fieldhouse, 'St. John and Savoy in the War of the Spanish Succession', *English Historical Review* 50 (1935), 278–284; Derek McKay, 'Bolingbroke, Oxford and the Defence of the Utrecht Settlement in Southern Europe', *English Historical Review* 86 (1971), 264–284; Symcox, *Victor Amadeus*, 164–165.

Portugal, dominated—economically—by England.[14] This relationship was embodied in a convention (1713) which confirmed the commercial privileges enjoyed by English merchants in Sicily under the Spanish Habsburgs.[15] A new Anglo-Savoyard connection loomed, an integral part of a new political and commercial balance, both in the Mediterranean and in Europe more generally.

Political and Economic Tensions, 1713–1748

However, the new relationship did not flourish as expected. Faced with the determination of Philip V to overturn the Utrecht settlement in both the Mediterranean as well as across the Atlantic, the new Hanoverian regime in London, less indulgent of Victor Amadeus, preferred to appease Philip. Following the Spanish conquest of Sardinia (1717) and invasion of Sicily (1718), Victor Amadeus was obliged to swap Sicily for Sardinia, which did not have the same commercial or political importance and in turn decreased Victor Amadeus' standing in the eyes of Britain.

Victor Amadeus therefore sought to stimulate the economy of his mainland territories in order to underpin (through higher tax revenues) the new position he had achieved since 1690.[16] Economic growth could be achieved in various ways. These included equipping the Savoyard state with appropriate institutions, such as the *Consolato*, established (1720) to regulate trade in the Savoyard state, and developing a navy. The king also received proposals to break into the Atlantic economy by, for example, establishing a presence in Madagascar.[17] There were efforts, too, to

[14] Peterborough's dispatch of 16 October 1712 is cited in Venturi, 'Il Piemonte', 232–234; Bridget Cameron, *This Master Firebrand. A Life of Charles Mordaunt 3rd Earl of Peterborough 1658–1735* (Norwich: Michael Russell Publishing), 344.

[15] Solar della Marguerite, *Traités publics*, II: 276–284; Sclopis, *Relazioni*, 47; Symcox, *Victor Amadeus*, 163–166.

[16] For what follows, cf. Symcox, *Victor Amadeus*, 201–221.

[17] Cf. 'Replique a la Reponse de SM le Roy de Sardaigne' (1727), A[rchivio] di S[tato] di T[orino]/Materie di Comercio [MC], Categoria 3: Comercio in generale, mazzo 1/39; the *mémoire* sent by marchese d'Arvillars on Spain's Indies trade and the opportunities for Piedmontese silk, 5 May 1729, AST/MC/ Categoria 3, mazzo 1/47; and, 'Progetti del Cav Chancel per il stabilimento d'una compagnia che potrebbe introdurre il commercio nell'Indie', 12 July 1726, AST/Città e Contado di Nizza/Porto di Villafranca, mazzo 5/10.

stimulate domestic production and export of woollen cloths in Piedmont and restrict foreign cloth imports, including from England. Simultaneously, Victor Amadeus sought to protect Piedmont's crucial silk industry against nascent foreign silk industries. Here, too, England was cause for concern, not least because without the English demand, Victor Amadeus's states would continue to depend entirely on exports of silk to France. Typical of the way in which economic issues informed Savoyard diplomacy in this period were the instructions prepared for the cavaliere Ossorio before his departure as Victor Amadeus' representative in London in 1729. These devoted far more attention to economic matters (silk exports, cloth imports) than the instructions given any previous minister leaving for London.[18]

Relations between London and Turin in the 1720s had not been easy, not least because of Victor Amadeus' efforts to stimulate and protect the domestic economy. In 1722, the king banned the export from Piedmont of raw silk, provoking English protests.[19] From 1724 onwards he obliged local merchants—Piedmontese and foreign—to buy unsold Piedmontese woollen cloths.[20] In July 1726, Victor Amadeus raised the import duties on English woollen cloths. This provoked a storm of protest in Britain. In December 1726 a new English representative in Turin, Hedges (who had been sent to win the king for the Hanoverian alliance following the Austro-Spanish alliance of 1725), claimed that English cloth should enjoy preferential tariffs, in accordance with the treaty of 1669. The claim received short shrift. Hedges was told that the English had not complied with the treaty of 1669, that the latter had been overtaken by the treaty of alliance of 1704, and that the circumstances were very different from those of 1669.[21] Hedges, however, persisted in thinking that the treaty

[18] Instructions (1729), AST/Negoziazioni/Inghilterra, mazzo 1.

[19] Giuseppe Prato, *La vita economica in Piemonte a mezzo il secolo XVIII* (Turin: Società Topografico-Editrice Nazionale, 1908), 230.

[20] Edward Allen to duke of Newcastle, Turin, 28 February, 1 April and 11 November 1730, N[ational] A[rchives], Kew, State Papers [SP], 92/33; Luigi Bulferetti, 'I Piemontesi piu ricchi negli ultimi cento anni dell'assolutismo sabaudo', *Studi storici in onore di Gioacchino Volpe*, 2 vols. (Florence, 1958), I: 41–91 (46).

[21] Guido Quazza, *Le riforme in Piemonte nella prima metà del Settecento*, 2 vols. (Modena: Società Tipografico-Editrice Modenese, 1957), II: 266.

of 1669 remained valid and urged ministers in London to put pressure on Victor Amadeus by retaliatory measures against Piedmontese silk imports into Britain.[22]

Victor Amadeus' foreign secretary, the marchese del Borgo, affected to be unmoved by threats of reprisals. This was despite the fact that Hedges was able to show that the balance of trade between England and Piedmont favoured the latter precisely because of the value of its silk exports.[23] But the king of Sardinia and his ministers were also aware of a bigger economic and political picture. In Ossorio's instructions, Victor Amadeus hoped to exploit English anxieties about the country's trade in the Mediterranean and Levant to secure English backing for further Savoyard territorial gains in Italy as English politicians sought to accommodate the ambitions of Philip V. Victor Amadeus certainly did not abandon his protectionist measures. In July 1730, further duties were imposed on imported cloths, although these targeted primarily cloth imports other than those from England, while Charles Emanuel continued his father's policies, increasing those duties further in February 1731.[24] Thus, contrary to the hopes of English ministers at the end of the War of the Spanish Succession, the Savoyard state had not become a second Portugal for English commerce and the great gateway into Italy and beyond.

Despite these and other difficulties, in 1743 Charles Emanuel III joined Britain and Maria Theresa in the War of the Austrian Succession. Apart from the court of Turin's enduring anxiety regarding Spanish political and territorial ambitions in Italy, the king of Sardinia was attracted by the prospect of English subsidies and of territorial gains for himself. These latter included the acquisition of a coastal outlet at Finale in Liguria, which the emperor, Charles VI, had sold to the republic of Genoa in 1713. It was hoped, Nice still not being easily

[22] John Hedges to Newcastle, Turin, 14 and 28 December 1726, NA/SP/92/32, fos. 73–75.

[23] Hedges to Townshend, Turin, 5 April, 7 June and 5 July 1727, NA/SP/92/32, fos. 173–175, 208–210 and 229–230; Venturi, 'Il Piemonte', 240. Cf. also Allen to Newcastle, Turin, 28 February 1730, NA/SP/92/33, fos. 334–335. According to Allen, England imported wrought silks to the value of £120,000 p.a. and Piedmont imported English woollen cloths worth £70,000 p.a., a balance in Piedmont's favour of £50,000. Cf. Luigi Bulferetti, *Agricoltura, industria e commercio in Piemonte nel secolo XVIII* (Turin: Istituto per la Storia del Risorgimento Italiano, 1963).

[24] Allen to Newcastle, Turin, 26 August 1730, 7 October, 11 and 15 November 1730, 17 February 1731, NA/SP/92/33, fos. 440, 465, 476, 527. Cf. Quazza, *Riforme*, II: 268.

accessible from Piedmont, that Finale would become a successful trading emporium for the Savoyard state. As in the treaty of alliance of 1704, that concluded in 1743 not only confirmed the commercial privileges already enjoyed by British subjects in the Savoyard state but also promised more (by treaty) if the British wished.[25] However, no such treaty was pursued during the war, and although Charles Emanuel gained new territories, he did not secure Finale in the settlement of 1748. The sacrifice of the king of Sardinia's interests on that occasion was proof that the Savoyard state remained a secondary power.

Savoyard Policy in the Wake of the 'Diplomatic Revolution', 1748–1789

The War of the Austrian Succession and its aftermath represented a turning point for the Savoyard state. Besides failing to secure the desired Mediterranean outlet at Finale, the peace of 1748 and the Treaty of Aranjuez (1752) confirmed the establishment of the Spanish Bourbons and Austrian Habsburgs in Italy, halting Savoyard expansion. Despite receiving British subsidies and loans, Charles Emanuel III had accumulated a large war debt by 1748 that made for a more cautious foreign policy. In December 1755, on the eve of the Seven Years War, the British representative in Turin, the earl of Bristol, noted Charles Emanuel's determination to maintain the peace in Italy and to clear the debt.[26]

Another development confirmed for many in Turin the wisdom of a policy of neutrality. The 'rise' of the Savoyard state since 1690 had owed much to its control of the alpine passages between France and the Po valley, and its ability to exploit that control—selling its alliance to one side or the other—in the struggle between Bourbon France and Spanish and later Austrian Habsburgs helped shape international relations in Europe. However, the 'diplomatic revolution' of 1756 transformed international competition and undermined the strategic value of the Savoyard state which could no longer play France

[25] Matthew S. Anderson, *The War of the Austrian Succession 1740–1748* (Harlow: Longman, 1995), 125, 203; Richard Lodge, *Studies in Eighteenth Century Diplomacy 1740–1748* (London: John Murray, 1930), *passim*; Sclopis, *Relazioni*, 69.

[26] Earl of Bristol to Robinson, Turin, 27 December 1755, NA/SP/ 92/63.

and Austria off against each other.[27] For the next generation, down to the outbreak of the French revolutionary wars, Charles Emanuel III and his son Victor Amadeus III (1773–1796), would pursue a policy of neutrality, which was only briefly interrupted by joint military intervention with France against the radical regime in Geneva, an intervention which suggested that the Savoyard state was in some respects back in the French Bourbon orbit.[28]

During the Seven Years War, the court of Turin was very sensitive to French complaints of its Anglophile sympathies, and its permission to the British fleet to use Villefranche, as in previous conflicts.[29] In fact both Britain and France breached Savoyard neutrality during that struggle.[30] Whether to remain neutral or to intervene became a matter of debate in governing circles in Turin.[31] At the conclusion of the Seven Years War, Charles Emanuel III accepted a cash settlement in lieu of territory (i.e. of Piacenza), reflecting the new priorities in Turin.[32] Not surprisingly, in a coded criticism of the king's neutrality, in the spring of 1763 another British minister in Turin lauded the more adventurous conduct of the king's ancestors.[33] However, with the Austro-French alliance surviving the stresses of the war, the Savoyard court remained reluctant after 1763 to attempt a bolder course, an attitude strengthened by the desire of Joseph II to recover territories alienated by his Habsburg predecessors (including those acquired by the House of Savoy).[34]

[27] Geoffrey Rice, 'Lord Rochford at Turin, 1749–55: A Pivotal Phase in Anglo-Italian Relations in the Eighteenth Century', in: Knights Errant and True Englishmen. British Foreign Policy 1600–1800, ed. Jeremy Black (Edinburgh: John Donald, 1989), 92–112; Black, 'Development of Anglo-Sardinian Relations', 57–58.

[28] Christopher Storrs, 'Savoyard Diplomacy in the Eighteenth Century (1684–1798)', in: *Politics and Diplomacy in Early Modern Italy. The Structure of Diplomatic Practice, 1450–1800*, ed. Daniela Frigo (Cambridge: Cambridge University Press, 2000), 210–253: 212–213.

[29] Bristol to William Pitt, Turin, 9 March 1757, and Bristol to earl of Holdernesse, Turin, 20 July 1757, NA/SP/92/65.

[30] Bristol to Pitt, Turin, 7 September 1757, NA/SP/92/65.

[31] Bristol to Pitt, Turin, 14 August 1758, NA/SP/92/66.

[32] Domenico Carutti, *Storia del Regno di Carlo Emanuele III* (Turin: Eredi Botta, 1856), II: 96–167.

[33] Pitt to earl of Egremont, Turin, 9 April 1763, NA/SP/ 92/70.

[34] Viscount Mountstuart to Hillsborough, Turin, 3 December 1780, NA/SP/92/83.

Much of the energy which might otherwise have been channelled into an adventurous foreign policy was spent after 1748 in efforts to stimulate the domestic economy. Indeed, those decades saw Savoyard monarchs and ministers making great efforts to both expand and diversify that economy, and to make it less dependent on silk, which still in 1752 contributed almost 80 per cent of total exports.[35] Ministers in Turin were well aware of the dangers of such an unbalanced economy, Count Viry's instructions as envoy to London (1755) noting that if the British did not take Piedmont's silk, it would depend on the French alone. Those same instructions articulated concern, too, that the English might seek silk from elsewhere, including China and Persia, Viry being ordered to threaten heavier duties on English cloth imports into Piedmont to prevent this.[36] Count Borré de la Chavanne had been recalled from The Hague in 1749 to oversee a swathe of measures intended to transform the Savoyard economy and which included—with Finale now out of reach—efforts to make Nice more attractive to foreign shipping.[37] That same year Charles Emanuel III confirmed Nice's status as a free port.[38] The authorities also sought to develop the port facilities at neighbouring Limpia. More foreign consuls were

[35] Quazza, *Rifome*, II: 298; Prato, *Vita Economica*, 313.

[36] Istruzioni di SM al conte di Viry…, 16 July 1755, AST/Negoziazioni/Inghilterra, mazzo 1° d'addizione, no. 24.

[37] 'Progetto di Gio Nicola Morena di stabilire un commerzio tra il Regno di Napoli ed il Piemonte per via specialmente del portofranco nelle spiaggie di Nizza e S. Ospizio e porto di Villafranca, mandata dal conte di Rivera, 18 October 1749 and 4 September 1750. Colla risposta al d[ett]o progetto dal conte di Monasterolo' [1750?], AST/MC/Categoria 3, mazzo 2/23. Monasterolo concluded that although there was no immediate advantage to be gained from a trade treaty with the court of Naples, if Neapolitan ministers showed willing to conclude one, with the usual franchises, it should not be ignored, and the 'noise' it would make in Europe could only enhance the reputation of the new port and attract business there. But Savoyard policy-makers hoped to exchange territory with Genoa to secure access to another Savoyard enclave on the Ligurian coast, Loano. The Genoese were reluctant to cooperate. Louis Dutens to Hillsborough, Turin, 16 September 1780, NA/SP/92/83, but for continued interest on the part of the court of Turin in an exchange which might facilitate Anglo-Savoyard trade, cf. the instructions given the comte de Front as envoy to London, 24 November 1787, AST/Negoziazioni/Inghilterra, mazzo 1° d'addizione, no. 37.

[38] For the dues still payable at Nice, cf. Trevor to duke of Leeds, Turin, 11 November 1789, NA/Foreign Office [FO]/67/6.

attracted to Nice,[39] and a network of Savoyard consuls established abroad.[40] Efforts would also be made to encourage domestic production by imposing or increasing import duties, for example on vitriol (1786).[41] At last some effort was made to exploit the resources of the island of Sardinia. Chavanne also sent samples of Piedmontese wine to England in the hope—abortive at that point—of establishing a flourishing export trade.[42]

Ministers not only sought to stimulate foreign trade in Europe, they also hoped to break into the lucrative colonial trade. As early as 1748, for example, they received a project to establish a company at Nice which should secure the privilege to send one or two ships annually to Spanish Santo Domingo, supplying grain, and returning with sugar, indigo and cacao,[43] although this was unlikely to succeed given Spanish determination to exclude foreigners from the Indies. Portugal seemed a more promising partner. Indeed, it was hoped in Turin that in return for corn from Sardinia, Charles Emanuel III's subjects might secure colonial commodities from Portugal's global empire.[44] Unfortunately, nothing came of these hopes, not least because the king of Sardinia would not invest the necessary sums.[45] The accession of Victor Amadeus III revived hopes of greater trade with Portugal, the instructions prepared for Count Fontana, sent to Lisbon in 1774 to discuss a marriage between the Prince of Beira and the king of Sardinia's sister also envisaging a trade treaty.[46] However, these hopes too proved abortive and the closer political ties cultivated since 1762 between the courts of Turin and Lisbon had not been accompanied by closer economic ties by 1789. In fact, the Savoyard state was a potential rival to Portugal, especially in respect of efforts to promote wine

[39] Prato, *Vita Economica*, 318.

[40] Storrs, 'Savoyard Diplomacy', 242.

[41] Trevor to earl of Carmarthen, Turin, 12 May 1786, NA/FO/67/4.

[42] Rochford to Holdernesse, Turin, 5 January 1752, NA/SP/92/69.

[43] 'Progetto di stabilimento d'una Compagnia di Commercio nella Città di Nizza', 1748, incl. 'Mémoire concernant l'état actuel du commerce', AST/Materie di Commercio/Categoria 3, mazzo 2/5.

[44] Instructions for conte Giuseppe Maria Ferrero di Lavriano, 26 April 1762, AST/Negoz/Portogallo mazzo 1.

[45] Dutens to General Conway, Turin, 3 August 1765, NA/SP/92/71.

[46] Instructions, 1774, AST/Negoz/Portogallo, mazzo 1.

exports from Piedmont to England, which might compete there not only with French claret but with Portuguese wine.

While Charles Emanuel III and his ministers sought to stimulate foreign trade, they were reluctant to commit themselves to a trade treaty, which—as the king's comments on the Anglo-Russian trade treaty of 1766 reveal—they saw as the prelude to closer political ties. In 1766 the instructions prepared for Baron Viry de la Perriere before he left for London explained that his sovereign did not want to be bound by a trade treaty since it would not be to his states' advantage. Only one such treaty had been concluded hitherto—that of 1669—which was essentially about establishing the free port at Villefranche (Nice) but that agreement had never been implemented. Viry de la Perriere—and his successor Count Scarnafigi—were therefore to find out all they could about existing trades and any other which might be established between the two states but should avoid any proposal for a formal treaty.[47]

Scarnafigi's instructions of 1769 referred to a recent episode in which an English captain had claimed exemption from export duty citing the treaty of 1669. Indeed, the year 1768 had seen much discussion of that earlier agreement. In May 1768, Raiberti, the interim foreign secretary, and in a manner reminiscent of the arguments used by Savoyard ministers in the 1720s told the British representative, Potter, that the treaty of 1669 was very old and that England had not fulfilled its own obligations under that treaty. He added further that the privileges granted England in that treaty were allowable when the English alliance was necessary to the House of Savoy but not in the present state of affairs. This was no doubt a reference to the general situation of the Savoyard state, caught between the courts of Versailles and Vienna, but may also have reflected exasperation in Turin at the British government's failure to oppose the French acquisition of Corsica, which clearly had threatening implications for the court of Turin's position in Sardinia and for the overall balance of power in the Mediterranean.[48]

[47] Charles Emanuel III to la Marmora, Turin, 14 and 28 September, 1765, AST/LM/Inghilterra, mazzo 71.

[48] Potter to Shelburne, 7 May and 20 August 1768, Turin, NA/SP/92/73; Charles Emanuel III to Viry, 18 June 1768, AST/LM/Inghilterra, mazzo 40.

This reluctance to conclude a trade treaty with Britain continued to characterize Savoyard policy after 1768. Scarnafigi's successor in London, the marquis de Cordon, was also instructed in 1774 to deflect any proposals for a trade treaty. More specifically, he was told that while other nations had sacrificed trade for political ends, Britain had done the opposite, that Britain did not tie itself by trade treaties, and that Britain restricted foreign merchants in order to free and encourage trade. However, commerce might be the pretext for a treaty with political advantages for the court of Turin, which was the only circumstance in which Cordon should listen to any treaty proposals. Cordon's instructions also included a discussion of Britain's trade, since her commercial rivalries could have more serious consequences. In these circumstances, the court of Turin preferred to remain neutral and not commit itself to any alliances, commercial or political, in order to be free to seize its opportunity once the Austro-French alliance broke down as it expected it would.[49]

For their part, although British ministers urged fulfilment of the terms of the treaty of 1669, they were not themselves necessarily eager for a new trade treaty. In 1779, discussing the suggestion of Count Perrone (Victor Amadeus' foreign secretary, who had been the court of Turin's minister in London, and who was familiar with English economic writers and had written, in 1751, *Pensées diverses sur les moyens de rendre le commerce florissant en Piémont*[50]) to revive the project to export Piedmontese wines to England, the British *chargé*, Poyntz, suggested that if those wines were allowed privileged access in Britain, English manufactures should enjoy similar advantages in Piedmont.[51] However, the instructions prepared in London for another envoy, Mountstuart (1779)—sent to Turin to secure Savoyard

[49] Cf. the instructions for Cordon going as ambassador to the French court (1788), in *Il marchese di Cordon e Vittorio Amedeo III. Corrispondenza inedita e cifrata*, ed. Angelo Francesco Trucco (Alessandria: Società Poligrafica, 1909), xxxi–xxxii. And instructions for conte Montagnini di Mirabello on his being sent to The Hague (1778), in J. J. Poelhekke, 'De Sardinische Gezantschapsberichten uit Den Haag 1781–1787', *Mededelingen van het Nederlands Historisch Instituut te Rome*, 3rd series, 10 (The Hague, 1959), 280–281.

[50] Cf. Paola Dagna, 'Un diplomatico ed economista del Settecento: Carlo Baldassare Perrone di San Martino (1718–1802)', in: *Figure e gruppi della classe dirigente piemontese nel Risorgimento* (Turin: Istituto per la Storia del Risorgimento, 1968), 9–46.

[51] William Poyntz to Chamier, Turin, 11 December 1779, NA/SP/92/82/57.

intervention in the war against Britain's American rebels and their continental allies—spoke of a desire to encourage British trade with Piedmont but made no mention of a treaty.[52] Once in Turin, Mountstuart did discuss a commercial treaty with Perrone,[53] but the secretary of state in London, Lord Hillsborough, was discouraging. Some years later, in 1786, another British envoy in Turin, John Hampden Trevor, enclosing a proposal for the export of hemp from Piedmont to Britain, and noting that both Russia and Denmark had made abortive proposals for formal agreements intended to develop their own trade with Piedmont, thought it better for Britain not to conclude a trade treaty. While noting that the balance of the trade was unfavourable to Britain, he thought the nature of that trade was such that Britain had more to lose than to gain from a treaty.[54] Indeed, that trade was increasing, reducing the need for a treaty.[55] In consequence, the remarkable flurry of commercial negotiations of the Pitt ministry in the 1780s did not embrace the kingdom of Sardinia.[56]

The Abortive Russian Trade Treaty

The abortive Russian trade treaty referred to by Trevor was the nearest the court of Turin came to concluding a full-blown trade treaty in this period. It was a Russian initiative, reflecting the aspirations of an emerging Russia to establish a political and commercial presence in southern Europe and the Mediterranean. In 1770, the year in which Russian warships entered the Mediterranean having sailed through the English Channel, Cordon, then Savoyard representative at The Hague, was approached by Prince Dimitri Golitsyn, the Russian minister there, following Cordon's efforts to find a contractor who would establish a naval magazine at Cagliari on

[52] Instructions for John Stuart Lord Mountstuart, 13 October 1779, NA/SP/92/82.

[53] Mountstuart to Hillsborough, Turin, 1 April 1780, NA/SP/92/83/56.

[54] Trevor to Carmarthen, Turin, 25 July 1786, NA/FO/67/5/25. Trevor sent various papers to London regarding trade between Piedmont and Britain at the end of 1786 but made no suggestion of a treaty; Trevor to Carmarthen, Turin, 22 December 1786, NA/FO/67/5.

[55] Thomas Jackson to Fraser, Turin, 10 March 1787, NA/FO/67/5.

[56] John Ehrman, *The British Government and Commercial Negotiations with Europe 1783–1793* (Cambridge: Cambridge University Press, 1962).

Sardinia. Golitsyn suggested that the two courts should develop their commercial relations and also exchange resident ministers—i.e. establish full diplomatic relations—in view of their mutual interests.[57] Symptomatic of the caution of the court of Turin and of the way it could not disentangle commercial and political contact, was the reluctance of Victor Amadeus III to respond to the Russian initiative at a time when Catherine the Great was at war with the Ottoman Empire and an object of suspicion among the other powers. However, while this particular initiative—and the brief visit to St Petersburg of a Sardinian agent, the *cavaliere* Triqueti (1773)—had no immediate result, the growing Russian interest in expanding commercial contacts in Italy was evident.[58]

In the summer of 1782 a Russian *chargé* appeared in Genoa, with which the czarina was said to be trying for some time to conclude a trade treaty.[59] Renewed approaches were also made to the court of Turin. In part this should be seen as part of Catherine's efforts to expand her coalition of neutral maritime powers—the 'Armed Neutrality of the North'— against British attempts to impose its views on the carriage of goods in wartime, which was followed by the conclusion of various trade treaties, most of which incorporated the principles of the Armed Neutrality.[60] In fact, the Savoyard state still had no fleet to speak of. Efforts to build one had been made after 1713, but with limited success. The Savoyard state could not compete with any of the major maritime powers—Britain, France, Spain—or indeed of the second and third rank powers, and remained vulnerable to the Barbary corsairs of North Africa. Besides lacking a royal navy of any substance, the Savoyard state possessed little by way of a merchant

[57] Serguei Karp, 'Un manuscrit de Diderot porté disparu: les Observations sur le traite entre la Russie et le royaume de Sardaigne', in: *L'edition du dernier Diderot. Pour un Diderot électronique*, ed. Gianluigi Goggi and Didier Kahn (Paris: Hermann, 2007), 51–62: 56–58, with references to relevant materials in the Archivio di Stato, Turin.

[58] Cf. Mirella Mafrici, 'Le relazioni diplomatiche e commerciali tra il Regno di Napoli e l'Impero russo nel secolo dei Lumi', in: *Sulla diplomazia in età moderna. Politica, economia, religione*, ed. Renzo Sabbatini and Paola Volpini (Milan: Franco Angeli, 2011), 219–239; Furio Diaz, 'L'abate Galiani consigliere di commercio estero del Regno di Napoli', *Rivista Storica Italiana* 80 (1968), 887–892.

[59] Mountstuart to Charles Fox, Turin, 27 July 1782, BL Add Mss 36802.

[60] Isabel de Madariaga, *Russia in the Age of Catherine the Great* (New Haven, CT: Yale University Press, 1981), 383–6.

marine. Its vulnerability may have made the court of Turin a target for recruitment to the Armed Neutrality, not least because its neutrality was severely tested during the American independence struggle.

In 1778, the British representative in Turin, Poyntz, asked Count Perrone about the likely reply to any official request to Victor Amadeus III to close his ports to American privateers. Perrone's response was revealing. He said that in 1777, without being asked, his master had closed his ports in this way, unless ships were in distress, but that the publication of the recently concluded treaty between France and the Americans meant that the king of Sardinia must adopt a different policy. Perrone referred to his master's want of ships (and observed that Dutch rebel vessels had put into Spanish ports in the Dutch Revolt), adding that in the absence of a treaty between Britain and the kingdom of Sardinia the latter must scrupulously respect the king's declared neutrality.[61] This was not an easy task. In 1779 the French court rejected the claims of the court of Turin regarding the extent of its jurisdiction in coastal waters, declaring that only the coast—and not the whole bay of Cagliari—were Sardinian.[62] This followed a British complaint at the French seizure of a British ship at anchor in that bay in breach of Sardinian sovereignty.[63] For its part, the British government complained about the role of Nice as an entrepot for the passage of naval stores to Toulon, in breach of Victor Amadeus' declared neutrality.[64] Indicative of the greater distance between London and Turin at this time was Perrone's offer in January 1781 of Savoyard mediation between Britain and its enemies.[65] Towards the end of 1781, and after pressure was put on the king of Sardinia by the Armed Neutrality, Perrone spoke as if the kingdom of Sardinia was moving towards membership of that association.[66] Some months later, in May

[61] Poyntz to Chamier, Turin, 13 May 1778, NA/SP/92/82.

[62] Poyntz to Chamier, Turin, 4 September 1779, NA/SP 92/83.

[63] Poyntz to Chamier, Turin, 14 April 1779, NA/SP/92/83. Cf. a *mémoire* presented by Cordon regarding a Mahon privateer (which seized a French vessel in breach of Sardinian neutrality), May 1779 and Poytnz to Chamier, Turin, 19 May and 21 July 1779, NA/SP/92/83.

[64] Dutens to Porten, Turin, 25 July and 15 August 1781, BL Add Mss 36805.

[65] Mountstuart to Hillsborough, Turin, 20 January 1781, BL Add Mss 36802.

[66] Dutens to Porten, Turin, 14 November 1781; Mountstuart to Hillsborough, Turin, 28 November and 1 December 1781, BL Add Mss 36802.

1782, Victor Amadeus bridled when the British envoy appeared to complain at the apparent breach of the traditional close connection between their two states.[67] Not surprisingly, there was great joy in Turin in late 1782 following reports of the progress of the peace negotiations, not least because the war—and the threat of seizure at sea—had reduced silk exports.[68]

The court of Turin was also more attractive as a trading partner at this time. Victor Amadeus III was readier than his father to spend on the necessary improvements to the state infrastructure in order to stimulate trade. This really meant the Nice road. In 1767, a project to export Piedmontese wine to Britain had failed because Charles Emanuel III would not spend the large sums necessary to improve the road between Piedmont and Nice. In addition, in a state in which there was as yet no independent 'public sphere' and in which most political debate took place within rather than outside government, one in which defence was a key concern of monarch and ministers, there was a strong sense that improving communications between Piedmont and Nice would make the latter more vulnerable to foreign invasion, since Nice had so easily fallen to the enemy in the wars against France between 1690 and 1748. As early as 1769 the opposing views had been clear: military defence (and cost) against economic development.[69] However, the accession of Victor Amadeus—and the appointment of Count Perrone—improved the prospects of the road, which would go through the Col du Tende, facilitating more exports and imports and stimulating trade with Switzerland.[70] In the spring of 1780, the king of Sardinia approved the project. It was expected to cost £20,000 and to take four years to complete. The fears of the military that it would facilitate an invasion of Piedmont were met with the promise of new fortifications at the pass of Saorgio.[71] The 'development' lobby had triumphed.

[67] Mountstuart to Fox, Turin, 9 May 1782, BL Add Mss 36802.

[68] Liston to Grantham, Turin, 21 December 1782, National Library of Scotland [NLS], MSS 5524.

[69] Istruzioni di SM al conte di Scarnafiggi, 19 August 1769, AST/Negoziazioni/Inghilterra, mazzo 1° d'addizione, no. 30.

[70] Mountstuart to Hillsborough, Turin, 8 March 1780, NA/SP/92/83.

[71] Mountstuart to Hillsborough, Turin, 1 April 1780, NA/SP/92/83. Mountstuart was encouraged to discuss a trade treaty with a receptive Perrone.

By September 1780, work on the road was already advanced, Perrone arranging to have English merchants inspect it. There were already great hopes that the additional exports generated (£400,000) would ensure that exports more than balanced their imports.[72] In the spring of 1783 the road, which was just one of a number of projects to improve and stimulate the prosperity of the state at a time when Victor Amadeus III feared a war in the East and his own ability without foreign aid—subsidies—to survive it, was said to be nearly finished,[73] and a year later Trevor thought it would be completed that year.[74] In fact, this was far too optimistic, the tunnel through the mountains proving a substantial challenge.[75] Further progress may have been slowed by a cutback in spending on public works in 1785 to release military funds.[76] The final stage of the road, the cutting of a passage through the mountains between Limone and Nice, was still going on in the summer of 1786 but sufficient progress had been made to justify extravagant hopes of its impact on the commerce of Piedmont.[77]

Whatever the reason, or reasons, Victor Amadeus III responded more positively than did his father to Catherine the Great's approaches. The czarina was delighted to see from the *mémoire* that the king of Sardinia ordered to be prepared by way of reply that Victor Amadeus was disposed to encourage trade between his states and Russia.[78] By the spring of 1783 a draft trade treaty was circulating in Turin, the British representative there, Robert Liston, sending a copy to London.[79]

The draft project comprised four chapters. The first chapter outlined the state of Russia's trade with Italy, and vice versa, noting that Nice was a port of the second rank in terms of its trade with Russia (behind Venice, Genoa and Livorno which themselves traded indirectly); Turin, too,

[72] Dutens to Hillsborough, Turin, 30 September 1780, NA/SP/92/83.

[73] Robert Liston to earl of Grantham, Turin, 23 March 1783, NA/FO/67/3 and NLS, MSS fos. 39–46.

[74] Trevor to Carmarthen, Turin, 7 April 1784, NA/FO 67/4.

[75] Trevor to Carmarthen, Turin, 26 June 1784, NA/FO/67/4.

[76] Trevor to Carmarthen, Turin, 9 March 1785, NA/FO/67/4.

[77] Trevor to Carmarthen, Turin, 9 August 1786, NA/FO/67/5.

[78] Copy of letter from A. Bezborodka to unknown, St Petersburg, 5–16 June 1782, AST, Negoziazioni, Russia, mazzo 1.

[79] Liston to Grantham, Turin, 23 March 1783, NA/FO/67/3 and NLS, MSS, fos. 39–46.

along with most of the other eleven principal towns of Italy, was thought of as second rank, depending on Genoa, Amsterdam and Hamburg to connect it with St Petersburg. The routes between Russia and Italy were identified as via the Baltic or the Dardanelles. Article 4 listed the Russian commodities consumed in Italy, with figures showing that Russian exports to Italy were already considerable but suggesting the trade could be expanded. Article 5 listed the many Italian goods which could be exported to Russia (silk of all sorts, olive oil, rice, wine), a total of thirty-two commodities. The second chapter identified the defects or weaknesses of the trade between Italy and Russia at that point, including the profit absorbed by all the intermediaries, the uncertainty and want of confidence, for lack of correspondence. In the third chapter, the advantages which would follow for both Russia and Piedmont from rectifying these difficulties were outlined, after explaining why the king of Sardinia had been chosen rather than one of the other Italian sovereignties. The situation of his states, and his supposed love of the public good and of humanity, and superior understanding of commerce and government all made Victor Amadeus the sovereign best able to second Catherine's grand enterprise. While asserting that sovereigns should intervene and regulate as little as possible, it was admitted that the state sometimes did need to play a part. More specifically, one of the requirements for the success of the project was that Victor Amadeus 'faire accommoder' —sort out— the Nice road, without which the project would surely fail. That road, which was surely one of the key attractions of the Savoyard state at this moment, would reduce the costs of transport of goods from as far as Switzerland which would—it was anticipated—reach Nice and be carried from there aboard Russian ships to Russia (via the Baltic or the Dardanelles) without any intermediaries.

The fourth chapter contained specific proposals. The subjects of Victor Amadeus and Catherine were to enjoy most favoured nation status when trading in the other's states. A company was to be formed, its members (subjects of both princes) to enjoy various tax privileges. Consuls were to be exchanged. There was to be a direct trade between Nice and St Petersburg on Sardinian or Russian ships. In time of difficulty, escorts would be available. Individual merchants were to be identified who should initiate the trade. Finally, since Victor Amadeus III's states were unlikely to be able to supply all the Italian commodities identified, the merchants of Turin and Nice (and of Oneglia) should mobilize their contacts elsewhere to supply those which were lacking and if those contacts wished to they might be admitted to the new company. In that sense the scheme extended beyond the states and subjects of the king of Sardinia. Implicit of course was continuation of work on, and completion of the road.

The project inevitably loomed large in the instructions prepared in 1783 for the marchese di Parella, the first resident envoy dispatched from Turin to St Petersburg. Those instructions noted the earlier Russian approach to Charles Emanuel III and his failure to respond. But Russia had grown in importance since 1770, and could now decide the European balance. It was anticipated that the Russian ministers would want to discuss both the trade treaty and Victor Amadeus III's accession to the Armed Neutrality. Regarding the former, since the czarina appeared very keen, Victor Amadeus would conclude if it proved advantageous. A trade project had already been examined in St Petersburg by the council of commerce and sent to Turin for examination.[80] But the king of Sardinia was not convinced of the need for a trade treaty, pointing out that even without one Russian merchants enjoyed all the advantages that the czarina sought and that, as the comments made in St Petersburg made clear, according to Catherine's own regulations Victor Amadeus' own subjects enjoyed all the advantages they could hope to get by a formal treaty. However, if Catherine insisted on a treaty in very general terms the king of Sardinia was happy to do it. But there was some uncertainty in Turin about what commodities could be traded. Parella therefore also received a list of goods that Victor Amadeus' states could supply to Russia and of those which might be drawn from Russia. As for joining the Armed Neutrality, Parella was to say he had no orders on this, because the Savoyard navy and merchant marine were so small that the king had not expected to be asked to join.[81] Not entirely surprisingly, the Russian trade treaty project came to nothing. Instead, Catherine looked elsewhere in Italy and in January 1787 concluded a commercial treaty with the kingdom of the Two Sicilies, which had joined the Armed Neutrality in the summer of 1783.[82] But Catherine continued to press Victor Amadeus to join the Armed Neutrality.[83]

[80] 'Osservazioni sovra un progetto di trattato di commercio tra la Russia e gli Stati di SM Sarda oppure con tutta l'Italia o la Sicilia', AST, Corti Straniere, Russia, mazzo 1/45.

[81] Instructions for marchese Parella, 26 May 1783, AST/LM/Russia, mazzo 1/1.

[82] Mafrici, 'Le relazioni', 226–233; de Madariaga, *Russia*, 633.

[83] Trevor to Carmathen, Turin, 2 September 1784, NA/FO/67/4.

The Armed Neutrality might still offer an alternative to a British connection which puzzled the court of Turin. In December 1784 Victor Amadeus III observed to his then representative in London, Count Nomis di Pollone, that if, in the past, British ministers took a great interest in his territories and their advantage it was because of the usefulness to their trade such that they saw 'our' interests as their own, seeing that there was no power in Italy able to help them resist the preponderance that the House of Bourbon sought in Italy, and the likely exclusion of the English from trading in Italy and the Mediterranean to the advantage of the French. But, stated the king, things had greatly changed. The English had abandoned in large part the Levant and Mediterranean trades. They had lost the island of Menorca which better enabled them to maintain a presence in the Mediterranean and did not seem to greatly regret the loss. Nomis was ordered to find out more about just how British ministers saw the Savoyard state, and their attitude towards trade with the Levant and in the Mediterranean. In fact, Nomis' response revealed—contrary to thinking in Turin—that the English still had a considerable trade in the Levant and Mediterranean and therefore still took a great interest in the affairs of Italy, and those of the Savoyard state.[84] This was reassuring. However, while British commercial interests promised political advantages they also might also be disadvantageous. In January 1787, Victor Amadeus III observed that the British ministry was more concerned with the conclusion of commercial treaties than a system (of alliances?) which would ensure its survival in time of need. The king of Sardinia hoped that the English ministers would turn their attention to this important matter once Parliament had approved the recent (Eden) trade treaty with France.[85]

For their part, Savoyard ministers remained hostile to both the trade treaty of 1669 and the conclusion of a new trade treaty with Britain. In September 1787, Count Graneri, Victor Amadeus' representative in Madrid, commented on British negotiations there for a trade treaty with

[84] Victor Amadeus III to Nomis di Pollone, 4 December 1784 and 8 January 1785, the latter acknowledging receipt of Nomis to Victor Amadeus III, 21 December 1785, enclosing a 'state' of British trade in 1783, AST/LM/GB, mazzo 87.

[85] Victor Amadeus III to Nomis di Pollone, Turin, 27 January 1787, and Nomis di Pollone's relazione of 9 January 1787, AST/LM/GB, mazzo 88. The correspondence with Nomis di Pollone revealed the court of Turin's awareness of the trade treaties then being negotiated by the British government.

Spain. Apparently, Count Floridablanca was said to favour a treaty but not King Charles III, who claimed that the English knew more about trade than did the Spaniards and having tricked the French (a reference presumably to the Eden treaty) would also deceive the Spaniards. Graneri agreed with the king, and noted that Bernardo Ward, author of the *Projet Economique pour l'Espagne* (1762, but only published in Madrid in 1779), declared that it was not in Spain's interest to conclude trade treaties, especially with the English, and that reciprocity was merely an ideal, given the disparity in resources (number of ships and so on) possessed by the English. Graneri added that it was fortunate that the treaty concluded with the English of 1669 was of no value, not having been observed, because it meant that Victor Amadeus III could take, in respect of customs duties, the measures most convenient for the good of the (Savoyard) state.[86]

Alternatives to Treaties

The failure to conclude a full-blown trade treaty—with any power—by no means exhausted the possibilities for encouraging economic growth. While Victor Amadeus III and his ministers were suspicious of such agreements, efforts were made to improve relations with various powers, including for example the emperor of Morocco, whose passports allowed Sardinian subjects to trade with greater security in the Mediterranean.[87] The court of Turin also secured commercial advantages by agreements far less ambitious than that proposed with Russia. In October 1751, for example, a treaty negotiated with the authorities in Milan reduced customs duties on Milanese goods exported via Nice.[88] A trade treaty was also concluded with the duke of Modena, in 1753.[89] In 1789, Graneri was

[86] Graneri to Victor Amadeus III, San Ildefonso, 11 September 1787, AST/LM/Spagna, mazzo 93.

[87] 'Relazione d'un progetto di pace colle Potenze Barbaresche formato nella vista di facilitare l'introduzione d'un Comercio maritimo colla Sardegna e cogli Stati di Terraferma di SM', 1779, AST/MC/Categoria 3, mazzo 2/20; Mountstuart to Hillsborough, Turin, 9 May 1781, BL Add Mss 36802. A consul had been named for Morocco.

[88] Cf. 'Objections faites par le ministère sarde a Mons de Helfried', 20 September 1785, copy sent by Trevor to Carmarthen, Turin, 12 January 1786, NA/FO/67/5.

[89] 'Trattato di stabilimento di Commercio tra SM il Re di Sardegna ed il Duca di Modena', 14 February 1753, AST/MC/Categoria 3, m. 2/14 and Trattati Diversi, mazzo 30/16.

negotiating in Madrid to secure the exemption of the finest Piedmontese silks from heavy import duties in Spain.[90]

Equally important, the financial needs of the Savoyard state after 1748 meant that it was ready to allow other states to redeem the so-called *droit de Villefranche*. This duty, first imposed by Duke Emanuel Philibert (1558–1580), was levied on any ship below 200 tons which passed that way and was set at 2 per cent of the value of its cargo.[91] The imposition yielded revenue, but was expensive to enforce and triggered confrontations with other states. The French redeemed the obligation in 1753 and Great Britain (in return for £4,000) in 1754,[92] Christian VII of Denmark in 1785,[93] the kingdom of Naples in 1786,[94] and the Portuguese in 1787.[95] Some other states continued to pay; others (the courts of Vienna, St Petersburg and Stockholm) refused to do so.[96]

Unlike the abolition of the *droit de Villefranche*, that of the so-called *droit d'aubaine* did not involve any payment but simply a reciprocal declaration that it would not be exercised in the states concerned.[97] The *droit* was abolished on a reciprocal basis with France and Monaco (1760), the empress (1763), Parma (1766), the Elector of Bavaria (1772), and the courts of Madrid (1782) and Lisbon (1787).[98] In 1788 the court of Turin suggested reciprocal abolition to that of Berlin, but a convention was only

[90] Graneri to [Hauteville?], Madrid, 30 June 1789, AST/LM/Spagna, mazzo 93.

[91] Alice Blythe Raviola, '"Le tout-puissant": Carlo Francesco Vincenzo Ferrero d'Ormea nella corrispondenza degli ambasciatori francesi', in: *Nobiltà e Stato in Piemonte. I Ferreo d'Ormea*, ed. Andrea Merlotti (Turin: Zamorani, 2003), 249–277: 254.

[92] Dagna, 'Un diplomatico', 22–23; Sclopis, *Relazioni*, 99. The British Parliament would not pay. George II paid, but far less than Charles Emanuel wanted.

[93] Solaro, *Traités publics*, III: 484–488.

[94] Solaro, *Traités publics*, III: 489–495.

[95] Trevor to Carmarthen, Turin, 1 April 1786, NA/FO/67/5/11; Jackson to Fraser, Turin, 10 October 1787, NA/FO/67/5.

[96] Trevor to Carmarthen, Turin, 1 April 1786, NA/FO/67/5/11.

[97] Cf. Peter Sahlins, *Unnaturally French. Foreign Citizens in the Old Regime and After* (Ithaca, NY: Cornell University Press, 2004). In 1730, Victor Amadeus had rejected a petition from foreign merchants for the *droit*'s suspension; Allen to Newcastle, Turin, 1 April 1730, NA/SP/92/33, fol. 361.

[98] Sahlins, *Unnaturally French*, 355; Carutti, *Carlo Emanuele III*, II: 284; Solaro, *Traités publics*, III: 106–110, 251, 279, 480, 496–499.

concluded in 1797.[99] Diplomacy thus achieved instruments of a less grand nature than major trade treaties but nonetheless favoured the expansion of trade relations between the states concerned and both reflected and underpinned good political relations between them.

Conclusion

The standing in Europe of the Savoyard state was much greater in 1789 than in 1660. Its economy had also undergone great changes. Efforts had been made to diversify and expand that economy, generally initiated by the court of Turin, but occasionally (the scheme of 1695) by foreign courts. However, these had rarely succeeded such that, despite some expansion and diversification, the Savoyard economy was still dominated by silk production and export, and dependent on a very few markets,[100] while the island of Sardinia was still largely uncultivated in 1789 and considered by some a burden to be got rid of.[101] Monarchs and ministers were certainly alert to the need to adapt to changing economic and political realities, in Italy, the Mediterranean and beyond, before and after 1748. However, the king of Sardinia's subjects were not, as one observer put it in 1771, a commercial nation.[102] More important, it was almost impossible to separate the political and the commercial. The court of Turin was unwilling to conclude full trade treaties because it was reluctant in a volatile and dangerous environment to commit itself and

[99] Solaro, *Traités publics*, III: 564–67.

[100] In 1783, 562,000 lb of almost 1,000,000 lb of exported organzines went to France and just 56,000 to Britain; Prato, *Vita Economica*, 313–314. Cf. Trevor to Carmarthen, Turin, 12 January 1786, NA/FO/67/5, enclosing (ch. 10): 'Of the Commerce of the Country', for the impact of reduced British demand (1785) on silk prices.

[101] According to Trevor to Carmarthen, Turin, 12 January 1786, NA/FO/67/5, ch. 5: 'Sardinia', the court of Turin would willingly sell the island if there were a buyer, while Russian efforts to obtain a port there had been frustrated by the opposition of France and Spain. In 1786, an officer in Joseph II's service was surveying Sardinia, prompting speculation that Victor Amadeus might exchange it for territory on the mainland; Trevor to Carmarthen, Turin, 1 and 8 April 1786, NA/FO/67/5.

[102] Lynch to Richford, Turin, 29 September 1771, NA/SP/92/76. Cf. Trevor to Carmarthen, Turin, 12 January 1786, NA/FO/67/5.

believed that commercial ties had political implications.[103] On the other hand, the court of Turin's economic policy and financial difficulties helped ensure that a series of lower level and more narrowly targeted agreements were concluded with a number of states which did encourage trade while the same concerns saw the 'development' lobby triumph over the military in the case of the Nice road. These were less impressive achievements than those envisaged in the draft trade treaty with Russia of 1782–1783 but represented nonetheless progress of sorts towards the dismantling of some obstacles to commercial expansion.

Christopher Storrs is Reader in History at the University of Dundee. His research interests focus on early modern Imperial Spain and Italy and the history of international relations, war and state formation. His publications include *War, Diplomacy and the Rise of Savoy, 1690–1720* (1999), *The Resilience of the Spanish Monarchy 1665–1700* (2006) the edited volume *The Fiscal-Military State in Eighteenth Century Europe* (2009), and*The Resurgence of Spain 1713–1748* (2016).

[103] J. Holland Rose, 'The Franco-British Commercial Treaty of 1786', *English Historical Review* 23 (1908), 709–724.

Negotiating a Trade Treaty in the Imperial Context: The Habsburg Monarchy in the Eighteenth Century

Christine Lebeau

Count d'Hauterive, editor of the first collection of trade treaties, once said that 'there was only a small number of treaties of trade and navigation in the seventeenth century. Trade relations often depended on clauses inserted in political treaties. It was not until the Peace of Utrecht in 1713 that governments generally adopted the practice of separating trade and navigation treaties from political treaties.'[1] The eighteenth century was one of commerce as well as of the balance of power, as shown by the fact that the French envoy to the Congress of Utrecht, Nicolas Mesnager, submitted to Torcy a plan for achieving a

[1] Pierre Louis Auguste Bruno de Lanautte, comte d'Hauterive, *Recueil de traités de commerce et de navigation de la France avec les puissances étrangères, depuis la paix de Westphalie en 1648, suivi du recueil des principaux traités de même nature conclus par les puissances étrangères entre elles depuis la même époque* (Paris: P. J. Rey, 1834), IV: 1.

C. Lebeau (✉)
University of Paris 1 Panthéon-Sorbonne, France
e-mail: Christine.Lebeau@univ-paris1.fr

A. Alimento, K. Stapelbroek (eds.), *The Politics of Commercial Treaties in the Eighteenth Century*, DOI 10.1007/978-3-319-53574-6_13

balance of trade.[2] Montesquieu devoted the entire opening of the twentieth book of the *Esprit des lois* to the beneficial effects of trade, underlining that 'peace is the natural effect of trade'.[3] Albert Hirschman was also able to investigate the idea of *doux commerce* in Jacques Savary's *Dictionnaire de commerce.*[4] The preface of this work—a European bestseller—also linked the re-establishment of peace to trade: 'If the great empires were established by courage and by the force of arms, they were strengthened and maintained only by the sustenance provided by trade, labour, and the industry of the People.' The need for mutual trade, however, did not exempt the powers from seeking to 'push ever further and ever more ambitiously their commercial affairs'.[5] Finally, the entry entitled 'Treaty', stressed the importance for merchants to protect themselves against the risks of trade by conforming to 'the articles adopted by the Sovereign Powers'.[6] Hence trade, navigation and naval treaties were caught between the notions of *doux commerce* and 'jealousy of trade'.[7]

The *Autriche* section of Hauterive's collection of commercial treaties shows how the Austrians were less active in pursuing such agreements than France and Britain. So while the turn of the eighteenth century is often identified with the emergence of Austrian 'power', it might seem Austria

[2] On Mesnager's plan for Jean-Baptiste Colbert, Marquis de Torcy, minister of foreign affairs from 1696 and secretary of state from 1700, see Lucien Bély, *Espions et ambassadeurs au temps de Louis XIV* (Paris: Fayard, 1990), 574; Loïc Charles and Guillaume Daudin, 'La collecte du chiffre au XVIIIe siècle: le bureau de la balance du commerce et la production de données sur le commerce extérieur de la France', *Revue d'Histoire Moderne et Contemporaine* 58 (2011), 128–155.

[3] Montesquieu, *The Spirit of the Laws* ed. A. M. Cohler, B. C. Miller and H. S. Stone (Cambridge: Cambridge University Press, 1989), book XX, par. 2.

[4] Albert Hirschman, *Les passions et les intérêts* (Paris: PUF, 1980), 67–86. A wider discussion is included in Catherine Larrère, 'Montesquieu et le "doux commerce": un paradigme du libéralisme', *Cahiers d'histoire. Revue d'histoire critique* 123 (2014), 21–38.

[5] Jacques Savary Des Bruslons, *Dictionnaire universel de commerce, contenant tout ce qui concerne le commerce qui se fait dans les quatre parties du monde* (Paris: Héritiers Cramer, 1744), 1, preface.

[6] Savary, *Dictionnaire universel du commerce*, III: 482–483.

[7] Istvan Hont, *Jealousy of Trade. International Competition and the Nation-State in Historical Perspective* (Cambridge, MA: Harvard University Press, 2005).

did not use trade treaties to reach this status.[8] How then did Austria 'rise' in the ranks of the European state system?

Following a short military campaign, in the wake of the signing of the Peace of Utrecht, Emperor Charles VI too agreed to declare peace at the Treaty of Rastatt (1714), in which he relinquished control of the Spanish kingdoms while acquiring the formerly Spanish-held Southern Netherlands, Naples, Milan, Mantua and Sardinia. Sardinia was later exchanged for Sicily in 1720, while the Treaty of Passarowitz (1718) once again moved the border with the Ottoman Empire as far as Belgrade. It seems doubtful that the cost of this new political and military domination would be covered by the meagre fiscal gain. If by 1715 the Austrian monarchy had become a 'great balancing power [...], it was Austria's territorial position and commitments, rather than her resources, which made her a great power'.[9] Notwithstanding these political and territorial successes, the prevailing view is that of a monarchy still in the grip of a prohibitive economic system in which, for lack of merchants, the Habsburg domains maintained only a few trade relations.[10] However, such an interpretation is misleading because the treaties, or rather some of their clauses, were renewed, reintroduced or partially amended. The court of Vienna's late entry into competition with the great trading nations is worthy of consideration above and beyond the discussions

[8] Oswald Redlich, 'Österreichs Grossmachtbildung in der Zeit Kaiser Leopold I', in: *Geschichte Österreichs*, vol. 6 (Gotha: Perthes, 1921); Jean Bérenger, *Léopold Ier (1640–1705) fondateur de la puissance autrichienne* (Paris: PUF, 2004); Karl Vocelka, 'Glanz und Untergang der höfischen Welt. Repräsentation, Reform und Reaktion im habsburgischen Vielvölkerstaat', in: *Geschichte Österreichs 1699–1815*, ed. Herwig Wolfram (Vienna: Ueberreuter, 2001).

[9] Derek McKay and Hamish Scott, *The Rise of the Great Powers, 1648–1815* (London: Longman, 1983), 77.

[10] For the first half of the eighteenth century see Josef Dullinger, 'Die Handelscompagnien Oesterreichs nach dem Oriente und nach Ostindien in der ersten Hälfte des 18. Jahrhunderts', *Zeitschrift für Social und Wirtschaftsgeschichte* 7 (1900), 44–83; Heinrich Srbik, *Der staatliche Exporthandel Oesterreichs von Leopold I. bis Maria Theresia* (Vienna: W. Braumüller, 1907); Karl Přibram, *Geschichte der österreichischen Gewerbepolitik* (Vienna: Duncker und Humblot, 1907); Roman Sandgruber, 'Oekonomie und Politik: Österreichische Wirtschaftsgeschichte vom Mittelalter bis zur Gegenwart', in: *Geschichte Österreichs*, ed. Herwig Wolfram (Vienna: Ueberreuter, 1995). See Andrea Komlosy, 'Imperial Cohesion, Nation-Building and Regional Integration in the Habsburg Monarchy', in: *Nationalizing Empires*, ed. Stefan Berger and Alexej Miller (Budapest: Central European University Press, 2014), 369–427.

commonly focused on the relationship between the Habsburg's trade and Austrian cameralism.

In point of fact, while the emperor signed fewer trade treaties than the kings of France or Britain, the chronology of the treaties actually signed by Austria conceals as many claims and conflicts as it reveals. The study of the history of commercial treaties cannot be limited only to the available texts, since the context of their elaboration, implementation and reception must also be taken into account, as must failed negotiations and applications.[11] The development of the power of the House of Austria in fact makes it possible to shed light on certain aspects of trade agreements in areas of commerce that the history of international relations tends to ignore. Taking a broader approach, we might attempt to understand how treaties and commercial policies were structured, since the interests of merchants may have contradicted those of the prince. In any case, in the Imperial context, the diversity of actors and interests gave rise not to a demand for princely protection, but instead to the development of local diplomacy (*vor Ort*) into a new and complex mobilization of legal knowledge and practices, a system of double diplomacy in which there was also an influence from the peripheries on the centre.[12]

The Commercial Treaty: A Product of 'Jealousy of Trade'

While the Habsburg monarchy appeared to be an outsider in the development of Atlantic trade, the Viennese archives in fact reveal a perception of commerce quite different from the one found in dictionaries and treaties: 'Jealousy and division govern continually between particular traders; each seeks to gain to the detriment of the other; the foreign powers often incite these jealousies and divisions; they surreptitiously support some only to eventually undermine the whole. They introduce problems

[11] See Renaud Morieux, 'La nation et les intérêts. Les manufacturiers, les institutions représentatives et le langage des intérêts dans le traité de commerce franco-anglais de 1786–1787', in: *La société civile XVIIIe–XIXe siècles*, ed. Christoph Charle and Julien Vincent (Rennes: Presses Universitaires de Rennes, 2011), 39–74.

[12] Nadir Weber, *Lokale Interessen und grosse Strategie. Das Fürstentum Neuchâtel und die politischen Beziehungen der Könige von Preussen (1707–1806)* (Cologne/Weimar/Vienna: Böhlau, 2015).

only to silence their merchants and to trouble and divide them.'[13] In the Southern Netherlands, the Habsburg monarchy joined an active trading space traditionally linked to Spain and dominated, in terms of routes and traffic, by France and the United Provinces.[14] The layers of inherited commitments effectively gave the emperor little room to manoeuvre.

While commercial treaties must in the first instance be considered public documents, a private report commissioned by Count Kaunitz, the former minister plenipotentiary to the Southern Netherlands (1746–1748) and the Austrian negotiator of the Treaty of Aix-la-Chapelle (1748), sheds light on what lay behind them. The report, preserved in the private library of the emperor, attempts to summarize the Chancellery's point of view on the possibility of negotiations after the signing of the Treaties of Aix-la-Chapelle and of Aranjuez (1752). It also reads as a convenient information source for various extant texts and offers an insight into their use by contemporaries, which may give us a clearer understanding of a poorly defined subject. The report first lists the great peace treaties: the Treaty of the Pyrenees (1659) concluded with the French, the Treaties of Westphalia (1648) with the United Provinces and the Treaty of Vienna (1725) with Spain, all of which constituted a framework that had to be constantly renegotiated and clarified in a highly competitive environment. Commercial clauses were initially included within these, with Articles 5 and 6 of the Treaty of the Pyrenees granting the citizens of both sides freedom of movement on land and sea, and also including a provision reciprocally granting most favoured nation status to the two countries. The fourteenth Article of the Treaty of Munster contained the same provisions, and also closed off the navigation of the River Scheldt, an act later reaffirmed in the Barrier Treaty.[15] But during the eighteenth century it became the norm to use specific treaties of commerce. Thus a separate trade treaty complemented the Treaty of

[13] 'Verbesserung des Handels mit fremden Staaten durch Aufrichtung von Handelskompagnien', *Verschiedene Vorschläge* 349, Hofkammerarchiv (HKA), Vienna, fos. 905–912: fol. 907.

[14] Joseph Lefèvre, *Étude sur le commerce de la Belgique avec l'Espagne au XVIIIe siècle* (Brussels: Lamertin, 1921), 20.

[15] 'Tableau de l'Etat politique et civil des Pays Bas: ordonné par S. M. Marie Thérèse d'Autriche', Cod. Ser. n. 25874, Österreichische Nationalbibliothek [ÖNB], Vienna, fol. 102.

Vienna of 1725 between Austria, Spain and Sardinia—in which Charles VI renounced his claims to Spain in return for Spanish and Sardinian recognition of the Pragmatic Sanction—while the Barrier Treaty was followed by a trade treaty between Austria and the Southern Netherlands, much like the Treaty of Vienna of 1731 that marked the beginning of a new alliance between Austria and Britain after the emperor's agreement to abolish the Ostend Company.[16] Nevertheless, while the major peace treaties continued to inspire confidence, the outcomes of the various trade agreements were determined by the good or bad faith of the signatories. In consequence, in times of dispute nations had recourse to the former, such as when France banned goods from the Southern Netherlands in contravention of the Treaty of the Pyrenees or when Britain and the United Provinces took advantage of their administration of the Southern Netherlands between 1706 and 1715 to adjust tariffs to their own benefit. In these instances the Treaty of Vienna (1725) served as a reminder that subjects of the Southern Netherlands were to enjoy the advantages that were accorded to the subjects of the United Provinces under the Treaty of Munster in 1648 and the Treaty of Utrecht in 1714. For all that, the trade clauses inserted in the Treaties of Westphalia dealt mainly with respect of property and the movement of people and of goods on the River Rhine and on the sea. They gave a definition of war supplies and determined a set of entitlements that facilitated market activity, namely the guarantee of acquisitions and debts, the right to suspend trading when necessary, a commitment to the non-application of *escheatage*, and the right to own houses for commercial purposes: all of this without binding the contracting parties on the issue of tariffs. The Treaties of Westphalia ultimately established a *modus vivendi* that facilitated the movement of goods without restricting the trade of the territories of the Holy Roman Empire, which received both *jus foederis* and limited sovereignty, especially on taxation. The first attempts at signing trade treaties after the Treaty of Hubertusburg (1763) once more signalled a growing conflict that the laws of the empire could no longer contain. The reason for the low number of trade treaties signed by the emperor was the framework fixed by the Treaties of Westphalia, to which he was

[16] Tableau de l'Etat politique, fos. 119, 122.

committed, on behalf of the Habsburg states, until the Treaty of Lunéville (1801). This was also an indication of the strong sense of conflict that lingered in the period between the War of the Spanish Succession and the War of the Austrian Succession in a context of strong political and trade competition, especially with the United Provinces. These treaties established a system that considerably limited the ambitions of the emperor. In the *Essai politique sur le commerce*, Jean Melon noted how the Ostend Company, created by the emperor to make up for the loss of traffic due to the closure of the River Scheldt and to gain access to colonial trade, had triggered the jealousy of the maritime powers that 'all were ready to take up arms when the Emperor thought it necessary to suspend the charter'.[17] Trade negotiations in this sense were restricted by the dynamic of the political situation and its dynastic hazards. The European recognition of the Pragmatic Sanction, according to this logic, severely limited the possibility of commercial integration.

However, we ought not to limit our view of a political history of trade treaties to that which considers them the cherished instrument of the great powers, the guardians of the European system. While significant tools for negotiation, trade treaties also represented staging posts in the development of positive international trade law. The Spanish withdrawal from its alliance with France had admittedly facilitated the signing of the Treaties of Vienna in 1725. But the specific conceptual elements and detailed formulations in the trade and navigation treaty, drafted by the well-known lawyer and publisher Jean Dumont, would resurface a few decades later, to be integrated into the Treaty of Aranjuez of 1752.[18] The treaty of 1725 redefined the freedom of trade established in the Treaties of Westphalia: the definition of war supplies, of rights of haven, of the conservation of sequestered goods, of the intangibility of debts that must be honoured when war ended, all constituted essential markers. Furthermore, the individual rights of merchants were clearly laid out: consuls would be installed in all ports or cities of trade where it pleased the king or emperor to do so, the right of *escheatage* and the right to search the houses of merchants were

[17] Jean-François Melon, *Essai politique sur le commerce* (Amsterdam: Changuion, 1734), 75.

[18] Jean Dumont was the author of the *Corps universel diplomatique du droit des gens* (Amsterdam: P. Brunel, 1726–1731) and historiographer of Charles VI. Hauterive, *Recueil*, 'Autriche', 63–88.

rescinded, and legal charges could be brought only in the case of personal debt. Above all, the clause concerning the most favoured nation was calculated on the basis of the rate of import duties and export fees conceded to Britain in 1667 and 1670 and renewed in Article 3 of the Treaty of Utrecht, with the exemption of harbour duties and the *alcavalas* and *millones* levies on Spanish imports. The entry 'Treaty' in the *Dictionnaire de commerce* invites us to distinguish between the laws concerning the movement of goods and the protection of merchants and their property, and the more specific tariffs defined by agreement between sovereign powers.[19] While with each new treaty the most favoured nation clause had to be redefined in accordance with changed circumstances, the legal issues of transportation and of protection were couched in the same terms in different places and these, being widely known, would prove crucial to the development of the rights of merchants.

The report submitted to the Count of Kaunitz serves as a reminder that one should not confuse the signing of agreements with their actual application, since 'the observation [of the Treaty of Vienna] did not last long'.[20] Jealousy of trade operated on many levels, including the level of actual trade by merchants on the ground. The treaty of 1725 faltered when applied locally, as shown by an undated report written shortly after the signing and preserved in the archives of the Imperial cabinet.[21] The report praised the competition that reduced prices and increased quality. Its author, however, also highlighted the different ways in which the privileges and benefits of the most favoured nation clause could be interpreted by listing the duties levied and owed, product by product, and denouncing the ignorance of the clerks. He moreover outlined the problem of interpretation between Article 13, which established a unique duty of 10 per cent on the value of the goods and Article 18 of the 1725 Treaty, which promised equal treatment as the British traders. A proposal to

[19] Savary, *Dictionnaire universel du commerce*, III: 482.

[20] 'Tableau de l'Etat politique', fol. 118v.

[21] 'Raisons par lesquelles on démontre que l'Espagne ne souffrira pas de préjudice en accordant la diminution de la Taxe par un convenio pour les principales marchandises et fabriques des Etats de SMI et en donnant la pleine exécution à l'article 10ᵉ du traité dernièrement conclu avec S.M. Imple et Roïale, par lequel Sa Majesté Cath s'engage de donner aux sujets de Sa Majesté Imple et Rle tous les avantages, franchises et privilèges dont jouissent les nations les plus favorisées', Alte Kabinettsakten [AKA], Haus-Hof- und Staatsarchiv [HHSTA], Vienna, 36, Liste 3.

establish a *convenio* based on Article 18 of the tariff of 1716 (which had changed only slightly since the time of Charles II and was favourable to the hereditary kingdoms and the Southern Netherlands) and on Article 3 of the Treaty of Utrecht never materialized due to lack of political support for the treaty of 1725. In 1722, two proposals for a draft trade treaty had already been submitted to the Governor of the Netherlands, the Marquis of Prié: one prepared in Cadiz by Jacques Vermolen, the Flemish consul in Cadiz, and the other in Vienna. Both proposals agreed on the principles of free trade, of Habsburg equality with other nations, and the appointment of adjudicating judges. The first also asked that bills of exchange be negotiated in currency as per their intrinsic value on the day of negotiation, while the second demanded the right to four ships to trade with America in exchange for the renunciation of the Habsburg claim to the Spanish throne.[22] However, Dumont, who wrote the final draft, refused to consider either of the two demands. Despite this, trading did not cease and even prospered, thanks in particular to the presence of Spanish subjects in the Southern Netherlands and natives of the Southern Netherlands in Spain, as well as to the proximity of Dunkirk. Whatever the political uncertainties, Spain continued to be the main market for Belgian yarns, fabrics, hosiery and lace, while the treaty of 1725, whether partially applied or ignored completely, continued to form the basis of trade relations.[23] Statistics from this period testify to this growing integration.[24] The discrepancy between the political uncertainty and the reality of commercial practice is also partly explained by the tensions that could arise between the interests of the prince, the Habsburg territories and those of the merchants, due to the large distances and geographical complexity of the state.

[22] Lefèvre, *Étude sur le commerce de la Belgique*, 23.

[23] 'Mémoire sur ce qui par rapport aux Etats héréditaires de S.M. Impériale et Royale en Allemagne peut servir d'instruction à celui ou à ceux qui seront chargés de négocier, principalement en faveur des Pays-Bas autrichiens un Traité de commerce avec l'Espagne', Vienna, 16 November 1752, Kommerz 997, HKA, Vienna, fos. 95–102: fos. 95r–96.

[24] In the private library of the empress, see 'Essai d'observation sur le commerce interne qu'externe des Pays-Bas surtout relativement aux Provinces Unies, présenté à Sa Majesté Impériale et Reine le 15 janvier 1753'; 'Essai d'observation sur le commerce des Pays-Bas considéré dans son rapport avec l'Angleterre, présenté à Sa Majesté Impériale et Reine le 23 février 1753'; 'Notes sur le sisteme de commerce à établir entre les États de l'Impératrice Reine en Allemagne, les Pays-Bas et l'Espagne', AKA 53, HHSTA.

Commercial clauses or treaties always resulted in ultimately unsatisfactory compromises and never extinguished trade rivalries.[25] By being integrated with political negotiations, and even subject to the interests of the princes, they were the first legal instruments to contribute to the development of trade law and their importance was recognized, as evidenced by the involvement of lawyers as important as Jean Dumont. From this point of view, they were public documents whose development and application did not reduce the space for negotiation between the state and commerce.

From Public Text to Private Negotiation

The negotiation and application of commercial clauses and treaties generated Chancellery work that brought together the prince's representatives and legal experts and the merchants, and so we find that we must consider trade treaties from three angles. Jacques Savary said that he based a part of his *Dictionnaire* on the operational reports of merchants before and after the Treaty of Ryswick.[26] The Imperial archives reveal this very clearly, in particular with regard to negotiations with the Ottoman Empire, the diplomatic records of which are placed alongside those regarding trade.

The fact that commercial treaties set down both entitlements and obligations was repeatedly emphasized when dealing with the Ottoman Empire.[27] According to d'Hauterive, the emperor gained no more than the same rights enjoyed by the great trading powers. We must therefore briefly review the history of the treaties. From 1648, thanks to the reconquest of the kingdom of Hungary, several treaties contributed to the development of Austro-Ottoman trade. The Peace of Vasvár, signed in 1664, authorized the Austrians to trade on the Danube as far as Belgrade. In 1699 the Treaty of Karlowitz was accompanied by a commercial agreement that ensured 'free, safe, and peaceful' trade for the Ottomans,

[25] Henri Sée and Léon Vignols, 'L'envers de la diplomatie officielle de 1715 à 1730. La rivalité commerciale des puissances maritimes et les doléances des négociants français', *Revue belge de philologie et d'histoire* 5 (1926), 471–491.

[26] Savary, *Dictionnaire universel du commerce*, preface.

[27] Guillaume Calafat, 'Les Interprètes de la diplomatie en Méditerranée. Traiter à Alger (1670–1680)', in: *Les Musulmans dans l'histoire de l'Europe*, vol. II: *Passages et contacts en Méditerranée*, ed. Jocelyne Dakhlia and Wolfgang Kaiser (Paris: Albin Michel, 2013), 371–410.

a guarantee that matched the privilege granted in 1664 by the emperor to Catholic Armenians alone. The *Commerciorum et navigationis tractatus*, signed on 27 July 1718 alongside the Peace of Passarowitz, contained twenty articles governing shipping, the exchange of consuls, and trade.[28] Austria therefore gained the same commercial privileges previously accorded to other Christian nations and more besides: Austrian merchants obtained passports that allowed them to buy and sell whatever goods they wished (with the exception of weapons and gunpowder) throughout the whole Ottoman Empire for a single duty of 3 per cent, to be paid on entering that commercial zone. Eastern merchants, in contrast, had to pay 5 per cent duty in order to gain access to the Habsburg monarchy. It was in this context that the Imperial Privileged Oriental Company (*Kaiserliche privilegierte orientalische Compagnie*) was established, and an alliance was formed with Venice, permitting Vienna to declare Trieste and Fiume (Rijeka) free ports in 1717.[29] And here law and commerce collaborated: an order to respect trade with the Sublime Porte was inserted in the Third Book of the *Codicis austriaci* in 1719. With the support of the sultan, the Habsburg emperor also signed treaties with the Regencies of the Maghreb and of Tripoli in 1726 and 1749, and with Tunis in 1725 and 1748. These focused on the safeguarding of vessels sailing under the Austrian flag from attacks by pirates off the coast of Africa. In legal terms they were simply treaties of free navigation and thus the Treaty of Tunis, signed in 1725, was described as a 'treaty of full and reciprocal security of navigation separate from all trade'. Designed to bring an end to all hostilities and establish free navigation for Austrian registered ships 'on all seas and rivers, irrespective of all trade and without granting the right to enter the ports of their dependencies', the treaty recalled the commercial clauses included in the Treaties of Westphalia.[30] But close attention should be paid to the legal aspects. The treaty had in effect brought together the 'Emperor of the Romans' and the 'magnificent lords Pascha, Beig, Dais, Divan, and Aga of the janissaries and militia of the city and the Kingdom of Tunis',

[28] For a longer discussion of the context, see Charles Ingrao, Nikola Samardžić and Jovan Pešalj, eds., *The Peace of Passarowitz, 1718* (West Lafayette, IN: Purdue University Press, 2011).

[29] Franz Anton Mayer, *Die Anfänge des Handels und der Industrie in Österreich* (Innsbruck: Wagner, 1892), 28–30.

[30] *Instrumentum Pacis im Tunetario* (1725), Tunetana 1725–1732, HHSTA, Vienna.

with three commissioners of the sultan, 'Emperor of the Ottomans and of Greece', acting as mediators. Above all, it placed under the Austrian flag—not without equivocation—the 'German convoys, the inhabitants of the Austrian Netherlands, Sicilians, Neapolitans, Calabrese and their dependents, and those of Fiume and of Trieste situated along the Adriatic Sea and all others, of whichever nation and religion they may be'.[31] The treaties with the Barbary Regencies effectively distinguished between the Habsburg sovereign's capacity as emperor and his capacity as sovereign of his hereditary states, and it defined an Imperial standard that granted protection from armed attacks, a haven in the ports of the emperor in the case of necessity, and authorized the freeing of recognized Imperial subjects taken to Barbary ports by the enemies of the emperor. These treaties enabled a parallel development of trade on the Danube and of commercial activities from the port of Trieste. As the road from Vienna to Trieste and the route along the Sava were improved, fourteen consulates were established in the Ottoman Empire and seven in Italy and, by the mid-eighteenth century, the effect of competition from Trieste came to be felt in Marseille.[32]

The negotiations with the Ottoman Empire had effectively established a new area of Austrian expertise, and, significantly, Paul Masson saw the development of the port of Trieste, competition with Marseille and the creation of the Eastern Academy in Vienna as related factors.[33] While the emperor continued to invoke his 'science, full power, and authority belonging [to him] by the laws of sovereignty, of nature and of the people' in the letters patent of the Ostend Company, negotiations with the Barbary states were based on unprecedented consultation with local—that is, Sicilian—mercantile institutions.[34]

[31] *Instrumentum Pacis im Tunetario* (1725), Tunetana 1725–1732, HHSTA, Vienna.

[32] Traian Stoianovich, 'The Conquering Balkan Orthodox Merchant', *Journal of Economic History* 20 (1960), 234–313; Paul Masson, *Histoire du commerce français* (Paris: Hachette, 1911), 391–393.

[33] Masson, *Histoire du commerce français*, 393.

[34] 'Égard aux très humbles demandes et supplications de nos Sujets de nos Paï Bas, eu sur ce l'avis de notre Plénipotentiaire au Gouvernement d'iceux, de nôtre Lieutenant, Gouverneur et Capitaine général de nosdits Païs, et ouï sur le tout nôtre Conseil Suprême etabli les Nôtre Personne Royale pour les affaires des mêmes Païs, et en dernier lieu nôtre Conférence Ministériale', 'Lettres patentes d'octroy accordées par Sa Majesté Impériale et Catholique

The possibility of signing a trade treaty with the Barbary Regencies provides an insight into the attempts made by commercial administrators to move well beyond free movement and the clause of most favoured nation, as already mooted in the Treaty of Vienna of 1725. Contacts with the Sicilian authorities centred on ways to stabilize trade, what goods to exchanged, what ports to open, and on whether to introduce complete or partial freedom of trade. The Senate of Palermo proposed establishing free trade only on certain items, excluding cereals, salt and rice. While these goods were not primary objects of competition between nations, they needed to be shielded from price competition to guarantee the earnings of the peasant population.[35] Proposing an increase of customs duties on imports of canvas, wine, cloth and coffee, the Palermitan expert Francesco Agras pointed out the risk of rising imports of French and British textiles in shipments from Ottoman merchants on account of the commercial terms of the Treaty of Passarowitz. He acknowledged, however, the benefit of Messina participating in 'universal trade' and expressed the hope of seeing Genoese, Livornese, papal and even Dutch ships adopting the Imperial flag to gain protection from the Barbary raiders. Setting up a quarantine station in Trapani, the nearest port to the Barbary coast, was also discussed.[36]

Managing outlying provinces undoubtedly requires the backing of market and political leaders, as the Austrians themselves had discovered to their cost in the Southern Netherlands.[37] A trade treaty with the Barbary states had the capability of resolving the problem of pirates—Maltese and Barbary—who preyed on the Italians. But the issue was bigger than mere political control: the trade treaties shaped the purview of Imperial policy from the reign of Charles VI up to the establishment of the 'central' trade council. The emperor had to understand and reconcile potentially conflicting interests within the empire while, at the same time, exercising the dominion which the treaties of 1713 had given him over new trading areas and a wealth of skills and knowledge. The public and

pour le terme de trente années à la Compagnie generale à établir dans les Pays-bas Autrichiens pour le Commerce et la Navigation aux Indes', AKA 36, HHSTA, p. 2.

[35] 16 January 1724, 1 Barbaresken: Berichte, Weisungen, Varia, HHSTA, Vienna.

[36] 17 January 1724, 1 Barbaresken: Berichte, Weisungen, Varia, HHSTA, Vienna.

[37] François Antoine and Jean-Jacques Heirwegh, 'Le port franc d'Ostende', in: Lombardie et Pays-Bas autrichiens, ed. Bruno Bernard, *Études sur le XVIIIe siècle* 36 (2006), 99–109: 109.

negotiated texts of the treaties signed between 1718 and 1726—and preserved in the diplomatic and trade archives of Vienna—bear ample witness to this.

Inventing the Empire: The Plan for a *Universal-Kommerz*

Pierre Renouvin has warned against over-reliance on diplomatic history: 'The relations between governments are no longer the focus; what is important is the history of relations between people.'[38] The question here is which standpoint—of the states or of the negotiators—to adopt to view the process that (all being well) results in a trade treaty. The multifarious nature of this process was determined by the structure of Imperial politics. In the absence of a public debate on trade policy, the approach in what follows starts from the debate conducted within the administration that radiated into various institutions of the Habsburg monarchy. Avoiding an inward-oriented national focus, a broader geopolitical approach to the Habsburg monarchy is suitable to reconstruct, starting from the Treaty of Passarowitz, the numerous case-by-case dialogues between the authorities of the various countries under its rule.

The plan for Imperial 'universal trade' is older than was suggested by Grete Klingenstein, August Fournier and Karl Pribram. It actually took shape at the same time as the negotiation with the Barbary states and the negotiations with Spain, both discussed above.[39] John Brewer noted the 'specific interest groups [who were] entangled in the legislative fabric of

[38] Pierre Renouvin, Introduction générale', in: *Histoire des relations internationales*, vol. I (Paris: A. Colin, 1953), quoted in Robert Frank, 'Penser historiquement les relations internationals', *Annuaire français des Relations Internationales* 4 (2003), 42–65: 42–43.

[39] Grete Klingenstein, 'Kommerz und Aussenpolitik. Habsburgische Kommerzialreisen im Vorfeld der Diplomatischen Revolution, 1756', in: *Die wirtschaftlichen Auswirkungen der Türkenkriege. Die Vorträge des 1. Internationalen Grazer Symposions zur Wirtschafts- und Sozialgeschichte Südeuropas (5. bis 10. Oktober 1970)*, ed. Othmar Pickl (Graz: Im Selbstverlag der Lehrkanzel für Wirtschafts- und Sozialgeschichte der Universität, 1971), 55–70; August Fournier, 'Handel und Verkehr in Ungarn und Polen um die Mitte des 18. Jahrhunderts', *Archiv für Österreichische Geschichte* 69 (1887), 317–481: 332; Karl Přibram, *Gewerbepolitik*, 27. See Adolf Beer, 'Die handelspolitischen Beziehungen Österreichs zu den deutschen Staaten unter Maria Theresia', *Archiv für Österreichische Geschichte* 79 (1893), 401–669.

the State'.[40] But how did these entanglements operate in the Habsburg monarchy? In Vienna three groups of merchants—urban bourgeois traders (*Bürgerlicher Handelstand*), privileged merchants close to the court (*Hofbefreite*) and foreign staple traders (*Niederleger*)—represented the different branches of trade. While the first two groups engaged primarily in retail, the same was not true for the foreign staple traders, who were mostly from other parts of the Holy Roman Empire. While expanding steadily from the 1740s, this group nevertheless remained tight but also very close to the trade council. The trade in copper, the model of state commerce, revealed the porosity of the boundaries between commercial administration, trade and diplomacy. Used as a bargaining chip when negotiating British subsidies, this trade was managed by a small number of companies, including the Hilleprand Company, which was especially important under Charles VI.[41] The Hilleprand family, originally from Tyrol, were incorporated as a company and counted as members Peter Anton Hilleprand von Prandau, a councillor and then vice president of the Aulic Council from 1745 and director of the state debt (*Universial-Bancalität*) in 1748, his brother Johann Georg Hilleprand von Prandau, administrator of the Bank of Vienna, and Maximilian Emanuel Hilleprand von Prandau, director (liquidator) of the Eastern Company from 1731 and councillor of the Court of Finances. Those who made fortunes through monopolies and financial dealings seemed to be given a free hand in the central administration.[42] It is necessary, then, to understand what is meant by the central administration. Before the establishment of the *Universal-Commercien-Direcktorium* in 1746 under the leadership of Count Philipp Kinsky, who also received the presidency of the Ministerial Banco Deputation and, therefore, 'universal' control of commerce including that of the kingdom of Hungary,[43] and also before the widespread use

[40] John Brewer, *The Sinews of Power. War, Money and the English State, 1688–1783* (New York: Alfred A. Knopf, 1989), 248.

[41] P. G. M. Dickson, *Finance and Government under Maria Theresia 1740–1780* (Oxford: Oxford University Press, 1987), I: 163. P. G. M. Dickson, 'English Commercial Negotiations with Austria, 1737–1752', in: *Statesmen, Scholars and Merchants. Essays in Eighteenth-Century History Presented to Dame Lucy Sutherland*, ed. A. Whiteman, J. Bromley and P. G. M. Dickson (Oxford: Oxford University Press, 1973), 81–112.

[42] Dickson, *Finance and Government*, 160.

[43] ÖZV, 1907, III, no. 58, 55, 60; Dickson, *Finance and Government*, 261.

of the trade tribunals in 1763, trade was managed by competing bodies: the Council of War for the Ottoman and Mediterranean areas, the Council of Spain and Italy for the Netherlands, to which the trade councils of the individual Habsburg countries were added from 1714.[44] At the same time, the state Chancellery remained in charge of diplomatic relations and the Aulic Council (*Hofkammer*) retained control of finances and, more specifically, of revenues. In the context of strong administrative competition, the councillors and planners played an important role, as evidenced by the numerous projects with indeterminate outcomes preserved in the state archives. The planners whom historians have called the 'Austrian cameralists', are best known. Johann Joachim Becher, a native of Speyer, succeeded in entering the service of the Elector of Bavaria when he devised a plan to found a trading company and recruit partners in the United Provinces. His proposal led to the establishment of a trade council in 1666 under the auspices of the Aulic Council led by Georg Ludwig Sinzendorf, for the development of manufacturing and trade. However, the resulting silk company, granted a monopoly over wholesale trade and manufacturing and with agents in Venice, Lyon and Antwerp, was soon declared insolvent.[45] Becher's brother-in-law, Philipp Wilhelm von Hörnigk, achieved greater posterity thanks to his *Oesterreich über alles, wenn es nur will* (Austria Over All, If She Only Will), a book reprinted several times during the eighteenth century.[46] On his advice, an Eastern Company was established in 1667, but it ceased operations in 1683.[47] The ideas and proposals of Becher and Hörnigk depended on the mercantilist system which sought to increase state revenues by developing local manufacturing and preventing the outflow of money by controlling the trade in luxuries. The state therefore was expected to support the activities of merchants by granting privileges and organizing financial backing. These

[44] A. F. Pribram, *Das böhmische Kommerzkollegium und seine Tätigkeit* (Prague: Verlag für Geschichte der Deutschen in Böhmen, 1893).

[45] Mayer, *Die Anfänge des Handels und der Industrie*, 6–9.

[46] *Oesterreich über alles, wenn es nur will. Das ist: Wohlmeynender Fürschlag, wie mittelst einer wohlbestellten Landes-Oeconomie die kays. Erb-Lande in kurzem über alle andern Staaten von Europa zu erheben und mehr als einiger derselben, von denen andere independent zu machen* (1684).

[47] Helmut Hassinger, 'Die erste Wiener orientalische Handelskompagnie 1667–1683', *Vierteljahrschrift für Sozial- und Wirtschaftsgeschichte* 35 (1942), 1–53.

ideas remained influential under Maria-Theresa, both in theory through republications of Hörnigk's work in 1753 and 1764 by Rudolf Chotek, president of the trade council, and in practice, since the same regulations continued to exist and were regularly updated based on practical experience.

As regards Ottoman commerce, the boundaries between administration, trade and planning were even more blurred. The negotiators of the trade articles of the Treaty of Passarowitz are particularly noteworthy: Michael von Talman, the first permanent representative of the emperor to Constantinople in 1703 (he lived in that city until 1713, this being the critical period of the Great Northern War and of the Russo-Ottoman War that was waged at the same time as the War of the Spanish Succession and the Rákóczi rebellion), and Franz Anselm von Fleischmann, Von Talman's successor in 1716 (the year Austria entered into a coalition against the Ottoman Empire). From 1704, the Austrian negotiators sought to clarify Article 14 of the Treaty of Karlowitz, which guaranteed freedom of passage and security of trade, as well as to obtain a lowering of duties paid by Austrian merchants from 5 per cent to the 3 per cent paid by their French, English and Dutch counterparts, at a time when military successes and the alliance with Venice offered new opportunities.[48] Particularly when dealing with the Ottomans and the Barbary states, negotiators had to be doubly proficient: on the one hand, applying an 'art of negotiation' adapted to local conventions and enhanced by gifts, and, on the other, maintaining a spirit, if not of hostility, then at least of competition with the trading powers.[49] Such expertise obviously required a working knowledge of commerce, but what the administrators of the monarchy called the centre was, first and foremost, an Imperial laboratory: the testing ground of the empire itself.

The projects that justified and encouraged the negotiations with both the Barbary states and Spain derived from a number of regional perspectives which, taken together, provided a global prospect of Habsburg trade given that, as the anonymous expert has pointed out, 'Flanders has connections to the Adriatic ports and extends as far as all the countries of the Levant, of the Mediterranean, and of the Black Sea'. According to cameralist rationale, the development of trade and navigation fostered the

[48] The Venetians had previously enjoyed a monopoly of the transport of merchandise. Trieste was declared a free port in 1717, Fiume in 1719. Mayer, *Die Anfänge des Handels und der Industrie*, 28–30.

[49] Calafat, 'Les Interprètes de la diplomatie en Méditerranée', 382.

happiness of the citizenry while simultaneously filling the Imperial coffers.[50] There was, however, also a political vision of trade that became increasingly prevalent, as evidenced by the evolution of the schemes devised by Michael von Talmann after the Treaty of Passarowitz. One such plan, apparently formulated in around 1725, informs us that the draft treaty with the Barbary Regencies had been conceived as far back as 1712 in the kingdom of Naples and Sicily.[51] The list of products to be marketed highlighted the multiplicity of sources of profit for all parts of the Habsburg monarchy, and the twofold point of the exercise was clearly stated: to introduce 'universal commerce' with the Orient, Asia and Africa, as well as with Amsterdam, Marseille and Italy; and to achieve a positive balance between internal and external trade.[52] Talman furthermore proposed the creation of a universal *collegio* to take charge of developing trade and to set up a commercial bank to finance the merchants.[53] And, once the Ostend and Trieste Companies were established, a further aim was to 'drive the wealthy people of Hungary, of Austria, of Bohemia, of other hereditary lands, of Naples and of Milan to use their wealth in the Adriatic Company just as all the Southern Netherlands and lower Germany would use their own for the Flanders Company'.[54]

A series of papers based on the recommendations of Brussels and, in particular, a contemporary memorandum on the opening negotiations with Spain defined 'universal trade' as a medium:

> through which it is shown how the main merchandise, manufactures and commodities that we could send to Spain are taxed and the benefits that could result from said goods and commodities and from increased trade through the ports of Trieste and of Fiume through the trade treaty and the reduction of tax by a *convenio* to be signed with Spain for the removal of duties on the principal manufactures and commodities of His Imperial and

[50] AKA, 36, HHSTA, Vienna, 2.

[51] 'Vorschlag des Michael von Talmann wie die Räubereien der Afrikanischen Barbaren in Zaum gehalten werden könnte', *Verschiedene Vorschläge* 348, HKA, Vienna, fos. 885–904. Biography of Talmann in: Jovan Pešalj, 'Making a Prosperous Peace: Habsburg Diplomacy and Economic Policy at Passarowitz', in: *The Peace of Passarowitz*, ed. Ingrao, Samardžić and Pešalj, 141–157.

[52] 'Projekt des Michael von Talman', *Verschiedene Vorschläge* 422, fol. 37, fol. 40.

[53] 'Projekt des Michael von Talman', *Verschiedene Vorschläge* 422, fol. 31.

[54] 'Vorschlag des Michael von Talmann', *Verschiedene Vorschläge* 348, fol. 908v.

Royal Majesty, and how we could attempt to link the trade of the Hereditary Countries with that of the Netherlands.[55]

A treaty of commerce, like a company, was a policy tool developed even before the Treaty of Passarowitz, where the authority of the emperor was required to stimulate trade and to unite the Habsburg lands behind the traders who were seeking to discover new markets. Leaving aside the issue of top-down management or demands from below, negotiations ultimately involved all areas of the Imperial system. Following the Treaty of Aranjuez (1752), a committee was formed with the membership of delegates from Trieste and Fiume and of the merchants Winter and Guillaume Schamp from the Southern Netherlands.[56] The negotiators were supported by the state Chancellery in Vienna and the ambassador in Madrid. This was the 'universal' vision of a consistent and beneficial trade proposed to Spain:

> because the States of His Majesty only provided him with needed goods such as, above all, all types of items made from canvas, linen and iron, and could not prejudice the development and manufacture of wools and silks that that he seems to wish to establish in his Kingdoms, and takes in exchange only the raw materials and manufacturing which abound while many other nations accept only hard cash in exchange.[57]

[55] 'Mémoire par lequel on fait voir comment sont taxées les principales marchandises, fabriques et denrées qu'on pourra envoïer en Espagne et les avantages qui peuvent résulter aux dittes fabriques et denrées et à l'augmentation du commerce par les Ports de Trieste et de Fiume du traité de commerce en diminution de la taxe par un convenio à faire avec l'Espagne pour la levée des droits sur les principales productions et fabriques des Etats de S.M. Imp et Rle et comment qu'on pourra tacher de lier le commerce des païs héréditaires avec celui des païs bas', AKA 36, HKA.

[56] 'Mémoire sur ce qui par rapport aux Etats héréditaires de S.M. Impériale et Royale en Allemagne peut servir d'instruction à celui ou à ceux qui seront chargés de négocier', Kommerz 997, fol. 95r; 'Relation; Etat que fait M. Guillaume Schamp de la commission dont il a été chargé par Sa Majesté Impériale et Royale et Son Altesse Royale le prince Charles Duc de Lorraine', Kommerz Litorale 659, HKA, Vienna; 'Mémoire sur ce qui par rapport aux Etats héréditaires de S.M. Impériale et Royale en Allemagne peut servir d'instruction à celui ou à ceux qui seront chargés de négocier', Kommerz 997, fol. 95r; 'Relation et Etat que fait M. Guillaume Schamp de la commission dont il a été chargé par Sa Majesté Impériale et Royale et Son Altesse Royale le prince Charles Duc de Lorraine', Kommerz Litorale 659, HKA, Vienna.

[57] 'Mémoire sur ce qui par rapport aux Etats héréditaires de S.M. Impériale et Royale en Allemagne peut servir d'instruction à celui ou à ceux qui seront chargés de négocier', Kommerz 997, fol. 97v.

We should not content ourselves with reading this report only in terms of international relations and the French and British monopolies on trade in gold and silver. Within the monarchy, the negotiations with Spain raised the same question as that occasioned by the distribution of the tax burden: 'The directorate of trade demands for the hereditary lands of His Majesty in Germany only the equal of what it could receive for the Southern Netherlands.'[58] The domination had to maintain balance or 'proportion' between the Habsburg lands 'because the new links between several branches of trade in the hereditary lands as well as the longer reach with the Netherlands inevitably increases its trade and, by consequence, its import duties'. On the Imperial level, trade negotiations were ultimately seen as a communication process that not only formed links between various levels of administration, but also introduced practical considerations into decision-making and relegated the question of interests to the background in favour of the need to preserve the balance between the parties.

This chapter has attempted to consider trade treaties—whether as additions to major trade treaties, aspects of the competition between trading powers, or components of the administration of an Imperial structure—as objects of study in their own right. The fact that the emperor may have been a somewhat minor contracting power proved a convenient starting point for the examination of a wider communication process punctuated by trade treaties, whether these only reached a draft form or became settled agreements. By shifting the focus from treaty negotiations towards the broader plans, it has been possible to take into consideration a wider range of actors and greater levels of analysis. This approach has also revealed that the range of constituent elements of trade treaties was already well established by the early eighteenth century, even though these ingredients may have been applied very differently in accordance with local circumstances or the differing issues at stake. Moreover, it has become clear that this body of knowledge was held both by the Europe of the Treaties of Utrecht and the Europe of the Treaty of Passarowitz. Viewed from the inside, trade treaties—as *convenios* that may at first glance have merely been agreements or compromises between powers but in fact

[58] 'Mémoire sur ce qui par rapport aux Etats héréditaires de S.M. Impériale et Royale en Allemagne peut servir d'instruction à celui ou à ceux qui seront chargés de négocier', Kommerz 997, fol. 97v.

were also linked to the merchant council—ultimately emerged as powerful political tools that made it possible to restructure the composite monarchy as an Imperial dominion and to bridge the various faculties of the state.

Christine Lebeau is Professor of Modern History at the University of Paris 1 Panthéon-Sorbonne. A specialist in the history of the Austrian monarchy and the Holy Roman Empire her interests also include financial history and state practices in the eighteenth century. Her key monographic publications include *Aristocrates et grands commis à la Cour de Vienne (1748–1791). Le modèle français* (1996), *L'espace du Saint-Empire. Du Moyen Age à l'époque moderne* (2004) and *Images en capitale: Vienne, fin XVIIe–début XIXe siècles* (2011).

French Representations of the 1786 Franco-British Commercial Treaty

Pascal Dupuy

The Anglo-French commercial treaty of 1786 has been the subject of numerous studies since the nineteenth century.[1] This sizeable literature, however, has hardly exhausted either the subject or its impact. This chapter will examine one neglected aspect of the treaty's reception, seeking to take account of the representations and broader image of the treaty from the French side as a complement to earlier work that examined strictly satirical representations of the treaty from the British perspective.[2] Without attempting to study the whole of the extant body of sources

[1] Most significantly, Mary M. Donaghay, 'The Anglo-French Negotiations of 1786–1787' (unpublished thesis, University of Virginia, 1970). By the same author 'A propos du traité commercial franco-anglais de 1786', *Revue d'Histoire Diplomatique* 101 (1987), 371–374 and 'The Exchange of Products of the Soil and Industrial Goods in the Anglo-French Commercial Treaty of 1786', *Journal of European Economic History* 19 (1990), 377–401; Orville T. Murphy, 'The Fatal Anglo-French (Eden) Commercial Treaty of 1786', in: *The Diplomatic Retreat of France and Public Opinion on the eve of the French Revolution* (Washington, DC: Catholic University of America Press, 1998), 63–79.

[2] Pascal Dupuy, 'Image et images des Traités', in: *Le négoce de la paix. Les nations et les traités franco-britanniques (1713–1802)*, ed. Jean-Pierre Jessenne, Renaud Morieux and Pascal Dupuy (Paris: SER, 2008), 11–124.

P. Dupuy (✉)
Department of History, University of Rouen, France
e-mail: pascal.dupuy@univ-rouen.fr

A. Alimento, K. Stapelbroek (eds.), *The Politics of Commercial Treaties in the Eighteenth Century*, DOI 10.1007/978-3-319-53574-6_14

published in France in this period, this chapter takes soundings in three principal areas with the aim of gauging the impact and measuring the stakes perceived in the French public sphere. First, we examine pamphlets published in the immediate aftermath of the treaty, considering the image they presented of the treaty itself and the British more generally, who are treated tendentiously as the cause of the economic crisis that struck France after the agreement was signed. Next, we consider the legislative debates of the French National Assembly, in which, from June 1789, references to Britain were commonplace, affording a glimpse of the attitudes of the French political elites regarding Britain's 'prosperity', which was largely associated with its commercial success. In these discussions, the treaty was widely denounced as being part of an aggressive and 'imperialistic' British policy aimed at weakening France at a time when French politicians were imagining a more harmonious diplomatic and commercial balance of power between the two countries.[3] This ambiguous and somewhat anguished position, which was expressed periodically in outbursts of invective, is similarly apparent in a third body of sources, the graphic representations of the treaty that oscillated between optimism and happiness only to transform themselves, above all with the onset of war, into a unilateral condemnation of the 'Englishman', presented as an archetype of the dishonest trafficker and trader. This perspective, which drew on themes of French patriotism evident since the middle of the eighteenth century,[4] would be developed particularly under the Consulate at a time when Britain had become the sole European adversary of the Franco-Napoleonic model. It should be added, finally, that all of these sources, despite their diversity and varied impact, cannot be considered as an absolute testimony of French 'public opinion', but rather provide an indication of 'published opinion', which was itself merely one segment of the views held at the time. Still, these sources are not of any less interest for that.

[3] See the chapter by Marc Belissa in this volume.

[4] See Edmond Dziembowski, *Un Nouveau patriotisme français, 1750–1770. La France face à la puissance anglaise à l'époque de la guerre de Sept ans* (Oxford: Oxford University Press, 1998).

The First Wave of Pamphlets: A Shared Treaty

The first matter that concerns us is the wave of pamphlets that accompanied the implementation of the treaty. There were various types of these, but we will focus here on pamphlets published by official bodies, including the deliberations of the Normandy provincial assembly and of various chambers of commerce, above all that of Normandy, which was one of the most active in the discussions involving the treaty.

It is true that the treaty hit Normandy hard, since the region had already been significantly weakened by both a long-term crisis and a more recent and acute one, and scholars often emphasize the damage caused to the region by the Treaty of Eden (1786). It is also true that official bodies and contemporary observers, as well as later historians, have provided figures and statistics that throw into relief the economic, commercial and industrial problems that led to social conflict in Normandy. As is widely known, French imports of British goods had begun to rise sharply even before the signing of the treaty: from 16 million *livres* in 1784 to 23 million in 1786 and 27 million the following year. These figures, in fact, include only official transactions, to which must be added illicit trade and contraband that by their very nature are difficult to quantify, but were significant. This rapid growth in imports took place amidst an economic crisis that provoked social tensions and demands, and the implementation of the trade treaty was widely identified as the cause. Simultaneously, opposition to the treaty also represented political antagonism towards the French ministers of the crown who were held 'responsible for the slump in business',[5] a downturn that in truth stemmed from deeper structural causes that were deliberately downplayed.

In response to the protests of the chambers of commerce of Rouen and Amiens, the authorities conceded that production would suffer the consequences of these massive imports in the short term, but argued that over the long term British competition would benefit the industries of Normandy and Amiens in that it would allow them to privilege quality, the only guarantee of prosperous trade and industry.[6] However, it is

[5] Guy Lemarchand and Claude Mazauric, 'L'opinion vis-à-vis de la Grande-Bretagne en Haute-Normandie (1787–1793)', *Etudes Normandes* 4 (1983), 27–35: 28.

[6] What follows is largely inspired by Jeff Horn's excellent study, *The Path Not Taken. French Industrialization in the Age of Revolution, 1750–1830* (Cambridge, MA: MIT Press, 2006), 51–87.

important to stress, as a number of historians have done, that Picardy, like Normandy, found itself at this juncture in a period of economic downturn, a situation that the treaty would temporarily but profoundly accentuate. Thousands of men were without work in Picardy, with trade slowing down and the textile industry in collapse. At Troyes, in Champagne, the authorities grew alarmed at the presence of some 9,000 unemployed men on the outskirts of the city—a dangerous situation, in the view of the intendant of the region. Clearly, the treaty was not solely responsible for the explosive social situation and the economic slump, which can be traced to a number of factors external and internal to the state and its administration. The inability to raise taxes on products imported from Britain, or to defend France against the policies of the British state, which were partially protectionist and fiddled with the application of clauses of the treaty, would only aggravate the situation. According to authorities, 185,000 workers and artisans in the textile industry had lost their jobs by the end of 1787.

It was in this atmosphere of crisis that the Chamber of Commerce of Normandy entered the fray by publishing its reflections on the treaty with Britain. One finds within them a mixture of fairly balanced assessments based on economic realities and studies on the ground, along with widely shared expressions of classic Anglophobia:

> The Englishman, an indefatigable and ruthless observer knew perfectly well before the treaty the state of our capacities and resources, and so, in comparing them to his own, easily worked out their relative weakness and insufficiency. He took note of our fields without sheep, while his own were covered; He examined our wool, and found it of poor quality and more expensive than his own; He found our greatest factories and establishments without machinery (*mécaniques*) and forced to use expensively prepared materials; and he remarked on the considerable number of little workshops where the glory of improvement and innovation meant nothing [. . .]. He saw, in the end, all his own superiority and advantage when he decided to undertake a treaty with us. And if we go back to all the advantages that the English obtained, in exciting our silk trade and forcing us to admit, without reserve, their woollen garments, we can say, without a doubt, that it was not at all in vain that the Lords, in giving their sanction to this treaty, assembled on balls of wool.[7]

[7] Lemarchand and Mazauric, 'L'opinion en Haute-Normandie', 29.

However, these texts, as the extract cited here attests, did not simply condemn 'perfidious Albion' in a discourse that would be sure to be condoned and understood by its readers. Instead, they denounced above all the timorous policy of the French monarchy, which was incapable of protecting technical inventions and revealed itself unable to defend both the traditional and innovative products by which French industry took stock of its advance. Moreover, alongside instances of classic Anglophobia, one can find traces of Anglomania that valorize, in a more or less anachronistic manner in this time period, the supposed interventionism of the British government with respect to economic matters.[8] The commentators reproached French manufacturers for not producing quality machinery to match that of the British, and worried that the British, thanks to the treaty, would be able to attract the most qualified French workers and steal their 'production secrets'. It is for these reasons that it would be false to claim that the chambers of commerce of Rouen and Amiens unanimously condemned the treaty, for in fact they desired more of what the treaty provided, not less. As Jeff Horn explains, these texts can be read as 'extended "white papers" that recommended a bevy of new policies designed to help them compete' and to render competition more balanced and fair.[9] Despite outward appearances, the condemnation of the treaty gave voice to a number of realistic and concrete proposals designed to enable France to catch up with Britain and to compete with her on equal terms while still benefiting from the traditional prowess of solid French manufacturing. Through these reflections, the bourgeoisie at the head of the chambers of commerce hoped to be consulted in the future regarding matters of trade, demanding a level of recognition that the French Revolution would soon grant them. All the more so because a number of sectors of the French economy were not affected by the decline, and on the contrary experienced a veritable expansion in the aftermath of the treaty. This is the case, for example, with wine production, spirits, coal and iron. Although northern and north-west France suffered enormously, the rest of the country did not, which suggests that the treaty cannot provide a valid and definitive explanation for the ills suffered by France in this period, which are held to have contributed to the revolutionary upheavals of the summer of 1789.

[8] Lemarchand and Mazauric, 'L'opinion en Haute-Normandie', 29.

[9] Horn, *The Path Not Taken*, 74.

However, among the general population of the north and north-west of France, and especially among workers and artisans, the treaty continued to be linked to unemployment and economic distress. The Norman *Cahiers de Doléances* provide a ready indication of this sentiment, in large part reiterating the general condemnation of the treaty, while frequently adding disparaging references to the technical machinery that had been introduced into France from Britain. 'Of the 332 *Cahiers de Doléances du Pays de Caux*, 48 or 14.4% make reference to the treaty of 1786', and all of these condemn it without reservation, blaming the treaty for the economic crisis and for the ruin of the textile industry.[10] The *Cahiers* attacked the introduction of 'machinery' (*mécaniques*) with particular insistence, holding it responsible for the crisis, and alleging that these technical innovations had enriched a small number of entrepreneurs while ruining the great majority of those working in the textile industry. Machinery had been the object of multiple attacks before 1789 and its presence in France was always ascribed to the treaty of 1786. One finds such protests in the remonstrance of the *Parlement* of Rouen that was presented to the king on 3 May 1788, or in the condemnation by the third estate of the city of Elbeuf of 'ministers misled in their imagined speculations who signed, against all complaints, the disastrous treaty with Britain, the death warrant of French manufacturers, which disposed of, in one fell swoop, the subsistence of a numerous class of citizens'.[11] Such resentment is summed up by a passage in a text drafted in March of 1789 in Rouen, in which the 'fourth estate' indicates that the 'treaty made with England was a murder attempt on commerce', and rails directly against *mécaniques*, explaining that 'they couldn't exist without uprooting the unfortunate people and throwing them into destitution'.[12] In some ways, this premonitory text announced the upheavals of the summer of 1789—the riots, the vandalism and attacks on machinery, and the social conflicts—that broke out throughout France, but particularly in Normandy, and that recently have been re-contextualized with brio by François Jarrige.[13]

[10] Lemarchand and Mazauric, 'L'opinion en Haute-Normandie', 29.

[11] Lemarchand and Mazauric, 'L'opinion en Haute-Normandie', 30.

[12] *La mort du Tiers Etat ou plaintes que présentent au Roi les bourgeois de la ville de Rouen, au nom des malheureux de toute la Province de Normandie* (Rouen, 1789), 19–29.

[13] François Jarrige, *Au temps des 'tueuses de bras'. Les bris de machines à l'aube de l'ère industrielle (1780–1860)* (Rennes: Presses Universitaires de Rennes, 2009).

In Rouen and its vicinity, enraged workers invoked the treaty more or less directly, and above all vented their frustration by attacking machines.

Nevertheless, it is necessary to emphasize, in the wake of the work of Renaud Morieux, that alongside these social movements and the sometimes ambiguous condemnations of the British character, commerce between France and Britain continued to prosper and, with it, so did the sizeable movement of contraband. The Channel was never, even in periods of war, watertight,[14] and the populations of the coast were seldom more receptive to the propaganda of authorities than they were to the popular complaints of the interior.

The treaty and the image conveyed of it on the eve of the Revolution reveals divergent aspirations that blend with larger recriminations, plebeian and secular, that in turn connect with the tumultuous political context of the 'pre-Revolution'. Defended by notables, even if they were themselves ready to bring up a number of the treaty's shortcomings, and attacked by the people, the treaty was in the end judged characteristic of the trickery of the British people, whose mercantile principles and commercial aspirations were admired as much as they were feared.

References to Britain in the Legislative Debates

From 17 June 1789 to 1 February 1793—that is, from the birth of the French representative regime to the declaration of war between Britain and France—references to Britain, British society and British politics in the French parliamentary archives (*Archives Parlementaires*) occur 265 times. But the thematic breakdown is especially interesting, given that half of the references concern politics, 15 per cent financial and fiscal matters, 13 per cent military affairs, and a mere 13 per cent are devoted to matters of justice and commerce, the principal subject of the treaty and of our investigations. If the overwhelming majority of the references concern politics, as these figures suggest, we can nevertheless note that invocations of the British model of government are present in virtually all aspects of the work and reflection of the French representatives. In fact, references to Britain were not confined to a privileged domain, but appear in the discourse of the representatives as a

[14] See Renaud Morieux, *Une mer pour deux royaumes. La Manche, frontière franco-anglaise (XVII–XVIIIe siècle)* (Rennes: Presses Universitaires de Rennes, 2008).

natural *topos*, raising envy and fear in matters as varied as public finance, commerce, judicial reform and the organization of powers, to say nothing of the direct evocation of British history since Cromwell, and its laws and political system. In the face of these regular and abundant references to Britain, one deputy declared on 16 April 1791 that, 'we have often spoken here of the English, of their laws, their customs, their practices. But it seems to me that we could speak of them even more, when it concerns their Navy.'[15] One could multiply the examples of references to British history, past and present. The country served as a kind of beacon whose light could either illuminate or blind, instruct or damn, depending on the perspective of the deputy. But if references to Britain appear during the entire period under consideration, they are particularly numerous under the Constituent Assembly, which accounts for 70 per cent of the interventions, with a frequency of six to seven monthly mentions over the twenty-eight months that this body met.

Regarding the economic and financial domain, the discussions around Necker's project to transform the *Caisse d'escompte* into a National Bank on the model of the Bank of England are at the origin of lively debates. Other discussions which made reference to the British model of financial management also took place between September and May of 1791, touching on such issues as the liquidation of the public debt, the creation and form of the *assignats*, the reform of the salt tax (*gabelle*), as well as those on property and tobacco. However, where economic matters were concerned, it was above all commerce and British prosperity that fed the imaginations of the French deputies. For the majority of deputies in the Assembly, who were liberals *avant la lettre*, somewhat in the manner of Voltaire's *Lettres Philosophiques*, the commerce that had so enriched Britain had likewise contributed to 'render them free, and this freedom in turn had expanded commerce; it was on this foundation that was built the grandeur of the state. It was commerce that established little by little the naval force that made the English the masters of the world.'[16] If British agriculture and industry fascinated the deputies and prompted them to cite British success as an example in these areas, this did not make British commerce, however fascinating it may have been, any less a subject of fear for the French representatives. Thus, Delattre, in a report on navigation that was printed

[15] Anon., 16 April 1791, *A(rchives) P(arlementaires)*, XXV: 147.

[16] Voltaire, *Lettres philosophiques* (Paris: Bordas, 1988), 88.

by order of the Assembly in September of 1791, reminded his colleagues of the strength of British commercial power, which had spread over the oceans of the world and was maintained by a protectionist state:

> British sailors became the object of great attention; the nation multiplied the number of its ports, workshops, and arsenals, and provided everything that it could to encourage the construction of ships and the improvement of navigation—favours, bonuses, incentives, lights, beacons, buoys—help of every kind was lavished on the British navy and merchant marine.[17]

For his part, the Duke de la Rouchefoucauld-Liancourt, in his *Opinion sur l'administration des colonies*, associated British commerce, 'which expands every day', with the success of its manufacturers, 'who have reached such a point of activity and perfection that they can undersell every manufacturer in Europe competing in the same sector'.[18] Yet behind the fascination with British success there often lay feelings of hostility among the deputies, along with jealousy and bitterness that rested on the conviction that the British did not respect the rules, and even when they did, the rules themselves were skewed to their advantage. But this observation was most often combined in equal measure with reflections on, and criticisms of, the actual economic station of France in the face of British competition, along with suggestions on how to improve it. This was true of a report by Joseph Dupré, entitled *Moyens d'exciter l'industrie et de détruire la mendicité*, which was appended to the Assembly's session of 27 October 1790, and protested against the decay of French national industry, which was the principal source of work for the country, invoking the example of Britain, its manufacturers, and the 'decided superiority that the English have obtained over us in all the mechanical arts'.[19] The Abbé Maury, for his part, in a speech delivered on 1 April 1790, criticized French commerce, while asking:

> Who are we to give these people [the British] lessons in wisdom? We, who have frivolous needs, whose commerce is devoted to luxury, that object of corruption, above all in this capital?; we, who are nothing but agents of the

[17] *AP*, XXXI: 203–204.
[18] *AP*, XXXI: 293.
[19] *AP*, XX: 63.

> English in India; we, who taught them perhaps the secret of making a state flourish? It is good to point out to you that England is taking 320 million a year out of India.[20]

As can be seen, references to Britain were used on several different levels: to pursue a goal or to push an agenda, but at the same time to sound a note of caution and distrust. The virtues of the British model—so often invoked—did not, clearly, generate unanimity among the French deputies. In this one finds the dual effect of Anglomania, but also of the Anglophobia aroused by numerous authors towards the end of the century in France. Although the rivalry with Britain in this period was a military one, its foundations still remained largely commercial in nature. The theme of the cupidity of the British merchant accordingly was reported as a generic vice of the whole of Britain. Thus Louis de Boislandry, in the context of an important debate on customs duties for goods entering and leaving the realm that began at the end of November 1790 and continued until February 1791, evoked the treaty of commerce of 1786 in denouncing the 'greed of English merchants' and its consequences. 'They have been obliged,' he affirmed, 'to sell their merchandise at a 30–40% loss to unload it. Forced sales, in this way, along with degraded prices, have been prejudicial to our manufactures who could support such unequal competition.'[21] The practice of 'selling at a loss' was condemned by all the deputies and by public opinion, and was a regular *topos* of discussions related to trade. The deputies denounced the recourse to such practices, which were considered unfair and disloyal. Associated with the industrial and agricultural might of Britain, they allowed 'perfidious Albion' to weave a network of commercial relations from which she alone could profit. And so, in the midst of a report on the rise in cost of colonial goods, Georges Caminet, a Lyonnais trader elected to the Legislative Assembly, summed up the sentiment of the French representatives with respect to British commercial policies: 'England always has in view the double project of favouring its own goods and destroying those of other countries.'[22] Evoking the bonuses accorded to the export of certain products—above all, refined sugar—the

[20] *AP*, XII: 514–515.

[21] *AP*, XXI: 145.

[22] *AP*, XXXVII: 613.

speaker warned his colleagues of the danger of an eventual suppression of the import duties on these commodities: 'Let us not believe that it is fanciful to think that, if we suppress our import duty on refined sugar, England would raise its subsidies for the same sugar. We've seen this nation make much greater sacrifices for its trade. We have seen how, after this long and foolish war against the United States, England determined the owners of British merchandise, which were vainly spread out across the markets of the new world, to sell at a loss and then indemnify them for the resulting losses.'[23] Here, as in the speech of Boislandry cited above, Caminet evokes British commercial practices that suppressed any notion of fair trade, while stressing the persistent hostility between the two nations. British policy, according to him, was essentially motivated by the desire to weaken France: 'and all that with the unique goal of removing French competition and holding on to its status as the sole provider of American markets, as before—a goal in which it has succeeded, unfortunately, only too well'.

In addition, the denunciation of British commercial practices as 'imperialist', as we would say today—above all with respect to competition with France—gave rise to some lively criticisms in the Assembly. Once again, the fears expressed by the deputies in a majority of cases revealed as much admiration for British maritime power as fear since, although their commercial success was undeniable and their trade thriving, this was due to 'monopolistic' policies carried out in the spirit condemned by the deputies, which weakened France and were in stark contrast with the principles of humanity and fraternity espoused by the Assembly. In the same way, British domination over its vast colonial empire was presented as an assault on the rights of man, just like the British treatment of its vassal, Ireland, which was viewed with sympathy of the majority of the Assembly, most likely because of its adhesion to Roman Catholicism. In the course of a discussion on the commerce of the West Indies, Louis-Charles Gillet de Jacqueminière summarized the opinion of a number of representatives on the question of British domination of trade: 'If England has prospered in that part of the world, it is because the English [West India] Company is sovereign—or rather, despotic—there; it is because it enslaves more than 20 million people, on whom she raises more than

[23] *AP*, XXXVII: 613.

30 million [pounds] in taxes.'[24] These discussions reveal the roots of Anglophobia, such as it existed in the eighteenth century in France, and as it had been used in certain noble and diplomatic circles with the aim of justifying French intervention on the side of the American 'insurgents'. This was a question of ending British dominion of the seas at the same time as supporting the American patriots. The Count of Custine thus declared in May of 1790, in a debate on the right of war and peace, that British policies were aimed, without exception, at 'universal monarchy', so ironically reversing a charge that had often been levied against France and Louis XIV in particular.[25] The Abbé Maury developed a similar point of view in declaring, apropos the Family Compact uniting France and Spain: 'France would not know how to abandon its most faithful and solid ally. [. . .] Our loyalty, as much as our interest, obliges us to stay by the side of this power that would be clearly compromised if it were isolated, and whose ruin would leave England master of all the seas.'[26] Not only would a Spanish defeat increase British power, but it would allow Britain to concentrate its naval and military forces on France, putting her in great danger. A speech by Jean de Dieu-Raymond de Cucé de Boisgelin on 21 May 1790, sounded the same note,[27] but the archetype of this kind of analysis could really be found in Choiseul's *Mémoire historique*, which sought to bring an end to the Seven Years War. The foreign minister did not hesitate to reinterpret history, accusing Britain of 'having aimed from 1755 to incite a general war against France and [. . .] to flatter itself that it could renew the famous "league" formed against Louis XIV'.[28]

Swirling around these discussions of flourishing British commerce at the beginning of the French Revolution was, of course, the question of the military rivalry between France and Britain that was developing anew. In this context, Guillaume Michel, a deputy of Morbihan, delivered a speech

[24] *AP*, XII: 513.

[25] *AP*, XV: 528.

[26] *AP*, XV: 565.

[27] *AP*, XV: 636.

[28] Etienne François de Choiseul, *Mémoire historique sur la négociation de la France et de l'Angleterre de puis le 26 mars 1761 jusqu'au 20 septembre de la même année* (Paris, 1761), 4. On this *Mémoire*, Edmond Dziembowski, 'Les négociations franco-britanniques de 1761 devant le tribunal de l'opinion: le Duc de Choiseul et la publicité de la diplomatie française', in: *Le négoce de la paix*, ed. Jessenne, Morieux and Dupuy, 50.

in May 1792 that pleaded for the construction of a French naval port on the Channel, the sole means, in his view, to fight effectively against eventual British assaults that already seemed imminent. He recalled that in 1692, 'after the infamous battle of the Hougue, France saw all its naval forces dispersed and almost completely annihilated in a single day'. Similarly, during the Seven Years War, the British 'burned all the establishments of the naval city outside the town [Saint Malo], along with those that were not under the protection of the batteries'. The speaker concluded that 'it is for lack of a port on the Channel that the English have an absolute empire over the sea and dominate our coasts, which, in times of war, are the curse of our navy, our navigation, and our trade'.[29]

As can be seen, the commercial and military rivalries were closely associated in the minds of the French deputies, as they had been since the beginning of the eighteenth century, in particular during periods of tension between the two countries. Nevertheless, at the beginning of the Revolution there was a swell of appeasing words spoken in the French Assembly about Britain. The representatives hoped to take inspiration from British success, even if British commerce was often the object of lively criticism and reservation. The *Nootka Sound* affair, the debates taken up in France around the question of war and peace, and then those that followed the declaration of war in April 1792 were all discussions that predicted an inevitable conflict with Britain, little by little transforming the commercial rivalry into a military rivalry, both of which derived, in the end, from identical motivations. Thus, in taking up the defence of the Spanish in 1790, Jacques Antoine Marie de Cazalès declared that if the Assembly did not come to their aid, Britain, after defeating her Spanish enemy, would attack the French.[30] For many deputies, regardless of their individual philosophical and political convictions, it was a matter, after an initial movement of sympathy for British reformism, of resuscitating and then maintaining a current of Anglophobia with deep roots in the eighteenth century. The deputies' feelings of Anglophobia were moulded in the reality of the Revolution and revived in the political and diplomatic context of the time. The principles of general sovereignty—from the rights of peoples to the exercise of national sovereignty—did not sit well with British 'imperialism' and commercial domination. Visual representations

[29] *AP*, XLIII: 75.

[30] *AP*, XV: 640.

and satirical images, which were largely subject to the opinions of the public, would take up this refrain with brio.

From the Glory of Commerce to Military Rivalry

The commercial treaty of 1786 was represented in images produced in France in a rather traditional manner. With the goal of celebrating the achievements of the crown, a largely allegorical iconography was developed in order to give the treaty more symbolic depth in keeping with well-established allegorical formulas and conventions. This was the case with the red chalk drawing celebrating the *Traité de commerce entre la France et les Etats-Unis, signé le 6 février 1778*. As pointed out above, this treaty, together with the American Revolutionary War, generated vengeful feelings towards Britain and the British. Thus a satirical etching, probably produced in 1780, entitled *Le destin molestant les Anglais* shows Charles-Henri d'Estaing (1729–1794), a hero of the French intervention in North America, offering a palm to the personification of America, who holds a staff topped by a liberty cap. Behind her, an allegory of Fame celebrates the 'exploits of the hero of France', who holds three fierce animals in chains representing the peoples of Great Britain. Around these three figures, casks, bundles and barrels attest to the development of commerce between the two countries, to the detriment of Britain.

Concerning the treaty of commerce of 1786 itself, we should draw attention to the vignette that introduces the actual treaty, and then another, from a year later, which graced the *Arrêt du conseil d'Etat du roi* that specified some of its provisions.[31] The two vignettes celebrate the supposed benefits for France of the accord between the two countries. Focusing on the content of the first, since the second is less original and based on earlier examples, it can be seen that the central motif is comprised of cornucopias and interlacing forms. The motif is topped by a French crown featuring the fleur-de-lys and framed in roses, which are one of the symbols of the throne of Britain. The emblematic flowers also feature further down, having been included as ornamental foliage. On both

[31] *Arrêt du conseil d'état du Roi, par lequel Sa Majesté, en exécution du traité de navigation et de Commerce, conclu entre Elle et le Roi de la Grande-Bretagne, le 26 septembre 1786, déclare que tous les ports, terres, états, villes, lieux et rivières de Sa Majesté en Europe, seront dès-à-présent ouverts aux sujets de Sa Majesté Britannique* (Paris, 1787).

sides of the central motif, one finds numerous images symbolizing the wealth brought about by commerce and navigation—the caduceus; barrels, pots and metallic boxes used to transport breadfruit trees; masts, struts and sails; and rolls of fabric. The association of these elements and the horn of abundance is typical of the allegorical images of the late eighteenth century, and underlines the hope placed in the treaty by the French authorities who imposed it on their people in the expectation of prosperity and peace on the seas—outcomes that would not come about.

Belonging to the same genre, although representing a different perspective, is the great painting, now lost, by Anicet-Charles-Gabriel Lemonnier, dedicated to the 'Genius of Commerce'. Lemonnier, an artist from Rouen, was well recognized and respected in the Old Regime, and received praise and commissions from official artistic circles.[32] In 1786 he was commissioned to complete a painting on the theme of the 'Genius of Commerce', most likely by the banker Lecouteulx de Canteleu. Lemonnier produced a sketch in 1787 dealing with freedom of trade: Neptune is charged with announcing to Mercury the freedom of the seas, represented by 'the flags of all the world's commercial places, to which a small genius has just brought together the flags of the thirteen states of America'.[33] Without doubt this painting, in the eyes of the man who commissioned it and the masonic lodges that apparently also played a part in its creation, refers in some way to the spirit of the treaty of commerce that was then being negotiated between Britain and France, along with the particularly strong ties between traders from Rouen and America. Nevertheless, in the time that elapsed between the initial sketch presented in 1787 and the completion of the work in 1791 (which we know from an engraving by Jean-Charles Levasseur, the original picture having disappeared), the work was subjected to numerous alterations and touch-ups, which testify to the increasingly difficult relations between France and Britain, in particular with respect to the treaty but more generally regarding the form of diplomatic relations that the Constituent Assembly hoped to bring about between the two nations. In effect, the final painting abandoned the emphasis on the liberty of the seas and accentuated its symbolic effects to stress the free commercial relations

[32] Christine Le Bozec, *Lemonnier un peintre en révolution* (Rouen: Publications de l'Université de Rouen, 2000).

[33] Le Bozec, *Lemonnier*, 50.

between France and America, the latter of which appeared as 'enlightened, full of hope and joy, an Eden of the future', in contrast to a sombre Africa, which was 'incapable of feeding its own progeny'.[34] One finds in this painting the interests of its principal commissioner, but also the economic preoccupations of men of the Enlightenment, which from 1789 were every bit as prevalent as the proclamation of liberties, of which the liberty of commerce was one of the most important. Nevertheless, the artwork makes clear that the newly freed commerce should not be subject to a single nation, Britain, and a single group of men, British merchants and shipowners, as the wave of pamphlets published in the wake of the treaty also insisted.

After a brief moment of enthusiasm and optimism, the reality of the treaty began to dawn in the minds of French men and women, especially those from Normandy and Picardy, as the economic crisis took hold. The breaking of machinery[35] referred to above, along with the social movements of French artisans and workers added to the wave of denunciations of the commercial accord, which was interpreted as uniquely favourable to British trade. A caricature circulating in France on the eve of the Revolution, just a few days before the fall of first minister Étienne Charles de Loménie de Brienne in August 1788, summarized these sentiments perfectly. In the centre of a square, in front of the building of the *Caisse d'escompte* and an assembled crowd, Commerce, in the form of Mercury dressed in a nightshirt, hangs from the gallows. Written on the noose are the words 'Caisse d'escompte', which allude to the 70 million *livres* advanced to the king after the collapse of stock prices and the three days of panic that ensued. Still attached to the feet of the hanging figure, the weights ('Export Duties', 'Ministerial Loans', 'Privileges' and 'Companies of Commerce') pull down the lifeless body, representing the empty royal treasury. The latter is also symbolized by an open cash box and by the extravagances of the ministers which indicate the impediments to trade, just like the strip that ties the hands of Mercury, on which one can read: 'Treaty of Commerce'.

With the onset of the French Revolution, the image of the treaty and of Britain would fade against the background of the vast satirical production dealing with revolutionary events. Patriotic caricature had other targets to mock. To be sure, the war in 1793 would rekindle the anti-British flame in

[34] Le Bozec, *Lemonnier*, 50.

[35] J.-P. Alline, 'A propos des bris de machines textiles à Rouen pendant l'été 1789: émeutes anciennes ou émeutes nouvelles?', *Annales de Normandie* 1 (1981), 37–58.

pamphlets and images produced during the Convention period, as Sophie Wahnich has shown.[36] It was only at the end of the century, at the time of the Consulate, however, that one would see the reappearance of repeated satirical attacks on the British, incarnated by John Bull, George III or William Pitt, who were all associated with British trade. The images rejoiced in the imagined difficulties of the British. An example of this is a French caricature of 1801 (Fig. 1), which expressed the same desire to thwart the British stranglehold on maritime trade. The caricature was prompted by the formation of the 'League of Neutrals' (Russia, Denmark and Sweden) that would soon become the 'Quadruple Alliance', with the adhesion of Prussia. But, as is well known, following Britain's reprisals and its military response, Russia withdrew from the alliance and was soon followed by the other members, who thereby acknowledged the maritime supremacy of Britain. Produced before this development, the caricature, announced in *Le Citoyen français* on 7 February 1801, was evidently created in the context of a reaction to this supremacy. The image is more of a caricature in intention than in form. The principal figures resemble one another: from left to right one finds the Czar, the King of Denmark, Pitt, George III, the King of Sweden and the King of Prussia. The four allies sought to tie up the British on their island along with the product of the embargo, with each figure expressing their resolve to no longer tolerate British aggression. George III seems to doubt the benefits of Pitt's aggressive policy, and the latter repents of the high grain prices he has provoked within his own country. Under the image of the title, moreover, there is a significant detail: the British crown and coat of arms (three golden lions) are upside down. In the background an allegory of Fame proclaims the new maritime code of law, which is applauded by four figures symbolizing the continents (from left to right, Africa, America, Asia and Europe). Their presence signifies the universal acceptance of the freedom of the seas.[37]

In the same way, the resignation of William Pitt, who formed the subject of very few caricatures in Britain itself, generated the interest of printmakers in France, one of whom produced a print (Fig. 2) entitled *Conseil de George III et désolation de M. Pitt*. In the centre we see George III and Pitt, both of whom resemble their official portraits for the

[36] Sophie Wahnich, *L'Impossible Citoyen, l'étranger dans le discours de la Révolution française* (Paris: Albin Michel, 1997).

[37] See Philippe de Carbonnières, *La Grande Armée de papier. Caricatures napoléoniennes* (Rouen: Publications de l'Université de Rouen et du Havre, 2015), number 5.

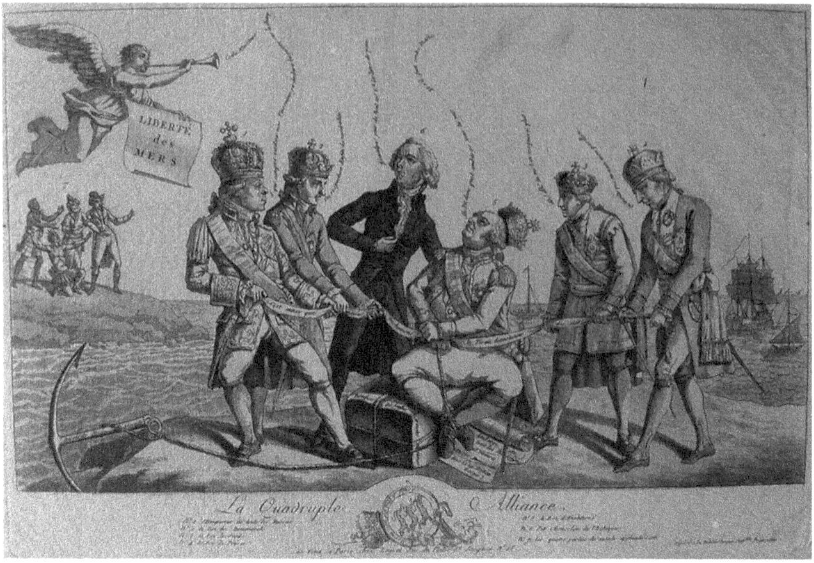

Fig. 1 Anonymous, *La Quadruple Alliance*, Paris, 1801, Private collection

most part. The monarch is dismissing his first minister on the grounds that the international economy was not favourable to Britain and because the country had been struck by an unprecedented bankruptcy. The scene is situated in a port ravaged by economic decline, while in the distance ports that were formerly allied to Britain are in flames and so lost to British diplomacy and commerce. In the face of this situation, Pitt is sacrificed and dismissed, held responsible for the British collapse. In a similar, but even more vigorous style, Pitt's dismissal is the subject of another image in which George III sends his prime minister packing with a furious kick (Fig. 3), and the legend, as is often the case in French printing, uses a pun: *George se dépitte et signe enfin la paix générale*. Clearly this caricature[38] also evokes the Peace of Amiens, which was not to the taste of William Pitt. In fact, French caricaturists were very sceptical of this treaty, which they saw as merely a way for Britain to stall and gain time. Thus, in the *Conseil de George III et désolation de M. Pitt*, George III explains to Pitt that he will

[38] Anon., *George se dépitte et signe enfin la paix générale*, coloured engraving (Paris, 1802).

Fig. 2 Anonymous, *Conseil de George III et désolation de M. Pitt*, Paris, 1801, Private collection

reinstate him in two years when the economy has bounced back. In other caricatures, the British monarch, who has lost his diplomatic heft (thanks to the balance of power), curses the peace that has enabled the 'Union of Europe'.[39] In these images, George III is represented with daggers and silver, symbols of the attitude of Britain, which arms and finances the other countries of Europe against France. But at the same time, the images rejoice that at last, thanks to Bonaparte and the peace, the freedom of the seas has been restored (Fig. 4).

Other authors were less candid, with one pamphleteer declaring: 'French citizens—you are too confident. Don't count on peace with England. It is possible that the defection of her allies forces her to talk of peace. It is possible that the Minister King [Pitt] who rules her will make use of this language. But it is a veil of deception, which England has employed before to hide her hideous designs and to ensure her final success. It is the mask with

[39] Anon., *L'inégalité juste*, coloured engraving (Paris, 1801).

Fig. 3 Anonymous, *George se dépitte et signe enfin la paix générale*, Paris, 1802, Private collection

which she seeks to fool the people again by making a show of peaceful intentions in order to have the time to manufacture daggers to arm the French against each other.'[40] The dagger here served as a further allusion to the royalist assassination attempt of Bonaparte on 10 October 1800, an act in which some observers saw the hand of Britain.

As opposed to British caricaturists, who received the peace treaty with indulgence, their French counterparts were much more circumspect. The government sponsored plays that appeared in the days following the signature of the treaty (25 March 1802) and extolled the glory of Bonaparte who was said to have granted the peace to Britain. As one of

[40] Anon., *Aurons-nous la paix avec l'Angleterre?* (Paris, 1801), 4.

Fig. 4 Anonymous, *L'inégalité juste*, Paris, 1801, Private collection

these declared, 'When Bonaparte wants to triumph, he pardons.'[41] Before the Peace of Amiens and the dismissal of Pitt—events that French engravers tended to associate in an almost unilateral fashion—French caricaturists, from the beginning of the Consulate, had presented the British situation as desperate, teetering on the brink of financial and commercial collapse. An anonymous engraving (Fig. 5), entitled the *Situation de l'Angleterre au commencement du 19e siècle*, shows Britannia buried beneath the 'unpaid bills of the Navy and the Banks', losing her crown in the storm blowing from above. The ships aligned behind her depict the slowing of commerce and rats invade the port. At Britannia's feet, the English lion is also being smothered by the pile of debts that allude to the country's precarious financial situation. When the peace treaty was finally signed, numerous images depicted the situation as merely temporary, with Britain only adhering to the clauses of the accord grudgingly and with difficulty. Thus two images (Figs. 6 and 7) that function as a pair make use of a dreamlike sleep to present their message. The two engravings play off each other, portraying British maritime supremacy as utopian, a chimera guides the boat in which Britain is sat carrying the trident of Poseidon, in contrast with the liberty of the seas, which allows each country to trade freely wherever it likes, without being submitted to British demands, as the tricolour flag of a French ship testifies. In the first image 'George', the King of Britain, is asleep, while he is awake in the second. However, both show him trampling the Treaty of Amiens underfoot, an explicit allusion to the bad faith of the British and their readiness to ignore the provisions of the treaty, which they considered to be nothing more than a temporary respite. In both images, allegorical figures guide the king. In the first, Error, a woman whose eyes are blindfolded according to iconographic convention, takes advantage of the king's sleep to present him with the chimera of British commercial hegemony, depicted in a cloud. In the second, Truth, with the aid of a mirror, stands before the awakened king, and chases away the clouds of his utopian dream.

When the treaty was eventually broken, French engravers and printmakers continued to formulate their themes around the freedom of the seas and freedom of trade. As an example, we could cite an engraving (Fig. 8), dating probably from June 1803, which comments satirically on

[41] *La Fête de la Paix ou les élèves de Saint-Cyr à Maringo* [*sic*], July 1802. Quoted in Jean-Paul Bertaud et al., *Napoléon, le monde et les Anglais* (Paris: Autrement, 2004), 50.

Fig. 5 Anonymous, *Situation de l'Angleterre au commencement du 19e siècle*, Paris, 1801?, Private collection

Fig. 6 Anonymous, *Le rêve de George*, Paris, 1803, Private collection

the embargo of French vessels and the renewal of conflict. The image evokes the expedition of an army corps to Hanover led by General Mortier. A fat British merchant is knocked down by a French soldier, who holds a sabre in one hand and a map of Hanover in the other. His red epaulettes identify him as a member of the grenadiers, an elite infantry unit. Behind him, the presence of a ship suggests the liberty of the seas and the menace of crossing the Channel.

The British man resembles both John Bull, the personification of the British people, and an British merchant. Falling down amidst a ham hock and a mug of beer, his foot treads on the Treaty of Amiens. He holds a map of Malta and a broken oar, sign of the impending end of his maritime supremacy. A large turkey (Dindon in French), a possible allusion to *Georges Dandin* (a play by Molière), contemplates the scene, and on the wall an animal engraving emphasizes the same message as the engraving as a whole, showing a lion, the symbol of courage, taking down a lion, the animal that figures on the British crown. The caricature is powerful both in its expressive

Fig. 7 Anonymous, *Le réveil de George*, Paris, 1803, Private collection

dynamism and its central message, affirming that the resumption of hostilities will end in the victory of liberty and courage, brought about by the trim and muscular French warriors who will topple their fat and sated British opponents, perfidious and untrustworthy in all their insolent opulence.

All of these engraving insist, like many others, on the tyranny of the seas exercised by the British navy and provide indications of assurance, hope and confidence for the future. This was the message of a former royalist, the Count of Montgaillard, who, thanks to Joseph Fouché, was converted under the Consulate into a committed Bonapartiste. 'France is the only nation', he explained, 'that can repress the maritime despotism of Great Britain and confine it to just limits. France is the only nation that can restore Europe to tranquillity.'[42] The engravings of this period take up this

[42] Comte de Montgaillard, *De la France et de l'Europe* (Paris, 1804), 58. Quoted in Bertaud et al., *Napoléon, le monde et les Anglais*, 59.

Fig. 8 Anonymous, *La Brouille,* Paris, 1803?, Private collection

patriotic and military refrain, suggesting that Britain, after the Treaty of Amiens, did not respect its engagements with respect to the evacuation of Malta, and that France, now that war had resumed, would finally be able to institute the freedom of the seas. Hence, a print poking fun at George III's indigestion depicts the British king forced by France to return his dinner composed of 'Malta, the freedom of the seas, and the security of nations'.[43] These sentiments can also be found in written propaganda of the time, such as those by Joseph Diacon:

> You should give back Malta and fortify yourself. To satisfy your hatred, you play with the credulity of nations. How has England behaved since the peace? What vile means has it not employed to defame France and injure its first magistrate? All the brigands vomited up by the republic

[43] Anon., *L'indigestion de George*, coloured engraving (Paris, 1803–1804?).

> have been welcomed on England's shores and incited to return to commit new crimes here.[44]

If the metaphor of indigestion and colic was often used in these images (and also, as we just saw, in texts), this was because it also played on numerous stereotypes of the diametrically opposed cuisines of the two countries, which fed in the case of Britain a man whose bulk was too great, whose outlines were too large, a fat man loaded down with lard, who ate too much and too badly.

In the end, from 1786 to 1804, the images that made reference to Britain did so by evoking the freedom of commerce that Great Britain refused to apply to the seas. Aiming to please the different French regimes, but also to give expression to patriotic attitudes that were in the end quite traditional, the images produced in France, whether allegorical or satirical, played on a series of venerable oppositions, using commercial and peace treaties as evidence and examples of the perfidy of Britain.

Conclusion

In 1795, a pamphlet written by a 'publicist', as the author identified himself, presented the reasons for the rivalry between France and Britain.[45] The chief cause, he argued, was the French Revolution, fomented by none other than William Pitt, who sought to sow chaos in the country, to incite civil war (the Vendée), and to destroy the French navy in order to 'assure that his country would dominate the oceans' and conserve the 'sceptre of the seas'.[46] To persuade his readers, the author established a detailed list of all the British colonies around the world, which he presented as being under the control of tyrants working in the pay of Britain to support its commerce and industry. The author concludes that France must lend its support to the 'united Irishmen whom Pitt fears so much' and destroy the government of

[44] Joseph Diacon, *Guerre à l'Angleterre*, puisqu'elle le veut, ou Réflexions sur la mauvaise foi du gouvernement anglais, Paris, Chez Lefort, 1803, page 7.

[45] *Coup d'œil d'un publiciste sur l'ambition, la politique du cabinet de Londres, et sur le projet de la descente en Angleterre* (Amsterdam, 1795).

[46] *Coup d'œil d'un publiciste sur l'ambition*, 8–11.

London with a French 'landing' on British soil.[47] These actions would allow 'the entire universe' to reclaim 'the freedom of the seas'.[48]

Two years later, Ambroise Henry Arnould published his celebrated *Système maritime et politique des Européens pendant le XVIIIe siècle*, which urged the French navy to rival that of Britain and so to re-establish the balance of trade in France's favour. To that end, after having summarized the history of the maritime systems of the great European powers of the age, Arnould devoted the final two chapters to the case of Britain and France. According to him, the French maritime system was weakened throughout the eighteenth century, and thus it was necessary and indispensable to transform Paris into a veritable 'maritime city'. He called on French legislators to direct the 'fermentation of minds' in a national and patriotic direction: 'Call upon all men of all parties to put as much ardour into rebuilding the country along these lines as they have expended in destroying the institutions of 14 centuries.'[49] This bellicose spirit, which justified itself through a patriotic call to establish a genuine military-maritime policy, can be found in two episodes studied by Edmond Dziembowski,[50] concerning the private donation of ships in France in 1761 and 1782, which were made, in both cases, with the aim of thwarting British naval power. Both episodes, which were largely directed by the authorities, reveal the new expansionist definitions of patriotism in France and testify to the will to lead the population to participate more actively in public life. For Arnould, and then for Napoleon as he was caught up in the continental blockade, this patriotic sentiment, tied to concrete measures, would serve to strengthen French balance of trade, 're-establishing' a freedom of the seas that until that point had been compromised by the superiority of the Royal Navy. Balance—whether of trade, of politics, or simply of technology—occupied greatly the

[47] *Coup d'œil d'un publiciste sur l'ambition*, 49–52.

[48] *Coup d'œil d'un publiciste sur l'ambition*, 55.

[49] Ambroise Henry Arnould, *Système maritime et politique des Européens pendant le XVIIIe siècle* (Paris, 1797), 288.

[50] Dziembowski, *Un Nouveau patriotisme français*, 458–472 and by the same author, 'Les enjeux politiques du patriotisme français pendant la guerre d'Amérique: les dons de vaisseaux de 1782', in: *Du patriotisme aux nationalismes (1700–1848). France, Grande-Bretagne, Amérique du Nord*, ed. Bernard Cottret (Paris: Créaphis, 2002), 43–73.

imagination of French artists and in particular French caricaturists. Treaties of commerce, which should have permitted a certain equilibrium between the two rival nations, ought to have established the perfect equality symbolized by the balance of scales. But, in fact as in image and representation, the scales always tilted to one side, rarely attaining a balance. From 1786 to 1804, the representations of French commentators discussing or evoking the Treaty of Eden and the freedom of the seas arrived at similar conclusions, even though hope had reigned for a brief time before being dashed as an illusion. These representations reflected, in the end, more of a mindset geared to propaganda than an expression of truly independent judgements. With the empire, this liberty of the sea would soon disappear, only to be reactivated by Napoleonic propaganda, 'an Anglophobia' that the beginning of the twentieth century and the First World War would finally render increasingly sterile.

Pascal Dupuy is an Associate Professor at the Department of History at the University of Rouen and member of the *Groupe de Recherche d'Histoire*. His research interests range from political history to the cultural representation of political debates in popular publications and satirical images. Among his key publications are *Talleyrand. Un camélon politique* (2012), *Caricatures anglaises. Face à la Révolution et l'Empire (1789–1815)* (2008) and the co-edited volume *Le négoce de la paix. Les nations et les traités franco-britanniques, 1713–1802* (2008).

Haiti's Commercial Treaties: Between Abolition and the Persistence of the Old Regime

Paul Cheney

In the modern sense of the term, political revolution is inseparable from those deep social transformations that irrevocably cut peoples off from their past or, as Reinhart Koselleck writes, "the social revolution must write off the past and create its substance out of the future."[1] The Haitian Revolution was the world's first successful mass slave uprising, which surely places it among the most radical ruptures that occurred during the Age of Revolutions (*c.*1776–1830). Before the French Revolution and the civil wars that led to the proclamation of Haitian independence in 1804, Saint-Domingue was an old regime society in which servitude and racial hierarchy were taken for granted. Haitian nationalism was grounded in the abolition of chattel slavery, which was proclaimed by an act of the French National Convention in 1794. French nationalism itself had a similar origin, grounded as it was in the abolition of feudal forms of servitude and privilege in August 1789; the bedrock principles of civic

[1] Reinhart Koselleck, "Historical Criteria of the Modern Concept of Revolution," in: *Futures Past. On the Semantics of Historical Time* (New York: Columbia University Press, 2004), 55.

P. Cheney (✉)
University of Chicago, USA
e-mail: cheney@uchicago.edu

A. Alimento, K. Stapelbroek (eds.), *The Politics of Commercial Treaties in the Eighteenth Century*, DOI 10.1007/978-3-319-53574-6_15

equality were enshrined in the Declaration of the Rights of Man and Citizen in the same month. Although Haitian nationalism was founded on the self-determination of freed slaves—ideologically, as decisive a break from the old regime as one might care to imagine—Haiti could not "create its substance out of the future." The past determined the choices of its ruling elites in a number ways, and rigid insistence on the caesura of independence obscures economic, social, and political continuities with the old regime that can be summed up in a single word: the plantation.[2]

The old regime plantation was more than a site where servile labor produced tropical export commodities such as sugar, coffee, indigo, and cotton; as Phillip Curtin has argued, it was instead a "complex"—a widely ramified economic and political system that tied together regions, people, and institutions across at least three continents.[3] Within Haiti, the elites that rose to dominance during the revolutionary decades sought to revive the plantation complex. Despite the ostensibly disruptive ideology of anti-slavery, these elites relied upon coerced labor to man the sugar plantations in the newly independent Haiti; these same elites did not seek to break entirely with the European imperial powers that held the plantation system in place. Within an existing international division of labor, they sought terms of trade that would guarantee them a more favorable share of the surplus produced on Haitian plantations. In this respect and others, new Haitian elites resembled nothing so much as the white planter elite of old regime Saint-Domingue that they replaced.

The commercial treaties that are the subject of this chapter, and of this volume more generally, governed more than exchange; they regulated entire systems of accumulation. Therefore, they provide a useful vantage point from which to view the persistence of the old regime in independent Haiti, since neither plantation production nor international networks of commodity exchange could survive without the

[2] For a recent work that explores continuities of the Haitian Revolution with the old regime in ways that are influential for this chapter, see Malick Ghachem, *The Old Regime and the Haitian Revolution* (Cambridge: Cambridge University Press, 2012).

[3] On the features of the "mature" plantation complex, Philip D. Curtin, *The Rise and Fall of the Plantation Complex: Essays in Atlantic History, 2nd edition*, (Cambridge: Cambridge Univeristy Press, 1998), 10–13. On terms of trade, Jean Tarrade, *Le Commerce colonial de la France à la fin de l'ancien régime. L'évolution du régime de "l'Exclusif" de 1763 à 1789*, 2 vols. (Paris: Presses Universitaires de France, 1972), 2: 547–55.

other. Surplus was generated on the colonial plantation and the terms of trade that operated in the world beyond it determined the division of this surplus between planters, merchants, and the state. This division, in turn, influenced patterns of investment and, thus, colonial economic development. While metropolitan officials attempted to impose trade regimes in the colonies, their overseas subjects did not passively accept the terms offered to them. Whereas commercial treaties are typically understood as agreements concluded *between* sovereign states, in what follows I broaden the notion of a commercial treaty to include trading regimes—usually consecrated as law, and often modified in practice—*within* imperial systems. Far from vitiating the comparison between the colonial and the early national periods, the juxtaposition between nominally independent sovereign states that concluded commercial treaties on their own behalf and colonies negotiating terms of trade with their imperial masters furnishes essential categories of analysis for what follows.

Calls for independence in the Spanish Empire were the endpoint of a process, as Jeremy Adelman has argued, in which loyal colonial subjects sought concessions in the domain of colonial trade. What is sometimes wrongly termed creole nationalism during the pre-independence period in places like New Spain was nothing other than an attempt to devolve sovereignty over matters touching on production and exchange into local hands.[4] In this context, negotiation over imperial terms of trade, what Adelman has termed the "search for sovereignty," should be thought of as a kind of unofficial commercial treaty between metropole and colony. In the Spanish Empire, colonists repeatedly sought to modify the convoy system that governed trade between Cadix and New Spain; the Navigation Acts, which regulated the division of surplus at the same time as it concentrated high-value manufactures in the metropolitan center, caused friction in the British Empire. From 1717, metropole–colony relations in the French Empire were governed by the Exclusive (*l'Exclusif*) which

[4] Jeremy Adelman, *Sovereignty and Revolution in the Iberian Atlantic* (Princeton, NJ: Princeton University Press, 2006), introduction and Chapter 1. For another exploration of the problem of sovereignty and economic independence, specifically in the Haitian context, Fick, Carolyn E. "Revolutionary St. Domingue and the Emerging Atlantic: Paradigms of Sovereignty." In *The Haitian Revolution and the Early United States: Histories, Textualities, Geographies*, edited by Dillon, Elizabeth Maddock and Drexler, Michael J. (Philadelphia: University of Pennsylvania Press, 2016), esp. pp. 25–27 and 40–41.

stipulated, with some minor exceptions, that goods flowing in and out of colonies like Saint-Domingue must be carried by French merchants operating out of French ports. From its inception, the *Exclusif* was a constant object of renegotiation, and each concession colonists won can be thought of as a piece of sovereignty wrested from imperial hands.

As the Haitians quickly learned, nationhood did not end the colonial search for sovereignty. Long after independence, they were still unable to negotiate non-secret commercial treaties with Britain because the USA and France refused to recognize Haiti's sovereignty. Until French and US recognition (1825 and 1862, respectively), Haiti's commercial treaties with many nations consisted of secret protocols and tacit understandings with those countries that did not want to risk offending imperial hegemons. So, from the early eighteenth century to well beyond independence, the relationship between Haiti's plantation complex and the wider world of exchange was determined by a highly variable set of factors. National sovereignty competed with imperial sovereignty, and the fact of increasingly creolized elites did not point inexorably to nationalist independence movements.

Rents, Production, and Nation

Over the course of the eighteenth century, the French monarchical state negotiated with its collaborators and critics over terms of trade within the French colonial empire. An edict of 1717 opened up trade to all French merchants trading out of most Ponant (Atlantic) ports at the expense of chartered trading companies, but established the *Exclusif* as a way of funneling profits to the metropole and tax receipts to the state. The French undertook the reform of 1717 partly in response to complaints that chartered monopoly trading companies hurt production by artificially limiting supplies of slaves and other capital goods. However, it is significant that the edict itself only mentioned "frequent controversies" arising between merchants over the division of rents which "might have the effect of preventing our subjects from extending a commerce that is useful and advantageous to the realm"[5] As the century progressed, the crown modified its longstanding tendency to conceive of its economic advantage in

[5] France: Conseil du Roi, "Edit du Roi portant règlement pour le commerce des colonies françoises, donne à Paris au Mois d'Avril 1717."

terms of merchant profit, and began to entertain much more explicitly the problem of colonial production.

When the *Exclusif* came under intensive scrutiny in the wake of the Seven Years War in 1765, administrators had already begun to experiment with the argument that the well-being of the colonial plantation economy—production—should have priority over the rents that merchants and the state reaped from it. In 1765, at the behest of Minister of the Navy Antoine de Sartine, First Secretary Jean-Baptiste Dubuc drew up a proposal for reform of the *Exclusif.* Tellingly, Dubuc was a native of the island of Martinique and a descendant of one of the families that had led an uprising of elite creoles on that island in 1717.[6] Proponents of reform hoped to allow molasses and tafia (rum) to be exported directly from the sugar islands in foreign bottoms—thus increasing planters' profits relative to those of French merchants—and also sought permission to receive slaves, wood, cattle, and subsistence goods directly imported in non-French ships. In fact, this proposal for a widespread reform would have merely represented the generalization of a set of decrees sent to the governors of Guadeloupe and Martinique immediately following the end of the British occupation during the Seven Years War. Islanders had been only too happy under their British occupiers, whose ships brought them slaves in plentiful numbers along with sufficient wood and victuals to keep expanded plantation operations running smoothly. Underlying these concessions on the Windward Islands was the reality of widespread, politically dangerous planter discontent that had made these islands such easy prey for the British in the first place: "these excessively prohibitive laws strike at our colonists' property, the ownership of which becomes useless because of the impossibility of cultivation [...] the colonists only invest their money and their efforts under the just and natural condition that they be supplied and that they find an outlet for their produce." At issue were plantation profits, of course, but the natural jurisprudential language employed here hinted at the broader political stakes in this discussion: "prohibitive laws without measure and limit

[6] Jacques Petitjean Roget, *Le Gaoulé* (Fort de France: Société d'histoire de la Martinique, 1966). Some of the issues discussed in this paragraph and the next are covered in Paul Cheney, *Revolutionary Commerce. Globalization and the French Monarchy* (Cambridge, MA: Harvard University Press, 2010), Chapter 6.

contradict our civil laws."[7] Excessively harsh terms of trade strained the social contract, which could lead to the forcible renegotiation of imperial sovereignty witnessed between Great Britain and the thirteen colonies of North America.

A broad set of reforms enacted starting in 1784, after the conclusion of the American War of Independence (1776–1783), rebalanced merchant–planter relations and, in so doing, cleared the way for the sugar and coffee boom in Saint-Domingue that lasted all the way until 1791. Many elements of the 30 August 1784 *arrêt*, fashioned by Secretary of the Navy Charles Eugène Gabriel de La Croix de Castries, were simply restatements of the propositions advanced in 1765 by Dubuc. The importation of wood and foodstuffs in foreign bottoms was allowed, as was the duty-free export of molasses to the USA for the manufacture of rum; the 1784 *arrêt* went beyond the 1765 proposals by designating five entrepots for foreign trade on the islands (one each in Martinique and Guadeloupe, and one in each province of Saint-Domingue); already in May 1784, Bayonne and Loirent were added to the list of French free ports, making four alongside Marseille and Dunkirk.[8] Although the direct importation of slaves into Saint-Domingue by foreign vessels envisioned by Dubuc was not conceded in the August 1784 *arrêt*, de Castries issued an *arrêt* four months later intended to restrain planter brutality and to encourage slave natality on the islands.[9] If ceding this part of the valuable slave trade to foreigners was a political impossibility, the French colonial administration nevertheless sought a solution, on the demand side, to a chronic undersupply of slave labor that threatened to choke off the growth of the plantation complex.

The War of Independence changed the context of negotiation between colony and metropole in two fundamental ways that assured success for de Castries' reforms; earlier, by contrast, Dubuc's 1765 proposal had been

[7] Jean-Baptiste Dubuc, "Sur l'étenduë & les bornes des loix prohibitives du commerce etranger dans nos colonies," 1765, France, Archives Nationales, Colonies, F2b/7. For a discussion of this memoir and the surrounding politics, see Tarrade, *Commerce colonial*, 1: 242 *passim*.

[8] For these details, see Tarrade, *Commerce colonial*, 2: 547–55.

[9] Yvan Debbasch, "Le Marronnage: essai sur la désertion de l'esclave antillais," *L'Année Sociologique* (January 1961); Gabriel Debien, *Les Esclaves aux Antilles françaises, XVII*^{e}*–XVIII*^{e} *siècles* (Basse-Terre: Société d'histoire de la Guadeloupe, 1974), 485–90.

beaten back by heavy lobbying organized by merchants through their chambers of commerce. First, as Malick Ghachem has cannily observed, the *arrêt* of August 1784 "legalized the American Revolution" in the French colonies by ceding on many of the trade issues that had provoked unrest in the thirteen colonies of British North America.[10] The threat of national self-determination helped to focus the minds of administrators, like de Castries, charged with mediating the interests of planters, merchants, and the imperial state. The example of the American Revolution meant that the division of surplus could no longer be conceived of as a technical issue apart from the broader problem of colonial self-rule. Second, the French state seemed to have learned from the post-Seven Years War stalemate. Rather than waiting for interested parties within the French Empire come to terms, measures of trade liberalization that were long sought after by the French colonial administration were incorporated into its treaties with foreign powers.

Acts of sovereign power short-circuited domestic lobbying and presented desired reforms as *faits accomplis*. Thus, the Treaty of Amity and Commerce signed between France and the nascent USA in 1778 required France to maintain its colonial entrepots and a free port in France (Articles 29 and 30). The Treaty of Versailles (20 January 1783), which ended the war between France and Great Britain, can be seen as part of the same reform movement. Article 18 stipulated that the two powers would conclude a new trade agreement by the end of 1786, and Controller General Charles Alexandre de Calonne used this provision to negotiate a trade pact, the Eden–Rayneval Treaty of 1786, which forced wholesale liberalization on key French sectors like the textile industry.[11] The political conjuncture in the final decades of the old regime made treaties of trade—whether formal or informal—essential tools of economic reform when a domestic consensus was lacking.[12] But if one of Calonne's goals in advancing the Eden Treaty

[10] Malick Ghachem, "'Between France and the Antilles': The Commercial Assimilation of the American Revolution in Saint-Domingue, 1784–1785," *Harvard Atlantic History Seminar: Working Paper Series* WP # 99026 (1999).

[11] On the American War of Independence and reform movements in France, see Paul Cheney, "A False Dawn for Enlightenment Cosmopolitanism? Franco-American Trade during the American War of Independence," *William and Marry Quarterly*, 3rd ser., 63 (2006), 463–88.

[12] On this treaty, see the suggestively titled Chapter 3, "Foreign Policy as Industrial Policy," in Jeff Horn, *The Path Not Taken. French Industrialization in the Age of Revolution, 1750–1830* (Cambridge, MA: MIT Press, 2006), 51–87.

was to push for a single customs zone within France, the West Indian plantation complex required forms of legal particularism that would persist well beyond Haitian independence.

Particular Laws

In his sweeping essay on the international history of the American Declaration of Independence, David Armitage has argued that Haiti represents an exception to the rule of American influence on subsequent declarations all over the world. The USA proclaimed peace and amity with the wider world, abjuring the ambition to spread revolution beyond its borders and proclaiming itself "open for business" among the trading part of the brotherhood of nations. In contrast, according to Armitage, Haiti's Declaration underlined the country's encirclement by hostile powers and presaged the bloody campaign of extermination against whites that took place shortly after its pronouncement in on 1 January 1804.[13] But the relations that Haiti sought with the wider world—and the internal economic order corresponding to it—are better understood by setting this extraordinary proclamation aside, and instead beginning with the constitution promulgated in 1801. In fact, this document only announced to the world the de facto independence the colony enjoyed since 1798, when Toussaint Louverture brokered the evacuation of the British from the western province of Saint-Domingue. Napoleon and the rest of the world took it for what it was: Toussaint Louverture's declaration of independence from the French.

The first article of the constitution proclaims Saint-Domingue a part of the French Empire "subject to particular laws"—laws which are then set forth as a plan for autonomous government in subsequent articles. Despite Saint-Dominguan autonomy, which included a separate legislature, the historical novelty of the formulation "particular laws" should not be overestimated. This article, in fact, reasserts the position developed by the National Assembly in 1791 by which the French colonies would be subject to an "external" regime imposed by the metropole while so-called "internal" governance would be left to the colonies themselves. What this meant in 1791 was that the metropole would still impose terms of trade through

[13] David Armitage, *The Declaration of Independence. A Global History* (Cambridge, MA: Harvard University Press, 2007), 115–16.

the *Exclusif*, but that the civil status of persons could vary from the norm of universal civic equality established within the hexagon.[14] Slavery could persist within the French Empire by dint of "particular laws" needed to ensure social order and productivity in the colonies, whose climate and social structure differed so wildly from the metropole, where the profits of this exception would continue to flow.

Under the old regime, Saint-Domingue and the French Antilles in general enjoyed "particular laws" in a twofold sense. First, the variations in privileges they enjoyed were simply part of the uneven political topography of the French monarchy that was abolished along with the "feudal" servitudes and privileges in August of 1789. Despite the ambitions of the absolutist state, provinces could differ widely in exemptions, burdens, and forms of administrative tutelage; in this sense, the colonies were merely far-flung provinces within the French monarchy. Second, despite the Code Noir (1685), which pretended some sort of royal purview over the treatment of slaves, plantations were, by design, veritable islands of despotism unreachable by the norms of civil law; this legal void is what guaranteed the functioning of the slave system and its profitability.[15] When the French National Assembly decreed the possibility of "particular laws" for the colonies that contravened the universal principles articulated in the Declaration of the Rights of Man and Citizen (henceforth, DDHC) (1789), it did so in order to maintain the despotic rule of slave owners on the countryside. Political discrimination against free people of color (*gens de couleur*), in any case, fully countenanced by the DDHC, was entirely subordinate to this primordial goal. The abolition of slavery in 1794 ostensibly put an end to inconsistent application of the DDHC between the colonies and the metropole. In point of fact abolition was never applied in the French East Indies, and remained a dead letter in Guiana and, due to the British invasion, in Martinique. The spotty observation of the DDHC in the colonies compared to the metropole became—officially at least—an aberration, a state of exception without underlying constitutional support. Among other things, Napoleon's authoritarian

[14] See Cheney, *Revolutionary Commerce*, Chapter 7.

[15] Yvan Debbasch, "Au Coeur du 'gouvernement des esclaves': la souveraineté domestique aux Antilles françaises (XVIIe–XVIIIe siécles)," *Revue française d'histoire d'outre mer* 72/266 (1985), 31–54.

constitution of the year VII (1799) reintroduced the principle that "particular laws" might apply to the French colonies—a signal of his intention to constitutionally reimpose slavery where it had been abolished as a matter of fact *and* law.[16]

After Haitian independence was proclaimed in 1804, all constitutions announced categorically the abolition of slavery, but "particular laws" for the maintenance of the plantation complex nevertheless had a long afterlife. Article 172 of the constitution of 1806 announced that "The police of the countryside will be subject to particular laws"—a system of constraint that we will discuss in more detail below. As François Blancpain has described it, well after achieving independence Haiti remained a society with a dual law, a law of liberty and equality inherited from the French Revolution and applied to the (largely light-skinned) bourgeoisie, and another authoritarian system applied to rural dwellers charged with generating agricultural surplus. Particular laws on the countryside constitute an essential continuity between the old regime and the revolutionary and even post-revolutionary periods.[17] This dual law was equally in force during Haiti's period of informal independence (1798–1803) under Toussaint Louverture.

Toussaint Louverture's constitution of 1801 is less expansive than its successors on the subject of foreign commercial or political relations. Like Napoleon Bonaparte, he had no inhibitions about conducting a freelance foreign policy as a general—a fact witnessed by a secret treaty concluded for the evacuation of the British from Saint-Domingue in 1798, which included a provision for free trade between these powers. Although Louverture's silence about Haiti as an independent international player was no doubt intended to mollify his French audience, he nevertheless sought to assure plantation owners of their future role in the Saint-Dominguan economy. He did so despite the fact that many had proven themselves politically unreliable during the civil war that had raged almost

[16] The actual text of Article 91 reads "The regime of the French colonies is determined by special laws." For French constitutions since 1789, see http://www.conseil-constitutionnel.fr/conseil-constitutionnel/francais/la-constitution/les-constitutions-de-la-france/les-constitutions-de-la-france.5080.html. All references to Haitian constitutions come from Louis-Joseph Janvier, *Les Constitutions d'Haïti (1801–1885)*, vol. 1 (Paris: C. Marpin et E. Flammarion, 1886).

[17] François Blancpain, *La condition des paysans haïtiens. Du Code noir aux codes ruraux* (Paris: Karthala Editions, 2003), 176.

continually since 1791. In order to resume management of their plantations, many would have to return from forced or voluntary exile.[18] Once the war came to an end, both French and foreign absentee owners could reclaim their rights (Articles 59 and 60)—including rights to sequestered plantations. When previous governments had contracted with third parties for the exploitation of abandoned or sequestered properties, the Louverturian regime would respect current leases. But if plantation owners came back to Saint-Domingue to press valid claims on properties managed by the government or its delegates, the constitution encouraged owners and current leaseholders to come to some sort of understanding (Article 74). In a word, a newly independent Saint-Domingue would not hand a *causus belli* to dispossessed planters who might seek foreign aid to recover their property. Taken together with the provision for free trade between Saint-Domingue and Britain and the USA in the secret treaty of 1799, normalization with potentially hostile powers seems to have been the dominant note of the Louverturian regime. Louverture gave even further proof of this when he refused to execute the orders from the Directory (the French executive from 1795–1799) to invade Jamaica.[19]

Treaties signed by Toussaint Louverture that led up to the 1801 constitution broke with the *Exclusif* by establishing free trade with the USA and Great Britain, but the underlying program embodied in the June 1799 secret accord with Brigadier Thomas Maitland had nothing to do with unrestrained free-trade cosmopolitanism.[20] Although the British and Americans wanted access to all Saint-Dominguan ports, Louverture saw to it that only Cap Français and Port Républicain (Port-au-Prince) were

[18] Manuel Covo, "Commerce, empire et révolutions dans le monde atlantique: la colonie de Saint-Domingue, entre métropole et Etats-Unis (ca. 1778–ca. 1804)" (Thèse de doctorat, histoire, EHESS, 2013), 624–41.

[19] Letter of American Ambassador Edward Stevens to British Brigadier General Thomas Maitland, Gonaives, Saint-Domingue, 23 May 1799. Reprinted in "Letters of Toussaint Louverture and of Edward Stevens, 1798–1800," *American Historical Review* 16/1 (1910), 73–76.

[20] Louverture, Toussaint and Maitland, Brigadier General, "Convention secrète entre l'honorable brigadier général Maitland et le général en chef de Saint Domingue, Toussaint-Louverture, 13 Juin 1799," in *Histoire d'Haïti*, ed. A. dolphe Cabon (Port-au-Prince: Petit Séminaire Collège Saint-Martial, 1937), 96–98. For the American agreement, "Letters of Toussaint Louverture and of Edward Stevens, 1798–1800." This is a point emphasized by Manuel Covo, "Commerce, empire et révolutions," 694–95.

included in the Maitland Accord (Article 3). Another provision (Article 6) excluded American and British merchants from the coasting trade. A later regulation of 8 May 1801, in which Toussaint Louverture adjusted tariff levels and implemented new procedures for foreign merchants, makes more explicit the economic logic underlying the Maitland Accord. Without tight surveillance, fraud would multiply, and tariffs would go unpaid: "a government cannot exist without contributions [. . .] it is my intention to favor Trade by all legitimate means, but it is equally legitimate to assure the Republic the collection of taxes."[21] The structure of tariffs Louverture established was intended to favor an export-oriented plantation economy heavily dependent upon foreign markets for subsistence goods. Whereas most imports would pay 10 percent duties, flour, biscuit, salted meats, and fish, as well as construction wood, would only pay 6 percent (Article 4). On the whole, imports were favored over exports, which were taxed at 20 percent, but Article 7, which prohibited the export of specie, was meant to ensure that foreign merchants stimulated the plantation economy by leaving Haitian ports laden with sugar, coffee, indigo, and cotton. Encouraging free trade did not mean that Louverture would relinquish traditional prerogatives of sovereignty or the equally traditional cut of plantation surplus that the state appropriated through taxes.

Internally, the Louverturian constitution sought to reestablish an economy that resembled as closely as possible the old regime system of production while still respecting the abolition of slavery and the equality of all citizens (Article 3). The colony of Saint-Domingue remained "essentially agricultural" (Article 14), and as under the old regime its commerce "consisted uniquely in the products of its soil"; it could, therefore, "not suffer the slightest interruption of work." Toussaint Louverture's rural code restrained planters insofar as it prescribed rest days and accorded one-quarter of the product (less expenses . . .) to citizen cultivators. Nevertheless, while ostensibly respecting abolition, the main thrust of the rural code was meant to intensify Saint-Domingue's "cultivation and commerce," the subjects of Articles 14–18 of the 1801 constitution. Former slaves were re-baptized "cultivators," and affected for revolving one-year terms of service on their

[21] Paris, Archives Nationales, Colonies, CC 9B, 18, "Règlement Toussaint Louverture, Général en Chef de l'Armée de Saint-Domingue," 18 Floréal, An 9.

former plantation.[22] Changing employers required the permission of the planter in conjunction with local military officials, and vagabondage laws severely limited freedom of movement in the countryside. Although Toussaint's rural code prohibited the use of the whip, cultivators viewed the ensemble as brutal and constraining.[23] Given the resemblance of these strictures to old regime slavery, it is perhaps unsurprising that Toussaint Louverture and, later, Jean-Jacques Dessalines, sought to buy slaves from Jamaican traders in order to replenish the ranks of Haitian *cultivateurs*.[24] As under the old regime, the Louverturian system relied fundamentally on extra-economic coercion to maintain productivity.

Toward a Slave Society without Slaves?

Toussaint Louverture's attempts to revive the plantation economy of the old regime without formal recourse to slavery registered some real material successes. In 1794, combined sugar and coffee production in Saint-Domingue stood at a mere 1/24 of 1789 levels; by 1800–1801, they had climbed to about one-third of pre-revolutionary peaks.[25]

[22] Paris, Archives Nationales, Colonies, CC 9B, 18, "Règlement rélatif à la culture, Toussaint Louverture, Général en Chef de l'Armée de Saint-Domingue," 20 Véndemiaire, an 9. The règlement de culture is reprinted in Victor Schoelcher, *Vie de Toussaint Louverture* (Paris: KARTHALA Editions, 1982), 427–32.

[23] For the brutality of this system, see the testimony in Great Britain Parliament House of Commons, *Parliamentary Papers, 1780–1849*, vol. 24, Communications Received at the Foreign Office Relative to Hayti (London: HMSO, 1829), 91–94. On the continuities with the *ancien régime*, see Sabine Maginer, "Le Régime de Toussaint Louverture en 1801: un modèle, une exception," in: *Rétablissement de l'esclavage dans les colonies françaises, 1802. Ruptures et continuités de la politique coloniale française (1800–1830)*, ed. Yves Bénot and Marcel Dorigny (Paris: Maisonneuve et Larose, 2003), 109–26.

[24] Philippe R. Girard, "Jean-Jacques Dessalines and the Atlantic System: A Reappraisal," *William and Mary Quarterly* 69/3 (2012), 549–82; Julia Gaffield, "Haiti and Jamaica in the Remaking of the Early Nineteenth-Century Atlantic World," *William and Mary Quarterly* 69/3 (2012), 583–614: 600.

[25] Yves Bénot, *La Démence coloniale sous Napoléon* (Paris: La Découverte, 1992), 29, citing contemporary figures. This blanket figure hides important variations among types of exports: 1801 in comparison to 1791 was (in terms of weight) a mere 2 percent for clayed sugar, 20 percent for muscavado, 63 percent for coffee, and 336 percent for syrup. Source: calculations from A. Cabon, *Histoire d'Haïti* (Port-au-Prince: Petit Séminaire Collège Saint-Martial, 1937), 95, citing statistics compiled by the British.

Nevertheless, these efforts were ultimately undermined by their contradictions. First, absentee planters in France, many of them of a royalist political bent, could simply not credit the possibility of a functioning plantation system without the yoke of slavery; these planters had the ear of an increasingly reactionary Napoleon Bonaparte, who for this and other reasons—including Toussaint Louverture's rejection of French commercial hegemony—ordered the ultimately unsuccessful reinvasion of the island in 1802.[26] The invasion of Saint-Domingue by the French army put all the more pressure on military and economic elites to generate the sort of plantation revenue that could support a successful war effort. Second, the refusal of many ex-slaves to return to their former (or any) sugar plantations continually compromised these efforts at reconstruction, and hence the project of national independence that plantation revenues were supposed to finance. Ex-slaves reaffirmed in their own way French planters' incredulity that a profitable plantation complex was consistent with abolition, and their resistance frequently destabilized successive Haitian regimes. Toussaint Louverture's attempt to push back the French invasion was nearly derailed, for instance, by an uprising of ex-slaves led by his adopted nephew, General Moyse.[27] The material requirements of Haitian independence, at least in the way that its elites conceived of them were fundamentally at odds with the organizing ideology of Haitian nationalism: the abolition of slavery.

This basic contradiction would continue to reproduce itself in the early national period, and to define its political and commercial relationship with the outside world. From the perspective of its elites, Haiti had the worst of both worlds. Internally, regimes never really succeeded in resuscitating for any length of time the punitive labor regime that the sugar plantation complex was based upon; Haiti's ex-slaves took abolition to mean that they could return to the land as peasant smallholders, growing subsistence crops for their own account and participating episodically in the market economy by cutting dyewood and picking coffee beans in the hills.[28] The

[26] For an excellent account, see Bénot, *Démence coloniale*, Chapter 2.

[27] Etienne Charlier, *Aperçu sur la formation historique de la nation haitienne* (Port-au-Prince: Les Presses Libres, 1965), 185–87.

[28] The literature on this subject is vast. See for instance Sidney Mintz, *Caribbean Transformations* (Chicago, IL: Aldine, 1974); André-Marcel d'Ans, *Haïti: paysage et société. Hommes et sociétés* (Paris: Karthala, 1987); Blancpain, *La condition des paysans*

ultimately futile attempts to bring the Haitian peasantry to heel help to account for the disproportionate share of military expenses as a share of total of public expenditures—around 50 percent up to 1860 and 25 percent thereafter.[29] Externally, after a brief honeymoon of collaboration with the USA and Britain while the Haitians threw off their French masters, Haiti was isolated by imperial powers with interests in the West Indies. Haitian nationalism, which was grounded in the abolition of slavery, simply aroused too much fear among the slaveholding powers in this region.[30]

The commercial isolation of Haiti came only in stages. Canny negotiation by Toussaint Louverture with the Americans and the British meant that during its period of de facto independence, Saint-Domingue freed itself from the constraints of the *Exclusif* imposed by its nominal imperial master, France.[31] As Philippe Girard has carefully documented, the first leader of an officially independent Haiti, Jean-Jacques Dessalines, pursued a commercial policy designed to protect the interests of the new planter class, consisting largely of military leaders like himself, who sought competitive markets for the sugar, coffee, and cotton it produced, as well as easy access to capital goods, subsistence items, and even African slaves to fill the depleted ranks of black republican *cultivateurs*.[32] Ceding to the planter lobby from the southern USA, which sought to weaken a potential vector of slave rebellion, Thomas Jefferson promulgated a commercial embargo against Haiti in 1806. Americans (and the French merchants who used them as straw men) continued to trade with Haiti, but even after the lifting of the official embargo in 1809, American non-recognition made any commercial agreement between the two countries, which would have facilitated trade to Haiti, impossible. In this atmosphere, fearing to offend other great powers,

haïtiens; Michel-Rolph Trouillot, "Caribbean Peasantries and World Capitalism," *New West Indian Guide* 58/1–2 (1984), 37–59; Johnhenry Gonzalez, "The Fruits of Destruction: Violence, Land, and the Making of the Haitian Peasantry, 1802–1826" (PhD thesis, University of Chicago, 2012).

[29] V. Bulmer-Thomas, *The Economic History of the Caribbean since the Napoleonic Wars* (Cambridge: Cambridge University Press, 2012), 162–69.

[30] This is another point that is well documented in the literature. See most recently Ashli White, *Encountering Revolution. Haiti and the Making of the Early Republic* (Baltimore, MD: Johns Hopkins University Press, 2010).

[31] Maurice A. Lubin, "Les Premiers rapports de la nation haïtienne avec l'étranger," *Journal of Inter-American Studies* 10/2 (1968), 277–305.

[32] Girard, "Jean-Jacques Dessalines and the Atlantic System."

Britain only concluded secret, semi-official agreements with Haiti.[33] Complicity between the great powers was such that the Treaty of Paris (1814) made no official mention of Haitian independence and a secret accord made at the Congress of Vienna (1815) stipulated that in the case of a French re-invasion, British ships would be allowed to continue to trade in Haiti. It was in this context that British merchants utterly dominated Haitian trade, which was disadvantaged by being forced to compete on unequal terms with British colonial produce in British markets.[34]

Early Haitian constitutions reflected the dual bind of Haiti's leadership, caught between a restive post-abolition workforce and foreign governments who, wary of the intentions of these same ex-slaves and their leaders, continued to isolate and ignore them. These constitutions seem to have been intended as much to reassure foreign states as to provide a structure of governance. Before its official recognition by France in 1825, all Haitian governments sought to reassure foreign nations that they would not seek to spread the founding principle of black liberty beyond the confines of the island of Hispaniola. Other articles extended specific guarantees of safety to foreign merchants. Internally, these constitutions underlined the importance of agriculture and free markets to assure an outlet for plantation produce. And although the republican constitutions of Haiti were replete with guarantees of the sort found in their French models, the most long-lasting documents up until 1843 (those of 1806 and 1816) emphasized, as discussed above, that the countryside was to be governed by particular laws intended to bind cultivators to the sugar plantation.

Conclusion: Failure and Retrenchment

The complete failure of these attempts to discipline the Haitian workforce in order to maintain the sugar industry are captured in the summary of commodity exports below (indexed to 1789 as the base year).[35]

[33] On these last two points, see Lubin, "Les Premiers rapports de la nation haïtienne avec l'étranger." On French commerce through American straw men, see Silvia Marzagalli, *Bordeaux et les États-Unis, 1776–1815. Politique et stratégies négociantes dans la genèse d'un réseau commercial* (Geneva: Droz, 2015), 181–204.

[34] Bulmer-Thomas, *Economic History of the Caribbean*, 162–69.

[35] Sources: Commons, *Parliamentary Papers*, 24, Communications Received at the Foreign Office Relative to Hayti, 159; Cabon, *Histoire d'Haïti*, 95.

Selected Haiti Commodity Exports, 1789–1826 gross weight

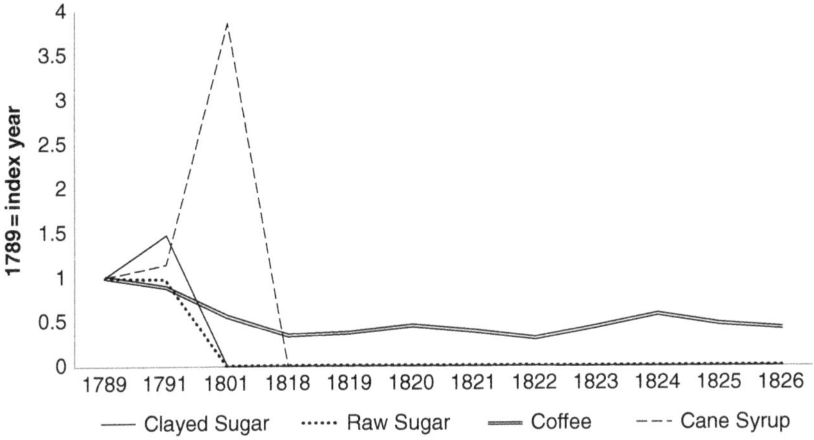

Laws restricting the division and sale of cane land and a decree of 9 March 1807 abolishing the export tax on all sugar products could not mitigate peasant aversion to the sugar plantation; foreign sales, following the curve of production, fell to virtually nothing by 1821.[36] Coffee harvesting and sale remained relatively stable over this period and left out of this chart is the explosion of dyewood exports, which from nothing in 1789, hovered between 1.9 and 8.3 million pounds per annum in the years 1801–1826. Dyewood production grew because, like the decentralized, "savage" method of coffee harvesting that proliferated in the mountains of Haiti after 1791, it could be combined with subsistence farming and it took place apart from the constraints and surveillance that defined the sugar plantation.

Despite the wishes of its elite, the peasant Haiti based on independent subsistence agriculture gained ground over the old regime system of vast sugar estates supporting a brilliant military-agricultural aristocracy. These were rival visions of Haitian nationalism itself. The first envisioned national defense paid for by profits generated by the plantation economy and realized on world commodity markets. The second, peasant alternative

[36] President Alexandre Pétion (r. 1806–1818) was more indulgent about land sales to peasants but nevertheless sought to keep large plantations on the great sugar growing plains intact. Blancpain, *La condition des paysans haïtiens*, 130.

was grounded in an equally defiant nationalism, but envisioned the division of lands and demographic growth that would create eager defenders of a Haitian nation. In comparison to the old regime, this second Haiti was to be relatively egalitarian and economically autarkic.[37] The virtual non-application of the rural codes and the steady division of lands under the presidency of Pétion (1807–1818) are proof that, for the purposes of its own survival, the elite of Haiti was, despite itself, ultimately forced to compromise with peasant Haiti. But this disagreeable expedient did not prevent mulatto elites from attempting to mold this new situation to their needs.

It is in this context that one should view Haiti's agreement in 1825 to pay a 150,000,000 franc indemnity to France in exchange for a cessation of the threat of re-invasion, diplomatic recognition, and improved trade relations. From a certain perspective, the indemnity paid to the former plantation owners of Saint-Domingue can be seen as a gentlemen's agreement between successive landholding elites. Presidents Pétion and Boyer not only represented these elites but belonged to them. For instance upon the general division of the Cul de Sac plain (Western Province) in 1812, the Ferron de la Ferronnays plantation—formerly consisting of 240 slaves—was granted to none other than Alexandre Pétion, and after his death in 1818 it was passed to President Boyer. The former owner of this plantation even seriously considered the possibility that President Boyer might want to legitimize his enjoyment of the property by purchasing it directly from him.[38] The proposition seems absurd, but in some sense, Haitian leaders did precisely what Ferron de la Ferronnays suggested, only on a wholesale level.

It was Haitian President Pétion who initially broached the idea of an indemnity in 1814.[39] Although he naturally believed that his countrymen had justly reclaimed their own freedom, Pétion was willing to negotiate with his erstwhile imperial masters to "sell us Saint-Domingue, as they sold

[37] Blancpain, *La condition des paysans haïtiens*, 176.

[38] Undated letter (certainly 1825), Pierre-Jacques-François-Joseph-Auguste Ferron de la Ferronnays (PJF) to President Boyer of Haiti. See also 16 December 1827, Ferronnays to Madame Mérillon (New Orleans). Private archive, Saint Mars la Jaille.

[39] Benoît Joachim, "L'indemnité coloniale de Saint-Domingue et la question des rapatriés," *Revue Historique* 246/2 (500) (1971), 363; Frédérique Beauvois, "L'indemnité de Saint-Domingue: 'Dette d'indépendance' ou 'rançon de l'esclavage'?," *French Colonial History* 10/1 (2009), 112–14.

Louisiana to the United States."[40] His successor Jean-Pierre Boyer was not thrilled about the outcome, but in 1821 he reinitiated discussions with the French, which led to the deal of 1825. The manner in which Haiti paid for the 1825 indemnity reinforces the impression that Haitian leaders sought a post-revolutionary settlement of land and labor, and a system of international exchange, that privileged the production and export of sugar. One year after this treaty was signed, Boyer issued yet another rural code, which Michel-Rolph Trouillot has argued, unintentionally functioned as an epitaph, rather than a new beginning, for the Haitian sugar industry.[41] As under the old regime, sugar export taxes remained low, and eventually the 25 percent government tax on production was lifted; by contrast, coffee producers were burdened by heavy export duties—generally about twice the rate of sugar exports—extracted to pay for the indemnity. This differential treatment had the explicit goal of favoring the industrial agriculture of the sugar plantation over small-scale coffee and subsistence agriculture. Such subsistence and capital goods as Haitians could not produce for themselves were subjected to heavy import duties, while luxury imports consumed by rich merchants and state officials went largely untaxed. In 1842 customs duties made up 98.2 percent of state revenues; surplus that was no longer being captured on the plantation was taken by state officials at the customs house. By the terms of the 1825 *Ordonnance* between Charles X of France and Haiti, France would pay exactly half the rate of customs duties as all other nations.[42] Haitians would naturally have preferred not to split these proceeds with the French, but this was not the state of play in the immediate post-independence world. Pétion and Boyer concluded agreements convenient not for the needs of a republic of peasant smallholders but for the aspirations of a militarized planter-aristocracy (and the merchant class that served them) that sought to reproduce the social conditions of the old regime without slavery.[43]

[40] "Extrait du journal de Dauxion," in Mission Dauxion-Lavaysse (1814–1815), France: Archives Nationales, Colonies, CC9 A 48. Cited in Beauvois, "L'indemnité de Saint-Domingue," 112.

[41] *Code Rural d'Haïti* (Port-au-Prince: Imprimerie du Gouvernement, 1826); Michel-Rolph Trouillot, *Haiti, State Against Nation. The Origins and Legacy of Duvalierism* (New York: Monthly Review Press, 1990), 60.

[42] Ordonnance, 17 April 1825, article 1. Reprinted in Cabon, *Histoire d'Haïti*, 334.

[43] Trouillot, *Haiti, State against Nation*, Chapters 1 and 2; see pp. 60–61 for figures. For further reflections on this episode, see Paul Cheney, *Cul de Sac: Patrimony, Capitalism and Slavery in French Saint-Domingue* (Chicago: University of Chicago Press, 2017), Chapter 7.

Paul Cheney is Associate Professor of History at the University of Chicago. He is a specialist in old regime France and its colonial empire, with interests in political economy, the history of political thought, and historical world systems theory. He has published *Revolutionary Commerce. Globalization and the French Monarchy* (2010) and *Cul de Sac: Patrimony, Capitalism and Slavery in French Saint-Domingue* (2017), a micro-historical exploration of the strengths and weaknesses of old regime capitalism in France's richest eighteenth-century colony.

What Trade for a Republican People? French Revolutionary Debates about Commercial Treaties (1792–1799)

Marc Belissa

The French Revolution obliged all contemporaries to reframe the question of trade and diplomatic relations between nations and to reconsider the existing paradigms of political economy. The links established from the time of Montesquieu between trade, *moeurs*, *esprit des peuples*, principles of government and national *constitutions* were re-examined in the light of social and political change since 1789. Consequently, the French Revolution was also a revolution of trade and many observers—economists, commercial directors, consular agents and others—asked themselves how a 'regenerated' France should set about rethinking its approach to commerce in the new European and global environment.[1]

[1] See Manuel Covo, 'Commerce, empire et révolutions dans le monde atlantique: la colonie de Saint-Domingue, entre métropole et Etats-Unis (ca. 1778–ca. 1804)' (Thèse de doctorat, histoire, EHESS, 2013). The ideas in the present chapter need to be seen in the general frame of the restructuring of Atlantic trade structures patterns in the course of the American, French and Haitian Revolutions.

M. Belissa (✉)
University of Paris Ouest Nanterre – CHISCO, Paris, France
e-mail: marc.belissa@u-paris10.fr

A. Alimento, K. Stapelbroek (eds.), *The Politics of Commercial Treaties in the Eighteenth Century*, DOI 10.1007/978-3-319-53574-6_16

The abolition of the monarchy in September 1792 modified the terms of these debates. For all contemporaries, the link between republicanism and international relations was self-evident: a republican nation could not trade in the way a nation of 'slaves of tyrants' had done. Accordingly, the need to replace the 'ancient diplomacy of the kings' with a 'commercial diplomacy' at the service of the people became a key point in the debates, as well as in proposed legislation, in the regulations issued or discussed by the Convention and then by the Directory and Legislative Council, in the works of economists, and in newspaper columns. The political disorder of the princes needed to be replaced by a rational trade order orientated towards national prosperity. Trade would then become the sole 'legitimate foreign policy' at the heart of a world freed from dynastic wars.

The revolutionary decade can be roughly divided into three periods. In the first, from 1789 to the declaration of war in April 1792, advocates of revolution considered how a regenerated France should rethink its international trade in accordance with its new 'constitution'. The regeneration of the old French monarchy passed through a redefinition of a national trade strategy under the direction of the legislature. For some advocates the Revolution presented the ideal opportunity for affirming a proactive policy to counter British maritime domination and to implement a reformed system of navigation between France and its colonies.[2] Others suggested a competitive alliance with Britain based on free trade. And yet others intended to introduce egalitarian policies based on respect for the reciprocal rights of all nations to participate in the 'general trade of mankind'. For everyone, business, power and international order were deemed to be elements of a new 'comprehensive trade system'. The 'balance of trade' and 'balance of powers' had to be reassessed in line with the regeneration of the nation.[3]

In the second period, from the abolition of the monarchy in September 1792 to the end of 1794, war—especially that against Britain which began in February 1793—dominated debates on the new 'trade diplomacy' of Republican France. The conflict between a revolutionary France and a monarchist Europe posed new questions that demanded original answers.

[2] See the first part of Covo, 'Commerce, empire et révolutions'.

[3] Marc Belissa, *Fraternité Universelle et Intérêt national. Les cosmopolitiques du droit des gens, 1713–1795* (Paris: Kimé, 1997).

Trade became seen as a weapon in the service of 'the side of freedom and humanity' that opposed tyranny.

Finally, starting from 1795 and up to the end of the Directory, French leaders tried to place the nation's trading power on a basis that reflected the power relations—notably territorial ones—that had arisen from the victory of the revolutionary armies and the creation of the sister republics. Various plans for trade treaties were developed, some of which were imposed on the countries with which the Directorial Republic entered into negotiations.

This chapter engages with the last two periods, which corresponded to the moment in which contemporaries were reconsidering the connections between republicanism and trade.[4]

G. J. A. Ducher and Commercial Diplomacy (1792–1794)

In 1789, the 'trading system' of the kingdom of France was conceived as being based on a series of treaties, some only recently signed. These were: the Family Compact that united the Bourbon dynasties of France, Spain and Parma; the 1786 Franco-British treaties of commerce; the 1785 treaty with the Dutch Republic and the 1778 trade and friendship treaty with the United States; those signed with the northern powers (Hamburg in 1769, Russia in 1787, etc.); and the trade agreements with the Levant.

The entries in the *cahiers de doléances* criticized in particular the Franco-British treaties of commerce and demanded a form of 'national' control to prevent any future signing of such a treaty. In the debate on the right of peace and war held in May 1790, the Constituent Assembly obtained the right to ratify them (Article 9 of the decree of 22 May 1790), but in the absence of a mechanism obliging the king to renegotiate existing treaties, such a supervisory right proved futile. Although the Assembly repeatedly asked his diplomatic committees to issue a report on the trade treaties, the requests were never followed up.

Despite such demands, most of the trade treaties of the Old Regime remained in force until the fall of the monarchy on 10 August 1792.

[4] The first period is discussed in Marc Belissa, 'Handel, Diplomatie und nationale Macht in der Französischen Revolution (1789–1799)', in: *Der moderne Staat und 'le doux commerce'. Staat, Ökonomie und internationales System im politischen Denken der Aufklärung*, ed. Olaf Asbach (Baden-Baden: Nomos, 2014), 229–250.

The treaties with Britain, the United Provinces and Spain were not formally rescinded until February and March 1793 when the Republic declared war on Britain, the Dutch Stadtholder and the King of Spain. From March 1793 until 1795, only the neutral powers (the United States, the Swiss Cantons, the Scandinavian states and the Ottoman Empire) retained commercial ties with France. Thus some trade treaties remained valid only in theory. In reality, the implementation of the clauses of those treaties depended on the goodwill of the neutral powers that the French Republic did not want to see falling into the coalition camp, but negotiations leading to new treaties were never actually opened.

Nonetheless, an important debate on the principles of republican trade continued in the Convention, in the committees and in the press. The main questions those discussions addressed were: How could the 'feudal' distinction between 'royal diplomacy' and 'national trade' be broken? How could foreign relations be 'republicanized'? What business dealings should the Republic maintain with other nations, 'free' or otherwise? How should France compete with Britain, the 'tyrant of the seas'?

One of the more prolific campaigners on these issues was the now largely forgotten G. J. A. Ducher,[5] erstwhile vice-consul and consul of France to the United States between 1783 and 1790, writer of a series of articles on trade and diplomacy in the *Moniteur*, adviser to Barère and to the Public Safety Committee from 1793, member of the Customs Commission in the years II and III. He was the chief exponent of the vision of a republican 'commercial diplomacy' and played a decisive role not only in the debates held by the Convention, for which he wrote numerous dissertations and reports, but also in the development of the trade and customs legislation proposed by the Marine and Public Safety Committees.

[5] On Ducher, the only existing study is Frederick L. Nussbaum, *Commercial Policy in the French Revolution. A Study of the Career of G. J. A. Ducher* (Washington, DC: American Historical Association, 1923). See also Allan Potofsky, 'The Transatlantic Political Economy: French "Interests" and the Debate Over the US Debt 1777–1795', *Transatlantica* 2 (2002); Allan Potofsky, 'The Political Economy of the French-American Debt Debate: The Ideological Uses of Atlantic Commerce, 1787 to 1800', *William and Mary Quarterly*, 3rd series, 63 (2006), 489–515 and Allan Potofsky, 'Le corps consulaire français et le débat autour de la "perte" des Amériques. Les intérêts mercantiles franco-américains et le commerce atlantique, 1763–1795', *Annales Historiques de la Révolution française* 363 (2011), 33–58.

It is difficult to identify the intellectual and economic networks to which Ducher belonged for little is known of his career prior to his appointment as consul to the United States. We know, however, that between 1789 and 1791 he was close to La Fayette (who acted as a pro-American lobbyist in Versailles), that he had a wide knowledge of the United States and its trade, and maintained links with pro-American Parisian circles and presumably also with the 'first' Jacobin Club. Moreover, some of the proposals he put forward in 1789 and 1790 were comparable to those of Charles-Claude de Peysonnel, member of the Jacobins and a prolific writer on business and international affairs, but a direct link between the two cannot be proved. Even so, since they both operated in the same circles (especially among the members of the Agriculture and Trade Committees of the Assembly) in late 1789 and early 1790, it is reasonable to assume that they knew and read each other. As with the above, it is not possible, given the paucity of the sources available, to ascertain whether Ducher maintained relations with members of the Balance of Trade Office.[6]

From June 1790 Ducher appeared before the Constituent Committees of Agriculture and Commerce to defend his ideas on Franco-American trade. Through his American experiences he had become conversant with the problems of transatlantic trade and the maritime laws of the European powers, and it was as a 'specialist' that he wrote a series of reports for the Assembly committees and the *Moniteur*. His articles and judgements helped to formulate the economic debate and commercial legislation of the period, especially under the Convention. Although his views were obviously not the only ones to be expressed at the time, they undoubtedly dominated the debate and exerted an influence on laws and regulations from 1793 onwards.

Also from 1790, Ducher was the legal representative of a trade protection system opposed to the elimination of customs barriers and free trade between the maritime powers and French colonies. Ill-disposed, as were many traders of the period, to the 1786 trade treaty between France and Britain, his objective was to set out a definition of national 'commercial

[6] Michel Beaud, 'Le Bureau de la Balance du Commerce, 1781–1791', *Revue d'histoire économique et sociale* 42 (1964), 357–377; Loïc Charles and Guillaume Daudin, 'Le Bureau de la balance du commerce au XVIIIe siècle', *Revue d'histoire moderne et contemporaine* 58 (2011), 128–155.

diplomacy' to provide a model for all nations wishing to end British 'tyranny' over world trade. France's 'commercial diplomacy' was meant to encourage other nations to develop their own navigation protection systems in order to overcome the domination of British 'despotism'. Rather than sign individual trade treaties, France needed to adopt a Navigation Act that would form the basis of its 'trading system'. Ducher outlined this idea in a publication addressed to the Constituent Assembly entitled *The Analysis of Commercial Laws*. Then, through his close relationship with La Fayette, he was able, thanks to the standing of the 'hero of two worlds', to present his ideas directly to the Committee of Agriculture and the Trade Assembly.

In February 1792 Ducher wrote his first article in the *Moniteur*. Between then and 15 June 1796 he wrote sixty-one texts, tirelessly making the case for a Navigation Act as the cornerstone of a new 'commercial diplomacy' in the service of nations, and also for the establishment of a powerful 'foreign' ministry uniting trade and diplomacy in the same administrative body.

Not long after the proclamation of the Republic, Ducher argued for the abolition of the distinction between diplomats and consuls, which he claimed were 'seignorial'. To his mind, consuls were just as much representatives of national interests as were foreign 'ministers', given that trade and diplomacy were expressions of the same reality:

> In this day and age our politics must be an extension of trade; France no longer has secrets to confide or to fear, the surveillance of our external relations must be entrusted to the same minister. [. . .] Foreign trade must be our first, I would willingly say our only foreign affair [. . .], however responsibility for trade treaties now rests with the Foreign Affairs Ministry, the level of customs levied in France belongs to the Ministry of the Interior, the collection of duties to the Inland Revenue, consulship and custom duties in the colonies to the Naval Ministry.[7]

He called for all those administrative functions to be grouped within a single ministry and, on 6 February 1793, he obtained his first success: a bill proposed by Barère transferred the Consular Office of the Navy to the Foreign Affairs Ministry.

[7] *Moniteur* no. 296, 20 October 1792, 'Consulats et affaires étrangères', 243.

However, Ducher's great cause was the preparation of a Navigation Act designed to underpin a new republican 'commercial diplomacy'. He believed that trade relationships between nations needed to be conducted directly, without mediation, and to be free and unconstrained by bilateral agreements as well as protected from the 'false powers' of Britain and the United Provinces. Countries had to be free to exchange their own 'national' products using their own 'national' ships. In effect, according to Ducher, by arrogating to themselves the role of transporting all the world's goods, the maritime powers, led by Britain, had appropriated the principal asset of ordinary people: their respective trade. Therefore, in order to turn trade into a public good, the people had to regain control of it by adopting protective legislation which excluded the British and the Dutch while encouraging direct and bilateral relationships. From this point of view, the Navigation Act proposed by Ducher tied in, in part, with the inconclusive debates of the 1750s on the struggle against Dutch intermediate trade,[8] albeit Holland was not considered the main trade rival during the Revolution, the main adversary being of course Britain. But, Ducher insisted, the Navigation Act was not meant to turn France into the 'new tyrant of the sea' in place of either Britain or the United Provinces, but rather to promote direct trade and honest, open relationships between different nations:

> Every nation must make the best trade laws for itself, and maintain direct relations with other nations [...] France does not demand and will not grant any commercial privileges; no nation will be either favoured or unfavoured by France. In the French sphere, all is frank; outside its limits, all is foreign, but all is regulated by justice and reciprocity. Individual trade treaties, those of the offensive and defensive alliances of the kings, and the balance of Europe have plagued the human species in all four corners of the world.[9]

[8] Antonella Alimento, 'La concurrence comme politique moderne: la contribution de l'école de Gournay à la naissance d'une sphère publique dans la France des années 1750–1760', in: *L'économie politique et la sphère publique dans le débat des Lumières*, ed. Jesús Astigarraga and Javier Usoz (Madrid: Collection de la Casa de Velázquez, 2013), 213–228.

[9] G. J. A. Ducher, 'Acte de Navigation' (12 February 1793) reproduced in Archives Parlementaires de 1787 à 1860. Recueil complet des débats législatifs et politiques des Chambres françaises, 1ére série, Paris, P. Dupont, 1867–1875, 72: 393.

According to Ducher, the connection between the 'European balance' and unequal 'trade treaties' was unjust, and he found himself participating in most debates on trade during the revolutionary period. His critique of the former notion was nearly always linked to his belief in the need to dismantle the latter.

The connection between the 'European balance' and unequal 'trade treaties' was not unique to Ducher, but was found in most trade discussions during the Revolution. The rejection of the former was nearly always thought to be linked to the extinction of the latter.

The adoption of the Navigation Act that Ducher desired was, however, far from smooth sailing. Indeed, many deputies within the Convention feared that adopting such a law in wartime would only cause neutral countries to distance themselves from France and thus isolate the country even more. Others argued for the maintenance of existing treaties in order to strengthen French trade in the North. Furthermore, some Girondins had not yet given up the idea of a reconciliation with Britain based on a fair free-trade system and it was not until their fall on 30 May and 2 June 1793 that the obstacles standing in the way of a vote on the Navigation Act were finally removed, although the Girondins were not the only party involved.

The first act was played out on 1 March 1793 with the denunciation of the Franco-British treaty of 1786 and the ban of British merchandise in France. Ducher had undoubtedly played an advisory role in the drafting of the decree by the trade committees and general defence, but it was the deputy Blutel who reported to the Convention and succeeded in having the text passed in the session of 16 March.

Soon after, Ducher's influence was confirmed by the creation of a new office in the heart of the Ministry of Foreign Affairs. Indeed, in the spring of 1793, the minister Lebrun proposed the formation of a new body that would combine the consuls and diplomats of the Republic who had not been able to occupy their posts because of the war. They were to be a think-tank to advise on the principles supporting the republican trade treaties that would replace those ratified by the monarchy. Additionally, the office of 'consular and political litigation' was established in April 1793 at the request of Ducher.[10] The plan to form a 'Ministry of the Exterior' to unite trade and diplomacy appeared to be making headway.

[10] Nussbaum, *Commercial Policy in the French Revolution*, 130.

Nevertheless, because customs matters were still outside the 'Ministry of the Exterior' to which he thought they should belong, Ducher continued to insist on the need to consolidate trade and diplomatic affairs in a single administration. On 7 May he published an article in which he proposed the creation of a subsection for foreign trade within the Ministry of Foreign Affairs as well as a 'central office' for non-domestic customs. He also opined that the administration of the merchant navy should be removed from the military navy and brought into the same ministry, along with matters covered by trade agreements and relating to the practical administration of maritime trade.[11] In the same text he bluntly denounced the trade agreements of the princes: 'It is neither in the dignity nor in the interest of the French people to strike up any particular treaty of alliance or trade with any power.' As the Republic desired nothing more than an absolute reciprocity of commercial rights, it must take care not to sign any treaty whatsoever. On 30 May, the 'Trade and Diplomatic Office' was created, with Ducher evidently a member, albeit his position does not seem to have been formalized.

The fall of the Girondins opened up new perspectives,[12] and on 9 June Ducher wrote an article reaffirming that the Navigation Act should serve as the foundation of 'commercial diplomacy'.[13] According to this, French negotiators had to explain to any power wishing to enter into a trade relationship with the Republic that they must adopt their own Navigation Act, similar to the French one, as a necessary precondition to the establishment of a mutually open and profitable agreement. An initial report was put forward by the deputy Marec to the Convention on 3 July, which was debated on 19 July.

In the end, Ducher's tireless efforts were rewarded with the Convention's adoption of the Navigation Act of 21 September 1793.[14]

[11] *Moniteur* no. 127, 7 May 1793.

[12] Covo, 'Commerce, empire et révolutions', II: 389 shows that the fall of the Girondins was not the only factor favouring Ducher's projects. Other actors, less visible, such as the Parisian Americans, the delegates of the Antilles and the interested shipowners equally played a decisive role. The collation in favour of a Navigation Act was large, but also very heterogeneous in its interests.

[13] *Moniteur* no. 160, 9 June 1793.

[14] For the text in English, see *American State Papers: Documents, Legislative and Executive, of the Congress of the United States* (Washington, DC: Gales and Seaton, 1833), I: 316–323.

The date was not insignificant, since, for Ducher, and for Barère, who served as the representative of the Committee of Public Safety, the Act amounted to a renewed proclamation of the Republic made in the sphere of trade and diplomacy. Barère said that it announced to the world the freedom of French and European trade and of the seas. Some days later, on 3 October, Ducher exulted in the link between 'the defeat of the old diplomacy' and the triumph of 'trade diplomacy'. The French Revolution destroyed the old diplomacy based on family alliances and the deceptive equilibrium of powers, bringing down an axeon this diplomatic 'feudalism'. The final blow had to be dealt. French diplomacy, he repeated, had to be 'restricted to business relationships'.[15]

The Act responded to Ducher's three major priorities: to make an airtight separation between the British and the French (while fighting for the 'gallicization of shipping'[16]), to eliminate the intermediary trade and redistribution of French foodstuffs by the British and the Dutch, and to rally the secondary powers (especially the United States) around a project for the general independence of trade.[17] While the Act did indeed outline these principles, legislation had to be drawn up in order for them to be applied. Ducher drafted a plan in forty articles, inspired by the American federal laws of 1789, which Barère presented to the Convention on the 17 Vendémiaire of year II (8 October 1793). Ten days later it was adopted. The Committee of Public Safety tried to use the Navigation Act in its ongoing negotiations with the United States, but these floundered.

The adoption of the Navigation Act was the starting point for an intense legislative and regulatory activity to which Ducher contributed as a member of the Customs Commission created on 8 October 1793. The 'Ministry of the Exterior' that he desired was practically a reality, although it did not formally bear that name. The former consul called for it to undertake a number of new tasks, including the monthly

[15] *Moniteur* no. 276, 3 October 1793.

[16] The different forms of fraud used to 'franciser' ships have been studied by Silvia Marzagalli, *Les boulevards de la fraude. Le négoce international et le blocus continental, 1806–1813* (Villeneuve d'Asq: Presses du Septentrion, 1999). See also Éric Schnakenbourg, *Entre la guerre et la paix. Neutralité et relations internationales, XVIIe–XVIIIe siècles* (Rennes: Presses Universitaires de Rennes, 2013).

[17] Covo, 'Commerce, empire et révolutions', II: 391.

publication of general foreign trade statistics of the Republic and of an updated list of the trade treaties, conventions and commercial and fiscal regulations then in force. This programme was accepted by the Assembly on 28 October 1793 and Ducher continued to exercise great influence at the heart of the Customs Commission, notably helping to shape the new Customs Code that was adopted on the 4 Germinal of year II (24 March 1794).

Despite these duties, Ducher still found time to write about his favourite subject in the *Moniteur*, which on 5 December published an article of his under the simple title of 'Commercial Diplomacy'. In this he renewed his refrain: 'The French Republic would dishonour its own creation if it does not recant all policies except that of courage, all diplomacy except that of commerce, the natural link between nations, the most solid base for their prosperity, the most powerful means to maintain or recover their political freedom.'[18] On the eve of Thermidor, he once again returned to the meaning of French 'commercial diplomacy', which was not intended to substitute the 'British tyrants of the seas', but to create 'a new European balance that would establish in its powers this independence, this equality of rights that exist between the citizens of France and this equality of maritime freedom, this proportion of trade that each one of them holds in nature'.[19] It would thereby establish equality in the commercial order between nations, just as the French had established it in the civic order. Individual trade treaties were an expression of *privileges*, while Republican trade promoted *equality* and *reciprocity*.

Commercial Treaties and National Power (1795–1799)

With the Battle of Fleurus (26 June 1794) and the victories in Holland (January 1795) and on the Rhine, the prospect of the defeat of Revolutionary France faded away. The treaties of Basel in the spring of 1795 signalled the failure of the first coalition and the withdrawal of Prussia and Spain, marking the return of France to the diplomatic stage. The United Provinces became the Batavian Republic and signed a treaty of alliance with the French Republic which was extended territorially with the

[18] *Moniteur* no. 75, 15 Frimaire Year II (5 December 1793).

[19] *Moniteur* no. 268, 28 Prairial Year II (16 June 1794).

annexation of Belgium, ratified on the eve of the separation from the Convention, and the occupation of the left bank of the Rhine. Soon the victories in Italy and Switzerland greatly extended 'the side of freedom' with the foundation of the Cisalpine and Helvetic Republics, while the fight against Britain and Austria continued. The issue of 'trade diplomacy' was then presented in a new context in which the French Republic planned to make use of its military victories to gain market dominance with its allies and/or with the powers with which it made peace.

According to republican commentators, this 'commercial diplomacy' had to form the basis for the Republic's foreign policy. The alliance with the Batavian Republic aimed at strengthening 'gallicized' trade on the Rhine to gain market dominance with its allies and/or with the powers with which it made peace.[20] Similarly, the Franco-Spanish alliance was viewed from the perspective of France's commercial development. The Spanish were not only summoned to open their markets fully but also to put pressure on Portugal to renounce the trade privileges accorded to Britain. The creation of the Italian Republics and the establishment of trade relations with the Cisalpine Republic in 1797 pointed to a potential new 'gallicized' commercial space in the western Mediterranean, while Italian patriots like Matteo Galdi favoured a Franco-Italian free market and the expulsion of the British trade from the peninsula.[21]

The debate on trade relations and the adoption of a Navigation Act by the sister republics (or at least by the Cisalpine and Batavian Republics, the only ones that lasted long enough) is a subject that has sadly been ignored by historiography. Indeed, to my knowledge, there are no Italian or Dutch books devoted to it. Although the works of Anna-Maria Rao on Italian patriots such as Galdi mention certain developments in their analysis of the regenerated Cisalpine trade,[22] the internal debate of its institutions is unknown to us. Raymond Kubben's work on Franco-Batavian relations tackles the questions of peace and of the alliance, but very little work exists

[20] For instance *Moniteur* no. 201, 21 Germinal Year V (10 April 1797), 803. The article by Eschassériaux, 'De la Hollande et de ses colonies'.

[21] Anna Maria Rao, 'Républiques et monarchies à l'époque révolutionnaire: une diplomatie nouvelle?' *Annales Historiques de la Révolution française* 296 (1994), 267–278: 273.

[22] Rao, 'Républiques et monarchies', 273.

on the debate relating to Franco-Batavian trade relations.[23] We do know, however, that Ducher encouraged the Dutch to produce a Navigation Act identical to the French one in order to expand the sphere of republican trade closed to Britain.[24]

In their discussions and proclamations French leaders insisted on the elimination of all exclusivity between nations. The programme embodied in Ducher or the deputy Joseph Eschassériaux under the banner of 'commercial independence'[25] saw this as the fundamental principle of economic relations, just as 'political independence' was the key concept of diplomatic relations. 'Political independence' was also important to Ducher, and implied the rejection of guarantees, of exclusivity, of the status of most favoured nation designed to exclude other countries, of limits placed on navigation and so forth.

For some republicans, French diplomacy had to set itself the objective of convincing those powers that wished to sign a trade treaty with the Republic to accede to a declaration of the maritime rights that would counter British trade tyranny. In 1797 Barère declared that France had to become a 'moral maritime power' based on freedom of the seas, equality of all nations and respect of the rights of the people.[26] France had already set an example by ratifying the Navigation Act of 1793.[27] By this proclamation, it had made a call for freedom to other nations 'by stirring them to imitate it and so recover their maritime rights'. This was not enough: after having liberated the continent, the French Republic had to 'finally proclaim and make plain the principles of the rights of nations and the independence of the seafaring nations'.

[23] Raymond Kubben, *Regeneration and Hegemony. Franco-Batavian Relations in the Revolutionary Ear—A Legal Approach, 1795–1803* (Leiden: Brill, 2011). On the neutrality debate, Koen Stapelbroek, 'The Dutch Debate on Commercial Neutrality (1713–1830)', in: *Trade and War. The Neutrality of Commerce in the Inter-State System*, ed. Koen Stapelbroek (Helsinki: COLLeGIUM: Studies Across Disciplines in the Humanities and Social Sciences, 2011), 114–142.

[24] Nussbaum, *Commercial Policy in the French Revolution*, 298.

[25] *Moniteur* no. 165, 15 Ventôse Year III (5 March 1795), 596–599, treating the session of 13 Ventôse Year III (3 March 1795) and issue 33 of 3 Brumaire Year III (24 October 1794), Ducher's article 'Diplomatie régénérée'.

[26] Bertrand Barère, *La Liberté des mers* ou le gouvernement anglais dévoilé, in 8°, 2 vol, Paris, 1er ventôse an VI.

[27] Barère, *La Liberté des mers*, I: 161.

For Barère, the alliance between France, the Batavian Republic, the Ligurian Republic, the Cisalpine Republic, and Spain already constituted a *commission de marine* whose mere presence on the ocean would oblige the restitution of all maritime rights.[28] By proclaiming the rights of nations, the French Republic 'by the freedom of the sea, only seeks the return to natural law, the maintenance of the law, the property of each nation, the interests of each power'.[29] It would not act as an ambitious power, as a rival to the British, and thus the 'General Republic of Europe' would of necessity side with the French camp. The fundamental principles of this association would be the freedom of the seas, the liberalization of trade and industry, the abolition of slavery and of trafficking of black people, and finally the proscription of privateering.[30]

'Commercial diplomacy' was not only manifest as a programme, but was also an influence present in the negotiations and treaties signed with the powers by the Thermidorien Convention and the Directory. However, the writings of the foreign affairs minister show that it was thought of more as a strategic imperative in the short and medium term. The idea that the Republic had to use the military context to impose the most favourable conditions for French trade and to exclude British goods from many countries is to be found in the records and projects of ministerial offices. In a diplomatic report of Fructidor year II, analysed by Marcel Reinhard, the trade imperative was clearly asserted: peace must provide the opportunity to conclude 'treaties as much commercial as political, in which trade would be both the aim and the means of politics'.[31] He argued that

> business interests are perpetually present in the thoughts of Republican negotiators. The kings, in their ignorance and in that of their advisors [...] were happy with what was called glory. The Republicans instead

[28] Barère, *La Liberté des mers*, I: 163. The meaning of the expression 'commission de marine' used by Barère is not quite clear. Does it represent an attempted merger of commercial and naval politics of the French Republic and its allies? Or simply the idea that the alliance between the Franco-Hispano-Italo-Batavian forces would inspire the Brits to tone down their ambitions?

[29] Barère, *La Liberté des mers*, I: 172.

[30] Barère, *La Liberté des mers*, I: 381.

[31] Marcel Reinhard, 'Les aspirations de la bourgeoisie française à l'hégémonie', in: *Mélanges Pierre Renouvin* (Paris: PUF, 1966), 88.

> considered the wealth, the prosperity, the labour, of the greatest number of their citizens. Substantial trade ensures all of that, it is the support and ally of substantial agriculture.

These same objectives—the ban on British goods, preferential (or no) import duties rights for French goods—were found in the treaties of 'friendship, navigation and trade' prepared by the Minister of Foreign Affairs Charles Delacroix, perhaps with Ducher's participation,[32] between December 1796 and spring 1797.[33] The text had five sections respectively entitled: 'Of national friendship', 'Of navigation', 'Commercial relations', 'Of consular jurisdiction' and a final one on the civil and political rights of the citizens of the contracting nations. The first established different methods of arbitration for trade activities, the second summarized the principles of navigation of neutral countries, the third sought to establish a form of trade, customs and fiscal reciprocity, and the final two detailed the duties of consuls, notably in relation to the civil state.

Designed as a proposal to be made to all allied or conquered powers, the treaty served as a template that was adaptable to circumstances. In a letter of the 13 Nivôse Year V to the Minister of Justice, Delacroix spoke of a 'project for a friendship, navigation and trade treaty whose general prescription could be applied to all pacts of this kind to be made with the nations who reconcile or ally themselves with the Republic'.[34] Initially set out as a proposal to be made to Spain during negotiations of the Treaty of Basel, the draft treaty clearly aimed to bring about a dominant position in local markets by capitalizing on the military and diplomatic momentum. In a report to the Directory on the subject of the planned commercial treaty with Spain, Delacroix stated bluntly:

> That it is the moment to negotiate this important act during the initial warmth of our liaisons with Spain after this lengthy current war. It guarantees us an advantage over our allies that is not counterbalanced by any foreign influence [...] It is about taking advantage of the present moment to ensure an advantageous and permanent rate for our products and to gain an advantage on the English, our rivals, in setting the consumption of our manufactured products

[32] Nussbaum, *Commercial Policy in the French Revolution*, 311.

[33] See Georges Dejoint, *La politique économique du Directoire* (Paris: Rivière, 1951), 161–223.

[34] Archives Nationales [AN], BB/16/713, bb 609.

> on a solid footing during the interruption of their trade in Spain. When the maritime peace is secured, the channels opened up will be filled by us.[35]

While trade treaties were part of the agenda of all the Directory's negotiations, very few of the texts were ultimately adopted. In all the peace treaties with the European powers, clauses concerning trade were on the whole limited to deferring future negotiations for the establishment of new specific trade treaties and the restoration of trade relationships 'on the basis of where they were before the current war' (Article 6 of the Basel treaty). For example, in the Treaty of Saint-Idelfonse agreed between France and Spain on 19 August 1796, Article 15 stated: 'A trade treaty will be concluded very shortly, from bases that are equitable and reciprocal to both nations, that assures each one, with its ally, a marked preference for home-grown manufactured products, or at the very least equal benefits to those enjoyed in their respective states as the most favoured nations.'

Despite these optimistic formulae, future negotiations were difficult. In the majority of the treaties signed by the Directory, only a few specific clauses were true to the republican trade programme. In the peace treaties signed with Württemberg and Baden, the Directory imposed the free trade of all French merchandise on the two states, without any obligation other than the payment of toll fees on traffic.[36] By contrast, in the negotiations with Spain, for example, the Spanish refused to ban British goods and the Directory had to content itself with restored trade relations. Likewise, France did not propose this type of treaty to the Batavian Republic for fear of competition in the redistribution of colonial products but was content with the freedom of navigation on the '*Trois Fleuves*'.

In the end, the two treaties with the Duchy of Parma of 1796 and the Cisalpine Republic of 1798 were the only ones to meet the requirements of the template trade treaty formulated by Delacroix and the Directory. Of the sixteen articles of the treaty with the Duke of Parma of 5 November 1796, six were dedicated to trade issues, regulating dealings between France and the Duchy, including the right of transit of their respective merchandise. French manufactured products would be free to enter and

[35] AN, F/III/69, Rapport au Directoire exécutif, 12 floréal an V (1 May 1797).

[36] Roger Dufraisse, 'Les relations économiques entre la France et l'Allemagne', in: *Deutschland und die Franzosiche Revolution* (Munich: Artemis, 1983), 232.

leave the Duchy without any customs duty other than those paid by other trading partners. France became the most favoured nation, and could freely import agricultural products and silk from the Duchy. The trade treaty with the Cisalpine Republic of 21 February 1798 included fifteen articles establishing an end to trade prohibitions and limiting the respective customs tariffs, while a secret article called on the Italian Republic to ban the entry of any British merchandise that was also prohibited in France.[37]

To be sure, the concrete results of the Directory's 'trade diplomacy' were, as we have seen, negligible. Even so, the importance of the subject in negotiations and diplomatic correspondence shows that it was a fundamental theme in the political reflection of the government.

Conclusion

Neither the Navigation Act that was supposed to underpin a republican trade system nor the 'commercial diplomacy' of the Directory were a great success. Manuel Covo has recently called the former a 'complete waste of time'. The Directory was never really able to integrate its allies—not even its Antillean colonies—despite their being theoretically treated as departments, in the broader republican trade system. It is true that the Navigation Act was not conceived to be implemented in wartime but rather when peace prevailed. It therefore did not come into force until the eighteen months of peace between the Treaty of Amiens and the resumption of war in 1804. Nonetheless, the importance of the debate on this subject during the Revolution amply demonstrates that contemporaries were conscious of the turmoil caused by the American and French Revolutions to the balance of power in trade in Europe, both within the colonial empires and between the European nations themselves, and so they looked for political solutions to those problems.

The activities of Ducher are symbolic of these issues as well as the tensions and dead ends of the political and economic debate. Defining the programme of a Ducher or a Barère remains problematic: was it in continuity with the reflections of the mid-eighteenth century to make the Navigation Act and 'trade independence' instruments to create a trading space that excluded Britain while making France a unifying control force?

[37] Jacques Godechot, *La Grande Nation* (Paris: Aubier, 1956), 449.

Or was it rather a real reciprocal alternative trade project? The policies devised by the Directory tend to suggest that the first objective was imposed in practice, but that does not necessarily mean that it was what the initial ambitious plans of Ducher or Barère had intended. It is nevertheless clear that the matter was subsequently settled by Napoleon, who clearly chose to orientate his economic policies towards bringing about the hegemony of France over her trading partners.

Here it is quite clear that the destiny of 'republican trade' was not played out only in Paris in the heart of the assemblies nor even in the committees. As Manuel Covo has ably demonstrated, the debate on republican trade took place just as much, if not more so, in Philadelphia, in Port-au-Prince and in Bordeaux as in Paris, and people integrated into Atlantic networks and their local branches played crucial roles in the success or otherwise of the attempts to redefine trade in a 'regenerated' France. The issue of trade treaties and its complications during the revolutionary era in this sense formed a representation of the broader context of the redefining of Atlantic 'empires' that took place in the same period.

Marc Belissa is an Associate Professor and Directeur de Recherches in Modern History at the University of Paris Ouest Nanterre—CHISCO. He has published numerous books on the eighteenth century, the Enlightenment and the French Revolution, including *Fraternité Universelle et Intérêt National, 1713–1795* (1998), *Repenser l'ordre européen, 1795–1802* (2006) and with Yannick Bosc, *Robespierre, la fabrication d'un mythe* (2013).

Index

A. Alimento, K. Stapelbroek (eds.), *The Politics of Commercial Treaties in the Eighteenth Century*, DOI 10.1007/978-3-319-53574-6

E

F

I

U

www.ingramcontent.com/pod-product-compliance
Lightning Source LLC
Chambersburg PA
CBHW042030200926
51615CB00028B/2
9783319535739